Selling Electronic Media

Selling Electronic Media

Ed Shane

Foreword and Discussion Points by Michael C. Keith

**Focal
Press**

Boston Oxford Auckland Johannesburg Melbourne New Delhi

Focal Press is an imprint of Butterworth–Heinemann.

Copyright © 1999 by Butterworth–Heinemann

Ⓡ A member of the Reed Elsevier group

♾ Recognizing the importance of preserving what has been written, Butterworth–Heinemann prints its books on acid-free paper whenever possible.

 Butterworth–Heinemann supports the efforts of American Forests and the Global ReLeaf program in its campaign for the betterment of trees, forests, and our environment.

Library of Congress Cataloging-in-Publication Data
Shane, Ed.
    Selling electronic media / Ed Shane ; foreword by Michael C. Keith.
      p.   cm.
    Includes bibliographical references and index.
    ISBN 0-240-80327-2 (alk. paper)
    1. Selling—Mass media.   I. Title.
  HF5439.M267S49   1999
  384.5'068'8—dc21   98-41464
                                                               CIP

British Library Cataloguing-in-Publication Data
A catalogue record for this book is available from the British Library.

The publisher offers special discounts on bulk orders of this book.
For information, please contact:

    Manager of Special Sales
    Butterworth–Heinemann
    225 Wildwood Avenue
    Woburn, MA 01801-2041
    Tel: 781-904-2500
    Fax: 781-904-2620

For information on all Butterworth–Heinemann publications available, contact our World Wide Web home page at: *http://www.bh.com*.

10 9 8 7 6 5 4 3 2

Printed in the United States of America

To Jack Biles
Your humor and insight are greatly missed.

Contents

2   The Sales Process   44

4   Sales Management   185

7   Selling Cable Advertising   313

8   Selling Radio Advertising   346

9   The Interactive Interim   394

Foreword

Michael C. Keith

Well, here it is! At long last, we have a single volume that comprehensively and eloquently captures the true essence and meaning of the world (and it is a world) of electronic media sales, and—not surprising to me or anyone else who knows him—it is written by Ed Shane. This estimable carbon-based life form, this gentleman among those who are not always so gentlemanly, had the good and right stuff to make it happen. Of course, it goes without saying (but I will say it anyway) that I am enormously pleased with the results of Ed's Herculean efforts, yet I am also very envious of his singular achievement.

My latter reaction is made all the more poignant and profound since I was originally slated to be his co-author, which would have meant sharing in this book, his latest glory. Alas, other obligations prevented my participation. My loss, however, is Ed's gain. For after reading his text for the second time, I realize that I would likely have impeded—perhaps even impaired—the brilliant flow of his protean pen and the powerful originality of his thinking. Besides, one does not stand in the way of fate (lest one be flattened), and it is now amply evident that it was Ed's destiny to write the definitive book on this complex and intriguing topic. It was for him alone to do.

Reflecting on my professional life, which admittedly I do more and more these days, particularly on momentous occasions and stellar events (and I now rank this book as one of them), it makes complete sense that Ed Shane would be the person to bring this tome's subject matter into the newest electronic age and the new millennium. Indeed, he had all the talent, experience, and expertise needed to reinvigorate the existing canon of published discourse on electronic media sales. His three-plus decades as a broadcaster and consultant, as well as media observer and scholar (he is the creator of several important industry studies and books), made him the perfect individual to meet the task head-on and, in fact, the likeliest of all of us to triumph.

Thus it hardly seems necessary or desirable to say anything further, since everything the reader needs or wants to know about electronic media sales awaits him or her in the following pages of this extraordinary volume. So make way for the "word"—*the last word*—as imparted by someone who is clearly the master of this unique domain.

Preface

These are the phrases I heard most as I collected the interviews and the research materials for this book:

- Merging and converging
- Explosive growth
- Unprecedented change
- Digital future

I start with them to get them out of the way. They're givens now in the electronic media environment, not the surprises they were in the year or two after the U.S. Congress affirmed the changes that were already in the wind.

This project began just over a year after the Telecommunications Act of 1996 took the limits off of broadcast ownership. Radio companies were allowed to acquire as many stations as they could handle if they followed the limits established for each marketplace (eight stations in the largest markets, fewer in smaller markets). Television's ownership was also unfettered as long as TV companies did not cover more than 35% of the U.S. population. There were even relaxed rules within the rules.

Wall Street had been in an upward spiral already because the robust 1990s economy in the United States buoyed stock prices. Media companies, especially broadcasters, were heroes in the financial community because of their newfound opportunities to create larger entities and to build asset value. CBS offered "one-stop selling" that included advertising on its television network, its radio and television stations, two cable channels, and an outdoor company they owned. Chancellor Media offered a new national radio network, local TV stations, hundreds of radio stations, and their own entry into outdoor advertising. Clear Channel Communications expanded from radio and television into outdoor advertising in the United States, Europe, and Asia.

With the consolidation of broadcasting and the proliferation of media as a backdrop, I was asked to make sense of the constantly morphing landscape to help students learn about selling electronic media. At the same time, I hoped to provide a book for those already selling electronic media who wanted to review the basics in light of all those phrases above.

There were strong hints that this new approach would be effective:

- *Advertising Age* reported that new media companies found salespeople in short supply: DoubleClick had 14 openings for salespeople; EarthWeb had 10; Yoyodyne said it would hire "anyone who meets its standards even without a specific opening."

- *Tuned In* quoted CBS radio chief Dan Mason: "The supply of radio salespeople is very low for the demand. If I were at a major university now and teaching broadcasting students, I would do everything I could to discourage them from standing in those long lines for programming jobs and encourage them to seek the opportunities that a radio sales career could provide."
- Ron Alridge, publisher and editorial director of *Electronic Media* told me, "If I were a TV GM, I'd find the best radio salespeople in my market and teach them television. They already know how to compete."

That insight told me that Focal Press was on to something with this book idea. There was a need for qualified sellers at the real-world level. This book is an attempt to fill that need and to address it in real-world language.

What Is Sales?

The most succinct definition of sales that I've heard is "identifying and satisfying customer needs profitably." In Chapter 1, you'll learn that there's more to that definition: selling must be profitable for both the seller and the buyer.

Sellers of "click here" banners on Web pages know that the mechanics are different from selling commercial time on radio. Selling television's six o'clock news is not the same as selling a concert promotion on MTV. I could go on with the differences, and I will—that's what this book is all about. Yet the basics of selling don't vary. You'll learn the basics and how to apply them to each electronic medium.

In Chapter 1, a television station owner worries that "everybody wants to be in everybody else's business" as she defines over-the-air television's sales challenges against direct satellite, cable, and telephone company delivery of programming that was once the province of the networks.

A radio sales trainer reminds us in Chapter 5 that the future of electronic media faces a diminishing resource: advertisers. There's lots of advertising, he says, but consolidation in businesses from banking to home improvement to office supplies means fewer individual advertisers.

You'll learn that there are basics to the sales process, no matter what you're selling:

1. Prospecting
2. Qualifying
3. Needs analysis
4. Presentation
5. Answering objections
6. Closing
7. Relationship management

One salesperson might put greater emphasis on one of those steps and not another, but no salesperson can argue with the essentials.

The people you'll meet in this book know that from time to time they must rethink their sales methods. They know that customers and buying habits change constantly, and they believe that sellers have to do the same.

If there's a bottom line to the comments from the selling experts you'll meet in this book, it's that the biggest change in selling in recent years is the shift from emphasis on the product to a focus on the customer. You'll discover in Chapter 2 that you need to immerse yourself in knowledge about your prospect and your prospect's industry.

Using This Book

Sales trainer Tom Hopkins urges his sales "Champions" to reread sales books one year after they've completed them the first time. I hope you'll apply Hopkins' idea to this book, too. Hold on to it when you finish and add a note to your calendar to pull it out for review. The passage of time and the development of new selling skills will offer you insight as you read the same chapters in a whole new light.

Master seller Zig Ziglar called his *Secrets of Closing the Sale* "the book you never finish," urging his readers to read and reread the text. First, Ziglar said, move through his book quickly, highlighting ideas. Next, read with a notepad to commit ideas to writing. Ziglar even offers advice on what to look for in your *fourth* reading!

Selling Electronic Media is designed to fill the gap between curricula in mass media and curricula in the business school. Because of my industry background, I cannot help but write from an industry perspective rather than from an academic perspective. I hope that focus makes this book useful to you whether you're a student entering the field for the first time or already selling advertising in television, cable, radio, or the new and emerging forms of electronic media.

Opportunities for selling new media are being invented as you read this. Direct Broadcast Satellite (DBS), Radio Broadcast Data Systems (RBDS), interactive multimedia, videotext, and selling in the virtual marketplace all hold promise. They will morph and morph again into forms we haven't yet imagined.

Because change is the essence of electronic media, I had to make decisions on where to include certain topics. I've linked traditional media—television with television, cable with cable, radio with radio. Some ideas are combined because a synergy already exists, especially the combinations of pages on the World Wide Web with virtually all traditional media. For example, TV programs have Web pages, radio stations use hyperlinks to the artists they play, and newspapers are networked in cyberspace. There are lots of shared opportunities.

There is a discussion in the book about what to call sellers of electronic media. Some organizations use the term marketing executives. Advertising agencies have long used the titles account managers or account executives. Radio and television stations have their own job titles. I use the words seller or salesperson for simplicity's sake. I also follow as my sources lead me. If they have a specific title for the sellers in their organization, I'll use it in their comments.

A word about the use of gender in the quoted material: there are quotations and excerpts from texts that use the pronoun "he" and the word "salesman" because that's the way things were when they were written. Obviously neither selling nor buying is a gender-specific activity, and I've approached this book with that attitude.

Acknowledgments

Undertaking a project like this book is a reminder that it cannot happen on its own. Michael Keith at Boston College began this process and engaged me as co-author. Later he encouraged me to take it on as a solo effort when his work on two other book projects took him away from this one.

Michael is prominent in the book, providing the Foreword and allowing quotation from his prolific industry writings.

The Review Highlights and Discussion Points at the end of each chapter were developed and written by Michael to give students an opportunity to test their knowledge and to give instructors a useful springboard for classroom conversation and review. Michael made even greater contributions behind the scenes, guiding me through my first textbook assignment as both advisor and reviewer.

Marie Lee at Focal Press was kind enough to see the merits of my previous books and to give her go-ahead to the project. Marie and Focal's Terri Jadick led me through the day-to-day minefields of preparing the book for you. Their patience enhances the book's usefulness.

The electronic media industry leaders who have given of their time and expertise add a wealth of insight that one author cannot. I thank them sincerely, and acknowledge them throughout the text.

Some went above and beyond to help me, and I'd like to say a special thank you to them.

Ron Alridge of the trade magazine *Electronic Media* provided background on the electronic media landscape. ("Big E, big M," he would say, referring to his publication. To Ron, this book is "Little E, little M.")

Gary Fries, president of the Radio Advertising Bureau (RAB), opened the doors of RAB's Dallas headquarters and gave me remarkable access to RAB archives. The RAB's Mike Mahone, Roann Hale, Andy Rainey, and Amy Wills were of invaluable assistance.

Diane Sutter of Shooting Star Broadcasting helped me bridge the gap between my radio roots and the knowledge I had to gain in the merging and converging television industry. She has worked in both fields, and her insight and guidance are appreciated.

Ed Cohen, director of research at Clear Channel Communications, let me pepper him with niggling little questions as I tapped his expertise in television, radio, research, and academia to check facts and theories.

Thanks especially to the Shane Media staff for their patience while I focused more on this project and less on them. Lizzy Waggoner knows the contents of this book forward and backward, having seen each word a million times. She's a great safety net for fact errors, double key strokes, and stray spaces. Jon Lutes added charts and graphs to several dense text pages. Katie Key tracked down visuals from networks and publishers and assisted in assembling text.

A special word of thanks to my wife and business partner, Pam Shane. Her direct contribution includes reviewing text and editing to make me look smarter. Her additional contribution is more than 27 years of allowing me to test philosophy and theory on her before it was written or spoken to less sympathetic outsiders. She was patient enough to miss all but a few innings of Astros' spring training in 1998 while I was at the keyboard. That was a tremendous sacrifice.

I hope you'll find this book a useful addition to your electronic media career. It'll be fascinating to watch the merging and converging, the explosive growth, and the unprecedented change of the digital future—together.

Ed Shane

1

The Selling Environment

What Is Selling?

The first "sales training" I ever received came in 1968 when I was named program director of a radio station in Atlanta, Georgia. The general manager who hired me showed me a poster of "the man in the chair," the grumpy old codger shown in Figure 1-1. The expressionless stare was chilling; the caption was as brutal as the man's eyes.

"The man in the chair" began as an ad campaign for *Business Week* and other McGraw-Hill publications in 1958. It was named one of the top ten ads that year by *Advertising Age*. The campaign was updated in 1968, again in 1979, and yet again in 1996, with different people in the chair. Ultimately, it was translated into French, Russian, German, Italian, and Chinese.

In my 1968 experience, I heard the message in plain English. The problem with selling, my new boss explained, is that not every prospect makes it as easy as the "man in the chair."

"Easy?" I asked.

Yes. The "man in the chair" ad could refer to any product. Further, it contained a straightforward litany of objections, ready to meet with information from a well-prepared seller.

Why did I need to hear that? I had just taken a job as a product guy at a radio sta-tion. I was not expected to sell advertising time, was I? Frankly, I hoped not. All of my exposure to selling anything prior to that day had been observing high pressure sales types who had tried to sell my parents something they didn't need and couldn't afford. In my mind, "sales" was charged with negative perceptions and evoked visions of diamond pinky rings and clouds of cigar smoke from overweight men who tricked people out of their savings.

My new boss called those salespeople "vultures" and said he didn't think his sales staff acted that way. As I worked with them, I discovered that he was right. That staff cared about their customers and worked hard to make sure the clients got benefits from advertising on our station.

My boss told me that my job was to understand the challenges that my sta-tion's salespeople were facing when they hit the streets every day. Also, I was to join the sales reps to meet with clients and talk about a product I knew better than the salespeople did.

Later, I would learn much more about sales—information that sellers in every field call "the basics," but I didn't know that then. Who knew then that prospecting and qualifying, analyzing needs and develop-ing solutions, continuing service after the

"*I don't know who you are.*

I don't know your company.

I don't know your company's product.

I don't know what your company stands for.

I don't know your company's customers.

I don't know your company's record.

I don't know your company's reputation.

Now—what was it you wanted to sell me?"

MORAL: Sales start **before** your salesman calls—with business publication advertising.

McGRAW-HILL MAGAZINES
BUSINESS•PROFESSIONAL•TECHNICAL

FIGURE 1–1   The Man in the Chair. A classic statement
about sales and selling, originally an ad for
Business Week magazine. © McGraw-Hill
Companies. Used with permission.

sale, and building relationships would be so important? Sure, the sellers did. Now the programming guy would know, too.

I was fortunate to have been given a taste of the basics of selling early in my career. I felt I had been brought into an elite circle that gave me insight into the business. This insight led to my understanding of the way media works—not just radio, but media generally. It deepened my desire to be a student of media.

Ultimately, it also led to the opportunity to carry a list, to manage radio stations, and to found and manage my own company, Shane Media Services. Our core business is programming and research consultation, but we exist in the selling and marketing environment. Everybody does.

What Have You Sold Today?

You don't have to be a professional sales person to answer the question above. If you have human interaction of any kind, then you'll "sell" something every day.

> Ask the boss for a raise, and you're selling the company on what you think you're worth.
>> Ask for a date, and you're selling the idea of togetherness, creating a need for companionship, with you as the solution to that need.
>> Ask a friend to do you a favor, and you're selling the benefits of friendship and reciprocity.

The answer to "What is selling?" is "Everything is selling."

Almost every environment exists because somebody with sales skills matched a need with a product or a service that fulfilled that need. Vehicles, cosmetics, hospitals, roller coasters you name it—a sales person created or sold a certain product that provided a solution to a specific problem.

In its typical definition, *selling* connotes economic exchange, not day-to-day human interaction. For sellers in electronic media, for example, the exchange is dollars for advertising time or message space.

"Selling is the mechanism that drives the economy," said Charles Futrell, professor of marketing at Texas A & M University, to the *Houston Chronicle*.[1] "It's matching what you're selling to a customer's needs in a professional manner." Futrell teaches selling at A & M's Lowry Mays College and Graduate School of Business. The name of the school speaks volumes. Mays, founder and chairman of Clear Channel Communications, a media company that spans the globe, funded a *business* school, not a media school.

Mays talks about various forms of media as conduits from the advertiser to the viewer or listener. As sellers of advertising in electronic media, we're sellers of the advertiser's product. Mays explains: "We view ourselves as being in the business of selling automobiles, tamales, toothpaste, or whatever our customers want to move off their shelves. That culture, whether in radio or television, has served us well and keeps our focus where it should be, and that's on the customer."[2]

Zig Ziglar calls selling "a transference of feeling. If I (the salesman) can make you (the prospect) feel about my product the way I feel about my product, you are going to buy my product." In *Secrets of Closing the Sale*,[3] Ziglar added: "In order to transfer a feeling, you've got to have that feeling." This is a very positive definition of selling, because it assumes that the seller is so enthusiastic about the product that the prospective buyer catches the euphoria.

There is a "process" to selling that guides behavior in a desired direction, culminating in the purchase. "The path to a sale is through uncovering client needs and satisfying those needs with product benefits," say Charles Warner and Joseph Buchman in the classic textbook, *Broadcast and Cable Selling*.[4] Warner and Buchman divided buyers into two groups—customers and prospects. "Customers" have already bought what you have to sell, and they need to be nurtured or resold. "Prospects" require information about your product, explanation of benefits, and evidence about expected results.

The last thing a prospect wants to be is "a prospect." That makes him or her sound like a target, not a person. Sales trainer Tom Hopkins reminds us that not everyone wants to be sold. Negative perceptions about selling are a reality to millions of people. "It arises from the actions of the minority of salespeople who believe that selling is purely and simply aggression," Hopkins writes in *How to Master the Art of Selling*.[5]

"Eventually all such vultures will be driven out of sales by the new breed of enlightened salespeople who qualify their prospects, care about their customers, and make sure their clients get benefit from their purchases that outweigh the prices paid." In that statement, Hopkins gives us his definition of "sales."

"Selling never changes," says Mark McCormack, author of *What They Don't Teach You at Harvard Business School*. "There are no fads in selling, only basics," he wrote.[6] There are tools that become fads—cell phones, palmtop computers, a fax machine in the car, software to make your computer's memory sharper, your client information more accessible, and your presentation more powerful. But tools don't persuade the customer to commit. That's the seller's job.

Are You Selling or Are You Marketing?

Selling is trying to get someone to buy something. It's the successful presentation of your product or service in such a way that your client sees the benefit of the purchase. The best salespeople make selling an art.

Marketing is also an art. Marketing means creating conditions by which the buyer is convinced to make a purchase without outside persuasion. Marketing involves developing a product or service that is perceived by customers to fit their needs so precisely that they *want* to buy it.

While this book has the word "selling" in its title, you'll necessarily read a lot about marketing and its big-picture, long-term view of moving people toward making their own decisions. In relation, selling is the day-to-day, shorter-term concept of moving goods and services. You can see they're dependent upon each other.

There is a difference between sales and marketing, and I've heard the differences expressed a hundred ways. Let's start with just a few:

"Marketing is strategy; selling is tactics."
"Selling is finding a need and filling it; marketing is finding a *perceived* need and filling it."
"Selling is product-focused; marketing is customer-focused."

"Marketing differs from sales in the sense that it involves creating a desire for the product that is related to emotion, image, or desire rather than practical need," says Allen Shaw, President of Centennial Communications.

Gary Fries, President of the Radio Advertising Bureau, told me,[7] "When I use the marketing approach, I save all the great reasons to advertise on my station and start right off focusing on the client. I spend my time asking clients about *their* industries, *their* specific businesses, *their* competitive advantages and disadvantages."

The effective seller moves from marketing to selling and back again, often in the course of a few minutes. Depending on where you are in the sales process, you might find yourself either in a very customer-focused needs analysis (marketing) or asking for the order (selling). As quickly as you change hats, you must change back again.

In a 1990 study by the American Marketing Association, published as *Marketing 2000 and Beyond*, the change from selling to marketing was apparent:

As to perspectives, more members of the sales force will see themselves not as selling a product or commodity, such as plastic or telephones, but as total problem-solvers. They will be a part of a marketing team assisting customers in solving their problems efficiently and in generating satisfaction. They will be expected to bring additional services and capabilities to customers. They will help customers capitalize on their business or personal opportunities and to readily overcome hurdles and difficulties.[8]

There's a complete outline of the sales process in Chapter 2. You'll discover that product-focused presentations have a

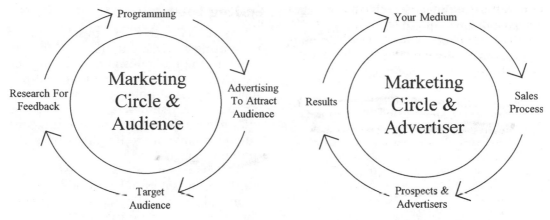

FIGURE 1–2 The lines between selling and marketing are blurred. To me, marketing is a circle that starts with the product, advertises to attract users, then measures feedback from those users to reshape the product. Then again, so is selling. There are two circles here, one for each of our targets: the advertiser and the end user—our viewers and listeners.

valuable place in the sales process, but that customer-focused selling makes the difference.

New Realities

Television is new to the marketing aspect of selling. Sales people in TV often find that their clients have been treated as "targets," not customers. That situation is a holdover from just a few years ago when TV had such a powerful lock on advertising dollars. It wasn't until the mid-1990s that TV caught up to the newspaper in the amount of advertising revenue it controlled. As an industry, television had not focused on customer needs as well as radio and cable both did.

That issue was reflected in a 1993 interview with Robert M. Ward, Director of Advertising Services for the Miller Brewing Company: "It is a real tribute to radio that it has delivered media value and promotion value long before it was perceived by many people as important. You're now seeing the television industry, particularly the networks, with declining HUT [Households Using Television] levels, scrambling for business."[9]

Today's reality for television is an increase of media outlets competing for dollars and a concurrent decline in share. The whole concept of selling television changed to a customer focus out of necessity. "TV is still trying to figure it out," says Diane Sutter, formerly Vice President of Shamrock Broadcasting, and later President and CEO of Shooting Star Broadcasting and owner of KTAB-TV in Abilene, Texas. "They're learning problem-solving for the advertiser and value-added selling, like promotion ideas," she told me.

In other words, marketing. Marketing starts, lives, and ends with your customer. "Marketing is making something happen," says sales trainer Ken Greenwood. Sellers in the marketing environment "have to be comfortable in problem-solving." He calls it "an opportunity-enabling environment" enabling your customer to take advantage of an opportunity to advertise on your medium.

You can see how the line between sales and marketing is very blurred. That's good for us as sellers, because it's good for our customers. When it comes to marketing, what *you* want is unimportant. It's what your customer wants that matters. The customer is at the core of the definition of both marketing and sales.

Peter Drucker's view is that "the customer *is* the business." (My emphasis.) Drucker says in *Managing for Results*:[10]

1. What the people in the business think they know about customer and market is more likely to be wrong than right. There is only one person who really knows: the customer. Only by asking the customer, by watching him, by trying to understand his behavior can one find out who he is, what he does, how he buys, how he uses what he buys, what he expects, what he values, and so on.
2. The customer rarely buys what the business thinks it sells him. One reason for this is, of course, that nobody pays for a "product." What is paid for is satisfactions. But nobody can make or supply satisfactions as such—at best, only the means to attaining them can be sold and delivered.

Drucker breaks down complex concepts into simple ideas: "A good deal of what is called 'marketing' today is at best organized, systematic selling."

Defining Sales

The most succinct definition of the word "sales" for sellers of electronic media comes from Diane Sutter:

Selling is identifying and satisfying customer needs profitably. Profitable for you, profitable for them.

That's the definition I'll use throughout this book because it reflects the customer-orientation of marketing as well as the product-orientation of selling.[11] Sutter told me that this definition is a product of her training and her observation of the evolution of various selling styles. Sutter first heard a similar definition from Steve Marx, President of the Center for Sales Strategy, based in Tampa, Florida. Marx traces the idea to Don Beveridge who became a media sales trainer after years with Mobil Oil. Whatever the origin of the specific words, today's selling is a win/win proposition: a win for the seller, and a win for the customer, too.

Selling Intangibles

I once worked with a bright woman in the accounting department of a radio station who quit the radio business claiming she "couldn't count barrels" in that job. Previously she worked at a paint warehouse. When she needed to know what was sold and what was not, she simply had someone conduct an inventory. In other words, she "counted barrels."

Advertising time was very frustrating to her. There was nothing tangible for her to count when it came time to bill the clients. The announcers who read or played the commercials on the air made check marks on the station's official log, yet nowhere was there an "inventory" from which to deduct the commercials. The idea of intangibility was foreign to an accountant who was trained to think only in concrete terms.

In electronic media, all we sell are intangibles: airtime, impressions, ratings points. Not even adding descriptive terms like "households," "persons using television," "cume audience," or "hits" relieves the intangibility. None of these "products" is as easy to count as barrels. *Intangible*, however, should not be mistaken for *unreal*. In *Selling Radio Direct*, Michael Keith argues that broadcast time sellers "do not sell something immaterial. . . . Quite the reverse, airtime is very real and very concrete." Without airtime for commercials, there would be no response to the advertising message.[12]

You've probably shopped at stores where the owner displays a newspaper or magazine ad in the store window or on a bulletin board. That's the owner's way of showing the tangible value received for an advertising dollar. "To the extent that a . . . commercial cannot be held or taped to a cash register, it is intangible," writes Keith. "However, the results produced by a carefully conceived campaign can be seen in a cash register."

Selling electronic media is different from retail sales or business-to-business selling. Our customer does not walk away from the selling transaction with something to wear, to eat, or to drive. Electronic media can only motivate the customer to purchase the wearable, the edible, or the driveable.

You can measure results from advertising in a variety of ways: the number of new customers, increased image for a product or service, or votes at the polling place. You can be assured also that your customer will measure results in a tangible way.

Fairfax Cone, of the Foote, Cone & Belding ad agency, said, "Advertising is what you do when you can't go see somebody." He said it in the time of the door-to-door salesperson, who presented brushes or cookware to women in their homes. The more difficult it became to knock on doors and make personal calls, the more important advertising became. Newspapers, magazines, radio, and TV then made the sales calls instead.

Electronic media as a whole is a powerful advertising tool because it commands the close attention of its users.

- Television and cable carry product demonstrations directly into the home

and create demand. Video advertising offers compelling and memorable visual images that remain in the viewer's memory. (That's why video is so effective in building brands.)

- Radio creates a bond with its listeners because they can imagine so much about the personalities that they hear but don't see. Radio's ability to target by demographic group and lifestyle means that messages are perceived as direct communication, often in the vernacular of the listener.

- Interactive media and online services engage the consumer in a one-on-one exchange. If used properly, the messages can be specifically targeted to that one individual. Regular Internet surfers know the mesmerizing effect of linking from Web site to Web site, looking for one more piece of information, one more graphic. It's a terrific environment for subject-specific advertising.

As a seller of traditional electronic media— TV, cable, radio—you'll have a unique

---

WHAT'S IN A NAME

For the sake of simplicity, I use the terms "seller," "salesperson," and "salespeople" throughout this book. That's about as generic as you can get. You'll find, however, that no media organization uses those words or phrases on a business card.

Instead, some organizations use the term "Marketing Executive." Others call their salespeople "Account Executives" or "Account Managers" because advertising agencies use those phrases for their client representatives.

The following sampling of real-world titles is designed to be illustrative, not comprehensive:

- NBC's cable and international salespeople are "Account Executives." So are sellers of E! Entertainment Television, CBS Television, CBS's Eye On People, Lifetime, A & E, and The History Channel.
- Turner Sales employs "Sales Planners" to sell advertising on CNN, CNN-SI, Headline

News, and The Airport Network. The same is true for Nickelodeon, Nick At Nite, and TV Land.

- Sellers of The Weather Channel and its sister network, The Travel Channel, are "Account Managers."
- Kaleidoscope (the "Health, Wellness, and Ability" channel that began as a channel for the disabled) uses the phrase "Marketing Manager."
- The CBS radio stations in Houston, Texas, employ "Account Managers," and one seller is designated as the "Senior Account Manager."
- I heard a commercial on our local classical music radio station looking for "Advertising Consultants."
- The Radio Advertising Bureau (RAB) offers a study course for "Certified Radio Marketing Consultants." Radio sales people who successfully complete the course use "CRMC" on their business cards like an academic degree.

advantage: everybody knows what those forms of media do, how they work, and how they deliver an audience. People may not know your specific outlet, but they'll have firsthand knowledge of the medium itself. Your job as a salesperson is to

demonstrate the impact of your medium as an advertising vehicle.

One important fact to keep in mind as you embark on a career as a seller of electronic media: You can't flatly sell anybody anything. You must help them discover that they need it.

The Case for Advertising

I wonder how many people I've sat with in focus groups or in one-on-one research interviews. At some time during each project, the subject turns to advertising. Either I'm measuring the effectiveness of my client's commercials or getting a sense of my client's place in an increasingly cluttered advertising environment.

Despite the number and variety of ads we're exposed to, no one admits to liking commercials. We've done research in markets as large as New York and Los Angeles and as small as West Point, Nebraska, and the response is the same: "Commercials don't influence me." Oh, but they do!

The enormous expenditure by advertisers to attract the attention of those consumers shows just how influential commercials really are. Approached without the face-value questions, most respondents in research projects will report brand awareness, product trial, and product affinity. But if told that their product choices are due to advertising, they'll argue. Immunity to advertising is one of humankind's most comforting self-delusions.

"Half the money I spend on advertising is wasted, and the trouble is I don't know which half," said Lord Leverhulme (later quoted by department store magnate John Wanamaker, who now gets the credit for the phrase).[13] Each man would have been comforted by today's media measurement. They would have seen the cause and effect relationship between advertising and purchase levels.

Advertising is impossible to separate from the economy as a whole, especially the uniquely American economy of abundance. In an economy based on scarcity, total demand is usually equal to or in excess of total supply. Thus every producer sells everything that's produced. When supply outstrips demand—as in the U.S. economic system, for example—advertising fulfills an essential function: moving merchandise from the manufacturer to consumer.

In a 1953 lecture at the University of Chicago,[14] Yale University's David M. Potter explained his views on the role of advertising:

> In a society of abundance, the productive capacity can supply new kinds of goods faster than society in the mass learns to crave these goods or to regard them as necessities. If this new capacity is to be used, the imperative must fall upon consumption, and the society must be adjusted to a new set of drives and values in which consumption is paramount. . . . Clearly it must be educated, and the only institution we have for instilling new needs, for training people to act as consumers, for altering men's values and thus for hastening their adjustment to potential abundance, is advertising.

Advertising existed long before the United States did, yet the United States took an early and commanding lead in using advertising to fuel the nation's economic growth. Popular forms of media have a rich history of subsidy by advertisers who want access to consumers who use that media. An NBC-TV executive expressed it this way: "We deliver eyeballs to advertisers."

What Business Are We In?

If focus on the customer is the basis for sales in electronic media, then Clear Channel's Lowry Mays answered the question "What business are we in?" earlier: "In the customer's business." Yet, as we discussed earlier, it's impossible not to say that you're in television or cable or interactive sales, isn't it?

That brings to mind the famous *Harvard Business Review* article by Theodore Levitt, who taught us that the railroads didn't stop growing because passengers didn't want to travel.[15] The railroads let other means of transportation take their customers away. Railroads perceived themselves to be in the railroad business, not the transportation business.

Some other examples:

- Charles Revson's company sells cosmetics, but Revson claims that he sells "hope" to buyers of his Revlon products.
- A hardware representative once said that his product was quarter-inch drill bits, but all his customers ever wanted were quarter-inch holes.

The core business of electronic media, then, is helping clients achieve their sales and marketing goals. We're in the advertising business, but we should be selling "hope" and "holes."

"Advertising is communication—mass produced, a brain child of our mechanized civilization." That statement is from a 1953 article in the trade publication *Printer's Ink*.[16] It continued in grandiose prose to rhapsodize about new discoveries that contributed to the "betterment of health and home" and about new methods of distribution of goods. The report stated the case for advertising in a defensive tone. I don't know if there had been a specific attack that prompted it or if the journal was answering criticism that has surrounded advertising from the beginning.

Calling advertising "the most economical way of bridging the gap between the man with an idea and the man who can benefit by buying it," *Printer's Ink* listed twenty-four "basic accomplishments of advertising." Here are a few of them:

- Advertising makes possible better merchandise at lower prices.
- Advertising helps cut the cost of distribution.

- Advertising pre-sells known brands.
- Advertising creates markets.
- Advertising speeds the introduction of new products.
- Advertising reaches prospects who won't see a salesman.
- Advertising establishes friendly relations with the public.
- Advertising helps stabilize a business.
- Advertising smokes out new prospects.
- Advertising foots the bill.

The last item, of course, makes the case for advertising in electronic media: Advertising pays the bills, allowing a constant flow of entertainment and information. Every time you sell a minute of airtime, a sponsorship of a Web page, a concert event for TV, or a scrolling announcement on a local cable channel, you're fueling the economy. In 1973, *Variety* reported that by a margin of 5–1, Americans judged television commercials as "a fair price to pay for being able to view the programs."[17]

There are three beneficiaries of the advertising you sell:

1. *Consumers.* Advertising is a terrific information source, saving time and trouble in shopping, comparing brands, and testing results. Brand advertising especially has given the consumer standards for measuring product against product.

2. *Business.* Advertising cuts selling costs and saves time for sales representatives.

3. *The economy.* Advertising sells products, which keeps distribution moving, which stimulates the supply of goods, which keeps workers at their jobs, which provides spending power to respond to advertising.[18]

The Story of Advertising

The earliest advertisements in English are still with us. They're not radio or TV commercials; they're not banners on Web pages. They are people. People named Smith and Goldsmith. People named Wright, Miller, Weaver, and Baker. Their surnames are the occupations of long gone ancestors.[19] Before the rise of England's domestic trade, people were known by their ancestry ("Tom, Dick's son" became known as "Tom Dickson"). Other names were derived from where people lived ("John at the wood" became "John Atwood").

With the increase of trade came the need for identification with the products or services each person could provide. Skills passed from parent to progeny, and so did names. Trade and advertising were born together, and they've remained together.

Well-known historical figures from the colonial period of the United States believed in advertising. George Washington distributed "trade cards" that offered his services as a surveyor. Paul Revere did the same for his silversmith business. Trade cards were oversized business cards that were lavishly illustrated. Professional men and tradesmen handed them to the public to drum up business.

As commerce progressed, advertising expanded to signage. A pub called "The Angel and Harp" created a sign that offered its name using both words and pictures. Customers who could not read knew that seeing a representation of an angel and a harp indicated a place to stop for a pint of ale or a night of rest.

Signage became the principal medium for advertising during the founding years of the United States. "Bill posters" would spread their signs against fences and anchor them with a glue-like whitewash applied with a large broom or brush.

Still considered classics of American advertising are the hyperbolic posters for P. T. Barnum's American Museum. There he displayed oddities like the midget General Tom Thumb, extravagant "Wild West Shows," and true talents like the soprano Jenny Lind. Barnum was an imaginative showman, and his contribution to advertising cannot be denied. It was Barnum who said, "If a man has not the pluck to keep on advertising, all the money he has already spent is lost."

Surprisingly, when newspapers became popular in the late eighteenth and early nineteenth centuries, advertising was considered less than respectable. Termed "puffing," advertising was thought to be the province of patent medicines, elixirs whose pitchmen wove tales of curative powers. There was even a feeling among newspaper and magazine publishers that advertising violated the integrity of their journals. Not even the potential for revenue could temper prejudice against advertising. Merchants themselves needed persuasion not only that advertising was worth spending money on, but also that such open and brazen hawking of wares was not disreputable. Those who chose to advertise fought an uphill battle against publishers who felt that advertising was a sign of commercial distress, the last step before bankruptcy.

Harper's magazine took such a negative attitude towards advertising that it once rejected $18,000.00 (an enormous sum in the 1800s) for a series of ads from a sewing machine manufacturer. *Harper's* chose instead to advertise its own books on that page.

In 1841, a Philadelphian named Volney B. Palmer founded what appears to be the first advertising agency.[20] The field was looked upon with such disdain that Palmer was forced to sell real estate, coal, and firewood to make a living. Palmer described himself as a "newspaper agent" rather than an advertising agent. He made it clear to advertisers that he worked for the publishers, not for them. The advantages of his services were savings of cost and time in trying to contact a variety of publishers. One-stop shopping.

Also in the 1840s, a New Yorker named John L. Hooper was soliciting advertising for Horace Greeley's *New York Tribune*. Often, when Hooper sold an ad in the *Tribune*, his customers asked him to place the same ad in other papers. Hooper was pleased to oblige, but Greeley frowned on the idea of giving away revenues that he thought should be funneled into the *Tribune*. So, Hooper resigned and became an advertising agent.

Although Palmer and Hooper were pioneers, today's major ad agencies trace their heritage not to them but to a Boston company founded by George P. Rowell. Rowell gave up his job as an advertising solicitor for the *Boston Post* in 1865 to begin an organized approach to the disarray of newspa-

SAY IT WITH SLOGANS

Another of advertising's early success stories is an Englishman named Thomas J. Barratt, who in 1865 became a partner in the small firm that manufactured Pear's Soap. At the time, Pear's spent about £80 a year on advertising. Within a decade, Barratt had increased that amount to more than £100,000 a year.

The message was simple: "Pear's Soap." No slogans, no explanations, no benefits, no features. Just repetition of the name in newspapers, magazines, posters, and billboards. Barratt's intention was a conditioned response: the idea of "soap" conjured the brand name "Pear's."

It worked. Pear's became the most widely known commercial product in the world. Later, Pear's added slogans, as did all advertisers in the future.

Early slogans were simple: "The Best," "Guaranteed Invaluable," and "Pleasant to the Taste." They seem primitive by today's standards, yet they were useful mnemonic devices that helped the public remember the product.

The word "slogan" comes from the Gaelic *sluagh-ghairm*, a battle cry. The word that once stood for the fierce yells of warriors carving each other with claymores now stands for "a phrase used in order that the prospect may become favorably disposed toward the article for sale."

By the 1880s, there was a widespread fondness for slogans. It developed to the extent that slogans were the only message communicated in advertisements. Using slogans was an advertising milestone. They added power to the message, but they also added power to the craft. In fact, for the first time, advertising was acknowledged as a craft. It had grown from simple announcements to true sophistication.[21]

per advertising. At the time, newspaper circulation figures were largely unverifiable, rate cards showed what the publishers hoped to get for their ads rather than the value of the space, and commissions could vary from zero to as much as 75% of the rate. Rowell sensed opportunity.

His solution was a package service: he calculated realistic estimates of newspaper circulation and then guaranteed the publishers cash payments. Each idea was a surprise—the former a rude deflation of circulation figures, the latter a welcome relief to papers that struggled for collections. Rowell bought newspaper space at what we would call "wholesale" rates and resold it to advertisers at retail. Publishers were enthusiastic because they were guaranteed payment and because Rowell assumed the risk. In small towns and rural areas, subscription fees had often been paid in eggs, vegetables, or hay, so cash for advertising was very attractive.

Every new idea Rowell had was considered an innovation:

- He became a space wholesaler for small newspapers.
- He began a flat 25% commission structure.
- He announced a policy of working only for the advertiser, not for the newspaper.
- He collected all his data about circulation figures and made it public in *Rowell's American Newspaper Directory*, which first appeared in 1869.
- He founded *Printer's Ink*, a crusading trade magazine for the advertising industry that lasted well into the twentieth century.[22]

Those who came after George Rowell began in earnest to shape American advertising. N. W. Ayer's agency, founded in 1869, grew large enough to buy Rowell's agency in the 1890s. Another agency established in the 1860s, Carlton and Smith, was bought in 1867 and renamed by James Walter Thompson. In order to secure a line of credit, Thompson claimed to have been a commodore and hero in the Union Navy during the Civil War. The story was as hyperbolic as the advertising Thompson would write, but it was based in truth: Thompson's assignment during the war was shoveling coal on a Union steamship.

The advertising agency came into existence because both publishers and advertisers needed help to sort rates, write effective copy, and make deals. In *Advertising in America*, editor Poyntz Tyler gives this perspective on the development of the ad agency: "In a larger sense, the agency's chief service in this early period was to promote the general use of advertising, and thus to aid in discovering cheaper and more effective ways of marketing goods."

Pioneers of Persuasion

The admen who brought the industry into the twentieth century are described by David Ogilvy as the "six giants who invented modern advertising":[23]

Albert Lasker (1880–1952). First an employee, later the owner of 95% of Lord and Thomas in Chicago. The agency became "Foote, Cone, & Belding" when three top employees renamed it a month after Lasker retired.

Stanley Resor (1879–1962). When he became head of J. Walter Thompson, the agency billed $3,000,000. When he retired 45 years later, it was the biggest agency in the world, with billings of $500,000,000.

Raymond Rubicam (1892–1978). He and a co-worker resigned from the N. W. Ayer agency in 1923 to form Young & Rubicam in 1923. Ogilvy claims Young & Rubicam ads have been read by more people than any other agency's ads.

Leo Burnett (1891–1971). Feeling that Chicago was more "real" a town than "mythical" New York, Burnett established the Chicago school of advertising to "talk turkey" to the majority of Americans. By the time of his death, his agency was the biggest in the world outside of that mythical town. His legacy is a list of all-American icons: Tony the Tiger, the Jolly Green Giant, and the Pillsbury Doughboy.

Claude C. Hopkins (1867–1932). From his typewriter at Lord & Thomas, he made many products famous, including Pepso-dent toothpaste, Palmolive soaps, and six different automobiles. He invented sampling by coupon and developed copy research.

Bill Bernbach (1911–1982). Known as "the Picasso of Madison Avenue," his goal was to raise advertising to an art. Bernbach achieved that goal with television commercials that showed monkeys manhandling American Tourister luggage, Volkswagen ads advising "Think Small," and the classic confession from Avis Rent-a-Car: "We're #2. We Try Harder." (Bold added for emphasis.)

David Ogilvy assembled that list, but did not include his own name. Ogilvy was also one of the giants. In *The Image Makers* by William Meyers, he's been described as "a dotty Englishman" who flunked Oxford, sold ovens door to door in Scotland, apprenticed as a chef in Paris, then wandered to America for a wartime post with the British government. He opened a U.S. branch of an English ad agency, then bought the firm and renamed it Ogilvy and Mather.

Treating Ogilvy's story here with just a paragraph or two is counter to the Ogilvy philosophy. He was a fanatic for long text. The more he told, the more he sold, he said. Testament to that philosophy are dense, copy-laden print ads that explained products in minute detail. A mid-1950's layout for Rolls Royce automobiles contained 719 words with a 19-word headline!

He wrote in *Ogilvy on Advertising*: "When I write an advertisement, I don't want you to tell me that you find it 'creative.' I want you to find it so interesting that you *buy the product*."

Brand Identity

Advertising, of course, sells more than just the product. It also sells image—the combined total of the impressions, promises, perceptions, and experiences with a product or service. All those factors weave information about a brand into the consumer's mental storehouse. There are so many factors that contribute to brand image, including what happens when a consumer opens a package or calls a toll-free customer service number.[24]

The Association of National Advertisers (ANA) separates "brand image" from "brand identity." *Brand identity* is a specific combination of visual and verbal elements that help to achieve recognition of the brand and differentiation from other brands. The components of brand identity, according to the ANA, are:

- The name of the brand
- Logos, such as the Nike swoosh symbol or the Coca-Cola lettering
- Symbols, such as Mickey Mouse or Ronald McDonald
- Slogans and messages
- Color, such as the IBM blue
- Package configuration, such as the Campbell's red and white soup can label
- Product configuration, such as the original Coca-Cola bottle

"Of all the things that companies own, brands are far and away the most important and the toughest," said Jim Mullen, whose agency produced brand advertising for BMW, Colgate, and Hewlett-Packard, among others. "Founders die. Factories burn down. Machinery wears out. Inventories get depleted. Technology becomes obsolete. Of your three forms of intellectual property—brands, patents, and copyrights—only one can never expire."

Mullen told *Reputation Management* magazine that his favorite brand is Morton's Salt:

> Morton's Salt has a huge share of the American market, as much as 50% of all salt sold. Moreover, Morton's Salt costs about a nickel more per box than other salt.
>
> In order to understand the dynamics of its brand, Morton's has conducted a fair amount of research. In focus groups, chemists have explained to consumers that salt is the lowest technology product in the world. Salt is salt: one molecule of sodium combined with another of chlorine to make sodium chloride. There is no such thing as premium salt, no designer salt, no salt seconds, just salt.
>
> When this was explained to consumers and then they were asked how many would still buy Morton's, half remained loyal to the brand.

WELCOME TO ANIMAL PLANET
THE ALL ANIMALS, ALL THE TIME TELEVISION CHANNEL.
Animal Planet is the only television channel where you always come face-to-face with the most fascinating creatures on Earth. Extraordinary entertainment from the people who bring you the Discovery Channel.

All animals. All the time.™
www.animal.discovery.com

© 1997 DCI

FIGURE 1–3
They say pictures of animals sell books, but these are here to reinforce branding. Animal Planet is an extension of the Discovery Channel, another well-branded network. Consistent with the Animal Planet theme, the ad slick they sent me was printed on recycled paper. Courtesy Animal Planet. Used with permission.

The focus groups were pushed further. Not only is salt salt, the moderator told them, but Morton actually co-packs about a third of the salt sold under other brand names. When the consumers were queried again about their purchase intentions, the same 50% indicated a preference for Morton's.

Why? Because these people aren't buying salt, they're buying trust.[25]

Branding is as old as the signage on the pub I described earlier or the silversmith's stamp on the back of an ancient goblet. The message in the stamp was that the consumer could rely on the product. Advertising carries as much of the brand message today as the product itself does, and brands are reinforced by their exposure in our commercials.

In American advertising, a brand is considered a business asset. Financial analysts measure pricing of brand name items against the average price of unbranded competitors, and then they multiply by the number of units sold. The result is the billion dollar valuation of brands from products such as vodka, cereal, or chewing gum. For example, Wrigley's Spearmint is one of the most famous brands in America. It has survived virtually unchanged since 1893.

How many other brands have lasted for decades? Quite a few: Campbell's, Coca-Cola, Del Monte, General Electric, Gillette, Goodyear, Kodak, Ivory, and Nabisco. *The Advertiser*, a publication of the ANA, noted that these brands, including Wrigley's, were number one in their fields in 1923 and remained number one well into the 1990s.

The dictionary defines "brand" as "to mark indelibly as proof of ownership." It also means "a sign of quality." Marketer Larry Light, who chairs the Coalition for Brand Equity, adds to the definition: "A brand is a trademark that differentiates a promise associated with a product and identifies the source of that promise."[26]

CBS was the first major broadcaster to brand itself, both on the air and in its corporate communications. Lou Dorfsman, the former CBS Vice President and Creative Director imposed the "CBS eye" logo on everything. A typeface that Dorfsman developed ("CBS Didot") was applied to everything from ads for network TV shows to the type on menus in the CBS dining rooms. Dorfsman even won a fight with the New York City Fire Department over the design of "exit" signs in the CBS building.

Branding for CBS was "unity of design" under Dorfsman's watchful eye. "Watchful" is an understatement: The ANA called Dorfsman the "image czar" because of his vigilance of the CBS brand icons. (If you enjoy graphic arts, please see the beautiful book, *Dorfsman & CBS* by Dick Hess and Marion Muller, a retrospective of Dorfsman's terrific work.)[27]

Branding in those days (the 1950s through the 1980s) did not apply specifically to the programming on any TV network. The network schedules were comprised of a broad variety of shows, known as "horizontal programming." A sitcom would be followed by a music special, then a news program, then a documentary. There was no overall theme to the shows. (In the era of CBS founder William Paley—that network maintained a level of such high quality programming that CBS was called the "Tiffany network.")

FIGURE 1–4   This benign frog face is a radio station brand in more than twenty markets. Sinclair Communications' chairman Kerby Confer originated the K-FROG, BIG FROG, and FROGGY concept. Branding is supported on the air with disc jockey names like "Hopalong Cassidy," "Ann Phibian," and "I. B. Green." This particular logo is from KFRG, San Bernardino, California, and is used with permission.

FIGURE 1–5
The CBS "look" continues as the "eye" logo is applied to CBS cable ventures. TNN (The Nashville Network) and CMT (Country Music Television) are the remaining CBS cable channels in the United States. This ad was created when CBS also owned a controlling interest in the TeleNoticias news network that serves Latin America. Courtesy CBS cable. Used with permission.

Advertising and Electronic Media

Electronic media is traced to the 1830s when Samuel Morse tapped out dots and dashes over telegraph wires. His first "Morse code" message traveled 200 feet. His work opened communications over long distances and tied the growing United States together. In 1875, Alexander Graham Bell accidentally stumbled across the secret of transmitting voice over the same type of wires, giving birth to the telephone.

The man credited as the "father of radio" is Guglielmo Marconi, who transmitted across the Atlantic in 1901. His message—the letter "S" in Morse Code—was sent from a base station in Wales to St. John's, Newfoundland.[28] In its earliest days, radio was used primarily by the military for ship-to-shore communications.

Radio's early literature is full of tales of experimentation, some of it commercially motivated. In 1910, John Wanamaker installed a transmitter in his Philadelphia department store and broadcast a radio show. The first "advertiser" on radio was a record retailer in Wilkinsburgh, Pennsylvania, who provided discs for Dr. Frank Conrad, the Westinghouse engineer who had been experimenting with station 8XK. Dr. Conrad broadcast music supplied by the store during the summer of 1920. By September, the Joseph Horne Company, a Pittsburgh department store, was advertising in the newspaper that receivers for Dr. Conrad's programs could be purchased at their store.[29]

Because of the positive response, Westinghouse officials became so confident of the new idea that they quickly authorized a license application and broadcast that fall's presidential election returns on their newly christened KDKA.

The next year Westinghouse produced the first popular-price home receiver (about $60, not including headsets or speakers) and established radio stations in cities where it had manufacturing plants—East Springfield, MA; Newark, NJ; and Chicago, IL. The stations were broadcasting not to sell advertising, but to sell radio sets.

General Electric, AT & T, and RCA quickly followed suit, selling their own radio sets on their own stations. David Sarnoff, founder of RCA, used the airwaves to sell what he called a "radio music box." In 1922, sales reached $11,000,000. The next year they more than doubled, reaching $22,500,000. By the third year sales were at $50,000,000.

Audience growth was just as steady. The power of the new medium was felt immediately. Radio was blamed for a 30% decline in magazine subscriptions and for a 90% drop in record sales. By the end of 1922, there were more than 200 radio stations broadcasting to over 3,000,000 radio homes. In 1923, radio licenses totalled 600, but no one had determined just how the stations could support themselves.

AT & T's New York station, WEAF, inaugurated a policy of continuous broadcasting with a rate card based on time: ten minutes for $100. In one of the first sponsored programs, 5:15 p.m. on August 28, 1922, there was a discussion of the advantages of apartments developed by the Queensborough Corporation in Jackson Heights, New York. The Radio Advertising Bureau identifies the copy writers as Robert and Albert McDougal, and the sales person as George Blackwell.

WEAF's breakthrough did not cause advertisers to flock to radio. Newspapers, billboards, and handbills remained the favored media. Secretary of Commerce (later President) Herbert Hoover didn't help matters when he predicted "the American people will never stand still for advertising on American radio." Fortunately for electronic media, he was wrong. By the late 1920s, radio became as inexorably linked to the concept of advertising as newspapers had been.[30]

A cigar commercial was the origin of the CBS we know today. There were several attempts at creating a network to compete with the fledgling, but successful, National Broadcasting Company (NBC). The competition NBC liked best was its own combination of Red and Blue Networks, designed to give variety to broadcasting but keep the profits in house.

In 1927, United Independent Broadcasters took a run at NBC, but soon ran out of money. To get an infusion of cash, United sold operating rights to Columbia Phonograph Company, which changed the network's name to "Columbia Phonograph Broadcasting System," hoping to increase publicity for its recordings. Within weeks, Columbia discovered the mistake of its investment and sold the rights back to United.

In stepped William Paley, the 27-year-old son of a Philadelphia cigar maker. Business at Congress Cigar Co. had dropped off because of the rising popularity of cigarettes, and Paley began to advertise "La Palina" cigars on WCAU, the local Philadelphia station. Sales jumped from fewer than 400,000 cigars a day to over a million.

Feeling that radio "was an astounding business," Paley bought a controlling interest in the new network to peddle daddy's cigars. Within two years, he turned a profit with CBS and was in radio for the long run.[31]

Radio became the advertiser's dream as it linked the nation in the 1930s with variety shows, orchestras, comedians, and daily dramas that reflected real-life stories. Those dramas became known as "soap operas," because of the advertising aimed at women who were not in the work force at the time.

Prominent companies begin to reallocate substantial portions of their print advertising budgets for radio because radio advertising worked. Expenditures on radio increased from $20 million in 1928 to $165 million in 1937. The numbers are scant by

SIGNS OF THE TIMES

As new stations took the air, their call signs reflected the names or slogans of other companies who used radio for commercial ends:[32]

WEEI, Boston—Edison Electrical Institute

WGL, Fort Wayne—"World's Greatest Loudspeaker" (Magnavox)

WOW, Omaha—Woodmen of the World (Insurance)

WGN, Chicago—"World's Greatest News-paper" (*The Chicago Tribune*)

WMT, Waterloo, Iowa—*Waterloo Morning Tribune*

WBRE, Wilkes-Barre—Baltimore Radio Exchange

KRLD, Dallas—Radio Labs of Dallas

WLS, Chicago—"World's Largest Store" (Sears)

WLAC, Nashville—Life and Casualty (Insurance)

---

today's standards, but remarkable considering the nation was weathering the Great Depression. A McGraw-Hill book called *Radio As An Advertising Medium* reported that *all* of radio's (network) advertisers in 1936 repeated their buys in 1937. "These former doubters discovered that radio was a very concrete way to market their products," says Michael Keith in *Selling Radio Direct*.[33]

Seeing Is Believing

Advertising as we know it today is steeped in our images of television. The turning point is marked in 1954 when a group of Ted Bates & Company executives met at a Manhattan restaurant to discuss a headache remedy. Rosser Reeves, head of Bates at the time, drew the outline of a man's skull on one of the restaurant's linen napkins. Inside the skull were three boxes. One contained a crackling lightning bolt, another a creaky spring, the third a pounding hammer. In his mind's ear, Reeves heard a cacophony of lightning bolts, coiled springs, and hammering sounds ending with an announcer saying:

"Anacin—for fast, fast, *fast* relief!"

The doodles were animated on film as the first "real" television commercial. Before that time, ads on television were

largely product demonstrations performed live on camera.

William Meyers writes of Reeves in *The Image Makers*: "With his ability to harness the immense power of television, Rosser Reeves transformed advertising almost overnight from low-keyed salesmanship into high-powered persuasion. Known along Madison Avenue as 'the blacksmith,' he believed that commercials should be mind-pulverizing. To be effective, they had to bludgeon people into buying."[34]

Within seven years, Reeves' Anacin commercial had made more money for American Home Products than *Gone With the Wind* had grossed for MGM studios in a quarter of a century. He developed aggressive campaigns for M & M's candies, Viceroy and Kool cigarettes, and Minute Maid orange juice, among others.

Reeves is also credited for the first TV advertising for a presidential candidate. His ads for the 1952 Eisenhower campaign were attacked as "Machiavellian" because they sold the candidate like toothpaste. This concept is so commonplace now that it's hard to believe there was ever such an outcry.

Television changed the way advertising agencies did their work. In the heyday of radio, agencies produced programs and paid for the network time to air them.

FIGURE 1–6   A ventriloquist's dummy in a top hat and tails dominated Sunday nights in America during the late 1930s. This graphic, based on C. E. Hooper radio reports showed more than 80% of the nation's ears were tuned to "The Edgar Bergen and Charlie McCarthy Show."

Because of the shortage of prime time hours on network TV, NBC and CBS retained full control of their programming in TV's formative years. (ABC-TV followed suit, but long after NBC and CBS television networks were established.)

A 1956 issue of *Fortune* magazine called television "a fearful headache" for agencies:

> Ideally, they would like to be in on the production of more shows; they would like to have something to say about which shows get on the air; they would like some firm assurances that shows would be allowed to stay on the air so long as the sponsor was happy with them. They would like, in short, to have as much influence in TV as they did in radio during the great days of that medium in the 1930s.[35]

As it turned out, those early fears were unwarranted because ad agencies quickly learned to work within the structure of the new medium. Rosser Reeves' commercial for Anacin proved that TV was not a headache at all. Television provided a remarkable canvas for advertising's cre-ative people. The power of the medium made commercials extremely effective.

It's surprising to discover that on the earliest TV broadcasts commercials were banned by law. According to rulings issued by the Federal Communications Commission (FCC) in 1936, a television station was for "research and experimentation." They could make an announcement of a sponsor and show the product or the logo, but that was all.

TV broadcasters were not allowed to solicit commercials or to charge additional rates for sponsorships that were re-transmitted (for example on a network). "The generous advertising dollars that have built broadcasting to its present greatness are closed to television at the present writing," lamented *Radio As An Advertising Medium* in 1939.

The radio networks at the time felt television was no threat to them. Lenox Lohr, President of NBC, said "You can't watch television while you are eating, dressing, playing bridge, or doing odd jobs around the house." Founder William Paley of CBS, echoed the sentiment: "It will not, I believe, undermine or replace present broadcasting."

Lohr's remarks seem ludicrous today as television permeates so many of life's activities. Strictly speaking, Paley's remarks were more prophetic, because new media do not displace previous media, they only add to the media mix.

After a hiatus for World War II, television as a commercial entity made a hearty run at radio in the early 1950s, and won the battle for the eye, the mind, and the leisure time of the American people. Since then, radio has been unable to regain the share of national advertising dollars it attracted before the arrival of TV.

Today's Television Environment

In the wake of Hurricane Andrew, which devastated southern Florida in 1992, Sears stores used radio to advertise television antennas as part of the "clean up" after the storm. A Sears executive explained the campaign saying, "Television is so much a part of life that people probably think about it before they get their roof back on."[36]

That's a provocative statement about a pervasive medium. There's no question that American television is a dominant cultural force. As Neil Postman put it, "There is no audience so young that it is barred from television. There is no poverty so abject that it must forgo television. There is no education so exalted that it is not modified by television."[37]

Postman (and so many others) warn us about "amusing ourselves to death" by letting modern media trivialize life, culture, and information. As early as the mid-1970s, there were books and articles arguing for the elimination of television. In the 1960s, FCC commissioner Newton Minnow called the television medium "a vast wasteland."

Media critic Sut Jhally calls television "the dream life of our culture" in a documentary called "The Ad and the Ego." In the same video, critic Jean Kilbourne complains that television ads "tell us who we are and who we should be."

Personally, I like the approach taken by Tony Schwartz. He's not afraid to call electronic media "the second God" in an analogy of how media influences our lives and shapes our beliefs. "Media are all knowing," he writes. "They supply a community of knowledge and feelings, and a common morality."[38]

The reason I like Schwartz is that he makes his living by shaping advertising that effectively uses electronic media. Unlike the critics who complain and offer no solutions, Schwartz feels we all have a responsibility "to use the second god as a social instrument in the hands of society."

Schwartz understands that the most effective commercials "do not tell us what to do or how to react. They present carefully chosen stimuli that evoke certain inner connections and elicit the desired behavior or reaction." Using AT & T commercials as examples, Schwartz says, "The spots did not *direct* people to make long distance calls. They made them *feel* like doing so." He also admits that some commercials "offend us by shouting at us and trying to pressure us into buying."

Despite its proponents, every new medium experiences its share of criticism. In one of the earliest media criticisms, Socrates told the story of King Thamus evaluating the "inventions" of the god Theuth: numbers, calculation, astronomy, and writing. Thamus warns that those who take up writing will "cease to exercise their memory and become forgetful," using "external signs" instead of their own internal resources.[39]

For another example, Gutenberg's invention of the printing press was hailed as a new medium that distributed printed words around the globe. Simultaneously, it was decried for giving each person the power to interpret words without help, thus undermining the authority of both church and state.

Even though advertising has its critics, there is little doubt that it has helped to shape our economy. Television advertising shapes our culture and our world view; it has expanded from largely descriptive product demonstrations on the first flickering black and white screens to the Anacin-type "made for TV" commercials to today's impressionistic and evocative imagery. Tony Schwartz calls the language of video imagery "the new grammar."

Neil Postman complains that "the television commercial is not at all about the character of products to be consumed. It is about the character of the consumers of products. Images of movie stars and famous athletes, of serene lakes and macho fishing trips, of elegant dinners and romantic interludes, of happy families packing their station wagons for a picnic in the country—these tell nothing about the products being sold. But they tell every-

thing about the fears, fancies and dreams of those who might buy them."

Another common complaint about commercials in electronic media is that we are unable to avoid them easily. In the newspaper, we can turn the page or divert our attention to another article or another ad. In radio, TV, and cable, commercials are intrusive. Unless we lower the volume, turn off the set, or zip and zap with the remote button, we cannot skip the commercials. Online advertising borrows from TV with interstitial ads that pop up at the

FIGURE 1–7   The network that claims to be "34% Better Than Real Life," complete with classic TV shows and vintage commercials. "Here in TV Land, we call 'em 'retromercials,'" says the TV Land presentation kit. Used with permission. MTV Networks.

TABLE 1-1 U.S. Advertising Volume

All things considered, the TV networks did well in 1997, especially given basic cable's increased audience. Cable received the benefits— high double digit increases in advertising revenues.

These figures are the most-anticipated numbers of any year. Robert J. Coen, Senior Vice President, Forecasting for McCann-Erickson Worldwide is advertising's official scorekeeper.

Medium Dollars	1996 Millions of Total	% of Dollars	1997 Millions of Total	% of Changes	%
Newspapers	38,402	21.9	41,670	22.2	+ 8.5
Magazines	9,010	5.1	9,821	5.2	+ 9.0
Farm pub.	297	0.2	325	0.2	+ 9.0
Television	42,484	24.3	44,519	23.8	+ 10.5
Radio	12,269	7.0	13,491	7.1	+ 10.0
Yellow Pages	10,849	6.2	11,423	6.1	+ 5.3
Direct mail	34,509	19.7	36,890	19.7	+ 6.9
Business papers	3,808	2.2	4,109	2.2	+ 7.9
Outdoor	1,339	0.7	1,455	0.8	+ 8.7
Miscellaneous	22,263	12.7	23,827	12.7	+ 7.0
National total	103,040	58.8	110,232	58.8	+ 7.0
Local total	72,190	41.2	77,297	41.2	+ 7.1
Grand Total	**175,130**	**100.00**	**187,529**	**100.00**	**+ 7.0**

The McCann-Erickson U.S. advertising volume reports represent all expenditures by U.S. advertisers—national, local, private individuals, etc. The expenditures, by medium, include all commissions as well as the art, mechanical, and production expenses that are part of the advertising budget for each medium.

Source: Robert J. Coen, McCann-Erickson Worldwide. Prepared for *Advertising Age*, May 18, 1998.

end of interactive segments. These ads, too, are virtually impossible to avoid.

However, some people don't want to skip commercials. Nick at Nite's TV Land, for example, promises to "put a sparkle back into television" by running 24 hours of classic TV shows every day. TV Land also runs classic commercials. They call them "retromercials," interrupting original programs like "The Sonny and Cher Show" or "The Ed Sullivan Show" with the Oscar Mayer song or a squeeze of the Charmin roll by Mr. Whipple.

Tony Schwartz says, "A commercial can have extraordinary power when it makes people conclude that it is putting them in touch with a piece of reality." TV Land takes that idea one step further in a mocking way by claiming that their classic programming and commercials are "34% better than real life."

A seller of television, cable, and interactive media must bear in mind that forms of visual media have created their own context. In many cases, the framework of a television program is television itself. That means that the commercial you sell fits into three contexts:

- The need or desire on the part of the consumer
- The context of advertising
- The context of television

Sociologists and critics will add more, I'm sure, but that's not my task in this book. There's no question of the impact of television and visual media. That's why they're so desirable for distributing advertising messages.

Closing Arguments

Advertising has shown itself to be virtually recession-proof. It has consistently outpaced inflation in its percentage of growth year to year. Some of that growth is a result of the growth of individual media. From 1985 to 1990, for example, the explosive rate of television advertising revenues were roughly equal to overall advertising increases.

Mass products can reach mass audiences quickly with broadcast television, while targeted media—radio, cable, magazines, and interactive media—reinforce the message to specific audiences.

Repeating something that we discussed earlier: Advertising creates markets. As you'll see in the next section, there are a lot of venues for advertising in electronic media.

The Electronic Media Environment

You should have seen my office during the preparation for this book! It was the metaphor for the explosion of media options available to consumers. My floor was littered with media kits from national cable networks, TV syndicators, regional news and sports channels, radio stations, TV stations, and TV and radio networks. Some were extremely elaborate:

- The media kit for Nick At Nite had a navy blue cover with flocked faux velvet, stamped with gold caricatures of old-time TV favorites and Nick at Nite's slogan, "Classic TV You Can Trust."
- Nickelodeon's main network sold itself with a green plastic pouch (the color of Nick's slimy "Gak") with what looks like kids' artwork showing through.
- A translucent notebook held E! Entertainment Television's audience research data, showing how an advertiser can mix and match programming to develop theme-based or demographic-based campaigns.
- CNN combined all their services—CNN, The Headline News Network, CNN-fn, CNN-Interactive, and the Airport Chan-

nel—in one presentation "pouch," a bright red cardboard envelope.
- Westwood One radio networks sent a 64-page, magazine-style catalog of all their programs: from CBS, NBC, and Mutual News and Shadow Traffic reports to talk shows like G. Gordon Liddy and "Imus in the Morning" to weekend music specials.
- Superstation WGN introduces the parent company and all its holdings (newspapers, TV and radio stations, *The Farm Journal* magazine, and the Chicago Cubs baseball team), then outlines programming, target demographics, and national reach.
- American Movie Classics (AMC) has an oversized folio with classic movie posters on the front and stills from classic films inside.
- The Houston Astros present prospective advertisers with a pocket-sized kit with details about the Astros Radio Network and signage in the ball park.

Presentations by local radio stations ranged from reams of statistics about audience reach to photographs of live broad-

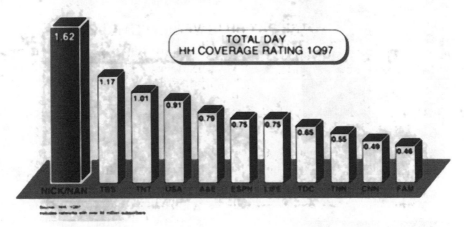

FIGURE 1-8   Too bad you can't get the sense of fun from
the Nickelodeon presentation kit in a green
plastic pouch that says "kids" (without having
to read the graphics that actually say
"Superkids"). Here's Nickelodeon in black
and white, showing their household rating.
Used with permission. MTV Networks.

casts with disc jockeys, mascots, and
wheels of fortune that listeners spin to win
prizes. One small town station spent more
time on its broadcast power than on
whether anyone took advantage of that
power to actually listen.

Next to the big guys, the local radio station packages looked, well, local. I knew at
once that radio sellers could learn a lot
from the collection on my office floor. See
the discussion of selling radio, in Chapter
8, where I'll share those thoughts.

The cable systems and networks are
selling to a national audience, thus they
need the elaborate printing jobs and creative shapes of their presentation pack-

ages. They have to dazzle the national
agencies and national advertisers every
day, and those buyers have seen it all. Most
of them work in New York, although some
are based in Chicago, Los Angeles, Atlanta,
or Dallas—media centers on their own.
With all the competition, it can be difficult
to get their attention.

When Lee Masters was president of E!
Entertainment Television, he called the
national buyers "highly sophisticated and
highly educated. No matter how much
they talk about qualitative (information),
they're concerned about quantitative."
After all, buyers demand proof of strong
ratings. For that reason, sellers at the

ENTERTAINMENT TELEVISION®

FIGURE 1–9
Logos are supposed to make a statement. This one does it with exclamation. So does the network it represents. You'll read about E!'s selling in this chapter and the next. In Chapter 3, you'll read about E! as an example of "signaling" to create a more efficient buy for advertisers. © E! Entertainment Television, Inc.® Used with permission.

national network level must be skilled analysts as well as skilled sales people. Masters called it "using the numbers to think about numbers. Our seller has to know Nielsen, Simmons, MRI. They're selling information and research."

"Ultimately, every buy comes down to demo," Masters said. "Really good sales people want to develop terrific relationships with the buyer, but the buyer takes almost a factory approach." He refers to selling a network like E! as "putting it out to bid."

The New Landscape

The media kits on my office floor told stories beyond the audiences each facility could deliver:

- NBC combined CNBC, MSNBC, and "the big network."
- E!, Court-TV, CNN, CBS, Warner Brothers, and lots of others referred to their interactive divisions. Some offered joint presentations.
- A cluster of Watertown, New York, radio stations plugged their Web sites.
- Cox Interactive Web sites combined news, weather, and local data from a Cox-owned TV and radio station, like *accessAtlanta.com* and WSB Radio and TV.

These are but a few examples of the merging and converging of the electronic media environment.

Every day, there are reminders of how fluid electronic media is as an industry: trade magazines, daily faxes, memos about company performance, sales projections of your medium against competing media. They carry stories of companies emerging from nowhere, ideas taking shape overnight, and mergers changing the competition to cooperative, co-owned properties. You'll read about the radio industry's consolidation, and about the new environment for television as HDTV expands both bandwidth and the number of channels. You'll follow Internet startups sprouting like weeds along the information superhighway.

FIGURE 1–10   A key theme of this book is the merging and converging of media. There's hardly a better example than NBC's extension to cable with CNBC business news and to MSNBC's news coverage on both cable and the Internet. Courtesy of NBC Cable Networks, Ad Sales Department, April 1998. © 1998.

As CEO Diane Sutter of Shooting Star Broadcasting says, "Everybody wants to be in everybody else's business." She's referring to new media being created by combinations of older technologies: content is distributed over the air, by digital broadcast satellite, by cable, by phone lines to cyberspace. Sutter reminds us that "there's never been a new medium that transplanted an old medium. They just added on."

Historically, whatever the next medium was, it added advantages to the last medium. So far, no new medium has eliminated the last medium. Mary Meeker put it this way in *The Internet Advertising Report*, which she wrote for the Wall Street research and investment firm, Morgan Stanley & Co:

Typically, new media have done some key things better than older media. For example, newspapers were better than town criers because the information was recorded; magazines were better than newspaper because they focused on national issues (and had cool pictures); radio was better than magazines because it was live and timely; television was better than radio because it was live, timely, and had cool pictures; and we contend that the Internet is better than television because it provides live, timely, viewable, and often storable information and entertainment when viewers want it, with the powerful addition of interactivity.[40]

Not only are new media additive, but often cooperative. Radio in the 1940s was pleased

What does MSNBC stand for?...

NBC NEWS on Cable
with more information, detail and coverage, 24 hours a day

FIGURE 1–11   Another answer to the question, "What does MSNBC stand for?" is the marriage of Microsoft Network and NBC television. The joint venture gave NBC a new cable channel and a strong Internet presence at *www.msnbc.com*. Courtesy of NBC Cable Networks, Ad Sales Department, April 1998. © 1998.

to recreate Hollywood films and cross-pollinate its stars, just as early television put pictures to the already popular radio comedy and variety shows.

Merging and converging is evident everywhere. Today's TV networks extend their reach with cable and Internet presence. NBC-TV, for example, presented its 1997 World Series post-game analysis not on the major network but on its CNBC cable channel. CBS recycled classic TV programming on its "Eye on People" cable channel. Each of the major networks and most of their key programs maintain Internet sites with interactive polls and promotions. WEB-TV is both a weekly program for over-the-air television and a full Internet domain, supported by Microsoft.

Twenty-First Century Radio

Radio's deregulation in 1996 yielded unprecedented consolidation through mergers of the largest radio companies into market-dominant clusters. Small companies that couldn't compete against the mega-operators were ripe for acquisition.

The trade publication *Radio & Records'* first headline after the passage of the Telecommunications Act of 1996 was "Let the deals begin!"[41] The lead paragraph was prophetic: "Buy, sell, or get out of the way."

Radio Business Report showed 71.4% of radio stations in some consolidated arrangement in the third quarter of 1998, either co-owned with other stations in the market or contracted to a local marketing agreement.[42] The mergers of radio companies and acquisitions of new properties

NBC Leadership

America's #1 News Network

- **NBC News Programs Dominate Network News Ratings**
  - *Today*
  - *NBC Nightly News with Tom Brokaw*
  - *Meet the Press*
  - *Sunrise*
  - *Weekend Today*
- **Dateline NBC: The Most Successful Primetime News Magazine**

FIGURE 1–12   Both CNBC and MSNBC trade on a very recognizable brand—the NBC Peacock—to carry the message of "NBC leadership." Courtesy of NBC Cable Networks, Ad Sales Department, April 1998. © 1998.

was so intense that the daily publication *Inside Radio* added a weekly edition called *Who Owns What* as a scorecard for consolidation.

Radio stocks showed 100% gains in the years immediately following the Telecommunications Act of 1996, while the Standard and Poors 500-stock index increased only 42%.

As *Business Week* noted, the excitement pushed the stock prices of industry leaders like Clear Channel Communications to more than 18 times the estimates of 1998 cash flow.[43] The magazine questioned whether radio could keep its advertising boom alive by grabbing a larger share of Madison Avenue budgets. Radio answered with a resounding "yes!"

Radio's share of the advertising pie was level at about 6% through the television years. In the 1990s, the share crept toward 7% once consolidated radio companies focused their selling power and increased radio's sellable inventory.

"Companies that owned 'A'-level stations bought 'C'-level stations," said Gary Fries, President of the Radio Advertising Bureau (RAB).[44] "That elevated the industry with better programming and better selling." Fries credits consolidation of ownership with allowing failing stations to add new, niche formats—jazz, for example—"to raise the level of good, quality inventory."

Fries admitted that radio's revenue renaissance was a product of timing. "Radio opened new inventory during a strong economy. If it had happened in 1989, we might not see the same results." In his estimate, only 70% of radio inventory is utilized, but he acknowledges that overnights and some periods of weekends prevent the medium from selling 100% of inventory.

Can radio increase its share of the total advertising dollar? "Raising the percentage is policy" at RAB, says Fries. "The mission of RAB is growing the business. Seven percent is nothing more than a milepost.

Radio can see 7% in their minds. When the industry hits 7% overall, we raise the milepost and try for $7\frac{1}{2}$."

Radio revenues from 1997 reached $13.646 billion dollars, $1.2 billion dollars more than the previous year, according to RAB figures. (Note that RAB figures differ slightly from McCann-Erickson's "official" statistics in Table 1–1.)

Born
January 5, 1998

On January 5th, AMFM Radio Networks signed-on as the biggest RADAR network debut in decades.

We are proud to be on-the-air with the great affiliate stations of
Chancellor Media Corporation and Capstar Broadcast Partners.

A New Network For A New Millennium

FIGURE 1–13   The launch of AMFM was one of the largest new network debuts ever. Before AMFM, network radio reached about 65% of the United States AMFM's launch took that number to "the mid-80s," according to Senior Vice President David Kantor. Courtesy Chancellor Media. Used with permission.

Twenty-First Century Television

The Telecommunications Act of 1996 also allowed television companies to expand when the previous limit of 14 stations was eliminated and the coverage cap of 25% of American homes was lifted to 35%. *Broadcasting & Cable* reported that the nation's top 25 TV-station groups owned or controlled 36% of the 1,202 commercial stations on the air in 1997, up from 33% in 1996, and 25% in 1995.[45]

While television broadcasters did not have the ability to own multiple stations in one market, there was a proliferation of local marketing agreements (LMAs), allowing companies to control the advertising sales of one other station. The coverage caps are adjusted for stations under LMA contract and for UHF stations.

"Are the networks showing their age?" was the headline in *Digital Home Entertainment* magazine in its first 1998 issue.[46] An editor's note indicated that the original headline was to have read, "The Death of Network TV," but that the situation was not so clear-cut.

National television networks faced erosion of shares as new media outlets challenged them. In 1987, affiliates of ABC, CBS, and NBC captured 71% of the prime time audience. Cable had but 14%. By the end of the 1996 season, the combined share for ABC, CBS, NBC, and Fox had declined to 61% and cable's total share had grown to 38%.[47]

In the summer of 1997, basic cable achieved a 40 share in prime time against only a 39 share for the traditional "Big Three"—ABC, CBS, and NBC.

The founder of USA Networks, Kay Koplovitz, told the Television Critics Association that year that broadcasters "conceded the summer" to cable, leaving "viewers available for easy pickings." *Cable World* magazine reported that new cable networks added to the cable pie without cannibalizing established services like CNN, ESPN, TNT, or USA.

The decline of network viewing was accelerated by services like DirecTV, PrimeStar, and other suppliers who delivered programming directly to the consumer, bypassing the local station or local cable operator.

Even in the face of declining shares, national TV networks commanded the highest prices ever for thirty-second commercials on leading programs. *Seinfeld* for the 1997–98 season demanded $575,000 per thirty seconds, up 5% from the previous season's unit rate, and advertisers paid the price. *Advertising Age* called the price increase "modest," because "it demonstrates that there are inflationary ceilings to what even the most coveted network inventory can command."

Once comedian Jerry Seinfeld decided to end the production of the program, rates skyrocketed to as high as $2 million per thirty seconds for the farewell episode.[48] Syndication prices for the *Seinfeld* program also increased, with a New York station paying $300,000 per episode in 1998 for programs it could not air until after the year 2001.

Television pondered whether digital delivery would either improve the picture on existing channels at home or split the signal to provide more programming on additional channels. The long-time promise of high definition television (HDTV) had been movie-quality pictures with a movie-shaped screen.

As a financial seminar convened in Los Angeles in August 1997, there was doubt about the way HDTV would finally appear.[49] ABC-TV President Preston Padden suggested to Kagan Seminars' "Digital Television Summit" that his network might offer multiple digital signals, including subscription programming channels, rather than fulfilling the big screen dreams of home theater enthusiasts.

"Padden was saying, 'We might not even need cable,'" said Ron Alridge, Publisher of *Electronic Media*. "The NAB went into cardiac arrest. [NAB President] Eddie Fritts had sold the Senate on the need for HDTV, and the Senate was saying 'Now it's different.'"

Different indeed! Instead of beautiful, clear, almost 3-D pictures with a larger screen configuration, HDTV loomed as a means for broadcast television to get multiple income streams that had been eluding the industry. The term "multicasting" was coined almost immediately to describe the new idea.

Thanks to Padden's new thinking, a new set of questions arose about digital TV:

1. Would the digital stations get "must carry" status for a presence on cable systems the way over-the-air television had?

2. Could stations using multicasting create an all new pay-per-view business?

3. How would digital TV's ability to transmit large amounts of high-speed data affect the design of the next generation of television sets, Internet appliances, and computers?

The first question can't be answered quickly. It took years before the Supreme Court rendered its initial "must carry" ruling that required local cable systems to include all local broadcast TV stations regardless of their audience levels. The high court saved stations owned by Paxson Communications from being excluded from local systems because they carried only infomercials. The guaranteed distribution gave birth to Paxson's PaxTV network.

Question two is a little easier. Sinclair Communications was among the first to announce multicasting on the stations it owned—one channel for free TV and the others available as pay services with "an inexpensive set top box."

At the National Association of Broadcasters convention in Las Vegas in April 1998, CBS and NBC announced that their networks would carry HDTV programming in prime time using "1080i," HDTV's original "interlace" technology.[50]

Fox had already announced plans to experiment with "720p," the technology called "progressive." Speaking for Fox, Andrew Setos of News Corp., Fox's parent company, said "There is only one interlace format. In progressive, there are three resolutions, three frame rates, and two aspect ratios. We like the progressive environment because it allows us to respond differently to each project."[51]

ABC backtracked from Preston Padden's earlier position on full-time multicasting and decided to transmit HDTV in prime time with some multicasting in other dayparts. Padden said the network would "decide later" on just how much programming would be in true HDTV.

In each case, the networks said they wanted the public to have time to compare systems. "The key is the benefit to viewers," Fox's Setos said. "This is part of the creative process—finding out what the viewers want. This will be driven by viewers, not by arbitrary technology matters."

Question three had an answer, too: at 1998's @d:tech Internet trade show, Ann Winblad of Hummer Winblad Venture Partners offered a vision of data broadcasting via the new HDTV spectrum. She predicted personal computers equipped with "rabbit ears" antennas to receive the signals.

"A lot of people have cable TV solely because they can't get clear reception any other way," said Brent Butterworth of CFG Labs in *Home Theater* magazine. "But with digital TV, people who get a marginally watchable picture right now will suddenly get a *perfect* picture."

In an article illustrated with a cute bunny rabbit on top of a TV set, Butterworth reviewed antennas—yes, "rabbit ears"—to get ready for the digital revolution. Rabbit ears are the telescoping rods that can be twisted and turned to a multitude of angles in order to receive television pictures clearly. Most rabbit ears were considered antiques and curios until Direct Satellite Broadcast made them popular again. DBS didn't deliver local over-the-air stations at first, so the rabbit ears antennas were hauled out of attics and basements by consumers who wanted the same choice they had with cable.

Surprise! The best way to receive the all new HDTV signals was by using the same old rabbit ears.

The Next Mass Medium?

Does the proliferation of Internet activity accelerate the decline of network TV shares? Internet "early adopters" apparently abandoned TV for online experience, according to a 1997 study by BJK & E Media Group. That led the news media to report that, yes, online activity affected TV viewing. Looking deeper into the numbers, BJK & E found that leaving TV had more to do with the early adopter's lifestyle, which didn't include much TV in the first place.[52]

MediaCentral, the online address of Cowles Publications,[53] cited a proprietary study by J. Walter Thompson advertising: even if early adopters had cut back dramatically on their TV viewing, it still would have had negligible impact on TV usage levels overall. Then Nielsen reviewed its people meter panel from October 1997 and found that, yes, there was a decline in TV usage in Internet households during certain times of day.

Nielsen's "PC Ownership Study" was based on the Nielsen Television Index (NTI) database of 5,000 metered households. From 10:00 a.m. to 4:30 p.m., Internet households in Nielsen's sample watched 25% less television than the total TV universe. Prime time showed less impact with only 4% less TV. Other key dayparts experienced erosion as well: mornings (7:00 a.m. to 10:00 a.m.) and afternoons (4:30 p.m. to 6:00 p.m.) were down 17% in Internet-wired homes.

ABC, Fox, NBC, and WB had higher ratings in Internet households than in the total TV universe. Writing for the online magazine *Ad Talk* at *www.adtalk.com* Richard Morgan suggested that those networks used "their Internet savvy to stave off erosion by aggressively cross-promoting their on-air and online synergies."

About 50% of U.S. companies had their own Web sites at the end of 1997, according to MediaCentral. Of those with Web presence, 66% used them for advertising, marketing, and public relations functions. And it goes beyond the big national advertisers. When Frank, the Exxon dealer across from my office, invited me to log onto his Web site, he underscored how online media has insinuated itself into the culture.

Adding to the blur, traditional media established its presence on the World Wide Web. NBC added *msnbc.com* and cross-promoted from the main network. Newspapers added online editions. Radio and

TV stations, movie studios, the music industry, and virtually every national and regional TV show maintained a Web site.

Internet-based advertising began at a very low base, but grew exponentially from the start. Morgan Stanley's *Internet Advertising Report* predicted that the Internet could be "the next mass medium." The *Report* showed that the benefits of obtaining information and entertainment via the Internet are "too compelling" when compared to traditional media: "Advertisers will find it tough to resist the opportunity to nab new eyeballs."[54]

The key difference in Internet delivery of content against traditional media is that receivers are already in place. Earlier in this chapter, we read that retailers had to sell radios in order to get an audience for their broadcasts. With the Internet, the infrastructure already exists. The estimated 165 million personal computers worldwide await only a modem and a connection to the World Wide Web.

The Internet showed the most rapid consumer adoption among electronic media. Radio took 38 years to reach 50 million users, according to Morgan Stanley. Tracking TV from 1950, it took 13 years to hit the 50 million mark. National cable took 10 years (tracked from the launch of HBO). The Internet? Morgan Stanley estimated five years.

The Internet Advertising Report added: "When adoption of a new medium has been faster, the flow of advertising revenues has increased more quickly." In 1995, Internet-based ad dollars were $55 million. That jumped to $300 million in one year. Other Internet dollars show similar exponential growth. Netscape in 1994 supported $14 million per quarter. By fourth quarter 1996, that number had jumped to $115 million. "So, things move quickly in the Internet world," the *Report* understated.

The U.S. Department of Commerce reported in April 1998 that traffic on the Internet was doubling every one hundred days.[55] At that time, there were an estimated 100 million people online. The Commerce Department report said that the digital economy was growing at double the rate of the overall national economy and

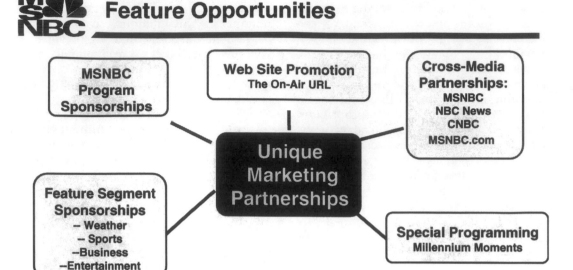

FIGURE 1-14   Analysts reviewing Nielsen data from the fall of 1997 said that NBC's extension to MSNBC helped the main network retain viewers in Internet households. NBC cable sellers offered other opportunities to tap the NBC branding. Courtesy of NBC Cable Networks, Ad Sales Department, April 1998. © 1998.

represented more than 8% of gross domestic product. (Compare that to 3.1% represented by the auto industry.)

Newspaper and Print

Don't let the growth of new media distract you from a key fact: print ads still command huge shares of the national advertising dollar. It was not until 1995 that television surpassed print's share of revenues, according to figures from the Television Bureau of Advertising (TVB).

Newspapers have the advantage of being a visual medium with direct impact when the consumer is ready to shop. Food prices, real estate listings, new car sections, and want-ads are typical examples of the power of newspaper advertising.

However, newspaper circulation is on the decline; in most markets, circulation is less than 50% of households. During the 1990s, however, the cost of newspaper advertising remained the same or in-

creased, protecting the newspaper's share of the pie. If there's an objection to newspaper advertising other than price, it's the medium's inability to target efficiently. There's no question, however, that newspaper remains a formidable competitor for advertising dollars.

The magazine industry shares the newspaper publishers' concerns about maintaining readership. People are not reading as much as they did in previous years. Reaching 18–34 year olds is especially difficult with print, even print targeted to those age groups.

On the positive side, 94% of adults say they read one or more magazines and spend about 5% of their time with the medium, according to a Simmons study.[56]

In contrast to newspapers, magazines are highly targetable. There are thousands of specialty magazines that allow advertisers to target demographically, by product affinity, or by lifestyle. How narrow? Think first of all the magazines you read or scan personally, then imagine the wall of publications at your neighborhood bookseller. There are more than 11,000 possibilities:

- *Razor's Edge* (for devotees of bald women)
- *Southeast Dragster* (for regional racing fans)
- *Audubon* (for nature enthusiasts)
- *Masthead* (for Canadian magazine publishers)
- *New York Teacher* (explanation unnecessary)
- *Lightwave* (a fiber-optics journal)
- *Tattoo* (dermagraphics meets demographics)
- *Double Bass* (for stand-up musicians)

You get the idea. There's real targetability.

Both newspapers and magazines promote the benefits of strong visuals, portability, and enough space to allow an expanded story to be told. Magazines can execute remarkable visual displays thanks to modern printing procedures. Newspapers are not so lucky: the coarseness of newsprint limits the aesthetic appeal of newspaper displays.

How can you as a seller of electronic media sell against the newspaper? There's ammunition for you at Appendix A.

Product Life Cycles

Each medium is a product. Like a product, each medium has a life cycle that can be measured in defined stages:

Introduction
Growth
Maturity
Saturation
Decline[57]

How can we tell, to use Peter Drucker's words, "when tomorrow's breadwinner turns into today's breadwinner and goes on to become yesterday's breadwinner?" Drucker's answer is to examine the cost of

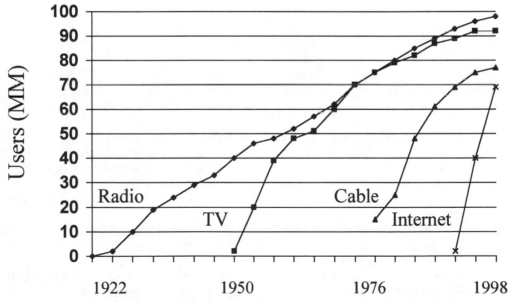

FIGURE 1–15 On a graph of adoption curves, the line representing the Internet hardly curves at all. Radio took 38 years to reach 50 million users, TV about 13, national cable 10. Morgan Stanley's *Internet Advertising Report* predicted five years for the Internet.

NEWSPAPER PERFORMANCE REPORT
CIRCULATION, PENETRATION, REACH AND FREQUENCY ANALYZER
9/2/97

Newspaper(s):   THE DALLAS MORNING NEWS (Morning)   Market: Dallas-Ft.Worth, TX

Metro Population (Adults 18+)	Metro Households	NDM+RTZ Circulation	Market Penetration	% of Market Not Reached	Readers per Copy	Average Daily Readers
3,243,600	1,772,671	421,344	24%	76%	2.195	924,850

TRENDING DATA

YEAR		METRO HOUSEHOLDS		GROSS CIRCULATION		ADVERTISING COST	
		NUMBER	% CHANGE	NUMBER	% CHANGE	SAU RATE	% CHANGE
1992	Base Yr.	1,605,500	0.0%	454,232	0.0%	$ 192.79	0.0%
1993		1,640,500	2.2%	504,313	11.0%	$ 213.03	10.5%
1994		1,651,400	2.9%	513,854	13.1%	$ 233.80	21.3%
1995		1,677,500	4.5%	515,571	13.5%	$ 280.33	45.4%
1996		1,723,400	7.3%	494,226	8.8%	$ 305.56	58.5%
1997	Estimate	1,772,671	10.4%	489,338	7.7%	$ 326.95	69.6%

NOTES:

NEWSPAPER REACH

	1st Day	2nd Day*	3rd Day*	4th Day*	5th Day*
Number of Persons Reached by Newspaper	924,850	1,072,826	1,146,814	1,202,305	1,230,051
Newspaper's Reach Rating (% of Population)	28.5	33.1	35.4	37.1	37.9
Frequency	1	1.7	2.4	3.1	3.8

FIGURE 1–16   Even more graphic than the decline in national circulation of newspapers is this analysis of the trends for the *Dallas Morning News*. Dallas area households increased by 10.4%, circulation dropped by 7.7%, and rates went up 69.6%! I've prepared more information to help you sell against newspapers at Appendix A. This information was prepared by the Radio Advertising Bureau and used with permission.

further increments of growth against results.[58]

At its introduction a product requires many more resources than it can hope to return. Development and testing must be paid for, so must advertising to announce the product to potential consumers. However, once the product reaches "Growth," each new dollar invested produces many dollars in return.

It's at the point of "maturity" (shown in Figure 1–17) that trouble begins. "When the product reaches maturity and becomes today's breadwinner," Drucker writes, "the incremental acquisition to be gained by additional input goes down sharply; where the cost of incremental acquisition reaches or exceeds the additional revenue that can be acquired, a product becomes yesterday's breadwinner." In other words, the market for the product is at "saturation," and "decline" is imminent.

It's not easy to spot the changes in the cycle. Some products have cycles that last only a short while. Fads, like the "pet rocks" of the 1980s come and go quickly. Other products are designed for long life but are preempted by innovation. Look at Windows 3.0 as an example. It was the personal computer standard until something newer came along.

Other products last for ages. Peter Drucker uses the example of aspirin as a product that has lasted for almost a century even in the highly innovative, constantly changing field of over-the-counter pharmaceuticals. Coca Cola, Campbell's soup, Eastman Kodak, and Goodyear are among a list of brands that have stood the test of time, ranking number one in their categories in 1923 and again in 1993, according to the ANA. An important point: every product and every mass medium was at "Growth" at one time or another.

Tom Peters and Robert Waterman pick up the product life cycle discussion in *In Search of Excellence*:

> After experiencing continued growth for a while, managers in the industry come to believe that continuing growth is assured. They persuade themselves that there is no competitive substitute for their product, and develop too much faith in the benefits of mass production and the inevitable steady cost reduction that results as output

rises. Managements become preoccupied with products that lend themselves to carefully controlled improvement and the benefits of manufacturing cost reduction. All of these forces combine to produce an inevitable stagnation or decline.[59]

Peter Drucker uses the example of mass circulation magazines in the Unites States in the 1950s. The signal of trouble, he says, was a "sharp rise in the cost of incremental acquisition of new subscriptions. To raise their circulation further, magazines suddenly had to spend more than they got back in additional subscription fees."

Each electronic medium can be viewed in terms of its place in its life cycle:

- *Radio*: The oldest electronic medium, it has reinvented itself several times. First, radio was disrupted by the introduction of television; but it survived the challenge by stretching individual music programs into 24-hour formats.

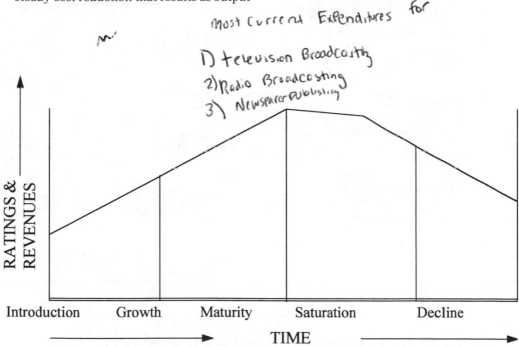

FIGURE 1–17   The product life cycle comes clear in this graphic by Shane Media's Jon Lutes. Each electronic medium has a place in the cycle. Radio and TV are mature. Cable is still growing. New media are at the introduction and growth stages.

MEDIA HABITS
Total Persons

Average Weekday Share of Time Spent with Each Medium

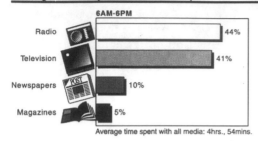

6AM-6PM

Radio	44%
Television	41%
Newspapers	10%
Magazines	5%

Average time spent with all media: 4hrs., 54mins.

6AM-Mid

Radio	33%
Television	54%
Newspapers	8%
Magazines	5%

Average time spent with all media: 7hrs., 45mins.

Competitive Weekly Reach
(percent exposed to medium)

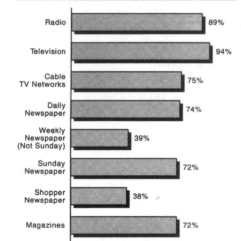

Radio	89%
Television	94%
Cable TV Networks	75%
Daily Newspaper	74%
Weekly Newspaper (Not Sunday)	39%
Sunday Newspaper	72%
Shopper Newspaper	38%
Magazines	72%
Outdoor	62%

Media Exposure Prior to Purchasing

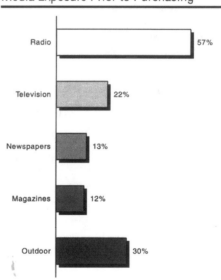

Radio	57%
Television	22%
Newspapers	13%
Magazines	12%
Outdoor	30%

Percent of Shoppers Reached by Medium Within 1 Hour of Largest Purchase
(Respondents reporting any purchase within 24 hours prior to contact)

1-B

Media Targeting 2000 — conducted by The Arbitron Company in cooperation with the Radio Advertising Bureau

Total Persons Media Habits

FIGURE 1–18   Overall, television commands the most time from American consumers, although radio claims a lead in the daylight hours. This analysis of media habits shows the reach of key media. It's from *Media Targeting 2000*, conducted by the Arbitron Company in cooperation with the Radio Advertising Bureau. Used with permission from each organization.

TABLE 1–2 Cable, New Media Lead Pack
Combined communications industry media gross expenditures
(in billions) and compound annual growth rate.

Industry	1996 Spending	Projected Growth Rate (Thru 2001)	Projected 2001 Spending
Television broadcasting	$34.4	5.0%	$44.0
Radio broadcasting	$12.3	9.1%	$19.0
Subscription video services	$34.3	10.1%	$55.5
Subscription video adv.	$6.8	17.1%	$14.9
Filmed entertainment	$32.3	7.0%	$45.4
Recorded music	$12.5	5.6%	$16.5
Newspaper publishing	$53.2	6.3%	$72.3
Daily papers–adv. rev.	$38.2	7.1%	$53.8
Consumer book pub.	$16.3	5.5%	$21.2
Consumer magazine pub.	$16.2	6.0%	$21.6
Consumer mag. adv.	$9.0	7.9%	$13.2
Business mag. adv.	$6.5	8.2%	$9.7
Interactive digital media (all)	$8.5	17.3%	$18.8
Cons. online/internet serv.	$4.2	24.6%	$12.7
Total spending	**$290.7**	**7.6%**	**$419.6**

Source: Veronis, Suhler & Associates, reported in *Advertising Age* July 28, 1997.

- Cable networks like CNN and MTV borrowed radio's strong, cohesive positioning by using 24-hour vertical programming, just like radio's individual music formats. Radio adapted with new niche formats like soft AC, Jazz, and a variety of permutations of rock.
- Nonetheless, radio is a very mature product, at the point of saturation. It shows maximum penetration.
- *Television*: Increased competition prompted the medium to re-tool its programming into demographic niches, still broader than radio's tight focus. TV's broad-based, "all things to all people" approach could not compete with narrowly drawn cable channels.

- Like radio, TV is a very mature industry, at the point of saturation.
- *Cable*: Newer on the scene and still growing. Figures from 1998 showed sustained growth of cable shares against the traditional TV networks, and advertising revenues for cable were also on the rise.
- Cable penetration still has room for growth, although it's not expected to reach 100% like radio and TV.
- A subset of options under cable is what the TVB calls "alternate delivery system television households": Satellite Master Antenna Systems, Microwave distribution, and Direct Broadcast Satellite (DBS) dishes.
- *New media*: The newest of the electronic media is interactive, online, and mul-

timedia—"new media" as I'm calling them in this book since a specific name hasn't emerged in the convergence of resources that is creating the new landscape.

- New media are at the position of introduction and growth. That growth in terms of advertising revenue is exponential. The remarkable flexibility of new media may mean that reaching the point of maturity is a long way off.

Mature media like broadcast TV and radio are expected to grow in advertising revenues regardless of eroding audiences. There's no hint that advertising will not continue at a robust pace. A 1997 forecast by Veronis, Suhler & Associates projecting the communications business through 2001 expected the industry's growth rate to outpace that of the U.S. gross domestic product.

Combined, the communications industries should grow 7.6%, reaching $419.6 billion. Television shows the smallest percentage of projected growth, consumer online services the largest. (See Table 1–2.)

Review Highlights and Discussion Points

1. If you have human interaction of any kind, you will sell something every day.
2. The answer to "What is selling?" is "Everything is selling."
3. Lowry Mays talks about media as conduits from the advertiser to the viewer or listener, while Zig Ziglar calls selling "a transference of feeling."
4. The process of selling guides behavior in a desired direction, culminating in the purchase.
5. The last thing a prospect wants to be is a prospect. That makes the prospect sound like a "target," not a person.
6. The best sales people make selling an art. Marketing is also an art. However, there is a difference between sales and marketing.
7. The effective seller moves from marketing to selling and back again, often in the course of a few minutes.
8. Product-focused presentations have a valuable place in the sales process, but *customer*-focused selling makes the difference.
9. Sales people in television often find their clients have been treated as "targets," not as customers.
10. As an industry, television had not focused on customer needs as well as radio and cable had.
11. Today's reality for television is an increase of media outlets competing

for dollars and a concurrent decline in share.
12. According to Peter Drucker, "the customer *is* the business."
13. Broadcast executive Diane Sutter states a major premise of this book: "Selling is identifying and satisfying customer needs. Profitable for you, profitable for them."
14. Michael Keith writes that broadcast time sellers "do not sell something immaterial. . . . Quite the reverse, airtime is very real and very concrete."
15. Electronic media are powerful advertising tools because they command such close attention by their users.
16. The job of the sales person is to determine the impact of a medium as an advertising vehicle.
17. Despite what some people might think, commercials are very influential.
18. Advertising is impossible to separate from the economy as a whole, especially the uniquely American economy of abundance.
19. The core business of electronic media is helping clients achieve sales and marketing goals. We are in the advertising business, but we should be selling "hope" and "holes."
20. *Printer's Ink* listed 24 "basic accomplishments of advertising."
21. There are three beneficiaries of the advertising you sell: consumers, business, and the economy.

22. The earliest advertisements in English are still with us. They are not radio and TV commercials; they are not Web pages. They are people's names.

23. Signage was the principal medium for advertising during the founding years of the United States.

24. In 1841, a Philadelphian, Volney B. Palmer, founded what appears to be the first advertising agency.

25. Most of today's major ad agencies trace their heritage to a Boston company founded by George P. Rowell.

26. The N. W. Ayer and J. Walter Thompson ad agencies emerged in the late 1800s.

27. David Ogilvy names Albert Lasker, Stanley Resor, Raymond Rubicam, Leo Burnett, Claude C. Hopkins, and Bill Bernbach as the "six giants who invented modern advertising."

28. Advertising sells image—the combined total of the impressions, promises, perceptions, and experiences with a product or service.

29. Branding is as old as the sign on the pub described in advertising's history or the silversmith's stamp on the back of an ancient goblet.

30. In American advertising, a brand is considered a business asset. Financial analysts measure pricing of brand name items against the average price of unbranded competitors, then multiply by the number of units sold.

31. Electronic media's ancestral chart includes, among many others, the names of Samuel Morse, Alexander Graham Bell, Guglielmo Marconi, Frank Conrad, and David Sarnoff.

32. In 1922, WEAF inaugurated a policy of continuing broadcasting with a rate-card based on time.

33. That same year, there were more than 200 radio stations on the air.

34. Initially, Herbert Hoover, Secretary of Commerce, objected to advertising on American radio.

35. By 1928, two national radio networks had made their debuts: NBC (red and blue) and CBS.

36. Advertising as we know it today is steeped in our images of television.

37. Rosser Reeves transformed advertising almost overnight from low-keyed salesmanship to high-powered persuasion.

38. Television changed the way advertising agencies did their work.

39. Commercials in the earliest TV broadcasts were banned by the FCC.

40. Television supplants radio as the top home entertainment medium after World War II.

41. Critic Jean Kilbourne complains that television ads "tell us who we are and who we should be," while astute media observer Tony Schwartz calls the electronic media "the second God."

42. Neil Postman laments that "the television commercial is not at all about the character of products to be consumed. It is about the character of the consumers of products."

43. Advertising has shown itself to be virtually recession proof.

44. Lee Masters, former President of E! Entertainment, called national buyers "highly sophisticated and highly educated" and very *quantitative* in their orientation.

45. The current electronic media environment is best characterized as "merging and converging."

46. Television and radio will continue as "hot" media buys into the twenty-first century, while the audiences for network broadcasts will likely continue to decrease in a climate of hyper-niching and fragmentation.

47. Digital technology will play a more central role in broadcast signaling, although its applications will continue to be a subject of much discussion and debate.

48. The news media report that Internet activity impacts TV viewing, while online advertising is on the upswing.

Chapter Notes

[1] Charles Futrell was quoted in "Careers in Sales: High motivation, energy mean success in sales career" by Alice Adams, *Houston Chronicle*, November 3, 1996.

[2] "Selling tamales" is a metaphor Lowry Mays uses regularly to keep his sellers customer-focused. He was interviewed by *Radio Ink*, August 19–September 1, 1996.

[3] Zig Ziglar's book, *Secrets of Closing Sales*, was reprinted in a collection called *Reaching the Top*. New York: Galahad Books, 1997.

[4] Charles Warner and Joseph Buchman paved the way for sellers of electronic media with *Broadcast and Cable Selling*. 2nd ed. Belmont, CA: Wadsworth, 1993.

[5] Tom Hopkins teaches you how to become a "Champion" in *How to Master the Art of Selling*. New York: Warner Books, 1982.

[6] Mark H. McCormack's *On Selling* is a collection of his experiences at selling and being sold. West Hollywood, CA: Dove Books, 1996.

[7] Gary Fries interview with Ed Shane, September 18, 1997.

[8] William Lazer, Priscilla La Barbera, James M. MacLachlan, and Allen E. Smith were considered "futurists" when they published *Marketing 2000 and Beyond*. Chicago: The American Marketing Association, 1990.

[9] Robert M. Ward of Miller Brewing was interviewed by *Radio Ink* magazine for their feature "Advertiser Q and A," May 19, 1993.

[10] Peter Drucker's customer focus was never more apparent than in *Managing for Results*. New York: Harper and Row, 1964.

[11] Diane Sutter of Shooting Star Broadcasting defined sales for me in an interview on June 20, 1997. She credited Steve Marx , President of the Center for Sales Strategy in Tampa, Florida, and former Mobil Oil executive Don Beveridge for shaping her definition of selling.

[12] Michael Keith's *Selling Radio Direct* is a quick refresher course. Boston: Focal Press, 1992.

[13] The line about 50% of advertising being wasted is usually attributed to John Wanamaker. David Ogilvy set us straight in *Confessions of an Advertising Man*, New York: Dell, 1963.

[14] David M. Potter's speech, "Advertising: The Institution of Abundance" was originally printed in the *Yale Review*, Autumn 1953, then collected in the book, *Advertising in America*, edited by Poyntz Tyler. New York: The H. W. Wilson Co., 1959.

[15] Who hasn't quoted Theodore Levitt's "Marketing Myopia" from the *Harvard Business Review*, July–August, 1960?

[16] The case for advertising is made in "What Advertising Is . . . What It Has Done . . . What It Can Do" from *Printer's Ink*, May 15, 1953, and part of Poyntz Tyler's *Advertising in America*, cited earlier.

[17] *Variety* was quoted in *The Advertising Age History of Television*, Spring 1995. Available online at *www.adage.com*. Click on "Features."

[18] The beneficiaries of advertising were named in "Advertising: Its Contribution to the American Way of Life," by Bruce Barton in *Reader's Digest*, April 1955, and reprinted in *Advertising in America*.

[19] Surnames as advertising is from editor Poyntz Tyler's preface to *Advertising in America*.

[20] An excerpt from Ralph M. Hower's *The History of an Advertising Agency* (Cambridge, MA: Harvard University Press, 1949) was also printed in *Advertising in America*.

[21] More history, including more of the Pear's Soap story, can be found in Frank Rowsome, Jr.'s *They Laughed When I Sat Down*, New York: Bonanza Books, 1959.

[22] William Meyers adds historical insight in *The Image Makers*, New York: Times Books, 1984.

23 The "giants," as listed by David Ogilvy in *Ogilvy on Advertising*, New York: Crown, 1983.

24 The discussion on branding comes from "Brand Identity: Maximizing a Key Asset in a Changing Business Environment" by Anita K. Hersh and John Lister in *The Advertiser*, Spring 1993. That's the magazine of the Association of National Advertisers.

25 I like the Morton's Salt story. It's from "Reinventing Advertising," *Reputation Management*, March–April, 1995.

26 Larry Light's definition of "branding" appeared in *Direct Marketing* magazine, March 1997.

27 I referenced *Dorfsman & CBS* by Dick Hess and Marion Muller, New York: American Showcase, Inc., 1987. That book and *Ogilvy on Advertising* should be part of every seller's media library.

28 Marconi's letter "S" in Morse Code was cited by the Radio Advertising Bureau in its study course, *Welcome to Radio Sales*.

29 There are plenty of historical texts about the early days of radio and television. A fine story of radio's origins is Tom Lewis' *The Empire of the Air*. New York: Harper Collins, 1991.

30 Michael Keith presents an overview of radio's beginnings in *The Radio Station*, 4th ed., Newton, MA: Focal Press, 1997.

31 The roots of CBS are from Ben Gross's *I Looked and I Listened*, New Rochelle, NY: Arlington House, 1954, and from Moguls: *Inside the Business of Show Business*, by Michael Pye. New York: Holt, Rinehart and Winston, 1980.

32 The call letters and their commercial origins are from *Broadcasting*, August 6, 1984.

33 Figures for network advertising revenues are from Warren B. Dygert's *Radio As An Advertising Medium*, New York: McGraw-Hill, 1939, and Michael Keith's *Selling Radio Direct*, cited previously.

34 Rosser Reeves's commercial for Anacin is clear in my mind's eye, but clearer thanks to William Meyers' *The Image Makers*, cited previously.

35 The "fearful headache" was described by Daniel Seligman in "The Amazing Advertising Business," *Fortune*, September 1956, reprinted in *Advertising in America*.

36 The Sears executive was Ralph Hoch, National Manager, Advertising and Visual Marketing, quoted in "Shopping America for Sears Media Buys," *Radio Ink*, November 16, 1992.

37 Neil Postman's *Amusing Ourselves to Death*, New York: Penguin Books, 1985, will help you maintain perspective.

38 I've always wanted to be Tony Schwartz, but the job is taken. His *Media: The Second God* (the "g" is lower case in the book) is a must-read. New York: Random House, 1981.

39 King Thamus evaluating Theuth's inventions was quoted in Postman's *Technopoly: The Surrender of Culture to Technology*. New York: Vintage Books, 1992. If you really want to dig deep, see Plato's *Phaedrus*. If Plato doesn't put things in context for you, try George W. S. Trow, *Within the Context of No Context*. New York: Atlantic Monthly Press, 1997. He's the source of the contextual references for commercials.

40 The problem with the Internet is that once you write something, it's quickly out of date. Not so with *The Internet Advertising Report*, written for the investment house Morgan Stanley by Mary Meeker. New York: Harper Business, 1997.

41 *Radio and Records'* headline appeared February 16, 1996.

42 The consolidation figures appeared in *Radio Business Report*, October 12, 1998.

43 "Radio stocks can't play this tune forever" was Robert Barker's article in *Business Week*, September 8, 1997.

44 Gary Fries' comments are from an interview, September 18, 1997, when we were both at the National Association of Broadcasters' annual Radio Show.

45 The "Top 25" statistics for television ownership are tracked by *Broadcasting and Cable* magazine. The figures cited are from "Television's Revamped Leadership," April 6, 1998.

46 "Are the Networks Showing Their Age?" The answer was "Yes, but . . ." in Rob Sabin's article in *Digital Home Entertainment* magazine, January/February 1998.

47 The year 1997 was truly a breakthrough for national cable networks with their big summertime shares against the traditional TV networks. The report was in *Cable World*, July 28, 1997, by Will Workman. Healthy shares for cable continued through 1998, according to the Cabletelevision Advertising Bureau (CAB).

48 The costs for Seinfeld were in every newspaper in the nation by the time the finale actually aired. Early references were in *Advertising Age*, February 23, 1997, and January 5, 1998, long before Jerry Seinfeld even decided to end the program.

49 Ron Alridge of *Electronic Media* covered the Kagan Seminar and offered me details of that and so much of the new media landscape in an interview on November 18, 1997.

50 Which network chose what digital transmission standard was covered in a special edition of *Broadcasting & Cable* produced for the National Association of Broadcasters convention, April 8, 1998.

51 Fox's Andrew Setos was quoted in *Television Digest*, April 6, 1998.

52 Richard Morgan's "The Buzz" appears in the online magazine *AdTalk* at *www.adtalk.com/buzz.htm* and usually has information like the BJK & E study before anybody else. The posting wasn't dated, but I downloaded the information on November 12, 1997.

53 Cowles publications maintains a Web site, < *www.mediacentral.com* >, for excerpts from their magazines, including *Cable World, American Demographics*, and other business publications.

54 *The Internet Advertising Report* was cited previously.

55 "Net use doubling every 100 days" is a remarkable statistic. That was the headline in *USA Today* on April 16, 1998, when the Commerce Department report was released.

56 Figures on adults reading magazines are from the Radio Advertising Bureau.

57 There are many renditions of product life cycle charts. This one is adapted from one used by Burns Media Consultants in their media seminars in the early 80s when I was one of their seminar leaders.

58 For more on products and their properties, see Peter Drucker's *Managing for Results*, cited earlier. Chapter 4, "How Are We Doing?" is especially helpful.

59 The now classic business book, *In Search of Excellence*, by Thomas J. Peters and Robert H. Waterman. New York: Harper and Row, 1982.

Taking It Further

Here are a few Web sites that relate to this chapter and additional reading not included in the Chapter Notes.

www.adage.com—*Advertising Age* magazine

www.amazon.com—Online bookseller

www.bh.com—Link to Focal Press through Butterworth-Heinemann, the parent company

www.broadcastingcable.com—*Broadcasting and Cable* magazine

www.emonline.com—*Electronic Media* magazine

www.mediacentral.com—Cowles publications site with access to editorial content from their media magazines: *American Demographics, Cable World, Promo*, and others.

Additional Reading

Auletta, Ken. *The Highwaymen: Warriors of the Information Superhighway*. New York: Random House, 1997.

Barnouw, Erik. *The Sponsor: Notes on a Modern Potentate*. New York: Oxford University Press, 1978.

Barnouw, Erik. *Tube of Plenty*. New York: Oxford University Press, 1982.

Brown, Les. *Television: The Business Behind the Box*. New York: Harcourt Brace Jovanovich, Inc., 1971.

Clancy, Kevin J., and Robert S. Shulman. *The Marketing Revolution*. New York: Harper Business, 1991.

Head, Sidney W., and Chrisopher H. Sterling. *Broadcasting in America: A Survey of Electronic Media*. Boston: Houghton Mifflin, 1987.

Lesly, Philip, ed. *Lesly's Handbook of Public Relations and Communications*, 5th edition. Lincolnwood, IL: NTC Business Books, 1998.

Lichty, L. W. and M. C. Topping (eds). *American Broadcasting: A Source Book on the History of Radio and Television*. New York: Hastings House, 1975.

Ries, Al, and Laura Ries. *The 22 Immutable Laws of Branding*. New York: HarperCollins, 1998.

Ries, Al, and Jack Trout. *Positioning: The Battle for Your Mind*. New York: McGraw-Hill, 1981.

Ries, Al, and Jack Trout. *Marketing Warfare*. New York: McGraw-Hill, 1986.

Ries, Al, and Jack Trout. *Bottom-Up Marketing*. New York: McGraw-Hill, 1989.

2

The Sales Process

"The man in the chair"—that poster I described in the first chapter—jogged me out of my mindset as a programmer and turned me into a salesperson. The more time I spent with sellers, the more I realized that selling was not actually new to me; it was what I did every day.

Selling had already been a valuable tool for me. I used selling to convince a woman to marry me. I received a commission on performance of my radio station because I had sold the boss on my abilities. I had sold an auto dealer on a better price for that green Pontiac with the white racing stripes. (Don't laugh; it was the 1960s. Racing stripes were groovy. Pontiacs were, too.)

Who sells? Once again, here are the words of one of the nation's leading sales motivators, Zig Ziglar: "Everyone sells and everything is selling."

To demonstrate, Zig uses the story of a shoe-shine stand at Lambert Field in St. Louis. One man called himself a "shoeologist" because he was so proud of the work he did. When Zig stopped by the stand, he knew that Johnny (the "shoeologist") could convince Zig to buy the best shine.[1]

"Nice shoes," Johnny would say, and he'd get Zig into conversation about how comfortable they were. Then Johnny would brush against Zig's pants leg. "This is one of the most unusual pieces of cloth I've ever felt," he'd say, and Zig explained about the rare fabric in his suit.

"You know, it just seems like a shame!" Johnny told Zig. "A man will spend over a hundred dollars for a pair of shoes; he'll spend several hundred dollars for a suit of clothes, and all he's trying to do is look his best. And then he won't spend another dollar to get the best shine in the world to top everything off!" Zig, of course, upgraded his shine.

But selling is more than shoe shines or advertising messages. Selling is involved in all of human activity. Your first date was a sale: making a presentation, showing the benefits of the evening, delivering what was promised, and building the relationship beyond the first sale.

Ask your boss for a day off, and you're making a sale. You're presenting the facts ("It's been a long time. . . ."), explaining the benefits ("Boss, you'll get a renewed, energized employee. . . ."), and asking for the order ("Is Friday good for you, boss?"). After the payoff, you as the salesperson are obligated to deliver on the promises made so that the relationship grows.

Who Should Sell?

Even though everybody sells, not everybody has the temperament needed to be successful at selling. All of the electronic media sellers I talked to in preparation for this book had a similar response when I asked them what makes a successful salesperson: drive and desire. More than money, it's that desire to win on a personal level.

Some salespeople put their emphasis on researching their customers. Others make lots of calls, increasing their opportunities for more sales. Still others are closing specialists who know how to ask for the order and get it. Whatever their individual strengths in the selling process, the common thread among successful sellers is a belief in themselves and the will to win. If you don't have it, you can't be successful in selling.

Most lists of attributes for winning salespeople begin with the word "attitude." Make that "positive attitude," and you've found an essential quality for any salesperson. There are so many variables in selling—distractions and disappointments on the road from prospecting to closing—a positive frame of mind is essential.

Call the Dallas-based offices of the Ziglar Corporation, and you'll hear nothing but positive remarks and can-do attitudes. Ask "How are you today?" and Zig's assistant Laurie Magers bubbles, "I'm terrific and getting better." That upbeat attitude is infectious.

Ziglar associate Jim Savage was a scout for the Washington Redskins in the 1970s, looking for football superstars, in his words, "someone who can play immediately and can be a great player in the league." To make his scouting job easier, he created a ratings sheet to score each player. For the Ziglar Corporation, Savage adapted his scorecard for sales "superstars."[2]

The first score on Savage's list is *attitude*. You'll hear from most successful sales trainers and recruiters that attitude is the little thing that makes the big difference. Other attributes of the effective seller are discipline, attention to detail, organizational skills, ability to listen, and persistence. See Figure 2–1.

"Most people are under the impression that knowledge will lead directly to success or that to have the 'better mousetrap' is tantamount to having a lock on the market," says television sales trainer Martin Antonelli. When he cites attributes needed for selling, discipline is at the top of his list.[3] Persistence and positive attitude are not far behind:

On discipline: "Without it, especially self-discipline, there can never be a maximization of potential. There are too many variables and distractions to make success likely without the aid of a plan of action and execution of that plan."

On persistence: "Winners look for ways to get the job done. If one approach doesn't work, another will. The loser looks for reasons to rationalize failure to him/herself and to superiors."

On positive mental attitude: "This involves the individual suggesting to him/herself that things are going to go well. It is a frame of mind, an attitude. It sets the stage for success."

The Antonelli Media Training Center in New York conducts 8-week courses to prepare salespeople to sell spot advertising for national television and cable networks and for the syndication marketplace.

You read Lee Masters' comments in Chapter 1 that sales of a national network like E! Entertainment Television requires analytical skills to present schedules to buyers who are "highly sophisticated."[4] Sellers at that level need all the attributes you'll read about in this chapter and then some: tenacity, flexibility, exacting preparation. In addition, they need a thorough knowledge of the national network business and of advertising nuances like pricing and scheduling. And of course they need to be skilled negotiators.

Putting Customers First

New selling strategies make us redefine phrases like "product knowledge," which used to mean "knowledge of the product being sold" but in the new selling environment means, "the advertiser's product."

The new message of selling is that *the customer is the center of the selling relationship*. The newest sales and motivation books have less to say about clever closing techniques than they do about mutual respect, collaboration, trust, and honor. Words like "partnering" and phrases like "Zen selling" make it clear that there's a new mindset to selling. The "ask for the order" paradigm is a thing of the past. No longer is sales a matter of coercion, manipulation, or out-thinking the prospect.

That philosophy underscores the definition of sales that I'm using as the theme of this book: Selling must be profitable for both the seller and the buyer.

Sharon Drew Morgen's *Selling with Integrity* adds a step to the selling process, suggesting that salespeople should act as "buying facilitators." Morgen urges salespeople to carry their personal values—including spiritual values—to work with them. In the buyer facilitation method, the seller takes responsibility for supporting the buyer in discovering the best solution to his or her problem, whether or not that solution is what the seller is selling.[5]

In a now-classic 1964 article in the *Harvard Business Review*, "What Makes A Good Salesman," David Mayer and Herbert Greenberg call "empathy" and "drive" the two essential qualities for a salesperson.[6] Empathy is the ability to feel what another person feels. As Mayer and Greenberg explain, "A salesman simply cannot sell

FIGURE 2–1
The words in these four classified ads indicate what it takes to be a seller: "Born salespeople." "Highly motivated." "Makes things happen." "Entrepreneur." Is it you? You'll find out in this chapter. Courtesy WBEB, One On One Sports, WXYV, and WRCX. Used with permission.

SUPERIOR SELLERS

Here are the factors that make truly superior salespeople, according to Martin Antonelli, president of the Antonelli Media Training Center in New York City:

Discipline
Organization
Persistence
Positive mental attitude
Independence

Self-confidence
Self-control
Resilience
Hard work
High energy
Product knowledge
Anticipation and planning
Constant learning
Understanding why people buy

COVEY'S SEVEN HABITS OF
HIGHLY EFFECTIVE PEOPLE

A popular book among salespeople is Steven Covey's *The Seven Habits of Highly Effective People*. The Covey Leadership Center serves *Fortune 500* companies and smaller operations, too, with training and seminars in leadership.[8]

Part of the Covey Center thesis is what he calls the "character ethic": integrity, humility, fidelity, temperance, courage, patience, industry, simplicity, modesty, and the Golden Rule. These are basic elements, but they are not seen in the success literature of the last 30 to 50 years.

Covey's "Seven Habits of Highly Effective People" are as follows:

1. Be proactive, moving from "There's nothing I can do" to "Let's look at alternatives." This step involves taking control of our feelings and our choices.

2. Begin with the end in mind. "The course of least resistance gradually wastes a life," Covey says.

3. Put first things first. Peter Drucker said, "First things first and one at a time."

4. Think WIN/WIN. This is another way to express the definition of "sales."

5. Seek first to understand, then to be understood. This is another reminder of the word "empathy" in the selling process. Covey recommends "empathetic listening."

6. Synergize. "Creative cooperation," Covey calls it. "The essence of synergy is to value differences—to respect them, to build on strengths, to compensate for weaknesses."

7. Sharpen the saw. This idea includes clarification of personal and spiritual values; service to the community; reading, planning, and other mental upgrades; and exercise, nutrition, and physical health.

Covey calls Habits 1 through 3 "private victories" and Habits 4 through 6 "public victories." Habit 7 is the principle of "balanced self-renewal."

---

well without the invaluable and irreplaceable ability to get powerful feedback from his client through empathy." Zig Ziglar calls this moving "from your side of the table to the prospect's side. Realistically that is where the sale is going to be made."

In his book *The Radio Station*, Michael Keith quotes radio sales manager Charles Friedman on the subject of empathy:

> You really must be adept at psychology. Selling really is a matter of anticipating what the prospect is thinking and knowing how best to address his concerns. It's not so much a matter of out-thinking the prospective client, but rather being cognizant of the things that play a significant role in his life. Empathy requires the ability to appreciate the experiences of others. A salesperson who is insensitive to a client's moods or states of mind usually will come away empty-handed.[7]

Is It You?

With these thoughts in mind about the qualities that make a winning salesperson, are you the person? Can you identify enough of these attributes in yourself to achieve success selling electronic media?

The good news, as Zig Ziglar says, is that everyone has every one of the qualities to be successful. How much of each quality you have will determine how much success you'll meet in selling (or any field, for that matter).

Just to make sure you're right for the job, the company that hires you is likely to give you a test that yields a psychological profile. Some of the tests yield catchy, even silly, marketing department-generated names for the high-performance sellers they identify:

- One company uses a list of 60 words and phrases to separate "power runners" (good sales candidates) from "walkers" (not so good).
- Another developed a "Comprehensive Personality Profile" to separate "race horses" from "plow horses." "Race horses," they claim, make nearly three times the average monthly sales commissions.

There are so many testing services, it's not practical to list them all. I've encountered sales organizations that used handwriting analysis as a testing procedure, with pretty good results. All the testing systems have merit because they help the employer know how well suited you are for the job.

Wilson Learning, of Eden Prairie, Minnesota, was the first service I became familiar with, thanks to radio's master seller, Ken Greenwood. Wilson Learning pioneered consultant selling for the insurance industry with its "Counselor Salesperson" program. The success of that approach enabled Wilson Learning to profile and train sellers in many fields. Greenwood added dimensions to the Wilson Learning concept and applied the systems to electronic media.

To give you a feel for the testing procedure, I've chosen two profiling tests, one from the Omnia Group of Tampa, Florida; the other from the H. R. Chally Group of Dayton, Ohio.

The Omnia Profile

The Omnia profiling system has been adopted by electronic media companies such as Cox Television and Saga Communications. Omnia has processed more than 150,000 profiles for industries of all kinds, and they claim 93% accuracy. The service rates 14 behavioral characteristics and displays the results as a graph and as text. See Figure 2–2.

Using the data, Omnia separates sellers into two easily definable groups and then further subdivides each group (again using catchy names).

True Sales Personalities

1. *The Persuasive*, also known as the Entrepreneur, is an aggressive competitor

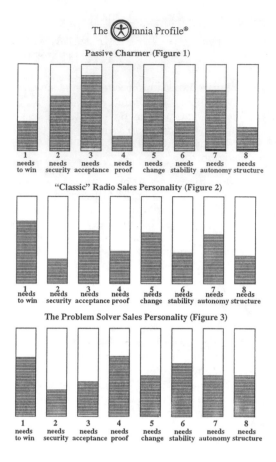

FIGURE 2–2
"Check all the words you think other people at work use to describe you" is the first instruction in the test that yields these Omnia profiles. The candidate chooses from 82 words, then faces another list of 82 for self description. There are more than three types of sellers, but you can see that the scores for each of these three examples are radically different. ©1997, The Omnia Group, Inc. Used with permission.

who sells through relationship-building, persuasion, and charm. (See Figure 2–3).

2. *The Problem Solver*, also known as the Operations Personality, is an aggressor who needs to win (like the Persuasive), but who sells by providing a practical solution to a client's technical problem.

3. *The Persistent*, also called Patient, has the qualities found in Persuasives and Problem Solvers, but adds superior listening skills, team orientation, and the patience that gives this title its alternate name.

Faux Sales Personalities

1. *The Passive Charmer*, also known as the Professional Interviewer, has all the friendly, outgoing charm that a salesperson needs, but is too cautious and security-conscious.

2. *The Technician*, also known as the Researcher, is well-informed but needs to have things right more than to win.

Mary Ruth Austin, Omnia's vice president for marketing and communication, claims that a third of sellers in broadcasting lack the need to win that defines the true sales personality. When the best salespeople are profiled, she says, the results show high marks in the need-to-win column and low marks for needing security.[9]

"The most common 'faux sales person' on the job today is the Passive Charmer," Austin says in a report that Omnia uses as a sales tool. "Poised, articulate, impatient, independent, and impressive, the Passive Charmer looks and sounds *exactly* like your best billers during the interview. The sales director becomes convinced that this candidate can sell airtime to aliens." But it won't happen, she says.

The problem? Austin explains that the Passive Charmer "loves making calls and meeting new people but just can't ask for the order." Passive Charmers fear that customers won't like them if they try to make the sale. "No" is a personal affront to the Passive Charmer.

In Austin's words, "There are only two ways to tell whether that glib, good-looking guy in your office is a Passive Charmer or a real salesperson—profile him before you hire him or hire him and see if he can sell."

The H. R. Chally Group

The H. R. Chally Group is unique because they were established through a 1973 U.S. Justice Department grant to measure candidates for law enforcement. Early in their work, they realized that the same testing could be applied to sales and management people.

Every three years, Chally compiles a "World Class Sales Benchmarking Study" to document what customers want from sellers and what skills are critical for salespeople to possess. They use the database of their own clients (AC Delco, Johnson & Johnson, Pepsi, UPS, and an impressive list of more than 250 others) to classify sales types and to develop measurable standards for improvement.

In 1991, Chally chairman Howard Stevens and writer Jeff Cox published *The Quadrant Solution*, a "business novel" based on customer and sales types uncovered by H. R. Chally testing.[10] As the title suggests, there are four quadrants that customers and sellers fit into. A customer from a specific quadrant is best served by a salesperson who fits the same profile.

The novel's central character, David Kepler, is manager of product development for a company in sales trouble. In a classic use of the fictional device, Kepler unfolds a cocktail napkin to demonstrate his quadrants. On the left is a measure of complexity of the customer from "low touch" at the lower left to "high touch" at the upper left. See Figure 2–4.

At the bottom is a measure of customer experience. On the left is "high tech" (a customer with less experience with the product or service) and on the right is "low tech" (more experience). Using the cocktail napkin as a visual aid, the hero explains customer orientation, marketing, and, of course, how to turn the fictional company around.

While the novel is an interesting and refreshing approach to the business book, a better source for our purposes is Chally's *How to Select a Sales Force That Sells*.[11] It demonstrates more clearly than the novel how the purchase quadrant, the customer quadrant, and the seller quadrant relate to each other.

Truly new products are typically purchased by technical experts who need the newest technology to remain expert or by what Chally calls "gateswingers" who have never used the product. The gateswinger needs the product to be simple to under-

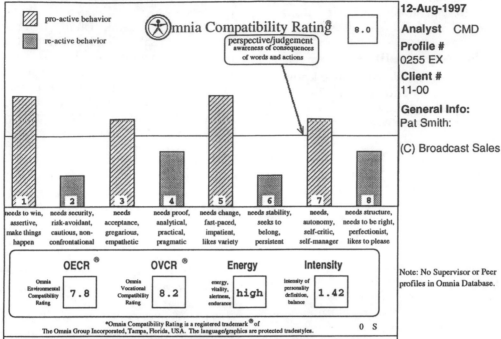

Pat's profile results are rather similar to your expectations for this position and she is fully recommended. Her "entrepreneur" pattern depicts an aggressive, outgoing, efficient and decisive individual. Ambitious, confident and competitive, she seems eager to take the initiative, to put numbers on the board and be amply rewarded for her efforts. Enthusiastic and personable, she should find it easy to build the relationships necessary to be successful in broadcast sales. A good networker, she can easily win the confidence of others and comfortably persuade them to give her their business. She enjoys juggling multiple responsibilities, clients and appointments, and has a good sense of urgency for meeting deadlines. She is rather independent and self-managing, but should respect your rules/regulations. Her over response to the profile may be due to job hunting stress or an attempt to make a favorable impression on you; before proceeding, be sure to carefully verify all application data, including her sales track record/closing ratio. To realize her full potential, Pat needs 1) an upbeat boss who provides plenty of verbal praise/encouragement, 2) autonomy and independence, 3) frequent challenges and opportunities to prove herself, 4) potential to advance and/or earn incentive pay, a way to keep score of her wins, and 5) short term goals to help her stay on track [leads that are slow to develop may lose her interest].

FIGURE 2–3   "Pat Smith" is not her real name, but the profile reproduced here is real. This is how The Omnia Group reports on sales candidates after their testing. ©1997 the Omnia Group, Inc. Used with permission.

FIGURE 2–4
This is the first in a series of quadrant diagrams that actually should be overlaid. Read the text and check the next few figures and maybe you can do the overlay mentally. From *The Quadrant Solution* by Howard Stevens et al. ©1991 H. R. Chally Group. Published by AMACOM, a division of American Management Association (*http://www.amanet.org*). All rights reserved. Excerpted by permission of the publisher.

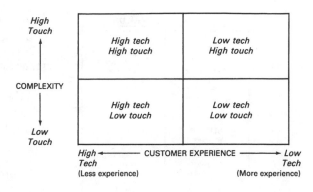

stand yet exciting enough to be on the cutting edge. New product buyers are in the lower left quadrant. See Figure 2-5.

A "new system buyer" is a real user but an inexperienced buyer. Once this buyer becomes knowledgeable, the buyer moves from the upper-left quadrant to the upper-right quadrant of the purchaser matrices.

Commodities buyers are in the lower right quadrant. These customers are so totally experienced with a product or service that purchase and usage are standardized and routine. The example the H. R. Chally Group uses is: "When was the last time you asked how to use an electric pencil sharpener?"

Combine the complexity/experience chart (Figure 2-4) with the purchase type chart (Figure 2-5), and you have Figure 2-6.

Finally, the seller is matched to the individual needs of the customer. In a section on understanding the four types of salespeople, Chally reminds us that there is no "universal" salesperson. "Every pro baseball player must throw, catch, and hit. Yet what it takes to be a great hitter or a 20-game-winning pitcher are dramatically different."

Matching the right salesperson to the right customer requires four types of sellers, and Chally divides them this way: closer, consultative, relationship, and display sellers.

- *Closer*. All salespeople must use closing techniques. But the "closer" term used here describes a personality type, not closing skills. The closer must quickly establish a prospect's emotional desire and

need for the product or service. Closers are good at demonstration sales and high-tech vanity sales, according to Chally.

- *Consultative*. Some people call this "IBM selling" because it's the approach taken by big-ticket and high-technology sellers. It also works best for intangibles like media. The sales environment requires patient, interpersonal contact, or "consultation," with the customer.

MARKET (PURCHASER) TYPES

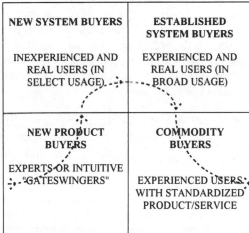

FIGURE 2–5
Now you see the purchaser type and how each relates to the "complexity" and "experience" matrices in Figure 2-4. The dotted line through the middle represents the product life cycle from introduction to maturity. From *How to Select A Sales Force That Sells*, ©1997, The H. R. Chally Group. Used with permission.

FIGURE 2–6
A pattern begins to emerge as you look at these quadrants. The "customer needs" are outlined on the same matrices used in Figures 2–4 and 2–5. ©1997, The H. R. Chally Group. Used with permission.

- *Relationship.* The sale is largely dependent on the relationship between the seller and the customer. A "good" relationship will generate some business eventually. This type of seller can move to a competitor and take a client list along. Stock brokers are good examples.
- *Display.* There's little personal involvement in display selling. Most display sellers (retail clerks, bank tellers, catalog order takers) get paid even if they don't make the sale.

Figure 2–7 shows how the four sales types match the purchase types and customer needs in quadrant segmentation. You can imagine overlaying each chart on the previous one to arrive at how certain types of sellers match with customers. An outline of the personal characteristics of each type of seller appears in Figure 2–8. The profile from testing by the H. R. Chally Group is several pages long. You'll find a sample in Appendix C.

What's Expected of You?

As a seller of electronic media, your primary objectives are

1. Developing new business

2. Maximizing revenues
3. Retaining current business

That's not a job description, but an overview of your job goals.

There's no simple list of duties that will cover every sales job, but here are typical examples:[12]

- To prospect for potential advertisers
- To provide solutions to advertisers
- To create value for your medium
- To create a competitive advantage for your medium
- To process orders
- To assure schedules are run as ordered
- To assure that billing is handled properly
- To monitor other media in your marketplace
- To understand customers' industries and their goals
- To execute your organization's sales strategies
- To answer to management
- To set personal goals as well as company goals
- To work on goal-getting as well as goal-setting

You'll work within a sales department under a person whose title may be sales manager, director of sales, or marketing manager. There are other titles you'll encounter, depending on the organization you're working for. Your manager will outline your job specifically and set the strategies for your selling effort. Those decisions

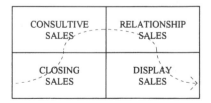

FIGURE 2–7
Matching the right salesperson to the needs of the customer requires understanding of the four types of sellers identified by the H. R. Chally system. ©1997, The H. R. Chally Group. Used with permission.

Personal and Biographical Characteristics of the Four Basic Sales Types			
Closing	**Consultive**	**Relationship**	**Display**
1. Extroverted 2. Energetic 3. Optimistic 4. Strong work ethic 5. Competitive 6. Success image but less likely to save frugally 7. "Positive mental attitude" 8. Highly self-confident	1. Career-oriented (especially into management) 2. Status and image conscious 3. More academic 4. Self-confident 5. Independent and self-developmental 6. Team-oriented 7. Not impulsive or "extreme" risk-taking	1. Strong work ethic (feel guilty if doing nothing) 2. Self-sufficient 3. Independent (don't like to be bossed) 4. Cooperative 5. Patient–traditional, conservative right-leaning 6. Strong and rigid value system (school of hard knocks)	1. Low career ambition 2. Easily bored (need to have something to do) 3. Enjoy people 4. High physical energy level 5. Impulsive 6. Work tends to revolve around home and other goals

Sales Type Summary			
Type	**Style**	**Primary Skills**	**Personality Strengths**
Closing	Theatrical & Confident	• Build Emotion, Enthusiasm • Give "Permission" to Buy • Create Urgency	• Handle High Failure Rate • Handle Personal Rejection
Consultive	Expert & Competent	• Demonstrate Technical Competency • Professional Credibility • Systemized & Organized • Answer Objections	• Handle Confrontation and Negotiate • Handle Personal Rejection
Relationship	Dependable & Loyal to Customer	• Demonstrate Product Knowledge & Customer Knowledge • Customer Advocacy • Time & Territory Management	• Patience • Persistence
Display	Responsive & Service-Oriented	• Congeniality • Demonstrate Product Knowledge • Energy & Stamina	• Handle Boredom • Handle "Social Fatigue"

FIGURE 2–8 Here's a quick overview of each of the four basic sales types profiled by the H. R. Chally Group. It's from *How to Select a Sales Force That Sells*, ©1997, The H. R. Chally Group. Used with permission.

may be made as part of a team that includes corporate leaders, or with you and your colleagues in the sales department. Often it's a two-step process: first, corporate management and local sales managers set strategy, then the selling staff adds plans for tactical implementation of the strategy.

There is no single structure that works for every electronic media selling team, so you'll find each sales department is slightly different. Structural differences are based on a variety of factors: the medium itself, the company that owns the facility, specific needs of the advertising community, the size of the market, and choices made by local sales management. (We will further discuss sales management in Chapter 4.)

The Stages of Selling

Writing in *High Performance Selling*, sales trainer Ken Greenwood outlines four stages of a salesperson's career:

1. *The Novice*. New sellers are faced with learning their own product and the industry in general. This is the point at which presenting, planning, and prospecting are most important.Novices learn to keep good records, to set a high activity level, and to believe in what they sell. "All basic, fundamental things," Greenwood says.

2. *The Learner*. This is the level at which salespeople begin to listen rather than talk, to explain the presentation rather than simply make it. They understand buying criteria. They gain confidence and a better understanding of the selling process.

3. *The Competent*. Sellers at this level become less product-oriented and more aware of solving problems for the buyer. They are able to find options and alternatives. They begin to negotiate. This is also the point at which their versatility becomes more apparent.

4. *The Professional*. The account is a customer, not just a sale. Salespeople at this level know their accounts well enough to forecast buyer needs and to combine accounts in promotional activity. They have a commitment to being professional and a deep belief that their services are needed. At this stage, the salesperson thinks like an independent contractor or a private business person.[13]

"Someplace between the learner stage and the competent stage," Greenwood says, "high performers make a transition. At first they are very much like the fiddler on the roof, scratching out a living and balancing on the ridgepole. On one side are their ego and their ego strength—what they want. On the other side are empathy and an understanding for what the buyer wants."

There's that word "empathy" again. Understanding what the buyer wants makes the customer the center of the selling process. As we saw in Chapter 1, focusing on the customer blurs the traditional lines between selling and marketing.

Personal Marketing Plan

"Dear Ed Shane: One of the secrets of doing business profitably—and doing more of it—is selling yourself first." The letter was designed to introduce me to a special price on Hewlett Packard printers. The premise was that my letters have to look good in order for me to sell myself. When I saw "sell yourself first" at the top of the letter, I thought how ironic it was that such a message would arrive as I was writing this chapter on personal marketing, which is, in effect, selling *you* as a product.

Before you sell any product, you have to sell yourself. You sell yourself as a product

---

ALL I KNOW

Allen Shaw's career took him from radio programmer to leader of several major broadcast companies. He formed Centennial Communications to operate his own stations. When I asked him to contribute to this book, he sent me a note that said, "This is all I know!" Here is his input.[14]

The basics of selling:

1. Know what your product can do for the buyer.

2. Know how the buyer will benefit from your product.

3. Prepare your presentation with thought, logic, and personal charm.

Qualities of a successful salesperson:

1. Desire to succeed.

2. High degree of empathy with potential clients.

3. Integrity and credibility.

4. Hard work ethic.

5. Optimism—nonreactive to rejection.

If that's all Allen knows, it may be enough!

when you pitch the sales job. You sell yourself as product when you make the appointment with a prospect to show that big presentation. Politicians do it. Entertainers do it. CEOs do it. No matter what business is involved, everybody can take advantage of a personal marketing plan.

Today's customer-oriented, service-driven marketplace demands personal marketing—positioning yourself the way you'd position a product. That means attention to packaging and sampling, just like a product. Being good at selling your product and being good at selling yourself are two different aspects of selling. You need to master *both*.

Your public image will be either enhanced or diminished in everything you do, whether you're on a golf course, at a restaurant, in a meeting, or doing charity work. In *Personal Marketing Strategies*, Mike McCaffrey writes that by actively participating in a charitable organization, you will be perceived as a doer, and that will transfer to your image as a seller. "Having already 'established' yourself in their minds as competent and easy to work with, their perception of you can easily be transferred over into business concerns."[15]

McCaffrey suggests that a seller becomes an activist or a doer in charitable, civic, social, or political organizations. From my own experience, it's important to find activities or outlets you enjoy. If you're giving your time, you'll want to be with pleasant people and working for an organization you truly believe in, something in line with your personal values. Once you've found the right fit, you can look for people who can help—contacts to enhance your selling.

Goal-Setting

One of the pioneers of electronic media, David Sarnoff, founder of RCA, left us a powerful quotation about the effects of goal-setting: "A life that hasn't a definite plan is likely to become driftwood."

If you want to succeed in any endeavor, you must have a plan. You need to know what you want to accomplish so you'll know you've done it. That's what goal-set-ting is all about. Most people spend more time planning their vacations than they do their lives. When it comes to life goals, they substitute wishes instead. "I want to be happy" or "I want to be rich" is as close as many get to the idea.

For the seller, only the most specific goal-setting works. Goals that are vague or poorly developed yield vague or poorly developed results. Break your broad view into short-term goals—daily, weekly, monthly, yearly—to provide benchmarks of your successes.

"If it's not in writing, it's not a goal," says Tom Hopkins. "The day you put your goal in writing is the day it becomes a commitment that will change your life."

Hopkins calls the sellers who take his training "champions." For his sales Champions, he outlines these rules for goal-setting:

1. Put your goals in writing. "An unwritten want is a wish, a dream, a never-happen."

2. Make your goals specific. "If it's not specific it's not a goal," Hopkins says, "Broad desires and lofty aims have no effect. Until you translate your vague wishes into concrete goals and plans, you aren't going to make much progress."

3. Goals must be believable. Hopkins quotes his mentor, sales trainer Doug Edwards: "If you don't believe that you can achieve a goal, you won't pay the price for it." Let me take that a step further: If you don't believe you can achieve a goal, then you won't.

4. An effective goal is an exciting challenge. If your goal doesn't push you beyond where you've been before, it isn't going to provide a challenge or change your lifestyle.

5. Adjust your goals to new information. "Set your goals quickly and adjust them later if you've aimed too high or too low," Hopkins advises. Goals are often set in unfamiliar territory. As we learn more about realities, we adjust goals down if they're unbelievable or up if they're too easy.

PERSONAL MARKETING STRATEGIES

Here are ten strategies for marketing yourself from Shane Media's *Power Selling Tactics*.[16]

1. *Become the CEO of your own career*. Develop your own strategic plan—short-term and long-term goals for yourself. Where are you now? Where do you want to be in 1 year, 5 years, 10 years? Set up a logical, meaningful way to measure each goal.

2. *Make connections*. Some people can help you achieve your goals, while others cannot. Learn who belongs to which group and target your personal marketing campaign to those who can help. Depending on your goals, these people may include the president of your company, the mayor, or the head of a civic group.

3. *Get things done*. Be the person who people rely on to take an additional assignment or to volunteer on weekends. Achievers move forward because they make everybody else's job easier.

4. *Make the boss look good*. This strategy is a corollary to number 3. Getting things done and getting ahead mean doing it within the system. Personal marketing means treating the boss like a client.

5. *Be visible*. Be seen where your clients and connection list are seen. Go outside your organization into professional, civic, and cultural circles. High visibility keeps the caliber of your performance high, because you're being watched by high-caliber people.

6. *Make appearances*. The local service clubs (Rotary, Exchange, Lions) need panelists and speakers. Offer topic ideas and volunteer to address local groups about your medium specifically and advertising in general. The most important part of a speech is the 15 minutes immediately afterward when you make contacts and collect business cards.

7. *Publish*. It sounds daunting, but it's not. Industry trade publications regularly look for fresh perspectives. Your local paper accepts editorial essays (often called "Op/Ed" for "Opinion and Editorial"). Don't overlook the weekly suburban papers and the entertainment freebies. Letters to the editor get recognition, too.

8. *Get third-party support*. Ask for introductions or testimonials from your connection list and from groups you've served or addressed. People like to help. They also like to hear reports of how valuable their help really was.

9. *Offer help*. You should reciprocate—provide introductions and offer leads. In marketing terms, this exchange is called giving free samples. Offer information to newcomers to the business. Share your skills.

10. *Research your personal packaging*. It's "dress for success" and more. Your clothing should fit your target audience and give them confidence in you as a product. Even before they see your clothing, however, they see your face. In marketing terms, the face is your "label." You may not be able to change its features, but you're in charge of its expressions. Make sure your face communicates what you want to say about your self-esteem.

---

6. Dynamic goals guide your choices. If you've set your goals properly, they'll show you which way to go on most decisions.

7. Don't set short-term goals for more than 90 days. Once you've developed experience in setting short-term goals, you might set them for a longer or shorter time. To begin, use 90 days as the limit so you can keep your interest high and see measurable results in just three months.

8. Balance long-term and short-term goals. Create enough short-term goals so you can measure progress while waiting for the payoff period of the long-term goal.

9. Include your loved ones. Let the family know what you're trying to achieve so they can cheer you on.

10. Set goals in all areas of your life. Goals are not just about money and new cars. Set goals for your health, for your exercise plan, for your family life, and for your spiritual life. Goals work when they're *used*, so make good use of them in all areas of your life.

11. Goals must harmonize. If your goals fight with each other, you lose. As Hopkins says, "Use your goals program to get rid of frustration, not to create it."

12. Review your goals regularly. Long-term goals can only be achieved if they are the culmination of your short-term goals. New goals should rise out of previous goals that you've achieved.

13. Set vivid goals. I like Hopkins' use of the word "vivid," because it conjures a clear and concise picture of something concrete. He tells the story of seeing a corporate jet parked next to the commercial airliner he was on, so he wrote in his book, "Ten-year goal—jet." Sure enough he achieved the goal, ten years to the day.

14. Don't chisel your goals in granite. Be ready to change if you have to. Hopkins followed the story of the jet with a story of his first fuel bill, for $882.00. At that rate, his jet would cost him $30,000 a month, so he sold it immediately.

15. Reach into the future. "The whole idea of setting goals is to plan your life rather than to go on bumbling along, muddling through, taking it as it comes," Hopkins says.

16. Have a set goal for every day and review results every night. This discipline will save you a lot of frustration. You'll find yourself able to feel good about little events. My wife, Pam, attended a seminar whose leader suggested using a Post-It® note to write one key accomplishment each day, then stick it on the mirror so it'll be there to motivate you the next morning.

17. Train yourself to crave your goals, which reinforces the earlier point about making goals vivid. By visualizing what you want, you make the possibility real and motivate yourself to achieve it.

18. Set activity goals, not production goals. "How many prospecting calls will I make today?" not "How many packages will I sell?" Even if your sales slump, your activity will be stimulated by your goal-setting.

19. Make luck work for you. "Winners understand that luck is a manufactured article," Hopkins writes. "They think in terms of good things happening to them and make themselves good-luck-prone."

20. Start now. The only way to elaborate on those two important words is to repeat them: start now.

Hopkins recommends setting aside 10 minutes a day for 21 days to work on goals and to revise them. After that, he says, "Two minutes a day plus one hour a week will keep you flying toward the immensely greater and richer future that the goal-setting system will deliver."[17]

Goal setting is a process: setting, reaching, and revising goals. Dennis Conner, the skipper of several U.S. entries in the America's Cup sailing race, says, "I don't know if this process ever becomes automatic. You have to keep working it out. When you get good at the process of setting goals and meeting them, you get good at the art of winning."

In *The Art of Winning*, Conner advises, "Make your goals central to everything you do, so everything else shapes itself around them. You become so committed to your goals that, finally, you become committed to the commitment itself."[18]

Time Management

If "time management" is a misleading title, I apologize. We cannot actually manage time; we can only manage ourselves and, therefore, use the time at our disposal effectively. Effective self-management enhances relationships and achieves results. We tend to call it "time management" anyway, most likely to give us the sense of controlling time.

No one has enough time, yet every one of us has as much as there is. It's the one resource that is distributed equally no matter who you are. The great paradox is that I can't think of one of my friends or acquaintances who hasn't said, "Where does the time go?"

Steven Covey captures time management with one phrase: "Organize and execute around priorities." That's in line with the third of Covey's "Seven Habits of Highly Effective People": "Put first things first."

There are four generations of time management, according to Covey, each building on the one that came before. First,

WHAT YOU SEE IS WHAT YOU GET

Watch a major league pitcher closely. First he checks the runner on first base. Then he checks the signs given by the catcher: Fast ball? Change up? Then the pitcher withdraws into himself until the windup and the pitch.

Most pitchers could probably get the ball over the plate with their eyes closed. They've practiced so much. They've measured that 60-foot, 6-inch space so often in their mind and in reality.

If you're a basketball fan, think of a player at the top of the key with a shot open. There's no time to measure distance, trajectory, or velocity. The best players know how to sink a shot from the top of the key, from the free-throw line, and from virtually any place on the court. Even with their eyes closed, they have a good chance of hitting the hoop.

Athletes work on that kind of visualization regularly. They win the mental game long before they take the field for the physical equivalent. Every pitch, swing of the bat, forward pass, or backhand stroke accomplished in practice hones the skill needed for the game.

Salespeople, too, have a powerful tool in visualization. When you *see* yourself as a successful seller, when you *see* yourself reaping the rewards of your work, you condition your mind to accept the skills you have. Visualization allows you to move effortlessly through the sales process, because you've already covered that territory in your mind.

Coupling visualization with positive self-talk gives you an even stronger psychological make-up. You can create a positive, successful attitude for yourself that permeates your entire being by using affirmations. As the word suggests, "affirmation" involves "affirming" or reinforcing your positive thoughts. The idea is to use repetition of positive messages to your subconscious in order to purge negative or self-defeating messages.

An affirmation consists of three elements:

1. *Statement*. It's called "self-talk" because you're saying positive things to yourself.
2. *Imagery*. Visualization of a scene in a positive, successful way.

3. *Emotion*. Experiencing the scene and hearing the self-talk in a way that is felt deeply.

"When you use affirmations," former NBC public relations expert Mike McCaffrey says, "you are providing your subconscious with positive inputs. Your subconscious accepts that input, your self-image changes and grows, and your comfort range expands."

Things that once seemed overwhelming or out of reach come into your control because you've conditioned your response mechanism to accept positive outcomes.

Affirmations are visualizations of the future, but expressed in the present tense. Your subconscious works only in the present, so your communication with it must be there, too.

Let's say your goal is to drive a new sports car within a year. Your affirmation would not be to say "I want" or "I will." Rather, you tell yourself, "I enjoy driving the Jaguar XK8." You visualize yourself in the car, driving the streets you drive today. See yourself squeezing the wheel, adjusting the seat for your comfort. In other words, *experience* it in your own mind.

Don't do it once. Do it every day for several minutes a day until the thought of the car becomes part of you. That makes your goals not only alive on your planner, but also alive in the deepest reaches of your subconscious.

This isn't daydreaming. It's an effective exercise in positive mental conditioning.

Here are other affirmations:

"I like meeting new people and making friends."

"I'm very proud to be a salesperson."

"I produce $_____ sales volume annually."

"I consistently earn $_____ every year."

The sales volume and income affirmations should state your *goals*, not your actual volume or salary. Remember, use future outcomes stated as present-tense facts for your subconscious.[19]

there were notes and checklists, an effort to recognize the many demands placed on our time and energy. Second came calendars and appointment books, an attempt to look ahead and schedule the future. Third was adding priorities, clarifying values, and comparing the relative worth of activities to those values.[20]

"While the third generation has made a significant contribution," Covey writes, "people have begun to realize that 'efficient' scheduling and control of time are often counterproductive. As a result, many people have become turned off by time management programs and planners that make them feel too scheduled, too restricted . . ."

That led Covey to the fourth generation of time management, which focuses on results, not on time. He developed the time management matrix I've adapted for Figure 2–9. The two factors that define any activity are *urgency* and *importance*. "We *react* to urgent matters," Covey says. "Important matters that are not urgent require more initiative, more proactivity. We must *act* to seize opportunity, to make things happen."

His point, of course, is that we are easily diverted into responding to the urgent, not the important. As long as you focus on the urgent *and* important matters in Quadrant I, they dominate your life.

Covey notes that people overwhelmed by Quadrant I often escape to Quadrant IV: "That's how people who manage their lives by crisis live." Others spend time in the "urgent, but not important" activities of Quadrant III. Covey concludes that people who spend time almost exclusively in Quadrants III and IV "basically lead irresponsible lives."

In Covey's mind, Quadrant II is the heart of effective personal management: things that are not urgent, but are important. "It deals with things like building relationships, writing a personal mission statement, long-range planning, exercising, preventive maintenance, preparation—all those things we know we need to do, but somehow seldom get around to doing, because they aren't urgent." The things that make a difference in your life will most likely fit into Quadrant II.

One of my favorite remarks in management literature is Peter Drucker's categorization of activities into "priorities and posteriorities." Priorities are generally set by pressures to get things done. Drucker says that pressures favor yesterday. "They always favor what has happened over the future, the crisis over the opportunity, the immediate and visible over the real, and the urgent over the relevant." He advises, that in addition to setting priorities, you set "posteriorities," that is, decisions about what *not* to do.[21]

Drucker reminds us of the circus juggler who keeps many balls in the air, but for only 10 minutes at a time. Most people can do two tasks at once, but few, he says, can do three tasks simultaneously. (He calls Mozart the only exception.)

Your System

There are a number of time management systems that contain day planners, calendars, priority lists, and other aids to assist the seller in keeping first things first. Most started as paper-based calendar books like Franklin Planner,™ Day-Timer,® and Day Runner.® Many have been adapted to computer software. (Franklin and Covey Leadership merged their companies to offer "life leadership products" as opposed to "time management systems.")

One thing I've noticed is that no one system fits every need. Some sellers use the Franklin system with a fervor approaching religion. They begin with seminars on time management and follow with a ritualized use of Franklin planners, note pads, and reminder cards to capture ideas and check off accomplishments. Others can't stand the Franklin system and opt instead for the Day-Timer system.

I found that neither of those suited me personally, but somehow portions of the Day Runner system did, so I mixed and matched to suit my airplane and briefcase lifestyle. There are a few systems that are designed specifically for media and advertising professionals, but that's still no guarantee they'll fit your specific needs.

Most of the prepackaged time management systems available offer a variety of formats, from pocket-sized to $8\frac{1}{2}$" × 11" binders.

Covey's Quadrants

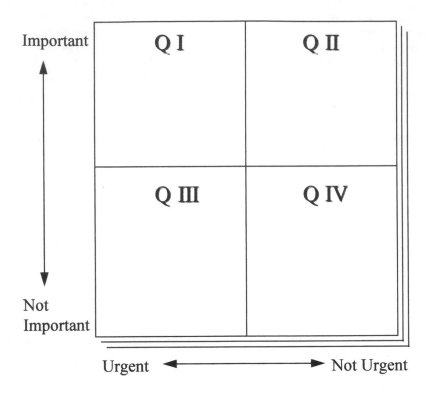

FIGURE 2–9 "We react to urgent matters," says Steven Covey. That's why most people tend to live in Quadrant I. If you don't have important and urgent matters nagging you, then you might live in Quadrant III, because urgency will get you. The ideal is life in Quadrant II, taking care of long-term, important issues.

They also allow you to mix and match to accommodate your specific needs. Some add touches like pictures of polar bears, mountains, beaches, and golf courses that not only personalize the planner but also remind the user of goals or motivators.

It comes down to personal taste. The key is to use *some* system and make it your one-stop reference for goal-setting, goal-getting, scheduling, and personal record keeping.

Psychology

"There is no fool who is happy, and no wise man who is not," said the Roman philosopher Cicero. In the centuries since, there has been considerable study of the plight of the unhappy fool, but little attention given to what makes us happy.

The magazine *The Futurist* published a special report called "The Science of Happiness" and noted that psychological literature between 1967 and 1995 included 5,119 abstracts mentioning anger, 38,459 mentioning anxiety, and 48,366 mentioning depression. In the same period there were only 1,710 mentioning happiness, 2,357 mentioning life satisfaction, and 402 mentioning joy—a 21:1 ratio of negative to positive.

In the report, authors David G. Myers and Ed Diener cite four traits of happy people:

1. Happy people like themselves. They have high self-esteem.
2. Happy people feel personal control. They feel empowered rather than helpless.
3. Happy people are optimistic.
4. Happy people tend to be extroverted.

As sellers, we might equate money with happiness, but money is simply a means to an end, not an end in itself. If we create an appropriate environment for our clients' messages, our clients get results, our advertising is paid for, we receive a commission, *then* we use that income for "life management" or "life leadership," as the time management people call it.

In *How to Master the Art of Selling*, Tom Hopkins admits that money is important, so much so that it's first among his "six motivators" and is related to many of the others. Here's a rundown of those six motivators:

1. *Money*. "Money is good as long as what you earn is in direct proportion to the service you give," says Hopkins. "All that money can do is give you opportunities to explore what will make you happy."

2. *Security*. Abraham Maslow tells us that the average human being strives daily to supply physical needs. Hopkins equates this with security, but he relates it also to money: "In a primitive society, security might be a flock of goats; in our society, security is something bought with money." (For more on Maslow's hierarchy of needs, see the discussion of needs analysis.)

ENHANCING HAPPINESS[22]

When people are asked to describe the best part of their favorite activity, the surprising answer is "designing or discovering something new."

In his book *Creativity: Flow and the Psychology of Discovery and Invention*, Mihaly Csikszentmihalyi of the University of Chicago says that people as diverse as dancers, rock climbers, and composers "all agree that their most enjoyable experiences resemble a process of discovery."

Csikszentmihalyi is considered a pioneer in "happiness research" and offers these suggestions for enhancing your own personal creativity and happiness:

1. Try to be surprised by something every day.
2. Try to surprise at least one person every day.
3. Write down each day what surprised you and how you surprised others.
4. When something strikes a spark of interest, follow it.
5. Recognize that if you do anything well it becomes enjoyable.
6. To keep enjoying something, increase its complexity.
7. Make time for reflection and relaxation.
8. Find out what you like and what you hate about life.
9. Start doing more of what you love and less of what you hate.
10. Find a way to express what moves you.
11. Look at problems from as many viewpoints as possible.
12. Produce as many ideas as possible.
13. Have as many different ideas as possible.
14. Try to produce unlikely ideas.

These tips on happiness were part of a special report, "Science Pursues Happiness" in *The Futurist*, September–October 1997.

3. *Achievement.* Hopkins divides people into two groups: achievers and nonachievers. He claims that "almost everyone wants to achieve, but almost no one wants to do what's necessary to achieve." That's why achievers make up only 5% of the world, according to Hopkins. No salesperson can succeed without a desire for achievement.

4. *Recognition.* Hopkins feels people will do more for recognition than for anything else, even money. That's why, he says, kids do cartwheels in their back yards—so their parents will pay attention.

5. *Acceptance by others.* Everyone wants to be liked, but that's not quite what Hopkins is saying here. The key, he says, is to "surround yourself with the people most like the person you want to become." Work to gain *their* acceptance. Remember that you'll demand more approval from the world than the world is willing to give.

6. *Self-acceptance.* More important than the acceptance of others is self-acceptance—what Hopkins calls "calcium for the bones of our personalities." Self-acceptance is "the state of being your own person. You have arrived exactly where you want to be."

You and Selling

You'll be put in a position to do the work long before you're paid for it. Sellers may start with a draw or salary, but they soon shift to commission. The trend in electronic media is toward spending more on commission than on salaries. (There's more on salary and commission in Chapter 4.)

Before the commission comes, you'll make presentation after presentation, you'll do the consulting, you may write the advertiser's commercial message—all for free. Closing simply affirms the work you've already done.

First-year salespeople spend more time learning than earning. You learn the medium you're selling, then you learn about the prospect's business. High-learn equals low-earn.

Chris Lytle of the Lytle Organization calls sales "a series of defeats punctuated by profitable victories." In school, an "A" grade might be 90 to 95%. In sales, it's more like 25%. Successful salespeople learn to handle rejection. "No" is not personal. Successful sellers tell themselves that every "no" is just a way of getting closer to a "yes."

The good news is that hard work is rewarded.

The Sales Cycle

It was July, and I had been given my first assignment as a salesperson in Houston. This was my opportunity to show what I could do as a seller, moving beyond the sales support role I played as head of the programming departments at radio stations. Where should I start? Or, better yet, how could I start with a win? I'd rather come home with my first sale to build my own confidence and to show the station they'd made a good investment in me as a seller.

I remembered talking a few months earlier with Buddy Brock, a Houston band leader who also ran a talent agency. In passing, he had said to me how he wished he could start booking Christmas parties in the summer so he'd know how his year would end. Nobody in Houston, Texas,

thinks about Christmas in July, but I called Buddy and reminded him of the conversation. Yes, he would be interested in a radio campaign that sold Christmas bookings in the heat of summer. My first close!

"If You Can't Close, You Can't Sell" is the title of a chapter in Charles R. Roth's *Secrets of Closing Sale*s, a classic in the sales field.[23] The premise of the book is that a salesperson should try for closing from the beginning of every sale. "Make every call a sales call," it says, and describes a seller who asks for the order on first handshake.

There's no denying that every sale must have a close. That's the moment when the prospect becomes a customer by saying "Yes!" To understand the dynamics of closing (and to use Roth's "Master Closing Formula," which I'll describe later), you have to begin at the beginning and follow the steps toward closing:

1. Prospecting
2. Qualifying
3. Needs analysis
4. Presentation
5. Answering objections
6. Closing
7. Relationship management

Those seven steps are the sales cycle. At any one time, you'll have a number of clients at a variety of points in the sales cycle. This is why salespeople are looked upon as independent managers of their own jobs. Only the salesperson knows for sure where each customer is in the cycle. So you must take charge of the process personally.

So much has been written about the sales cycle that you'll find lots of different words to describe those seven basics. Here are a few examples:

- *Selling Power* magazine combines "prospecting" and "qualifying" under "call preparation." I prefer to keep them separated.
- Michael Keith, writing in *Selling Radio Direct*, equates "prospecting" with "list building." I agree and have adapted some of his ideas on the subject.
- I prefer to separate "qualifying" from "needs analysis," even though one begins to dissolve into the other. I tend to take the word "qualifying" literally and

remind myself that there are some prospects we just shouldn't sell. (I'll explain that idea later.)
- In Charles Warner's classic textbook, *Broadcast and Cable Selling*, "prospecting and qualifying" are termed "researching and targeting." That also assumes the step of "answering objections," which I prefer to separate out so you can see how objections are a natural part of the sales process.
- You might see "negotiation" as a separate element of the sales cycle. I include it as part of closing. If you're at the point of negotiation, the sale is emotionally closed. Only the terms of the sale are still in question.
- I feel the same way about "servicing" accounts. Getting the paperwork done, the order processed, and the commercial copy prepared is part of closing. Otherwise sellers of electronic media could not deliver their product, and, technically, there'd be no close. Servicing and implementation is a bridge between closing and relationship management.
- "Relationship management" begins the process all over again by helping us retain clients. Repeat business keeps us all gainfully employed.

You'll find that the seven points I've listed are contained in every list, regardless of what they're called and regardless of how many entries there are in the list. The specific words I have chosen to use are the result of letting electronic media selling experts guide me. (See Figure 2–10.)

The Perfect Customer

"In sales, you get the customers you deserve," says Mark McCormack, author of *What They Don't Teach You at Harvard Business School*.[24] If you don't believe this, McCormack suggests you look at your company's top producers. Who do they sell to? Who are their prospects? How do their customers stack up against yours in terms of power, friendship, integrity, and decisiveness?

McCormack describes the perfect customer as (a) a friend, (b) a decision-maker, and (c) someone who likes what is being proposed and will form an alliance with you as the salesperson to overcome the forces of resistance. That description reinforces the definition of selling presented in Chapter 1: when the buy is right, the customer needs no convincing. Closing has to be profitable both for your company and for the customer.

The Sales Cycle

FIGURE 2–10 The steps of the sales cycle in order. I've tried to indicate that each flows into the next. The line from Relationship Management back to Prospecting means you should follow the arrows, then start again.

How can you identify "the perfect customer"? Here are Mark McCormack's guidelines:

1. *The customer talks, you listen.* The customer describes the problems *and* the solutions. From the beginning, you know if there's an internal conflict that affects the sale. The sure sign the customer is a friend is if *you* are included in the solution.

2. *The customer needs you; you don't abuse it.* Not only are you needed, but you're trusted, too. You don't over-promise. You don't overspend. In McCormack's words, "You have to bend over backwards to be *less fair to yourself*." (McCormack's words, my emphasis.)

3. *When the customer says no, you still feel good.* If there's no interest, that's clear immediately. The customer respects your time. If there's interest but rejection follows, that's also clear. The perfect customer prepares you for rejection so you don't lose face. You never feel that you've been stiffed.

4. *The customer makes you better.* If the customer has high visibility or exalted status in the community, the prestige rubs off on you. The fringe benefits of associating with some customers often outweigh the commissions, especially if you learn to do your job better or to reach a personal goal.

The Numbers Game

Perfect customers or not, you can separate your prospects into five categories:

1. Those who don't believe in advertising.

2. Those who believe in advertising but don't believe in the medium you're selling.

3. Those who believe in your medium but not specifically in your outlet— your station, system, or network.

4. Those who have used your outlet in the past and were dissatisfied with the results.

5. Those who've had no problems at all with your outlet.

Your sales manager or sales director will advise you to limit the time you spend trying to convince the people in category 1 to change their minds. It can be done, but it's a long, frustrating process. You'll have more success selling category 2 than you do category 1, more selling, 3 than 2, and so forth. You find yourself longing for prospects in category 5, but those are few and far between.

First and foremost, sales is a numbers game. A seller in the insurance business needs the names of 40 friends, friends of friends, coworkers, and relatives in order to get ten appointments. From ten appointments, an insurance salesperson is likely to get four sales. If that sounds like a lot of contact for little return, Tom Hopkins tells us that in all of selling, the average is closer to 10 to 1. Ten prospects yield one appointment. Ten appointments yield one sale.[25]

In baseball, a batter with 30 hits is not very good, unless that's measured against 100 at-bats. Now you've got a .300 hitter! That's how big league managers decide whom to send to bat against an opposing pitcher.

Direct marketing experts declare victory with a 2% response rate to a database mailing. They know response is the first step to conversion. The statistics help them know what to expect.

You can look at the percentages in one of two ways: as daunting because they tell you there's lots of work to be done, or as an incentive because you know that once you've made the fourth call, your chances of closing are higher on the fifth. Like the baseball manager, you play the percentages.

All successful businesses use percentages to guide decision-making. Mutual funds lure your money with projected annual yield. You'd rather establish an account that yields 18% than one that pays 5%, right?

Percentages are an easy-to-grasp way of expressing ratios, where one number divided by another gives each a perspective. As Tom Hopkins explains in *How to Master the Art of Selling*, ratios that help you manage your selling business are serious stuff. Here are the ratios Hopkins urges sellers to track:

- Prospecting calls/hours spent prospecting
- Prospecting calls/appointment made
- Appointment/sales
- Hours worked/money earned
- Prospecting calls made last month/income this month

In Hopkins' words: "If you're not keeping track, you're not steering your ship." He looks at the selling process as a constant increase in the numbers in your ratios:

By making one call a day, you're meeting about 30 people a month, so you're closing about three sales a month. Now what's going to happen if you decide to make two calls a day?

Your sales go up to six a month, and your income doubles.

Suppose you elevate your performance level again, and start making four calls a day?

Your sales go to 12 a month and your income doubles again. So if you were making $1,000 a month off three sales before, now you're making $4,000 a month off 12 sales—and feeling very good about yourself.

Hopkins doesn't ask us to double our effort immediately, only to add one call a day. He knows that every prospecting call does not yield a sale. Yet more calls equals more chances for closing. What Hopkins is telling us is that we must set our goals high enough to keep ourselves challenged, yet solidly rooted in reality so we can have a reasonable chance to achieve them. He's also telling us to constantly raise the bar to achieve the next level of success.

Your sales director or sales manager sets goals for you each week, each month, and each quarter. For each of the steps in the selling cycle, be ready to set specific goals for yourself, too.

SALES IS A CONTACT SPORT

Make 12 phone calls a day, averaging 5 minutes each, and you spend about one hour per day talking to clients and prospects. Increase daily contacts to 20 or 25, and business will pick up fast.

Here are five practical steps to getting your contact rate up. They're from Phil Broyles, a sales consultant to the financial industry:

1. *Have a daily contact goal—keep score.* Set a goal of 25 contacts per day, outgoing and incoming, both current clients and prospects. Use a daily worksheet or your calendar to keep score. Daily tabulation of calls completed will quickly help you develop the habit of meeting daily call goals.

2. *Prepare a "call today" list.* Before you leave each day, make a list of people to call the next day. Arrive at the office at least an hour before you start making calls. Use that time to decide which names you'll call. To contact 25, you'll need a list of at least 50. Your list should include people you didn't reach on previous days, ongoing clients, and fresh prospects.

3. *Use your calendar aggressively.* Your calendar is a basic prospecting tool; with your daily call log added, it helps you create each day's call list. In addition to appointments, you should schedule follow-up calls. As soon as you reach a prospect, note the

next step on your calendar. Don't wait until the end of the day.

4. *Block out contact time.* Schedule specific blocks of time, 60 to 90 minutes, that are reserved *only* for contacting prospects and clients. Then you can get on a roll and stay on it. In the same way, reserve afternoons or mornings that you will use only for in-person calls. Working with blocks of time lets you meet daily contact goals because you're focused on accomplishing a specific task in a specific time frame.

5. *Avoid distractions.* Use the contact time you've scheduled for that purpose only. Have your calls held. Schedule other time for paperwork, presentations, and so forth. If you must attend to something while calling, use the time you're on hold to scan, sign, or discard papers. In a normal day, you'll save and use 20 to 30 minutes this way.

Broyles exhorts salespeople to take action. It's characteristic of top producers to spend substantially more of their time talking with clients and prospects.

Another suggestion from Broyles: Follow the "10 before 10" rule. Contact at least ten people before 10 a.m. to ensure reaching your daily contact goal—and your monthly sales goals.

From *Research* magazine, April 1991.[26]

Step One—Prospecting

Where do potential customers come from? They start as prospects—potential advertisers. Just as the insurance seller starts with family, friends, co-workers, and others who might need insurance coverage, your first step is to cast the net to see who needs advertising.

First, every business needs to advertise. Not every business needs to advertise in electronic media, so your task is to develop lists of those who might and then to qualify them—see if they are, indeed, prospects for your medium.

If they already advertise on television, radio, cable, or interactive media, then they're already prime prospects. They've been sold by somebody. Your job is to convert them to your specific service as part of their overall media mix. Start with the basics; for example:

- *For sellers of local Web sites*: Who's already represented with banners on local city pages or click-throughs on regional home pages? Who's on manufacturer sites of retail pages?
- *For radio spot sellers*: Who's on the air at other stations?
- *For TV time sellers*: Who's advertising on the other channels? On local cable? On radio?

Those are your first prospects, and they're already predisposed to your message.

Now let's look closer at competing media as prospecting tools.[27]

Newspaper

Newspapers still take the lion's share of advertising from most markets. Newspapers not only tell you who's in business, but also how much money they're spending on advertising. The larger the ad, the more they spend. Big display ads are important qualifiers. When an advertiser can afford to buy one or more full pages in the newspaper, chances are there's cash for other media, too.

The business section of the local paper is a perfect place to begin prospecting. What new deals have been cut? What land has been sold and to whom? Does it mean a new business is about to open?

National newspapers like *The Wall Street Journal* and *USA Today* carry regional and local news and advertising. Look especially in the *Journal*'s "Marketplace" section. Read the editorial copy and the advertising content. Read beyond the institutional ads and find the small displays about new openings, new assignments, and help wanted.

When reading your hometown paper, don't stop reading at the business sections. Check real estate, food, entertainment, and sports sections, too, for advertisers who prefer to link themselves with a reader's activities or specific lifestyle.

In the Sunday papers, look for coupons and coupon books (known as FSIs in newspaper language for "free-standing inserts"). Those four-color glossy coupons mean more to you than a few cents off at the grocery store. They could be a lead to a new promotional campaign or a new retailer. In other words, a prospect.

Local want ads are early indicators of pending openings. When a store begins to hire staff, the grand opening can't be far behind. Look also for out-of-town companies soliciting personnel.

Suburban papers carry press releases from every new business in the community. You should subscribe to every weekly in your trading area. Don't overlook the want ads.

Newspaper advertisers have long been considered targets for radio salespeople, because an advertiser can divert a portion of a newspaper schedule to radio and still see the ad in print.

Radio

Virtually everyone in America listens to the radio during the average week: 76.5% of persons aged 12 and over listen every day, 95.1% listen every week. Radio's ability to target demographically and geographically attracts businesses of all types.

It's not as easy to go prospecting on radio as it is in the newspaper, because advertisers on radio are not so neatly compartmentalized. You can't tear out a prospect's advertisement to get the address, so you may have to do some research. By scanning the dial and making notes of all the commercials you hear, you can begin to create a list of potential clients who use the medium.

Local cable sellers target radio advertisers, arguing that commercials on cable cost about the same as radio and have the advantage of adding pictures to make the message more effective.

Cable

Cable reaches 68% of all U.S. homes and even more (81%) of households with an annual income of $60,000 or more. Like radio, cable is considerably more targetable than over-the-air television because specific channels provide content that is geared to specific demographics, affinity, or lifestyle.

Because cable systems make their money on subscriber fees, not all local operators sell advertising. Most major markets have "interconnects" that sell advertising on several cable systems as one package. The Cable Advertising Bureau (CAB) lists 109 interconnects covering markets as large as New York and as small as Dothan, Alabama.

Even with interconnects, some markets cannot be covered with one buy. Baltimore, for example, requires several interconnects to reach both the city and suburban areas. Utica, New York, has one cable operator; its neighboring city, Rome, has yet another.

If the cable operator in your area does carry advertising, it's another opportunity for prospecting. Area advertisers who buy cable might use inserts in CNN, TBS, or USA programming in place of local TV commercials because cable costs less.

Because of the low cost, cable has been called "discount television" by some national advertisers. So advertisers who use scrolling cable messages or banners may not be as lucrative as prospects, because they spend so little to get their exposure. The important point for you to consider is that they've shown a commitment to advertising in electronic media.

Television

Over-the-air television reaches 98% of U.S. households, and the average viewer spends more than 7 hours a day with the TV turned on. The good news for sellers of TV advertising is that the medium reaches huge portions of the mass audience with a single exposure. Pictures, sound, and motion are all factors in television's potential to attract attention for an advertiser.

The bad news is that TV shares are declining in the face of new competition from cable, new networks like Fox, UPN, and WB, and online usage that steals time once spent with TV. Production costs, too, create anxiety for TV advertisers. A typical 30-second spot for a national advertiser might cost more than $250,000 just to produce. Airtime increases that cost dramatically.

Advertisers on local television are good prospects for media salespeople who can demonstrate how to use the same dollars more efficiently, targeting consumers directly.

Yellow Pages

The phone company is kind to sellers. Not only do they give us our best tool for contact—the phone itself—but each year they issue an encyclopedia of local business, the Yellow Pages. Any business that has more than the standard listing of name, address, and telephone number pays for the privilege. That means when you see a display ad in the Yellow Pages, you've found a business willing to spend money on advertising.

To make things even easier, the Yellow Pages are organized by category, so you can identify immediately what a company does. In the Phoenix Metro Yellow Pages for 1997, there were 136 pages with the heading "automotive." That included the dealers, the car washes, muffler shops, and wrecker services.

Stories abound about first-time sellers who are handed the Yellow Pages and told to sell something. I've been asked whether those stories are myth or reality. Believe me, they are reality. The Yellow Pages is called "the prospector's Bible" for a reason.

Outdoor Displays

I know salespeople who keep notebooks or recorders in their cars. When they see a sign announcing construction of a new business, they make a note. More importantly, they make a call, asking who's building the new business and where the owner can be reached.

Any business that uses outdoor advertising is a prospect for electronic media. Billboards aren't cheap, so even one outdoor board indicates a substantial commitment. The advantages of outdoor advertising include the ability to be seen by large numbers of consumers. The disadvantage is that those consumers are often traveling at high speeds, so the copy on a billboard must be brief to be effective. Electronic media sellers have the opportunity to demonstrate that their form of media can fill in the gaps in a cogent outdoor message.

The Internet

Most companies have an online presence for public relations purposes. They want their customers to have access to information they cannot provide in brochures. By checking search engines like Yahoo! or Infoseek, you can discover categories of potential advertisers.

Look also for local and regional advertisers who sponsor banners on city guides like *accessatlanta.com*, *sidewalk.com*, *bayinsider.com*, and *nbc-in.com*, which creates local Web sites for broadcast TV stations affiliated with NBC.

Trade Publications

Every industry has one or more trade publications. They offer a wealth of leads. They're not only excellent for list-building, they also make you seem smarter to a retailer who knows you've been doing your homework on an industry other than your own. This is the customer focus that is so important in selling electronic media today.

The Supermarket

Neighborhood "shopper" publications provide leads, especially for forms of media that target geographically—radio and cable, for example. Sellers of new interactive media create prospects from "local" advertisers who want to create a marketplace beyond the store on Main Street. Does it matter to the retailer where orders originate? An order and a valid credit card number are enough of a payoff in the new wired economy. A retailer shouldn't care that customers come from another part of the globe via cyberspace.

While I'm on the subject of shoppers, don't take the next trip to the supermarket for granted. After squeezing the produce and stocking up on prepared meals, scan the end-of-aisle displays and the "shelf talkers" (those little signs on the shelves). They may tell you about a selling opportunity, a new product, or a special promotion.

Stop at the grocery store bulletin board if there is one. Among the listings of babysitters and free kittens are often business cards, notices of hiring, and other possible leads.

Brochures and Flyers

That neon flyer placed under your windshield wiper at the mall may lead to a sale. Don't throw it away until you pursue the potential. Could the business become an advertiser?

While I was waiting for a client to pick me up at a hotel in Midland, Texas, a man in the lobby handed me a flyer about job openings at the new Computer City store opening soon. No, I didn't want to interview for a job, but I *did* want that flyer. I gave it to my client so one of his salespeople could use it as a lead.

A brochure or flyer at the cash register of a retailer you trade with might be your next appointment for a presentation.

Direct Mail

Direct mail, the most targetable nonelectronic advertising medium, can zero in on geography, product affinity, previous purchases, potential interest, or lifestyle activities. The greatest advantage of the medium is that each consumer can be addressed as an individual.

A letter directed to you is a sales lead if it's from a retailer or service provider who works in your trading area. If you sell local advertising, say on radio, television, or cable, the coupon mailings that come each month in ADVO or Carol Wright packages may be good prospecting for you.

Your pitch to advertisers who prefer to use mail should be that direct mail has traditionally low-response rates, and consumers perceive the stuff as "junk mail" even if they read and respond.

Government Offices

The county clerk, the secretary of state, the city permit office, or any government agency that accepts new filings should be contacted. The secretary of state has files of newly created corporations. Your city hall issues building permits. Your state alcohol and beverage agency controls liquor permits. Your county clerk files real estate transfers.

Some states require fictitious names filings before a new business can even get a bank account. That's the law in Texas, and every 10 years when I refile the name of my company with the county clerk, I get a flood of calls and mailings from sellers who think we're a new business.

Handshakes and Referrals

Insurance sellers know that sales begin at home. Don't overlook the prospecting value of your personal network. Who in your personal circle is a prospect? Friends, family, school friends? Even if they can't buy advertising, they might lead you to a prospect they know.

Think of members of your immediate family who might help. Do they work with a company that advertises? Do they know someone who does? After you examine the immediate family, check the extended family, in-laws, cousins, and family members by marriage. Again, look for opportunities. If they advertise or influence advertising, put them on your prospecting list.

If you have no personal network, then create one. Offer to speak to a business breakfast club. Better yet, join several. Network at any organization meeting, especially service clubs. Where business people gather is your opportunity to make contacts, collect business cards, and build your list. You can also trade potential prospects with sellers in other industries.

Tom Hopkins tells the sales "Champions" in his training sessions that referral prospects are the easiest to close. He claims you'll spend half as much time selling the referred lead as compared to the company-generated, nonqualified lead.

Your Own Operation

All radio and TV stations and some cable outlets get news releases by mail, fax, and e-mail. Ask your news director to pass along any release that has commercial implications.

Radio and TV stations and some cable channels use commercials or promotional announcements to advise advertisers of the benefits of running a schedule. The premise is that if the advertiser is already watching or listening to that medium, there's a predisposition to using it for advertising, too.

You'll read Cheryl Vannucchi's sales pitch later in this book. I found her on the "Santa Rosa 6" cable TV channel in Sonoma County, California, while I was there working with a client. As a seller for the local cable channel, Cheryl was part of a TV commercial inviting businesses in Sonoma County to advertise on the local system.

If you're selling for an Internet company, the one-to-one opportunities of interactive media seem to be made for prospecting. Many commercial home pages include an "advertise here" message to let users know there are availabilities.

Running Dry?

"You never lack leads," says Roann Hale, vice president of the Radio Advertising Bureau (RAB). She conducts sales meetings for RAB member stations and helps salespeople stay alert for new advertising dollars. She tells members of her training sessions that "the sky is the limit" when it comes to leads and opportunities. It's true for all electronic media selling.

List Building

Each salesperson has a "list," a collection of clients and potential clients exclusive to that seller. It's called a list because it's usually written down. Exclusivity is an unwritten rule.

A new salesperson may get a list that looks impressive at first because it's long and filled with business names. The new seller's first list is often nothing more than a catalog of dormant accounts. Michael Keith recalls in *Selling Radio Direct* that his first list was two pages long and contained 75 area retailers.[28]

His first impulse was, "Good Lord, I'll be rich in no time at all!" His glee was dampened when Keith's sales manager informed him that only two of the 75 were active accounts. After attempting to turn his prospects into customers, Keith dubbed the list the "Dead Sea Scroll" and proclaimed the accounts "beyond dormant to moribund. They had been neglected for too long or horribly mishandled" by previous salespeople.

It's a lesson that every sales representative must learn: how to build an account list, usually from scratch, using all the prospecting and networking techniques you can muster.

Don't be surprised if another sales representative on your staff also attempts to "claim" an account you've discovered.

Every seller in your department is busy exploring prospects and making lists, so duplication is inevitable. Most sales organizations work on a first-come, first-serve basis, and the arbiter is the sales manager.

"Claiming" an account is done only with the sales manager's approval. A new advertiser or prospect might be added to a seller's list for a short period of time to see whether the seller can generate interest. If the first salesperson to claim the account fails to make progress, the sales director may assign the account to another representative, hoping that a different approach might bear fruit.

Generally, once a seller is assigned a client or finds and claims a new prospect, other salespeople in the same department are expected to stay clear of that business, not to make calls or otherwise compete with the first seller for that account. Again, the sales manager is the referee.

A list may be defined geographically—the northwest side of town, the southeast region of the United States, or all of the state of Georgia, for example. It may be defined by category—auto dealers or finance companies. Most lists, however, are catch-alls of clients assigned by the sales director, combined with prospects uncovered by the seller. A seller who calls on gift shops might also call on unrelated businesses such as restaurants and hardware stores.

The growing customer focus in electronic media selling makes the category-based list both popular and lucrative. Hiring sellers who become specialists in the customer's industry makes advertisers more comfortable. The seller who reads *Automotive Weekly* has a better chance of striking a responsive chord with an auto dealer than the seller who simply walks in with a rate card in hand. Rapport breeds revenue.

Lists are most effective when worked diligently. Sales trainer Chris Lytle likes the idea of a limited number of accounts on a seller's list, with maximum contact:

> Let's assign 200 accounts to Jones and 50 accounts to Smith and require each of them to make 10 calls a day. At the end of the month, Jones and Smith have each made

THE BEST TIMES TO REACH PROSPECTS

Sales consultant Irwin Pollack offers this list of opportunities to make contact with decision makers:

Retailers
Appliance stores: Tuesdays, Wednesdays, midday.

Bicycle shops: Wednesdays, early mornings. Check for possible days off.

Bridal shops: Early mornings.

Car dealers: Tuesdays, Wednesdays, midday.

Computer stores: Midmorning. Avoid Mondays.

Convenience stores: Before 1 p.m.

Department store advertising directors: Early mornings, late afternoons.

Fast food stores: Between 10 and 11 a.m.

Florists: Early morning.

Food brokers: Before 9:30 a.m. Late Friday afternoon.

Furniture stores: Avoid the end of the week.

Golf stores: Midweek, early afternoon. Rainy days.

Home improvement stores: Midweek, 2 to 4 p.m.

Jewelers: Early morning or late afternoon. Avoid Thursdays.

Pet stores: Early week, midday.

Produce/fruit stores: End of the week. From 9 to 11 a.m. is your best shot.

Shopping mall managers: Mornings.

Sporting goods stores: Midweek, early afternoon.

Supermarket managers: Between 11 a.m. and 2 p.m., Mondays and Tuesdays are best.

Toy stores: Between 1:30 and 3 p.m. Early in the week.

Wine retailers: Decision makers are usually in on Saturday mornings. Tends to be a side business, with the decision maker working one morning or day per week.

Women's specialty shops: Before 11 a.m.

Entertainment
Amusement park directors: Before 2 p.m.

Bars/night club owners: Late in the week, late afternoon.

Cruise companies: After 10 a.m. and before 4 p.m. Early in the week is better.

Restaurant executives: Before 11:30 a.m. Avoid Mondays (deliveries).

Services
Accountants: Between the 12th and 20th day of each month.

Bankers: Before the bank opens for transactions (usually 9:00 or 10:00 a.m.)

Barbers/beauticians: Mondays.

Brokers: Before the New York stock market opens.

Convalescent home owners: Between 1 and 3 p.m.

Daycare centers: Late afternoon.

Dentists: Before 10:00 a.m. Check for days off.

Photographers: Midmorning.

Dry cleaners/launderettes: 2 to 4 p.m.

Eye care centers: After lunch.

Health care/hospitals: Midday. Avoid Mondays.

Housekeeping services: First thing in the morning.

Lawyers: Before 10 a.m. or after 4 p.m. Check for trial appointments.

Photo developers: Late afternoon.

Real estate executives: Midmorning, midweek.

Service departments (auto dealers): After 3 p.m.

Tanning salons: Midmorning, rainy days.

Business-to-Business
Copy centers/printers: Early afternoons.

Couriers: Late afternoon.

Office supply/furniture stores: End of the week, late afternoon.

Recruitment directors: Mondays, Thursdays, or Fridays.

Irwin Pollack is president of the New Hampshire-based Radio Sales Intelligence. Pollack conducts sales and management seminars for state associations, broadcast clusters, and individual radio stations along with providing consulting services for both broadcast companies and local owners. He can be reached via *www.irwinpollack.com* or by calling (603) 598-9300.

200 sales calls. Jones has made one call each on 200 accounts. By "concentrating the force" of sales calls against the target group, you can bet that Smith outsold Jones. Jones has a bigger list, but Smith has more sales on the books.

Farmers have used this principle for years. It's more profitable to increase the yield from the same acreage than buying more fields.[29]

Cold Calling

I remember a story in *Selling* magazine about an insurance seller who would stalk prospects, sneak though back doors, dodge receptionists, lurk in parking lots—anything to deliver a sales pitch. The magazine dubbed the man the "king of cold calls" and congratulated him on his prowess.[30]

The story troubled me when I read it, because that's exactly the kind of thing that gives salespeople a bad name. I'm not against cold calling, but I am reluctant to encourage you to act like such a vulture.

The term "cold calling" means walking into a prospect's place of business unannounced—cold. There's also the fact that cold calling sends chills down the spines of some of the heartiest salespeople. The idea has been called "less than professional" and "downright rude." In the eyes of some retailers and most agency buyers, it's more professional to set up an appointment by phone, then proceed with the sales call during the scheduled appointment.

Appointments are not easy to get, as you'll see in the next section. But unless the phone rings off the wall with new business at your place, you'll find yourself making cold calls, knocking on doors, and hoping for a friendly ear.

Be prepared for rejection. Few prospects have time for interruptions, especially at peak hours of the day. Many targets of cold calls think only in terms of how to get rid of the intruder.

Imagine for a second that you are the target of a cold call. You're a shop owner or a business manager. A salesperson has walked in unannounced. There are two questions going through your mind:

1. What is this about?
2. How do I get rid of this problem?

As the salesperson, it is your job to keep the prospect as far away from the second question as possible. Through careful choice of words, you can do it. Begin by answering that first question—"What is this about?"

Always begin the conversation by stating the purpose of the call in words the buyer wants to hear. The typical buyer doesn't necessarily care what *we* want, or what *we* need or what *we* would like.

For instance, don't say, "I dropped by to introduce myself and my company." The prospect will simply think, "Who cares? I have work to do."

Another wrong approach is "I came by to tell you about a new promotion our company has just introduced." Expect your target to think, "If it is something I want, I would have already called you."

Houston-based sales trainer Rick Alan, of Rick Alan and Associates, puts it bluntly:

> It is no big mystery why many buyers think salespeople are all alike. Let's face it, many of us sound alike. Whether we like it or not, we are an interruption to the buyer. I'm not saying we're not a worthwhile interruption, but we are an interruption. It is up to us to create value in what we are saying and to increase the buyer's curiosity to hear our message.[31]

Here are two possible ways to make the interruption work for you and for your prospect:

> "I came by to talk with you about generating more customers for your business."
>
> "I came by with an idea that could possibly give you an edge over your competition."

As Mark McCormack suggests, "Have a pretext. It doesn't have to be a profound or persuasive reason, but it has to be slightly more compelling than 'I want to sell you something.' That's not a pretext. That's a subtext—which is usually left unspoken."[32]

A good pretext is a visit to someone in a new job, saying "congratulations" or "welcome to the community." For that reason, newly opened businesses get a lot of cold calls. The owner or manager might even be pleased that you discovered the establishment.

Another pretext is "being in the neighborhood," for example, calling on another account and stopping by other businesses on the same street or in the same shopping center. "Our advertising campaign can help your business the same way it did Monica across the street at the Boulevard Bistro. She had a sellout on Thursday night."

Mark McCormack adds one more pretext: "Invite them to something." His business is involved in sporting events, so there's always a big-name golf or tennis match on his schedule.

What's your invitation? Here are a few ideas:

- If you sell for a TV station that sponsors an annual bridal show, you might offer an invitation.
- As a radio seller, you might invite a prospect to the premiere of a new movie you're sponsoring or to a concert your station is presenting.
- Your cable system may be participating in a business-to-business show at the convention center.
- New media sellers will know about demonstrations and workshops introducing new software. Invite a prospect.

If you walk in the door as a breath of fresh air for prospects, you're less of an infringement on their time.

"I don't know anyone who will admit to enjoying the cold-call process," says Mark McCormack. "It's intrusive. It's fraught with rejection. It's psychologically draining, especially if you're calling 100 people a day and 99 of them won't even agree to see you in their office."

Don't take rejection personally. There's a lot of rejection in cold calling. The payoff is also very low. It takes a lot of cold calls to generate welcomes warm enough to translate into appointments. Your most productive prospecting will be done by telephone.

Keeping Track

As a salesperson, you're likely to have 100 or more accounts on your list—some active advertisers, others inactive, but prospects nonetheless. Every one will represent potential earnings. To know where you stand with each client and prospect, keep a record of all calls, whether in person or by telephone. It's easy to forget what happened on a call at the end of the day when you've made additional calls that same day. As Michael Keith says in *Selling Radio Direct*, "A record of the call will put you back on point. When preparing a record of a call, the more detail the better." Keith uses this example:

> Bennington Floor Covering—contacted 5/11. Presented TAP Plan. Client says not interested until late July. Wasn't too impressed with TAP approach. Listens to 'Bill Bannon Show.' Maybe have Bannon visit on next call. Offer plan in show. Call back in mid-July. Gets co-op dollars and buys in combo. Not happy with newspaper. Likes station. Solid prospect. Mail new inserts from media kits and drop off dozen (station) magnets. Stick with this one.

A status report like that one should be kept for every client, so you'll have a quick and easy reference. If the client's an active advertiser, the file should include plans you've offered the client previously as well as the one being used currently.

Your file is not complete without your advertising contracts and the schedules the client bought. It should also include past contracts, affidavits, and credit check information from your research on the client. As we work through the sales process, you'll conduct a needs analysis for each client. That information should be part of the client file, too.

Records management software programs will make the job easier. Database management software designed for sellers captures the essential information and gives you the flexibility to customize data fields for your own needs.

www.IRTS.org

GETTING BY THE GATEKEEPER

Gatekeepers are secretaries, assistants, receptionists, administrators—anybody charged with defending the decision-maker's schedule. As the first line of defense against time-eating intrusions, most gate keepers screen out salespeople's calls. And they take their role quite seriously.

Gate keepers can make or break a sale. They may not sign the checks, but they wield enormous power over salespeople.

How you play the gate keeper determines whether they throw open the door and lead you straight to the decision-maker or short-circuit your most persuasive pitch before it even rolls off your tongue.

There are two basic approaches for getting to the decision-maker: (1) face the gate keeper at the front door, make him or her an ally, and try to reach the decision-maker with the gate keeper's support; or (2) make a run for the back door, avoid the gate keeper, and attempt to reach the prospect on your own. Most salespeople choose the front-door approach. The indirect route can work, but it's risky.

The Front Door Approach

Here are some ways to build prosperous relationships with gate keepers:

- *Watch your attitude*. Be friendly but not sugary, confident but not cocky.
- *Be honest.* Fibs will make your nose grow before they increase your sales.
- *Personalize the relationship*. Find out and use gatekeepers' names, and gather as much personal information about them as possible.
- *Sell the gate keepers.* If you show gatekeepers how they and their companies can benefit from your product, they will be more likely to push for you. It can only better their standing in the company if they recommend a winning product.
- *Ask for help.* Gate keepers are wired. They can give you the inside scoop on their companies' needs and goals, and clues about the best time to call the decision-maker.

- *Show appreciation*. "Thank you" is obvious, but don't stop there. Compliment gatekeepers personally for their help and suggestions, and pass that praise on to their bosses.
- *Try the occasional stunt*. Creativity and humor can help build bonds with gate keepers and their bosses. Wear an appropriate costume or deliver a mystery package that gets attention from everyone in the prospect's office.
- *Patience, patience, patience*. Don't expect to see results overnight. It may take months, or years, to get through the door.

The Back Door

When all else fails, you can try these measures to get you in the back door:

- *Time it right*. Call before 8 a.m., during lunch, or after 5:30 p.m.; try not to be obvious why you're doing so.
- *Direct dial*. Find out the prospect's phone number and call direct.
- *Try a special delivery*. Creative mailing is a proven back-door method.
- *Choose your words carefully*. Misleading words set up an antagonistic feeling.
- *Hold your cards close to your vest.* Slight evasions can also help get you through, but they can backfire if gate keepers catch on.
- *Use food as bait.* Bring in lunch or arrange to have it delivered.
- *Patience, patience, patience*. You've heard this before. Keep trying.

Regardless of the path you pick, be forewarned: gate keepers are not going to disappear. As businesses get leaner, the gate keeper's power to influence—even to choose—services and products for their companies is on the rise.

Also note that gate keepers often get promoted. One who has little buying power today could very well end up holding the pen some time down the road.

Adapted from Shane, *Media's Power Selling Tactics* for *Tactics: Sales*, April 20, 1998.

Using a Database

My company markets its services primarily to radio stations. To be effective, we maintain our own database of targeted prospects and potential clients. We also buy databases from list marketers who specialize in electronic media, although we find our own information preferable to that we get from outsiders. (After all, who can define the target better than we can?)

One of those list marketers called me to solicit a buy, and he began by asking me if I knew his company. Yes, I did, I said. I told him we'd used his databases, but it had been a few years. (In fact it had been 5 years.)

"Let me get my files," he said. A remark like that is the beginning of the end of the conversation for me. I asked myself quick questions about his selling approach:

Why wasn't his file open when he called me?

Why did a database company use its own product so badly?

Why did he wait 5 years to call?

The reason we weren't using his product, I told him, was that he didn't have specific names available in the database. We were much better served by scanning trade magazines and having our own people keep up with changes at stations.

His reply was that all a salesperson has to do is to call the prospect and ask the receptionist for the manager's name before asking to talk to the person.

I told him that no one representing my company could afford to be caught so unprepared. The research on whom to call comes first, before the call. I want the receptionist to know our people are prepared, too. That ended the conversation. He expected our sellers to treat our prospects as casually as he had treated me. No one can afford to sell that way.

There are many contact management and sales automation software systems available. So many, in fact, that *Selling Power* required five pages just to list all the systems they reviewed in the November 1997 issue.[33]

Each month there are new releases with new features. The basic element of any sales software is the customer database and fields for information about contacts, histories, pricing, and so forth. Time management pages and word processing are also basic. The least complex systems are called "contact managers" or "account managers" because that's what they help you do.

It doesn't require a sophisticated system to include e-mail, faxing, map makers for retail selling, and basic order processing (although most electronic media outlets have their own system for order processing).

Systems that work on a local area network or an intranet allow for sales analysis, inventory control, changing grid levels (pricing) when inventory becomes tight, and other tools that are more the province of the sales manager or sales director than the individual salesperson. Those systems are generally called sales force automation (SFA).

The favorite contact management software systems for some years were ACT! and Goldmine. They are not identical, but similar, with the benefit of lots of fields, many that can be designed by the user for specific purposes. (A friend of mine in the music industry retooled his ACT! pages to show top-40 chart positions and other pertinent information about his artists as well as the basic needs for customer data he had as a seller.)

A step up from those systems is the SalesLogix system, which falls between contact management and the high-end sales force automation systems. SalesLogix contains an online sales library, automated processing of routine tasks, and custom reports on the whole sales team that the sales manager can access.

There is proprietary software designed for each electronic medium, too, which allows integration of Nielsen and Arbitron ratings information.

Step Two—Qualifying

We never want to say this to the customer, but some customers are better for us than others. The best example is a customer who spends a lot of money buying advertising. One of the mistakes first-time sellers often make is concentrating on advertisers whose budgets are too small. No matter how hard you work, you can't increase the amount of money the customer is willing (and able) to spend.

Customers who pay their bills on time are better customers than those who stall and make excuses. Those who pay on time are back month after month or season after season, and you can count on their advertising expenditures. Checking credit rating and payment history will be near the top of your list as you qualify potential advertisers.

Because the purpose of business is to create customers, bear in mind that not all customers are the same. Which customers do you want to sell to? The good ones, of course. But how do you know who the good ones are? You know by *qualifying* your prospects.

Qualifying is information-gathering. It's the step at which you begin to build a file on your prospect. Charles Warner and Joseph Buchman call qualifying "the single most important step of selling because it is in this step that you *begin your relationship with your customer*." (Their emphasis.) They feel that 15% of your average month should be spent qualifying prospects.[34]

You'll notice a point at which qualifying begins to merge with needs analysis. It's difficult to create clean lines of demarcation in the sales process. A good job of qualifying yields a head start on needs analysis. Proper needs analysis is often its own closing technique. Given Warner and Buchman's feeling that qualifying is the beginning of relationship-building, that's a head start on the work you'll do after the close.

Tom Hopkins links qualifying directly to closing. He says salespeople "try to close the wrong people too often and too hard. In other words, they don't fail to close, they fail to qualify." It takes the same amount of time to present your story to ten unqualified prospects as it does to ten qualified prospects. The difference is you can work toward closing only with those who are qualified.

Hopkins says you'll close one qualified prospect for every one that gets away, and you'll lose nine unqualified sales for every one you close. Remember that closing rates vary. Hopkins' figures are based on selling generally, not on selling electronic media. The principle remains the same.

Getting to the Right Person

Getting your foot in the door is only half the battle, as the saying goes. Make sure your foot's in the right door. All your efforts will be for nothing if you don't present your story to the person with the power to make the buy.

Here's a rule for qualifying prospects: "Don't take no from someone who can't say yes." Bill Burton, president of the Detroit Radio Advertising Group and self-described "cheerleader" for sellers, was the first person I heard say that. I'm sure it was said long before Bill, but he deserves credit for saying it repeatedly to sellers who call on the auto industry in Detroit.

If the prospect has no authority to buy, you're wasting your time making a presentation. If your prospect has no budget, you're also wasting your time. It might be that the prospect cannot buy until next year's budget is approved or until an existing contract ends. You need to know that. Consultant Harry Spitzer says 65% of all sales calls are made to the wrong person. The key is getting to the person who makes the buying decision.

It doesn't hurt to ask, "Are you the person who makes the final decisions on your company's advertising?" If the answer is "no" ask, "Who is that person?" If you are businesslike, most of the people you encounter will help you by giving you the name of the person you need to approach.

Tom Hopkins has two very effective questions he recommends using to get to the right person. One is direct: "Who, in addition to yourself, makes the final decision?" You'll find some prospects want to feel important, so they wait until the last minute to tell you that they can't make the decision. Asking the direct question early in your qualification process saves you both time and frustration later.

Hopkins' other question is less direct, but opens the conversation to additional information: "If we are fortunate enough today to find the right schedule for you, would you be in a position to proceed?" The phrase "If we are fortunate enough today" takes the pressure off, because you indicate you're not going for the close then and there. That might open the prospect to say something like, "No, before we go any further, I'll have to get my partner's approval."

Again, don't take "no" from a person who can't say "yes."

Checking Resources

A key qualifier you must determine for any potential advertiser is the ability to spend money. Does your prospect have the dollars required to commit to an advertising plan you develop?

If you were a network cable seller calling on my company, you'd discover that we can afford a schedule on Nickelodeon's sister channel, TV Land, but a schedule on the main channel is out of the question.[35] The cost is far beyond our means. As a seller, you should have qualified me by finding out about my resources. For a big schedule on the big network, I'm a terrible prospect. You'll be disappointed that my money will run out far faster than your schedule will.

Fortunately, I'm a good credit risk, so that's not a problem when you call on me. Just direct me to the lesser network, where I'll get fewer viewers but good response, and you'll help me spend my limited resources wisely.

Credit is not the only issue here. If you were actually trying to sell me advertising on Nickelodeon, you'd have missed an important step in qualifying: making sure that my service fits your audience. Most of my advertising is business-to-business ad-

vertising within the electronic media industries, so neither network would be exactly the right fit. If one were better than the other, it would be Nick At Nite because it reaches adults.

Qualifying requires matching the business to the medium so that the category works for the seller and for the buyer. Simple examples include soft drinks on MTV, beers on ESPN, homebuilders and grocery stores on adult contemporary radio, and banks and auto dealers on news/talk stations.

Can They Pay?

Some of your prospects will not be very credit-worthy. That may lead you to reject them as potential advertisers or to limit them to paying cash in advance before their schedules run. Asking for money up front can be very uncomfortable, but it's necessary to ensure that you're able to collect. After all, that's how you're paid.

Checking credit is usually left to the business office, not to the individual salesperson. As a seller, you need to know from your business office just what a prospect's credit rating is. As Warner and Buchman put it in *Broadcast and Cable Selling*:

> In general, it's a good idea to use managers as a buffer and to let them take the heat or blame for decisions that could offend or upset a prospect for that is one of the things for which managers are paid. The important thing is to conform to good business practice while leaving the door open for further approaches.

Note that some advertisers—night clubs, concert promoters, and other entertainment businesses—are often required to pay cash in advance for their advertising. Generally, they're used to it, because they pay in advance for other services, such as bands and performers. Asking them for money up front is not so troublesome as asking the same thing of a prospect who isn't able to pay or who isn't accustomed to paying in cash in advance.

Remember that a prospect who cannot pay you is not a prospect at all!

Saying It Again

Let me repeat the importance of qualifying. Your most successful work in sales will be the result of using your time effectively, so think of qualification as a time management tool. The more time you spend qualifying your prospect, the less time you waste making presentations to the wrong people. As Tom Hopkins puts it, "Qualification is the key to high production."

Getting in the Door

Qualifying eases the way to needs analysis, which continues the sales cycle's information-gathering process. In order to conduct a needs analysis, you've got to get in the door, to see the prospect face to face. In order to get in the door, you may have to fight for an appointment.

The easiest and most logical way to see your prospect is to make a phone call and ask. If you already know the person, that's probably all you'll need to do. Most of your prospects, however, will be people you don't know. Rather than offering you a gracious invitation to sell them, they'll be more like the grumpy old codger you met at the beginning of this book. Remember the caption on the poster of the "Man in the Chair"?

> I don't know who you are.
> I don't know your company.
> I don't know your company's product.
> I don't know what your company stands for.
> I don't know your company's customers.
> I don't know your company's record.
> I don't know your company's reputation.
> Now—What was it you wanted to sell me?

That's a tough audience to face! The good news, of course, was that the old codger at least sat still for an appointment with the seller he was addressing.

If you work for a well-known media outlet—the leading TV station, a high-profile cable operator, or the radio station with the number-one morning show, for example—that alone might get you in front of your prospect. Your medium is already perceived to be of value, and that value transfers to you.

Yet even the most valuable medium can't get you in to see a prospect who isn't predisposed toward using that medium for advertising. Worse, some prospects have an aversion to advertising itself, regardless of medium.

You may also encounter former clients who have been disappointed by your outlet or by your competition. It's difficult to convince them that the appointment you want will be anything but a waste of their time.

The Telephone

Get ready. One of the most disturbing aspects of selling is that during your career you'll make thousands of phone calls trying to set appointments, with only a few callbacks. Even so, the telephone is your best organizer and time saver.

"Agency buyers and retailers are busy people," says sales trainer Pam Lontos. "They don't want salespeople just dropping in on them with an attitude of, 'Drop what you're doing, I'm here to sell you advertising.' It shows no respect for the client's time. And it's hard to sell someone you've annoyed," she warns.

Further, Lontos believes that setting an appointment by phone "improves your chances of getting the sale." If you've made the appointment, the client has set aside time to listen to what you have to say. You've also demonstrated respect for the client's time.

Here are her tips for setting appointments successfully:

1. Ask for the owner, president, or senior manager. Don't ask for the person in charge of advertising because that person might not be the decision-maker.

2. Start at the top. If your first call is to a person who can't make decisions, it's difficult to go over that person's head without antagonizing them. If your first meeting is with the top person, you can go back to them if you don't get results from a subordinate.

3. Use the name of the person at the top. If the CEO or president refers you downward to an advertising manager, say so and use the top person's name.

4. Top decision-makers use receptionists and assistants to screen calls. Call early (before 8:30 a.m.) or late (after 5:30 p.m.) to bypass the gatekeeper.

5. Find out if the decision-maker is in before you ask to speak to that person. It makes it difficult for someone to say that your target's not available after saying the target is in the office.

6. Show confidence and energy in your voice. Sound like someone of authority who deserves to be put through.

7. Use first names, yours and theirs. It makes you sound like a friend.

8. Get the secretary's first name and use it. Make the secretary your friend.[36]

Lontos advises against leaving messages, assuming that the prospect will say something like, "Oh boy! Another salesperson!" My feeling is that leaving a message can't hurt, and it may even help. You still have to keep calling until you can get through to the person you want, so leaving a message is hardly the end of the process. I look at a stack of telephone messages as a measure of persistence on the part of a seller.

If you decide to leave a message, be creative with it. Arouse enough curiosity that the prospect wants to call you back and find out what your evocative message is all about. Kerby Confer, who built Keymarket Communications and merged it into Sinclair Communications, would call prospects and tell them he had "the big idea for their business." Prospects responded to the message because with Kerby it was never a ploy. He delivered with promotion and advertising ideas that won him business and made money for his clients.

Lontos suggests at least 30 calls a day, all made in a short period of time, say between 9 and 10 a.m. "Thirty calls should result in reaching 15 people, which should yield 8 appointments. With practice, your ratio of appointments to calls should improve." Lontos uses the tally sheet in Figure 2–11 to count calls and appointments. That helps her measure the ratio.

"Once you start your 30 calls, don't stop until all are done," she advises. "These calls go fast if you don't stop or go for coffee in between. When you get an appointment, dial another number immediately. Call back at the end of the day to reach all the people you couldn't get in the morning."

Step Three—Needs Analysis

We've defined selling as "identifying customer needs profitably. Profitable for you, profitable for them." Your job as a salesperson, then, is to use all the tools at your disposal to help your prospects and clients solve their advertising and marketing problems in a mutually profitable way.

Tool number one is your own medium and the audience your programming attracts. Tool number two is your own knowledge of the client and the client's business. Your success as a seller will be in direct proportion to your demonstration of your knowledge of the client's product, service, and customers.

The RAB's introductory course for radio salespeople, *Welcome to Radio Sales*, has a section that applies to anyone selling any electronic medium:

> It stands to reason that the more we know about what they (the clients) really care about—how their industry works, current trends in their industry, major concerns for their industry, emerging profit centers in their business, who their customers are likely to be—the more time they'll be willing to spend with us . . . and the more likely they'll be to openly sharing information about their specific concerns and problems.
>
> To gain this critical knowledge, we no longer can get away with walking into an account, completely ignorant of his or her business, and saying "Tell me all about the _____ business." Why?
>
> **1.** Most prospects have neither the time nor the inclination to teach you (and

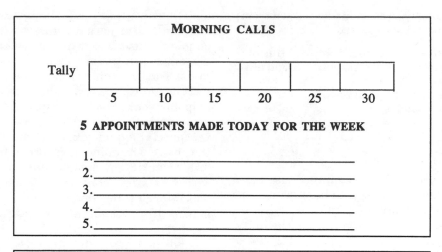

MORNING CALLS

Tally

5	10	15	20	25	30

5 APPOINTMENTS MADE TODAY FOR THE WEEK

1._____
2._____
3._____
4._____
5._____

TODAY'S APPOINTMENTS AND COLD CALLS

<u>Appointments</u>   <u>Cold Calls</u>

1._____   1._____
2._____   2._____
3._____   3._____
4._____   4._____
5._____   5._____
                               6._____

AFTERNOON CALL BACKS

<u>Client</u>   <u>Appointment</u>

1._____   _____
2._____   _____
3._____   _____
4._____   _____

3 APPOINTMENTS FOR TOMORROW

1._____
2._____
3._____

FIGURE 2–11 Can you make 30 telephone calls a day? That's Pam Lontos' recommendation. She says 30 calls equals 15 contacts and 8 appointments. Here's her tally sheet for appointment calls. Courtesy Lontos Sales & Motivation, Inc., Orlando, Florida (407) 299-6128. Used with permission.

every other salesperson who calls on them) about their business; and

2. They will not see you as a true professional who deserves their time and ultimately their trust.

Without *prior* knowledge of the prospect's industry, you simply will be perceived as just another rep trying to sell them something instead of a valued resource.[37]

There are two steps to gaining that prior knowledge: (1) doing your homework, and (2) asking questions. Without the homework, you may never get to ask the questions.

You should go into your appointment armed with no less than the prospect's company history, some idea of business cycles in that industry, and a sense of the competition for the prospect's customers. Sales trainer Chris Lytle suggests starting a client interview with a fact about the client's industry. For example, you might be calling on an electronics retailer and open the interview with the following:

The Electronics Industries Association says in their year-end reports that audio product sales grew about 22% last year compared to a 3% increase in color TV sets. What percentage of your sales came from audio?

Your question about the prospect's specific store is based on the homework you've done. Where do you look? Read the local newspaper, *The Wall Street Journal*, trade magazines from the client's field, and annual reports from the client's company. Watch the local TV news and talk to receptionists, secretaries, and assistants. The more you know before you meet with the prospect, the greater your ability to impress them.

In order to learn specifics about any company, you need to ask questions. For example, IBM sales representatives have a list of 103 questions to ask prospective clients. Xerox sales reps ask as many as 137.

Harvey Mackay, author of *Swim with the Sharks Without Being Eaten Alive*, arms the salesforce of his Mackay Envelope Corporation with a 66-question customer profile.[38] The questions in the "Mackay 66" are de-

tailed and even personal. They include medical history and marital status, how much alcohol the customer drinks or whether the customer has an aversion to those who drink. The list even includes moral and ethical questions to be considered in a relationship between Mackay Envelope and its customer. Mackay's sellers don't ask their prospects the questions directly. They get the answers by doing their research.

Former NBC public relations practitioner Mike McCaffrey compares the needs analysis interview to a doctor-patient relationship.[39] In *Personal Marketing Strategies*, McCaffrey reminds us that a physician "spends no time at all pointing to diplomas or boasting about cures." Instead, "the doctor probes with questions because it is necessary for his diagnosis."

McCaffrey believes that "the single most effective selling tool you have is the ability to ask questions well," and he calls asking questions a "highly learnable skill."

When you ask questions, you take control of the conversation, because you define who is going to talk and what the subject is. If you ask a prospect what their business offers that the competitor can't or won't offer, it's unlikely that the subject will involve anything but the answer to your question. If the prospect rambles or repeats, you can maintain control with an interruption:, "You just triggered another question . . ." Questioning gives you credibility.

Back to McCaffrey's analogy to the doctor and patient: As the doctor asks more probing, perceptive questions, the patient's confidence grows. "The most successful sellers do not need to tout themselves," McCaffrey says. "When they ask incisive, perceptive questions, pretty soon the buyer gets the message: 'This guy knows what he's doing.'"

RAB has five tips to insure a successful consultancy call or needs analysis interview:

1. Resist selling! Remember: the goal is to gain information that will help you make the big sale.

2. Memorize as many of the questions as possible, and be sure to ask them in the proper order.

3. Be sure to customize or tailor the questions with client industry research.

4. Take copious notes during the interview so you can remember to include key findings in your subsequent presentation—and to show the prospect you're really listening.

5. Don't hesitate to be enthusiastic about the prospect, the business, and your ability to help solve key marketing problems.

There are differences of opinion about "taking copious notes." In *Broadcast and Cable Selling*, Warner and Buchman recommend against taking notes, saying it makes people nervous and unwilling to open up. They suggest instead making detailed notes *after* the interview.

I prefer taking notes, because I was a reporter early in my career and the habit stuck with me. I don't write *everything* down, but I capture key words that help me fill in detail later. Using key words takes only a moment and you don't lose focus on the prospect and what's being said.[40]

I remember a salesperson who took notes on a laptop computer and tried to input every word I said during a needs analysis interview. It drove me nuts! So much so, I asked him to stop typing and start listening.

On another occasion, *I* was the one asking the questions in a needs analysis interview, and I decided to rely on my memory rather than taking notes. While I perceived no problem, the client admitted that she had a terrible memory and it worried her that mine might be as a bad as hers. She begged me to take notes on the conversation!

RAB NEEDS ANALYSIS
CONSULTANCY INTERVIEW QUESTION GROUPINGS

1. NUTS AND BOLTS
Hours
   a. Peak hours?
   b. Best day(s)?

Sales and special events
   a. Dates and names of all major sales events?
   b. Two strongest sales events and why they are the most successful?

Financing:
   a. Bank cards accepted?
   b. Revolving plan?
   c. 90 days same as cash?

2. MARKET POSITION
Business advantages
   a. Why do customers come to you?
   b. What do you offer that competitors can't or won't?
   c. What makes your business unique? (positioning)

Major competitors
   a. Who are your competitors?
   b. Why do customers go there?
   c. What is their largest competitive advantage?

What is your single greatest competitive advantage?
What is your single greatest competitive disadvantage?

Overall image
   a. Currently: (low price, large inventory, service, none, etc.)?
   b. Desired: (low price, large inventory, service, etc.)?
   c. What is biggest misconception consumers may have of your business?

What is the biggest marketing problem you face today?

3. CUSTOMER PROFILE
Customer demographics
   a. Gender ratio:
      Currently: Male _____ %
                 Female _____ %
      Desired: Male _____ %
                 Female _____ %
   b. Age:
      Currently: 18–24, 25–34, 35–44, 45–54, 55–64, 65 +
      Desired: 18–24, 25–34, 35–44, 45–54, 55–64, 65 +

Continued

RAB Needs Analysis *(continued)*

Customer income
  a. Currently: Under $20K, $20–40K, $40–60K, $60–75K, over $75K
  b. Desired: Under $20K, $20-40K, $40-60K, $60-75K, over 75K

Marketing area
  a. Currently: (Regional, local, neighborhood)
  b. Desired: (Regional, local, neighborhood)

4. MEDIA PERCEPTIONS

Rank by order of importance to your business (1 = most important; 7 = least important).
  a. Outdoor _____
  b. TV _____
  c. Radio _____
  d. Newspaper _____
  e. Direct mail _____
  f. Magazines/trade publications _____
  g. Telemarketing _____
  h. Other _____ Describe _____

Tell me about the medium you ranked #1.
  a. What do you like best about that medium?
  b. What do you like the least about the medium?
  c. If you could, how would you change or improve that medium?

Tell me about the medium you ranked #2.
  a. What do you like best about that medium?
  b. What do you like least about that medium?
  c. If you could, how would you change or improve that medium?

By percentage, how do you allocate your advertising dollars.
  a. Outdoor _____
  b. TV _____
  c. Radio _____
  d. Newspaper _____
  e. Direct mail _____
  f. Magazines/trade publications _____
  g. Telemarketing _____
  h. Other _____ Describe _____

How often do you advertise in the following media?
  a. Outdoor _____
  b. TV _____
  c. Radio _____
  d. Newspaper _____
  e. Direct mail _____
  f. Magazines/trade publications _____
  g. Telemarketing _____
  h. Other _____ Describe _____

Approximately how much is your annual advertising budget? $_____

5. FUNDING OPPORTUNITIES

Co-op funds/special vendor support:
  a. The major sources of advertising support I've uncovered are . . .
  b. What are other possible sources of cooperative advertising funds?
  c. Are you taking advantage of discretionary vendor support?

6. CREATIVE PREFERENCES

What style of radio commercial would best depict your business?
  a. Comedy
  b. Straight read
  c. Highly creative
  d. Lots of sound effects
  e. Slice-of-life
  f. Other

OTHER QUESTIONS

Do you have an agency?

Who are the others involved in planning and implementing advertising program?

Could we both benefit from my asking these questions of others?

SUGGESTED INTERVIEW CLOSE

"Thank you for giving me the opportunity to meet with you today to learn more about you and your business. Over the next few days, I'll be comparing the information you've shared with sales and marketing data our research department is collecting on your industry. As we conduct this custom research, should I be looking for information on any other areas of specific interest to you?

"Let's get together on (day–date–time) to review our findings and explore your marketing options."

From *Welcome to Radio Sales*, a study course for sellers by the RAB. Used with permission.

NEEDS ANALYSIS GOALS

Whoever said, "You don't get a second chance to make a first impression" was thinking about the needs analysis interview.

Here are the goals for your first meeting:

1. Establish rapport.
2. Build trust.
3. Discover opportunities.
4. Assess attitudes.
5. Measure expectations.
6. Develop a partnership.
7. Arrange for a presentation.

Psychology

Remember Peter Drucker's view that "the customer *is* the business"? In Chapter 1, I quoted from Drucker's *Managing for Results* that there is only one person who knows what the customer wants and that's the customer. "The customer rarely buys what the business thinks it sells him. One reason for this is, of course, that nobody pays for a 'product.' What is paid for is satisfactions. But nobody can make or supply satisfactions as such—at best, only the means to attaining them can be sold and delivered."

The word "satisfactions" indicates "needs" that would be satisfied. When the word "needs" is introduced, the first name that typically comes to mind is Abraham Maslow's, not Peter Drucker's. In his ground breaking 1954 book, *Motivation and Personality*, Maslow theorized that you and I are motivated by a desire to satisfy several needs at once.[42]

He established this hierarchy that flows from bottom to top:

1. *Self-actualization*. Realization of individual potential.
2. *Esteem*. The need for respect from others and competence of self.
3. *Social relationship*. The need to belong, to be loved.
4. *Safety and security*. A predictable, controlled environment.
5. *Physiological needs*. Food, clothing, shelter, air, and water.

Maslow took the world even deeper into his theory in *Toward a Psychology of Being*, "It is a basic or instinctual need if (1) its absence breeds illness, (2) its presence prevents illness, (3) its restoration cures illness. . . ."

I'm not going to develop a theory that selling electronic media might prevent or cure illnesses, nor am I going to turn this into a psychology text. But selling includes a good deal of psychology, and you're better at needs analysis if you recognize the complex motivations that cause people to buy.[43]

As the 1980s turned into the 1990s, several former Apple Computer staffers were recruited by Marc Porat of General Magic, a Silicon Valley company, to develop software for wireless computing. To stimulate his Apple corps to "change the world one more time," Porat had them investigate three basic "domains" or needs of humans:

1. Keeping track of words and pictures that belong to you. "It's very personal; it's very intimate."

2. Maintaining relationships between you and other people. This could be based on interactions with family, friends, workers, or people who have only a brief role in your life, such as an insurance agent or an electronic media salesperson.

3. Obtaining information you require quickly, whether it relates to business, entertainment, or home repairs.[44]

Porat's three needs were part of a speech to a conference called "Wireless Mobile Computing" in 1990 and were reported in the newsletter *Mobile Data Report*. Porat's approach was termed "touchy-feely Applespeak" by his detractors. To others, what seemed vague was dismissed as a company that did not want to give away its secrets.

I use Porat's list because the items address a world that has solved Maslow's basic safety, security, and physiological needs, even if it hasn't distributed the solution to everyone. In an affluent, information-based society, people often think first of their connection to themselves, and that's where General Magic found its psychology.

The basis of sales psychology is that needs are learned and can be triggered externally; thus good sellers develop an eye for clues that tell them how to react.[45] Warner and Buchman offer specific examples for sellers of electronic media:

- Photos of the prospect and important people indicate a need for *recognition*. You might suggest that the prospect appear in commercials.
- If the prospect keeps you waiting and fields phone calls during your interview, there's a need for *dominance*. Pitch the dominance a schedule will give the prospect's business.
- Intelligent, probing questions about the advertising you sell means the prospect needs *understanding*. Include lots of facts and figures in the presentation.
- Sports analogies indicate a need for *achievement*. Position your medium as a means to win, to beat the competition.
- A bare desk indicates a need for *order*. Show that you're the salesperson with an eye for detail.

Larry Wilson of Wilson Learning identified four reasons why people don't buy: no trust, no need, no help, no hurry. As a result, Wilson introduced the idea of consultant selling to the insurance industry. Wilson's systems were licensed and adapted for electronic media by Ken Greenwood, CEO of Greenwood Performance Systems.[46]

Greenwood teaches the "social style" concept, a two-dimensional way to look at needs and expectations—why people respond to each other as they do. (See Figure 2–12.) One dimension is assertiveness, the other is responsiveness. The horizontal axis shows assertiveness from "asking" at the left to "telling" at the right. The vertical axis shows responsiveness, with people at the bottom and tasks at the top.

Greenwood cautions that there is no "best" social style and no "right" place to be in the quadrants. "Each style has strengths and weaknesses," he says. "When you learn to recognize the social style of a prospect or customer, you can tailor your sales process to those needs and expectations."

Asking Questions

Today's selling environment is as much about questioning and listening as it is about presenting and closing. Your presentation is better targeted if your questioning skills are sharp and your listening skills honed.

In *Selling with Integrity*, Sharon Drew Morgen describes how "the seller takes responsibility for supporting the buyer in discovering the best solution to his or her problem." Morgen equates questions with "supporting the process of discovery."[47]

Greater discovery comes with open-ended questions, the ones that cannot be answered with a simple yes or no. Usually open-ended questions begin with who, what, why, and how.

IBM salespeople use the worst-best method, a specific set of open-ended questions: "What do you like best about this particular product?" They follow that with "why" questions to make sure they understand the prospect's attitude toward the product that's likely to be replaced by an IBM. Once they've exhausted the "best" sequence, the questions turn to "What's worst about this product?" That's followed by additional "why" questions to probe feelings.[48]

The objective of questioning is not to sell, but rather to find out what the prospect needs. "If you arrive at that point," says Mike McCaffrey, "you are likely to make the sale. The good seller first

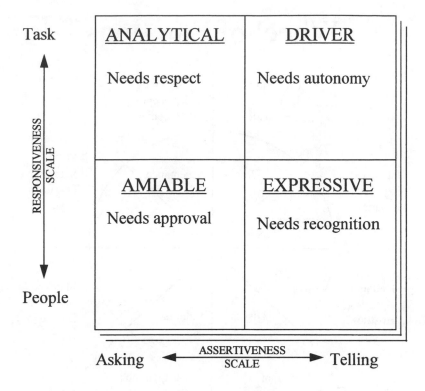

FIGURE 2-12 Ken Greenwood teaches the "Social Style" concept, pioneered by Wilson Learning. The styles fall into quadrants formed by matrices of responsiveness and assertiveness. Learn to recognize the social style of your prospect or customer and tailor your selling accordingly.

seeks to find problems rather than sell solutions."

Here are open-ended questions McCaffrey suggests as examples to evoke revealing discussion:

- What is your thinking on . . . ?
- I'd like to better understand your thinking on . . .
- Would you elaborate on that?
- Why are you taking this action?
- What are your greatest areas of potential growth?
- What are the reasons for this?
- Where has your company been? Where is it now? Where is it going?
- If you could step back and be objective, what would you say are your greatest strengths?

- If there was one area that might be strengthened, what would it be, and why?
- What would you say are your biggest concerns?
- What do you think needs to be done to improve the situation?
- What are some of the indications that make you feel you could use help?
- What takes up most of your personal attention? Why?
- What are the real reasons you are considering a change? Elaborate.

McCaffrey says the response to the final question is the best clue to the prospect's "emotionally charged beliefs, opinions, positions, and justifications." (See Figure 2-13.)

Wheel of Emotions

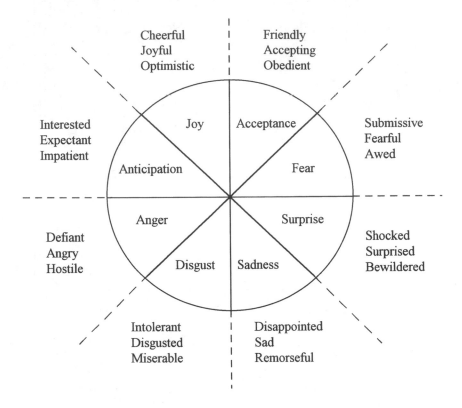

FIGURE 2–13 *The Marketing Revolution* by Kevin Clancy and Robert Shulman introduced me to this wheel of emotions. They applied it to research for consumer products, but I think it also applies to needs analysis. As you read your customer and the reasons for a purchase, look for a motivation based on any of these emotions.

There's a danger here, however. Some salespeople collect more information than they can ever use, and it gathers dust in a computer database or a paper file. It's important to transfer questions into action. You'll see later in this chapter that the information you collect must be used as a well-targeted presentation that demonstrates to the prospect that you've not only asked your questions, but you've also understood the answers.

Ken Greenwood puts it this way: "The PURPOSE of asking questions is to gather information that fills a gap between what you know about a buyer and what you need to know. The PROCESS of asking questions is to connect questions so that the buyer wants to reveal information. . . . The PAYOFF for the seller is insight into the buyer's product and personal needs."

By using questions effectively, you as a seller can position your offering of an advertising plan as a solution that fits both sets of needs the buyer has demonstrated, product and personal.

I like questions that open discussion to the prospect's hopes and goals. For example, "Where are you trying to go?" or "What are you trying to achieve?" It's even fair to ask directly, "What's your vision?" The answers are valuable.

There are three inviolable rules in question-asking, according to Harold Bausemer, president of the Sales Group of Boston: "One, never ask a question that the client cannot answer. Two, never ask the same question twice. Three, never ask more than one question at a time."[49]

Listening Skills

You may develop the best questioning skills on the planet, but it counts for nothing if you can't listen to the answers. The fifth of Stephen Covey's *Seven Habits* is "seek first to understand," and understanding requires listening. "Empathic listening," Covey calls it, because doing it right creates empathy with the person you're listening to.[51]

"Most people do not listen with the intent to understand," says Covey, "they listen with the intent to reply. They're either speaking or preparing to speak."

When you're busy thinking about what to ask next, you're not hearing what's being said at the moment. Covey calls that being "filled with our own autobiography. Our conversations become collective monologues, and we never really understand what's going on inside another human being."

The Wall Street Journal called Americans "a nation of blabbermouths" in an article that lamented the passage of the pause.[52] "People think that listening is boring," said an Atlanta communications trainer. "It's more fun to talk. There's the old joke, the opposite of talking isn't listening, it's waiting to talk."

The *Journal* assigned the blame to three areas:

- Radio and television, because people combine their listening with other activities
- The fast-paced world where we're mentally saying, "Get to the point."
- The public opinion that listening is considered innate. It's not. It's a skill that must be learned and practiced.

Sales expert Ken Greenwood tells a story about the upbringing of a young girl. Mother says, "Guess what, Sarah said her first

---

BETTER QUESTIONS

By changing the way you word a question, you can change your results and gain more usable, valuable feedback. Here are approaches to changing a question so that it promotes more and better responsiveness. These are adapted from *Sales Questions That Close the Sale* by Charles D. Brennan, Jr.[50]

Basic question: Do you make the final decision?
Better: Describe the selection process and how this compares to the way you handled this process in the past.

Basic question: Do you have money in the budget?
Better: Tell me the budget process you go through and how that compares with other areas you fund.

Basic question: Where does your company want to be 6 months from now?
Better: Explain the path your company is going to take in the next 6 months and the factors that will lead you in that direction.

Basic question: Is there anything I can do to help close?
Better: Tell me the role I can play in assisting you in the buying process.

Basic question: What area would you most like to improve?
Better: Describe the areas you would most like to improve and the reasons that you identify these issues over others.

word today." A few years later, mother picks up Sarah at nursery school and is told, "Sarah said her little stand-up speech today very well." The story takes Sarah through high school, where she becomes valedictorian. Greenwood supposes that Sarah "in her entire life, was never praised for listening, only for talking. In fact, in her teens she probably heard that great line: 'Now, listen to me, young lady!'"

How do we apply that to sales? Greenwood puts it this way: "Salespeople who are good listeners focus on the other person, really give them their full attention. Thus the novice salesperson is likely not to pay attention. They merely wait for their time to talk."

A 1957 article in the *Harvard Business Review* gave early support to listening as a skill for salespeople:

> *How* a salesman talks turns out to be relatively unimportant because what he says, when it is guided by his listening, gives power to the spoken word. In other words, the salesman's listening becomes an on-the-spot form of customer research that can immediately be put to work in formulating any sales talk.[53]

Empathic listeners paraphrase what's being said. Suppose for a moment you're the seller of broadcast TV advertising for a station in Chicago. You're conducting a needs analysis with an auto dealer in Napierville, which is well west of the Loop and in the center of populous DuPage County. You might say something like this:

> So, reaching only DuPage and Kane Counties is important to you. You're worried about the wasted coverage of our Chicago signal over Cook County. Do I understand you correctly?

That's a sign that you're really listening and striving for understanding of the client's needs. The prospect responds this way:

> No, viewers in northwest Cook County might drive out to my dealership, I just hate to waste my money on the Loop and people as far away as Will County.

Now you're not only on the same wavelength, but you've also received useful information from your prospect that will help you create an advertising plan.

TEN STEPS TO STRATEGIC LISTENING

1. *Look the speaker in the eye.* Your client should have your undivided attention. Eye contact is the surest way to demonstrate it.

2. *Block distracting thoughts.* Last weekend's party or next weekend's ski trip may be more fun to think about than this sales call, but clear them from your mind.

3. *Ask questions.* Unless they're off the wall or redundant, questions show the speaker that you're listening and that you care about what's being said.

4. *Concentrate on what's being said.* Listen to word choices. Are the images abstract or concrete? Is the attitude positive or negative? You'll get an insight into your client's thinking.

5. *Listen between the lines.* Is something being said beyond the words you take at face value? Listen for clues about the company, industry, and hierarchy.

6. *Don't interrupt the train of thought.* Even if your client wanders off the subject,

it's okay. A change of subject might provide new information you need.

7. *Listen with an open mind.* Defer judgment just as you would in a brainstorming session. You're after information. You can form opinions later. If opinions arise now, they'll get in the way.

8. *Stay focused.* Don't allow yourself to daydream. Humans listen at a rate of 400–600 words per minute, but speak at only 200 words per minute. It takes a special effort to pay attention to the slower pace.

9. *Clarify.* Use sentences that begin with "I." For instance, say "I'm confused," instead of "You confused me." Or say "I didn't catch what you said about deferred payment," and not "You glossed over payment."

10. *Make notes.* Key words and phrases will help you reconstruct the conversation. Ask the speaker's permission to make notes. Most people are flattered by that question.

"Being a good listener does not necessitate being a passive listener," says public relations expert Henry C. Rogers in *Rogers' Rules for Success*. "If you are a good listener, you will give as well as take. If you are listening intently, questions will come to mind. When the speaker pauses, ask them. Even though you may allow (the speaker) to carry the bulk of the conversation, an occasional relevant comment makes you an active participant."[54]

Creating Solutions

Remember, advertisers are not buying advertising, they're buying a business solution. That's why you spend so much time in your needs analysis digging for information about the prospect and the prospect's product or service.

Your homework and your interview yields an outline that shows both the prospect's needs and clear ideas about how your medium gets the prospect's message to the target audience. You're ready to become a partner with your prospect, to affect the conversion from prospect to client.

The needs analysis also gives you direction for your proposal and presentation. The presentation is your face-to-face demonstration that you've created a solution that will bring your prospect more business.

Step Four—Presentation

The sales presentation is here—it's show time!

Most good sellers like the presentation part of the sales cycle the best. It's an opportunity to demonstrate just how attentive you were during the needs analysis and just how well you understand the problems your prospect wants solved.

It's also the way to answer the prospect's key question: "What's in it for me?" By answering that question, you become a partner with your prospect, and you set the stage for closing the sale.

Presentation is making a case for your medium in a face-to-face meeting with your prospect. Your job is to let the prospect—the buyer—know that advertising with your operation will do one or more of the following:

- Solve the buyer's problem
- Save the buyer money
- Increase sales for the buyer
- Raise the buyer's stature in the community
- Make the buyer's work easier

You can tell I like Mark McCormack, because I quote him all the time. Like everybody else, I discovered him with his first book *What They Don't Teach You at Harvard Business School*. Until I read McCormack, I knew nothing about the International Management Group, the company he founded, which manages the business affairs of golfers Arnold Palmer, Gary Player, and Jack Nicklaus, as well as other sports greats.

In *McCormack on Selling*, he includes a section called "How Anyone Can Make Me Buy," which offers good advice on how to sell a man who knows how to sell. McCormack is also a buyer at IMG, so he looks at sellers from a buyer's perspective. First, the essentials:

- Belief in your product
- Belief in yourself
- Seeing a lot of people
- Timing
- Listening to the customer
- A sense of humor
- Knocking on old doors
- Asking everyone to buy
- Following up after the sale with the same aggressiveness you demonstrated during the sale

"I'm sufficiently insulated at our company nowadays that I don't have to see sales people off the street," McCormack explains, so not all of the essentials apply to people he sees personally. Those that do, however, he takes very seriously. For example, he doesn't want to be just another sales call. "Like most people, I don't enjoy the feeling that I'm just a name and number on someone's massive checklist of people to call. Lump me in a crowd and you won't get my money. Make me feel unique, as if I'm the first person you've ever called on with your product or service, and you will."

"Common sense will tell you to step back and look at my business. What does our company do? Who do we deal with? Who have we bought from in the past? How have we grown? What do we need? Common sense will tell you to talk to people who know me," he continues.[55] It's the homework you learned in the discussion of needs analysis.

Why They Buy

Research from Learning International shows three key reasons why customers buy.[56] They have nothing to do with price, rather, with the quality of sellers:

1. Business expertise and image
2. Dedication to the customer
3. Account sensitivity

Yet sales trainer Chris Lytle notes that clients still say, "Your rates are too high." Clients give us rate objections because they have trouble articulating why they aren't buying. "Very few clients will tell you, 'You are an inept, insensitive person dedicated only to selling . . . and unwilling to offer me any expertise or guidance,'" Lytle says. Instead, they let you down easy.

You cannot avoid objections, as you'll see. However, if you've done your homework properly, you can overcome objections that are nothing more than a diversionary tactic.

Your Attitude

A key step in any presentation is believing in yourself. If you demonstrate no faith in your own ability to sell, your prospect will develop none. When your nerves tell you it can't be done, remember Henry Ford's words, "If you think you can, you can. If you think you can't, you're right."

Make your anxiety work for you, not against you. It's natural to be nervous before a presentation. By channeling your anxiety, you help yourself stay sharp and ready for anything the prospect might ask.

Use your nervous energy to rehearse out loud one last time. Give yourself a quick motivational speech. Harvey Mackay (the man who taught us to *Swim with the Sharks Without Being Eaten Alive*) told the story of a seller in the mining industry who wrote at the bottom of each day's schedule of calls the word "astonish." It was a reminder to be ready for every call, every presentation.

Give yourself the same benefit. Think back to the article about visualization, "What You See Is What You Get." Picture yourself closing the sale, for example. Visualize the handshakes or the pats on the back when you report the victory to your sales manager. Mentally write the amount of your billings on a blackboard or whiteboard for all to see.

Repeat these silent affirmations before your sales call:

- I am here to help.
- I go the extra mile.
- (Prospect) is the most important person in the world.
- Closing is a very natural, mutual conclusion for me.

Remember that affirmations are tools for subconscious image impression. Using a positive assertion about yourself and your selling situation is a specific way to program yourself for success. Your subconscious will believe whatever you tell it, so why not feed it positive, productive messages?

Recall from earlier in this chapter that the critical factor about affirmations is to say them in present tense, as if they've been achieved. (This is the significant difference between affirmations and goals.) Say the words aloud, see the results in your mind, and *feel* the results.

With affirmations you give yourself the inner strength and the resolve to keep going. Selling is all about keeping going. By the way, that means going back again, too. Sales consultant Harry Spitzer gathered these figures from sales management studies:

- 48% of salespeople make one call and quit.
- Of those remaining, 25% make two calls and quit.
- Of those remaining, 12% make three calls and quit.
- Of those remaining, 15% make four calls and quit.
- The clincher: 89% of sales to new accounts are made *after the fifth* call![57]

Credibility

You're not only delivering a presentation, you're developing mutual trust with the prospect. Without that trust, the sale breaks down. Your prospect should expect you to demonstrate your trustworthiness, competence, objectivity, and expertise throughout the selling process.

Lester Wunderman, "the pioneering father of direct marketing," reminisces in his book, *Being Direct*, about a needs analysis early in his advertising career. Wunderman asked what results the prospect had enjoyed previously, but the man said he wouldn't even share that with his ad agency. The two agreed on an exchange of letters that guaranteed confidentiality. Wunderman agreed not to divulge the prospect's financial details if the prospect would agree to keep Wunderman's proposals and pricing a secret. Each said yes, and Wunderman was able to show the prospect a way to attract new business.[58]

Not every prospect will be so private, yet you'll need to demonstrate that your prospect's business secrets aren't going to be heard all over town. The best way to build trust is to be honest. Begin by telling the truth. Prospects have uncanny antennae that can detect false claims and phony flattery (although, as *Selling Power* puts it, "A fake smile is better than a sincere frown").

Sell the Benefits

Make no assumptions when it comes to your prospects' needs and concerns. Tell your prospect why they are going to benefit from buying advertising on your medium. (See Figure 2–14.)

The fact that you've got the largest 18–34 female audience in town is good, but remember the advertiser's main concern: "What's in it for me?" It's not just the size of the audience but how you can deliver that audience to that advertiser.

For instance, radio stations often make the mistake of using their wattage as a selling point. The prospect doesn't care how powerful the station is. The benefit is that the advertising can be heard all over town or across two states. It's the same message, but expressed in advertiser language.

For a proposal that puts the prospect's needs first, see Figures 2–15 through 2–18.

There are exceptions. Some presentations you make as a seller will be product-focused, not benefit-focused. Professional buyers at advertising agencies, for example, expect product-based presentations that talk about ratings numbers because it makes their jobs easier. Product-based selling works well when selling a one-time event like the Super Bowl or the Olympics. The advantage: one presentation covers many prospects.

Get to the Point

Time and attention are the chief currencies of the twenty-first century. No one has time to waste, and attention is divided among too many stimuli. If your prospect has enough money to spend on advertising, you can assume he or she has a full and pressured calendar. Time is money, and wasting either will be a strike against you.

The way to get the customer's attention is to provide helpful information that demonstrates your expertise. Narrow your focus to just a few important points and stick to them. Make sure everything you say sets up your key point, then supports and illustrates it. Complex and complicated are out, simple and effortless (for the buyer) are in.

Business writer Howard Upton reinforces that: "Ask IBM for details on a consumer product, for instance, and you will

In October, Market Volatility Drove Viewers Seeking Information to CNBC

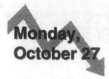

The Market Collapses Viewers Flock to CNBC

Monday, October 27

- Dow Jones Industrial Average fell a record 554 points.
- Trading curbs were imposed at 3:30pm, halting trading for the day 30 minutes early.

- Viewers turned to CNBC in record numbers. Business Day averaged a .58 rating and 368,000 HHs — more than double our record 3Q average.
- CNBC viewership peaked from 3:30–3:45pm with more than one million HHs tuned to the network!

The Market Recovers Viewers Flock to CNBC

Tuesday, October 28

- On Tuesday, October 28, the market recovered as a record 1.2 billion shares were traded during the day.
- The Dow experienced its greatest single-day point gain ever, rising 337 points.

- CNBC's audiences increased over the previous record-setting day. CNBC Business Day averaged a .68 rating and 429,000 households.
- CNBC Viewership peaked between 10:00–10:15 am during which time the Dow hit bottom and then started its ascent.

As a CNBC Advertiser, You Are Always There When Investors Have the Most at Stake.

FIGURE 2–14 The product focus is CNBC's report on a volatile stock market. The benefit to the advertiser is that viewer levels surge when there's big news. Courtesy of NBC Cable Networks, Ad Sales Department, April 1998. ©1998, NBC Cable Networks.

receive a printed piece covering that particular product. Period. Moreover, the IBM brochure will be clearly written."

Upton, former CEO of the Petroleum Equipment Institute, saw his share of sales presentations:

> Skilled salespeople limit their presentation to the specific product in question and concentrate on explaining how that product will benefit the particular customer. They avoid distractions and refrain from confusing the customer with information overload.
> "Successful salespeople . . . dispense customer information in measured amounts—neither too little nor too much. They realize that there is, after all, as much

business peril in providing too much information as there is in not providing enough.[59]

Presentation Tips

Has the client heard it all before? Most clients have been exposed to basic sales pitches before yours. Since that's the case, you'd better come up with a new angle.

Your presentation will stand out if you have interesting (but brief) stories to tell. The stories should not be about you. Rather, make them success stories about similar advertising campaigns for similar clients or targeted for the same audience your prospect desires. Nothing is so con-

---

WRITING FOR SUCCESS

When writing a sales presentation, you need to win approval for the advertising program that you're suggesting. Follow these guidelines both to get read and to get the buy:

- State up front exactly what you're proposing.
- Follow with supporting reasons that show customer benefits.

- Use the client's own words from previous meetings.
- Describe the results of choosing your proposal as specifically as possible.
- Use short, clear sentences that communicate well.
- Keep the entire presentation short.

A SPECIAL PRESENTATION FOR...

Hometown

Furniture

Exclusively prepared for:

Alice Smith, Managing Partner
Hometown Furniture

FROM BILL JONES
WXYZ RADIO
MAY 1995

FIGURE 2–15

Start a proposal from the client's point of view. This prototype makes the client's logo the largest item on the page, demonstrating that the subject of the proposal (and all the conversation that follows) will be the client. Note that the station information is in relatively small type. Developed by Mike Mahone of RAB for *Welcome to Radio Sales*. Used with permission.

vincing as hard evidence that other people have done the same thing you're asking the prospect to do. When somebody tells you that you're making a smart decision, it gives you comfort, right? That's what testimonials are all about: other people offering reinforcement. Here are some examples of targeted testimonials:

- BET presents a list of its clients to show a potential advertiser that their product will fit well into the current group of advertisers.
- Letters from satisfied customers fill the pockets of presentation kits from many local cable operators who sell local advertising.
- RAB canvassed its membership to collect 1,100 case studies and testimonial letters to show the power of radio.

Talk about colorful: Twentieth Television sends photos of agents Fox Mulder and Dana Scully to potential *X-Files* advertisers. Bound behind the slick photo are ratings comparisons of *X-Files* against ABC, CBS, NBC, and Fox prime time schedules to entice ad agencies to support *X-Files* in off-network syndication.

In another example, potential advertisers on TBS and TNT receive fat binders with elaborate pull-out pockets holding photos of stars and data about programming on the two networks.

National networks have the most elaborate graphics because they hope to sway advertisers who've seen just about everything. But local media can do the same on a lesser scale: Some of Forever Broadcast-

WHAT YOU TOLD US ....

1. **You're concerned about the competition**

   A. Primarily competition from other furniture stores

   B. Also increased competition from area department stores

   C. And, to a lesser degree, competition from discounters and others

2. **You'd like to increase your business by ...**

   A. Continuing to reach and influence your primary customers — middle-age women, primarily age 30-50

   B. Developing sales opportunities with new consumer segments

3. **You want to create a unique market position for Hometown Furniture**

   A. In the mind of the consumer

   B. In your advertising and marketing

FIGURE 2–16
The first section of the proposal takes its language from the consultancy interview or needs analysis. The three points will become the foundation of the entire proposal. Section 2, "The Research Shows . . . ," positions you as a valuable marketing consultant and partner, not just another media seller. Courtesy Radio Advertising Bureau. Used with permission.

THE RESEARCH SHOWS...

1. **You have a tremendous amount of tough competition!**

   A. The yellow pages list over 116 competitive retail locations
   1. 40 full-line furniture stores (34% of sales)
   2. 32 department stores (28% of sales)
   3. 18 discount stores (18% of sales)
   4. 26 other retailers advertising furniture items (Home Testing Institute for *Furniture Retailer* - 1994)

2. **The best way to increase business is with multi-faceted marketing**

   A. Continuing to focus on adult women
   1. Over 52% of furniture buyers are women, generally age 30-44, primarily married with children (Simmons 1994)

   B. Attracting customers from emerging (and virtually untapped) consumer segments like singles and empty-nesters
   1. 39% of furniture buyers are unmarried (Home Furnishings *Executive* 1994)
   2. 39% of furniture is purchased by adults age 45+ (same)
   3. Empty nesters, age 55+, account for 17% of furniture buyers (Simmons)
   4. 55+ buyers spend the highest percentage of their disposable income on furniture (U.S. Dept of Labor - 1995)

3. **Creating a unique market position or selling proposition is an important key to attracting new customers**

   A. As interest rates rise, new and existing home sales are slowing. Hometown Furniture growth must come from new markets not necessarily dependent on the purchase of a new home.

ing's radio stations call themselves FROG-GY and include color photos of their "Mr. Froggy" mascot in the presentation packages.

Give Your Numbers Impact

It's hard to digest numbers, so give them perspective. In other words, relate numbers to something your prospect can visualize. For instance, a cable seller on Chicago's west side might describe suburban DuPage County as "a population equal to Indianapolis." The quarter-hour share for a Houston radio station might be "standing-room-only at the Astrodome."

Design easy-to-read charts and graphs to illustrate your figures. I hate to give newspapers credit, but *USA Today* does a terrific job with the graphics they use to show polling results. The artwork adds to the understanding of the numbers behind the percentages.

Country Music Television uses Arbitron ratings for the country format on radio as a selling tool for the cable network. The CNN Airport Network uses an index of frequent travelers against the U.S. population to demonstrate the income potential of its audience.

Cable systems in markets 100 and smaller use Arbitron's "RetailDirect Lite" to show advertisers qualitative data about viewers: banking services used, beer and soft drink consumption, plans to buy automobiles, grocery expenditures, and ten other qualitative categories. Cable sellers

WHY YOU NEED RADIO...

1. **You'll stand out from the competition on Radio.**

   A. You'll reach your best customers — 95% of all women listen to Radio each week. (RADAR Fall 1994)
   B. You'll reach your best prospects — 78% of all women listen to Radio over three hours every day. (RADAR Fall 1994)
   C. Your commercials stand alone, away from the competition on Radio. (as compared to side-by-side placement in the newspaper)
   D. You not only will improve your advertising reach, but also build message frequency (repetitive exposures) with cost-efficient Radio.

2. **You'll increase your business with Radio...**

   A. By continuing to influence women, married age 30-50 — Radio reaches 97.6% of women each week. (RADAR Fall 1994)
   B. By efficiently reaching new consumer groups and/or niches with the right selection of highly targeted stations — one out of four loyal Radio listeners will buy furniture within the next 12 months. (Media Audit 1994)

3. **You can create a unique market position with more than one consumer segment with highly selective Radio!**

   A. Build a program to target affluent young singles who account for approximately 9% of all furniture sales. (Home Furnishings Executive - 1994)
   B. Build a program to target empty-nesters who have a high degree of disposable income and account for 17% of all furniture sales. (Home Furnishings Executive - 1994)

FIGURE 2–17

Before a prospect considers your operation, you've got to sell your medium and its benefits. Here, the benefits of radio are outlined. Only then does the presentation turn specifically to the seller's station. Courtesy RAB. Used with permission.

WHY YOU NEED "MEMORIES—AM 600'

1. **You'll stand out from the competition on Memories AM 600!**

   A. Your commercial messages will stand alone on WAXY Radio — We guarantee at least 12 minutes competitive separation!
   B. Your commercial messages will stand out with your exclusive sponsorship of high-interest WAXY news & weather sponsorships!
   C. Your commercial messages will reach a market that, until now, has been virtually ignored by many of your toughest competitors

2. **You'll increase your business by advertising regularly on WAXY...**

   A. By continuing to reach your primary market of adult women, age 25-54...37% of Memories AM 600's audience! (Simmons National Format Average - 1995)
   B. By tapping into the highly lucrative "empty-nester" market — 59% of WAXY's audience is age 55+.

3. **You'll create new, unique, profit-building market position with the help of marketing experts at Memories 600 AM!**

   A. You'll be able to take full advantage of the unique relationship and unparalleled influence WAXY has with its listeners of all ages.
   B. Your new "empty-nester" marketing opportunity will be less volatile than other consumer markets because:
      1. They have a very high level of disposable income.
      2. Their furniture buys are less likely to be tied to the purchase of a new home.

know who's a potential user of the prospect's product, and they have the numbers to demonstrate the fact.

Make sure the numbers you use tell the story, not garble the issue. Best to keep figures to a minimum and use them to illustrate a point, not as the point in themselves.

Some prospects want numbers, numbers, numbers in their presentation. Your needs analysis should uncover that information. As an example, I presented a new music format to two partners who owned a chain of radio stations in the Southeast. My needs analysis showed that one was the creative force in the company, the other was a CPA and numbers cruncher. My presentation for them had two parts: one with lots of audio and visuals of modern rock bands, designed specifically for the creative partner, the other with stacks of research tables for the analytical partner.

Use Questions

If you've taken journalism courses, you know the "Who, what, where, when, why, and how?" question sequence. The same open-ended questions work well in the selling setting, too. They encourage thoughtful answers in full sentences, not just a word or two. Questions encourage participation.

Questions help you secure agreement as you proceed through the presentation. Look for nonverbal signals that indicate whether you've connected. In sales, communication is *your* responsibility. If the

FIGURE 2–18

Your client is buying more than a schedule, so sell solutions. Use a page to demonstrate how your commercials will solve the problems that were the basis for the entire proposal. Then, in the last section of your presentation, cover the details and get the client's approval. Courtesy RAB. Used with permission.

HOW YOUR MESSAGE ON WAXY WILL GENERATE SALES...

1. Each Hometown Furniture Message on Memories AM 600 will be carefully crafted to:

   A. Stand out from the advertising of any area competitor;

   B. Increase sales by calling for specific consumer action;

   C. Build and fortify a unique market position for Hometown Furniture.

2. Each of your commercial messages will talk directly to adults 55+ who, for whatever reason, now have their home to themselves.

3. While targeting "empty nesters," your commercial messages will not alienate other consumer segments, such as women 30-50.

4. Your WAXY copy will change every week, but the basic creative approach and underlying message will not! Repetition and consistency is the key to advertising success.

5. Sample Hometown Furniture commercial message.

THE DETAILS — YOUR NEW WAXY RADIO MARKETING PROGRAM...

1. Weekly News Sponsorships —
Monday:	10am & 4pm
Tuesday:	6am & 5pm
Wednesday:	noon
Thursday:	8am & 6pm
Friday:	noon

   Start date:_____ Weekly Investment: $_____

2. Weekly Weather Sponsorships —
Monday:	6:10am
Tuesday:	3:40pm
Wednesday:	7:40am
Thursday:	11:10am
Friday:	5:10pm
Weekend 10-pack Rotator	

   Start Date:_____ Weekly Investment: $_____

3. Sale and Special Event "Drive Schedule"

   - Thirty 60-second commercial announcements per broadcast week; Total Reach/24-hour equal distribution scheduling

   - Event dates:_____

   - Investment per Event: $_____

---

client is not listening to you, it's not the client's fault, it's the presenter's fault.

If you're not connecting with the client, address the issue right away. Questions like "Am I really on target for you?" and "Is there something else you would like to hear about?" underscore your sensitivity to the client's response.

Questions work in both directions. You learn more about the prospect's needs with your questions. Let the prospect ask, too, so you can fill in all the details that lead to closing.

Let the Customer Say "No"

Customers have a need to say no. It helps them maintain a sense of dignity and control. As Mark McCormack puts it, "No customer wants to be regarded as a pushover." He suggests prefacing a great idea with a few lesser ones.

A better technique is offering several proposals that differ in price: one large, one medium, one small. Amy Bly and Robert Bly of the Center for Technical Communication call it "The Rule of Three."

Before you sit down to bargain, you should have three figures or positions fixed firmly in your mind:

The maximum—the highest figure. The most you dare ask for without "blowing away" (the client).

The minimum—the bottom line. The lowest figure you'd settle for.

The goal—a realistic figure you have a good chance of getting. The goal is probably between 50 and 75 percent of the maximum.[60]

If you use the three-step proposal, you should construct the one with the lowest cost so that it shows clearly how much better the medium- and high-cost proposals are in comparison to it.

Tom Hopkins calls this procedure "bracketing-up for money" and the "triplicate of choice." Buyers often pick the middle price, especially if they're buying tangible products (like office equipment) or services (insurance, for example). The natural response is the middle, in an attempt to avoid seeming either extravagant on the one hand or cheap on the other.[61] See Figure 2–20 for a promise to recommend only the right plan.

Keeping Your Prospect Involved

When my wife and I were trying to decide on a new vacuum cleaner, the woman at the shop greeted us with a container of sand, which she threw on the floor. She handed Pam the business end of the Hoover "Wind Tunnel" vacuum we had seen advertised during Houston Astros games. Once Pam finished, she handed the machine to me, and in no time, the floor was clean. Now *that*'s involving the prospect!

Copier sellers do the same type of thing: they hand you a sheet of paper to feed into the machine. Sellers of telephone systems plug in the phones so prospects can push the buttons, hear the rings, and check the audio quality. Buying a new sofa? You wouldn't buy without sitting on it, would you? A new mattress? I bet you'd stretch out on it and bounce on the edges before you'd buy!

You get the idea. Involvement techniques are like the auto dealer's test drive. If a car seller gets a prospect behind the wheel, there's "effective selling control," to use Tom Hopkins' words. The more the prospect touches and feels the merchandise, the better the opportunity for a sale.

The difficulty in selling electronic media is that there's no vacuum cleaner to suck up strewn sand and no ability to "get behind the wheel." Our intangible forms of media are made more tangible with ideas, however—recorded commercials from radio stations, storyboards from TV stations, and promotional tie-in opportunities.

Media kits like the ones I described earlier in the chapter also make our products more tangible. Media kits contain market and audience information, descriptions of programming, personality profiles, coverage maps (for radio, television, and cable), rate cards, testimonials, and press clippings.

Says Michael Keith in *Selling Radio Direct*, "Media kits do not sell a client, but they can certainly aid in this objective. Promotional materials say a lot about a station. They reveal it."[62]

A flashy, fun media package says the medium is flashy and fun. Nickelodeon's materials reflect the whimsy of a kids' network and the nostalgia of its sister networks, Nick At Nite and TV Land. (See Figure 2–19.) The Weather Channel uses an austere, factual presentation peppered with remarks designed to catch the reader's attention, such as "If hell freezes over, you'll hear it here first."

Media kits are designed for the salesperson to use as visual aids to bring the medium alive in the prospect's mind during a presentation. An effective seller uses parts of the media kit as integral elements of the presentation to inform and involve the prospect. For example, bringing out a profile sheet when you're describing your medium gives you the chance to physically hand something to your prospect.

The A&E network's presentation requires the prospect to unfold the kit itself and then open a cardboard tab to remove spiral-bound books and program information. USA Network puts its presentation in a black folio that looks like the box for a movie script. Prospects are involved immediately because they must remove an elastic band to open the folder.

A good salesperson doesn't work directly from a media kit, Keith says. "Select in advance what parts of the packet you'll employ. During a presentation, don't dig through your pouch of materials like a circus clown does his bottomless, gag-filled satchel. You'll just look silly." Don't take Keith's "satchel" remark as a cue that you shouldn't use tools, including gags, that enhance your presentation. His point is that you want to *plan* what you use.

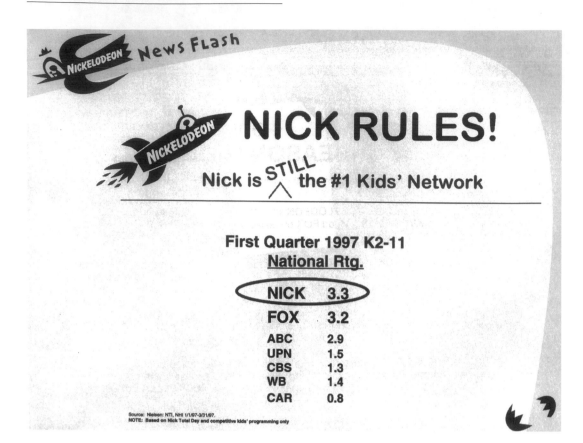

FIGURE 2–19 A flashy, fun media kit says the medium is flashy and fun. The green plastic pouch that holds Nickelodeon's presentation is the color of the slimy Gak that Nickelodeon splashes on unsuspecting kids. Even mundane ratings information is presented with flair and attitude. Used with permission. MTV Networks.

When Kerby Confer, Chairman of Sinclair Communications' radio division, speaks to audiences about creativity, he often tells stories about his "big deal pen." Out of his pocket comes a huge pen—probably 2 feet long. When he was a station salesperson, Kerby would put the pen on the edge of the desk and roll it toward his client. "I've brought the big deal pen, because I feel today's the day you'll sign the big deal you've been looking for," he'd say. The client got involved immediately, trying to catch the rolling pen. Kerby got attention and earned a reputation for creativity and confidence.[63]

Powerful Words

Words. Choose the right ones and you open doors. Mark Twain said it best: "A powerful agent is the right word." He added a modifier for effect: ". . . those *intensely* right words."

Practice using the best possible words to convey your meaning while portraying transactions in the most positive terms possible. It's not *what* you say but *how* you say it that can make a difference between a sale and no sale.

Tom Hopkins uses the term "rejection words" for words that remind buyers that this is a selling situation—you're making a sale to them. That may trigger fear. "Rejec-

THESE GUARANTEES ARE THE FOUNDATION OF OUR BUSINESS

1. We promise not to sell you a plan of action that we do not think will work. We guarantee to ask questions that help us match our strengths to your needs and challenges. At **FROGGY 98**, we listen as much as we talk.

2. We guarantee to never personally attack our competitors. We will, however, make strong observations and valid comparisons to provide you with the resources to make a decision in your best interest. Serving you effectively requires that you know where we stand with regard to the competition. We pledge to be candid and honest.

3. When we tell you that we will be back with an idea, that means no more than four working days. And when you need a change of copy, you get "same day" service. Business changes quickly and you will always be a priority at **FROGGY 98**.

4. We pledge to listen as much as we talk. In order to serve you, we need to get YOUR views and ideas. What is important to you is important to us.

FIGURE 2–20 Ethics are alive and well! The radio stations owned by Forever Broadcasting include a pledge to their advertisers about how the stations will conduct business.

tion words really work well," Hopkins says. "They let you scare your prospects so much that most of them will reject you and your proposition."

Here are samples of rejection words and their preferred alternatives:

Rejection Word	Preferred Word
Buy	Own
Commission	Fee for service
Contract	Paperwork, agreement, worksheet
Cost or price	Total investment
Deal	Transaction, opportunity
Down payment	Initial investment
Monthly payment	Monthly investment
Pitch	Presentation, demonstration, plan
Sell, sold	Become involved with the program
Sign	Okay it, approve it, endorse it, authorize it

DOS AND DON'TS FOR PRESENTATION

Do . . .
- Research the advertiser.
- Be prepared.
- Know all you can.
- Have a relevant plan in mind.
- Be enthusiastic.
- Think positive.
- Display confidence.
- Believe in yourself and your product.
- Smile.
- Exude friendliness, warmth, and sincerity.
- Be human and accessible.
- Listen.
- Be polite, sympathetic, and interested.
- Tell success stories. Provide testimonial material.
- Think creatively. Look for the novel approach.
- Know your competition.
- Maintain integrity and poise.
- Look your best. Check your appearance.
- Be objective and retain proper perspective.
- Pitch to the decision-maker.
- Be courteous to everyone you encounter.
- Ask for the order that will do the job.
- Service the account after the sale.

Don't . . .
- Pitch without a plan.
- Criticize or demean client's previous advertising.
- Argue with the client.
- Talk cost up front.
- Bad-mouth the competition.
- Talk too much.
- Brag or be overly aggressive.
- Lie, exaggerate, or make unrealistic promises.
- Smoke or chew gum in front of the client.
- Procrastinate.
- Be intimidated.
- Make a presentation unless you have the client's undivided attention.
- Use jargon unknown to client.
- Lose your temper.
- Ask for too little. Never undersell a client.
- Oversell a client.
- Fail to follow up.
- Accept *no* as final.
- Pitch after the client is sold.

From *Selling Radio Direct*, by Michael C. Keith. ©1992 Focal Press and used with permission.

Alternate words don't change the fact that a sale is being made. They simply soften the effect on the buyer and help to reduce the triggers that send red flags up during the selling process. Those red flags make the buyer cautious, which may stall the momentum and turn into an objection.

Consider just one of the examples above, the word "investment." What do you do when you invest? You put your money to work to bring income or other benefits. That's why "investment" is a better choice than "cost," "price," or "payment." Use your vocabulary to create *value* in the prospect's mind.

The decision-making process is often more emotional than rational. By choosing the right words you tap the emotional side of your prospect. As an example, a question using the word "think" prompts a rational response. Instead of trying to get someone to accept an idea you've proposed by saying "What do you think?" try these approaches to trigger an emotional response:

"How does it sound so far?"

"Feels pretty good, doesn't it?"

"Does this look like a winner to you?"

Appealing to the senses helps you gain acceptance for your proposal.

Use "pedestal words" to raise the other person to a level above the ordinary. Here are ten examples:

"May I?" Asking permission implies authority.

"As you of course know . . ." implies vast knowledge.

"I'd like your advice . . ." suggests superior wisdom.

DRESS UP A PRESENTATION

Here are a few creative ideas to enhance your next presentation.

Ask the station engineer for a 3-inch piece of wire used in your outlet's operation. For radio and television, it should be from the transmitter. For cable, it should be from the operations center or the headend. Get the technical number of the wire.

Attach the wire to the cover of your presentation with a caption that says "This 3-inch piece of 3DHMX wire can connect you to the biggest audience in (area covered)." Or "This piece of wire plugs you right into *your* target audience."

***

List the total reading time on the cover of a presentation, especially one that will be read when you're not present. This lets prospects know you're concerned about their time.

***

Use the prospect's logo on the cover of the presentation. It adds a personal touch and places the focus where it belongs: on the prospect's business. Get the logo from letterhead or a print ad and scan it.

***

Add the script for a commercial as the last element of a presentation. When you write the copy, include two or more throw away lines—something the client can scratch without damaging the creative concept. When the client gets to that part of the proposal, offer a pen for corrections.

***

Send a postcard once a week to a prospective client that states qualitative information, special promotions, or ratings that specifically target the client's audience. For example, "KXXX listeners bought 100 Hondas in December." After four or five weeks, call and ask for an appointment.

***

Give a client a tape caddy containing a copy of their commercial. A place to store their audio commercials provides a "scrapbook" similar to what many people use for newspaper ads.[64]

"I'd sure appreciate it if . . ." implies that the prospect has the power to refuse or grant.

"You are so right." A pat on the back.

"Spare time from your busy life" implies the prospect is a busy and therefore important person.

"Because of your specialized knowledge." Implies skill, professionalism.

"A person of your standing." No one knows just what "standing" means but everyone believes—or hopes—he or she has it.

"I'd like your opinion." People on pedestals are supposed to have opinions, so if an opinion is asked, the person is immediately put on a pedestal.

"Please." The great lubricator of human relations.

Do these words work every time? No, of course not. Yet they beat the alternatives every time.

The power of "the intensely right word" is demonstrated by Tom Hopkins when he reminds us that no one ever says, "Wait till you see what a salesman sold me today." Instead, you'll hear, "Wait till you see what I bought today." Hopkins' explains:

> When people talk about *what I bought today*, they're really saying, "Wait till you see the new status-raiser that I own as of today. They've done something. Now they want everyone to admire their wisdom, style, and power—and they won't willingly share the glory with the salesperson who closed them.[65]

Most buyers don't want to admit that something other than their own choice entered the decision to buy. "Owning" a product or service allows them to maintain the dignity of their desires and decisions. "Buying" the same service means they've been unduly influenced.

In customer-focused selling, the sales process should be transparent so that the buyer makes the decision to own. As the seller, you're a facilitator who creates a logical link between the customer's need and the solution you sell.

In the next section, you'll see that the link is not always logical. Nor is it always smooth. But you'll also learn techniques to neutralize your prospect's defense mechanisms.

SALES PRESENTATION CHECKLIST

After giving a sales presentation, replay the meeting by yourself, completing the following checklist. At the end of the week, look over your sales presentation scores to pinpoint strengths and weaknesses.

Name of business: _____

Prospect name: _____

Describe the Prospect

____ Good-natured	____ Angry	____ Know-it-all
____ Open-minded	____ Religious	____ Curious
____ Apathetic	____ Timid	____ Tense
____ Egotistical	____ Skeptical	____ Cynical
____ Enthusiastic	____ Cautious	____ Relaxed
____ Procrastinator	____ Analytical	

Cold Calling

Did you make the prospect comfortable?	___ Yes	___ No
Did you get the prospect to talk?	___ Yes	___ No
Did the prospect like you?	___ Yes	___ No
Did the prospect want to hear about your station?	___ Yes	___ No
Did the prospect show interest in the medium?	___ Yes	___ No
Did the conversation flow smoothly?	___ Yes	___ No
Do you know what the prospect wants or needs?	___ Yes	___ No

Presentation

Evaluate your performance on a scale of 1 to 10, with 1 meaning poor and 10 meaning outstanding.

____ Aura of excitement
____ Professional manner
____ Conversation focused on the prospect
____ Your answers were intelligent
____ Your answers were confident
____ The prospect was persuaded

Questions and Objections

List the two most important questions your prospect asked.

1. _____

2. _____

Briefly list the prospect's main objections to your presentation. _____

_____

_____

How did you reverse their objections? _____

_____

Continued

Sales Presentation Checklist (continued)
Closing the Sale
How many trial closes did you make?   _____

How did the prospect respond to these closes?   _____

_____

After testing the sales climate with trial closes, how many times did you
attempt to close?   _____

After your first close, what did the prospect say and what was the reaction?

_____

Did the prospect buy?   _____

If you didn't clinch the sale, why do you think the prospect didn't buy?

_____

Evaluation
Rank these elements of your selling plan from 1 to 10, with 1 being the weakest
and 10 being the strongest.
_____ Identifying the prospect
_____ Cold call
_____ The presentation itself
_____ Answering questions
_____ Handling objections
_____ Closing the sale
_____ Getting leads from the prospect
_____ Creating a relationship

Step Five — Answering Objections

The seller's dream is to make a presentation to a potential customer and immediately hear the words, "I'll take it!" More often, the seller experiences a rude awakening: "Your rates are too high!" Get used to it. This will not be the last time you hear that sentence if you're serious about selling.

Part of your presentation should prepare the customer to hear the price or a range of prices. Examples of what other schedules cost in your medium help to ease the way. Choose your examples with care, and be prepared to help raise the customer's sights.

Price, you'll discover, is the easiest objection for a prospect to articulate. As you read in the last section, there's often a deeper reason for not wanting to buy. It's your job to probe for the true reason and to answer it with the benefit inherent in the schedule you're proposing or the medium you're selling. That way you neutralize the objection and win the business.

An objection is simply an expression of your prospect's concern about advertising.

On the surface, the objection seems to be a reason *not* to buy what you're selling. You might even take an objection as *rejection*. Don't. As Tom Hopkins puts it, "You don't lose to objections, you win by handling objections." (See Figure 2–21.)

The objections you encounter are likely to fit into one of three categories:

1. An unspoken request for more information or clarification
2. A defense mechanism on the part of the prospect
3. A stalling technique

The good news is that objections can be resolved to the benefit of both prospect and seller. As Hopkins says, "Any active sales person will discover most of the built-in objections within the first month. A built-in objection is one that the prospect will give you nearly every time. After a few months in the business, the sales people will say, 'I always get hit with that objection.'"

" *I don't know who you are.*

I don't know your company.

I don't know your company's product.

I don't know what your company stands for.

I don't know your company's customers.

I don't know your company's record.

I don't know your company's reputation.

Now – what was it you wanted to sell me?"

Sales start **before** you call—with business-to-business advertising.

The McGraw·Hill Companies

Financial Services. Information and Media. Educational and Professional Publishing.
© 1996, by The McGraw-Hill Companies, Inc.

FIGURE 2–21 "The Man in the Chair" states his objections clearly and openly for sellers. Your prospect may not be so easy to read. This is the 1996 version, less confrontational than the original (see Figure 1–1) and more in tune with today's selling style. ©1996, McGraw Hill Company. Used with permission.

Let that give you hope. It's a positive sign if you know in advance what objections are going to arise while you're selling. That gives you the opportunity to prepare not only your presentation but also your response to objections. Until you learn to handle objections adroitly, you cannot reach your potential as a seller.

Objections Versus Conditions

The example I used earlier, "Your rates are too high," is typical of an objection. However, what if a prospect says instead, "I can't afford to advertise on TV"? That's a *condition*, not an objection.

The difference between objections and conditions is that objections can be overcome but conditions cannot. A condition is a valid reason for not buying, and it's a reason for the salesperson to walk away.[66]

Conditions should be discovered in the qualifying process. The major aim of qualifying is to determine whether there are conditions that make the sale impossible. Yet even the most skillful seller will sometimes overlook a signal in the qualifying process, thinking that it's an objection that can be overcome.

When that happens, take Tom Hopkins' advice: "Treat it like an objection. That is, try to break it down. If it doesn't break down, it's a condition, and you'll need to develop the ability to swallow hard and then quickly and courteously disconnect from that prospect."

If the prospect truly cannot afford to buy TV time, you, as a smart TV seller, should bow out. The reason to do it gracefully and to be pleasant about it is that the condition may someday be removed. If that prospect grows the business and the advertising budget, you'll want to pitch again!

Walking away shows the difference between the old-style "close-at-all-costs" selling methods and today's customer-oriented sales. (See Figure 2–22.) By saving the prospect a needless (and harmful) expenditure, you show respect and therefore win respect. The prospect's doors are more likely to be open to you when the time is right.

FIGURE 2–22
I like the fact that this ad uses the phrase "salespeople that don't know what the word NO means." It weeds out candidates who can't or won't give all they can. Used with permission of Chancellor Media's WAXQ.

When the Customer Says "No"

My company once published an article titled, "Selling Begins When the Customer Says NO." We didn't invent the phrase; we adapted it from selling literature that had been used for years. The phrase is essential to maintaining a positive attitude while you're selling. It's a given: you *will* encounter objections.[67]

Objections need to be dealt with before you can move forward in the selling process, and addressing each objection specifically and completely gives your sale momentum. Your job is easier if you prepare in advance. Consider the following guidelines:

- *Expect the objection*. If you anticipate it, you'll be in control when the objection occurs. If you are caught off guard and hesitate before answering, the prospect will think you agree. You can forestall the objection by anticipating it and including it in your presentation. It's best to address recurring objections early, so you appear objective and candid. That enhances credibility.

- *Understand the objection*. When a potential customer has stated an objection, make sure you understand the comment. An answer that doesn't satisfy the customer's need distances you from the close. Use open-ended, probing questions. Don't ask, "Do you watch CNN?" Ask, "How do you think advertisers evaluate their schedules on CNN?"
- *Reconfirm the objection*. Restate the objection and position it as a benefit. Then ask if your statement is correct. Compliment the prospect for being so astute: "That's a good point you've made."
- *Address the objection*. Once the prospect agrees, you have eliminated the objection. Now you are ready to counter the objection with another benefit. Empathize with the prospect: "I understand how you feel about our station's teenage audience.The real value is the adult females we deliver, too."
- *Close the sale*. As soon as you have an agreement, try to close. The longer you wait, the more opportunity the prospect will have to come up with objections. (We'll cover trial closes in the next section.)

Planning and preparation are the primary ways to deal with objections. According to *Selling Power*, there are four universal difficulties salespeople face when they deal with objections:

First, sales people discuss the problem instead of possible solutions. Accept the fact that the client is unhappy for a few moments, then deal with the facts and the negative emotions will quickly vanish.

Second, sales people overreact by blowing the problem way out of proportion. Don't automatically assume that every objection is a major hurdle. Determine the true extent of the objection before you negatively prejudge your chances for making the sale.

Third, sales people often assume that the problem has been dumped in their laps and they must be the only ones who have to find the solution. That's not true. Customers often come up with their own solutions, providing you ask them for their ideas and suggestions for coming to an agreement.

Finally, sales people tend to ignore the customer's concerns instead of confronting the objection. While ignoring a fake objection is a good strategy, real objections should be addressed quickly. You don't want a genuine objection to smolder until it bursts into leaping flames.[68]

Ken Greenwood sees an evolution in the art of handling objections. In what Greenwood calls "old-style selling," there was a simple format:

You presented; they raised objections. You handled the objections and you closed. They raised another objection, you turned it into a question, and you closed. In the scheme of understanding the sales process, objections fit neatly between the pitch and the close.[69]

The fit is not nearly so neat now, because objections can arise anywhere in the process, even as early as when you're trying to set an appointment with a prospect. Greenwood suggests that each of the four levels of sales expertise recognizes objections differently and handles them in different ways.

Novices, Greenwood explains, feel that an objection is a personal rejection. In their minds, they, themselves, are being rejected, not the proposal. "Out of this . . . mindset comes the idea that you 'overcome objections,'" he says.

Second-level sellers, learners, feel their idea or product is being rejected, not themselves. "They transfer the objection from personal to product," he explains.

Level-three salespeople—the competents—consider objections part of the sales process. "Often in their call planning," Greenwood says, "they will do a little brainstorming or visualizing and anticipate objections they might encounter. They plan their presentation to eliminate as many objections as possible."

Greenwood's fourth and highest-level sellers, which he calls both "consultants" and "cocreators," put the emphasis on the customer and the customer's needs in such a way that the objection is separated from buyer and seller. The objection, therefore, is without ownership and can be stated in third-party language:

"So the reservation is the lack of guarantee, right?"

"The issue here seems to be change, and change is often difficult."

"The implication is clearly made that the issue, the problem, the reservation (all words used instead of objection), is a neutral problem that we ought to consider," Greenwood says. You'll find your own approach to handling objections will evolve along with your selling skills.

Addressing Objections

I've taken Ken Greenwood's lead in not using phrases like "overcoming objection." Instead, I like to use "neutralizing," "handling," and "addressing" objections. Selling electronic media is not a confrontation, rather a consensus that leads to a solution for the buyer.

Here are some typical objections you'll encounter and a brief discussion of how to handle each one.

"Your rates are too high."

Probe to discover what the prospect is using for comparison. Another electronic medium? The newspaper? Find something the prospect is doing that may have high rates, such as an expensive location or a large, impressive sign. Remind the prospect that the money was well spent.

Compare the value. Stress that the prospect will be buying much more than an advertising schedule, such as the numbers reached, or the characteristics of that audience. Instead of the cost of the schedule, emphasize the cost of reaching individual customers and how it compares to other media.

Quote success stories from other advertisers. Remember that if price is the objection, then you haven't made the case for the *value* of your medium or the schedule you're selling. Remind your prospect that you don't set the rates, your advertisers do. Rates are based on supply and demand. The fact that rates are high means that inventory is almost sold out.

As a general rule, put off discussion of price until the very end of a presentation, so you have an opportunity to demonstrate value that supports the price. The truth is, the only way to know if a price is too high is to quote it and ask the prospect to pay it.

"I don't have the budget."

Try to discover the prospect's advertising budget during the qualifying process. Use the information (or your best estimate) to show the affordability of your schedule and demonstrate how your medium will reach potential customers.

Look for co-op or vendor money to augment the prospect's limited budget. Tell the prospect how much assistance your organization or your industry group (TVB, CAB, RAB) can offer in securing vendor programs. (See Chapter 5 for more about co-op advertising.)

"My budget's already spent."

If you've estimated the prospect's total budget you'll know if that's true. That means you've got a condition, not an objection. If so, prepare for the future by learning when the prospect commits the budget.

For example, a prospect says there's no budget and two days later you see a full-page ad in the local paper announcing an annual October sale. You file the information for the following year. In *August*, talk to the client about the sale.

"I only buy newspaper."

Quote the statistics about newspaper readership: there's been a steep decline. Tell the client that buying your schedule helps to offset the decline. Newspaper reaches old, established customers. New customers are tuned to electronic media.

Suggest that the client refer to the newspaper ad in commercials on your outlet. "See our ad in today's paper" reinforces the print and reaches the people who won't read it.

"I tried cable (or TV or radio) and it didn't work."

Probe for more information. You may find that the prospect bought too short a schedule or targeted the wrong demographics. Maybe the commercial was poorly written or executed. Explore the likely causes of disappointment and explain how you will do things differently on the client's behalf.

Use facts and examples to demonstrate the effectiveness of using your medium to reach the prospect's potential customers.

"You can't guarantee results."

This calls for success stories and testimonial letters. If your qualifying and needs analysis uncovered friends of the prospect who have been advertisers on your medium, ask the prospect to call and learn firsthand about their results.

Network television sellers guarantee the size of audiences for their programs. If the shows don't meet a certain level, the advertiser gets additional spots in other programs to make up for the shortfall. (See "Upfront Buying" in Chapter 6.)

"I've been advertising on Channel 2 for years. I don't want to change."

Find out when the prospect first advertised with Channel 2 and what influenced that decision. Reinforce the success the decision brought the prospect. Then ask how the prospect's business will grow from this point on. You're offering the means to reach an audience beyond Channel 2's audience—new customers or a different mix of customers. It may be advantageous to compare costs.

"I'll think it over." "Let me sleep on it."

The prospect may actually want to think about it, but it sounds more like a stalling device to me. Don't allow "thinking it over" until you've probed to find out what they're going to think about.

Summarize all the benefits you've presented that received a positive response. "The timing is right for your grand opening, right?" "You like using 30-second spots, right?" "You've already agreed that the cost is in line."

Go back through all the yes answers you've received to ferret out that final no. Then answer it. The client may not want to sleep on it after all.

"Your cost per point is too high."

As you'll learn in Chapters 3, 4, and 5, cost-per-point (CPP) and cost-per-thousand (CPM) selling is the norm at agencies, especially those that buy national advertising. Sellers at the national broadcast, cable, and radio networks sell almost exclusively on a CPP or CPM basis. Automated systems like Maximi\$er (see Figure 2–23) for radio or TVTrak for television allow you to hone in on the audience your buyer wants to reach.

Zero in on demos: the automated systems create demos that are not typical Arbitron or Nielsen demo breaks. Change dayparts by spreading the schedule into other hours. Radio and cable sellers target geography.

"I'm buying around you."

The customer is saying, "I don't need your outlet," and you're being challenged to prove that it's not true. What can you show that demonstrates to the prospect that your operation is essential to the buy? Do other outlets being bought deliver the audience composition that mirrors the market? Or the prospect's product?

"I don't see media sales people."

What you need is something other than media to talk with the prospect about. If you've done your homework, you know about the customer's business or about something personal that gives you an opening discussion. Call with an idea for the church fund-raiser that's so close to your prospect's heart. That gets you in the

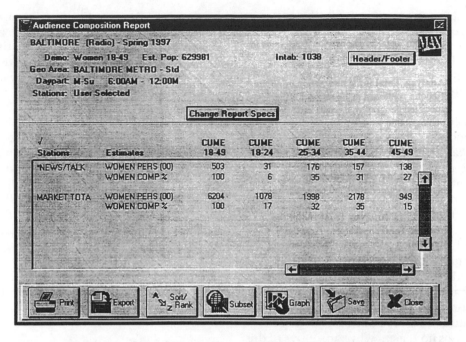

FIGURE 2–23 Create your own dayparts and custom reports with software that uses ratings data to tell the story. Television and cable sellers have similar tools. This one is Maximi$er from Arbitron, showing the comparison of women listening to News Talk radio to the Baltimore market overall. Courtesy the Arbitron Company. Used with permission.

door and begins a relationship that could blossom into a sale.

"I'm not interested."

That's a sign the seller has not created interest. According to *Selling Power*, the best response is, "There's no reason why you should be interested until I show you how it can help you make money and solve problems."

Transactional Business

Some selling situations are better described as "buying situations." You might find there's nothing you can do to change the buyer's mind, and there's no way to overcome what you would classify as an "objection." You may even get the order, but you get no more than the buyer intended to give you.

This situation arises in the advertising agency setting, where decisions are made about market coverage and media placement long before the buyer is involved. A media planner or media director makes the decisions and hands it off to the buyer for execution. If the process starts long before the buyer's in the picture, it's even longer before salespeople from various media are called in to make presentations.

This is called "transactional selling," because it's more a transaction than the give-and-take of the "consultant sale." In transactional selling (as it applies to electronic media), there's little input by the seller. This is a situation that requires matching the buyer's cost-per-point target rather than using a more persuasive selling technique.

Lee Masters of E! Entertainment Television put it this way: "Selling national cable, ultimately, every buy comes down to demo. No matter how much [the national agencies] talk about qualitative, they're concerned about quantitative." In other words, how large is your outlet's audience in the target they're after?

Compare it to cashing a check at a bank's teller window. The human teller is unnecessary in the transaction. Banks discovered this fact long ago and introduced ATMs and debit cards, reducing the numbers of face-to-face transactions and saving enormous sums of money. Does that mean the electronic media seller is unnecessary in the transactional sale? If the buy is made on a CPM or CPP basis, it's virtually a computational function. As E!'s Masters said, "The buyer takes almost a factory approach. Selling skills come into play if [the buyer] is on the fence. If somebody is buying seven [networks] deep, selling skills determine how much I will get and at what price."

There's no reason why some buys of this nature could not be done in a purely computational way, with the agency's target matched to a database of each medium's performance. In fact, it's been attempted with online buying services as *www. buymedia.com.*

How much transactional selling will you encounter? Ken Greenwood admits there's no research on percentages of transactional against consultant selling, but his estimate is that consultant sales accounts for about 60%. "The figure may even be higher," he says. "It's certainly true in advertising, insurance and real estate, heavy machinery and high-tech."

At the local level, there's less transactional selling than at the national level. You'll find more in large markets than in small markets, because large markets tend to have more business that flows through advertising agencies. Agencies are covered in more depth in Chapter 5.

Cheryl Vannucchi of Cable One in Santa Rosa, California, and Jennifer Baird of CNN in Chicago are both sellers of time on cable, but their jobs are at opposite ends of the selling spectrum. Vannucchi works completely in the realm of consultant selling, working with direct accounts like real estate brokers, restauranteurs, and bridal boutiques in Sonoma County. Baird, on the other hand, sells CNN, Headline News, and CNN's Airport Channel and interactive services primarily to advertising agencies in her midwest region. Both women use their personal selling skills, but Baird spends more of her time in transactional selling, especially for the main network. "The benefits of CNN are known," she says, "so the buyers know how to buy it. For the extension networks [Airport Channel and the interactive services] there's a lot more selling. That takes relationship building."

In transactional selling, you're more like a commodity broker than a consultant seller. That's not a value judgment; that's a fact. It takes a keen analytical sense to judge the research information that's required to present your commodity, that is, your medium, effectively.[70]

Rejecting Rejection

Addressing objections is a natural part of the selling process. Tom Hopkins calls objections "rungs of the ladder to sales success." Master seller Zig Ziglar calls them "the key to closing the sale."

There's a story that motivational speakers use about Thomas Edison's work on the invention of the light bulb:

> The biggest challenge Edison faced was finding a filament that would burn long enough to make the light bulb practical for use. Before he solved the problem, Edison conducted over a thousand experiments and wrote detailed notes on each one of them. None of them produced what he was looking for: a device to light a room electrically.
>
> He developed a filament that worked for an hour or so. Next, he found one that worked for a full day. Next a week's worth of light. Finally, the longer lasting bulb that makes us wonder how we could live without his invention.
>
> Someone asked Edison, "How did you feel, failing over a thousand times?"
>
> His answer: "I did not fail a thousand times. I learned a thousand ways it wouldn't work."

A true story? I hope so. It's a perfect story for sellers who face both objections and sales that are not made. A nonsale can be considered as either a failure or a step to the next sale. It's your choice.

A final note about objections: some customers have a need to say no. It helps to maintain their dignity, as I mentioned earlier, and it also helps them assure themselves that they're not pushovers. You might find yourself pitching a few bad ideas before you pitch your excellent idea, just to get "no" out of the buyer's system. Or, you may have to go back again and again. As Mark McCormack puts it:

> I'll go back to a potential client with another proposal, and yet another. I'll do all sorts of things—send them newspaper clips, personal notes, invitations to events to let them know I value them, that there are no hard feelings, and that I still think we can do business together.
>
> After spending so much time getting to know a potential customer, I'd be foolish to take his first or second or third no as a cue to cross him out of my life permanently. The way I see it, as the customer's no's accumulate, my odds of getting a yes increase.[71]

Getting to "yes" means closing. That's the next step in the sales process.

Step Six — Closing

No one is happier than I am that selling and marketing are merging. The day of the high-pressure hard sell is long gone, because today's customer is so savvy. But not every salesperson knows that.

A few years ago I was shopping for office space to see if my business would be better served from a different location in Houston. One rental agent drove me nuts, trying to close on virtually every comment I made: I said I liked the view, so he went for a close that had to do with the view: "You could be enjoying those trees every day, Mr. Shane. Will you put your desk in this corner or that one?" I commented on the carpeting, and he said, "Think of those rich blues greeting you every morning when you arrive, Mr. Shane. Shall I have the rest of the carpeting done in the same shade or a compatible gray? Finally, I had enough of his transparent closing techniques, and each time he tried one of the prepackaged closes, I asked where he learned it. "What do you mean?" he asked me. "That sounds like Charles Roth," I'd say, "but you're not being subtle enough." Or, "That's Tom Hopkins' 'Little Questions Close' isn't it? That's not what Tom meant." Or "That's Ken Greenwood's 'Alternate Close,' right?"

The real estate salesman was not pleased. I don't blame him, but "going for the close" in such a clumsy way was absurd. He had read the right books but he interpreted them the wrong way. He recited the words and phrases he had memorized rather than guiding me naturally and easily through the steps, allowing me to make the sale for him. Needless to say, he didn't close. He didn't even get to an effective needs analysis. Now that I think about it, I'm not sure he was even aware of what I wanted. He was so dead-set on closing at the wrong time.

What's the right time? The right time is when all the questions have been answered and when all the objections have been discussed and resolved. In other words, when the prospect is ready. The first sign may be the point of negotiation. When the prospect is ready to talk price, you've entered the closing phase.

You'll remember from my introduction to the sales process that some sales experts list negotiation as a separate step in the sales cycle. My feeling is that when negotiation begins, the close is in sight. Just the minor details are left to work out. (Of course, I admit that they don't seem "minor" at the time!) That's why I include the negotiation process here, as the first topic of conversation in the closing section.

I must increase sales now! (repeated many times, arranged in two columns)

Sign up here —

©1991 The Competitive Advantage

FIGURE 2–24 This is not an affirmation, it's a mandate. When I first saw this graphic in the newsletter *The Competitive Advantage* in 1991, I clipped it and saved it. When I need a motivator, I pull it out and post it where I can see it. The same idea might work for you, too. Thanks to *The Competitive Advantage*, 1101 King Street, Suite 444, Alexandria, VA 22314. 1-800-722-9221.

Many people look on negotiating as an unpleasant, stressful chore to be avoided at all costs. Because they're not comfortable with the idea of negotiating, they feel they get the short end in bargaining sessions.

It's true that the word "negotiation" conjures confrontation and risk-taking. You'll even read about "opponents" and detect an adversarial tone in some literature on negotiation. To me that's the wrong approach. It indicates that there will be a winner and a loser when the negotiating is over. To be effective, you need to negotiate so that both sides win. You win the order, and your customer wins the best advertising schedule.

Think of negotiation in the same way you thought of sales at the very beginning of this book: if everything is selling, whether you're asking for a raise or deciding on a movie for the weekend, then everything is negotiation, too. That raise requires negotiating with the boss. The movie is the result of discussion about whether to go to a 30-screen cineplex or watch a video at home. It's all negotiation.

Gerard Nierenberg, who wrote the first book on the formalized process of negotiation, *The Art of Negotiating*, says, "Whenever people exchange ideas with the intention of changing relationships, whenever they confer for agreement, then they are negotiating."[72]

In his book, *It's Negotiable*, Peter Stark discusses a San Diego State University seminar on negotiation:

> [T]he following question was posed to participants: How often do you negotiate—often, seldom, or never?
>
> Surprisingly, over 36 percent of the respondents answered seldom or never. However, this was a trick question! The correct answer is always. Everything in life is negotiated, under all conditions, at all times: from asking your significant other to take out the morning garbage to merging into a freeway lane in rush-hour traffic, from determining what time to schedule an appointment with a client to deciding which 11:00 o'clock news program to watch with your family—every aspect of your life is spent in some form of negotiation.[73]

Negotiation takes place throughout the sales process. The moment you meet your prospect, negotiation begins. You'll negotiate for an appointment, for information, and for a chance to make a presentation.

In the discussion on presentation, I suggest "The Rule of Three" from Amy and Robert Bly. Before you bargain, have three figures fixed in your mind: (1) the maximum, which is the highest figure, the most you dare to ask; (2) the minimum, which is the lowest figure you'll settle for; and (3) your goal, which is the figure you have the best chance of getting.[74]

In an article published by the Center for Technical Communications, the Blys say: "It pays to be optimistic and aim high when setting your maximum. When negotiating, try for your goal but be prepared to accept any offer between the minimum and the maximum. In some cases you may be surprised to find that the maximum is approved without argument."

On the other hand, you might also find that the customer wants to spend something less than your minimum. It's very important to know your minimum—how low you will go. Be prepared to walk away from any figure that's a penny lower.

The Blys suggest that *you* set the rules in negotiation:

> The person who controls the negotiation is usually the one who has set the guidelines. . . .
>
> To do this, say, "Before we get started, I'd like to go over the situation as it stands, and outline what we hope to accomplish here."
>
> Then go on to state things as you see them. The other person will generally agree, interjecting only to make a few minor modifications to what is basically your point of view. Thus, when you begin to negotiate, you're in control of the situation—because you defined it.

Key elements to success are being prepared and being able to choose the time and place. You can control the preparation, but often you cannot control the venue. Your prospect will likely be an agency or a retailer who will want you at their location for your negotiation.

That makes it essential that you plan your negotiating strategy in advance. What type of order do you want to get? Are you going for rate? For the largest amount you can get? For share of budget?

In your planning, you need to know what concessions you're willing to make and what you'll give up in order to move the process forward. Good negotiators suggest letting your concessions get smaller and smaller as you go along so you give the impression that there's nothing more to give. Hold on to those items you've decided to give up until critical junctures in your negotiation talks. If you surrender something too early, you look too easy, and it makes the other side greedy for more.

Victoria Ruttenberg, a Washington, DC–based lawyer who advises on negotiation, suggests role-playing in practice sessions so you can anticipate the other party's tactics. "Not just what position they're going to come up with, but why. And not just the business reason why, but what else is driving them."[75]

Like any management skill, negotiation can be learned. If you enjoy dealing with other people, and you're committed to creating a win-win outcome, it'll be easier for you. The fact that you want to be a seller says you enjoy solving problems and coming up with creative solutions. Approach negotiation with that attitude, and you're on your way to closing!

If You Can't Close, You Can't Sell[76]

You'll remember that line from reading it earlier. It's a chapter title from *Secrets of Closing Sales*, by Charles B. Roth and Roy Alexander. The book is a sales classic that has guided more than 200,000 sellers since it was first published in the 1940s. It introduced Roth's "master closing formula," which you'll learn in just a few pages. His formula, along with countless "closing techniques" that can be memorized and rehearsed are all effective tools for the seller.

In the wrong hands, "closing techniques" are as dangerous as they are effective in the right hands. Rehearsal, repetition, and study are essential, but only if they make the close a natural part of your sales process. By reading closing formulas and memorizing phrases, you make the process second nature.

The reason for rehearsal and memorization is to prevent your having to think about it when the time comes. Here's a nonsales scenario as an example:

> You're driving at 60 miles per hour, and a car cuts in front of you. There's no time to articulate the situation, but if there were, you might hear yourself saying, "That's a Volvo S-70, moving 55 degrees to the right. I'm going 88 feet per second. It will require 12 pounds of pressure to my brake pedal to stop about three feet shy of a collision."

Instead, without the slightest hesitation, your brain communicates with your hands and feet: Hit The Brakes! And you do.

The more you drive, the more practice you get. Repetition prepares you for quick reaction to dangerous situations. The same is true in sales. The more you practice the language of closing, the easier it is to say the right words without thinking about them. If you've prepared yourself for closing the way you prepared yourself to meet objections in the last section, your response will come naturally, smoothly, and—most importantly—at the appropriate time.

Financial sales trainer Bill Good says that every salesperson needs at least six different closes "memorized and instantly available."[77] There are more than six in the coming pages, and you must assimilate them into your own personal style. The minute you spew canned closes like a robot, you run the risk of blowing the sale, just like the hapless real estate seller I mentioned earlier.

What Is Closing?

Sales trainers will tell you that closing is everything, but like a fine wine, closing is better in its own time. A salesperson who beats a customer into verbal submission is not going to get much repeat business. That's old-style selling. Yet it's still true that "If you can't close you can't sell."

Closing is the payoff for all the work you've done: the prospecting, qualifying, needs analysis, presentation, and answering objections. As sales trainer Chris Lytle puts it:

> You do the consulting for free. You do the commercial for free. You write the proposal for free. All of that may take hours, and you may or may not get paid for it. When the client says, "yes," you collect commissions for the schedule's duration.[78]

Since closing is the payoff, closing is perceived as the glamour part of the sales process. It's the one point in sales when you want to shout "Yes!" for everyone to hear. Zig Ziglar insists that "the close is no more, or no less, important than any other phase of the sales process." He makes his point by reminding us that if there's no prospect, there's no chance to close. If there's no presentation, there's no close. And so forth through the selling steps.

Ziglar's right, of course. All the steps in the sales process are equally important because together they create the atmosphere that solves the buyer's problem with the solution the seller offers.

In *Personal Marketing Strategies*, Mike McCaffrey calls closing "the natural conclusion," because that's the point in the sale when you and the buyer want something agreeable to each of you. "There should be nothing dramatic about the natural conclusion, or close," McCaffrey says. "It should be as its name implies, *natural*. Closes are not climaxes, nor should they be. As a part of a total sequence of events, closes should be the mutually satisfactory result or outcome of the whole selling presentation."

Before we study closing techniques, let's review some rules for getting to the "natural conclusion":

1. *Assume you will close.* Go into your presentation *expecting* to make the sale.

McCaffrey calls this "an attitude of assumptiveness." The seller approaches the situation with confidence, as if, using McCaffrey's words, "it would be unnatural if you didn't reach a mutually satisfying conclusion." Expecting to close makes you *ready* to close. You take the appropriate materials, you watch the prospect's closing signals, you stay cool and confident even though your adrenaline is pumping.

2. *Summarize needs and wants.* What surfaced during your needs analysis and your presentation? All the problems, concerns, and situations you uncovered that led you along the path to a sale should be recapped. McCaffrey advises that this step should take only a minute, long enough to let the prospect know that you've listened, and that you've matched your solution to the needs.

3. *Summarize solutions.* During your presentation, you reached agreement on specific solutions your advertising schedule will provide the prospect. This summary is confirmation that you've matched solution to need. Next, emphasize that advertising is a solution, and your proposal is the best solution to the prospect's problems.

4. *Help prospects fantasize.* In the previous section, you read powerful words that help to create a positive mood for the prospect. Take that a step further—encourage the prospect to visualize their commercial message on the air. Speak in the present tense as if the schedule has already been bought. Talk about *when* the prospect sees the commercial, not *if.* You're selling adjacencies to show-business, so involve the sponsor in the show business aspect of your medium.

5. *Close early.* It works especially well when the benefits are already known or are easy to explain. "There's a :30 available in the 11 O'Clock News, and I knew you'd want it." Some salespeople go for the close moments after the first handshake. "I'm here to get your order, provided I can prove its value to you."

6. *Ask for the order.* You'd be surprised at how many salespeople go through a presentation and never ask for the business.

They're afraid of rejection or afraid of appearing pushy. It happens more with newcomers to sales than with veterans, but no one's immune to the tendency.

You don't have to say the specific words, "May I have an order, please?" but it helps. You want to communicate to your prospects that you want their business. I find that saying something like, "We're ready to get this schedule on the air when you give the go-ahead" is a good signal to the client.

I also like to say to a prospect, "My staff is eager to get to work on your project." It indicates commitment of all the company's resources, and in our case it happens to be true.

7. *Shut up!* Tom Hopkins adds these two most important words at closing. Ask a question that prompts a close. Give the prospect a chance to answer your question and commit to the buy. It may lead to an awful silence, but the minute you talk, you take the pressure off the prospect.

The Master Closing Formula

Closing seems so simple when you look at short list of rules from *Secrets of Closing Sales*. Here is Charles Roth's "master closing formula":

1. Make every call a selling call.
2. Try early in every sale for a close.
3. Close on every resistance.
4. Keep trying time after time.

On the surface, Roth's formula sounds like the old days of adversarial sales, where the seller won and the buyer lost. It's true that Roth first put his ideas together in the 1940s when that was the attitude of too many sellers. However, the "master closing formula" holds up in today's customer-focused selling, too.

Obviously I don't recommend twisting the arm of the buyer on first meeting (or ever). Showing a sense of purpose in your initial call and in your needs analysis interview sets the tone. By approaching every call as a sales call, you offer something that you can close on later.

Dickie Rosenfeld, the long-time general manager of Houston's KILT stations, accused sellers of being "visitors" when they didn't try to close. Charles Roth calls them "loafers" and "goodwill ambassadors." Not very flattering words.

The idea of closing "on every resistance" is a way to keep you selling even in the face of blustering objections. Some prospects are willing to say, "No sale, I'm not interested" just to test you. Your best response may be to ask for the order, because they don't expect it. It won't work every time, of course.

When sellers take full advantage of Roth's closing formula, they add closing techniques to their arsenal of selling strategies, maneuvers that have been tested by sales professionals in a variety of fields. As I said before, the power of the techniques is in knowing them so well that they're second nature to you. They must sound as if they've come from you personally, not from this book or a sales seminar.

Closing Techniques

Remember the real estate seller I used as an example at the beginning of this section? You sure don't want to sound as shallow and mechanical as he did. Closing techniques must be sincere and transparent to the customer.[79]

Sales books and sales seminars are full of "closes." Some of them leave me cold because they don't sound real. Consider, for instance, the "secondary question close." It's a statement of the decision, followed by another question that involves the buyer at another level. The tip-off of a secondary question close is the opening phrase: "The only decision we have left is...." That's followed without a pause by the phrase "by the way" and a choice between two other options. Here's an example:

"The only decision left is when you'll start benefiting from the JX7546 gizmotron. By the way are you going to use it in the new plant or in the existing warehouse?"

"I see that the only decision left is when to start our janitorial contract. By the way will you clean the main factory first or use the service at your home?"

Maybe I just can't hear myself saying those words. Not surprising, some salespeople do better with one technique and not others.

Assimilate the techniques that fit your personality, then make them second nature. When the situation arises, you'll be able to recognize it, say the words naturally, and close naturally. Finally, match the proper technique to your prospect's style and pace. Here are some different closing techniques.

The Direct Close

This is basically asking for the order. Use a question or phrase that yields agreement: "Can we go ahead with this schedule?" or "Let me write this up so you can be on the air Thursday night."

The Deadline Close

You are about to be sold out. The special package rate ends Friday. The rates go up on the first of next month. Tell your prospect they should buy now before the deadline arrives. One key to the deadline close is there's no bluffing or you'll lose trust.

The Choice Close

Following the "rule of three," you've offered three options for scheduling. Now follow with a question: "Which package do you prefer, the first, the second, or the third?" Prospects feel less trapped when they have several choices to consider. Tom Hopkins calls this close the "triplicate of choice."

The Ben Franklin Close

Remind the prospect that Benjamin Franklin, "a founding father and a wise man," would make his decisions by drawing a line down the center of a blank sheet of paper and listing the reasons for and against the decision. (Franklin wrote "reasons for" and "ideas opposed," according to Zig Ziglar.)

In the "for" column list a key benefit, preferably one that is emotion-based, "You like our morning show," for example. Then begin the "against" list with the objection you heard most during the presentation. Some sellers complete the "for" list first. Some alternate. You as seller should bring out the objections. It proves you were listening. Anyway, if you don't, the prospect will, so take charge.

Don't number the points as you make the list, but total them at the end of the process. If you've done your job there will be more in the "for" column than in the "against" column. Analytical, fact-oriented prospects will appreciate the approach. It makes the seller seem fair and objective.

This technique is also called the "balance sheet close" and the "t-account close."

The Higher Authority Close

Before you visit your prospect, you know there's a specific question coming, so you prepare with a little help from an important friend.

Contact a well-known client who had the same question during one of your presentations. Look for a client who is satisfied with the performance of your schedule and who accepted your answer to the objection or question you anticipate. The client needs to have a high enough profile to be "the higher authority" in the eyes of your current prospect.

When the questions arise, write them down. When the list is complete, ask to use the phone on your prospect's desk. "You know Jim Johnson at Hondaland, don't you?" (Even if the prospect doesn't know him personally, you've chosen someone who is seen and heard regularly.) Place the call and let Jim Johnson answer the prospect's questions.

This is a situation where preparation is vital. The higher authority must know your call is coming and must be willing to field it for you.

The Make-Me-an-Offer Close

If the prospect makes you an offer, there's an intention to buy. Save this technique for late in negotiation, because it usually results in some sort of concession.

If you can keep it from being a price concession, all the better, such as: "You know this plan is right, so make me an offer on something other than price, and I'll see what I can do." Or "Make me an offer of how many promos you want and I'll see what I can do." Or "Make me an offer of how you'd like to participate in the promotion and I'll see what I can do."

The Three Questions Close

Zig Ziglar teaches his own salespeople to use this close when they're selling Ziglar training:

1. Can you see how using this sales training course would increase your sales?

2. Are you interested in increasing your sales?

3. If you were ever going to start increasing your sales, when do you think would be the best time to start?

Replace "sales training course" with "schedule" or "promotion" and the questions apply to selling electronic media.

Speaking of questions, I've seen sales books that recommend taking a customer's question and turning it into your own closing question. For example, the customer says, "Could we run Monday through Thursday?" The sales technique suggests asking, "If I schedule it that way can I get the order?" It sounds like a neat tactic, but what if the customer's answer is no? Then you've lost the order.

A better approach would be when the customer asks, "Could we run Monday through Thursday?" you answer, "Absolutely!"

Acceptance Mode

One of the key elements in closing is to accept that you've closed. Be quiet. Leave promptly. Mark McCormack calls it shift-

ing to acceptance mode: "After scratching and clawing their way into the customer's heart and mind, they can't stop to relax and enjoy their victory. . . . They don't know how to take yes for an answer."

You may be tempted to summarize the discussion, but don't do that. You'll sound as if you're renegotiating the deal. Worse, you may bring up objections that had been neutralized and make them real in the client's mind again. There's nothing to gain from lingering at the site of your triumph. Leave the customer as soon as common courtesy allows.

After you've reached a commitment for the sale, compliment your customer on their wisdom in choosing your plan, pick up your materials, close your briefcase, shake hands, and depart.

Mark McCormack says, "This body language sends a message of closure and finality to the meeting. The sooner you leave, the sooner you know you've wrapped up the sale. There's nothing you can say to improve on yes, so why try?"

After the Sale

You sold the big account. The campaign was a big success. Why, then, didn't the client call and tell you how wonderful a job you've done? Because you were doing the job you were expected to do. After all, you promised fair value for the client's dollar. You promised to reach the right audience. You assumed success. Your commission is on the way. That may be all the thanks you get.

Even if the client raves about the job you've done, keep the words of Harvey Mackay in mind: "Don't expect gratitude to last any longer than it takes for the recipients to say they're eternally grateful."

It's Mackay's tongue-in-cheek way of saying you've got to earn new gratitude every day. That requires going beyond the sale to implementation, to relationship building.[80]

By "implementation," I mean getting the order processed and the copy into production. Sometimes that means giving facts about the advertiser to a copywriter or creative director. Sometimes that means that you will write the commercial message yourself.

There's a file to be established and maintained for bookkeeping and billing purposes. Whatever the situation, there's paperwork to be done—a lot or a little, depending on your organization.

Closing's not the end of the process. Some even say it's only the beginning.

Consider closing like a baseball power hitter who smashes a hanging curve ball and launches it out of the park. The crowd leaps to its feet! It's a home run! Yet what if that player rounded second base, crossed third, and went directly to the dugout? If he doesn't touch home plate, he doesn't score.

For sellers, closing is the long ball out of the park, but after the sale comes the contract, the paperwork, the copy, the scheduling, the execution of the order. That's the equivalent of touching all the bases. If your attention to follow-up is not as focused as your attention to the sales process, you haven't scored.[81]

Servicing your account is the first step toward relationship building. Building and managing relationships will put you in line for repeat business. It means you and your client have reached a level of mutual trust and respect.

Since sales is a matter of solving problems for your client, service after the sale links you as the seller to the solution. *You* become the differentiation between your schedule and a campaign on another medium.

The Commercial as Service

At some point in the sales process, you'll have to guide your client through the most effective use of the commercial message you're selling. Somewhere between "closing" and "servicing" is the copy phase. At this point, the deal may be done, but there's no real closure until the commercial is written and produced to the client's satisfaction.

During the needs analysis, you've gathered information about the client's business. You've also taken the first step toward assembling information that will ultimately become a part of the commercial. Depending on your medium, you need to know how best to attract the ear, the eye, or the click-through.

If you're selling for a major national network, your client's agency has commercial material already produced, either a campaign with several related messages, or one commercial that gets the message to the listener or viewer.

In markets dominated by agency buying, your client may have a message already prepared by another radio or TV station, by a copy service, or by the advertising agency. Radio and TV stations sometimes (but not always) have a writer on staff to take the information you collect from your client and turn your sale into a persuasive commercial.

The smaller the media outlet, the more likely you are to do most of the follow-up work yourself. Local radio salespeople often write commercials for their clients. Some radio sellers are also on-air performers and they voice the commercials, too. That's not generally a requirement, because the typical radio station has announcers who can take the salesperson's copy and produce a commercial with background music, sound effects, and other enhancements. Some stations appoint a production director who supervises development and conceptualization of commercials, called production.

Local cable system salespeople are often called on to use a still camera to take slides that will be part of a client's commercial. Other small-market cable and TV salespeople find themselves learning to use video equipment to develop or enhance a customer's commercial because there's insufficient staff to handle the job.

The larger the market, the more likely the station or system is to have full-time commercial production assistance. Major-market TV stations may have such good production talent on staff that they create a profit center making and producing commercials for a variety of local advertisers.

If you're selling to an advertising agency, you'll find the services vary from agency to agency. Some large agencies—especially those whose business is national in scope—create, write, record, and distribute commercials for their clients. Others write copy that the station or cable system must produce before airing. Some agencies are simply buyers who place the commercial time through a seller at an electronic media outlet and expect the outlet to do all the creative and production work.

One of Shane Media's marketing directors joined our company from a TV station in Orlando. As a salesperson there she not only called on clients, she also wrote copy for her customers and occasionally acted in their commercials. One client used the kitchen at the salesperson's house as the set for a series of commercials. Now that's service after the sale!

Writing Copy

There are some very good books on copy and production. Any attempt to add to that information is misplaced here. So I'll skim a few basics instead.

To write a commercial message effectively, you need to know that consumers don't buy soap, they buy "skin you love to touch." They don't buy lipstick, they buy "kissable lips." They don't buy mattresses, they buy "a good night's sleep."

You'll also need to know the essential commercial criteria for your medium. Writing a 15-second video message calls on skills not needed for a 60-second radio spot. How many "click here" buttons do you see in an hour on the World Wide Web? The successful seller knows how to motivate the surfer to click.

Commercial messages in cyberspace have a different set of rules. *Wired* coined the term "netiquette" to remind online users about unsolicited commercial messages, among other new media manners.

I've mentioned David Ogilvy often enough to let you know I'm a fan of his philosophy and his work. He wrote the definitive rules for commercials:

1. Identify your brand early in the commercial.
2. Identify it often.
3. Promise the listener a benefit early in the commercial.
4. Repeat it often.

"Ninety commercials out of a hundred do none of these things," Ogilvy said.[82]

In a speech to the Association of National Advertisers in the fall of 1991, Ogilvy reminded the group of an important premise about copy: "We sell or else." He claimed that too much emphasis is placed on art, not enough on increasing sales. In other words, agencies want to win awards, while their clients only want to sell merchandise.

"If you spend your advertising budget entertaining the consumer, you are a bloody fool," Ogilvy told the advertiser group. "Housewives don't buy a new detergent because the manufacturer told a joke on television last night. They buy it because it promised a benefit."

So there's one more rule if you're writing the commercials for your customer: don't let the commercial get in the way of selling your client's product.

You're Still Not Finished!

Before I address the specifics of building and managing relationships with your customers, there's one more step your operation may require of you as part of servicing the account—collecting the money due for the advertising schedule.

You'll remember in the discussion of needs analysis about asking for money in advance when a prospect was not financially qualified to buy on credit. Money's always a sensitive issue, and asking for it is even more delicate. All sellers must face the fact, however, that you won't get your commission if your client doesn't pay the bill. That means working on collections should be a part of the sales process.

When your client signs the order or contract, say right then, "Our terms are 30 days." If done in a proper, professional tone, you won't risk either business or respect. Most businesses tend to pay the people they think are most important first and wait on the rest. When you discuss it during the sale, you stress the importance of prompt payment.

Sales consultant Irwin Pollack suggests other techniques to assure your company is paid and you get your commission:

Collections Cycle

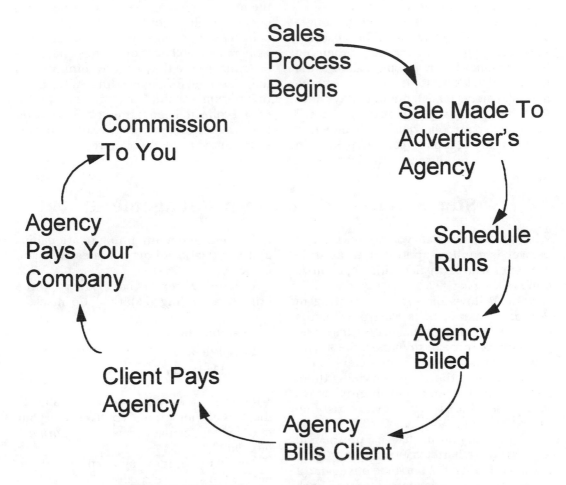

FIGURE 2–25 When it comes to billings versus collections, collections usually wins. By that, I mean that most operations pay on money collected, not on dollars billed or booked. You don't get paid until your company gets paid. Here's how the collections cycle works. It underscores the importance of qualifying your prospect.

- Don't wait 60 days before calling delinquent advertisers. On the second or third of each month, salespeople need to call advertisers with a reminder.
- Once an advertiser has extended past the 60-day mark, send a Western Union Mailgram to demand payment. The Mailgram envelope indicates urgency.

- Recognize that most advertisers follow a consistent payment pattern. For example, they always pay between the 20th and the 28th of the month. If you detect a break in the pattern, act quickly to collect what's due.[83]

Most operations have credit and payment policies. Some are formalized, written procedures. Others exist only as guidelines that are communicated verbally to advertisers. Collections procedures are instituted by the sales manager, sales director, or other management-level people.

Advertising agencies typically take longer to pay than direct accounts because the agency must first bill its client and then collect the money before passing it along to the media outlet. It's not unusual for agency payments to arrive 60, 90, even 120 days after the schedule runs. (See Figure 2–25.) You'll find more about collections in Chapter 4.

When my company consulted KILT in Houston, I'd often wait in the lobby for a meeting, intrigued at the sight of KILT salespeople rushing through a small door just behind the reception desk. That was the mail room, and the sellers were checking to see which of their clients had sent checks so they could walk them to the bookkeeper personally. KILT salespeople were responsible for collections and wanted to make sure they got the commissions they deserved for their selling. At the time, that station was the Houston market leader and collected approximately $58,000 on a typical business day. No wonder the sales staff wanted to get their share!

Step Seven—Relationship Management

What's the easiest sale you can make? The answer is a follow-up sale to an existing customer who's satisfied with what you've done in the past.

John Fellows of Giraffe Marketing in Portland, Maine, feels electronic media doesn't keep enough customers. "It's no secret that keeping customers is the key to growth, satisfying your customers is the key to keeping them, and servicing them above the norm (more importantly, above their expectations) is the key to satisfying them."[84]

We've seen how to change a prospect to a buyer: work hard to get to closing. Then the job is to turn the one-time buyer into a customer—someone who comes back again and again because buying your medium works.

That's why I separate "servicing" from "relationship building." Building relationships goes far beyond the sale and the paperwork. The idea here is to strive for renewal from the moment you close the sale. Keeping clients is as difficult as closing them the first time, and I like to give it its own emphasis. Regis McKenna, the marketing expert whose work with Apple Computer won him national fame, says, "Service is not an event; it is the process of creating a customer environment of information, assurance and comfort."[85]

That's why I call it "relationship management." Take a pro-active approach to developing and maintaining relationships and you'll find follow-up sales easier to come by.

Creating customers boils down to three criteria, according to Mark McCormack:

1. Communication
2. Service
3. Added value

"How well you handle these is a reliable indicator of how long you'll keep your clients," McCormack says (in *McCormack on Selling*).[86]

For instance, it's easy to communicate before the sale. We're alert. We're able to explain everything to the prospect. We return calls promptly because we're focused on the selling process. After the sale it's even more important to communicate with your client. "Are you accessible?" McCormack asks. "Do you listen as well as hear? Do you accept as a given that the client's priorities are different and more important than your own priorities? Most important, do you work overtime at explaining why?" Most salespeople fall short after the sale, not during the sales process.

McCormack uses the word "service" as one of his three criteria. As you've seen at the end of the previous section, it's an important one. "Servicing the account" is a catch-all phrase that means anything from a simple "thank you" note to giving your customer advice on buying other media. It also means working through billing problems for your client, sending articles about the client's business, and, basically, keeping in touch.

"Service is not a sometime thing," says Murray Raphel. "It is an ongoing, never-ending, always-increasing, necessary way of doing business." Raphel developed the Gordon's Alley pedestrian mall in Atlantic City and conducts direct marketing seminars. Here is an example of customer service from Raphel's retail experience:

> We had a basic, must-learn, always-used phrase in our retail shops whenever a customer was unhappy. First . . . we listened. Because that's what the unhappy customer wants you to do. Not interrupting. Not commenting. Just listening. Then, when the complaint is fully described and the conversation stops, simply say, "Tell me what you want and the answer is yes."
>
> If the color in the shirt ran in the washing, they could ask for a new shirt, and/or their money back, and/or money for gas for driving to our store . . . whatever they wanted. And it was given with our apologies and thanks.
>
> Here's what happened: the customer was first confused, then bewildered, then amazed, and then, often, apologetic! They were so used to and ready for a confrontation that they simply could not accept such an easy solution."[87]

The first point is vital and familiar: listen. And listen *all the way through* your client's comments.

You won't always hear complaints, because customers are more likely to complain to someone other than you. When they do tell you what's wrong, listen with empathy and understanding. Take it as a good sign, not as trouble.

Respond to problems and concerns after the sale the same way you would during the sales process. Consider any question or concern from a client the same way you would as you answer and neutralize objections. If a client describes a problem to you, look at it as an opportunity to create service beyond expectations.

Ask the Customer

Media outlets often survey their clients to better understand how to cement relationships. Donn Seidholz, Triathlon Broadcasting's market manager in Omaha, commissioned focus groups of Phoenix advertisers during 1993 while he was general sales manager at that city's KMLE radio station.[88]

The research began with questions about the Phoenix broadcast industry in general, covering radio and television stations. Once general questions were answered, the study got specific about the way KMLE handled customer relations.

The project was a cooperative effort with KMLE's national rep firm, McGavren Guild, which used the idea at other stations it represented at the time. *Radio Only* magazine documented the results:

> Foremost the attendees were in agreement that the AEs with which each of them dealt were the sole eyes and ears of the radio station they represented. A station could have the best reputation in town, but that meant nothing if the rep that they worked with wasn't following through and wasn't taking care of them.
>
> They felt that many AEs were in contact with them only when they needed something. They want to learn about changes in format or personnel directly from the AE for that station—not through the rumor mill. They do not like to be taken for granted by an AE after they had dealt with them for a while—the old phone call once every 3 months when they think a buy's going to come up.
>
> Clients had a real problem with incorrect statements in billing: preempted spots, spots that ran out of time, spots running that they didn't order. They said many radio stations do a poor job of resolving these problems. However, they felt that it wouldn't really even be a problem if only they were informed of it before they got their bills. It creates hours of extra work for them to try and rectify, so they would much rather hear about it from the AE beforehand.
>
> Conversely, they didn't want their time wasted by AEs who telephone or drop in with no specific agenda. They don't like to be pressed for information about buys

that will take place or what percentage of a buy a particular media rep receives.

A similar study conducted by Regional Reps Corporation of Cleveland reflected many of the same concerns on the part of advertisers.[89] The company's Stuart Sharpe says the most consistent frustrations reported by his customers deal with billing— "late billing, incorrect invoices, waiting interminably for credits and corrected paperwork. These are consistent complaints, along with finding out, long after the schedule ended, that spots didn't run or ran outside of the dayparts ordered." Another criticism deals with response time. Sharpe said advertisers told him, "There are always changes in orders and it takes too long for a salesperson to get back to us."

Paperwork may be the most boring part of selling, but you can tell from these studies that advertisers rely on prompt, accurate follow-up to the sale. Getting the paper trail in order, advising the client about billing details up front, and getting sufficient information to create a commercial— are all a part of servicing the account and vital to building the kind of deep, trusting relationships that bring your clients back again and again.

Mark McCormack's third criteria for creating customers is added value. He calls added value the toughest of the three to measure and deliver, "because what constitutes added value in your mind (i.e., extraordinary service that is way beyond the call of duty) may be standard procedure in one client's mind and totally unnecessary in another's."

You'll face that dilemma often. As McCormack relates, "Some clients come to us simply to increase their income. Measuring added value is a numbers game with them: How much did they earn before they came to us, and how much are they earning with us? They don't care about all the extraordinary service we provide. It has no value to them. Other clients come to us precisely for that service."

The point is that before you can add value to a relationship with a client, you have to learn what the client *really* values.

The phrase "added value" in electronic media often means promotion or merchandising in addition to an advertising schedule. As you'll read in the direct and retail selling discussions in Chapter 5, added value can also mean bringing useful ideas to your customer.

When Diane Sutter, CEO of Shooting Star Broadcasting, was general manager of radio stations in Pittsburgh, her staff would conduct brainstorming sessions for clients. "The group included my chief engineer, who was very good at it; our sales people, and production personnel. We did lots of work with the Pittsburgh Pirates marketing team. On another occasion an agency was pitching an account and asked us for help. They won the account thanks to our brainstorm session," Sutter says. Her group learned systematic brainstorming tactics from a professional trainer.[90]

"Spots are easy," she says. "Everybody has spots to sell. Relationships are more difficult." Yes they are, but they're worth the time and effort.

Relationship-Building Tactics

The phrase "out of sight, out of mind" was recorded as early as the fifteenth century (by Thomas à Kempis). It could have been said about a sales representative who didn't stay in touch with a client. The twenty-first century corollary is "What have you done for me lately?"

The following tactics are designed to keep your customer at the forefront of your mind, and to keep you constantly in the customer's thoughts and (hopefully) in the budget:

Let the Customers Know Why They're Smart to Do Business with You

Advertisers want to be assured that they've made the right decision when they use your medium to reach their customers. Your task is to reinforce the wisdom of that decision.

If a positive article is published about you, your company, or your medium in the local press or the trade magazines, send a

SHANE MEDIA

Please tell us how important each of these factors is to your decision to advertise on WXXX. Circle one number on the 1 to 10 scale below each topic. "1" means "Not Important" in your decision-making, "10" means "Very Important."

RATINGS
       1   2   3   4   5   6   7   8   9   10

SALES PERSON, ACCOUNT EXECUTIVE
       1   2   3   4   5   6   7   8   9   10

COST PER COMMERCIAL
       1   2   3   4   5   6   7   8   9   10

COST PER POINT
       1   2   3   4   5   6   7   8   9   10

FLEXIBILITY ON RATES
       1   2   3   4   5   6   7   8   9   10

KNOWLEDGE OF QUALITATIVE INFORMATION
       1   2   3   4   5   6   7   8   9   10

CREATIVE IDEAS
       1   2   3   4   5   6   7   8   9   10

VALUE-ADDED PROMOTIONS
       1   2   3   4   5   6   7   8   9   10

STATION PERSONALITIES
       1   2   3   4   5   6   7   8   9   10

TIMELY INVOICES
       1   2   3   4   5   6   7   8   9   10

ACCURATE INVOICES
       1   2   3   4   5   6   7   8   9   10

QUALITY OF COPY OR PRODUCTION
       1   2   3   4   5   6   7   8   9   10

LONGEVITY OF STATION SALES STAFF
       1   2   3   4   5   6   7   8   9   10

STATION'S STANDING IN THE COMMUNITY
       1   2   3   4   5   6   7   8   9   10

FIGURE 2-26 How do you know you're doing a good job? Ask! Shane Media developed this questionnaire for our client stations to assess their impact with their advertisers.

Revenue Flow Manager

Account Executive: _____ Date: / /199____

Decisions To Buy A Schedule - Likely This Week

Agency	Client / Account	Month of	Month of	Month of	1-10	Next Step	What's your game plan?	% Time

Decisions To Buy A Schedule - Later This Month

Agency	Client / Account	Month of	Month of	Month of	1-10	Next Step	What's your game plan?	% Time

Developing / Pending	Monthly Totals			
Revenues	Probable $			

Next Step: A = Relationship   D = Make Presentation
B = Needs Analysis   E = Gain Commitment
C = Develop Proposal   F = Confirm Sale

Revenue Forecast

Months	Goals	Sold-to-Date +	Probable $	= Projected	Status + (-)	Goals to Add This Week
Month of _____						
Month of _____						
Month of _____						

Your Best Suspects		% Time	Qualified Prospects		% Time
Client / Account	New	Possible Month	Client / Account	New	Possible Month

FIGURE 2–27 You keep building relationships to keep your revenues up. Warren Wright of Twenty-first Century Communications introduced me to this "revenue flow manager" to keep track of what's likely this week and this month. Notice column 6 has a 1–10 scale to determine how likely a buy really is. Courtesy Warren Wright. Used with permission.

copy to your customer. If your company wins an award or other recognition, let your customer know. Seize every opportunity to portray your operation in a leadership position.

Keep Customers Informed about Themselves

Just as important as keeping the customer informed about your company is being a fact-gathering service for the customer's own business. If you hear that a competitor is moving into the mall, let your client know. It'll show your concern. If there's time, put the information in writing and send it by messenger or fax, along with source material like an article from an out-of-town newspaper.

If time is tight, call and inform the customer by telephone. Pay close attention to your client's print ads and those of the client's competitor. If you detect a shift of position by the competitor, let your customer know quickly.

Deliver Bad News as Soon as You Can

A radio station in Kansas City changed from its rock format to country music during a live broadcast from a local merchant's store. The salesperson on the scene had no idea the change was coming and had to be the bearer of bad news. The big question, of course, was whether the broadcast should continue. The client said yes, willing to pay for the new audience.

In this particular case, the news was too late. Better for the station to have announced its plans so the salesperson could get the news to the merchant in a timely manner. If it's possible to provide news to your client without compromising confidentiality, by all means do what you can.

Give Your Customer Ideas

Show the client how to improve business operations beyond advertising. Salespeople are constantly inside all types of businesses, and there are basic systems that work, regardless of the product. Without divulging trade secrets or proprietary information, pass along helpful, time-saving tips. For example: "Charlie at Jones Motors found a new software package that keeps track of that type of sales tax. Why not call him and see if it would apply to your store?"

Demonstrate Continuing Interest

Advertising agencies and PR firms use internal "call reports" that are filed with the client within 24 hours of every contact. A one-sheet call report describes what was said, and what was promised. That may be too much paper for the average advertiser, but don't overlook an appropriate substitute.

Would a copy of the production order show the client you're efficient behind the scenes? Would the client like extra copies of the script? An audio- or videocassette of the commercial? A note by fax with specific times a TV, radio, or cable schedule will run? You'll know best what to provide each client.

Ask Your Customers for Their Opinions

The finest form of flattery is asking "What's your opinion?" Those words show you value a person's ideas. It's easy to hand out tickets to sports events and concerts, but the effect is not nearly as strong as letting someone be the expert. Most people don't have sufficient opportunities to talk about their ideas. Anyone who creates that situation makes a friend. The questionnaire at Figure 2–26 does exactly that.

Give Your Customers Your Home and Cellular Phone Numbers?

Don't print the numbers on your business card. Instead, when you present the card, turn it over and write them on the back. It'll seem special and private. Also make sure that the client has the names of key people at your operation in case they need to get to someone when you're not available.

When you're working after hours, let the customer know. If the timing is right, call and say, "I'm here at home working on your account," and use that as an introduction to a question, a comment, or an idea.

Use the Customer's Product

If your client runs a clothing store, buy your clothes there. If the customer sells toothpaste, make sure you and your family use that brand. If the customer sells hats and you don't wear hats, make an exception. If it's possible to go a few steps further down the distribution chain, do business with your customer's customers. If you drive an Acura, park it around the corner when you call on the Ford dealership. Don't bite the hand that feeds you.

Let the Client Take Credit for Your Ideas

You worked hard to close the account and the clincher was the positioning line you wrote for the client's commercial. Now you see the slogan in print and hear it on other radio stations. The client's first TV campaign will feature commercials built around the new slogan. You hear about the client's press conference to describe the slogan to the business editors of the local papers and writers for industry trade magazines.

Your response? Bite your tongue and congratulate the customer for his wisdom in positioning his business so well.

Stay in Touch with the Client When Commercials Aren't Running

Off season, between flights, imply that you like your customers because they are who they are, not because of the money they spend with you and your outlet. In other words, treat them as individuals, not as a client category.

Do not forget anyone who has done business with you. Send birthday cards, anniversary cards, and notes about special events like a new baby or wedding in the customer's family.

Give Your Customers Sales Leads for Their Business

Hand out your customer's business cards to your contacts. Suggest that friends frequent the client's place of business. It only takes one sale that's traced directly to you to make your client take notice.[91]

The 80:20 Rule

For most companies, customer retention means big money. Some large companies report as much as 95% of their profits coming from long-term, repeat customers, according to *Direct Marketing*.

The 80:20 rule, first postulated by the nineteenth-century economist Vilfredo Pareto, suggests that 80% of your business comes from 20% of your customers. There's a variation on the 80:20 rule in every selling situation.

Is it always 80:20? No. The numbers vary, industry by industry, medium by medium, and media outlet by media outlet.[92]

At QVC network, for example, 4% of their customers account for 64% of their profits. At Sears Canada, 10% of customers represent 40% of sales. Another 40% of customers account for only 30% of sales. (See Figure 2–28.) Some customers are more valuable to us than others because they buy more.

The more often customers come back to you, the easier it is to serve them. The reasons are probably obvious:

1. Basic information has already been collected.

2. Copy points and positioning statements are known: earlier campaigns can be continued.

3. Your accounting department and the client's accounting department have a working pattern.

4. Customers who get solid returns on their investment are less price-sensitive than new prospects.

5. Financial projections are easier to make when there's history to trace.

"If you ain't P1, you ain't @#$!"

% of Diaries vs. % of Quarter Hours

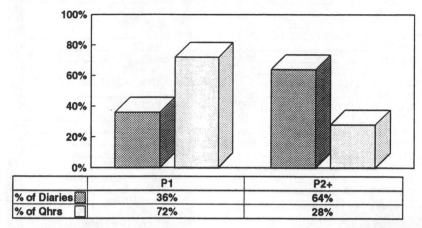

	P1	P2+
% of Diaries ▦	36%	64%
% of Qhrs ☐	72%	28%

ARBITRON
Consultant Fly-In

FIGURE 2–28 Adding to the 80:20 theory is Arbitron's finding that 38% of diaries account for 72% of average quarter hour (AQH) listening. That amount of listening defines the "P1" (Parallel 1) listener, the person who listens most to any radio station. Compare that to P2 listeners: 64% of diaries account for only 28% of quarter hours. Courtesy the Arbitron Company. Used with permission.

Repeat business is more profitable than new business, because it costs less to sell someone who is already sold. Some sources claim it costs five times as much to acquire a new customer as it does to service an existing customer.

In the rapidly expanding economic environment of the past few decades, there has been a tendency to seek new business, often at the expense of existing business. The rush to develop asset value in many new electronic media companies (especially the consolidated radio companies) caused the same thing. Sales departments were forced into "conquest marketing"—conquering new business rather than building relationships among existing customers.

Chris Lytle helps his electronic media clients put a dollar value on customer re-

tention with his "Churn Calculation Worksheet."

Here's how Lytle explains the listings you see on the worksheet in Figure 2–29:

On the surface, you see a sales increase of $6,935 from one month to the next. We know how much the salesperson billed—but look at how they did it. Only five advertisers repeated from one month to the next. Twelve advertisers are no longer on the air. They have lost 75% of the advertisers and 76.6% of the billing from the previous month.

Are you still happy about the increase in sales?

As a rule of thumb, a business will lose 25% of its customers in a year. Some move away. Some choose to do business with the competition. It is one thing to lose 25% of

Churn calculation worksheet

STEP 1
My accounts on the air last month

Name/Company	Amount Billed
AABKO Mortgage	$ 800
American TV	2,357
Arnold's Soda Shop	445
Betsy's Box of Gifts	520
Chi-Chi's	1,200
Don the Muffler Man	660
Fortune Magazines	410
Hardy Hardware	777
Joe's Pizza	480
Linkon Auto Parts	1,600
Menson's Auto	910
New Horizons Health	1,466
Newstand Daily	600
Schwegler Lanes	2,250
Sunny Savings & Loan	1,222
What's New Books	560
Why Knot Cafe	500

Total sales last month **$16,757**

STEP 2
My accounts on the air this month

	Name/Company	Amount Billed
R	American TV	$ 1,550
R	Arnold's Soda Shop	610
	Best Buy Wholesale	1,187
R	Chi-Chi's	550
	Civic Center Playhouse	650
	Coliseum Tickets	2,280
	Fantasy Gifts	218
	The Tire Changer	456
	J. J. Maxx	1,200
R	Joe's Pizza	250
R	Linkon Auto Parts	965
	Madison Magazine	440
	Momma's Deli	1,206
	Olds World Auto	4,800
	Our Own Hardware	882
	Park Towne Civic Group	610
	Parker Pen & Card	800
	Pet World USA	580
	Remax Realty	3,656
	Rugs from Tibet House	802

Total sales this month **$23,692**

STEP 3   Identify repeat business.
STEP 4   Add up the dollars billed THIS month to businesses that are carryovers from LAST month. This is your REPEAT BUSINESS.   **$3,925**

STEP 5a

Total of last month's billing		$16,757
Less repeat business	(-)	3,925
= TOTAL DOLLAR CHURN		$12,832

STEP 5b

% of billing churned*
.7657 = 76.6%

$16,757)‾ $12,832
Last month's $ sales / Total $ churned

STEP 6a

No. of accounts on air last month		17
Less no. of repeat business accounts	(-)	5
= TOTAL NO. OF ACCOUNTS CHURNED		12

STEP 6b

% of accounts churned*
.7058 = 70.6% *

17)‾ 12
No. of accounts on / Total accounts
air last month   churned

*Should be less than 20%

FIGURE 2–29 A business will lose 25% of its customers in a year's time. Sales trainer Chris Lytle of the Lytle Organization looks at business month-to-month to examine what's lost. His Churn Calculation Worksheet allows sellers to put a dollar value on customer retention. ©1998 Chris Lytle. Used with permission. Phone: 800-255-9853 or 608-284-1284.

your clients in a year. It's altogether something else to lose 70% of them in a month.[93]

Are there any businesses that do not need to worry about relationship building and customer retention? The souvenir seller on the beach has no reason to believe customers will return. You can probably think of a few others. But why try?

Electronic media sellers can't be casual about customers. Customers are your company's most treasured asset. They not only pay for advertising time, but if you listen to them, they tell you how to sell them again.

What Makes Customers Mad

There are as many reasons for losing a customer as there are customers to be lost. Here are a few broad categories.

- *You don't deliver.* The schedule's not what the customer ordered. The price isn't what you promised. Nothing happened on time.
- *Sell and walk syndrome.* Customers don't want the salesperson to disappear after the sale. A good customer is buying into a personal relationship as well as into an effective advertising medium.
- *Changes in personnel.* Clients hate breaking in new salespeople, especially if they've been served well. It's worse if they've been served badly, because they

expect the new seller to be no better than the first.

- *Lack of contact.* A corollary to the sell and walk syndrome. Ad agency founder Fred Poppe puts it this way: "When you're out of sight, you're out of mind. And you will soon be out of pocket." Poppe also outlines two essentials for relationship management: "Contact" and "More contact."
- *Ignoring details.* You never know which tiny detail is crucial to the customer until you've overlooked it. The customer won't.
- *Getting caught.* Whatever it may be that you don't want the client to know about, expect the client to find out. Avoid sharing secrets, gossiping about the client, changing the client's schedule. The client *will* find out.[94]

The most serious of all sins against customers is not knowing when they're mad. Business writer Terry Varva says 91% of unhappy customers will never again buy from the company that dissatisfies them.[95] Worse, they'll announce their dissatisfaction to at least nine other people.

I found an appropriate comment about relationship management in an article by Lois Geller in *Direct Marketing*: "When companies are interested in keeping customers for a long time, it is because they intend to be in business for a long time."[96]

HOW TO DEVELOP REPEAT CUSTOMERS BY MARK H. MCCORMACK

1. SELL THE MARKET, THEN THE PRODUCT.

In the sports marketing business, our company is regarded as a pioneer and the market leader. So part of our sales effort has always been educating customers about sports. Before we try to sell them our brand of sports marketing, we have to get them excited about sports in general. We're willing to take our chances on whether they eventually do business with us. Experience has taught us that if a company becomes dedicated to sports, we'll pick up a little or a lot of their

business. Customers come back to us because of the market we're in, not because of our market share.

2. SERVICE FIRST, SELLING SECOND.

The moment a customer buys into one of our projects, we're faced with a dilemma: Do we service the sale? Or while he has his checkbook out, do we try to sell him something else?

The tendency in our company is to devote all our efforts to servicing that sale and max-

Continued

How to Develop Repeat Customers
(continued)

imizing the benefits for the customer and ourselves. This is not all that bad. It's a lot easier to go back to a customer with a certified success behind you than without one.

3. SHARE THE WEALTH WITH YOUR PEERS.

In our organization we put a premium on interdivisional cooperation. That's often the key to generating repeat business. A customer who is already doing business with our golf division may not have the budget or the need for more golf projects. But this same customer may be intrigued by a concept from our tennis or winter sports division. It's my job as a manager to encourage colleagues to share the wealth with their peers.

Unfortunately, this is not as easy as it sounds. There's a part in all of us that gets possessive with a customer or client. We don't want someone to dilute our relationship, or become a better friend of that customer, or siphon funds from our profit center, or take the credit for our spadework. A compensation system that recognizes and rewards cooperation—that shares the wealth with those who share, if you will—will usually cure this problem.

4. USE THE CALENDAR.

In the right hands, a calendar is a sales tool.

Nearly every customer has some dates during the calendar year when he is more willing or able to buy and, consequently, most vulnerable to a sales effort. Florists, for example, know that people buy flowers around certain holidays. So they remind their customers (with advertisements, flyers, and letters) and get their repeat business several times a year—each year.

A similar pattern exists in corporate sales. Fiscal years vary among corporations. But nearly every company is more willing to buy at the beginning of the fiscal year, when the coffers are full, than at the end.

5. THINK SMALL TO GET BIG.

When it comes to generating repeat business, there are several compelling reasons to think small. Small sales are easier to close, easier to service, and far less risky to your reputation. Mess up a small deal and the customer may forgive you. Mess up a big deal and the customer may not be around to buy again.

I find it's helpful to think of customers as revenue streams. If you start with a trickle, the flood will come later.

For example, I have a reputation for asking big numbers. But some of my best sales have been very small. I once called on a company about an expensive client-entertainment concept. Minutes into our discussion, it was apparent that their plans weren't nearly as grandiose in scope as I had imagined. So I shrunk the proposal, suggesting that they take four people to a prize fight and let us arrange the evening for them. They agreed. To me that's a success. It gives us a foot in the door at their company, gets them used to seeing our face, and starts them thinking of us as a business resource. If we do our job well, we may never have to call on them again. They will call us.

6. DON'T SELL RELIABILITY SHORT.

No matter how well you master the five points above, when all is said done there's no magic to winning repeat customers. The successful executives in our organization are the people who deliver what they say they will deliver when they say they're going to deliver it at a cost that they originally quoted. That's a rare combination. Customers will rush to do business over and over again with people like that.

I've never met Mark McCormack, but I've read so much of his material, I feel I know him. This is reprinted from Mark H. McCormack on Selling, *published by Dove Books. ©1996. Thanks to Geoff Hannell at Dove for permission to use Mark's excellent work.*

Review Highlights and Discussion Points

1. Selling is involved in all human activity.

2. Even though everybody sells, not everybody has the temperament to be successful as a professional salesperson.

3. Some salespeople put their emphasis on researching their customers, while others make lots of calls, increasing their opportunities for more sales. Still others are closing specialists who know how to ask for the order and get it.

4. Whatever their individual strengths in the selling process, the common thread among successful sellers is a belief in themselves and the will to win.

5. Most lists of attributes for winning salespeople begin with the word "attitude."

6. Other attributes of the effective seller are "discipline," "attention to detail," "organizational skills," "listening," and "persistence."

7. Tenacity, flexibility, preciseness, industry knowledge, self-confidence, resilience, and energy, are also on the list of attributes.

8. David Mayer and Herbert Greenberg call "empathy" and "drive" the two essential qualities for a salesperson.

9. In the new selling environment, product knowledge means the advertiser's product. The message of selling is that the *customer is the center of the selling relationship*.

10. The "ask for the order" paradigm is a thing of the past. No longer is sales a matter of coercion, manipulation, or out-thinking the prospect.

11. Wilson Learning pioneered consultant selling for the insurance industry with the Counselor Salesperson program, and Ken Greenwood added important dimensions to it for electronic media sales.

12. As a seller of electronic media, your primary objectives are (1) developing new business, (2) maximizing revenues, and (3) retaining current business.

13. The seller will work in a sales department under a person whose title may be sales manager, director of sales, or marketing manager.

14. Your manager will outline your job specifically and set the strategies for your selling. There is no single structure that works for every electronic media selling team.

15. Ken Greenwood outlines the four stages of selling as (1) the novice, (2) the learner, (3) the competent, and (4) the professional.

16. Before you sell any product, you have to sell yourself. Shane Media's *Power Selling Tactics* outlines ten key strategies for marketing *you*.

17. Sellers must set goals in order to be successful. Planning is essential. Goal setting is a process of establishing, reaching, and revising.

18. Effective self-management enhances relationships and achieves results. Says Steven Covey, "Organize and execute around priorities . . . put first things first."

19. A number of time management systems contain day planners, calendars, priority lists, and other aids to assist the seller in keeping first things first. Of course, no system fits every need.

20. As sellers, we might equate money with happiness, but money is simply a means to an end, not an end in itself.

21. Sellers may start with a draw or salary, but soon shift to a commission. The trend in electronic media is toward spending more on commission than on salaries.

22. First-year salespeople spend more time learning than earning. High-learn equals low-earn.

23. The steps toward closing a sale include prospecting, qualifying, needs analysis, presentation, and answering objections. That is the sales cycle.

24. "In sales, you get the customers you deserve," writes Mark McCormack, who also provides guidelines for identifying the perfect customer in his book *What They Don't Teach You at Harvard Business School*.

25. First and foremost, sales is a numbers game. Tom Hopkins tells us that in all of selling the average is 10 to 1. Ten prospects yield one appointment. Ten appointments yield one sale.

26. Phil Broyles cites five practical steps to getting a seller's contact rate up.

27. All potential advertisers start as prospects, and prospects are typically already advertisers in other media. This is a good place to begin the search for customers. Check out newspapers, Web sites, Yellow Pages, billboards, cable, radio, television, and direct mail.

28. Cold-calling means walking into a prospect's place of business unannounced—cold. When cold-calling, be prepared for rejection, and always prepare a reason—a pretext—for being there.

29. As a salesperson, you will likely have 100 or more accounts on your list—some active advertisers, others inactive—which require ongoing tracking. As Michael Keith writes, "A record of a call will put you back on point."

30. Maintain a database of targeted prospects and potential clients.

31. One of the mistakes first-time sellers often make is concentrating on advertisers whose budgets are too small.

32. Customers who pay their bills on time are better customers than those who stall and make excuses. Checking credit rating and payment history will be near to the top of your list as you qualify potential advertisers. Qualifying is information gathering.

33. All your sales efforts will be for nothing if you do not present your story to the person with the power to make the buy. The key is getting to the person making the buying decision.

34. Determine whether the potential customer has the ability to spend money on what you are proposing. Does the prospect have the dollars required to commit to an advertising plan you develop? Is the client creditworthy?

35. Qualifying eases the way to needs analysis, which continues the sales cycle's information-gathering process.

36. The telephone is the best organizer and time-saver, although a seller will make thousands of phone calls trying to set up appointments with only a few call-backs.

37. Pam Lontos suggests making at least 30 phone calls a day, all within a short period of time, say between 9 and 10 a.m.

38. The seller's job is to use all available tools to help prospects and clients solve their advertising and marketing problems in a mutually profitable way.

39. Mike McCaffrey believes that "the single most effective selling tool you have is the ability to ask questions well," and he calls asking questions a "highly learnable skill."

40. Sales trainer Chris Lytle suggests starting a client interview with a fact about the client's business.

41. Sellers would do well to become acquainted with Abraham Maslow's hierarchy of needs as a means of better understanding human nature and the client. These include self-actualization, esteem, social relationship, safety and security, and physiological needs.

42. Today's selling environment is as much about questioning and listening as it is about presenting and closing. A seller's presentation is better targeted if his or her questioning and listening skills are sharp and well-honed. The objective of questioning is not to sell, but to find out what the prospect needs.

43. There are three inviolable rules in question-asking, according to Harold Bausemer: "Never ask a question that the client cannot answer, never ask the same question twice, and never ask more than one question at a time."

44. Clients are not buying advertising; they are buying business solutions, which are the product of a seller's thorough needs analysis effort.

45. Presentations are an opportunity for sellers to demonstrate just how well they understand a prospective advertiser's problems.

46. Research from Learning International shows three key reasons why cus-

tomers buy: (1) business expertise and image, (2) dedication to the customer, and (3) account sensitivity.

47. A key step in presentation is believing in yourself. If you demonstrate no faith in your own ability to sell, your prospect will develop none.

48. Affirmations are tools for subconscious image impression. Using a positive assertion about yourself and your selling situation is a specific way to program yourself for success. With affirmations you give yourself inner strength and the resolve to keep going.

49. Eighty-nine percent of sales to new accounts are made after the fifth call.

50. Your prospect should expect you to demonstrate your trustworthiness, competence, objectivity, and expertise throughout the selling process.

51. Make no assumptions when it comes to your prospect's needs and concerns. Tell your prospect why they would benefit from buying advertising on your medium.

52. Get to the point of the presentation. Time and attention are the chief currencies of the twenty-first century.

53. Keep your presentation colorful. Have interesting (but brief) stories to tell.

54. Make sure the numbers in your presentation tell the story, not garble the issue. It is best to keep figures to a minimum and use them to illustrate a point, not as the point themselves.

55. Keep your prospect involved with the points of your presentation, and use media kits to make your product more tangible.

56. Keep the presentation moving forward. Do not get bogged down. Use powerful words to generate desired pacing.

57. Keep in mind that an objection by a prospective customer is simply an expression of concern about advertising. Do not take an objection as a rejection. Deal with it, then move forward in the selling process.

58. When the negotiations begin, the close is in sight. If you cannot close, you cannot sell.

59. Servicing the account is the first step toward relationship building. Part of the "service" for a client is getting the commercial copy written and produced.

60. Some electronic media outlets require salespeople to collect money due for the advertising schedules they sell.

61. Relationship management means creating repeat customers, not just one-time buyers.

62. Mark McCormack lists three criteria for customer retention: communication, service, and added value.

63. Advertisers rely on prompt, accurate follow-up to the sale. Getting the paper trail in order, advising the client about billing details, and getting information for the commercial are all vital to building deep, trusting relationships.

64. Customer retention means big money. For most companies a small number of customers accounts for a large amount of business. That theory is called the 80:20 rule, although the ratio varies industry by industry and medium by medium.

Chapter Notes

1   "Everyone sells," says Zig Ziglar. His take on the selling process and the story of the shoeologist can be found in *Reaching the Top*, cited previously.

2   Jim Savage's "Your Key to Winning and Success" appeared in the Ziglar Corporation's magazine, *Top Performance*, January/February 1989. I wanted to show you one of Jim's "scouting report" charts, so I called him at his Florida home. Unfortunately, he hadn't keep them.

3   Martin Antonelli's list of attributes was first published in *Broadcasting*, Febru-

ary 25, 1985. I clipped the article then and kept it in my sales file.

4   I interviewed Lee Masters of E! Entertainment Television on December 22, 1997. More from Masters appears in Chapter 7.

5   Sharon Drew Morgen takes a truly ethics-based approach in *Selling with Integrity*. San Francisco: Berrett-Koehler, 1997.

6   David Mayer and Herbert M. Greenberg wrote about empathy in "What Makes a Good Salesman" for the *Harvard Business Review*, July–August 1964.

7   Charles Friedman was quoted on the psychology of selling in Michael Keith's *The Radio Station*, cited previously.

8   Steven R. Covey's *The Seven Habits of Highly Effective People* is a must-read for any seller. New York: Simon & Schuster, 1989.

9   The booklet, "Finding and Selecting TRUE Salespeople," was published in 1995 by the Omnia Group, Inc., of Tampa, Florida. Mary Ruth Austin's "Faux Salesperson or Superstar?" is a separate report. ©1996 Omnia Group.

10 When I read a magazine ad for The H. R. Chally Group, I didn't connect the company to the book, *The Quadrant Solution*, which had been on my bookshelf for a while. The book, by Chally's Howard Stevens and writer Jeff Cox, is a novel, which is an unusual format for a business book. New York: AMACOM, 1991.

11 *How to Select a Sales Force That Sells*. 3rd ed. Dayton, Ohio: The H. R. Chally Group, 1997.

12 These are from Dave Gifford. There are several good articles by him in *The Radio Book, Volume One: Management and Sales Management*. West Palm Beach, FL: Streamline Press, 1995.

13 The stages of a seller's competence are outlined by Ken Greenwood in *High Performance Selling*. West Palm Beach, FL: Streamline Press, 1995.

14 Allen Shaw of Centennial Communications sent a personal note by fax when he heard I was collecting ideas for this book.

15 Mike McCaffrey with Jerry Derloshon. *Personal Marketing Strategies: How to Sell Yourself, Your Ideas, and Your Services*. Englewood Cliffs, NJ: Spectrum Books, 1983.

16 The Shane Media workbook, *Power Selling Tactics*, was published by our company in 1990 and is still available through the National Association of Broadcasters.

17 I'm so happy that Tom Hopkins gave me permission to use his material. His advice on goal setting is from *How to Master the Art of Selling*, cited previously.

18 Skipper Dennis Conner's *The Art of Winning: A Hands-On Plan for Systematizing Success*, written with Edward Claflin, was excerpted in *Success*, January/February 1989.

19 On the subject of affirmations and visualization, Tony Robbins is the best. He has written several books, but I recommend his *Unlimited Power* audio programs, available from Nightingale-Conant Corporation in Chicago. 1-800-323-5552.

20 Covey's time-management (or life-management) ideas are from *The Seven Habits of Highly Effective People*, cited earlier.

21 "Pick the future as against the past," says Peter Drucker, urging concentration on one thing at a time in *The Effective Executive*. New York: Perennial Library, 1967.

22 "Enhancing Happiness" was distilled from a special report in *The Futurist*, September/October 1997. The magazine drew from author Mihaly Csikszentmihalyi's *Creativity: Flow and the Psychology of Discovery and Invention*. New York: Harper Perennial, 1996.

23 Because of its age, Charles B. Roth's book, *Secrets of Closing Sales*, may seem heavy-handed and too focused on closing rather than building relationships. However, there are still a lot of basics to be gleaned from the book. I have the fifth edition, which Roth wrote with Roy Alexander. Englewood Cliffs, NJ: Prentice-Hall, Inc., 1983.

24 "The Perfect Customer" was adapted from "How to Recognize the Perfect

Customer" by Mark McCormack in the Southwest Airlines magazine, *Spirit*. May 1989.

25 Tom Hopkins' *How to Master the Art of Selling* was cited previously.

26 My neighbor Tom Vann, who manages a brokerage office, introduced me to Phil Broyles' columns, called "Tools of the Trade," written for financial sellers. Broyles' "Our Business Is a Contact Sport" appeared in *Research*, April 1991, and a Shane Media editor condensed it for our client newsletter, *Tactics:Sales*.

27 Where to go to find prospects came from a number of sources: The Radio Advertising Bureau's *Media Facts*; Michael Keith's *Selling Radio Direct*, cited earlier; Irwin Pollack's "25 Prospecting Sources"; Tom Hopkins; Chris Lytle; Jim Taszarek's *Large Market Radio Selling*; Cabletelevision Advertising Bureau's *Cable Facts 1997*; and the Television Bureau of Advertising.

28 Michael Keith's *Selling Radio Direct* was cited previously.

29 Chris Lytle's "concentrating the force" was part of his article, "A Whole New Ball Game," in *Radio Ink*, March 1, 1993.

30 Ideas from "The King of Cold Calls" and "How to Get Past the Gatekeeper," *Selling*, July/August, 1994.

31 At a Texas Association of Broadcasters meeting where I was a speaker, I met Rick Alan, who also did a seminar there. He allowed Shane Media to reprint some of his materials in our newsletter, *Tactics:Sales*, April 21, 1992.

32 Mark H. McCormack's *On Selling* was cited previously.

33 Sales automation software changes as quickly as new ideas are conceived. *Selling Power* publishes a software directory each year. I used the 1998 edition from the November/December 1997, issue. Also check SalesLogix online at *www.saleslogix.com*, a video sales meeting program at *www.cuseeme.com*, and GoldMine at *www.goldminesw.com*. (*Selling Power* is a great resource for sellers. Motivational expert Gerhard Gschwandtner is the publisher.)

34 Warner and Buchman's *Broadcast and Cable Selling* was cited previously.

35 Ted Kerley, a sales planner at Nickelodeon, assembled a "buy" for Shane Media on both Nickelodeon and Nick's TV LAND network. It's used as an example in Chapter 3.

36 Pam Lontos' tips for getting appointments appeared in "Dialing for Dollars: Get the Appointment, Then Make the Sale," *Radio Ink*, June 21, 1993.

37 The Radio Advertising Bureau's *Welcome to Radio Sales* is a basic course in selling as well as an introduction to the radio medium. It's published for member stations by RAB, 1320 Greenway Drive, Suite 500, Irving, TX 75038.

38 Harvey Mackay's *Swim with the Sharks Without Being Eaten Alive* is still one of the best business books ever, in my opinion. New York: William Morrow & Co., 1988.

39 Mike McCaffrey's *Personal Marketing Strategies* was cited previously.

40 On the subject of taking notes, there's the Warner and Buchman opinion. Then there's my opinion. So let's break the tie: in *Rogers' Rules for Success* (New York: St. Martin's/Marek, 1984), Henry C. Rogers suggests that taking notes flatters the person being questioned.

41 Peter Drucker's *Managing for Results* was cited before.

42 "Maslow" and "need" are said almost simultaneously because of Abraham H. Maslow's *Motivation and Personality*. 2nd edition, New York: Harper & Row, 1954. Maslow's *Toward a Psychology of Being*. 2nd edition, New York: D. Van Nostrand Company, 1968.

43 The serious student of needs should also consult Carl Jung's *Psychological Types*, Princeton, NJ: Princeton University Press, 1971.

44 Marc Porat's speech was covered in "Trying to Change the World," an article in *Mobile Data Report*, November 19, 1990. Dennis Waters, the publisher of *Mobile Data Report*, was the first radio person I knew who understood the impact of new media. When he couldn't convince anyone in radio to listen, he began newsletters like *Mobile Data Report and Microticker Report* for those who would.

45 The idea of looking for clues came from Warner and Buchman, *Broadcast and Cable Selling*, cited previously.

46 Larry Wilson is quoted by Ken Greenwood in *High Performance Selling*, cited previously.

47 Sharon Drew Morgen's *Selling with Integrity* was also cited previously.

48 The IBM questions are from Mike McCaffrey's *Personal Marketing Strategies*, cited before.

49 Harold Bausemer wrote "What's Your Focus" for *Tuned In*, July 1997.

50 *Sales Questions That Close the Sale* by Charles D. Brennan Jr., president of the Sales Development Institute. New York: AMACOM, 1994.

51 Steven Covey's *The Seven Habits of Highly Effective People* was cited before.

52 The article about listening in *The Wall Street Journal* was "The Crucial Question For These Noisy Times May Just Be: 'Huh?'" by Cynthia Crossen, July 10, 1997.

53 Listening is called "the unused potential" in "Listening to People" by Ralph G. Nichols and Leonard A. Stevens, in the *Harvard Business Review*, September/October 1957, reprinted in *HBR's Paths Toward Personal Progress: Leaders Are Made, Not Born* in 1982.

54 *Rogers' Rules for Success* was cited previously.

55 It's true. I'm a real fan of Mark McCormack. His *On Selling* is a great resource, as cited previously.

56 Chris Lytle quoted the Learning International research in "The Real Reason Clients Buy" in *Radio Ink*, October 4, 1993.

57 The data on the fifth call was collected by Harry Spitzer for Impact Resources in 1988. I first quoted the figures in Shane Media's *Power Selling Tactics*.

58 Lester Wunderman's book is not about electronic media, but it's sure fun to read. *Being Direct: Making Advertising Pay*. New York: Random House, 1996.

59 Howard Upton wrote "The Perils of Information Overload" for the "Insider's Digest" column in Southwest Airlines' *Spirit*, May 1990.

60 "How to Improve Your Negotiating Skills" by Amy S. Bly and Robert W. Bly of the Center for Technical Communications, Dumont, NJ. Find it online at *www.smartbiz.com/sbs/arts/bly60.htm*.

61 Tom Hopkins' "triplicate of choice" is in *How to Master the Art of Selling*, cited previously.

62 Michael Keith's *Selling Radio Direct* was cited before.

63 Kerby Confer does a terrific speech on creativity for broadcast groups. He always rolls the "big deal pen."

64 The ideas in "Dress Up a Presentation" are from Shane Media's *Tactics: Sales* information service for our radio station clients.

65 Examples of "rejection words" and "pedestal words" are from Tom Hopkins; Ken Greenwood, *Power Selling Tactics*, and from *Words That Sell* by Richard Bayan, Chicago: Contemporary Books, 1984.

66 If it doesn't break down, it's a condition, not an objection, says Tom Hopkins in *How to Master the Art of Selling*, cited previously.

67 "Selling Begins When the Customer Says NO" is from Shane Media's *Tactics: Sales*, October 27, 1992.

68 Discussing the problems, not the solutions is a caution from "Selling 101: The Seven Basics of Successful Selling," in *Selling Power*, June 1996.

69 "Old-style selling" is something to avoid. Ken Greenwood addresses how in *High Performance Selling*, cited previously.

70 Comments from Lee Masters of E! Entertainment Television, Cheryl Vannucchi of Santa Rosa's Cable One, and Jennifer Baird of CNN are from my conversations with each of them.

71 Mark McCormack's comment is from *On Selling*, cited before.

72 The classic text on negotiation is Gerard I. Nierenberg's *Art of Negotiating*, recently re-released by the International Center for Creative Thinking. Also see Nierenberg's *The Complete Negotiator* from Nierenberg and Zeif, 1986. Both are available through the online bookseller *amazon.com*.

73 Thanks to the Smart Business Supersite *www.smartbiz.com* I came across Peter

B. Stark's work on negotiation. *It's Negotiable*, San Diego, CA: Pfeiffer & Co., 1994.

74 The reference to Amy and Robert Bly was cited earlier.

75 The quotation from Victoria Ruttenberg is from "Most Things Are Negotiable: Here's How to Get Good at It" by Hal Lancaster in *The Wall Street Journal*, January 27, 1998.

76 "If you can't close, you can't sell" is the premise of *Secrets of Closing Sales* by Charles B. Roth and Roy Alexander, cited earlier.

77 Bill Good is based in Sandy, Utah, and operates a sales consulting firm for the financial industry. His articles on closing appeared in *Research*, in January and March, 1992.

78 Chris Lytle's comment about "doing the consulting for free" was in "Spec Work: A Novel Idea," *Radio Ink*, October 19, 1992.

79 Closing techniques are difficult to document. The ones I've chosen are combinations of reading and learning. Thanks to Zig Ziglar, Tom Hopkins, Charles Roth, Charles Warner, and Bill Good. Then add a long list of sellers in electronic media who have shaped my ideas and responses over the years. I've given specific credit where due.

80 In addition to Harvey Mackay's *Swim with the Sharks Without Being Eaten Alive,* cited previously, he also contributed *Beware the Naked Man Who Offers You His Shirt*. New York: William Morrow, 1990.

81 Every sales trainer uses analogies. I think the "long ball out of the park" is from Zig Ziglar. I chose it because I wrote this chapter during baseball season.

82 David Ogilvy's *Ogilvy on Advertising* has been cited elsewhere. The speech to the Association of National Advertisers was printed in ANA's magazine, *The Advertiser*, Summer 1992.

83 Irwin Pollack's advice is from one of his online sales tips, accessible at *www.irwinpollack.com*.

84 John Fellows wrote "Keep Your Customers, Grow Your Sales" for *Radio Ink*, February 1, 1993.

85 "Successful sales personnel develop customers, not just orders," says Regis McKenna in *The Regis Touch*, Reading, MA: Addison-Wesley Publishing, 1985.

86 Mark McCormack, *On Selling*, cited previously.

87 Murray Raphel is a columnist for *Direct Marketing*. This is from "Tell Me What You Want and the Answer Is 'Yes,'" which is a great title. It appeared in October 1996.

88 The KMLE customer study was documented by *Radio Only* in an article "What We Learned from Client Gripes," September 1993.

89 Stuart J. Sharpe of Regional Reps Corp. in Cleveland told the story of his customer study in the *Small Market Radio Newsletter*, September 1997.

90 Diane Sutter shared her Pittsburgh experiences during an interview with me on June 20, 1997.

91 "Relationship Building Tactics" are from *Power Selling Tactics*, Houston, TX: Shane Media Services, 1990.

92 Examples that support the 80:20 rule are from "The Marketing Manager's Job Is, Above All, to Make Sure That the Clients Are Satisfied" by Henry Whitney in *Direct Marketing*, October 1997.

93 Chris Lytle's "churn calculation worksheet" originally appeared in *Radio Ink*, March 29, 1993. Lytle updated the information and provided clarification for use in this book.

94 "What makes customers mad" was inspired by Mark McCormack and collected from all sorts of people. Fred Poppe, who led the Poppe-Tyson advertising agency for years, contributed *50 Rules to Keep a Client Happy*, a thin book (87 pages) worth many times its weight in insight. New York: Harper & Row, 1987.

95 Terry Varra's comment about 91% of unhappy customers is from *Aftermarketing: How to Keep Customers for Life Through Relationship Marketing*, Homewood, IL: Business One Irwin, 1992.

96 Lois Geller wrote "Customer Retention Begins with the Basics" in *Direct Marketing*, September 1997.

Taking It Further

Here are a few Web sites that relate to this chapter and additional reading not included in the Chapter Notes.

www.ama.org/index.html—The American Marketing Association site provides information and ideas for both the marketing and sales dimensions

www.amanet.org—The American Management Association. Their scope is much broader than sales, but they offer sales and sales training courses on CD-ROM plus a full catalog of business books through AMACOM Publishing

www.amcity.com—American City Business Journals, access to sales and business columns

www.covey.com—Steven Covey's site with time-management and life-management information

www.hoovers.com—A search engine for business information with background data on virtually any industry

www.imarketinc.com—A subscription-based online prospecting service with links to business and industry lists. While the site is national in scope, you'll find information specific to local areas, too

www.inc.com—*Inc.* magazine's site with tips for small business people—your customers

www.naa.org—A look at the other side from the Newspaper Association of America

www.peoplesuccess.com—Self-development books, tapes, and seminars from motivational experts

www.primenet.com/ ~ th—Tom Hopkins International

www.xmission.com—Another online resource for self-development and motivation

Additional Reading

Bayan, Richard. *Words That Sell*. Chicago: Contemporary Books, 1984.

Beckwith, Harry. *Selling the Invisible: A Field Guide to Modern Marketing*. New York: Warner Books, 1997.

Delmar, Ken. *Winning Moves: The Body Language of Selling*. New York: Warner Books, 1984.

Geraghty, Barbara, Michael Larsen, and Fred Hills. *Visionary Selling: How to Get to Top Executives and How to Sell Them When You're There*. New York: Simon & Schuster, 1998.

Good, Bill. *Prospecting Your Way to Sales Success: How to Find New Business by Phone, Fax, Internet and Other New Media*. Complete Revised Edition. New York: Charles Scribner's Sons, 1997.

Gordon, Josh. *Tough Calls*. New York: AMACOM, 1996.

Merrill, David, and Roger Reid. *Personal Styles and Effective Performance: Make Your Style Work for You*. Radnor, PA: Chilton, 1981.

Rackham, Neil. *SPIN Selling*. New York: McGraw-Hill, 1988.

Robbins, Anthony. *Awaken the Giant Within*. New York: Summit Books, 1991.

Schiffman, Stephan. *The 25 Habits of Highly Successful Salespeople*. Holbrook, MA: Bob Adams, Inc., 1994.

Schiffman, Stephan. *Closing Techniques That Work*. Holbrook, MA: Bob Adams, Inc., 1994.

St. Lawrence, Michael, and Steve Johnson. *If You're Not Out Selling You're Being Outsold*. New York: John Wiley & Sons, 1997.

Tronnes, Mike, ed. *Closers: Great American Writers on the Art of Selling*. New York: St. Martin's Press, 1998.

3

Research and Ratings

Before David Ogilvy founded Ogilvy & Mather advertising agency he was a researcher. He delivered the first paper on copy-testing in the history of British advertising. He ran the Gallup Audience Research Institute, which predicted the potential public appeal of motion pictures. And he led his agency to extensive use of research for its clients.

Ogilvy's research philosophy is simple: "Advertising people who ignore research are as dangerous as generals who ignore decades of enemy signals."[1]

Research is the key to any successful advertising venture, and "code" is a good analogy for research. The user has to analyze, dissect, and interpret it in order to make sense of it. There are plenty of texts that will help you learn market research and audience measurement; I've listed a number of them in the chapter notes and suggested reading. This chapter will show the application of research data in selling electronic media.

Ogilvy cited "18 Miracles of Research," including measuring the reputation of your company; estimating sales of new products; getting consumer reaction to new products still in the concept stage; positioning a product or service; and defining the target audience. "Research can tell you whether your advertising communicates what you want it to communicate . . . which of several television commercials will sell the most . . . how many people read your advertisements, and how many remember them," Ogilvy states. Ad agencies, especially national agencies like Ogilvy's, were early proponents of research that helped them understand why consumers behave the way they do. That type of research requires both data collection and a dose of psychology.

For example, in the late 1930s, the Plymouth automobile company geared its advertising toward women in a groundbreaking campaign. One magazine ad showed a young couple gazing longingly at a Plymouth under the headline, "Imagine Us in a Car Like That." Another showed a well-dressed woman next to a Plymouth, saying "My Car Fits Like a Glove." Plymouth reversed its previously negative sales figures by recognizing its customers.

The pioneering Plymouth campaign was the work of 30-year-old Ernest Dichter, a Vienna-born psychologist hired by Plymouth's agency, J. Stirling Getchell, Inc., to probe the hidden desires of auto buyers.[2] In 1987, at age 80, Dr. Dichter recalled the campaign in an *Adweek* special report: "You didn't need to be Sigmund Freud to realize that it was the woman who made the real purchase decisions for cars while the man pretended to."

That ad campaign may not have needed Freud but it did need Dichter, because statistics like that weren't available in the 1930s. Today, however, Detroit auto manufacturers can document that 81% of car purchases are directly influenced by women. Triggering buyer responses was a new technique in the 1930s. Targeting specific buying groups, however, was not. Most early audience segmentation was based on social distinction. The *Chicago Tribune* research department undertook a massive house-to-house survey in 1913. They combed residential districts to collect data that, when released in 1916, showed figures on rent, buying habits, and potential dealers for a variety of product lines in each district of the "Windy City."[3]

As an example of audience segmentation, Procter & Gamble's introduction of Crisco Oil in 1912 was aimed at railway chefs, immigrant Jews, and homemakers in the Southwest. Crisco saw the value of target markets, even though it wasn't called "targeting" at that time.

Today's marketer takes targeting and segmentation for granted. This comment in *Radio Ink* magazine from Stephen Smith, director of media planning and buying for American Express, is typical:

> There is a tremendous distinction between people who are oriented toward the services and benefits of being an American Express card member and people who do not see a need for those services and benefits. Even within the affluent segment there is a differentiation between people who are oriented toward a bank card and those who appreciate and have an interest in what American Express offers. I would describe that as psychographic and lifestyle driven. The more likely you are to be a frequent business traveler, the more likely it is that our services will be strongly appealing to you and that you will be a long-term card member.[4]

Qualitative Versus Quantitative

There are two main types of research—qualitative and quantitative. Collecting the information that gets deep into the means and motives of the consumer is *qualitative* research. It measures the "quality" of the information rather than the number of people who may feel or act a certain way. The numbers side of research—"How many people said *such and such?*" or "Who's number one?"—is *quantitative* research. It measures quantity: sheer numbers.

In selling electronic media, qualitative data is much more valuable than quantitative, although achieving a number-one position in a market or attracting a mass audience cannot be overlooked.

Former Group W executive Mike Burnette addressed the value of qualitative data in *The Truth About Radio Ratings*: "For the local retailer, that may mean explaining what your 6.2 share in women 25–54 really means in terms of potential customers. For a media buyer, it might mean showing that your exclusive cume is as large as the capacity of the local stadium."[5]

Quantitative research is often expressed in "rankers"—a rank order of scores on a particular question. Ratings numbers are most prone to bar graphs that stack number one at the top and the others below. While that's an easy way to make sense of the numbers, it's not an effective means of showing why the number one on the list became number one.

Measuring the Audience

Attention is such a limited resource that there's actually a scarcity. The media that wants our attention increases, yet the amount of attention we have remains static. That's the basis of ratings: a measurement of the attention the audience pays to programming. Specifically, a rating is the estimated percentage of the population that is listening to or viewing an advertisement or a program. However, the phrase "the ratings" often expands to mean percentage of population, share of persons using the medium, and the demographic and geographic breakouts, too. Knowing which stations or programs people pay attention to is obviously vital information for sellers who attempt to measure the actual behavior of a perceived audience, not just their opinions or intentions.

The A. C. Nielsen company originated television and national cable ratings. Another company, Nielsen Media Research, continues the work today. Since they're both named "Nielsen" and they both provide research and ratings, they're easily confused. Here's the story:

> A. C. Nielsen and the Cognizant Corporation were spun off in the 1996 split-up of the Dun & Bradstreet Corporation, which owned them both. Cognizant owned Nielsen Media Research at the split. (Later, Nielsen Media Research split from Cognizant and became an independent, publicly traded company in 1998.)
>
> A. C. Nielsen provides TV ratings and some radio ratings to media in countries outside the United States and Canada. A. C. Nielsen also offers other research services to consumer products and service industries worldwide.
>
> Nielsen Media Research provides television information for networks, stations, cable systems, syndicators, and advertising agencies in the United States and Canada.

The "Nielsen" referred to throughout this book is Nielsen Media Research. "The Nielsen Ratings" may mean one of many services provided by Nielsen Media Research, depending on the medium being measured. There are several Nielsen indexes, each measuring a specific audience or medium.[6] (See Figure 3–1.)

The Nielsen Television Index (NTI™) is network television's rating report. Established in 1950, NTI provides continuous audience estimates for all national broadcast network programs. Nielsen gathers information every day from approximately 5,000 households using an electronic "people meter" that instantaneously measures viewing.

The Nielsen Hispanic Television Index (NHTI), introduced in 1992, was the first electronic metered service to report Hispanic audiences on a national basis. NHTI uses the people meter with a sample of 800 Hispanic households in the United States.

The Nielsen Station Index (NSI™), established in 1954, is the local television station report. The NSI provides continuous metered measurement in 44 major markets and diary measurement in more than 200 designated market areas (DMA™). There's a Hispanic equivalent to NSI—the NHSI, or Nielsen Hispanic Station Index. It was established the same year as the NHTI to gather viewing information in 14 markets with significant Hispanic populations.

The Nielsen Homevideo Index (NHVI™) was introduced in 1980 to measure cable-delivered networks, pay cable, VCRs, video discs, and other television technologies. Data is collected through people meters, set-tuning meters, and paper diaries.

Nielsen Syndicated Service (NSS) was formed in 1985 to measure syndicated programming on both the local and national levels. NSS measures programs carried on at least five stations during the survey period.

Local cable channels seldom appear in NSI reports because they don't have high enough ratings to meet the minimum reporting standards. Cable sellers on the local level are often left to sell to local advertisers the success stories and the halo effect of the national networks.

The Radio Market Report is the Arbitron Company's radio equivalent of Nielsen's local TV station report, the NSI. For its radio ratings reports, Arbitron uses diary methodology to collect listening data in 268 markets. Arbitron was originally a provider of television and cable ratings, too, but it closed its television operation at the beginning of 1994. Radio was Arbitron's single most profitable revenue stream, and the marketplace would not support two television ratings services, so radio was Arbitron's logical choice. The company also provides services to cable, utilizing data collected in its radio surveys and through its ownership of Scarborough, a qualitative research company.

Arbitron had a national competitor for radio ratings, too. Birch/Scarborough studied listening with telephone recall methodology from the late 1970s until its demise in 1991. Scarborough existed on its

Boston, MA   May 1996
(Including Manchester, NH Area)
Metered Market Service

SPECIAL ETHNIC TREATMENT USED IN THIS MARKET
(See Page 3)

Nielsen Station Index

Nielsen

Viewers in Profile

Accredited by
Electronic Media
Rating Council ®

FIGURE 3–1 The Ratings. The front cover of the Nielsen
Station Index (NSI) for Boston. Since most
agencies and TV salespeople use the electronic
version of the NSI ("the tapes"), few see this
paper version ("the book"). Courtesy Nielsen
Media Research. Used with permission.

own for a while after Birch closed and before its acquisition by Arbitron.

Arbitron has seen one other competitor in recent years. Strategic Radio Research of Chicago expanded its custom research services to add syndicated AccuRatings. This service got a positive response from radio stations but a chilly reception by advertising agencies. As a result, Strategic withdrew AccuRatings in 1997 and turned it into a custom property for local stations called Accu-Track. This system is similar to ratings but is used more for programming than for advertising sales.

Another radio company, Willhight Research, Inc., was formed in 1982 to provide detailed ratings for medium- and small-market radio stations. The company has worked in more than 30 states, although most of its business is on the West Coast. The core client base is in the states of

Washington (Willhight's home is in Seattle), Oregon, Idaho, and Alaska. Willhight uses telephone methodology and limits its interviews to one person per household. The company promotes a sample guarantee in order to contrast its research with Arbitron.

All of these ratings services define their market areas by the U.S. government's Metropolitan Statistical Area (MSA), Primary Metropolitan Statistical Area (PMSA), or Consolidated Metropolitan Statistical Area (CMSA). The government designations, set by the Office of Management and Budget, are modified slightly by Arbitron and Nielsen, based on the needs of their subscribers.

Markets are typically defined in three ways: for radio, the Metro Survey Area ("Metro") and the Total Survey Area (TSA); for television, the DMA.

Television Ratings

In Chapter 1, I referred to television as a "dominant cultural force." Most people will admit that television is one of the most influential mediums of communication and entertainment. So it follows that television ratings should be an important indicator of advertising success. Brad Edmondson of *American Demographics* magazine sums up the power of television ratings:

> In the world of market research, it can cost millions of dollars to get incomplete answers to simple questions. Here are two: how many people watch television programs, and what are their demographics? Answering these questions earns Nielsen Media Research more than $300 million a year. Billions in advertising revenue depend on the answers, because the cost of a television ad depends on how many people watch it.[7]

Measuring TV audiences used to be a simple matter when the "Big Three" were the sum of the choices—ABC, CBS, and NBC. Now Fox makes it the Big Four. UPN, WB,

and Pax TV hope to make it the Big Seven. Cable television extends that from the Big 40 to the Big 500. Digital transmission adds even more.

The influence of cable and digital TV became more clear when the Nielsen ratings showed a nine point decline in the networks' share of prime time viewing from 1991 to 1996 and an equal and opposite increase for basic cable. (See Chapter 7 to learn of cable's ratings victories.) Since Nielsen was the only rating service measuring television, the networks cried foul. "I don't trust the numbers at all," said Don Ohlmayer, president of NBC's West Coast division in *American Demographics*. "They're trying to measure twenty-first-century technology with an abacus."

The feud between Nielsen and the networks began building when Arbitron left the TV ratings business. The contretemps came to blows in print in 1996 when ABC, CBS, NBC, and Fox announced in full-page displays in advertising industry trade magazines:

Our confidence in Nielsen is DOWN.

Each of the Networks has informed Nielsen that:

- The people meter sample is insufficient in today's TV environment.
- The in-tab sample rates for key demographics are the lowest in 10 years.
- Their national sample did not reflect the national demographic profile.
- There is a growing disparity between local overnight ratings and national ratings.
- Unexplained fluctuations in critical audience measurements are alarming.

The ad closed with "Nielsen is not responding adequately to the industry's concerns."

The networks' ads used virtually the same layout that Nielsen itself had used in a series of ads in the same magazines earlier. The Nielsen ads proclaimed, "Our service is UP" and used these statistics:

- National people meter sample increased to 5,000 homes.
- Record high cooperation in the national sample.
- Expanding metered market service —38 by 1997.
- Objective ratings for the competitive marketplace.

Each Nielsen advertisement ended with a quotation from an ad agency buyer expressing trust and confidence in Nielsen.[8]

To underscore their dissatisfaction with Nielsen, ABC, CBS, Fox, and NBC signed letters of intent to support a new ratings service proposed by Statistical Research, Inc. The new service, called SMART, also gained support from national advertising agencies.[9] After field testing in Philadelphia the networks decided against financial backing for SMART.

At some point, all rating services come under attack, especially when the numbers decline. However, the pressure has been especially intense over the last two decades. The network response described above is typical. Radio stations thrash Arbitron because of sample size and a variety of data errors. Disappointed fans blame TV program cancellations and radio format changes on the ratings. (They're right, but the ratings service is not to blame.)

Nonetheless, ratings are here to stay. As James Fletcher wrote in his *Handbook of Radio and Television Broadcasting*:

Regardless of the volume or direction of public outcry and regardless of the variety of shortcomings to which ratings are subject, there is little likelihood in the near future that the ratings will disappear or seriously diminish in influence. Among the more prominent reasons are these: (a) Ratings are the products of relatively small organizations, which (b) provide information otherwise unavailable, (c) at a low cost, (d) in response to stated needs of advertisers, but (e) under the close supervision of the industry.[10]

Fletcher points out that the essence of the ratings is delivery of large amounts of data at low cost:

There may be better ways to collect information from a respondent than the ways used by the ratings services, but none has survived in the marketplace. The reason has been that other methods do not provide so much information at such a low cost. Ratings reports are relatively inexpensive, especially when contrasted with the cost of custom field surveys of the same scope. The ratings are inexpensive for two important reasons: the data collection methods used by the rating services are usually efficient. A diary, for example, collects all of the viewing for a week; an aided recall interview collects a week of listening. A telephone coincidental interview, on the other hand, provides information from only one viewer or listener at one point of time, making the telephone coincidental at the other end of the cost spectrum, despite the fact that in other ways this method of data collection is probably superior.

The second reason for the relatively low cost of the ratings is the large number of customers who consume these research products. The largest customers of the rating services are national advertisers and advertising agencies, with networks and major production houses also providing major revenues. Reports sold to local stations mean additional revenue to the ratings service. And to the local station, even though the cost of a rating report is considerably higher than another book of equivalent length, the cost is much lower than for any other research package for which the station could pay. This fact explains both the appeal of these market reports to stations and the relatively slow speed at which changes desired by broadcasters are introduced into rating service procedures.

Broadcasters and advertisers alike have a vested interest in seeing that the ratings services remain responsive to the needs of advertisers.

Television Ratings

Nielsen Media Research surveys the 212 television markets in November, February, May, and July for four-week periods called "sweeps." The largest markets are surveyed seven times a year by adding sweeps in October, January, and March. Since the TV programming season begins in the fall each year, the sweeps year also begins in the fall.

The basic measure of television is done via the diary method. Diary-keepers write their daily viewing activities in a small booklet for one week. Each day is broken down into 15-minute periods, and diary-keepers are asked to write down which station and program they watched. They are also asked to enter the age and sex of all family members and visitors who may be watching. At the end of the survey week, diaries are mailed back to Nielsen for tabulation.

Nielsen people meters record TV-set usage in more than 5,000 households in large markets. Note that I use the phrase "TV-set usage." The meter records whether the set was turned on or off and to what channel it was tuned, not whether anyone actually watched the set. That's the source of the contentious response by the networks to Nielsen's report of the decline of shares.

In an article called "How to Read TV Ratings" in *American Demographics* magazine, NBC-TV researcher Horst Stipp reminds his readers, "Households don't watch TV, people do." He continues:

Many express amazement and concern about the 'finding' that Americans watch seven hours of TV a day. They don't! Nielsen finds that on most days in the average home, television sets are physically on and tuned to one channel or another for about seven hours.[11]

People meters automatically download their data to Nielsen via phone line. The company compiles the information daily and creates "overnights," which are ratings profiles of shows aired the previous night.

Nielsen data is released in printed form and is referred to as "the book." Stations, however, also use detailed Nielsen information delivered on data disks. Because the same data was once provided on reels of computer tape, the Nielsen data on disk is often referred to as "the tapes."

The television reports show the estimated audiences for stations in each market by sex and age and by time period.

Pros and Cons of the Nielsen Ratings System

The advantages of the diary include its ability to record large amounts of information at one time, thus reducing the cost of collection. The diary also reflects individual viewing behavior and gathers demographic data.

The downside of the diary is its reliance on people—a respondent may lie about viewing, fail to complete the entries, or fail to return the diary to Nielsen. Plus the diary is prone to inaccurate entries and illegible handwriting. James Fletcher adds to that list:

In the case of a television diary one person in the household typically reports the viewing of others, and evidence indicates that a housewife, for example, has a different rate of accuracy when reporting her own viewing and that of her children or husband. In an exploratory study at the University of Kentucky housewives were accurate in reporting viewing of their husbands as little as 16 percent of the time.

In addition, it is common for a householder to wait until the end of the viewing period to fill out the viewing reports for the entire week, reducing the accuracy of that diary as contrasted with a diary filled out as the viewing reported was going on.

The advantages of meters include the ability to record exact times that the set was turned on and off, and the exact channels to which it was tuned. Meters eliminate human reporting error and provide fast turnaround of the results.

The disadvantages include the fact that there's no way to tell if anyone is actually watching the metered set, there's no demographic information available, and meters are expensive technology. You can see in Figures 3–2 and 3–3 that demographic data is provided in the NSI report. That information comes from the diary-keepers rather than the metered sets.

At the end of this chapter, I've reprinted "Confessions of a Nielsen Family" from *American Demographics* so you can get an insight into ratings from the respondent's point of view.

Using Nielsen Ratings

Typical pages of the NSI report for Boston in May 1996 appear in Figure 3–2. All time periods are covered in the report, but for the sake of space, we'll focus on just a couple. (The NSI "book" is about half an inch thick as it is, and it's printed on very thin paper to reduce bulk.)[12]

Take a look at the two-page spread in Figure 3–2A. It shows prime time, Monday–Friday, broken into three views: 8 p.m.–10 p.m. at the top of the page, the full daypart, 8 p.m.–11 p.m., in the center, and 10 p.m.–11 p.m. at the bottom.

All the Boston TV stations are listed, along with a few out-of-town signals that play well in the Boston area. Next to the call letters of the stations are symbols for network affiliation: *A*, *C*, *F*, and *N* should be obvious. *I* means independent and *P* means public; *IU* is UPN, and *IW* is WB. Only ten cable channels received enough audience to be listed in the Boston book, beginning with WTBS (*T*) with the rest shown in alphabetical order.

The first two columns on the left are the ratings and shares in Metro households.

("Metro" in this usage means "Metropolitan Statistical Area.") The first two columns to the right of the station call letters are ratings and shares for DMA households. (Note that the columns themselves are numbered, with the space used for the call letters an imaginary 3, 4, 5, and 6.)

As you read across, you find trending of shares, with the most recent sweeps period first, then going backwards to the previous year. The large columns headed "Persons," "Women," and "Men" show ratings for the DMA. The last column under "Women" is headed "Wkg," indicating "working women."

The final eight narrow columns show where people live: in Metro Boston, in the Boston DMA (the "home" DMA), or in an adjoining DMA like Providence–New Bedford (Rhode Island), Portland–Auburn (Maine), or Hartford–New Haven (Connecticut).

Continuing across the second page, the same daypart hours apply and the same stations are on the list, but now you're reading households and people, not shares or ratings. In studying this figure, you need to think in human terms rather than in percentages and decimals. (Remember, however, that your agency clients will think in percentages.) The first column (column 52) shows the DMA households tuned to each station, followed by the four-week average from all the surveys in the area.

All the columns to the right of the call letters in Figure 3–2B represent numbers of people, broken into a variety of age and sex cells. Multiply any number by 1,000 to get the totals. So WABU's 65 persons 2+ should be read 65,000. The very last line of any time period is labeled "H/P/T" and shows the totals of households or persons, depending on what's in the column above.

A quick scan of the numbers shows you that WHDH was the market ratings leader in prime time during this survey. WHDH was beaten only in Women 12–24, and that's by WFXT between 8 p.m. and 10 p.m.

So what were they watching? Take a look at Figure 3–3, the NSI program averages. Because programs change each night on the traditional networks, the time frames are slightly different in this two-page spread, but they cover a period as close as possible to the charts in the previous example.

WHDH was winning with the NBC line-up, especially with the big numbers attracted by "ER" at 10 p.m. on Thursday. Just look at the second-to-last line in Figure 3–3A. In the line above that, you can see that Wednesday's "Law and Order" helped with the NBC ratings, primarily in older demos.

For convenience, at the back of the NSI is a program index that lists all programs in alphabetical order by day of the week, by which survey week they appeared in, and by share trending. You'll find a sample page in Figure 3–4. That particular example begins with several days of the syndicated "Montel Williams." From this chart, you can tell that the show is on WFXT at midnight and that it ran for four weeks of the survey period. This entry begins with Wednesday because Monday and Tuesday would have been on the previous page.

The example in Figure 3–4 also lets you see how a weekly program is listed. Find "Nanny" to see how it fared on CBS affiliate WBZ. Because the survey period covered the 1996 NBA basketball playoffs, you can see how special programming is listed by day and with the appropriate week noted. To find the average persons watching and their demographic characteristics, you'd have to turn to daily program averages, which are available in the NSI.

Cost Comparisons

Ratings are a most important element in setting prices for commercial time (the other key elements are demand and demographics). Good ratings and good shares in demos help you command high rates. The objective for buyers is to reach their target at the lowest cost of delivery. The objective for sellers is to make sure the cost reflects the value of the audience being delivered.

The total of all the ratings generated by each commercial in a schedule is the gross rating points (GRPs), pronounced *grips*.

Let's use the Boston NSI to calculate GRPs. Suppose your client wants to evaluate a schedule of ten commercials running Monday through Friday from 8 p.m. to 10 p.m. on WLVI and targeting Women 18 + .

The formula to use is

$$\text{GRPs} = \text{Rating} \times \text{number of spots}$$

Using Figure 3–2A, find the DMA rating for WLVI in the Women 18 + column—a2 rating. Multiply by 10, the number of spots, and you have 20 GRPs.

The same schedule on the same station targeting Men 18–34 would yield 30 GRPs, a 3 rating multiplied by the ten spots.

Now let's spread a campaign across several Boston stations using the DMA household rating. The advertiser who wanted ten spots on WLVI in the previous example might want to reach Men 18–34 on WLVI, WFXT, and WCVB with ten spots on each station. Here is how the total GRPs in such a campaign would look:

WLVI	3 rating × 10 spots	= 30 GRPs
WFXT	6 rating × 10 spots	= 60 GRPs
WCVB	4 rating × 10 spots	= 40 GRPs
	Campaign total	= 130 GRPs

The next questions is about value: how much will it cost to deliver a message to 1,000 people using your medium? The answer is expressed in cost per thousand (CPM). The M is from the Latin word *milia*, thousand, and is the source for the Roman numeral M for thousand. There's a standard formula for cost per thousand:

$$\text{CPM} = \frac{\text{Cost of the spot or schedule}}{\text{Number reached (HH or Persons)}} \times 1,000$$

Using the Boston NSI, refer to Figure 3–2B. Find the column showing Persons 18 + for WHDH in prime time, 8 p.m.–11 p.m., Monday through Friday. What's the CPM to reach Persons 18 + if I have $5,000 for the schedule?

There are 503,000 Persons 18 + tuned to WHDH during that period, so $5,000 divided by that number and multiplied by 1,000 gives you a CPM of $9.94.

To do the same calculation with working women, divide $5,000 divided by 132,000 and multiply the result by 1,000 fz for a CPM of $37.88. It's much more expensive to reach a narrower group, but often worthwhile if you are selling a product whose

DAYPART SUMMARY

BOSTON, MA (& MANCHESTER AREA)

METRO HH RTG (1)	METRO HH SHR (2)	DAYPART TIME(ETZ) STATION	DMA HH RTG (7)	DMA HH SHR (8)	IN MKT SHR (9)	SHARE TREND FEB '96 (10)	NOV '95 (11)	JUL '95 (12)	MAY '95 (13)	PERSONS 2+ (15)	12-24 (17)	12-34 (18)	18-34 (19)	18-49 (20)	21-49 (21)	25-54 (22)	35+ (23)	35-64 (24)	50+ (25)	WOMEN 18+ (26)	12-24 (27)	18-34 (28)	18-49 (29)	25-49 (31)	25-54 (32)	WKG (34)	MEN 18+ (35)	18-34 (36)	18-49 (37)	21-49 (38)	25-49 (39)	25-54 (40)	TNS 12-17 (41)	CHILD 2-11 (42)	CHILD 6-11 (43)	PERCENT DISTRIBUTION MET (44)	HOME DMA (45)	ADJACENT DMA #1 (46)	#2 (47)	#3 (48)	TV HH RATINGS IN ADJACENT DMA'S #1 (49)	#2 (50)	#3 (51)
		MON.-FRI. 8:00P-10:00P																																									
2	4	WABU+ I	2	3	5	1	1			1	1	1	1	1	1	1	2	1	2	1				1	1	1	2	1	1	1	1	1	1			62	93	6			1		
10	15	WBZ C	9	14	20	14	14	13	15	5	2	3	3	5	5	5	7	7	9	7	2	4	6	6	7	7	4	3	4	4	4	4	2	2	1	56	93	5			2		
10	15	WCVB A	9	14	20	15	16	14	18	6	4	5	5	6	6	6	7	7	7	7	5	6	7	7	8	7	5	4	5	5	6	5	5	4	5	57	93	5	1	1	2		
<<		WENH P	<<			1	1	1																												36	87		11				
10	15	WFXT F	8	12	17	13	12	7	10	5	7	8	8	7	7	6	4	5	3	6	9	10	8	8	7	7	5	6	6	6	6	5	7	2	3	66	93	6			2		
2	4	WGBH P	2	3		4	4	4	3	1				1	1	1	2	1	3	1			1	1	1	1	1	1	1	1	1	1				51	70	17	1	3	2		
2	2	WGBX P	1	2		1	1	2	1	1						1	1	1	1								1		1	1	1	1				68	86	14			1		
<<		WGOT I	<<																																								
14	21	WHDH N	14	21	30	22	21	17	19	9	8	10	10	11	11	11	10	11	10	11	8	11	12	12	12	11	9	9	9	10	10	10	7	3	4	52	89	4			3		
4	6	WLVI IW	3	5	7	5	5	5	6	2	2	2	2	2	2	2	2	2	3	2	2	2	2	1	1	2	2	3	2	2	2	2	2	1	1	60	92	7		1	1		
<<		WMUR A	1	2	2	2	2	1	2	1	1	1	1	1	1	1	1	1		1	1	1	1	1	1	1	1		1	1	1	1	1		1	5	85		3				
<<		WNDS I	1	1	1	1	1	1	1																			1								37	99						
3	5	WSBK IU	3	4	6	5	6	8	7	2	1	2	2	2	2	2	2	2	2	1	1	1	1	1	1	2	2	2	2	2	2	2	1		1	45	68	7	6	2	1	1	
1	1	WTBS T	1	1		2	1	1	1				1						1			1					1	1	1														
1	2	AEN	2	2		2	3	2	2	1			1	1	1	1	1	1	2	1			1	1	1	1	1	1	1	1	1	1											
1	1	DSC	1	1		1	1	1	1						1		1		1								1		1	1	1	1											
2	2	ESP	2	3		1	1	2	2	1	1	1	2	1	1	1	1	1	1	1		1	1	1	1	1	2	2	2	2	2	2	1										
1	1	FAM	1	1		1	1	NR									1		1	1						1																	
1	2	LIF	1	2		2	2	2	1	1	1	1	1	1	1	1	1	1	1	1	1	1	1	1	1	1	1			1	1	1											
<<		MTV	<<																														1										
2	3	NIK	2	3		3	3	3	2	1		1	1	1	1	1	1	1	1	1		1	1	1	1	1	1	1	1	1	1	1		3	3								
1	2	TNT	1	2		2	1	2	3	1	1	1	1	1	1	1	1	1	1								1	1	1	1	1	1	1										
2	3	USA	2	3		3	3	4	3	1	1	1		1	1	1	1	1	2	1	1		1	1	1	1	1	1	1			1	1										
65		H/P/T.*	67		46	68	69	58	68	45	35	42	43	46	47	49	54	51	58	53	37	45	48	51	51	51	48	41	44	45	47	47	36	19	24								
		8:00P-11:00P																																									
2	4	WABU+ I	2	3	5	1	1	1	1	1	1	1	1	1	1	1	2	1	2	1					1	1	2	1	1	1	1	1	1			61	93	6			1		
10	15	WBZ C	9	14	21	14	14	14	15	5	2	3	4	5	5	6	7	7	9	7	3	5	6	7	7	7	5	3	4	4	4	4	2	1	1	58	94	5			2		
11	17	WCVB A	10	16	22	16	17	16	19	6	4	5	5	6	7	7	8	8	8	8	4	6	7	8	8	7	6	4	5	6	6	6	4	3	3	58	93	5		1	2		
<<		WENH P	<<			1																														37	89		9				
8	12	WFXT F	7	10	14	11	10	6	8	4	6	6	7	6	6	5	3	4	2	5	7	8	6	6	6	6	4	5	5	5	5	5	5	2	2	64	93	6			2		
2	3	WGBH P	2	3		4	3	4	3	1				1	1	1	1	1	2	1			1	1	1	1	1	1	1	1	1	1				52	79	16	1	3	1		
1	2	WGBX P	1	1		1	1	2	1								1	1	1								1									69	87	13			1		
<<		WGOT I	<<																																								
15	23	WHDH N	14	22	32	23	23	18	20	9	8	10	11	11	11	11	11	11	10	12	9	12	12	13	13	11	9	10	9	10	10	10	7	2	3	55	89	4			2		
4	6	WLVI IW	3	5	7	5	5	5	6	2	1	2	2	2	2	2	2	2	3	2	2	1	1	2	2	2	2	2	2	2	2	2	2		1	62	92	7			1		
<<		WMUR A	1	2	2	2	2	1	2	1	1	1	1	1	1	1	1	1	1	1	1	1	1	1	1	1	1		1	1	1	1	1			5	84		4				
<<		WNDS I	<<			1	1																													37	99						
3	5	WSBK IU	3	4	6	4	5	8	7	1	1	1	1	1	1	1	2	2	2	1		1	1	1	1	1	2	2	2	2	2	2	1			46	70	8	5	2	1	1	
1	1	WTBS T	1	1		1	1	1	1										1								1	1															
1	2	AEN	1	2		2	2	2	2	1			1	1	1	1	1	1	1	1				1	1	1	1	1	1	1	1	1											
1	1	DSC	1	1		1	1	1	1																						1												
2	3	ESP	2	3		1	1	2	2	1	1	1	2	1	1	1	1	1	1			1	1	1	1	1	2	2	2	2	2	2	1										
1	1	FAM	1	1		1	1	NR									1		1																								
1	2	LIF	1	2		2	2	2	2	1	1	1	1	1	1	1	1	1	1	1	2	1	1	1	1	1	1				1	1											
<<		MTV	<<			1	1	1	1																								1										
2	3	NIK	2	3		3	3	2	2	1		1	1	1	1	1	1	1	1	1		1	1	1	1	1	1	1	1	1	1	1		2	2								
1	2	TNT	1	2		1	1	2	3	1	1	1	1	1	1	1	1	1	1								1	1	1	1	1	1	1										
2	3	USA	2	3		3	3	4	3	1	1	1	1	1	1	1	1	1	2	1	1	1	1	1	1	1	1		1			1	1										
64		H/P/T.*	65		45	66	66	57	66	43	32	39	42	44	46	47	53	50	57	51	34	43	47	49	49	49	46	40	42	43	45	45	30	14	17								
		10:00P-11:00P																																									
2	4	WABU+ I	2	3	5	1	2	2	2	1				1	1	1	2	1	2	1					1	1	1	1	1	1	1	1	1			58	93	6			1		
10	17	WBZ C	9	15	21	15	16	15	16	5	3	4	4	5	5	6	7	7	8	7	4	5	6	7	7	7	5	3	4	4	5	5	2	1	1	61	94	4			2		
12	20	WCVB A	11	19	26	20	21	18	22	7	4	5	5	7	7	8	10	9	10	9	3	6	8	8	9	8	7	5	6	7	7	7	2	1	1	58	93	5		1	3		
<<		WENH P	<<			1																														40	92		5				
4	6	WFXT F	4	6	8	8	6	4	4	2	3	3	4	3	3	3	2	2	2	3	4	4	3	2	2	3	3	3	3	3	3	3	1			58	92	7			1		
1	2	WGBH P	1	2		3	2	4	2	1							1	1	1	1						1	1				1					55	84	12		3	1		
1	1	WGBX P	1	1		1	1	1											1																	71	90	10					
<<		WGOT I	<<																																								
17	27	WHDH N	15	25	34	26	26	19	22	9	9	10	11	11	12	12	11	12	10	13	10	13	13	14	14	12	9	10	9	10	9	9	5	1	1	60	90	4			2		
4	6	WLVI IW	3	5	7	6	5	5	5	2		1	1	1	2	2	2	2	3	2		1	1	2	2	1	2	1	1	2	2	2	1			65	93	7			1		
<<		WMUR A	1	2	2	2	2	2	2	1				1	1	1	1	1	1	1			1	1	1	1	1		1	1	1	1				6	82		5				
<<		WNDS I	<<																																	36	99						
2	4	WSBK IU	2	3	5	4	4	8	6	1	1	1	1	1	1	1	1	1	2	1			1	1	1	1	1	2	1	1	1	1	1			50	75	8	3	2	1		
1	2	WTBS T	1	1		1	1	1	1										1																								
1	1	AEN	1	2		1	1	2	2	1					1	1	1	1	1	1						1	1	1	1	1		1											
1	1	DSC	1	1			1	1	1																																		
2	3	ESP	2	4		1	2	2	2	1	1	1	2	1	1	2	1	1	1						1		2	3	2	2	2	3	1										
<<		FAM	<<					NR																																			
1	2	LIF	1	2		2	2	3	2	1	1	1	1	1	1	1	1	1	1	1	3	2	1	1	1	1	1																
1	1	MTV	1	1		1	1	2	1		1	1									1							1					1										
2	3	NIK	1	2		2	3	2	2	1		1	1	1	1	1	1	1	1	1		1	1	1	1	1	1		1	1	1	1											
2	3	TNT	1	2		1	1	2	4	1		1	1	1	1	1	1	1	1								1	2	1	1	1	1	1										
1	2	USA	2	3		3	2	4	3	1	1	1	1	1	1	1	1	1	1	1	1	1	1	1	1	1	1						1										
62		H/P/T.*	60		44	61	61	56	61	38	27	34	38	41	42	44	50	48	55	48	29	40	43	45	46	45	44	37	39	40	41	41	18	4	4								

Nielsen has been advised that a station(s) conducted a special promotional activity.

#1=PROVIDENCE-NEW BEDFORD 556,960
#2=PORTLAND-AUBURN 344,410
#3=HARTFORD & NEW HAVEN 911,490

MAY 1996

FIGURE 3–2A The Daypart Summary from Nielsen's NSI for Boston, May 1996.

NSI AVERAGE WEEK ESTIMATES   **BOSTON, MA (& MANCHESTER AREA)**

STATION TOTALS (000)

AVG WK (52)	4 WK (53)	STAT TOTAL HH 000 (54)	DAYPART TIME STATION	HH (58)	PERSONS 2+ (59)	18+ (60)	12-24 (61)	WOMEN 18+ (65)	12-24 (66)	18-34 (67)	18-49 (68)	25-49 (69)	25-54 (70)	50+ (72)	WKG (73)	MEN 18+ (74)	18-34 (75)	18-49 (76)	25-49 (78)	25-54 (79)	TEENS 12-17 (81)	GIRLS (82)	CHILD 2-11 (83)	6-11 (84)
			MON.-FRI. 8:00P- 10:00P																					
19	39	419	WABU+	48	65	59	7	21	2	3	7	7	9	13	7	38	7	17	16	19	5	1	1	1
57	84	1303	WBZ	211	301	279	20	181	13	34	88	80	95	93	79	97	19	53	50	58	9	5	13	7
57	81	1310	WCVB	216	342	289	45	174	26	48	110	95	107	64	76	115	31	76	69	75	23	11	30	22
		133	WENH	10	9	9		4			1	1	1	3	1	5	1	2	2	2				
41	62	929	WFXT	182	303	252	77	152	48	78	127	96	103	25	77	100	50	84	71	74	32	18	18	16
19	40	491	WGBH	56	72	71	3	38	1	3	10	10	12	28	12	33	4	13	11	14	1		1	1
11	28	269	WGBX	28	33	32	2	12		2	5	5	6	7	4	19	3	8	7	10	1			
			WGOT	<<																				
67	85	1619	WHDH	335	555	494	85	284	44	92	188	161	181	96	130	209	79	147	125	139	35	17	27	19
26	54	593	WLVI	78	115	99	20	46	11	13	24	20	22	21	20	54	21	34	29	32	11	6	5	4
8	14	183	WMUR	26	42	34	8	19	5	7	14	11	12	5	11	15	4	11	10	11	4	3	4	3
5	14	119	WNDS	12	14	11	1	5		1	2	2	2	3	1	6	4	4	4	4			2	1
24	55	691	WSBK	88	127	115	17	52	5	14	29	25	29	23	24	63	21	39	32	36	7	2	5	4
9	22		WTBS																					
12	25		AEN																					
9	21		DSC																					
14	24		ESP																					
7	16		FAM																					
12	27		LIF																					
			MTV																					
12	23		NIK																					
9	20		TNT																					
17	35		USA																					
96	99		H/P/T.*	1290	1979	1743	285	989	156	297	606	513	579	382	443	755	245	488	425	476	129	63	107	79
			8:00P- 11:00P																					
22	42	495	WABU+	48	64	58	6	22	1	2	7	6	8	16	7	36	7	16	15	18	4	1	1	1
64	88	1450	WBZ	211	299	279	22	181	15	36	91	81	95	90	79	98	21	55	52	59	9	5	11	6
65	85	1513	WCVB	232	358	318	42	189	23	48	113	98	112	76	79	129	34	82	73	81	18	8	21	16
		157	WENH	9	9	9		4		1	1	1	1	2	1	5	1	2	2	2				
44	67	1022	WFXT	150	246	209	61	121	38	62	99	74	80	22	63	88	42	73	61	64	24	13	13	11
21	43	553	WGBH	48	61	60	2	33	1	3	9	9	10	24	11	27	4	11	10	12	1		1	
13	31	299	WGBX	23	26	25	2	10		1	4	4	4	6	3	16	3	6	5	7	1			
			WGOT	<<																				
73	87	1756	WHDH	340	555	503	87	295	47	97	197	166	187	97	132	208	79	147	122	136	32	16	20	14
32	59	730	WLVI	74	108	97	14	46	8	11	24	20	23	23	19	50	17	30	27	29	8	4	4	3
10	17	234	WMUR	26	40	35	6	19	4	6	14	11	12	6	10	15	4	11	10	11	3	2	3	2
		135	WNDS	10	10	8	1	4		1	1	1	1	2	1	5	3	3	3	3			1	1
31	62	884	WSBK	78	109	99	14	44	4	11	23	21	24	21	20	55	19	33	28	31	6	1	4	3
11	26		WTBS																					
14	27		AEN																					
11	25		DSC																					
17	28		ESP																					
7	17		FAM																					
14	30		LIF																					
			MTV																					
14	26		NIK																					
12	24		TNT																					
21	40		USA																					
96	99		H/P/T.*	1249	1885	1701	258	968	141	280	583	493	560	385	426	733	233	469	407	455	105	51	79	57
			10:00P- 11:00P																					
14	27	307	WABU+	47	60	57	4	25	1	1	5	5	7	20	8	32	5	14	13	15	2		1	1
43	71	957	WBZ	210	295	281	26	180	18	41	96	83	97	85	78	101	24	59	55	61	9	5	5	3
46	71	1055	WCVB	263	389	375	36	218	17	48	118	104	121	99	87	157	40	94	81	92	9	3	5	4
		62	WENH	8	9	9	1	4	1	2	2	2	2	2	1	5	2	3	3	3				
18	38	403	WFXT	84	131	123	28	60	17	30	44	30	33	16	34	64	27	49	41	45	6	3	1	1
8	21	196	WGBH	32	39	38	1	22	1	1	7	7	7	16	8	16	3	7	6	7				
5	13	107	WGBX	15	12	12		5					1	4	1	8	1	2	2	2				
			WGOT	<<																				
52	78	1218	WHDH	351	554	521	92	316	53	107	216	177	200	100	137	205	78	148	118	130	25	14	8	4
16	35	365	WLVI	67	94	91	3	48	2	7	23	22	26	25	16	43	11	22	22	23	2	1	1	1
0	13	142	WMUR	25	37	36	3	20	1	4	13	12	12	7	9	16	3	11	11	11				
		39	WNDS	7	3	2	1					1	1	1		3	1	1	1	1	1			
16	38	419	WSBK	59	73	69	8	28	1	5	12	12	14	16	12	41	14	23	19	21	3			
6	17		WTBS																					
6	16		AEN																					
4	12		DSC																					
13	22		ESP																					
			FAM																					
7	18		LIF																					
5	14		MTV																					
6	12		NIK																					
7	16		TNT																					
10	24		USA																					
89	96		H/P/T.*	1167	1695	1616	203	927	112	247	537	452	521	390	391	689	209	430	370	413	58	27	21	14

Nielsen has been advised that a station(s) conducted a special promotional activity.

MAY 1996

FIGURE 3–2B The Daypart Summary, continued. Courtesy Nielsen Media Research. Used with permission.

BOSTON, MA (& MANCHESTER AREA)

WK1 4/25-5/01 WK2 5/02-5/08 WK3 5/09-5/15 WK4 5/16-5/22

PROGRAM AVERAGES

METRO HH RTG	METRO HH SHR	STATION DAY PROGRAM	DMA HH RATINGS WEEKS 1	2	3	4	MULTI-WEEK AVG RTG	MULTI-WEEK AVG SHR	HUT	PERSONS 2+	PERSONS 18+	PERSONS 12-24	PERSONS 12-34	PERSONS 18-34	PERSONS 18-49	PERSONS 21-49	PERSONS 25-54	PERSONS 35+	PERSONS 35-64	PERSONS 50+	WOMEN 18+	WOMEN 12-24	WOMEN 18-34	WOMEN 18-49	WOMEN 21-49	WOMEN 25-49	WOMEN 25-54	WOMEN 50+	WOMEN WKG	MEN 18+	MEN 18-34	MEN 18-49	MEN 21-49	MEN 25-49	MEN 25-54	TNS 12-17	CHILD 2-11	CHILD 6-11
1	2		3	4	5	6	7	8	14	15	16	17	18	19	20	21	22	23	24	25	26	27	28	29	30	31	32	33	34	35	36	37	38	39	40	41	42	43
2		*R.S.E. THRESHOLDS 25+%*	*2*	*2*	*2*	*2*	*1*			*1*	*1*	*4*	*2*	*2*	*2*	*2*	*1*	*1*	*2*	*1*	*1*	*6*	*4*	*2*	*2*	*2*	*2*	*3*	*2*	*1*	*5*	*2*	*2*	*2*	*2*	*8*	*5*	*8*
1		*(1 S.E.) 4 WK AVG 50+%*	*1*	*1*	*1*	*1*	*LT*			*LT*	*LT*	*1*	*1*	*1*	*LT*	*LT*	*LT*	*LT*	*LT*	*LT*	*LT*	*2*	*1*	*1*	*1*	*1*	*LT*	*1*	*1*	*LT*	*1*	*1*	*1*	*1*	*1*	*2*	*1*	*2*
		9:00PM																																				
2	3	WSBK MON NOWHERE MN-UPN	1	2	2	2	2	2	71	1	1		1	1	1	1	1	1	1	1	1		1	1	1	1	1	1	1	1	1	1	1	1	1			1
1	2	TUE BORDERLINE-UPN	1	1	2		1	2	70	1	1	1	1		1	1	1	1	1	1	1			1	2	2	2		1	1	1					2		
1	2	TUE MNR ADJ SP-UPN				1	1	1	67					1			1											1			1	1	1	1	1			
3	5	WED SWIFT JSTC-UPN	3	2	3	2	3	4	67	2	2	1	1	2	1	1	2	2	2	3	2	1	2	1	1	1	1	3	1	2	2	1	2	2	2			
3	5	SAT SWIFT JSTC-UPN	2				2	3	55	1	1		2	2	1	1	1	1		2	1		2	1	1	1	1			2	2	1	1	1	1			
2	3	SUN STAR-VYGR2-UPN	1	1	1	3	2	2	69	1	1		1	1	1	1	1	1	1	1	1		1	1	1	2	1		2	1		1	1	1	1			
		9:30PM																																				
3	4	WABU+FRI RED SOX PREGME		2			2	3	62	1	1					1	1	2	1	3	1							2		2	1	1	1	1	1			
<<		SAT NEWHART		<<	<<		<<		58																													1
15	21	WBZ MON CYBILL-MON	14	14	14	14	14	20	71	8	10	4	6	7	9	9	10	11	11	11	11	6	8	11	11	12	12	13	12	8	7	7	8	9	8	4	1	1
15	23	WCVB TUE COACH-ABC TUE			12	15	13	20	67	9	10	5	8	9	11	12	12	10	12	7	12	5	10	14	15	15	15	9	12	7	8	9	9	10	10	3	5	6
12	18	TUE DANA CARVY-ABC	11				11	16	65	6	7	6	8	7	9	9	9	7	9	3	8	5	8	10	11	11	11	4	8	6	6	7	8	8	7	9		
16	22	TUE HOME IMPRV-TUE		16			16	23	72	10	12	13	12	12	12	13	14	12	13	12	14	13	14	14	14	14	16	12	8	10	10	10	11	10	11	11		
13	22	WED B WLTR ANNV SP	14				14	23	61	7	9	3	5	6	7	8	8	10	10	11	11	2	9	9	10	11	11	14	10	6	3	5	6	6	5	1	2	
8	12	WED FACULTY-WD-ABC		8			8	12	66	4	5	1	4	4	5	5	6	6	5	6	6		5	6	7	8	7	6	7	4	3	3	3	4	4	2		
9	15	WED J FXWTY WD-ABC			10		10	15	69	6	7	5	7	9	8	8	8	6	6	6	7	4	9	9	8	9	9	5	9	7	10	7	8	6	7	1		
9	14	FRI FMLY MTR-FRI				7	7	11	67	5	3	2	2	2	4	4	4	4	5	2	4		2	5	6	6	6	3	3	2	1	3	3	3	3	5	17	
7	11	FRI HANGN-COOP-FRI	7	7	7		7	11	62	5	4	7	6	5	5	5	5	4	4	3	5	10	7	6	6	6	6	3	6	4	3	4	5	5	4	9	7	11
12	17	WFXT SUN MARRD-CHILD-SP		9			9	13	69	5	6	8	10	11	8	8	7	3	3	2	3	3	5	4	5	4	4	1	3	9	18	11	11	10	10	5		
8	13	SUN MARRD-CHLD SPC	7				7	11	65	5	5	12	9	8	7	7	6	4	5	1	3	8	4	4	4	3	3	1	1	8	11	11	9	10	10	15		
12	17	SUN MRRD W-CHLD SP				10	10	15	69	6	7	3	6	7	7	8	9	8	8	8	5	3	4	5	5	4	5	6	5	10	9	10	11	12	13	3		
12	18	WHDH TUE J LAROQTTE-TUE	13	10	12	11	11	17	68	6	8	4	5	6	7	7	8	9	9	9	8	4	5	7	7	8	8	10	8	7	6	7	6	7	7	3		
26	36	THU CAROLN-CTY-NBC	24		24	27	25	35	71	17	20	16	22	25	24	25	24	17	19	10	21	18	26	26	27	27	26	11	23	18	23	22	23	23	22	11	6	8
2	3	WLVI WED UNHPPLY-AFT-WB	3	2	1	2	2	3	68	1	1	2	2	3	2	2	2	1	1		1	4	3	2	1	1	1		1	2	3	2	2	2	2	1		
<<		WMUR TUE COACH-ABC TUE			2	2	2	3	67	1	1	2	1	1	2	2	2	2	2	1	2	3	2	3	3	3	2		2	1		1	1	1	1	3	1	1
<<		TUE DANA CARVY-ABC	<<				<<		65																													
<<		TUE HOME IMPRV-TUE		2			2	3	72	2	2		2	2	3	3	3	2	2	1	2		3	2	3	3	3	1	3	2	2	3	3	3	4			
<<		WED B WLTR ANNV SP	2				2	3	61	1	1	2	1	2	2	2	2	1	2		1		1	2	2	2	2			2	3	3	1	2	1			
<<		WED FACULTY-WD-ABC		1			1	2	66								1	1	1	1	1						1	2										
<<		WED J FXWTY WD-ABC			1		1	2	69	1	1				1	1	1	1	1	1	1	1		1	1	1	1	1	1	1				1	1	1	1	
<<		FRI FMLY MTR-FRI				1	1	1	67				1									1	1													1	1	
<<		FRI HANGN-COOP-FRI	1	1	1		1	1	62	1	1	1	1	1	1	1					1	2	1	1	1				1	1	1	1	1	1	1			
1	2	WSBK TUE MOESHA SPC-UPN				1	1	1	66					1			1											1			1	1	1	1	1			
		9:45PM																																				
4	7	WABU+FRI REDSOX BSBL WD		5			5	8	60	3	3	3	2	2	2	2	2	4	3	6	2	2	1	1	1	1	1	4	2	5	3	3	2	2	3	2		
		10:00PM																																				
1	1	WABU+MON MATLOCK	1	1	1	1	1	1	59		1							1		1	1							1										
1	2	TUE MATLOCK	1		1	1	1	2	61									1		1	1							2	1									
2	3	WED MATLOCK	1	2	1	1	1	2	59	1	1							1		2	1							2										
2	2	THU MATLOCK	2	2	1	1	1	2	64	1	1						1	1	1	2	1						1	3	1	1				1				
1	*2*	*AV4 MATLOCK*	*1*	*1*	*1*	*1*	*1*	*2*	*61*	*1*	*1*							*1*	*1*	*1*	*1*							*2*	*1*									
<<		SAT SAVE-STREETS		1	<<	<<	<<		55																													
<<		SUN ECU	<<	<<	<<	1	<<		65																													
14	24	WBZ MON CHCGO HOPE-MON	12	12	14	15	13	22	59	7	9	5	6	7	9	9	9	10	10	9	11	7	9	11	11	11	12	11	10	7	6	6	7	7	7	3		
8	12	THU 48 HOURS-THU	7	6	8	6	7	10	64	3	4	1	2	2	3	3	4	5	5	7	5		2	3	4	4	4	8	4	4	2	3	3	3	3	1		
9	16	FRI NASH BRDGS-CBS	9	7			8	13	58	4	5	3	3	3	4	4	5	6	7	7	6	3	3	4	4	4	4	9	6	4	2	4	5	5	5	3		
11	19	SAT WALKR-RNGR-CBS	11	12	10	11	11	20	54	6	8	2	2	3	4	5	6	10	9	14	9	3	4	5	6	5	6	15	7	7	2	4	4	5	5	1	1	
20	31	WCVB TUE NYPD BLUE-ABC	18	19	17	17	17	29	61	11	14	10	11	13	14	15	15	14	16	13	14	9	12	14	15	15	15	13	13	14	13	14	15	14	14	4		1
11	18	WED PRMTM LIVE-WED		9	14	8	10	17	60	6	7	1	5	6	6	6	7	8	7	9	8	2	8	7	8	9	8	10	7	5	4	4	4	5	5		1	1
12	21	FRI TURNNG PT-BABY		14			14	24	59	8	9	6	6	6	7	7	9	11	10	12	12	9	10	11	10	11	12	15	10	5	2	4	4	4	5	6	2	
13	21	FRI 20-20-ABC	15		11	11	12	21	58	7	8	2	5	5	7	7	8	10	10	11	10	2	6	8	9	9	10	13	8	7	5	6	6	7	6	2	1	1
9	16	SAT AMR COMEDY-ABC		7			7	13	57	4	5	6	5	6	6	5	5	5	5	4	6	8	7	7	6	6	6	3	6	5	4	4	5	4	3	4	1	
7	13	SAT COMEDY-STR-ABC	5				5	10	52	3	3		1	1	3	3	3	5	5	5	3			2	2	2	3	5	2	4	1	3	3	4	3			
4	6	WFXT MON COPS	2	5	4	4	4	6	63	3	3	5	4	5	4	4	3	2	2	2	3	6	6	4	4	3	3	1	3	3	5	4	4	3	3	1		
4	6	TUE COPS	3	5	4	4	4	6	63	2	2	1	1	1	2	2	2	3	3	3	2	1	1	2	2	2	2	2	3	3	1	2	2	2	3	3		
4	7	WED COPS	3	4	5	6	4	7	62	3	3	5	5	6	4	4	3	2	2	2	3	7	6	4	3	2	2	2	4	3	5	5	5	5	4	1		
4	6	THU COPS	3	4	5	3	4	5	67	2	2	1	1	1	2	2	3	3	3	3	2		2	2	2	2	3	3	3	2		2	2	2	3	1		
5	8	FRI COPS	4	4	5	5	5	8	59	3	3	2	5	5	5	5	5	2	3	1	4	3	6	5	5	5	5	1	5	3	4	4	4	5	4	2	1	1
4	*7*	*AV5 COPS*	*3*	*5*	*4*	*4*	*4*	*6*	*63*	*2*	*3*	*3*	*3*	*4*	*3*	*3*	*3*	*2*	*3*	*2*	*3*	*4*	*4*	*3*	*3*	*3*	*3*	*2*	*3*	*3*	*3*	*3*	*4*	*4*	*4*	*1*		
4	6	SAT TALES CRYPT 1	4	4	2	3	3	6	56	2	2	2	3	4	3	3	3	2	2	1	2	2	4	3	4	4	3		3	3	5	3	3	3	3	1	1	1
1	2	SUN LAZARUS MAN	1	2	1	2	2	3	59	1	1				1	1	1	1	1	1	1			1	1	1	1	1	1	1		1	1	1	1			
2	*3*	*NOR LAZARUS MAN*	*1*	*2*	*2*	*2*	*2*	*3*	*61*	*1*	*1*				*1*	*1*	*1*	*1*	*1*	*1*	*1*			*1*	*1*	*1*	*1*		*1*	*1*		*1*	*1*	*1*	*1*			
9	15	WHDH TUE DATELINE-TUE	10	8	8	9	9	15	61	5	6	1	3	3	5	5	5	7	7	8	7	2	5	6	6	7	7	9	6	4	2	3	4	4	4	1		
15	25	WED LAW&ORDER-NBC	11	13	15	17	14	23	59	8	10	6	7	8	9	9	9	11	11	13	11	6	9	10	10	10	11	13	10	10	8	8	9	8	8	1	1	1
31	46	THU E.R.-NBC	28	28	25	30	28	44	64	18	21	20	24	27	25	26	25	18	20	13	25	24	32	30	31	30	30	16	27	17	22	20	21	21	20	12	2	2
13	23	FRI HOMICIDE-NBC	9	9	11	12	10	18	58	6	8	5	5	6	7	7	7	8	8	8	8	4	5	8	8	8	8	9	7	7	7	7	6	6	6	2		
1	2		3	4	5	6	7	8	14	15	16	17	18	19	20	21	22	23	24	25	26	27	28	29	30	31	32	33	34	35	36	37	38	39	40	41	42	43

Nielsen has been advised that a station(s) conducted a special promotional activity.

See Program Index for complete details of program start time, duration and weeks of telecast.

MAY 1996

FIGURE 3–3A Examples of the program averages from Nielsen's NSI for Boston, May 1996.

NSI AVERAGE WEEK ESTIMATES   **BOSTON, MA (& MANCHESTER AREA)**

STATION TOTALS (000)

Right margin (vertical): PROGRAM AVERAGES

TIME STATION DAY	HH	2+	18+	12-24	12-34	21-49	35+	W18+	W12-24	W18-34	W18-49	W25-34	W25-49	W25-54	W25-64/50+	WKG	M18+	M18-34	M18-49	M21-49	M25-49	M25-54	M25-64	T12-17	GIRL	2-11	6-11
(col no.) 58	58	59	60	61	62	63	64	65	66	67	68	69	70	71	72	73	74	75	76	77	78	79	80	81	82	83	84
	23	50	40	38	43	43	32	27	29	31	29	25	24	24	21	22	29	36	32	30	26	26	26	30	26	38	33
	6	13	10	10	11	11	8	7	7	8	7	6	6	6	5	6	7	9	8	8	7	7	7	8	7	10	9
9:00PM																											
WSBK MON	59	78	72	8	25	51	48	31	2	9	23	21	23	25	7	15	41	14	32	27	27	29	34	1		5	4
TUE	42	62	52	14	19	38	41	31	1	4	27	26	27	30	4	17	21	6	11	11	7	8	11	9		2	2
TUE	18	15	15		9	10	6	6			1	1	6	6	5	6	9	9	9	9	9	9	9				
WED	72	106	106	6	30	49	75	49	6	15	23	17	26	29	26	18	57	15	26	26	26	33	45				
SAT	47	64	64		29	29	35	20		15	15	15	17	17	5		44	14	14	14	14	14	18				
SUN	53	64	62	1	16	48	47	31	1	11	25	25	27	30	6	24	31	4	23	23	23	24	28	1	1	1	1
9:30PM																											
WABU+FRI	44	59	59		6	13	53	16						9	16	4	43	6	13	13	13	13	23	1	1	3	3
SAT	7	5	1	1		1	1	1									1										
WBZ MON	319	464	438	41	128	265	329	277	30	59	164	149	174	207	113	132	161	49	109	107	102	113	127	19	14	7	6
WCVB TUE	303	502	451	47	166	353	300	295	26	86	220	198	215	241	75	133	156	66	133	133	123	134	137	15	4	37	28
TUE	247	359	312	70	160	261	198	188	27	65	155	143	157	175	33	92	124	48	106	106	94	101	113	46			
TUE	354	578	536	133	239	344	340	313	67	112	209	161	217	217	104	89	222	84	152	152	110	143	158	43			
WED	325	427	406	26	105	218	306	272	12	70	145	133	148	204	127	113	134	29	80	80	72	74	98	6		15	3
WED	177	247	238	15	75	150	171	150	6	44	104	97	107	113	46	80	88	23	47	47	47	51	73	9			
WED	234	320	317	54	151	216	169	173	24	75	132	111	120	133	41	101	144	73	101	101	70	94	94	3			
FRI	165	318	158	27	60	125	125	103		17	81	81	85	103	21	40	56	17	43	43	43	43	51	27		133	71
FRI	159	298	203	68	111	154	130	127	51	54	99	75	81	84	28	63	76	19	64	64	59	59	59	38	26	56	51
WFXT SUN	192	291	269	79	197	207	94	86	20	45	72	52	52	52	14	38	183	130	158	141	120	133	133	22			
SUN	155	299	240	110	176	181	123	72	39	34	58	43	43	54	14	15	167	83	160	123	123	131	131	59			
SUN	231	363	340	35	127	221	233	124	24	38	75	58	75	75	49	54	216	70	146	146	146	175	200	19		4	
WHDH TUE	274	388	373	43	107	203	280	212	22	41	118	106	125	156	94	94	161	52	100	90	83	97	117	14	9	1	1
THU	582	1012	911	165	448	717	516	512	91	214	410	350	373	408	102	261	399	182	336	318	283	298	323	53	32	48	39
WLVI WED	41	73	64	24	49	49	21	32	19	22	31	16	17	17	1	14	32	21	31	31	28	28	30	6	4	3	
WMUR TUE	46	82	66	22	29	55	49	44	13	15	41	32	32	32	3	19	22	1	14	14	14	18	21	13	4	4	4
TUE	10	20	20	9	10	19	10	10	3		5	10	7	7		7	10	6	10	10	4	4	4				
TUE	51	111	104	8	48	84	61	49		28	42	42	49	49	7	36	55	15	42	42	39	52	52	5		2	2
WED	43	68	68	19	27	49	41	29		8	29	29	29	29			39	19	39	20	20	20	20				
WED	24	17	17	1	2	2	14	15	1	1	1		14	14	14		1			6	6	6	6	9	4	5	5
WED	31	42	33	4	4	18	33	19	4		11	11	11	14	8	13	13			6	6	6	6	9	4	5	5
FRI	14	21	13	4	10	8	6	4	4	4	4	4	4	4	4	10	5	3	4	4	4	4	4	4		4	2
FRI	18	37	30	14	20	20	13	17	9	9	14	7	7	9	3	8	13	8	11	11	8	8	9	3	2	4	2
WSBK TUE	17	14	14		9	9	5	5							5		9	9	9	9	9	9	9				
9:45PM																											
WABU+FRI	101	158	149	28	38	49	119	49	9	9	19	9	9	26	31	25	99	20	38	30	28	34	51	9			
10:00PM																											
WABU+MON	18	24	24		2	7	22	15				4	4	4	6	11	9	2	3	3	3	3	5				
TUE	25	23	23		2	5	21	20			1	3	3	5	7	17	7	3	1	2	2	2	2			2	
WED	26	30	29	1	1		4	29	19	1		1	1	4	5	18	5	10		3	3	3	3	1		1	1
THU	33	44	43	1	3	11	41	26	1		4	4	8	11	22	7	5	16	1	7	7	7	7	10	1	1	
AV4	26	31	30	1	2		7	29	20	1		3	3	5	11	7	17	5	10	1	4	4	4	4	5	1	1
SAT	9	2	2				2	2																			
SUN	4																										
WBZ MON	296	416	402	46	121	247	293	261	32	67	162	140	164	195	99	115	141	42	92	88	82	90	112	13	10	1	1
THU	151	207	202	6	38	89	167	122	2	18	51	50	58	83	71	43	80	17	41	39	39	42	60	3	1	2	1
FRI	173	242	229	29	55	124	187	134	14	25	64	52	61	98	71	69	94	17	65	65	60	71	78	13	3		
SAT	250	357	346	17	46	134	306	200	15	27	78	67	88	118	122	79	146	13	56	56	56	71	104	6	3	5	2
WCVB TUE	397	644	621	102	214	409	427	326	45	90	216	175	210	244	110	142	295	104	209	200	166	188	221	19	5	3	2
WED	236	337	329	16	100	182	231	205	10	64	119	111	121	161	86	79	124	35	69	64	63	70	92	1	1	6	6
FRI	308	438	402	59	116	198	310	284	44	75	156	126	166	193	128	128	118	17	57	57	50	65	76	24		12	12
FRI	290	414	401	22	91	210	317	247	13	46	129	119	137	186	110	90	154	38	90	84	84	91	118	7	4	6	4
SAT	158	245	226	60	98	146	143	129	38	55	103	74	80	91	27	47	98	27	61	61	46	46	53	15		4	4
SAT	121	162	162		13	80	149	79			32	32	38	52	47	25	83	13	48	48	48	48	68				
WFXT MON	91	160	156	52	85	118	74	78	29	44	63	35	35	38	15	28	78	39	63	62	42	44	48	3	1	1	1
TUE	90	117	107	11	27	58	91	49	7	5	28	28	30	38	21	27	58	11	31	30	30	39	43	11	7		
WED	99	160	154	47	92	113	68	49	7	35	46	57	23	25	33	20	77	40	67	67	59	60	62	5	1		
THU	80	103	97	6	26	50	77	47	2	16	23	23	37	37	24	28	50	4	27	27	27	39	42	6	2		
FRI	104	169	157	24	88	130	76	82	14	48	73	61	63	65	10	48	74	33	65	61	59	60	64	7	2	5	5
AV5	93	142	134	28	64	94	77	51	8	28	49	34	38	42	18	36	68	26	51	49	44	49	52	6	3	1	1
SAT	74	125	114	23	68	92	49	51	8	28	49	43	45	45	3	30	63	37	50	43	35	41	47	3	3	9	3
SUN	36	40	39		6	27	33	22		4	15	15	17	20	7	7	18	3	12	12	12	12	17			9	1
NOR	39	44	42		8	31	35	21		4	16	16	19	19	4	8	22	3	15	15	15	15	20			1	
WHDH TUE	209	285	280	17	63	148	223	176	12	40	99	90	101	129	77	64	104	17	55	53	52	58	77	6	3		3
WED	320	488	475	56	138	267	343	264	29	72	153	129	153	183	111	113	210	60	126	121	100	115	151	5	4	7	3
THU	652	1077	1003	201	504	745	555	624	123	270	480	390	431	469	144	301	379	178	309	293	254	272	299	56	33	18	12
FRI	238	365	355	47	109	213	252	207	20	45	126	109	123	144	81	80	147	57	98	90	75	85	103	3		3	2
(col no.)	58	59	60	61	62	63	64	65	66	67	68	69	70	71	72	73	74	75	76	77	78	79	80	81	82	83	84

Nielsen has been advised that a station(s) conducted a special promotional activity.

MAY 1996

FIGURE 3-3B The program averages, continued. Courtesy Nielsen Media Research. Used with permission.

WK1 4/25-5/01 WK2 5/02-5/08 WK3 5/09-5/15 WK4 5/16-5/22

BOSTON, MA (& MANCHESTER AREA)

PROGRAM INDEX

PROGRAM NAME	STATION	DAY	WEEK	START TIME	SHR TREND ¤ CUR SHR	FEB '96	NOV '95	MAY '95	NO. QUARTER HOURS WK 1	WK 2	WK 3	WK 4
MONTEL WILLM R	WFXT	WED	1234	12:00M	9	6	7	4	4	4	4	4
		THU	1234	12:00M	9	5	9	5	4	4	4	4
		FRI	1234	12:00M	8	8	8	4	4	4	4	4
		AV5	1234	12:00M	8	7	9	4	20	20	20	20
MORE-X-FILES	WFXT	FRI	3	8:00P	13	11	10	10			4	
MOSAIC	WLVI	SAT	1234	6:00A		X			2	2	2	2
MOTORWEEK	WBZ	SUN	1234	6:00A	9	10X	8	9	2	2	2	2
MOVIE	WABU+	MON	1234	8:00P	1	1	1	1	8	8	8	8
		TUE	1 34	8:00P				1	8		8	8
		WED	1234	8:00P	3		1		8	8	8	8
		THU	1 34	8:00P	1		1		8		8	8
		AV4	1234	8:00P	1	1	1		32	16	32	32
MOVIE TRAILER	WSBK	SAT	1234	8:30A	4	6X	6	6	8	8	8	8
MOVIE WATCH	WNDS	SUN	1234	3:00P	2	2X		2	8	8	8	8
MOVIE WATCH	WNDS	MON	1234	8:00P	1				10	8	8	10
		NOR	1234	8:00P	1	1	1		8	8	8	8
		TUE	1234	8:00P	1				8	8	10	10
		NOR	1234	8:00P	1	1X	1	1	8	8	8	8
		WED	1234	8:00P	2	1X	2	1	8	8	8	8
		THU	1234	8:00P		1X	1		8	8	8	8
		AV4	1234	8:00P	1				34	32	34	36
		NOR	1234	8:00P	1	1	1	1	32	32	32	32
		SUN	1234	8:00P	1	1X	1	1	8	8	8	8
		AV5	1234	8:00P	1				42	40	42	44
		NOR	1234	8:00P	1	1	1	1	40	40	40	40
MRDR-WROTE-CBS	WBZ	SUN	1234	8:00P	23	18	16	24	4	4	4	4
MRRD W-CHLD SP	WFXT	SUN	4	9:30P	15	13	11	12				2
MRS AMER CELEB	WNDS	SUN	1	10:00P		1			4			
MURPHY BRN-CBS	WBZ	MON	1234	9:00P	21	20X	21	19	2	2	2	2
MURPHY BROWN	WSBK	M-F	1234	11:30A	4	6	5		10	10	10	10
MURPHY BROWN B	WSBK	M-F	1234	11:00A	4	5	5		10	10	10	10
MUSIC&SPKN WRD	WMUR	SUN	1234	8:30A					2	2	2	2
MUTANT LEAGUE	WLVI	M-F	1234	8:00A	2	3X	3	5	10	10	10	10
MYSTRY-MLLNIUM	WBZ	WED	1	8:00P	9	12	11	12	2			
N H AUTO SHOW	WNDS	SAT	1234	9:00A		X			2	2	2	2
N H BAPTIST	WNDS	SUN	1234	8:00A					4	4	4	4
NANCY DREW MYS	WFXT	SAT	1234	2:00P	4	11	6	5	2	2	2	2
NANNY-CBS	WBZ	MON	1234	8:00P	23	22X	17	18	2	2	2	2
NASH BRDGS-CBS	WBZ	FRI	4	8:00P	11	11	11	15				4
NASH BRDGS-CBS	WBZ	FRI	12	10:00P	13	10	10	16	4	4		
NBA INSD STUFF	WHDH	SAT	1234	12:00N	6	5	6	6	2	2	2	2
NBA PLAYFF-SA2	WHDH	SAT	2	3:30P	5	6	9	11		10		
NBA PLAYFF-SU1	WHDH	SUN	2	12:45P	5	8	50	14		11		
NBA PLAYFF-SU2	WHDH	SUN	2	3:30P	7	7	29	12		8		
NBA PLAYFF-SU3	WHDH	SUN	2	5:30P	9	10	16	16		4		
NBA PLAYFF-SU3	WHDH	SUN	2	6:45P	9	10	11	13		5		
NBA PLYF SAT 2	WHDH	SAT	4	3:30P	8	6	9	11				10
NBA PLYF SUN 2	WHDH	SUN	4	3:30P	18	8	26	13				10
NBA PLYFF-SAT1	WHDH	SAT	3	1:00P	13	4	9	8			13	
NBA PLYFF-SAT2	WHDH	SAT	3	4:15P	9	7	8	12			7	
NBA PLYFF-SUN1	WHDH	SUN	3	12:30P	8	7	47	14			10	
NBA PLYFF-SUN2	WHDH	SUN	3	3:00P	11	8	31	13			12	
NBA PLYFF-SUN3	WHDH	SUN	3	6:00P	12	11	17	16			2	
NBA PLYFF-SUN3	WHDH	SUN	3	6:45P	15	12	13	14			7	
NBA PLYOFF-SA1	WHDH	SAT	1	1:00P	5	4	8	8	10			
NBA PLYOFF-SA2	WHDH	SAT	1	3:30P	6	7	9	11	11			
NBA PLYOFF-SU1	WHDH	SUN	1	12:30P	5	7	47	14	10			
NBA PLYOFF-SU2	WHDH	SUN	1	3:00P	6	8	32	12	11			
NBA PLYOFF-SU3	WHDH	SUN	1	5:45P	7	11	14	15	10			
NBA SHOWTM SAT	WHDH	SAT	1 3	12:30P	4	4	4	7	2		2	
NBA SHOWTM SAT	WHDH	SAT	2 4	3:00P	5	5	10	8		2		2
NBA SHOWTM-SPC	WHDH	SUN	2	12:00N	3	3	7	6		2		
NBA SHOWTM-SUN	WHDH	SUN	123	→ 12:00N	5				2	↓ 1	2	
		SUN	1 3	12:00N					2		2	
		SUN	2	12:30P						↓ 1		
		NOR	1 3	12:00N	6	3	7	6	2		2	
NBA SHOWTM-SUN	WHDH	SUN	4	2:30P	8	9	53	15				4
NBC MON-MOV	WHDH	MON	1234	9:00P	21	21X	20	19	8	8	8	8
NBC MOVIE-SAT	WHDH	SAT	1	8:00P	12	13	15	14	8			
NBC NITELY NWS	WHDH	MON	1234	6:30P	18	16X	18	16	2	2	2	2
		TUE	1234	6:30P	17	15X	16	16	2	2	2	2
		WED	1234	6:30P	17	15X	19	15	2	2	2	2
		THU	1234	6:30P	17	16X	21	18	2	2	2	2
		FRI	1234	6:30P	19	17X	19	18	2	2	2	2
		AV5	1234	6:30P	18	16X	18	16	10	10	10	10
NBC SAT-MOVIE	WHDH	SAT	3	8:30P	23	14	16	16			10	
NBC SAT-MOVIES	WHDH	SAT	4	9:00P	9	14	16	16				8
NBC SUN-MOV	WHDH	SUN	1234	→ 8:30P	26				↓ 8	10	12	↓ 8
		SUN	1	9:15P					↓ 8			
		SUN	23	8:30P						10	12	
		SUN	4	9:00P								↓ 8
		NOR	1234	8:30P	25	19	20	26	↓ 7	10	10	↓ 8
NBC-NWS SAT	WHDH	SAT	1234	6:30P	13	12X	14	12	2	2	2	2
NBC-NWS SUN	WHDH	SUN	4	6:30P	11	13	16	16				2
NCAA WM GYM CH	WBZ	SAT	2	3:00P	6	6	6	4		4		
NE AUTO CLSSFD	WNDS	SAT	1234	10:30A		X			2	2	2	2
		SUN	1234	10:30A		X			2	2	2	2
NEW HAMP BSNSS	WMUR	SUN	1234	12:30P		X			2	2	2	2
NEWHART	WABU+	SUN	4	1:30P	4		3	3				2
NEWHART	WABU+	SAT	23	9:30P		2		2		2	2	
NEWHART	WABU+	FRI	1	10:15P			2	2	1			
NEWS FOR KIDS	WHDH	SAT	1234	6:00A		6X	9	9	2	2	2	2
NEWS 4-LATE	WBZ	MON	1234	11:00P	18	18X	28	20	2	2	2	2
		TUE	1234	11:00P	13	14X	16	17	2	2	2	2
		WED	1234	11:00P	14	15X	13	17	2	2	2	2
		THU	1234	11:00P	14	15X	16	17	2	2	2	2
		FRI	1234	11:00P	12	11X	11	16	2	2	2	2
		AV5	1234	11:00P	14	15X	17	17	10	10	10	10
		SAT	1234	11:00P	17	15X	17	17	2	2	2	2
		SUN	1234	11:00P	19				2	2	3	2
		NOR	1234	11:00P	20	17X	19	19	2	2	2	2
		AV7	1234	11:00P	15				14	14	15	14
		NOR	1234	11:00P	15	15X	17	17	14	14	14	14
NEWS 4-NOON	WBZ	M-F	1234	12:00N	16	17X	16	16	10	10	10	10
NEWS 4-SAT	WBZ	SAT	1234	7:00A	13	16X	13	10	8	8	8	8
NEWS 4-SUN	WBZ	SUN	1234	8:00A	11	11X	10	10	4	4	4	4
NEWS 4-SUN	WBZ	SUN	1234	10:30A	9	10X	8	9	2	2	2	2
NEWS 4-5P	WBZ	MON	1234	5:00P	8	9X	9	13	4	4	4	4
		TUE	1234	5:00P	8	8X	8	14	4	4	4	4
		WED	1234	5:00P	8	8X	8	14	4	4	4	4
		THU	1234	5:00P	7	10X	6	13	4	4	4	4
		FRI	1234	5:00P	8	8X	8	14	4	4	4	4
		AV5	1234	5:00P	8	8X	8	13	20	20	20	20
NEWS 4-6AM	WBZ	M-F	1234	6:00A	17	14X	20	22	20	20	20	20
NEWS 4-6P	WBZ	MON	1234	6:00P	11	12X	14	13	4	4	4	4
		TUE	1234	6:00P	10	13	13	13	4	4	4	4
		WED	1234	6:00P	12	11X	13	13	4	4	4	4
		THU	1234	6:00P	11	13X	10	13	4	4	4	4
		FRI	1234	6:00P	9	12X	12	13	4	4	4	4
		AV5	1234	6:00P	11	12	12	13	20	20	20	20
		SAT	1234	6:00P	13	9	17	13	2	2	2	2
		AV6	1234	6:00P	11	12	13	13	22	22	22	22
NEWS 4-630PM	WBZ	SUN	1234	6:30P	16	16X	14	16	2	2	2	2
NEWSRADIO-SUN	WHDH	SUN	1	8:45P	19	18	18	21	2			
NEWS9 AT NOON	WMUR	M-F	1234	12:00N	5	4	5	3	10	10	10	10
NEWS9 AT 6	WMUR	MON	1234	6:00P	6	6	6	5	2	2	2	2
		TUE	1234	6:00P	7	6	6	3	2	2	2	2
		WED	1234	6:00P	6	7	6	4	2	2	2	2
		THU	1234	6:00P	6	7	5	4	2	2	2	2
		FRI	1234	6:00P	5	6	6	6	2	2	2	2
		AV5	1234	6:00P	6	6	6	4	10	10	10	10
		SAT	1234	6:00P	4	4	2	2	2	2	2	2
		SUN	1234	6:00P	3	3	3	2	2	2	2	2
		AV7	1234	6:00P	5	6	5	4	14	14	14	14
NEWS9 DBK 6	WMUR	M-F	1234	6:00A	7	9	4	7	10	10	10	10
NEWS9 DBK 630	WMUR	M-F	1234	6:30A	6	8	6	7	10	10	10	10
NEWS9 NT RPT	WMUR	MON	1234	11:00P	2	2	2	5	2	2	2	2
		TUE	1234	11:00P	3	3	3	3	2	2	2	2
		WED	1234	11:00P	2	4	4	5	2	2	2	2
		THU	1234	11:00P	2	2	2	3	2	2	2	2
		FRI	1234	11:00P	4	4	3	4	2	2	2	2
		AV5	1234	11:00P	3	3	3	4	10	10	10	10
		SAT	1234	11:00P	3	3	3	4	2	2	2	2
		SUN	1234	11:00P	2	2	3	4	2	2	2	2
		AV7	1234	11:00P	3	3	3	4	14	14	14	14
NEWS9 SUN	WMUR	SUN	1234	10:00A					2	2	2	2
NEWS9 5-A	WMUR	MON	1234	5:00P	4	3	3	2	2	2	2	2
		TUE	1234	5:00P	4	3	4	2	2	2	2	2
		WED	1234	5:00P	4	2	4	2	2	2	2	2
		THU	1234	5:00P	4	3	2	1	2	2	2	2
		FRI	1234	5:00P	3	4	2	3	2	2	2	2
		AV5	1234	5:00P	4	3	3	2	10	10	10	10
NEWS9 5-B	WMUR	MON	1234	5:30P	5	4	4	3	2	2	2	2
		TUE	1234	5:30P	4	4	4	2	2	2	2	2
		WED	1234	5:30P	5	4	5	2	2	2	2	2
		THU	1234	5:30P	5	4	3	2	2	2	2	2
		FRI	1234	5:30P	4	4	3	3	2	2	2	2
		AV5	1234	5:30P	5	4	4	2	10	10	10	10
NEWS9NT RPT RP	WMUR	SUN	1234	6:00A					2	2	2	2
NHRA PNZL NTLS	WMUR	SUN	3	2:00P							4	
NICK NEWS	WFXT	SUN	1234	7:00A		4X	5		2	2	2	2
NIGHT COURT	WLVI	MON	1234	12:30A	5	4X	4		2	2	2	2
		TUE	1234	12:30A	6	6X	5	3	2	2	2	2
		WED	1234	12:30A	5	5X	6	3	2	2	2	2
		THU	1234	12:30A	5	5X	6		2	2	2	2
		AV4	1234	12:30A	5	5X	5		8	8	8	8
NIGHT COURT	WMUR	SUN	3	1:30P							2	
NIGHT STAND	WCVB	SAT	1234	11:30P	8	8X	7	11	4	4	4	4
NIGHT STAND	WNDS	SAT	1234	9:00P				1	4	4	4	4
NINJA TRTL1 SA	WBZ	SAT	1234	9:30A	4	7	6	6	2	2	2	2
NINJA TTL CLSC	WBZ	SUN	12	7:00A	4	10	9	6	2	2		
NITELINE-MON	WCVB	MON	4	12:00M	13	11	20	9				2
NITELINE-MON	WMUR	MON	4	12:00M		3		4				2
NORTHRN EXPSRE	WABU+	M-F	1234	3:00P	3	3X	3	2	20	20	20	20
NORTHRN EXPSRE	WNDS	M-F	1234	11:00A		X			20	20	20	20
NOT JUST NEWS	WFXT	SAT	1234	6:00A	6	10X	8		2	2	2	2
NOTHNG BUT NET	WBZ	SAT	2	2:00P	3	4	4	3		4		
NOWHERE MN-UPN	WSBK	MON	1234	9:00P	2	5X	5	5	4	4	4	4
NTL GEO SP-NBC	WHDH	WED	3	8:00P	16	15	16	12			4	
NTL GEO-ASGNMT	WABU+	SAT	2	12:00N	4	2	2	3		4		

¤ 4-Week Time Period Averages

Nielsen has been advised that a station(s) conducted a special promotional activity.

MAY 1996

FIGURE 3–4 A page from the program index in Nielsen's NSI for Boston, May 1996. Each program has an alphabetical listing with shares and trends. Courtesy Nielsen Media Research. Used with permission.

message would be wasted on the larger audience. As I've said before, this thinking is new to TV, but you can tell by looking at the way the audience is sliced and diced in the Boston numbers that targeting is the only effective way to approach today's fragmented audiences.

Another cost comparison is cost per point (CPP) (and sometimes referred to as cost per rating point). The CPP formula is

$$CPP = \frac{\text{Cost of schedule}}{\text{GRP}}$$

Back to Figure 3–2A: If the schedule costs $5,000, and we're buying ten spots to reach Women 18+, Monday through Friday, 10 p.m.–11 p.m. on WBZ, we divide $5,000 by 70 for a CPP of $71.42. An advertiser may recoil at that figure, but the math works. Some-

times, the math is all an advertiser cares about.

Advertisers, primarily ad agencies, use CPP calculations for planning purposes. They compare costs among markets and plan how much to spend to reach the people they want in a specific market. Since CPPs are based on rating points (metro persons ratings in radio, DMA household ratings in television), the numbers increase with the size of the market. A "1" rating in New York City represents approximately 141,000 people. In Savannah, Georgia, the same "1" rating is only 2,300 people.

As a seller, you use CPM and CPP information to persuade agencies that they can meet their objectives effectively and efficiently by using your station in their advertising mix.

SPOTS AND DOTS

When you compare the cost of your shows to the agency's CPM or CPP target, you'll hear the phrase "spots and dots."

The program you're selling (or the time period) may have a 3 rating, but it's actually taken to tenths of a rating point in the tape (or detailed Nielsen information available on computer, not in the book). That means you might have a 3.1 or a 3.7 to present to the buyer, not just a 3.

You're selling *spots*. The buyer's looking at *dots*, or decimals.[13]

Radio Ratings

Four times a year in the larger markets, radio gets its report card: the Arbitron "book." The quarterly ratings report is printed in book format, thus the name. A large number of radio station users prefer to use Arbitron's Maximi$er data disk, which has far more data than the printed book contains. Maximi$er helps Arbitron users slice and dice their numbers to greater advantage.

Every Arbitron market is surveyed at least once a year in the spring, generally in April, May, and June (although start dates sometimes include the last few days of March). Some markets get two surveys per year, the spring book and the fall book, from mid-October to mid-December. The markets with four ratings periods per year are known as continuous measurement

markets, even though several weeks of the year—Christmas holidays, for example—are not actually surveyed.

Since radio is typically sold as a *local* medium, the Arbitron survey area definitions are specifically local. The Metro Survey Area (Metro) contains the primary geographic data used by Arbitron subscribers. Arbitron's "Metro" is an area defined by subscribers and often varies from the Metropolitan Statistical Area as defined by the U.S. Office of Management and Budget (OMB). Nielsen's view of "Metro," on the other hand, is the OMB definition.

Arbitron reports also include the Total Survey Area (TSA) and the Designated Market Area (DMA) used for television. Often the DMA covers such a large geographic area that it's impractical for radio use. The Los Angeles DMA, for instance, includes the Metro Survey areas of Los Angeles, Orange County, Riverside–San Bernardino, Ventura–Oxnard, and Santa Barbara. Similarly, Denver's DMA stretches to counties in Wyoming and Nebraska because they receive Denver television signals through mountain passes.

Arbitron uses the diary method to collect radio listening information. They send one diary for each member of selected households who are 12 years of age or older. In their diaries, respondents record the time they begin listening; the station call letters, station name, program name, or dial position; whether the station is AM or FM; and whether they listened at home, in the car, at work, or elsewhere. If there was no listening on a particular day, the diary-keeper is asked to check a box to indicate that information. (See Figure 3–5.)

When Arbitron decided to abandon its television ratings business at the end of 1993, radio benefited immediately. Arbitron added qualitative questions to the radio diary.

"The concept is to link ratings with buying and shopping behavior," said Arbitron president Steve Morris when the announcement was made about exiting television. "Our radio customers have been saying that, in order to develop a targeted capability of selling our product, they need to isolate not just the numbers and demographics but to provide a more precise audience profile that they can use as a real sales tool."

In 132 markets that are smaller in rank than number 100, Arbitron includes 25 qualitative questions at the back of the radio diary: employment status, newspaper readership, use of major cable TV networks, retail purchases and intentions, banking services used, fast food consumed, and others.

From Figures 3–6 and 3–7, you can tell that the layout of the Arbitron Radio Market Report is completely different from Nielsen's NSI. First, every section of the Arbitron book is organized by some demographic group: Persons 12+, 18–34, 18–49, 25–49, 25–54, and 35–64. The Persons trends are followed by Men and Women

sections, each of which has the same age classifications and an additional 12–24 demographic break. There's also a Teens 12–24 section. The demographic base of Arbitron's layout says that radio is a targeted medium.

The examples in Figures 3–6 and 3–7 are from two markets that are very different: Tampa–St. Petersburg–Clearwater, FL, and Utica–Rome, New York. The Tampa book, Figure 3–6, requires four pages to cover all the stations that received sufficient mention to be listed in the survey. The total length of the report is 215 pages.

Across the top of the page are columns for the full week's listening—"Monday–Sunday 6 a.m.–MID"—and a column each for the major radio dayparts. Each station has six entries, the most recent survey period first, which in this case is fall 1997. After that are the previous three survey periods, an average of a year's surveys (labeled "4 book" in Tampa, "2 book" in Utica), and the survey period from a year ago.

You can see that the largest cume and share on the sample page went to WFLZ-FM. (As a matter of fact, they led the market overall in that survey.) Closest on this page would be a tie between WAKS-FM and WCOF-FM. No other station in the market approaches the double-digit shares of WFLZ-FM in the other pages of the report for this age group.

The Utica–Rome report in Figure 3–7 takes only two pages to list all the stations because of the smaller size of the market. Even so, the data tables in the Utica Arbitron stretch to 197 pages. Right away you can see that two of the stations on the first page have double digits: WLZW and WFRG. That's often the case in smaller towns where listening is more concentrated among fewer stations.

Because there are so many radio stations and because most stations are targeted to a demographic group through the use of a specific music format, ratings are often small. In the Tampa book, you see that WFLZ-FM has an average 2.2 rating over the full week based on a four-book average. That's a much lower number than you saw with the leading television stations in the Nielsen NSI example.

THURSDAY

	Time		Station			Place			
			Call letters or station name _Don't know? Use program name or dial setting._	Check (✓) one		Check (✓) one			
	Start	Stop		AM	FM	At Home	In a Car	At Work	Other Place
Early Morning (from 5 AM) →									
Midday →									
Late Afternoon →									
Night (to 5 AM Friday) →									

SAMPLE

If you didn't hear a radio today, please check here. ☐

FIGURE 3–5 The Arbitron diary-keeper starts here. Thursday is the first day of the Arbitron week. Courtesy the Arbitron Company. Used with permission.

Listener Estimates/Metro

Target Listener Trends

Persons 18-49

	Monday-Sunday 6AM-MID				Monday-Friday 6AM-10AM				Monday-Friday 10AM-3PM				Monday-Friday 3PM-7PM				Monday-Friday 7PM-MID			
	AQH (00)	Cume (00)	AQH Rtg	AQH Shr	AQH (00)	Cume (00)	AQH Rtg	AQH Shr	AQH (00)	Cume (00)	AQH Rtg	AQH Shr	AQH (00)	Cume (00)	AQH Rtg	AQH Shr	AQH (00)	Cume (00)	AQH Rtg	AQH Shr
+WAKS–FM																				
FA '97	88	1460	.9	5.0	120	790	1.3	4.7	140	717	1.5	5.2	120	879	1.3	5.4	36	526	.4	4.9
SU '97	92	1370	1.0	5.4	136	762	1.4	5.6	134	692	1.4	5.2	113	782	1.2	5.3	47	449	.5	6.2
SP '97	104	1464	1.1	5.7	147	721	1.6	5.8	154	801	1.6	5.6	133	884	1.4	5.8	45	549	.5	5.8
WI '97	101	1597	1.1	6.0	156	906	1.7	6.5	146	831	1.5	5.7	132	952	1.4	6.1	43	492	.5	5.9
4-Book	*96*	*1473*	*1.0*	*5.5*	*140*	*795*	*1.5*	*5.7*	*144*	*760*	*1.5*	*5.4*	*125*	*874*	*1.3*	*5.7*	*43*	*504*	*.5*	*5.7*
FA '96	114	1589	1.2	6.7	169	1003	1.8	7.0	192	849	2.0	7.2	168	1029	1.8	7.7	35	424	.4	5.4
VBDN–AM																				
FA '97	8	111	.1	.5	2	32		.1	12	60	.1	.4	8	73	.1	.4	10	36	.1	1.4
SU '97	14	152	.1	.8	12	66	.1	.5	19	107	.2	.7	23	118	.2	1.1	5	56	.1	.7
SP '97	9	71	.1	.5	8	48	.1	.3	9	50	.1	.3	7	32	.1	.3	12	48	.1	1.6
WI '97	**	**	**	**	**	**	**	**	**	**	**	**	**	**	**	**	**	**	**	**
4-Book	***	***	***	***	***	***	***	***	***	***	***	***	***	***	***	***	***	***	***	***
FA '96	5	109	.1	.3		6			25	102	.3	.9								
VCOF–FM																				
FA '97	89	1474	.9	5.0	118	840	1.2	4.7	136	670	1.4	5.1	117	864	1.2	5.3	37	493	.4	5.1
SU '97	106	1572	1.1	6.2	134	803	1.4	5.6	188	827	2.0	7.2	145	992	1.5	6.8	33	439	.4	4.4
SP '97	123	1711	1.3	6.8	162	930	1.7	6.4	211	908	2.2	7.7	151	994	1.6	6.6	43	509	.5	5.6
WI '97	103	1622	1.1	6.1	127	896	1.3	5.3	169	808	1.8	6.6	152	1094	1.6	7.0	38	504	.4	5.2
4-Book	*105*	*1595*	*1.1*	*6.0*	*135*	*867*	*1.4*	*5.5*	*176*	*803*	*1.9*	*6.7*	*141*	*986*	*1.5*	*6.4*	*38*	*486*	*.4*	*5.1*
FA '96	121	1707	1.3	7.1	152	1000	1.6	6.3	231	908	2.5	8.7	163	1089	1.7	7.5	39	457	.4	6.1
VDAE–AM																				
FA '97	17	319	.2	1.0	15	120	.2	.6	47	153	.5	1.8	18	145	.2	.8	4	72		.5
SU '97	7	166	.1	.4	7	49	.1	.3	8	84	.1	.3	20	126	.2	.9	3	35		.4
SP '97	9	167	.1	.5	8	75	.1	.3	15	101	.2	.5	13	83	.1	.6	8	57	.1	1.0
WI '97	**	**	**	**	**	**	**	**	**	**	**	**	**	**	**	**	**	**	**	**
4-Book	***	***	***	***	***	***	***	***	***	***	***	***	***	***	***	***	***	***	***	***
FA '96	3	12		.2	5	12	.1	.2	6	12	.1	.2	6	12	.1	.3				
VDUV–FM																				
FA '97	23	284	.2	1.3	32	168	.3	1.3	44	190	.5	1.6	24	118	.3	1.1	5	53	.1	.7
SU '97	22	336	.2	1.3	32	164	.3	1.3	38	170	.4	1.5	26	161	.3	1.2	8	91	.1	1.1
SP '97	22	288	.2	1.2	29	154	.3	1.1	41	143	.4	1.5	26	162	.3	1.1	7	67	.1	.9
WI '97	25	351	.3	1.5	22	133	.2	.9	32	168	.3	1.2	42	212	.4	1.9	17	112	.2	2.3
4-Book	*23*	*315*	*.2*	*1.3*	*29*	*155*	*.3*	*1.2*	*39*	*168*	*.4*	*1.5*	*30*	*163*	*.3*	*1.3*	*9*	*81*	*.1*	*1.3*
FA '96	20	302	.2	1.2	23	148	.2	1.0	39	149	.4	1.5	24	141	.3	1.1	6	87	.1	.9
VFLA–AM																				
FA '97	59	822	.6	3.3	107	453	1.1	4.2	89	441	.9	3.3	76	506	.8	3.4	27	223	.3	3.7
SU '97	63	887	.7	3.7	84	443	.9	3.5	120	432	1.3	4.6	86	501	.9	4.0	34	219	.4	4.5
SP '97	61	859	.6	3.4	93	494	1.0	3.7	114	505	1.2	4.2	85	472	.9	3.7	24	231	.3	3.1
WI '97	59	834	.6	3.5	94	451	1.0	3.9	106	506	1.1	4.1	89	497	.9	4.1	19	161	.2	2.6
4-Book	*61*	*851*	*.6*	*3.5*	*95*	*460*	*1.0*	*3.8*	*107*	*471*	*1.1*	*4.1*	*84*	*494*	*.9*	*3.8*	*26*	*209*	*.3*	*3.5*
FA '96	63	769	.7	3.7	84	381	.9	3.5	122	486	1.3	4.6	78	425	.8	3.6	38	233	.4	5.9
VFLZ–FM																				
FA '97	206	3164	2.2	11.7	403	2069	4.2	15.9	258	1493	2.7	9.6	216	1786	2.3	9.7	93	947	1.0	12.7
SU '97	213	3161	2.3	12.4	397	1965	4.2	16.5	268	1597	2.8	10.3	229	1821	2.4	10.7	94	1085	1.0	12.4
SP '97	223	3164	2.4	12.3	403	2137	4.3	15.9	244	1588	2.6	8.9	247	1780	2.6	10.8	112	1081	1.2	14.5
WI '97	204	3128	2.2	12.0	360	1932	3.8	14.9	235	1707	2.5	9.2	232	1838	2.5	10.7	109	1108	1.2	15.0
4-Book	*212*	*3154*	*2.3*	*12.1*	*391*	*2026*	*4.1*	*15.8*	*251*	*1596*	*2.7*	*9.5*	*231*	*1806*	*2.5*	*10.5*	*102*	*1055*	*1.1*	*13.7*
FA '96	178	2925	1.9	10.5	301	1870	3.2	12.5	235	1493	2.5	8.8	202	1720	2.1	9.2	80	1028	.8	12.4
VFNS–AM																				
FA '97	7	111	.1	.4	12	82	.1	.5	4	54		.1	5	36	.1	.2	3	29		.4
SU '97	**	**	**	**	**	**	**	**	**	**	**	**	**	**	**	**	**	**	**	**
SP '97	**	**	**	**	**	**	**	**	**	**	**	**	**	**	**	**	**	**	**	**
WI '97	7	127	.1	.4	11	81	.1	.5	12	62	.1	.5	9	60	.1	.4	5	61	.1	.7
4-Book	***	***	***	***	***	***	***	***	***	***	***	***	***	***	***	***	***	***	***	***
FA '96	6	81	.1	.4	3	20		.1	4	29		.2	10	45	.1	.5	4	34		.6

* Station(s) not reported this survey.
* Listener estimates adjusted for reported broadcast schedule.
+ Station(s) changed call letters – see Page 13.
4-Book: Avg. of current and previous 3 surveys.
2-Book: Avg. of most recent 2 surveys.

FIGURE 3–6 Target Listener Trends for Persons 18–49 from the Tampa–St. Petersburg–Clearwater Arbitron. Comparing a Radio Market Report to Nielsen's NSI, it's apparent that radio thinks in demographics and targeting, not in programs. Courtesy the Arbitron Company. Used with permission.

Listener Estimates/Metro

Target Listener Trends

Persons 18-49

	Monday-Sunday 6AM-MID				Monday-Friday 6AM-10AM				Monday-Friday 10AM-3PM				Monday-Friday 3PM-7PM				Monday-Friday 7PM-MID			
	AQH (00)	Cume (00)	AQH Rtg	AQH Shr	AQH (00)	Cume (00)	AQH Rtg	AQH Shr	AQH (00)	Cume (00)	AQH Rtg	AQH Shr	AQH (00)	Cume (00)	AQH Rtg	AQH Shr	AQH (00)	Cume (00)	AQH Rtg	AQH Shr
WFRG-FM																				
FA '97	34	342	2.6	14.4	53	233	4.0	15.3	55	224	4.1	15.1	34	244	2.6	12.1	8	92	.6	7.7
SP '97	47	445	3.3	19.0	66	290	4.7	18.0	56	280	4.0	16.8	62	314	4.4	19.9	27	178	1.9	21.8
2-Book	*41*	*394*	*3.0*	*16.7*	*60*	*262*	*4.4*	*16.7*	*56*	*252*	*4.1*	*16.0*	*48*	*279*	*3.5*	*16.0*	*18*	*135*	*1.3*	*14.8*
FA '96	28	345	2.0	11.7	49	239	3.5	14.0	38	185	2.7	10.5	40	236	2.8	14.0	9	113	.6	8.3
SP '96	39	367	2.7	14.1	66	263	4.6	16.5	47	220	3.3	11.8	38	218	2.6	11.8	16	149	1.1	12.3
FA '95	49	403	3.4	19.1	74	297	5.1	19.4	67	262	4.7	18.2	60	286	4.2	19.7	17	149	1.2	13.3
WIBX-AM																				
FA '97	6	137	.5	2.5	12	87	.9	3.5	8	55	.6	2.2	3	49	.2	1.1	5	38	.4	4.8
SP '97	9	146	.6	3.6	15	100	1.1	4.1	13	82	.9	3.9	13	80	.9	4.2	4	44	.3	3.2
2-Book	*8*	*142*	*.6*	*3.1*	*14*	*94*	*1.0*	*3.8*	*11*	*69*	*.8*	*3.1*	*8*	*65*	*.6*	*2.7*	*5*	*41*	*.4*	*4.0*
FA '96	7	109	.5	2.9	8	64	.6	2.3	17	73	1.2	4.7	10	60	.7	3.5	1	17	.1	.9
SP '96	8	151	.6	2.9	17	98	1.2	4.2	15	79	1.0	3.8	9	64	.6	2.8		8		
FA '95	8	168	.6	3.1	19	108	1.3	5.0	9	51	.6	2.4	10	65	.7	3.3	3	38	.2	2.3
WKLL-FM																				
FA '97	19	266	1.4	8.1	22	144	1.7	6.4	26	153	2.0	7.1	23	175	1.7	8.2	14	127	1.1	13.5
SP '97	19	294	1.3	7.7	24	165	1.7	6.6	27	141	1.9	8.1	27	186	1.9	8.7	13	110	.9	10.5
2-Book	*19*	*280*	*1.4*	*7.9*	*23*	*155*	*1.7*	*6.5*	*27*	*147*	*2.0*	*7.6*	*25*	*181*	*1.8*	*8.5*	*14*	*119*	*1.0*	*12.0*
FA '96	19	291	1.3	7.9	27	137	1.9	7.7	25	179	1.8	6.9	19	172	1.3	6.6	12	134	.8	11.1
SP '96	20	290	1.4	7.2	24	150	1.7	6.0	26	178	1.8	6.5	25	180	1.7	7.8	15	127	1.0	11.5
FA '95	12	222	.8	4.7	17	119	1.2	4.5	12	124	.8	3.3	13	142	.9	4.3	11	108	.8	8.6
WLFH-AM																				
FA '97	1	20	.1	.4	2	16	.2	.6		6				6			1	3	.1	1.0
SP '97		16			1	9	.1	.3	1	13	.1	.3		3			1	2	.1	.5
2-Book	*1*	*18*	*.1*	*.2*	*2*	*13*	*.2*	*.5*	*1*	*10*	*.1*	*.2*		*3*			*1*	*2*	*.1*	*.5*
FA '96	2	22	.1	.8	3	16	.2	.9	5	19	.4	1.4	2	16	.1	.7		6		
SP '96	1	21	.1	.4	2	15	.1	.5	1	8	.1	.3	2	15	.1	.6		3		
FA '95		18			1	7	.1	.3		14			1	7	.1	.3				
WBUG-FM																				
FA '97	1	38	.1	.4	1	13	.1	.3	3	24	.2	.8	2	24	.2	.7		5		
SP '97	2	44	.1	.8	3	28	.2	.8	1	18	.1	.3	2	19	.1	.6	1	12	.1	.8
2-Book	*2*	*41*	*.1*	*.6*	*2*	*21*	*.2*	*.6*	*2*	*21*	*.2*	*.6*	*2*	*22*	*.2*	*.7*	*1*	*9*	*.1*	*.4*
FA '96	1	22	.1	.4	2	12	.1	.6	2	16	.1	.6	2	19	.1	.7	1	9	.1	.9
SP '96	1	26	.1	.4	1	10	.1	.2	1	16	.1	.3	1	19	.1	.3	1	6	.1	.8
FA '95		22				3				6				13			2	3	.1	1.0
WLZW-FM																				
FA '97	38	422	2.9	16.1	60	284	4.5	17.3	62	240	4.7	17.0	41	257	3.1	14.6	17	154	1.3	16.3
SP '97	40	449	2.8	16.2	57	236	4.0	15.6	66	240	4.7	19.8	47	243	3.3	15.1	17	131	1.2	13.7
2-Book	*39*	*436*	*2.9*	*16.2*	*59*	*260*	*4.3*	*16.5*	*64*	*240*	*4.7*	*18.4*	*44*	*250*	*3.2*	*14.9*	*17*	*143*	*1.3*	*15.0*
FA '96	43	458	3.0	18.0	59	261	4.2	16.8	72	268	5.1	19.9	49	267	3.5	17.1	20	176	2.0	26.9
SP '96	52	467	3.6	18.8	73	294	5.1	18.2	88	311	6.1	22.1	56	330	3.9	17.4	25	210	1.7	19.2
FA '95	40	450	2.8	15.6	63	305	4.4	16.5	70	262	4.9	19.0	45	273	3.1	14.8	14	148	1.0	10.9
+WODZ-AM																				
FA '97		7			2	5	.2	.6		2				3				3		
SP '97		3								3				2				2		
2-Book		*5*			*1*	*3*	*.1*	*.3*		*3*				*2*				*2*		
FA '96		20				4				4				4				4		
SP '96	1	22	.1	.4	1	7	.1	.2	1	15	.1	.3		6				3		
FA '95		13				10				10										
WODZ-FM																				
FA '97	9	189	.7	3.8	10	98	.8	2.9	11	70	.8	3.0	11	126	.8	3.9	4	76	.3	3.8
SP '97	12	227	.8	4.9	16	136	1.1	4.4	13	108	.9	3.9	17	148	1.2	5.4	8	82	.6	6.5
2-Book	*11*	*208*	*.8*	*4.4*	*13*	*117*	*1.0*	*3.7*	*12*	*89*	*.9*	*3.5*	*14*	*137*	*1.0*	*4.7*	*6*	*79*	*.5*	*5.2*
FA '96	8	177	.6	3.3	14	102	1.0	4.0	10	99	.7	2.8	9	103	.6	3.1	3	35	.2	2.8
SP '96	16	226	1.1	5.8	24	135	1.7	6.0	22	114	1.5	5.5	21	130	1.5	6.5	8	90	.6	6.2
FA '95	15	238	1.0	5.9	17	97	1.2	4.5	24	93	1.7	6.5	18	149	1.3	5.9	6	65	.4	4.7

** Station(s) not reported this survey.
* Listener estimates adjusted for reported broadcast schedule.
+ Station(s) changed call letters – see Page 13.
4-Book: Avg. of current and previous 3 surveys.
2-Book: Avg. of most recent 2 surveys.

UTICA-ROME   **ARBITRON** 38   FALL 1997

FIGURE 3–7 Target Listener Trends for Persons 18–49 from the Utica–Rome, New York, Radio Market Report. Courtesy the Arbitron Company. Used with permission.

Ratings, especially GRPs, are useful in mass-market television, but are difficult to use in radio because of the small size of the numbers. Agencies often compare radio to TV, which is unfair to radio. In radio terms, GRPs are determined by Average Quarter Hour persons multiplied by the number of spots. Because listeners use more than one station, GRPs may actually add up to more than 100% of the market.

Television sells households more often than not, and has only recently begun to target and sell specific demos. In contrast, radio has been a demo-targeted medium for several decades and gives the advertiser the opportunity to hone a specific message to a specific group. Radio sellers are much more likely to take qualitative information to a buyer in order to demonstrate how even a small audience matches the needs of an advertiser.

Let's use grocery shopping as an example and compare the Tampa–St. Petersburg and Utica–Rome markets again. In Figure 3–8, you see the profile of people in the Tampa market who have spent $100 or more on groceries, based on Scarborough information available for the market. If your station targets persons aged 35–44, there's a compelling story for a grocery chain. A station that targets the 25–34 age group could also attract a grocery buy.

In Utica–Rome, as seen in Figure 3–9, the profile itself looks a bit different because information was collected in the Arbitron "Qualitative Diary," not in the Scarborough questionnaire. The first useful difference is that grocery shoppers in Utica–Rome are older than in Tampa Bay. (You'll also notice the Utica report is on $125 spent on groceries, an indication of the difference in prices in the market.)

Arbitron provides other analyses in the printed report: Time Spent Listening; Listening Locations (work, car, home).

Online Ratings

When it comes to measuring Internet usage, there are more questions than answers. Advertisers ask the potential reach of Web advertising. They want to know how effective banners, sponsorships, and interstitials are. Does a certain copy approach work better than another? How many surfers are out there?

That last question is the most important of all. The answer, of course, is "a lot." An answer that imprecise is like looking at your speedometer and having it register "pretty fast" instead of "90 miles an hour."

Because new interactive forms of media are evolving so quickly, there are few definitive answers. Furthermore, new media and traditional media are merging in a way that could make separate and distinct measurement of online use irrelevant. As an example, NBC-TV's experiment with intercasting "The Tonight Show" creates the need for measurement of not only ratings for the broadcast but also feedback from the online information about Jay Leno's guests that is presented on specially equipped personal computers.

In early 1998, Nielsen Research announced a co-development project with Microsoft Corporation to extend the Nielsen ratings to computers. Nielsen wanted to be ahead of the technology curve so that media clients would not complain that there was no system in place to capture data about merging and converging markets. In the words of David Harkness, Nielsen senior vice president, "We look at the potential of the PC becoming another television outlet in the home."

Arbitron, too, launched an Internet measurement service with *Radiowave.com*, the interactive radio subsidiary of Motorola. In late 1998, the two companies announced an agreement to generate listener reports for radio stations and other outlets that stream audio programming on the Internet.[14]

There are other attempts at measuring online traffic. A monthly survey of Internet sites by RelevantKnowledge counts unique visitors to the most popular sites. On top of the list generally are *AOL.com*, *MSN.com*, *ZDNet.com*, *CNN.com*, and *weather.com*. Breaking news stories and sporting events alter the pattern. The U.S. mission to Mars put *nasa.gov* in the top ranks. The 1998 Winter Olympics was a stimulus for *CBSsportsline.com* and *CNNsi. com.*

Home Testing Institute (HTI) of Uniondale, New York, a research facility that relies on panels of consumers, claimed to have been "flooded with requests" for computer data by advertisers. That prompted HTI to establish a panel to participate in PC ratings. Everyone in selected households who uses a computer at work was provided with tracking software to log online usage. Monthly, HTI sends a retrieval disk to panelists, who transfer their usage data electronically and mail it back to HTI.[15]

"The first thing [advertisers] ask me is, 'Where's the audit?'" said Anna Zornosa, senior vice president of PointCast Network. "Until you have something audited, the media community doesn't accept it as real," she told *Advertising Age*. PointCast announced in the fall of 1997 that it would be audited by the Audit Bureau of Circulations (ABC), the organization known for documenting newspaper and magazine readership. ABC had about 80 Web clients at the time under the name of Audit Bureau of Verification Services, Inc. (ABVS).

Internet Profiles, Inc., the Redwood, California, company known as I/PRO, measures advertiser-supported activity on the Internet. Competitor NetCount was bought by I/PRO in late 1997, and their audits were combined to cover about 70% of online advertising. I/PRO generates the "pre-buy audit report," designed to verify traffic to Web sites. An I/PRO product growing in popularity is the post-buy report, which verifies ad views, page views, and click-throughs. When technology allowed Web sites to rotate banner advertising, the need for measurement followed immediately. Advertisers needed information on how many of their ads were actually being delivered.

"At a particular stage, clients are going to need to have some form of assurance that they got what they bought," confirmed Rishad Tobaccowala, president of Leo Burnett's Chicago-based interactive agency, Giant Step Productions. "They're going to need to find that data from someone besides the person who took their money."[16]

When the Internet Advertising Bureau announced a study that showed ad banners as effective vehicles for communicating brand messages, I wrote about it in a newsletter for my radio station clients. A California client circled the article and sent it back with a note, "That's like asking a barber if you need a haircut!"

Until measurement of new media becomes standardized and consistent, the barber is the only one to ask.

Beyond the Ratings — Qualitative Research

"I have a clear visual picture in my mind of consumers moving toward a product, moving away from it, or not moving at all." Judith Langer, president of New York–based Langer Associates, was addressing the Advertising Research Foundation's "Key Issues Workshop" in 1987.[17] Langer's focus group and depth interview work is quoted regularly because she puts a human face on otherwise cold statistics.

"My rule of thumb," she told attendees of the ARF meeting, "is that in a focus group of ten respondents, it is better to have a few excited about a product than have all ten feeling lukewarm."

Her words remain with me, because as a radio researcher, I look for passion in listeners—the desire to go back to the same station time and again. And you can only observe the passion face to face: it doesn't show on paper. You can measure it and distill it to statistics, but nothing beats hearing "a few excited" users.

If you sell television, cable, or radio, you'll use ratings information: cold, faceless statistics. They'll be your life and livelihood. Yet it is vital that while you sell numbers, you also visualize, as Langer did, the real people who use your medium.

SPENT $100+ ON GROCERIES

Target Persons: 752,585   Target Intab: 682
TAMPA-ST. PETERSBURG-CLEARWATER
Scarborough, Aug96-Jul97

Gender

50.4	% Male	49.6	% Female

Employment Status

Employed Full-Time	60.8%
Employed Part-Time	7.8%
Not Employed	
A Homemaker	8.9%
A Student	2.4%
Retired	14.8%
Disabled	3.6%
Temporarily Laid-Off	0.4%
Not Employed-Looking for Work	1.0%
Other	0.5%

Occupation

Administrative Support	13.8%
Executive, Administrative & Managerial	9.8%
Farming, Forestry & Fishing	0.4%
Handlers, Eqp Clnrs, Helprs & Lborers	1.2%
Machine Operators, Assemblers & Inspctr	1.5%
Precision Production, Craft & Repair	6.4%
Professional Specialty	9.3%
Sales	10.7%
Service	9.1%
Technicians & Related Support	3.2%
Transportation & Material Moving	3.2%

Education

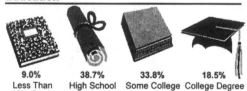

9.0%	38.7%	33.8%	18.5%
Less Than 12th Grade	High School Graduate	Some College	College Degree or More

Demographic Breakout

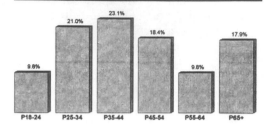

P18-24	P25-34	P35-44	P45-54	P55-64	P65+
9.8%	21.0%	23.1%	18.4%	9.8%	17.9%

Household Income

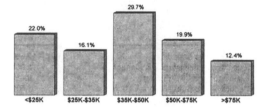

<$25K	$25K-$35K	$35K-$50K	$50K-$75K	>$75K
22.0%	16.1%	29.7%	19.9%	12.4%

Presence of Children Under 12 in Household

None	51.2%
One	22.6%
Two	16.9%
Three or More	9.3%

Home Ownership

Own	72.6%
Rent	25.2%
Other	2.2%

This report is based on Persons 18+ in SCB Tampa-St.Pete-Clrwter Radio Metro - Std

SPENT $100+ ON GROCERIES (Amount Spent on all Groceries Past 7 Days is $100 - $124 or $125 - $149 or $150 - $199 or $200 or More)

Estimates displayed are reported for % Composition.
©1997 The Arbitron Company and Scarborough Research Corp./VNU

ARBITRON
Q5

FIGURE 3–8 Grocery shoppers in the Tampa–St. Petersburg–Clearwater market are younger than those in Utica–Rome (Figure 3–9), and they are more likely to have children in the house. From the Arbitron Radio Market Report, fall 1997. Courtesy the Arbitron Company. Used with permission.

SPENT $125+ ON GROCERIES

Target Persons: 59,746   Target Intab: 207
UTICA-ROME
Qualitative Diary, Fall 1997

Gender

| 54.8 | % Male | 45.2 | % Female |

Employment Status

Full-Time	51.2%
Part-Time	15.9%
Not Employed	32.9%

Education

20.7%	24.2%	35.1%	20.0%
Less Than 12th Grade	High School Graduate	Some College	College Degree or More

Home Ownership

Own	84.9%
Rent	14.4%
Other	0.7%

Presence of Children Under 12 in Household

None	61.4%
1 Child	17.5%
2 Children	11.0%
3 Or More Children	10.1%

Demographic Breakout

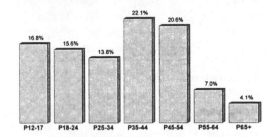

16.8% P12-17
15.6% P18-24
13.8% P25-34
22.1% P35-44
20.6% P45-54
7.0% P55-64
4.1% P65+

Household Income

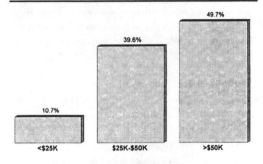

10.7% <$25K
39.6% $25K-$50K
49.7% >$50K

This report is based on Persons 12+ in UTICA-ROME METRO - Std

SPENT $125+ ON GROCERIES (Grocery Spending-Past 7 Days (HH) is $125 Or More)

Estimates displayed are reported for % Composition.
©1998 The Arbitron Company

ARBITRON
05

FIGURE 3–9 In Utica–Rome grocery shopping costs more than it does in Tampa Bay (see Figure 3–8). Shoppers are older and are more likely to be male. From the Utica–Rome Arbitron Radio Market Report, fall 1997. Courtesy the Arbitron Company. Used with permission.

Your client will demand more than ratings. Being number one means nothing to the client if the audience that makes you number one doesn't buy the product your client sells. Your client wants to get more money out of the schedule than the amount invested. Few retailers care if the medium they buy is number one or number 21, as long as the results make them number one.

That's the job of qualitative information: to add depth or quality to audience figures. James Fletcher offers these examples:

> Many potential sales have been lost because sales people could not alter a client's prejudice about the listeners of album-oriented rock, Top 40, or country and western radio formats. In television there are sometimes prejudices on the part of time buyers as to the desirability of various regional or local audiences. The unequivocal remedy to such adverse prejudice is solid research data as to qualities of the station audience which make it especially attractive to advertisers.[18]

Major advertisers conduct qualitative studies to guide sophisticated media campaigns. Networks develop qualitative audience research to arm their salespeople with information on the value of the audience to individual programs. Radio and TV stations in the largest markets either conduct their own qualitative studies or subscribe to services like Media Audit, Scarborough, and Simmons to prove that they have value beyond the ratings numbers.

With qualitative data, not only do we know who is watching or listening, but we also learn sociographic characteristics pertaining to income levels and social status; demographics, referring to age and gender; and psychographics, a measure of attitudes and lifestyle traits. One station may have middle-income professionals in its audience, another might have trade workers. The first station is better for advertising Volvos, the second for pickup trucks.

Researchers Bill Livek and Bill Engel of Symmetrical Resources, put it this way:

> With qualitative data, not only did we now know demographically who was watching,

but also the component sociographic characteristics of those demo groups. For example: One station might have middle-income men who are professionally employed, while another, within that same demo group, has a preponderance of trade workers. One station might appeal to the "Volvo" set while another is targeted at "pickups." At the same time, the data may show that there is no difference in the buying power of the "Volvo vs. pickup" audience.

> With qualitative data, there is a tool to show the difference between your 2 share and your competitor's. By the mid-80s, qualitative data began to take hold in the local market. Broadcasters began to see the advantage of extended demographic data such as income, occupation and education, as well as the importance of product usage data in providing stations with lower sociographic profiles ammunition to prove that their audience buys products.[19]

Most media outlets find it cost prohibitive to conduct their own qualitative studies, so they share information in syndicated research packages from Scarborough, Media Audit, Simmons, or other suppliers.

Simmons data, for example, targets products and services used by consumers in categories like automotive, electronics, households, sports and leisure, and others. A Simmons analysis for the Radio Advertising Bureau indicated that listeners to alternative rock formats tend to be two and a half times the national average in travel to Britain, twice the national average in attending theme parks, and three times the national average in snow skiing. Data like that can sway a buyer who may otherwise wince at the station's choice of music. When Arbitron collects radio listening in the smallest markets (markets number 100 and smaller), they also collect qualitative information about cable network viewing, fast food consumption, banking preferences, plans to buy automobiles, carpeting, furniture and appliances, and grocery expenditures. Arbitron calls the process the Qualitative Diary.

This data is packaged as RetailDirect and is provided to radio station subscribers to the Arbitron ratings report and in Arbitron's online analysis service, Maximi$er (a registered trademark of the Arbitron Company). In addition, the same data is sold to local cable systems as RetailDirect Lite to help systems sell to local advertisers.[20]

Qualitative information includes data collected in one or more of the following categories:

Activities	Work, hobbies, social events, vacations, entertainment, club and community activity, shopping, sports
Interests	Family, home, recreation, fashion, food and wine, media, personal achievement
Media Behavior	Light, medium, or heavy users of electronic media; local newspaper readership; magazine subscriptions
Recreation	Sports fans, sports participants, travel for recreational purposes, live theater, concerts, movies
Social Activity	Joiners who frequent the social scene or participate in clubs and organizations, home bodies who concentrate on do-it-yourself projects and gardening
Purchase Patterns	Recent purchases, intention to purchase, likely choices when the purchase time arrives
Opinion	Social issues, politics, business, education, products, culture, the future
Demographics	Age, sex, education, income, occupation, family size, rent or own housing, geography

"In broadcasting," James Fletcher says, "Because of the pervasive influence of the ratings, it has become the habit to equate demographics with age and sex." In general use, though, the additional elements listed above are all part of demographics.

Selling electronic media means selling the fragmented audiences that are the result of the explosion of media choices. Until recently, most marketing was mass marketing—dispersing one message that reached virtually everyone. No special effort was made to ensure that the message would appeal to everyone.

In "A Beginner's Guide to Demographics," *Marketing Tools Magazine* characterized mass marketing this way:

A great deal of money was spent pitching products and services to sections of the audience who didn't want or need them. In buying a prime time spot for its television ads, a motorcycle company would be paying to reach the housebound elderly as well as the young adults for whom their product was designed. A swimsuit manufacturer that ran an ad in a national magazine would pay a premium to reach the inhabitants of Nome, Alaska, as well as Floridians. Gradually, it was recognized that the "shotgun" approach is not an efficient use of marketing dollars.[21]

Mass marketing, as you've read so many times in this book, has given way to target marketing. That means knowing more about the customer than simply how many of them there are.

Targeting

"How important are ratings?" *Radio Ink* magazine asked Stephen Smith, of American Express. "Somewhat important," he an-

swered, "but we tend to place greater emphasis on target composition. We use a combination of traditional audience measurement and other research to look at the quality of the audience."

As I said earlier, targeting traces its history back to the early twentiethth century. In a textbook published in 1915, *The Business of Advertising* by Ernest Elmo Calkins, there was clear awareness of the use of different periodicals to target various populations: children, farmers, college students, and religious people. There were trade or class magazines such as those aimed at plumbers or Masons.

Joseph Turow at the University of Pennsylvania at Philadelphia studies Calkins: "He appreciated the targeting value of a small-town newspaper, saying that it gives local influence to the advertisements which it carries. And he suggested 'canvassing consumers' in different cities around the country in order to gather information for an ad campaign."

In *Breaking Up America*, Turow uses General Motors as an example of targeting and segmentation to differentiate products. Trying to work out of a sales slump in the 1920s, General Motors reorganized its strategy based on price segments. Chevrolet, Pontiac, Buick, and Cadillac were priced differently and advertised to buyers with different incomes.

"This sort of logic led manufacturers to support magazines and radio stations that reached the consumer segments they coveted," Turow writes. Radio at that time was more mass than segmented. Today radio is the ideal demographic and psychographic segmentation medium. Cable is close behind, with network television catching up quickly. Interactive new media breaks new ground daily in narrow segmentation, reducing some demographic and behavorial groupings to a relative handful.

The aim of the new targeting ability is to reach consumers with specific messages delivered in familiar, even specific language, about how products and services fit them personally.

Turow presented this analysis in *American Demographics* magazine after *Breaking Up America* was published:

Target-minded media help advertisers do this by building primary media communi-

ties formed when viewers or readers feel that a magazine, radio station, or other medium resonates with their personal beliefs, and helps them chart their position in the larger world.

Nickelodeon and MTV were pioneer attempts to establish this sort of ad-sponsored community on cable television. Owned by media giant Viacom, they are lifestyle parades that invite their target audiences (relatively upscale children and young adults, respectively) into a sense of belonging that ranges across a panoply of outlets, from cable to magazines, to books, videotapes, and outdoor events that their owners control or license.

The idea of these sorts of "programming services" is to cultivate a must-see, must-read, must-share mentality that makes the audience feel like they belong to a family, attached to the program hosts, other viewers, and sponsors. *Sports Illustrated* is no longer just a magazine; it is a cross-media brand that stands for a certain approach to life.

Some media are going a step further by making an active effort to exclude people who do not fit the desired profile. This makes the community more 'pure' and thereby more efficient for advertisers. *Signaling* is one way to do this. Simply put, signaling makes it abundantly clear that "this is not for everyone." "Beavis and Butt-head" filled this role for MTV during the mid-1990s, as did "The Howard Stern Show" for E! Entertainment Television. These programs had so much "attitude," they sparked controversy among people clearly removed from their "in" crowds. Executives involved with scheduling the shows hoped controversies surrounding them would crystallize the channels' images and guarantee sampling by the people they wanted to attract. The executives acknowledged they also expected "signature shows" would turn off viewers whom they didn't want in their audience.[22]

Another form of targeting goes beyond chasing undesirables away, or, as Turow says, it simply excludes them in the first place. *Tailoring* is the capacity to aim media content and ads at particular individuals. As Turow said, "With just a little effort (habit, actually), people can listen to radio stations, read magazines, watch cable programs, surf the Web, and participate in loyalty programs that parade their self-images and clusters of concerns. With no seeming effort at all, they receive offers from marketers that complement their lifestyles."

Just as media has changed since targeting and segmentation began, so has research. The statistical tools available to the researcher have grown tremendously over the years. The plunging cost of computation makes it both economically and logistically feasible to merge large databases and create new analyses in the merged files.

Researchers are now able to uncover relationships among demographic attitudinal, behavioral, and geographic elements of the population. Those relationships are called "clusters."

Clustering

If you've ever heard the saying, "Birds of a feather flock together," you already have a sense of clustering. By combining demographic data, a market can be grouped into clusters, also known as geodemographic segmentation systems.

Cluster systems take many demographic variables and create profiles of different individual or household characteristics, purchase behaviors, and media preferences. Most of the clusters used in media sales and analysis have catchy, descriptive names in an attempt to make them easier to remember. Examples are "Elite Suburbs," "2nd City Society," "HeartLanders," and "Rustic Living," all from Claritas' PRIZM cluster system.

Marketing Tools magazine said, "Cluster systems are especially powerful when used in conjunction with business mapping. Sophisticated mapping software programs easily link demographics to any level of geography (a process called geocoding). Some software can pinpoint specific households with neighborhoods from . . . customer data and then create schematic maps of neighborhoods by cluster concentrations."

To apply this concept to your selling, you might use cluster analysis and geocoding to show a prospect that your audience and the advertiser's customers are the same and that they live within a few miles of the advertiser's business.

The geographic element is the one thing that distinguishes clusters from psychographic segments. Another difference is that cluster categories are based on socioeconomic and consumer data, not attitudinal data.

Zip Codes

When mapping and media mix, ZIP codes often come to mind. When the U.S. Postal Service divided the nation with ZIP codes in 1965, it was done with mail delivery in mind, not geodemographic segmentation. Radio stations tend to use ZIP codes to segment likely Arbitron diary-keepers, but it is not an exact science.

In his 1988 book, *The Clustering of America*, Michael Weiss introduced the use of ZIP codes as a clustering device. Weiss told a human interest story rather than describing ZIP codes in statistical terms. His work introduced marketers to age, education, and buying segments originally developed by Claritas Corporation for their PRIZM database. As effective as Weiss was in describing clustering, among media sellers he is remembered for his ZIP code analyses.[23]

Here's the problem with ZIP codes: there are more than 36,000 of them in the United States. Multiply that by the fact that a single ZIP code can contain 35,000 addresses or more.

Use my ZIP code as an example. Here's what you'll find in ZIP 77063:

My comfortable but not expensive middle-class neighborhood.

The building where my offices are located.

The home of the owner of one of the city's top Mexican food chains.

Several apartment complexes, a few among the highest rents in town and one of the lowest as well.

A shopping area catering to natives of India and Pakistan.

A neighborhood of near-million dollar homes including Mary Lou Retton's house.

That's *not* segmentation!

In New York, because of the density of the population, ZIP codes are somewhat cohesive in terms of ethnic and socio-economic mix. In the smallest towns, there may be only *one* ZIP code, defying segmentation. That's why the cluster systems were developed.

The four major cluster systems are Claritas' PRIZM, Strategic Mapping's ClusterPlus (developed by Donnelley Marketing), National Decision System's MicroVision, and CACI's ACORN. Each of these vendors combines more than a half-billion individual purchase records, product, media, and lifestyle preferences, and Census Block Group demographic information. (See Figure 3–10). The data is sliced and diced to create an accurate portrait of the people in geographic units as small as block groups (the equivalent of neighborhoods) and ZIP + 4 codes.

There are 62 unique PRIZM clusters, organized into 15 broader social groups. Each group is identified by a group code, which denotes a basic neighborhood type: Metro Urban, Metro Suburb, Small Town, Rural. When linked to market data or to Nielsen and Arbitron ratings, PRIZM's geodemographic model produces descriptions of the audience.

Getting It Straight

Cluster analysis is often confused with psychographics. "Psychographics" and "lifestyles" tend to be used interchangeably, but there is a difference. "Psychographics" usually refers to a formal classification system that categorizes people into specific types based largely on psychological characteristics. "Lifestyle" is more vague. Generally, people are organized by attitudes or consumer behavior: "politically conserva-

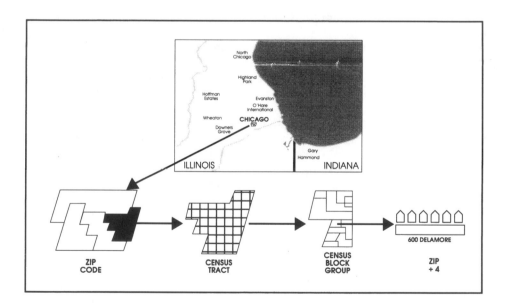

FIGURE 3–10   The ZIP code is a starting point, but not everybody in any given ZIP code is like everybody else. Take a Chicago ZIP code, reduce it to a census tract, distill it further to a census block group, and you still have another step. Reduce a map to ZIP + 4 and you've zeroed in on similar likes and dislikes. This map is from TransAmerica Marketing Services. Used with permission.

tive," for example, or "avid golfer." Cluster systems are based on purchase behavior ("own a cell phone") and demographics (age, sex, income, and education).

Vals™

"Hi, I'm Ed Shane, Actualizer/Achiever."

I don't suppose anyone introduces themselves that way, but we each fit into one of the eight psychographic segments in SRI Consulting's Values and Lifestyles (VALS) system.[24]

The VALS segmentation system sorts U.S. adults (18 and over) into eight distinct consumer groups, based on the way they answer the VALS questionnaire. VALS consumer groups are shown graphically on a matrix with two dimensions: self-orientation (the left-to-right axis) and resources (the top-to-bottom axis). The self-orientation axis moves from principle-oriented to action-oriented; the resource axis moves up from low resources to high resources. See Figure 3–11.

Self-orientation. People pursue and acquire products, services, and experiences that provide satisfaction and give shape, substance, and character to their identities. They are motivated by one of three powerful self-orientations: principle, status, and action.

- Principle-oriented consumers are guided in their choices by abstract, idealized criteria, rather than by feelings, events, or desire for approval and opinions of others.
- Status-oriented consumers look for products and services that demonstrate the consumers' success to their peers.
- Action-oriented consumers are guided by a desire for social or physical activity, variety, and risk taking.

Resources. "Resources" refers to the full range of psychological, physical, demographic, and material means or capacities to buy things, and to energy level. In the VALS system, resources are represented as a continuum from minimal to abundant. Resources generally increase from adoles-

cence and decrease with extreme age, depression, financial reverse, and physical or psychological impairment.

VALS was one of the original consumer segmentation systems based on lifestyle characteristics and is the only one still commercially available. According to literature from SRI Consulting:

> Traditional demographic consumer research techniques measure attributes such as age, gender, and income—an approach that is useful for understanding where people stand in society.
>
> A psychographic approach takes the analysis a step further, measuring people's attitudes and lifestyle characteristics. Such measurements are excellent indicators of how people are thinking and where they are going with their lives.

Here's a brief description of each VALS consumer type:

ACHIEVERS are successful career- and work-oriented people who like to, and generally do, feel in control of their lives. They value consensus, predictability, and stability over risk, intimacy, and self-discovery. They are deeply committed to work and family. Work provides them with a sense of duty, material rewards, and prestige. Their social lives reflect this focus and are structured around family, church, and career.

ACTUALIZERS are successful, sophisticated, active, "take charge" people with high self-esteem and abundant resources. They are interested in growth and seek to develop, explore, and express themselves in a variety of ways—often guided by a desire to have an effect or to make a change.

BELIEVERS are conservative, conventional people with concrete beliefs based on traditional, established codes: family, church, community, and the nation. Many Believers express moral codes that are deeply rooted and literally interpreted. They follow established routines, organized in large part around

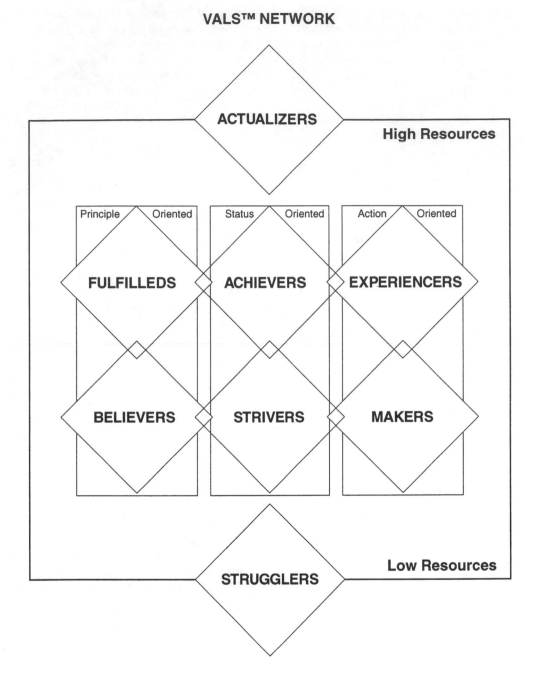

© 1998 SRI Consulting. All rights reserved. Unauthorized reproduction prohibited.

FIGURE 3–11 The VALS diamonds showing consumer groups on a matrix with two dimensions: self-orientation (left to right) and resources (bottom to top). ©1998 SRI Consulting. All rights reserved. VALS is a trademark of SRI International.

home, family, and social or religious organizations to which they belong.

EXPERIENCERS are young, vital, enthusiastic, impulsive, and rebellious. They seek variety and excitement, savoring the new, the offbeat, and the risky. Still in the process of formulating life values and patterns of behavior, they quickly become enthusiastic about new possibilities but are equally quick to cool. At this stage in their lives, they are politically uncommitted, uninformed, and highly ambivalent about what they believe.

FULFILLEDS are mature, satisfied, comfortable, reflective people who value order, knowledge, and responsibility. Most are well educated and in (or recently retired from) professional occupations. They are well-informed about world and national events and are alert to opportunities to broaden their knowledge. Content with their careers, families, and station in life, they tend to center their leisure activities around the home.

MAKERS are practical people who have constructive skills and value self-sufficiency. They live within a traditional context of family, practical work, and physical recreation and have little interest in what lies outside that context. Makers experience the world by working on it—building a house, raising children, fixing a car, or canning vegetables—and have enough skill, income, and energy to carry out their projects successfully.

STRIVERS seek motivation, self-definition, and approval from the world around them. They are "striving" to find a secure place in life. Unsure of themselves and low on economic, social, and psychological resources, Strivers are concerned about the opinions and approval of others.

STRUGGLERS have constricted lives. Chronically poor, ill-educated, low-skilled, without strong social bonds, elderly, and concerned about their health, they are often resigned and passive. Because they are limited by the urgent needs of the present moment, they do not show a strong self-orientation. Their chief concerns are for security and safety.

I have VALS-typed myself. That's why I introduced myself as an "Actualizer/Achiever." (To be absolutely correct, SRI Consulting would have me say: "I am most like an Actualizer, and I'm second-most like an Achiever.") To be classified, I answered a questionnaire (online at *http://future.sri.com/vals/valsindex.html*) with 35 general-attitude statements (e.g., "I dress more fashionably than most people.") Ten Internet-specific statements ("When on the Web, how frequently do you access the following: Content? Cool Sites?" etc.), and five demographic questions (gender, age, education, household income, and ZIP code). At the end of the questionnaire I was typed.

Based on the descriptions above, I like being an Actualizer (i.e., most like an Actualizer). Who wouldn't want to be classified as a "successful, sophisticated, active, take charge" person?

Using Research to Sell

Television time is often bought on the basis of households, because of the large numbers of households that watch the most popular shows. However, the changes I've described in the media environment have moved television sellers to create demographic profiles and qualitative profiles of their programs. This section includes some examples.

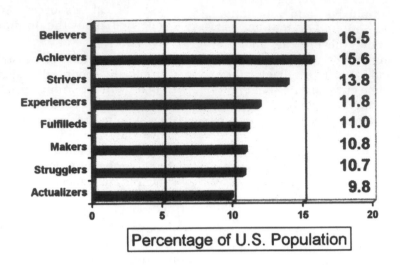

Distribution of VALS Types in the U.S. Population

	Percentage
Believers	16.5
Achievers	15.6
Strivers	13.8
Experiencers	11.8
Fulfilleds	11.0
Makers	10.8
Strugglers	10.7
Actualizers	9.8

Percentage of U.S. Population

FIGURE 3–12 According to VALS segmentation, there are more Believers among the U.S. population than any other VALS consumer type. Source: SRI Consulting. VALS is a trademark of SRI International.

(TNN). The Nashville Network, uses two balanced columns that describe twenty "viewer characteristics." Here are just a few:

(AMC). In focus groups, viewers describe American Movie Classics as a special destination, "a zone of ease and reassurance," and a "haven from stress." Those descriptions prompt AMC sellers to tell advertisers that their channel has a "special bond with viewers." AMC sells only a limited number of commercials—only two minutes per movie—and uses their proprietary research as a selling tool.

(20th). When 20th Television launched "Home Team" with Terry Bradshaw into the syndication market, there was no ratings history to draw on, except for Bradshaw's work on Fox and CBS NFL broadcasts. The syndicator turned to primary research to tell the story to stations and advertisers. Using focus groups conducted in Glendale, California, and in Phoenix, 20th showed positive response to the idea of the program and to Bradshaw's interviewing and hosting skills. In contrast to that approach, when there is a ratings

Shop at Wal-Mart.	Do not shop at Macy's.
Have bank accounts.	Do not use ATMs.
Go hunting and fishing.	Do not visit museums.
Drink coffee.	Do not drink bottled water.
Go camping.	Do not go to the beach.
Go to theme parks.	Do not go to live theater.
Purchase jeans.	Do not purchase tuxedos.

NICKELODEON IS HOME TO 58% OF ALL KIDS 2-11 GRPS FOR THE NEW SEASON

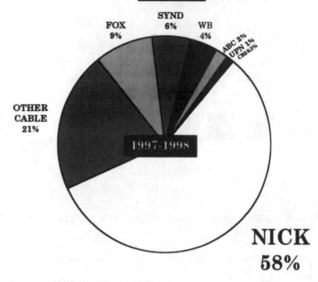

SHARE OF KIDS 2-11 GRPS
1997-1998

Source: Nielsen: NTI, NHI, 9/1/97-9/14/97; NSS, 9/1/97-9/7/97.
NOTE: Based on Nick Total Day and competitive kids' programming only
May not add to 100% due to rounding.

FIGURE 3–13 Nickelodeon sells using its share of audience.
Other Nickelodeon graphics are funny or
whimsical. This one is all business—the
business of research. Used with permission.
MTV Networks.

profile available, as there was for "The X Files" for example, the syndicator showed the program's power in its first run on Fox and against all other networks.

(WGN). WGN sells its impact with women 18–45 on weekends by ranking the top 15 cable networks. WGN's number five rank puts it behind Lifetime, USA, TBS, and TNT. To sell teens, WGN compares itself to MTV and points out that their teen programming out-delivers 80% of MTV's programs. For sports, WGN pits its Chicago Bulls basketball coverage against NBA games on both TBS and TNT.

(Tribune). Tribune Entertainment included in its sales materials for "The Geral-

do Rivera Show" a topline research report. One hundred women in Fort Lee, New Jersey, and in Chicago evaluated "the new Geraldo," after he toned down his daily talk show. He was then perceived as being sincere in his compassion for his guests and mature in his new clothing styles. Showing candor that's rare in our industry, Tribune included in the report recommendations from the researchers that said Rivera should not hug guests without their permission and that using a 900-telephone number was considered a "rip off."

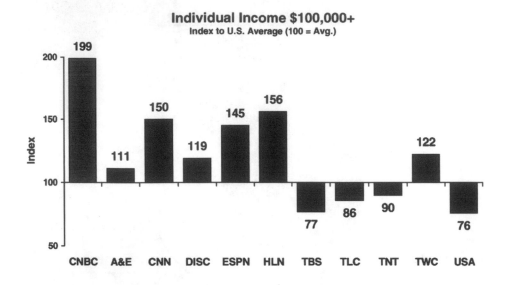

CNBC Viewers Are Affluent

Individual Income $100,000+
Index to U.S. Average (100 = Avg.)

To be read: CNBC viewers are 99% more likely (199 index) than the average adult to have individual employment income of
$100,000 or more
Source: MRI, Doublebase 1997

FIGURE 3–14 CNBC emphasizes audience quality in its sales material. CNBCviewers are almost twice as likely as the average adult to have an income of $100,000 or more. The way CNBC demonstrates that fact to potential advertisers is by publicizing these bar graphs, which compare the other major cable networks. Other CNBC graphics show stock transactions, doctoral degrees, and company executives. Courtesy of NBC Cable Networks, Ad Sales Department, April 1998. ©1998.

The Research Police

Advertisers need to know not only the ratings but also the reliability of the numbers that the ratings represent. Credibility is crucial since so much money rides on every decision. In 1963, Congress held hearings into the influence and shortcomings of the ratings services, and the result was the formation of the Broadcast Ratings Council (BRC). The BRC was to monitor, audit, and accredit the ratings services,

making sure that the ratings were "valid, reliable, effective, and viable," to use the words of the BRC charter.[25]

In 1982, the BRC was renamed the Electronic Media Ratings Council (EMRC) to reflect a connection with the services that tracked the cable TV industry. In 1997, there was another change of name, to Media Ratings Council (MRC), this time to "reflect the expansion of the auditing and assess-

CONSUMER PROFILE
Fax Machine Purchasers
PAST TWELVE MONTHS

Gender

73 % Male	**27** % Female

Income (Adults 18+)

Over $50,000	74%
$25,000-$50,000	21%
Under $25,000	5%

Occupation (Adults 18+)

Professional/Managerial	35%
Technical, Sales, and Administrative Support	23%
Service	7%
Precision Production and Craft & Farming, Forestry and Fishing	3%
Operators, Fabricators and Laborers	1%

Education

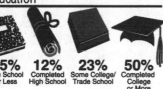

15% High School or Less	12% Completed High School	23% Some College/ Trade School	50% Completed College or More

Sociographic Shoppers Profile

Brand Loyal	24%
Cautious	52%
Venturesome	24%

Own Home   **71%**

Households with Children   **36%**

Average Weekday Non-Newspaper Readers   **29%**

Demographic Breakout

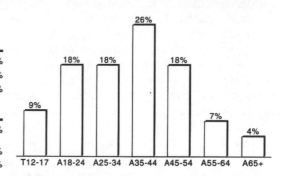

T12-17	A18-24	A25-34	A35-44	A45-54	A55-64	A65+
9%	18%	18%	26%	18%	7%	4%

Lifestyle Profile by PRIZM® Groups

GROUP	DESCRIPTION	
S1	Elite Suburbs	21.1%
C2	2nd City Centers	17.5%
U1	Urban Uptown	12.9%
T1	Landed Gentry	11.9%
S2	The Affluentials	10.5%
T2	Exurban Blues	7.5%
T3	Working Towns	5.9%
C1	2nd City Society	3.0%
R3	Rustic Living	2.9%
U2	Urban Midscale	2.4%
R2	Heartlanders	1.7%
S3	Inner Suburbs	1.6%
R1	Country Families	1.0%
C3	2nd City Blues	0.0%
U3	Urban Cores	0.0%

64-A   *Media Targeting 2000 — conducted by The Arbitron Company in cooperation with the Radio Advertising Bureau*   Fax Machine Purchasers Consumer Profile

FIGURE 3–15 Radio sellers use consumer profiles from *Media Targeting 2000*, a national study conducted by Arbitron and the Radio Advertising Bureau. Here fax machine purchasers are profiled for the salesperson about to call on an office products account. By matching a station's audience to the profile, a sale is more likely. Courtesy Arbitron and RAB. Used with permission.

ment process into multi-media measurement," according to the news release announcing the change.

Members of the MRC at the time of the name change were ABC/Disney, A&E Networks, Clear Channel Communications, Cox Enterprises, ESPN, NBC Network, NBC Stations Group, CNBC, CBS, Fox, and 35 other companies, including ad agencies and print and electronic media organizations.

The ratings services try to police themselves. Arbitron cites any station that refers to its diaries on the air. Nielsen issues a notice about contests and special promotions that Nielsen feeels may affect viewing. (See Figure 3–16.)

Another organization setting and monitoring standards for research is the Advertising Research Foundation (ARF). Founded in 1936 by the Association of National Advertisers and the American Association of Advertising Agencies, ARF is a nonprofit group in pursuit of more effective marketing and advertising communications. In addition to providing guidelines for researchers, ARF is able to combine its forces to conduct complex and expensive studies that its members could not undertake alone.[26]

At the ARF annual conference in 1998, there were eight research presentations devoted to online and interactive measurement. Some dealt with solving the problem of accountability for Web advertisers, others with the topic of using the Internet as a data collection method.

Last Words

I know sellers of media, electronic, and other, that reread *Ogilvy on Advertising* on a regular basis. It's a classic in the field. The hardcover version is a big, beautiful book full of color ads that Ogilvy or his agency produced. I recommend it to you.

Since I began this chapter with Ogilvy, I'd like to end it with Ogilvy:

> I admit that research is often misused by agencies and their clients. They have a way of using it to prove they are right. They use research as a drunkard uses a lamppost— not for illumination but for support.

FIGURE 3–16
Nielsen posts "Special Notes" like these in each NSI book to alert advertisers of attempts by stations to attract viewers with special promotions and contests. Arbitron does the same for its radio reports. Courtesy Nielsen Media Research. Used with permission.

```
CONTESTS AND SPECIAL PROMOTIONS

NIELSEN HAS BEEN ADVISED THAT A CONTEST WAS CONDUCTED BY THE
NATIONAL SYNDICATOR, MULTIMEDIA ENTERTAINMENT, INC., TITLED
'SALLY'S GETAWAY' DURING THE MONDAY-FRIDAY TELECASTS OF 'SALLY
JESSY RAPHAEL' FROM APRIL 25, 1996 THRU MAY 20, 1996.  THE
PROGRAM INDEX SECTION OF THIS ANALYSIS IDENTIFIES ANY LOCAL
STATION(S) CARRYING THE PROGRAM AND THE TIMES OF THE TELECASTS IN
THIS MARKET.

PLEASE CONSULT THE STATIONS FOR ADDITIONAL DETAILS.
```

```
CONTESTS AND SPECIAL PROMOTIONS

NIELSEN HAS BEEN ADVISED THAT A CONTEST WAS CONDUCTED BY THE
NATIONAL SYNDICATOR, KING WORLD PRODUCTIONS, INC., TITLED 'WHEEL
OF FORTUNE OLYMPIC GAMES SWEEPSTAKES' DURING THE TELECASTS OF
'WHEEL OF FORTUNE' FROM MAY 6, 1996 THRU MAY 22, 1996.  THE PRO-
GRAM INDEX SECTION OF THIS ANALYSIS IDENTIFIES ANY LOCAL STA-
TION(S) CARRYING THE PROGRAM AND THE TIMES OF THE TELECASTS IN
THIS MARKET.  THIS STATION(S) MAY OR MAY NOT HAVE AIRED THE
EPISODES THAT INCLUDED THIS CONTEST.

PLEASE CONSULT THE STATION(S) OR SYNDICATOR FOR ADDITIONAL
DETAILS.
```

```
NIELSEN HAS BEEN ADVISED THE FOLLOWING CONTESTS WERE CONDUCTED
DURING THIS MEASUREMENT PERIOD:

STATION WCVB-TV CONDUCTED A 'WATCH OPRAH EVERYDAY' CONTEST APRIL
29-MAY 22, 1996 DURING THEIR MON-FRI 4-5PM OPRAH WINFREY PROGRAM-
MING.

STATION WNDS-TV CONDUCTED A 'CRUISE INTO SUMMER' CONTEST AT
VARIOUS TIMES THROUGHOUT THEIR MON-FRI 4-8PM PROGRAMMING.

PLEASE CONSULT THE STATIONS FOR FURTHER DETAILS.
```

CONFESSIONS OF A NIELSEN HOUSEHOLD
BY JAMES C. RAYMONDO

"Go ahead, blame me for the deplorable state of television," wrote sociologist James C. Raymondo, in *American Demographics* magazine. Nielsen Media Research asked the Raymondo family to join the 5,000 metered households that generate the Nielsen Television Index.

The geographic unit most frequently chosen as a beginning point is the county. The United States has a manageable number of counties, it's easy to get a list of them, and there are estimates of how many households they have. The last fact is important because if the final sample is to be representative, a county's chance of being selected should be proportional to how many households it contains. For example, a county ten times the size of another should have ten times the chances of being selected.

Once a certain number of counties has been selected, depending on the desired completed sample size, the process continues with another random draw of smaller geographic units. The process continues until it reaches the level of geography small enough to locate individual households. In most cases, the stopping point is the census block.

Census blocks are geographic areas with physical boundaries. The simplest example is an actual city block surrounded by four streets, although railroad tracks, waterways, and any number of other things also act as boundary features. The advantage of census blocks is that once a sample of them has been chosen, researchers can compile lists of the housing units within each one.

My housing unit just happened to be one of those selected. Nielsen was more interested in my address than in me. If I had moved away during the two-year participation period, whoever moved in after I left would have been offered an opportunity to continue in the ratings survey.

After I agreed to participate in the ratings process, a group of Nielsen technicians visited my home to hook up the monitoring equipment to my TVs and VCRs. The television part is relatively simple. The technicians opened up the set(s) and place a small probe near the tuner that measures the frequency being emitted, thereby capturing the station to which the TV is tuned. The probe is connected to a transmitting device attached to the rear of the television set that sends the data along a cable to a small computerized storage device.

The monitoring equipment for a VCR is a little more complicated, because Nielsen wants to know whether you are recording a program or playing a tape. (Nielsen assumes that if you record a program, you intend to watch it, so taping a program has an impact on its ratings.) A simple radio probe cannot measure all of that, so the technicians solder about five or six wires directly to the circuit board inside the VCR.

Somehow this part of the process was not clearly explained beforehand, and I almost backed out when I saw the soldering iron come out. But the televisions had already been connected, and the technicians had traveled more than a hundred miles, so I allowed them to continue. It turned out that my fears were groundless. The wires for the VCR monitoring equipment do no harm at all. They are connected to a transmitter attached to the rear of the VCR, and the data are sent along the same cable as the television data to the computerized storage device.

In most cases, only two pieces of Nielsen equipment are visible to you or anyone who visits your home. The first is the meter that automatically captures the tuning information. This is a small electronic box measuring about five by seven by two inches with eight red and eight green lights across the front. The other is a small remote-control device with which you indicate who's watching at any given time. This is what turns the simple meter into a "people meter." The system can identify up to eight individual viewers in a household. Basic demographic data for each household member are supplied to Nielsen in a short questionnaire at the outset of the participation period.

When someone begins to watch TV, he or she punches in a personal code and the "OK" button. The light corresponding to the code number changes from red (not watching) to green (watching). When the person stops watching, they sign off by repeating the punch-in process. When visitors watch tele-

Continued

Confessions of a Nielsen Household
(continued)

vision, they can use any vacant code number and manually input their sex and age using controls on top of the meter.

This sounds a little easier than it really is. A few years ago, Nielsen added a feature to keep respondents more on their toes about logging off. Advertisers were concerned that people would often forget to indicate when they stopped watching thereby inflating shows' ratings and the cost of advertising. So now, you have to verify that you're still there by hitting the OK button every 70 minutes. Nothing explodes if you don't comply, but red lights blink at you in an extremely distracting and effective manner until you do.

Even this is not so bad. The biggest annoyance is that you also have to hit the OK button every time you change a channel, or the red lights continue to do their blinking thing. This wouldn't have been a big deal thirty years ago when you might change channels a total of two or three times in a typical evening. After all, you had to get up and walk across the room to change the channel and then adjust the rabbit-ear antenna for three or four minutes to get a clear signal. Contrast that with the remote-control, cable-ready, channel-surfing 1990s. It seems like you spend half your life reaching for the Nielsen remote to hit the OK button. After a few weeks, however, I got accustomed to the system. In fact, I found myself instinctively reaching for the Nielsen remote even when I was watching TV elsewhere, in hotels and other people's homes.

I think it is fair to say that no one ever got rich by being a Nielsen household, unless some unscrupulous television producer tried to bribe them into watching particular programs. Actually, security is extremely important to Nielsen. Those who participate in the ratings are instructed not to reveal their participation to anyone, except for family and friends who visit. Representatives from Nielsen call each household periodically to make sure that the household information is up to date and to see if there are any problems. One of the things they always stress is the importance of confidentiality. You are to notify Nielsen immediately if anyone approaches you with questions about your participation in the ratings.

In the absence of illegitimate compensation, there is little financial incentive to be a Nielsen household. In consideration for permitting people to come into your home and install their monitors, you receive a one-time $50 fee. As long as you are participating in the ratings process, you get a monthly fee of $2 per hooked-up television set and VCR. I had two sets and two VCRs, so I received the grand sum of $8 per month.

There are two other small means of compensation. About every six months, you can pick up one item from a small catalog of inexpensive items that probably range in value from $2 to $10. I ended up with a flashlight, clock, and small hatchet. Nielsen will also reimburse you for half of the repair charges to any television or VCR that needs fixing while its monitoring equipment is connected.

Viewing data for each day are transmitted from the hooked-up TVs and VCRs to a single computerized storage device, which is equipped with a modem and attached to a telephone line in the house. Once a day, usually between the wee hours of 3:00 and 5:00 a.m., the device dials a toll-free number and uploads the viewing data to a central Nielsen computer.

Reprinted from *American Demographics* magazine with permission. ©1997, Cowles Business Media, Ithaca, New York.

Review Highlights and Discussion Points

1. David Ogilvy developed the first paper on copy-testing in the history of British advertising, and he ran the Gallup Audience Research Institute, which predicted the potential public appeal of motion pictures.

2. Code is a good analogy for research. The user has to analyze, dissect, and interpret it in order to make sense of it.

3. Ad agencies, especially national agencies, were early proponents of research that helped them understand why consumers behave the way they do.

4. Triggering buyer responses was a new technique in the 1930s. Targeting specific buying groups was not. Most early segmentation was based on social distinction.

5. Today's marketer takes targeting and segmentation for granted.

6. Collecting the information that gets deep into the means and motives of the consumer is qualitative research. It measures the "quality" of the information rather than the numbers of people who may feel or act a certain way.

7. The numbers side of research is quantitative research. It measures quantity: sheer numbers.

8. In selling electronic media, qualitative data is much more valuable than quantitative, although achieving a number-one position or attracting a mass audience cannot be overlooked. The latter is most often expressed in "rankers" —a rank order of scores on a particular question.

9. A rating is the estimated percentage of the total population listening or viewing. A share is the percentage using a particular medium.

10. The A. C. Nielsen company originated television and national cable ratings and still provides TV ratings and some radio ratings to media in countries outside the United States and Canada.

11. The Nielsen Television Index (NTI) is network television's rating report. It provides continuous audience estimates for all national broadcast network programs.

12. Nielsen gathers information every day from approximately 5,000 households using an electronic "people meter" that instantaneously measures viewing.

13. The Radio Market Report is the Arbitron Company's radio equivalent of Nielsen's local TV station report, the NSI. Radio is Arbitron's single most profitable revenue stream.

14. For its radio ratings reports, Arbitron uses diary methodology to collect listening data in 268 markets.

15. The U.S. government defines market areas as Metropolitan Statistical Area (MSA), Primary Metropolitan Statisti-

cal Area (PMSA), or Consolidated Metropolitan Statistical Area (CMSA).

16. The ratings services define markets in three ways: for radio, the Metro Survey Area (Metro) and the Total Survey Area (TSA); for television, the Designated Market Area (DMA).

17. Nielsen ratings showed a nine point decline in the network's share of prime time viewing from 1991 to 1996 and an equal and opposite increase for basic cable.

18. James Fletcher observes that the essence of the ratings is delivery of large amounts of data at low cost.

19. Nielsen Media Research surveys the 212 television markets in November, February, May, and July for four-week periods called "sweeps." The largest markets are surveyed seven times a year by adding sweeps in October, January, and March.

20. The basic measure of television is done via the diary method. Daily viewing activity is written in a small booklet and is recorded for one week. These booklets are mailed back to Nielsen at the end of the survey week.

21. Nielsen data is released in printed form and is referred to as "the book." The television reports show the estimated audiences for stations in each market by sex and age and by time period.

22. Ratings help buyers reach their target audience at the lowest cost of delivery possible. Meanwhile the objective of sellers is to make sure the cost reflects the value of the audience being delivered.

23. Cost per thousand (CPM) and cost per point (CPP) are formulas employed by media buyers to ascertain the most efficient deployment of an advertiser's money.

24. Four times a year in the larger markets, radio gets its report card—the Arbitron "book," which is distributed in book form. Smaller markets are surveyed once or twice a year.

25. Arbitron uses the diary method to collect radio listening data. One diary is sent to each member of selected households who are 12 years of age or

older. Respondents fill in the diaries for one week and return them to the rating service for tabulation.

26. When it comes to measuring Internet usage, there are more questions than answers, and because interactive media is evolving so quickly, there are few answers of a definitive nature.

27. It is vital that while you sell "numbers," you also visualize the real people who use your medium. The job of qualitative information is to add depth to audience figures.

28. Major advertisers, the networks, and the local television and radio stations in the largest markets conduct their own qualitative studies to prove that they have value beyond the ratings numbers.

29. Using qualitative data, we not only know who is watching or listening but we also learn their sociographic, demographic, and psychographic characteristics.

30. Qualitative information includes data collected in one or more of the following categories: activities, interests, behavior, recreation, social activity, purchase patterns, opinion, and demographics.

31. The terms "psychographics" and "lifestyles" tend to be used interchangeably, but there is a difference: psychographics refers to a formal classification system that categorizes people into specific types based on psychological characteristics, while the term lifestyle is more vague, generally referring to attitudes or consumer behavior.

Chapter Notes

1   *Ogilvy on Advertising* was cited in Chapter 1.

2   Ernest Dichter's story appeared in *Adweek*, December 7, 1987.

3   "Hypersegmentation" is what Joseph Turow calls the tendency to exploit differences among individuals. The account of the *Chicago Tribune* research is from "Breaking Up America: The Dark Side of Target Marketing," *American Demographics*, November 1997. Turow is also the author of *Breaking Up America: Advertising and the New Media World*. Chicago: University of Chicago Press, 1997.

4   Stephen Smith of American Express was quoted in "American Express Charges Radio: 'Help Us Reach Our Target'" in *Radio Ink*, November 2, 1992.

5   Mike Burnette's *The Truth About Radio Ratings* was published in 1993 by *Radio Only* and was featured in that publication.

6   Nielsen abbreviations are from public relations materials supplied by Nielsen Media Research.

7   The terms NTI, NSI, DMA, and Nielsen Homevideo Index are all registered trademarks of Nielsen Media Research.

8   "Measuring television use in the 1990s is like trying to shovel smoke," says Brad Edmondson in "TV Execs to Nielsen: Get SMART, "*American Demographics*," October, 1997.

9   The ads from Nielsen Media Research appeared in *Advertising Age*, November 4 and November 11, 1996, and in other media publications during the same period. The networks' response ran in *Advertising Age* December 16, 1996.

10   "SMART" is an acronym for "System for Measuring and Reporting Television" proposed by Statistical Research, Inc. That led to the headline, "TV Execs to Nielsen: Get SMART" in "The Statmeister" column in *American Demographics*, October 1997.

11   I learn something every time I talk with Jim Fletcher of the University of Georgia. The best (i.e., most understandable) text on ratings and research I've ever read is Dr. Fletcher's material in the book he edited, *Handbook of Radio and Television Broadcasting*. New York: Van Nostrand Reinhold, 1982.

12   NBC researcher Horst Stipp also makes it simple: "Households don't watch TV,

people do." Stipp's "How To Read TV Ratings" appeared in *American Demographics*, March 1997.

13 Nielsen materials came from Nielsen Media Research, who were very helpful to me in this project.

14 The "Spots and Dots" story came from Ed Cohen, director of research for Clear Channel Communications.

15 Arbitron made its announcement of an Internet radio ratings service just in time for the 1998 NAB Radio Show in Seattle. RelevantKnowledge and Media Metrix agreed to merge inOctober, 1998.

16 Home Testing Institute asked me to be part of the PC Ratings panel, so I felt like an insider.

17 "Media buyers want more from Web site audits" by Kate Maddox appeared in *Advertising Age*, September 22, 1997, and contained the Zornosa and Tobaccowala quotations and the information from I/PRO.

18 I've kept a copy of Judith Langer's speech, "The Process of Insight: How Researchers Turn Qualitative Research into Marketing Insight," since she delivered it to the Advertising Research Foundation's Key Issues Workshop, July 15, 1987.

19 Jim Fletcher's work was cited above, as were Turow's and the article in *Radio Ink* that quoted Stephen Smith.

20 Bill Livek and Bill Engel founded Symmetrical Resources after Birch Radio

closed. The quotation is from "Increasing Station Profits: The Solution May Lie in the Tools You Use" in *Radio Ink*, November 30, 1992.

21 RetailDirect and RetailDirect Lite were described online at Arbitron's Web site. There's more about RetailDirect Lite in the Chapter 7 discussion of selling cable.

22 "A Beginner's Guide to Demographics" by Berna Miller appeared in *Marketing Tools*, October, 1995.

23 Joseph Turow's work was cited at the beginning of these chapter notes.

24 In addition to Michael Weiss' *The Clustering of America*, the discussion of ZIP codes owes credit to TransAmerica Marketing and to Ellyn Ambrose, who offered insights on mapping. Weiss's book is no longer in print.

25 The VALS™ Segmentation System information was supplied by SRI Consulting, which originated and perfected VALS. SRI asked to see the copy for this section and offered a few pointers, all of which enhanced the understanding of the material and did not impose anything I wouldn't have said myself.

26 BRC to EMRC to MRC: For early history, I relied on Jim Fletcher's book, cited previously, and on a news release from the newly renamed organization, "EMRC Is Now the Media Ratings Council (MRC)," October 23, 1997.

27 Advertising Research Foundation information was supplied to me by ARF.

Taking It Further

Here are a few Web sites that relate to this chapter and additional reading not included in the Chapter Notes.

future.sri.com/vals/valsindex.html—SRI Consulting, the people who developed VALS™

www.arbitron.com—Arbitron for Radio, Scarborough Qualitative, RetailDirect

www.ipro.com—Auditing services for Internet advertisers

www.nielsenmedia.com—Nielsen Media Research

Additional Reading

Advertising Research Foundation. *Understanding Copy Pretesting*. New York: ARF, 1994.

Alreck, Pamela L., and Robert B. Settle. *The Survey Research Handbook: Guidelines and Strategies for Conducting a Survey*, 2nd ed. Homewood, IL: Irwin Professional Publishing, 1995.

Beville, Hugh Malcolm. *Audience Ratings: Radio, Television and Cable*. Mahwah, NJ: Lawrence Erlbaum Associates, 1988.

Fletcher, James E. *Profiting from Radio Ratings: A Manual for Radio Managers, Sales Managers, and Programmers*. Washington, D.C.: National Association of Broadcasters, 1989.

Piirto, Rebecca. *Beyond Mind Games: The Marketing Power of Psychographics*. Ithaca, NY: American Demographics Books, 1991.

Pope, Jeffrey L. *Practical Marketing Research*. 2nd ed. New York: AMACOM, 1993.

4

Sales Management

The organizational structure of the specific sales department you'll work in is difficult to predict. The number of employees and the support level of any sales department is influenced by market size and by the volume of sales dollars that the organization generates. For instance, you'll find that some large-market television stations have a director of sales, a general sales manager, a local sales manager, a national sales manager, a retail sales manager, a co-op manager or coordinator, a research director, a sales staff of 15 or more employees, an army of sales assistants, and a traffic director.

On the other hand, in a small-market, owner-operated radio station, you might see the owner doing double- or triple-duty as general manager, sales manager, and seller, with three or four salespeople making calls to direct clients. Another radio station in that same market might be operated as part of a consolidated cluster, with a director of sales and a few individual sales managers for each of five or more stations.

A non-network UHF TV station in a large market may have a compact, modest sales operation, calling on direct customers much as a local radio station does.

Regardless of medium and market size, the key functions of the sales department are the same:

- Selling time to advertisers
- Delivering a targeted audience to advertisers at a competitive cost
- Developing promotions for advertisers
- Generating revenues for the company to operate competitively in its market
- Generating a profit for the company
- Adding to the asset value of the operation by maintaining advertiser support

The sales department and its management, therefore, are essential to the organization. In radio and television stations, the sales department provides most, if not all, of the revenues. At a local cable system, subscriptions are the largest share of revenues, but the contribution of the advertising sales departments is growing. Advertising is the primary source of revenue for some new media operations. For others, electronic commerce is the main source, and banner advertising is an additional revenue stream. Effective leadership of the sales department maximizes both revenues and profits. The director of sales (DOS) is a job function at the largest organizations, such as large-market television stations or clusters of multiple radio stations under one ownership. Most often, the director of sales coordinates the efforts of a group of sales managers. At television stations, there are so many layers of sales administration that the DOS provides to the company the sales overview it needs, while freeing the general manager from close scrutiny of day-to-day selling efforts.

The DOS for a radio cluster makes projections of market conditions and balances the selling efforts among the stations to make sure that each station maximizes revenue for the good of the entire group. A director of sales in the radio sector often reports to the president of the company or to a divisional vice president rather than to the local general manager.

If there is no a director of sales, then typically the general sales manager (GSM) is at the top of the department's chain of command. To be effective, the GSM must have a complete understanding of the ownership and management of the media outlet, of the marketplace and its competitive environment, of programming and the audience it reaches, of sales management techniques, and of the sales staff as individuals and as a team. The GSM's duties include:

- Answering to the general manager of the operation
- Organizing the sales department and setting departmental policies and strategies
- Recruiting, interviewing, selecting, and hiring sales staff
- Leading and managing the sales staff
- Preparing the sales budget
- Developing the rate card
- Controlling advertising inventory
- Coordinating with the business department on collections, credit checks on prospective clients, and processing delinquent accounts
- Developing the compensation plan for the sales staff
- Providing continued training and skills development for members of the sales staff
- Matching salespeople to accounts for maximum return
- Setting monthly, quarterly, and annual billing goals
- Monitoring and measuring the staff's achievement of the sales goals

- Conducting regular sales staff meetings[1]

The national sales manager (NSM) answers to the GSM. This job requires coordinating the sale of time to national and regional advertisers through the station's national representative (rep) firm. The NSM maintains contacts with local offices of regional and national accounts. In the larger markets, the NSM travels to cities where major agencies are located and makes calls with a seller from the rep firm.[2]

According to *The Small Market Television Manager's Guide II*, the key character traits for a successful NSM are adaptability, resourcefulness, tenacity, and a knack for problem-solving. The NSM is often called on to motivate the national rep firm to aggressively sell spot advertising on the local medium. (More on national representatives is discussed later in this chapter.)

The local sales manager (LSM) also reports to the GSM. As you can tell from the title, the job is primarily planning and administering local sales activities. The LSM has more hands-on supervision of salespeople and performs such tasks as assigning lists to the sellers, establishing sales quotas, and, in some outlets, carrying a client list and making sales calls.

Some sales organizations also have a co-op coordinator. Manufacturers often establish programs that reimburse retailers for all or part of advertising schedules that promote the manufacturer's products. That system is called cooperative advertising, or co-op. The co-op coordinator's job is to provide information to salespeople about the co-op advertising opportunities that may be available to their clients. In order to be reimbursed, the retailer must be able to be prove that the advertising actually ran, so the co-op coordinator also coordinates the paperwork for the retailer.

Thanks to efforts by TVB, RAB, and CAB to uncover cooperative advertising opportunities for their members, the co-op coordinator position has been implemented in many markets. (We discuss co-op advertising more in Chapter 5, including an outline of the co-op coordinator's job.)

Sharpening the Edge

To increase sales, increase the sales staff. That was the rule some years ago, before media multiplied and advertising revenues were divided into ever smaller pieces.

Television sales trainer Pat Shaughnessy calculates that between 1980 and 1992 at least one million additional 30-second commercial units became available for sale in most markets because of new radio, television, and cable outlets. As Shaughnessy says, "Just adding two more warm bodies to the local sales staff won't cut it anymore, because television sales departments are finding that it's taking a sales job to get the business rather than a schmooze job."

Writing in *The Small Market Television Manager's Guide II*, Shaughnessy urges training programs. Coming from a sales trainer, that advice may sound self-serving, but it is not. "The more your AEs know, the more intelligently they will speak and stand out in the crowd," he says. He is so right. The environment you've been reading about in this book demands top-quality sellers who keep up-to-date on their own industries and on the customer's business. Even the very best skills can be sharpened further.

Your first month or two at a new job may include a schedule of viewing video tapes and listening to audio tapes about selling. You'll review the basics, such as you've learned in this book, and you'll learn about the specifics of the medium you're selling.

Depending on the company you're working for, you'll study information either from an industry organization like TVB, RAB, or CAB or from a sales trainer with a structured program of specific learning goals. You may be lucky enough to be exposed to both.

Here are the types of things you might be tested on in the early weeks of your first sales position:

- Demonstrate the ability to start, stop, and revise a complicated order.
- Discuss the theory of positioning.

- Know what key pieces of information should be collected from every client.
- Demonstrate the ability to work with a rate card.
- Name the competitive media specifically, including call letters (if they apply) and key personalities, features, or programs.
- Know the population of the market, the three largest employers, and other economic factors.
- Demonstrate the ability to get an appointment by telephone.
- Show an understanding of the jargon of your medium and of key retail categories.[3]

Sales trainer Chris Lytle suggests dividing the first month of work for a new salesperson this way:

	Training	Selling
Week 1	95%	5%
Week 2	75%	25%
Week 3	50%	50%
Week 4	25%	75%

Training is not just for newcomers, however. Think of the most successful people in any field: dancers and singers rehearse constantly; baseball's best long-ball hitters take batting practice every day; a football player's life during the fall alternates between blocking exercises and viewing last week's game films.

In *High Performance Selling*, Ken Greenwood reports that 200 top-producing salespeople were asked what skills they wanted to enhance. Listening was at the top of the list, he says, followed by people skills, questioning skills, presentation, handling objections, closing, and post-sales implementation and service. "Years ago, that list was very different. Handling objections was the number-one request in a sales seminar, with closing skills following close behind," Greenwood says. That shift in priorities is an indication of how selling has changed and how much the need for training has increased.

Training and upgrade programs exist for sellers at every level of experience, income, and competence. There are also training services that help a staff develop new business, exploit promotional opportunities, or prepare for calls on categories of advertisers. Others focus on time management, selling ratings, negotiation, and so forth.

Sales trainers tend to attach acronyms and other mnemonic devices to their systems to make them easier to remember and understand. Here are some examples.

The SEES Formula. The letters SEES stand for Situation, Exploration, Explicit, and Summary. Ken Greenwood uses this formula as the basis of his Greenwood Performance System:

What's the selling *situation*?

Can I *explore* for complete information?

Yes, if I ask *explicit* questions.

Then I *summarize* for agreement and a close.

The PAPA Presentation. David Ogilvy originally used this idea for writing copy, and Ken Greenwood applies the idea to creating sales presentations. The letters PAPA stand for Promise, Amplification, Proof, and Action.[4]

Promise: This is how our proposal will solve the problem you outlined.

Amplification: Here's how the solution in my proposal will work for you.

Proof: This is why I'm so sure it will work.

Action: Would you agree?

The SKOAPP System. For years, students in media selling courses at the college level have been quizzed on those six letters, which represent Skills, Knowledge, Opportunities, Attitude, Preparation, and Persistence.[5] The University of Missouri's

Charles Warner says:
"S × K × O × A × P × P = Success."

Training Organizations

Well-known trainers in radio selling include Jim Taszarek's TazMedia, The Chris Lytle Organization, Norm Goldsmith, Dave Gifford, Irwin Pollack, and Roy Williams, among others. Pam Lontos began in radio and expanded to selling in general.

The Center for Sales Strategy began as an adjunct to New City Communications, a broadcast station owner. CSS President Steve Marx began as a radio programmer and later became a general manager for New City. (Marx developed Optimum Effective Scheduling for radio sellers. We discuss OES in Chapter 8.) As he and his staff trained sellers for New City's properties, other companies discovered they, too, needed the same services. In fact, when television sellers felt the pinch of new competition, they hired CSS to train their staffs in the customer-focus that Steve had taught to radio sellers over the years.

Pat Shaughnessy's AVI Communications should also be added to the list. AVI markets its Television Sales Training System with two courses, one for veteran salespeople and one for rookies.

The Antonelli Media Training Center mentioned in Chapter 2 is another resource for sharpening the edge, especially for TV sellers.

Wilson Learning, also discussed in Chapter 2, belongs on this list of trainers. They provide Social Styles workshops to improve interpersonal relationships in addition to training in negotiation and selling styles.

A few workshops outside electronic media are applicable here as well, including Tom Hopkins' Champions, Zig Ziglar's Top Performance, and the classic sales training from Dale Carnegie. They're all valuable investments for sellers at any level.

Remember the adage: No train, no gain.

Team Selling

Team selling became popular (if not downright fashionable) in the mid-1990s because of the intensification of selling efforts at all electronic media outlets. Team selling in some form has existed for quite a while, however. For instance, a salesperson is accompanied on a call by a sales manager, the general manager, or member of the creative staff. Pairing the seller with the GM or GSM adds clout to the call. It's especially effective if either of the managers has a relationship with the client and the salesperson doesn't. Another effective team-selling strategy is involving a writer, producer, or air personality on a call, which allows the client to see the depth of your operation's skills and resources. Outlets with co-op coordinators often pair a seller with the co-op specialist, which also shows the client that you'll work hard to get the money needed to cover a schedule.

When a rookie joins a sales staff, an experienced seller might be paired with the newcomer to create a team for a limited time. This approach is an effective way of letting the new seller experience by observation.

The new and fashionable sales teams are combinations of opposite, but compatible, strengths: the flashy seller paired with the buttoned-down pragmatist; the free-wheeling type with the cautious; the detail person with the creative; a young person with an older person; starters with closers.

Mark McCormack recommends team selling in *McCormack on Selling*: "It's like managing a baseball team. You don't get rid of a starting pitcher who can give you only seven good innings each time out. You find a relief pitcher who can shut batters down for the other two innings. Neither pitcher is very good alone. But together they achieve the desired result: You win."

Michael Carter, general manager of KPRT and KPRS radio stations in Kansas City, offered *Radio Ink* magazine a caution about team selling: "Don't surprise the client. If you are planning a team sales effort, let the client know so that when you show up as a team they won't feel intimidated."

Hal Smith, general manager of KSYG in Little Rock, offered advice in the same article from his earlier experience: "For any team sales call to be effective, there must be a purpose and plan. If the rep cannot answer the question, 'Why is this person with me?' or if both members of the team do not know their roles, then you will have an ineffective sales call that could cost the station a sale."[6]

The dearth of qualified sales personnel prompted some outlets to create teams of experienced sellers who don't want to work full-time. Job-sharing sales teams sell as one, but split the workload and the commissions. Ann Sedita and Carlene Swensson of KLIF-AM in Dallas are examples of how this concept works.[7] Each had been a successful sales representative for Dallas radio stations, and each had left a job to spend time with her family, but they both missed the business. Their solution was to pitch themselves as a job-sharing sales team to area radio stations. KLIF's General Manager, Dan Bennett, agreed to try the idea. Within three years, the cubicle that Sedita and Swensson shared at KLIF was lined with sales awards and plaques. "Would you rather have a full-time mediocre sales person or Ann and Carlene, who set records sharing a job?" asks Bennett. His choice was obvious.

The challenge was to make the arrangement seamless for KLIF clients. Sedita and Swensson had one business card with both names but one phone number and one fax number. They also shared voice mail. Swensson worked the first three days of the week and Sedita the last three. On Wednesdays, they scheduled new business calls so they could meet with prospects together. Swensson said she had to learn not to overwhelm Sedita the moment they were together on Wednesdays.

Both women told the *Dallas Morning News* that a key factor in their job sharing is also sharing a similar work ethic. They believe their individual strengths are different: Sedita is best at customer strategy, Swensson at creativity. As a KLIF client put it, "One'll pitch the ball, and one'll shag the fly."

Sales Meetings

Early in my career, I hated meetings. The more experience I gained, the more I realized it wasn't actually meetings I hated, it was *bad* meetings. I had attended too many unnecessary gatherings called by pompous, attention-hungry grandstanders who were nothing more than energy vampircs, sucking the life and enthusiasm out of anybody in attendance. When I had the opportunity to attend well-planned, agenda-driven, action-oriented meetings, I realized that meetings could be good experiences. I had confused the problems from bad meetings with the meeting process itself.

Statistically, television and radio salespeople are either in favor of sales meetings or are neutral toward them. A cooperative study by RAB and TVB showed that only 16% of radio sellers in markets 1–99 and 20% of television sellers in the same size markets did not like meetings.[8] Those who liked the meetings did so because they discussed sales strategy, had an opportunity to learn, and kept the sales staff united. The people who were not in favor of meetings felt their sessions went on too long, were not focused, and dealt with things that should be handled in individual meetings.

RAB's George Hyde says that lack of preparation by the sales manager was the leading complaint he heard from sellers at radio stations.[9] What can sales managers do? "Just because it's Monday at 8 o'clock, don't have a sales meeting. And before you even come to the idea of scheduling a departmental sales meeting, think about what you are trying to communicate." In other words, always have a purpose for the meeting. State it clearly, and post it on a white board or a flip chart in the meeting room: "This meeting is to discuss structure for selling the Business-to-Business Expo and to create sales packages."

The best meetings have a written agenda, because that shows there has been some thought given to the purpose of the session. Time management materials from the Charles R. Hobbs Corporation use the word "visible" when suggesting a written agenda. Making sure every participant *sees* the agenda makes the meeting more productive because they know what to expect and how to contribute.[10]

The Hobbs Corporation also suggests telling attendees not only when the meeting will start but also when it will end. Of course, that recommendation includes starting and ending on time, or even ending early. Another tip from Hobbs: "Hold meetings standing up to keep them short."

I witnessed first-hand the power of a well-organized and focused meeting when visiting one of my clients, KFRG in the Riverside–San Bernardino market in Southern California. This station traditionally brought clients into the sales department meeting so K-Frog sellers could learn more about the industries they sold. I remember being at the station at the end of a presentation by an Internet provider. The salespeople came out of the conference room energized because they had a new understanding of the mysteries of cyberspace. They were each trying to outdo the other with the new jargon they had learned in the meeting.

Here are some other ways to make sales meetings more meaningful:

1. To prevent your listeners and viewers from being seen as statistics in a cost-per-point equation, bring items that might be in a typical home: a bedside clock, for example. Have the sales staff tell the story of how that listener or viewer uses the clock so everyone can create the visualization of a real person, not just ratings numbers.

2. Ask a former salesperson from a competing medium to address the staff and tell how they sell against your medium. For example, if you're in cable, find out what the radio seller says to combat similar rates. Also, newspaper salespeople usually have a lot to say.

3. Bring people from other departments into the sales meeting to talk about what they do and how they contribute to the overall operation.

4. Sales departments often role-play to prepare for face-to-face meetings. Similarly, you can add a session of listening to telephone pitches so each seller can critique and be critiqued.

Compensation Plans

Selling has the rewards of the hunt (prospecting and closing) and also the reward of financial payoff. It's common to find sellers who are the highest-paid employees in their companies. After the major acting stars of network programming, sellers command the biggest paychecks. At local radio and cable operations, compensation for salespeople regularly outdistances that of the announce staff or technical staff.

The new environment of publicly traded media companies offers far more incentive than the "cottage industry" days just a few years ago. Consolidated broadcast companies and vertically integrated network operations are able to offer stock options, 401-K retirement plans, profit sharing, and other non-dollar motivators to their sales staff. While it is perfectly understandable that those benefits may be important to you, I want to focus on the direct rewards of selling—being paid for what you sell.

As a salesperson, you'll want at least enough money to enjoy a reasonable standard of living and a sense of security. Those needs will be balanced by those of your employer, who wants to keep you motivated to sell more, not to stop when your personal standard of living has been achieved. Therefore, incentives must be large enough to justify extra effort on your part.

You may find yourself wanting even more than a comfortable standard of living. Since electronic media sales is rife with stories of sellers who became wealthy, you may look at this field and want your part of the treasure. Your employer will attempt to balance that, too, making sure that incentive payments are in line with overall company expenditures.

Most of the world works on salary or hourly wages, but not salespeople. While there are sellers who receive only a salary, financial compensation for sales staffs usually includes some form of commission, usually a percentage of the amount sold.

Compensation strategies vary from company to company, and even from outlet to outlet within a company. Local market conditions are the most important factor in any compensation package. From market to market, you'll see differences, too.

The National Association of Broadcasters (NAB) reported "literally hundreds of approaches sales managers currently use to pay their sales persons and sales department support staffs" in a survey of radio stations released in 1994, *Successful Radio Compensation Strategies.*[11] Changes in the radio environment since then have likely added hundreds more. Add to that the sales operations of local television stations, national networks, and cable systems, and you have an unfathomable number of combinations. Putting aside the possible permutations, there are seven basic compensation methods.[12]

Salary Only

With a straight salary approach, the company assumes all the risk. The salesperson receives the same level of compensation whether he or she contributes to the company's business or not. Salary provides security but little incentive to produce additional sales. There's no "scoreboard" to track progress, and no ability to shape positive behavior.

Sellers on salary are generally excluded from being paid overtime. The Fair Labor Standards Act exempts employees if 80% of work time is "performed in soliciting sales or activities in conjunction with the sales function, such as writing sales reports," according to the NAB book, *The Small Market Television Manager's Guide II.*

Sales managers who do not service clients, co-op coordinators, and trainees are likely to be compensated on a straight salary basis. Few, if any, of the top sellers are paid only a salary.

Salary Plus Bonus

Another option is a salary combined with a bonus based on net revenues. Across all businesses, this is the most common compensation method, although not the most common in electronic media.

Salary plus bonus satisfies the salesperson's need for security while adding an incentive that rewards performance. It also accommodates lean selling times by allowing salespeople to live comfortably between heavy selling periods.

Straight Commission

With a straight commission, there are no guarantees! The salesperson assumes all the risk in this plan. The seller receives only commission and no other compensation. Straight commission can yield comparatively large paychecks, especially in the larger markets.

FIGURE 4–1
Single-rate commission plans are most often found in electronic media selling. Progressive-rate commissions are good motivators. Regressive rates are actually demotivators.
From *Successful Radio Compensation Strategies*, by Gerald Hartshorn. Reprinted with permission from NAB.

Typically there's one level of commission for selling a direct account and another for selling an account through an agency. Since standard agency commission is 15%, the reduced commission to the salesperson takes into consideration the lower net revenue.

Commission rates paid to sellers vary. Radio stations in smaller markets often pay 15%, although that number is not universal. Some organizations pay much less; large market television stations, for example, pay 1% to 3%. Some pay more, as much as 18% to 25%. There are almost as many percentage rates as there are media outlets selling advertising.

The advantages of the straight commission plan for the company are ease of administration and no fluctuation in percentages of sales costs because they are in direct proportion to revenues. The disadvantage to the company is that the straight commission plan does not help the company meet long-term strategic goals. Emphasis is placed instead on short-term billing. In some cases, salespeople sell as much inventory as they can for whatever price they can.

As you see in Figure 4–1, there are three types of commission: single, progressive, and regressive. Single commission pays a flat rate for all sales. Progressive plans allow the salesperson to earn more as he or she achieves higher sales numbers. Regressive commissions have lower rates as sellers make higher numbers.

Draw Against Commission

Draw against commission is the most popular pay plan at both radio and television stations. In this option, account executives establish their own minimum compensation, or draw, and receive that amount as long as their sales commissions meet the goal during the specified period, which is usually a week or a month. Commission is paid on all sales that exceed the draw. You might call this a loan against future sales.

Some media outlets provide a guaranteed draw, which means that compensation is paid even if the goal is not met. A

Commission Structure	Commission Rate	Strengths	Weaknesses
Single Rate	single rate for all sales	• easy to understand • easy to administer	• lacks motivational component for higher sales
Progressive	rate accelerates with higher thresholds rate reduces when goal is missed	• provides known, built-in motivation for higher sales • provides for performance-based commission rate	• thresholds can be set too high for motivation • somewhat harder to administer
Regressive	rate decreases with higher performance maximum income can be fixed	• allows for limits on commission paid	• lacks motivational component • unpopular with sales persons • requires careful administration

Comparison of Commission Rate Structures

guarantee usually remains in force for only a limited period, such as 3 or 6 months.

Salary Plus Commission

This plan provides some security for the seller and gives the company a chance to use the commission payments for motivation or reward. The average paycheck in this option is higher than in the salary-only option, but the ceiling is lower, which means that the salesperson will not get paid as much in the long run. That's good for the company because there's a cost savings.

CBS president and COO Mel Karmazin got the industry's attention when he was named to head the CBS-owned television stations. He immediately changed the compensation plan from salary plus commission to straight commission. "The reason to pay people a salary is to control the costs," he told *Broadcasting & Cable* magazine. He preferred that salespeople make "a ton of money at 3%" so the company would make "a zillion dollars at 97%."

Salary, Commission, and Bonus

This combination offers the security of a salary, the incentive of commission, and an extra motivation to reach some additional goal. Bonuses might be paid on attainment of a billing level over and above budget, on improved time management, on effective presentation writing, on the number of prospecting calls made, or on other, measurable criteria.

Some stations allow salespeople to name a skill they'd like to improve, and bonuses are tied directly to their improvement in that area. That allows each seller to develop in weak areas. Administration by the company is often difficult because each seller's situation and measurement criteria have to be defined explicitly and judged carefully.

Straight Commission with Bonus

This option is the same as the one above, but without the security of the regular salary. See Figure 4–2 for a comparison of

Comparison of Compensation Approach Characteristics with Typical Station Sales Positions

| Compensation Approach | Characteristics | | | Suitable for |
	Risk	Employee Security	Performance Motivation	
Straight Salary	Station	High	Low	Sales Researchers Sales Support Sales Trainees Jr. Account Executives
Straight Commission	Sales Person	Low	Very High	Experienced Account Executives Stations with limited sales support resources
Commission with Draw	Sales Person	Little	High	Experienced Account Executives Stations with limited sales support resources
Salary Plus Incentive	Shared by Station & Sales Person	Moderate	High	Experienced Account Executives Developing Account Executives Jr. Account Executives

FIGURE 4–2
An analysis of compensation plans from NAB's *Successful Radio Compensation Strategies*, by Gerald Hartshorn. Reprinted with permission.

a few of the more popular compensation plans.

Compensation Plan Objectives

Every compensation plan includes essential objectives, as outlined in a paper published by the University of Missouri's Charles Warner and James Spencer. A well-designed compensation system, they say, should include as many of these objectives as possible:

- Aid in meeting an organization's strategic objectives.
- Aid in communicating corporate goals, performance standards, and expectations.
- Tie compensation directly to current sales performance.
- Attract and hold good people.
- Keep salespeople's motivation high.
- Help in analyzing sales potential, planning account coverage, and allocating selling time.
- Be understood by salespeople.
- Be fair to employees.
- Be fair to the organization.
- Provide management control.

- Enhance teamwork and cooperative effort.

Notice that some of the basic compensation arrangements I outlined don't fulfill all the objectives.

In another study, Warner calls broadcasting "out of step with other industries" in terms of compensation.[13] His 1991 study of radio and television sales staffs reported that "approximately two-thirds of U.S. companies use a combination of salary and incentive compensation, which only 7% of radio stations and 13% of television stations do."

That study, funded by RAB and TVB, states that "the best performing companies always integrated the sales compensation plan with corporate goals and did not follow industry practices in designing and implementing their sales compensation plans. Also, the best performing compa-nies gave rewards that were based primarily on performance on desired sales activities rather than just on volume or total revenues, which straight commission systems do."

TV stations in the larger markets were more likely than smaller market stations to use payment systems other than straight commission. Warner suggests that radio, too, should look at more effective ways to pay sellers. Media broker Dick Chapin, of Chapin Enterprises in Lincoln, Nebraska, echoes that sentiment:

> Commission-based pay implies permission not to sell once commissions have satisfied financial goals. This explains why successful sellers "level out." The amount paid for sales is one thing, but the method of payment may be equally important. Worse, it signals that leadership doubts the product's value.[14]

New Approaches to Compensation

New compensation plans introduced since Telecom 96 use the basic approaches, but they show interesting mix-and-match combinations as well. Many add bonuses with one of two configurations: (1) the salesperson defines an area to work on, and a bonus plan is based on improvement measured by the sales manager, as defined in the salary-commission-bonus plan; (2) money is pooled so that all salespeople get a proportionate share if company goals are reached.

In the discussion of relationship management in Chapter 2, I describe a study conducted among Phoenix advertising buyers that examined all media sellers in the market, then focused on the staff of KMLE radio, which sponsored the study. The project did more than give KMLE input about servicing accounts. It also helped the station change its compensation plan.[15]

Donn Seidholz, then GSM for the station, posed the question, "How are you going to pay people to make decisions that are good for the customer if all they get paid on is what they put on the books? There may be situations where it's not in the client's best interest to take a particular order."

The result was that the station's salespeople began receiving 70% of their income up front with the understanding that to earn that 70% they must service their clients. The 70% was based on hitting budget figures, and the other 30% was paid as commission after the fact.

The 70/30 plan is based on techniques taught by Don Beveridge, a former Mobil Oil executive who worked as a sales trainer with New City Communications and the Katz rep firm. Beveridge applied his observations from Mobil and other Fortune 500 companies to broadcast sales.

Here are some other ideas that mix and match compensation styles.[16]

Incremental Performance Payoff. The baseline commission is 8%, beginning in the first month of the company's fiscal year. If the seller makes quota, the commission goes to 9% the second month, 10% the third, and so on. If the seller does not make the quota during a given month, then the commission goes back to 8% and starts again.

New Account Bonuses. The first new account of the month earns a $20 bonus, the second earns $40, the third $60, the fourth $80. Anything after the fourth new account nets $100.

Raise the Rate. This option raises not the open rate, but the lowest rate on the rate card. That means the "average" rate goes up without the sticker shock of a higher open rate.

Customer Retention Bonuses. "The most important customer is the customer we have on now," says Bruce Walden of LBJ-S, in Austin, Texas. (That's the radio and television company formed by President Lyndon Baines Johnson, hence the initials LBJ.) His company's compensation plan includes rewards for renewals.

Other Bonuses. This option includes bonuses to be paid on a variety of items, including collections, first-time calls (opportunity calls, not cold calls), the number of presentations made weekly, closing ratio, etc.

Incentive Pools

With an incentive pool, sellers are paid a base salary that may vary according to their experience, length of service, or other factors. The pool is the collected commissions for the entire team, combined so that each seller earns a share depending on his or her individual contributions.

Most operations that use the pool concept use factors other than billing to reward sellers. According to Charles Warner:

> Sales managers describe the behaviors for which they want to reward all members of the sales staff, and then they award pool shares based on performance on the listed behaviors, effort and activities. For example, a sales manager may want to reward salespeople for developing new business, getting high rates, and using qualitative research in written presentations. At the end of the month or quarter, the sales manager evaluates each salesperson's performance on the desired behaviors and gives the salesperson an appropriate share of the pool.

The pool concept rewards salespeople for selling the way the company wants them to sell and for reaching company goals, not individual goals. Thus, sellers are compensated for cooperation, not billing.

Incentive pools also reward nonsales personnel. Bruce Walden's system at LBJ-S provides a 2% reward when the team hits their goals. The traffic department, copywriters, and production department personnel all get a share. Walden told attendees at an RAB seminar that his staff thinks in terms of team first, "How do *we* get there? The group works together to cover for each other." If sales goals are exceeded by 5%, that's also shared with support staff.

The ideal compensation plan is one that rewards salespeople for achieving company objectives as well as individual goals. It's flexible enough to take into account individual differences among sellers on the same staff. The ideal plan is perceived to be ideal by the sales staff when they have input into the way the plan is formulated.

Sales Contests

Half of radio station managers interviewed by NAB said they used contests as part of their overall incentive plan. The larger the market, the more likely they were to use contests: up to 85% of stations in the top 20 markets.[17]

In the joint RAB-TVB study of sales departments, 66% of television sales departments reported using contests. Like radio, the figures were higher in the larger markets: 70% in markets 1–99 and 55% in markets 100 and smaller. The average number was two sales contests a year in large markets and three in smaller markets.

Using just a few contests a year makes them special and worth the competitive effort. Typically a sales contest might run from 4 to 6 weeks. Most don't last longer than a quarter because that makes them seem long-term, and they lose the urgency of the goals to be met.

"Contests are popular methods to temporarily increase new business development, build rates, sell promotional packages and remotes, and simply move more commercial units," according to *Successful Radio*

Compensation Strategies, the book that reported on the NAB survey.

Contests are short-term means of directing the efforts of the staff, increasing sales, and building morale. They provide little impact on long-term performance. For example, sales managers and directors of sales are warned not to expect contests to correct sales-force problems. (After all, that's what training is all about.)

According to the paper by Warner and Spencer that reported on the RAB-TVB study, "Salespeople like well-designed and well-administered contests and tend to view them as fun and extra motivators. (F)or contests to have any positive effect, they must be perceived to be fair (that everyone has an equal chance of winning) and should be based on some type of improvement goal, such as new business volume, rather than overall billing or revenue goals."

While not technically part of the compensation plan, some contest prizes are sufficient enough to augment compensation. Cash is not the most effective prize, because a cash prize has to be large enough to offset tax deductions; otherwise, the final check seems insignificant. The reward must be perceived by the participants as valuable enough to trigger positive response. Typical prizes other than cash are merchandise, travel rewards, and special recognition or privileges.

The greatest benefit of contesting among sellers is to make them feel like winners personally. They like to get recognition for good performance, and a contest makes the rewards instant and tangible. An engraved plaque is often more meaningful as a reward than cash or a prize that doesn't fit the winner's lifestyle or self-esteem. The best contests have prizes for everyone on the staff, from "grand prize" to consolation prizes.

Figure 4–3 shows the components of various compensation plans, including contests.

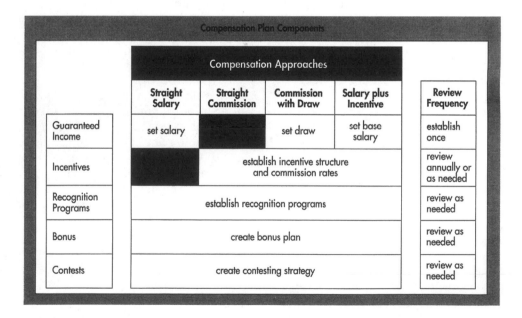

Compensation Plan Components					
	Compensation Approaches				Review Frequency
	Straight Salary	Straight Commission	Commission with Draw	Salary plus Incentive	
Guaranteed Income	set salary		set draw	set base salary	establish once
Incentives		establish incentive structure and commission rates			review annually or as needed
Recognition Programs	establish recognition programs				review as needed
Bonus	create bonus plan				review as needed
Contests	create contesting strategy				review as needed

FIGURE 4–3 The components of compensation plans and notes to the sales manager or sales director about approaches and timetables for review. From *Successful Radio Compensation Strategies*, by Gerald Hartshorn. Reprinted with permission from NAB.

Changing Plans

Some companies constantly modify their pay plans, looking for the right mix of incentive, motivation, and staff stability. NAB's *Successful Radio Compensation Strategies* offers advice:

> Before you create your station's pay plan, you will need to determine the plan's objectives in the form of a compensation strategy. You will need to ask yourself and answer questions such as, How much and what do we need to offer to attract the sales professionals who will benefit our station? What do we need to provide to keep the best sales professionals at our station? How much salary? What about incentives and perks?

Here are some reasons to examine or modify an existing plan:

- *To lower sales costs.* Some operations feel that the return on investment among sellers is not high enough, so the compensation plan is adjusted.
- *To keep from losing good people.* Good sellers are at a premium, and the best sellers are worth the most. Changing compensation plans prevents the top people from being lured away by other stations or other media.
- *To get rid of salespeople.* It sounds like a joke, but often a new owner or manager will alter the compensation package to see who's flexible, who's too comfortable, and who's going to be aligned with the new thinking.
- *To improve incentives.* Usually, plans are adjusted to keep the sellers motivated, to create incentives that prompt them to make more prospecting calls, and to sell more. Operations that aren't number one in the market often need to build incentives because rates are not high enough to be motivators on their own.
- *To stay competitive in the market.* Companies that pay too much find that more aggressive sales staffs hurt them in the marketplace. Those that pay too little find that their salespeople are lured away by competitors.

Billings Versus Collections

Commissions are sometimes paid on billings, that is, on orders written. Most often, however, commissions are paid on collections, so you don't receive your money until your company receives its money. By paying on collections, your organization takes the precaution that you don't sell advertising to an account that cannot pay the bills. (That's why checking credit and resources is so important in the qualifying phase of the sales process. See Chapter 2.)

On the other hand, paying on collections can be demoralizing to the salesperson. If you have to wait 45, 60, or 90 days to reap the rewards of your selling efforts, you might lose the incentive to sell more.

While it's better (for you the seller) to be paid on billings, that process requires an internal accounting system at your company. A strict tracking system must be in place to prevent salespeople from selling noncreditworthy accounts. Another concern is that payment on billings might tempt an unscrupulous seller to write bogus contracts to beef up compensation. If your employer decides to pay on billings and not on collections, you'll discover that someone in the organization is assigned to be intensely and aggressively vigilant to ensure that orders and contracts are both solicited and agreed on.[18]

Bogus contracts (sometimes called phantom contracts) create an ethical problem that is seldom talked about openly. Bogus contracting all too often happens when billing is the basis for compensation. The accountability systems that are required to combat the problem usually lead companies to pay on collections instead.

Beyond Money

The word "compensation" conjures visions of money, but sellers also seek rewards beyond financial remuneration. Approval, respect, and recognition are high on the list of employee hopes for any job. Salespeople seek even higher levels of recognition because they are so often put in situations of constant rejection. Sales managers and sales directors who reward individual achievement and who recognize both individual and team contributions help both their sellers and their organization.

When KVEN-AM and KHAY-FM in Ventura, California, were owned by NAB board member Bob Fox, the stations created a new car bonus for salespeople. Sellers who billed at a certain dollar level for three consecutive months received a company car. If they hit the next dollar plateau, a cellular phone was installed. Another incentive on the bonus schedule was Dale Carnegie-type career development courses. The station's goal was to attract top salespeople from other stations in Southern California, and they did.

A Marriott Hotels ad in *Selling Power* magazine emphasized motivation with non-dollar rewards: "People don't daydream about fancy pen sets or personalized luggage. But a vacation. That sets hearts and minds racing."

In the same issue (a special on sales motivation), Victoria's Secret placed an ad showing a model in a slinky black dress and offered "beautifully presented merchandise certificates" to use in sales incentive programs.

American Express Incentive Services suggested a bowling ball as motivation. "You don't think a new bowling ball could lead to inspiring work. Then you don't know Lisa in regional sales. But this ad isn't about bowling. It's about *choices*."[19]

Salespeople are individuals, so incentive and motivation plans should reflect that individuality.

Another important point about motivation is that those who respond to incentives like money, recognition, or hard goods must be self-motivated first, or there's no result. A sales staff that is unmotivated has either an attitude problem or a leadership problem, or both.

Master sales trainer Dave Gifford addressed that issue in an article in *The Radio Book*:

> Management can activate, not motivate, and management can change behavior, not attitudes. You have to hire attitudes. If you hire the right people in the first place, the argument as to whether or not you can motivate someone is moot.[20]

Marilyn Kushak, partner in WMAY, WNNS, and WQLZ radio stations in Springfield, Illinois, and the stations' vice president for sales and marketing, told attendees at a RAB meeting that her company uses job titles as motivation. A new seller is a "sales representative." If he or she reaches a certain dollar level in a year, the seller graduates to "account representative." The next step is "marketing representative," and finally, "senior marketing manager." Each level has its own base salary and bonus structure, creating a sense that, in Kushak's words, "It's not just a job, it's a career."[21]

TYPICAL INCENTIVES FOR SELLERS

Travel: Vacations, weekend getaways, ski trips

Automotive: Company car, discounted lease, gasoline allowances, oil changes, discounted auto insurance, a special parking spot identified with a sign, "Top Biller"

Entertainment: Dinners, club memberships, concerts, sporting events, theme park admission, a limo for a day

Personal: Child care, tuition, days off, a new briefcase

Home: Furnishings, home entertainment equipment, rent

Communications: Telephone and paging services, discounted long distance, cellular phone

Apparel: Clothing allowance, jewelry, accessories

Recognition: A champagne toast, a new job title, plaques and awards, a letter from the company president

Stock: A new addition to the list since only recently have major media companies become asset-rich entities

Cash: One size fits all!

Structuring Rates

We're lucky to be in the electronic media business, because our products are inexpensive to make. If you were selling any other product, pricing would be based on factors like cost of inventory and cost of production. The auto dealer, for example, estimates not only the cost per unit, but also the length of time the vehicle stays on the lot and the cost of delivery from the factory. The grocery store has to factor the cost of spoilage of fresh produce and meats. Retailers add costs of shoplifting.

For electronic media, once overhead costs are met—rent, salaries, and so forth—there's no additional cost for selling more advertising. Each dollar beyond overhead costs is profit. Since overhead costs can be kept stable, pricing can be projected from how much inventory is available to be sold. That's a good theory, but unlike the automobile or the fresh produce, a commercial message has no intrinsic value. As Charles Warner puts it, "It vanishes into thin air after 30 seconds. It is worth only what someone is willing to pay for it, and this willingness is guided by what alternative advertising opportunities are available and at what price."

It's our job as sellers to give the messages we sell their intrinsic value. To increase the worth of an advertisement, for instance, we must increase demand for the medium carrying the message. That's the easiest way to set pricing. When supplies are tight, prices go up. When supplies are plentiful, prices go down.

Again, that's a good theory. It works best in the general economy: when there's a shortage, somebody will simply produce more, and that ends the shortage. No automobiles? Ford increases production. A shortage of bread? A baker rushes to the rescue. The increase of supply eases demand and reduces prices again.

In electronic media, there's less flexibility in supply. You can back-order a sofa or a Ford, but you cannot buy time on yesterday's radio show or sponsor last night's online chat room. Furthermore, there are a finite number of TV and radio stations, and each has only 60 minutes to sell in the hour. Most of them set commercial limits that are much lower than that. It is virtually impossible for a broadcast outlet to increase the amount of time to sell the way newspapers and magazines increase their pages when advertising is heavy.

Digital delivery allows over-the-air television to expand the number of commercial units through multicasting. Cable systems increase the number of channels delivered. This expansion of inventory has the potential to inflate overall revenues by expanding the advertising base. Yet whether broadcast, multicast, or cablecast, the seller must wrestle with the length of the hour.

Inventory in electronic media can be compared to inventory in the airline industry. An airplane has a finite number of seats, and the airline wants each plane to leave the gate with a full load of passengers. That's why the best pricing is available on advance purchases. The later you buy your seat, the more it costs, even though the seat bought hours before the flight has no greater intrinsic value than the seat bought a month in advance.[22]

New media outlets are not so trapped by time and space as traditional electronic media. They are more like print in their ability to expand. Interactive media extends the advertising space available by using technology effectively, adding hyperlinks that extend their message-carrying ability.

Adding supply does not create demand by itself, even in the booming interactive media segment. Demand must be created through programming that attracts a large audience or by sellers who can demonstrate the effectiveness and value of a medium even if the audience is small. There's another problem with using supply and demand to establish rates in electronic media. Not every advertiser wants to buy at the time when supply is at its most flexible.

- Seasonal advertisers have seasonal sales patterns, and they plan their advertising accordingly. Land's End Direct Merchants, for example, focuses on Christmas with extra staff, extra phone personnel to take orders, and extra advertising.

- Auto dealers target end-of-model clearances and new model announcements in late summer and early fall.
- Florists are interested in Valentine's Day, Mother's Day, and prom time.
- Electronics retailers conduct inventory at the end of January and want excess merchandise out of the store before they have to count it.
- Local events like Minneapolis' Ice Festival, Sonoma County's Wine Harvest, or Houston's Livestock Show and Rodeo create retail and sponsorship opportunities for both advertisers and media outlets.[23]

The second and fourth quarters are the heaviest advertising periods. Various forms of media have traditionally attempted to attract advertisers in first and third quarters with lower rates, special packages, and other incentives to buy, like travel and contests. However, the majority of advertisers aren't moved by those tactics.

In January, television viewing levels are high, yet television advertising rates remain low. The product in electronic media is no different in January than it is in December. However, there is a preconditioned response in the media-buying community: "These are bad months for you guys, so we expect great deals."

The good news is at the other side of that equation: when advertising demand goes up, the rates also go up. That has not been a deterrent to advertisers. As demand squeezes inventory, even guidelines for efficiency like CPP and CPM are often discarded. Negotiating becomes a daily, almost hourly, affair to assure that advertisers get the access they need to the audiences they want.

There used to be a common complaint among broadcast sellers: the ratings leader was not the rate-card leader. The number-one outlet in town undercut rates just to get the buys. They fought for a big share of the buy, not a big share of the marketplace dollars. Salespeople from competing media would hear advertisers ask, "Why should I buy you at those rates when I can get number one for half that price?"

Consolidation of the radio industry helped. A company that owned several stations in one market could combine audiences to make a more effective buy for the advertisers. Demands for revenue increases by publicly held ownership motivated a number-one station to increase its rates to increase the company's asset value.

There are markets in which electronic media is traditionally underpriced, often suppressed by a dominant newspaper whose selling tactics undermine competitors. And there are still outlets that undervalue their commercial time in a scramble to pay off highly leveraged debt. They reduce costs for short-term gain instead of long-term value.

Just the opposite is true in some markets: certain stations or programs cost more because they always have. It happens most often in television where the station's community image creates higher value in the advertiser's mind. A radio station with a large at-work audience might command larger dollars for its midday programming than for the morning drive. A very popular radio morning show increases the value of the entire station. As another example, a well-respected news anchor raises the perception, and thus the value, of a TV station.

Revenue Projections

Commercial inventory exists to be sold. Unsold inventory is lost revenue, and that means lost forever. The NAB guide *Buying or Building a Broadcast Station* advises station owners to evaluate past, current, and projected rate-card pricing for network, national, and local commercials, then to review station logs for unsold and oversold areas[24]. That's how your sales manager or DOS will begin to structure the rates that you'll present to advertisers.

Here's a simple exercise to show how it's done.[25] Count the number of commercial messages you have available per hour. Multiply that figure by the number of effective hours of selling (18 hours a day for radio, for example). Then calculate the number of units in a week, then in a month, then in a year. Assume that every unit will not be sold, so apply a "sellout percentage" to the equation: 50% in this calculation to be conservative. To calculate the potential, multiply by the average rate for your medium, and you've got a revenue projection. For example:

14	commercials
× 18	hours
252	commercials per day
× 7	days per week
1,764	commercials per week
× 52	weeks per year
91,728	commercials per year
× .50	50% sellout
45,864	potential units sold
× $50	average rate of $50.00
$2,293,200	potential annual revenue

To increase revenues, you have two options: increase the sellout percentage or increase the average price per unit. If the sales director wants revenues to increase by 20% (from $2,293,200 to $2,751,840 annually), the sellout percentage has to increase to 60% or the average rate has to increase to $60.00.

It's possible to achieve a 70% sellout, and many calculations are based on that figure. (The RAB recommends using 70% as a standard to its members. Radio brokers calculate the value of radio properties using that number.) Here's the same math with a 70% sellout rate and no change in average rate:

14	commercials
× 18	hours
252	commercials per day
× 7	days per week
1,764	commercials per week
× 52	weeks per year
91,728	commercials per year
× .70	70% sellout
64,209	potential units sold
× $50	average rate of $50.00
$3,210,450	potential annual revenue

By selling 40% more commercials, you can increase the annual revenue projections accordingly.

Understand that a 100% sellout rate is a delusion. It will happen in certain periods of the year—May, for example, or around Christmas. Lean times in early January and those difficult-to-sell overnight periods prevent a 100% sellout. There's an axiom about being sold out: a 100% sellout situation means the rates are too low.

Figures 4–4 through 4–7 show a variety of quarterly reports that help you track sales and revenues.

The Rate Card

Commercial time is a perishable commodity. Yesterday is of no value to an advertiser. Once time has passed, it cannot be sold. In *Electronic Media Management*, Pringle, Starr, and McCavitt put it this way:

> This fact imposes on the sales department an obligation to manage its commercial inventory in such a way that it produces the maximum possible financial return.
>
> As a first step, the department must ensure that the rate is realistic, based on considerations such as the size or characteristics of the audience, market size, and competitive conditions. But inventory management also requires the development of

sales policies that will make time available and attractive to advertisers, and that will not result in audience tune-out.

The rate card describes pricing. Some say it sets the rate, but often the rate card simply suggests the opening rate for negotiation.[26]

Base rates depend on the size of the audience a program or medium will deliver. The bigger the audience, the higher the rates and the higher the demand on inventory. The higher the demand on inventory, the greater the sales organization's ability to increase rates. The average rate we saw in the pricing example is never shown on the rate card.

In most large-market radio stations and in all large-market television stations, rates are set by sales management on a daily, and sometimes hourly, basis. To stay up-to-the-minute, they use sophisticated software that counts "avails," which are sales

QUARTERLY PERFORMANCE REPORT

Sales Rep _____   Date ____/____/_____

Months: _____   _____   _____

Date Hired: ____/____/____

QUARTERLY TOTAL

	Budget	Actual	+ / -	%
Local Agency				
Local Direct				
TOTAL				

KEY RESULTS ACHIEVED

#		GOAL	ACTUAL	COMMENTS
1	Face to face sales calls			
2	Closing ratio: calls to closes			
3	Number of new business pitches			
	a) Agency			
	b) Direct			
4	Number of new business closes			
	a) Agency			
	b) Direct			
5	Quarterly AUR			

FIGURE 4–4 If I had said there would be paperwork, it might have scared you away! There will be some, but it's to your advantage to track your goals and your actual selling. "Budget" is sometimes called "goal" or "profit plan," depending on the company you work for. This report tracks results. Designed by Warren Wright of 21st Century Communications. Used with permission.

opportunities available at that moment. Pricing is based on demands on inventory and what the market will support. The goal is to maximize revenue, to ensure that salespeople get the best possible order for the best possible price.

The software creates an electronic rate card that may change by a dollar or two each time commercial inventory is sold or by larger amounts depending on days of the week. A commercial on Monday morning that runs between 6 and 10 a.m. on a popular radio station might cost $35. By Friday, demand on inventory could double or even triple the price of that same com-

QUARTERLY GAME PLAN - PAGE 2

Sales Rep _____   ___ Quarter, 199__   Date ___/___/___

SPECIFIC BUDGET GOALS

	Month #1	Month #2	Month# 3
Local Agency	$	$	$
Local Direct	$	$	$
TOTAL	$	$	$

	Month #1	Month #2	Month# 3
# of face to face calls			
New Business (# of accounts closed)			
New Business (Total $ closed)	$	$	$

Quarterly AUR	$	$	$

FIGURE 4–5 Some sales managers measure progress monthly. These forms are for quarterly use, but break out monthly increments. AUR means "average unit rate," an average of all the spots in your schedules, regardless of how expensive or cheap they are. Courtesy Warren Wright of 21st Century Communications.

QUARTERLY GAME PLAN - PAGE 3

Sales Rep _____   ____ Quarter, 199__   Date ___/___/___

MAJOR TARGETS & OPPORTUNITIES

VIP's TO WIN OVER

TO GROW PROFESSIONALLY

PROBLEMS TO RESOLVE

FIGURE 4–6 On this tracking sheet you have to be brutally honest with yourself. No dreaming or hoping allowed. The "Targets & Opportunities" may be new businesses opening in the area, seasonal buys, or projections toward next Christmas. From that, you plot whom you have to win. Then the tough part: how to grow *you*. Courtesy Warren Wright, 21st Century Communications.

QUARTERLY GAME PLAN - PAGE 4

Sales Rep _____   _____ Quarter, 199__   Date ___/___/___

1st; 2nd; 3rd; 4th (Circle one) **FORECAST WORKSHEET**

Client	Agency	Year			
		Actual 95			
		Projected 96			
		Actual 95			
		Projected 96			
		Actual 95			
		Projected 96			
		Actual 95			
		Projected 96			
		Actual 95			
		Projected 96			
		Actual 95			
		Projected 96			
		Actual 95			
		Projected 96			
		Actual 95			
		Projected 96			
		Actual 95			
		Projected 96			
		Actual 95			
		Projected 96			

Pg. Total Actual				
Page Total Proj.				

TOTAL (All pgs.)				
Proj TOTAL (of all pgs.)				

FIGURE 4–7 This form is designed to show the differences between one year's results and the next year's possibilities. Collect all your selling results for the previous year and put them in the "actual" blanks, then show what you project for the new year. Courtesy Warren Wright, 21st Century Communications.

mercial. But Saturday morning's rate might be only $10 because of lower demand.

Grid cards are written versions of the rate fluctuations found in the electronic cards created by software systems. Grid cards are inventory-sensitive, according to Michael Keith, writing in *Selling Radio Direct*:

This gives stations a considerable degree of rate flexibility. For example, if a station has five rate-level grids, it may have a range of between $20 and $50 for a 60-second spot.

Clients would then be given rates at the lower grid if the station had few sponsors on the air, thus creating many availabilities. As business increased at the station and availabilities became scarcer, the station would then ask for rates reflected in the upper grids. Gridding is based upon the age-old concept of supply and demand. When availabilities are tight, airtime is at a premium; it costs more.[27]

Figures 4–8 and 4–9 show two approaches to a rate plan.

TV LAND
FOURTH QUARTER 1997 / FIRST 1998
PLANNING COSTS
AD18-49

QUARTER	SUB BASE (000)	PROGRAMMING	DAY/TIME	HH (000)	AD18-49 VPVH	A18-49 (000)	A18-49 CPM	:30 UNIT RATE
4Q 97	21,000	ROS	6A-3P	67	0.687	46	$5.11	$235
		ROS	3P-3A	105	0.695	73	$7.19	$525
		ROS	3A-6A	55	0.782	43	$3.26	$140
1Q 98	25,000	ROS	6A-3P	80	0.688	55	$5.09	$280
		ROS	3P-3A	125	0.696	87	$7.18	$625
		ROS	3A-6A	66	0.788	52	$3.17	$165

RATES AND RATINGS VALID FOR 10 BUSINESS DAYS
PREPARED FOR ED SHANE
SHANE MEDIA SERVICES
2450 FONDREN RD
SUITE 112
HOUSTON, TEXAS 77063
713-952-9221 PH
713-952-1207 FAX
9/30/97

3:52 PM[Date],NI41PC.XLS

FIGURE 4–8 Printed rate cards gave way to specific rate plans generated by computers that study ratings and availabilities. Nickelodeon Sales Planner Ted Kerley assembled this plan, targeting adults 18–49 on Nickelodeon's TV Land network. Used with permission from MTV Networks.

Local cable and radio sellers will encounter the letters AUR, the average unit rate. A high-dollar sponsorship, such as commercials during ESPN's Sunday Night NFL games, might be combined with commercials in the early-morning repeat of "SportsCenter" to make the rates more favorable. The high rate for NFL plus the low rate for "SportsCenter," when divided by the number of commercials bought, yields the average unit rate.

Radio salespeople package a few spots in morning drive with a few spots in the evenings to create a favorable average rate for the client. If a spot in the morning show costs $250 and a spot at night costs $50, the AUR is $150 if one spot is bought in each daypart.

To bring the AUR down, increase the number of the lower-priced commercial. Five spots in the morning show at the $250 rate and ten spots at night at the $50 rate:

$$\begin{array}{rcl} \$250 \times 5 &=& \$1,250 \\ \$\ 50 \times 10 &=& \$\ 500 \\ \hline 15 && \$1,750 \end{array}$$

Divide $1,750 by 15 spots for an AUR of $116.67.

One strategy for increasing revenues is raising the AUR across the board. Find your lowest-price advertisers and create a pro-

SHANE MEDIA SERVICES
AND
NICKELODEON
4TH QTR 1997 PLANNING COSTS

QUARTER	ROTATION	NAT'L HH RTG	HH (000)	K6-11 (000)	NAT'L K6-11 RTG.	:30 UNIT COST	HH CPM	HH CPP	K6-11 CPM	K6-11 CPP
4TH '97	M-F 6A-9A	0.74	721	324	1.40	$13,425	$18.62	$18,122	$41.44	$9,595
	M-F 9A-2P	1.27	1232	329	1.42	$29,525	$23.97	$23,324	$89.74	$20,781
	M-F 2P-8P	1.67	1621	890	3.84	$37,875	$23.37	$22,740	$42.56	$9,855
	S/S 6A-8P	1.42	1384	762	3.29	$29,325	$21.19	$20,621	$38.48	$8,912
	PREMIUM	2.03	1975	1,180	5.10	$66,000	$33.42	$32,523	$55.93	$12,952
	SNICK	1.89	1838	1,233	5.32	$100,000	$54.41	$52,950	$81.10	$18,781
	PRIME	1.92	1868	1,308	5.65	$125,000	$66.92	$65,125	$95.57	$22,130

Nickelodeon Scatter is not guaranteed.
RATES AND RATINGS VALID FOR 10 BUSINESS DAYS

PREPARED FOR ED SHANE
SHANE MEDIA SERVICES
2450 FONDREN RD
SUITE 112   .
HOUSTON, TEXAS 77063
713-952-9221 PH
713-952-1207 FAX
9/30/97

9/30/97 3:50 PM NI41PC.XLS

FIGURE 4–9 Contrast the TV Land plan in Figure 4–8 with this rate plan from Nickelodeon's main network. Unit costs are higher because of a larger household count, a ratings profile, and the highly desirable K6–11 group, children. Used with permission from MTV Networks.

gram of easy-to-swallow rate increases over a year. Raise each a small percentage each quarter (with higher increases in the second and fourth quarters, and less in the first and third), and the average rates go up.

Inventory Management

If I keep saying that commercials are perishable and that inventory in electronic media exists to be sold, I'm being redundant on purpose. Since unsold inventory is lost forever, sellers and sales managers work hard to make sure that every avail is sold at the best price possible.

As you've seen already, maintaining revenue is a product of assessing and understanding demand. Maximizing revenue requires an additional step: manipulating supply in order to increase demand.

Managing inventory is a volatile process. As I said earlier, a 100% sellout situation usually says that rates are too low and that the outlet hasn't maximized inventory. Inventory management is more critical in television than in radio or in local cable. TV time is generally bought in narrow dayparts or specific programs. Miss a spot in the morning, and you can't make it up the next hour because of differences in target viewers for each show. In addition, the windows are fewer. Network avails change the local station's options. Television, therefore, requires more complex inventory management systems and extremely careful planning.

At local cable systems there are the same constraints on local avails because of network scheduling. Some desirable networks have no local selling opportunities (Country Music Television and American Movie Classics, for example). Many local systems rotate commercials among all the advertiser-supported channels.

Co-owned radio stations that are sold together can manage inventory effectively by packaging the inventory of all the stations in the local cluster. The leading rock station might want to preserve its high-price, high-demand inventory and let a less popular station in the cluster absorb commercials at a cheaper cost. The result is a greater share of the buy with no concessions from the powerhouse leader. The director of sales controls the packaging.

TEN RULES FOR RAISING RATES

1. Everybody understands the law of supply and demand. Climbing rates means that the medium is healthy and sought after. The advertising works. Business people must perceive that it has value.

2. Ease your good customers into it. The next order is at the current rate, but the one after that will be at a higher rate.

3. For a smaller advertiser, stair-step the increases over a mutually agreed upon period of time, like 6 months.

4. For the advertiser who's "always been with you," make the concession that "you'll be the last to be raised."

5. Don't raise all the rates at once.

6. Don't raise rates for every customer at the same time. Start with the lowest, least profitable list. If you lose them, you don't lose much.

7. If you can't raise the rate, raise the conditions. Hold the advertiser's lower rate if it's combined with other buys.

8. Make rate increases understood as part of the client relationship. Become such a resource that the client wouldn't dream of going elsewhere.

9. Make the client think you're the source of unique marketing ideas.

10. Don't even think about the B-word (bonus).

Adapted from Jim Taszarek's *Large Market Radio Selling.*[28]

In Chapter 8's discussion of selling radio, you'll learn about Optimum Effective Scheduling (OES), a formula for controlling inventory in radio while maximizing revenues.

Dayparts

Broadcast outlets divide their days into segments roughly defined by the amount of viewership or listenership at that time of day, thus the term "daypart."[29] Advertising rates for each daypart reflect the differences in the available audience. Scheduling strategies differ for the same reason.

It costs more for a commercial in television's prime time than it does for late fringe or overnights. Morning drive is radio's prime time, followed by afternoon drive at most stations. Those dayparts costs more than middays or nights at the typical station.

Television dayparts are more narrowly defined than radio dayparts and offer more strategic placement of commercials because of the differences from program to program:

> Early morning: 6 a.m. to 9 a.m.
>
> Morning: 9 a.m. to noon
>
> Afternoon: noon to 4 p.m.
>
> Early fringe: 4 p.m. to 6 p.m.
>
> Early evening: 6 p.m. to 7 p.m.
>
> Prime access: 7 p.m. to 8 p.m.
>
> Prime time: 8 p.m. to 11 p.m.
>
> Late fringe: 11 p.m. to 11:30 p.m.
>
> Late night: 11:30 p.m. to 2 a.m.
>
> Overnight: 2 a.m. to 6 a.m.

These times are Eastern Standard Times. Prime access, prime time, and late fringe are adjusted by one hour in the Central and Mountain Time Zones. You can find an expanded analysis of television dayparts, including available audiences and programming strategies, in Chapter 6.

In comparison to TV, radio dayparts are simple. Here are the configurations used by Arbitron in reporting listening:

> Morning drive: 6 a.m. to 10 a.m.
>
> Midday: 10 a.m. to 3 p.m.
>
> Afternoon drive: 3 p.m. to 7 p.m.
>
> Evening: 7 p.m. to midnight
>
> Overnight: midnight to 6 a.m.

(Radio dayparts are expressed in local time.)

In addition to that segmentation, stations tend to create their own dayparts based on market conditions or other factors:

- In large cities with sprawling freeways (Los Angeles and Houston, for example) afternoon drive might be extended to 8 p.m. by stations that know they can reach listeners in their cars.
- Towns with early-rising commuters prompt stations to begin morning drive as early as 5 a.m. The stations often begin their morning shows that early and begin premium rates at that hour.
- Music stations with large at-work audiences might structure dayparts around those listeners, creating an 8 a.m. to 5 p.m. workday daypart.
- Using electronic versions of the Arbitron ratings information, talk stations can create 2- or 3-hour dayparts that reflect a specific talk show.

Figure 4–10 shows a screen from a software program that helps stations to create dayparts.

FIGURE 4–10
If standard dayparts don't work for your client, create your own with software that reads your medium's ratings information. Arbitron's Maximi$er will calculate average quarter hour ratings for any sequence of hours, demos, or geographic areas.
Courtesy the Arbitron Company. Used with permission.

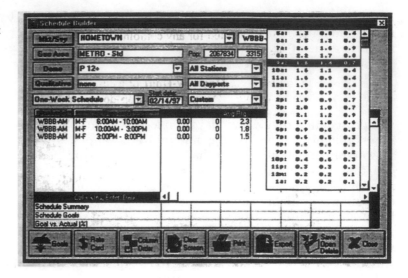

Unit Structure

A unit is a commercial message, regardless of length. In television, the standard length of commercials is 30 seconds, with 60-second spots costing twice as much as 30-second spots. When ad agencies discovered they could get their messages across in 30 seconds and still make an impression on consumers, they combined two sponsors into one 60-second package, and the piggyback commercial was invented. To protect revenues, TV sales managers increased the pricing on 30-second spots, and the TV standard changed from 60-second spots to 30-second spots.

The 15-second commercial was invented for the same reason—to protect revenues. In 1986, NBC was on top of both ratings and revenues. ABC was in the middle. CBS was at the bottom and had changed hands in what author Ken Auletta calls "the creeping takeover" in *Three Blind Mice*.[30] To bolster its revenue stream, CBS introduced the 15-second commercial, which sold for about half of the cost of the 30s. Publicly CBS said that because 15s were less expensive, new, smaller, advertisers would be attracted to network TV. In reality, they needed the cash.

Ad agencies responded as they had to 30s: they learned to create effective messages in 15 seconds. Some large advertisers were able to reduce their investment in television because they got the impact they needed from the less expensive 15-second spot.

While the 30-second commercial is still the TV standard, 15s reached as high as 35% of network inventory in 1990. The PreTesting Company, a media research firm, reported in 1997 that 15s were being negatively impacted by an increase in the number of messages in a commercial pod.

In local radio, the 60-second commercial is the standard; at the network level, it's the 30. The popularity of the 60 was maintained through effective pricing: most stations charged 80% of the 60-second rate for a 30-second commercial. The 60 is also considered more effective for communication of ideas through words and sounds, as you'll see in the discussion of radio commercials in Chapter 8.

The rise in popularity of FM music stations in the late 1970s caused radio to rethink the idea of scheduling commercial minutes. To reduce commercial interruption and to lengthen listening time, radio operators chose to limit the number of units they sold in an hour. Regardless of length, a unit was a unit, a commercial was a commercial. Soft rock or easy listening stations restricted unit counts to as few as eight per hour through the early 1990s. Rarely would a music station sell more than 10 or 12 units an hour.

That practice changed with the Telecommunications Act of 1996. The new rules allowed companies to combine multiple stations under one ownership. They also released radio from previous commercial limits. Needing increased revenues to pay high prices for radio properties, owners raised the number of units carried in the typical hour to as high as 16 on FM music stations, and double that on some talk-based AM outlets.

Plans, Discounts, and Packages

In most situations, the more advertising a client buys, the less the average unit will cost. Television, radio, and cable offer frequency discounts for buying multiple spots. For example, a message that costs $125 on a one-time basis might cost only $65 when purchased on an annual contract.

I've seen small-town radio station rate cards that open at $10 for a one-time commercial and offered a $2 rate for several hundred spots on an annual contract. The practice prompted the derogatory phrase, "dollar a holler." Early in its evolution, The Travel Channel cable network had a frequency discount that resulted in a $25 rate, uncommonly low for a national network.

For advertisers with limited funds, run-of-schedule (ROS) plans or best-time-available (BTA) plans make sense. The advantage of either plan to the advertiser is that rates are extremely low. The disadvantage is that there is no guarantee of the time the messages might run. When commercial loads are light, ROS and BTA commercials might get premium exposure. When loads are heavy, advertisers who choose ROS or BTA plans might find their messages running in the wee hours of the morning.

Most advertisers buy packages, a custom plan they create with their sales representative or a plan developed by the outlet to maximize both exposure and revenue. Soft demand for advertising in January and February prompts radio and television stations to create winter packages with low rates. Some winter packages add incentives like trips to Hawaii or to the Super Bowl for interested advertisers.

Packages that rotate commercials through various programs or dayparts are very effective for advertisers who want to hit a variety of audiences. In television, this is called a scatter plan, because the spots are scattered through various shows. A news scatter plan gives the advertiser both early and late news. A TV station might also construct a scatter plan with low-rated prime time positions and a very desirable prime show.

In radio, the same idea is called the total audience package (TAP or TAP Plan). Commercials rotate through all dayparts for exposure against all of the station's audiences. The rate for the TAP commercial is the average for all the dayparts it rotates through, so it is cost effective.

Any combination makes a good package. Targeting demographics is a typical approach. For instance, select programs or channels that deliver an audience of men 18–49, and you've created a package. Combine play-by-play sports with other sports-related programming like coaches' interviews or pregame festivities. Similarly, Saturday mornings and weekday afternoons yield kids' packages.

Figures 4–11, 4–12, and 4–13 show examples of unique packages, dayparts, and policies, respectively, developed by E! Entertainment Television.

clearly original
sales packages

- E! is a dual audience network with an evenly split adult 18-49 audience.

- Our vertical programming can be packaged to deliver a male or female skewing sales plan:

<u>Women</u>
- Fashion File
- The Gossip Show

<u>Men</u>
- Howard Stern
- Talk Soup

- E! can provide packages based on genre or "themed programming."

<u>Awards</u>
- Golden Globes
- Grammy Awards
- Academy Awards®
- Daytime & Primetime Emmys

<u>Seasonal</u>
- Haunted Hollywood
- Talk Soup Turkey
- Hollywood Moms
- Hollywood Dads
- Fall TV Preview

<u>Movies</u>
- Coming Attractions
- Behind the Scenes
- Summer Movie Guide
- Sundance Film Festival
- Cannes Film Festival
- Live Movie Premieres

<u>On E! Specials</u>
- Celebrity Weddings
- Celebrity Homes
- Most Eligible Bachelors
- Celebrity Cooking
- The World's Most Intriguing Women

FIGURE 4–11 Mix and match to reach the audience needed with sales packages from E! Entertainment Television. The client wants awards shows? E! accommodates. Specials? E!'s ready. ©E! Entertainment Television, Inc.® Used with permission.

policies and considerations

Dayparts

As a vertically programmed network with:

No kids block
No sports block
No women's block

E! Programming is designed to reach young adults
in every daypart. As such, E!'s dayparts are broad based and
defined as:

Morning	M-Su	6A-12P
Day	M-Su	12P-6P
Prime	M-Su	6P-12A
Late Night	M-Su	12A-3A
Weekend	S/S	6A-6P

Trailers

• E! accepts paid movie trailers as an element in our weekly
"Coming Attractions" show (unedited) and on "Howard Stern"
(edited to standard commercial lengths).

Planning Costs

• E's planning department can provide you with CPP's and CPM's.
These planning costs/efficiencies are subject to marketplace
fluctuations and are not guaranteed at times of media placement.

FIGURE 4–12 The software in Figure 4–10 creates specialized
dayparts. Here, E! Entertainment Television has
more efficient buys for advertisers. ©E!
Entertainment Television, Inc.® Used with
permission.

Commercial Lengths

•E! accepts
:15s
:30s
:60s
:45s
:120s

Note: Not :10s (unless partnered)

:30s are defined as standard units and E! does not guarantee clearing non-:30 -equivalent units.

Specials/Awards/Live-Events
•Due to scheduling and daypart programming distribution, all advertisers who purchase E! Specials/Awards/Live Events must air 6A-3A, and when necessary, out of flight.

Competitive Advertising Policy

• On a case-by-case basis, E! will or will not accept competitive advertising.
• In no case will E! clear day/date specific copy.

FIGURE 4–13 In the discussion about rate cards, I said that each operation sets its own policies. Here are just a few of the rules and regulations in the E! presentation. "Competitive advertising" means for other cable networks. "Day/date specific copy" means copy that says "tonight on" another network. © E! Entertainment Television, Inc.® Used with permission.

Terms and Conditions

Most operations have policies that govern the amount of time that can be purchased (whether 30- or 60-second increments or longer), the number of commercial breaks per hour, the number of commercials in a break, and the total number of commercial minutes in an hour.[31]

Policies are set according to the revenue objectives set out by management with two exceptions: (1) children's TV programs (targeted to viewers 12 and under) have a commercial time limit of 12 minutes on weekdays and 10.5 minutes on weekends; and (2) political candidates running for federal office have specific rights of access regardless of commercial limits imposed by broadcasters. They also are charged the lowest unit rate used by the station during the 45 days before a primary and 60 days before a general election.

A typical rate card includes the following information, usually printed in barely readable type on the back of the contract form:

- A brief policy statement concerning terms of payment and commissions
- A statement about acceptable content for the commercial messages
- Information about discount policies in effect
- Guarantees for rate protection (or lack thereof)
- Policies on cancellation

Most conditions vary by operation, but the ones shown here are fairly standard.

Salespeople are seldom reminded to read the back of the contract, so I'm reminding you: read the conditions your operation imposes. Reading and understanding the fine print will save you time (and money) later. For example, a schedule on a radio morning show might be cancellable, but if you've combined it with a noncancellable campaign in sports play-by-play, which condition overrides the other?

Most rate cards provide clients with a protected rate for a designated period of time. Should a client buy in September and rates increase in October, the client does not pay the new price until the end of the contract period.

Some conditions are violated or ignored by both parties to the contract, and that's accepted as standard practice. Radio stations, for example, often turn a blind eye to cancellation policies, opting instead to protect radio's image as flexible and responsive. Television stations are generally not as flexible and tend to hold to cancellation policies as stated in the contract.

Here are some other policies that might apply.

Product protection. Some outlets will not run spots back-to-back for competing products. Some will not run them in the same break as competing product messages. Advertisers vary in their opinions about this situation. Auto dealers are used to running side-by-side with their competitors in the newspaper auto section, so they are less sensitive.

Product acceptance. Some forms of media allow condom ads and some don't. Advertising liquor was in the news when Seagram's bought local radio and television commercials at some outlets that agreed to accept them. X-rated films and sexually oriented businesses are often the subject of copy acceptance policies.

Make goods. When a commercial does not run as scheduled or is aired improperly, the station "makes it good" with another time acceptable to the advertiser.

National Representatives

Put yourself in the place of an advertising agency buyer trying to place commercials for a national product on hundreds of local television stations and cable systems, thousands of local radio stations, and who-knows-how-many Web sites that accept advertising.

First, you wouldn't have time to research who listens to or watches each station to assure a client sufficient coverage and efficient pricing. Even if you could do the research, you'd face the daunting task of contacting each operation, negotiating a favorable rate, and placing the orders.

Nothing would get done if the system worked that way. Thanks to the national representatives concept, it doesn't. Reps, as they are called, are independent contractors who maintain selling staffs in cities where the largest national agencies have offices. The rep firms contract with local stations, station groups, or cable systems to represent them to the national and regional advertising community.[32]

The reps are responsible for selling national spot advertising, or "spot" as it's usually called. That includes advertising that is bought on a national basis, but not distributed by a network. (Although sometimes the same products are advertised using network schedules and in national spot buys.)

National spot advertising allows a national or regional advertiser to place schedules in a specific region of the country. In the case of television and cable, national spot allows an advertiser to buy one or more of the 211 Nielsen DMAs. Cable makes the process even easier with local interconnects, which are covered in Chapter 7.

How It Works

Most of the big agencies have offices in New York, Chicago, Atlanta, and Dallas. Others are located near their major clients, such as the concentration of automotive agencies in Detroit, entertainment agencies in Los Angeles, and those that cluster around Anheuser-Busch in St. Louis. (During the 1980s, advertising agencies decentralized their buying responsibilities and increased the number of regional offices in order to serve their clients better.)

If it's impossible for an agency buyer to keep track of all the individual media to buy, it's equally unlikely that broadcast stations, cable operations, and other electronic media outlets could maintain sales staffs in all those cities. The rep, therefore, is an extension of the local sales force. *Electronic Media Management* explains how the arrangement works:

> Rep sales are billed by the station to the agency, which deducts its 15% commission. From the balance, the station pays the rep a commission, as set forth in the contract between the two. It may range from 5 to 15% of the gross business offered (i.e., the amount billed to the agency).
>
> National and regional sales account for as much as 20% of a radio station's sales revenues and up to 75% of the revenues of a television station. For most television stations, they represent the largest single source of revenue. Selection of a rep, therefore, is an important decision. . . .
>
> The basic service offered by a rep company is the sale of national and regional advertising on stations it represents. Some of the larger companies also put together groups of stations to sell as a package in what are known as *unwired networks*. Sales are accomplished through rep account executives who make regular calls on media buyers in advertising agencies.

Radio stations rely on their rep firms for analyses of Arbitron ratings for their market and for the national overview. Reps often package research materials for individual radio formats, showing the strength of the country format, for example, or the benefits of smooth jazz.

For television stations, the rep maintains a program department so its clients receive information about new network programming, syndication, barter, specials, and pilots in production or in the planning stages. Stations also receive reports on ratings projections and performance.

Because they collect so much information, reps offer another key service to sellers: advice, including sales strategy, sales training, and development of rate cards. They also provide materials for presentation and sales promotion.

An effective relationship between a local station and its national representative company requires constant two-way communication. The NSM usually maintains contact with the rep firm, providing up-to-date market data and information on local programming. The NSM works with the rep's staff on rate cards and package plans that will be presented to advertisers.

Information is important; since sellers on the rep firm's staff represent so many different outlets, the more they know the better they sell. The NSM makes sure that the rep has clippings from local newspapers, video of local newscasts, audio of radio airchecks—anything that gives the rep a sense of what the station is all about.

The NSM at a TV station notifies the rep each week of that week's opportunistic inventory and supplies information about sports programming and other special events. Each quarter, the TV NSM should communicate low-rated, low-demand time periods that are available for placement of direct-response programming or infomercials.

GSMs or NSMs often travel to New York and other cities where their rep firms have offices to make face-to-face contact with the sellers who represent their stations. It's not unusual for a rep firm's staff to be addressed by the sales manager from one of their sta-

---

A DAY IN THE LIFE

The day starts at 7:30 and goes until . . . well, until it ends. "This is not a 9-to-5 job," says Melissa Weinberg, who sold for Katz Radio Group and was followed through a typical day by *Radio Only* magazine[37]. Here is Melissa's June 23:

7:30 a.m.   Prep time. She gathers ratings data from a terminal in her office and collects support materials from her stations.

8:30 a.m.   The daily sales meeting. On this day, the sales manager from KLOS, Los Angeles, shows a 60-page handout of station information to about 25 Katz salespeople.

9:30 a.m.   She takes a cab to Vitt Media to drop off a video of a Boston station's promotion for Clearly Canadian soft drinks, a Vitt client.

9:45 a.m.   She travels by subway to Popofsky Advertising to talk about local personalities to deliver commercials for their client, Vital K.

11:00 a.m.   Next she goes to Chiat Day Advertising for a meeting with their MTV marketing team and the sales team from Katz's New York City client station.

12:30 p.m.   She checks the office by phone before lunch with two buyers from Chiat Day, a media buyer from another service, a colleague from the Katz office, and the sales manager of a Boston station.

2:45 p.m.   She has an appointment with the Boston sales manager and buyers at Allscope Advertising.

3:45 p.m.   Melissa shares a cab with the Boston sales manager to two different appointments. Weinberg is at Backer Spielvogel Bates, where she meets with a newly promoted media buyer whom she's helping to learn the business.

4:30 p.m.   After walking back to the Katz office, she returns phone calls, first to East Coast clients, then working westward; most are from her radio station clients. Finally, she completes the interview with the reporter who has followed her all day.

tion clients; however, a seller for Katz radio said that she had the opportunity to meet people from only 10% of the 500 or so stations that her company represented.

Sellers who work for the reps often find themselves in precarious positions with the operations they represent. The stations want their reps to get the largest piece of business possible. They don't much care about the other clients on the rep firm's list. The agency buyer, however, may not want every station in the rep's package, so the rep gets the buy in some markets and not in others.

Buyers who deal with reps are more likely than not to have done their homework on the local markets they're buying, which is good because the rep seldom has the time to pitch each station individually the way local salespeople do. The rep seller's job is primarily to react to the buyer's request for avails and to get the highest percentage possible of advertising dollars.

If local outlets felt they were being slighted by their rep firms, the solution at one time was simply to change reps when the contract was up. That option was diminished with consolidation, which hit the rep business in the recession of the late 1980s and early 1990s. Many rep firms merged, leaving only two major national operations for radio, two for cable, and three for television. (Each medium has several regional rep firms.)

Options were reduced further in radio when Chancellor Media, a major station group owner, purchased the rep firm Katz Radio Group in 1997. When Chancellor also entered the radio network business in 1998 with its AMFM Networks, ABC Radio announced it would no longer allow Katz to represent its owned and operated stations. That left ABC with only one option, Katz competitor Interep.[33]

An unusual aspect of the rep seller's job is that there's seldom an opportunity to go to closing. When a buyer is ready to place business in a specific market, all the reps who have outlets in that market will be called in to make their presentations. Typically the buyer calls in the order *after* all the presentations have been made. This doesn't mean the rep seller cannot or should not ask for the order. It does, however, mean that the rep seller experiences delayed gratification.

There's very little time for prospecting for new business, since most of the agencies are established operations. Yet sales development is an important job for the seller who represents small market TV stations. Writing in *The Small Market Television Manager's Guide II*, Paul Morrissey, senior vice president and director of sales for Petry Television, recommends four steps for his client stations:

1. Develop an in-depth television market presentation that can be positioned effectively against other media (radio, cable, newspaper, etc.) for your specific market.

2. Create, with the assistance of your national representative, value-added promotions and merchandising opportunities that can be presented at the agency (buyer, planner, or account executive) and client level.

3. Establish and maintain constant qualitative contact with local key advertisers and key decision makers located at both the agency and client level.

4. Review with your national representative the various ways other stations around the country are tackling sales development.

Small markets are at a disadvantage in national spot sales because a disproportionate share of national dollars goes to the top 25 markets. Even more is concentrated in the top ten markets.

Morrissey suggests promotions, sports and specials, and local event sponsorships as new revenue enhancement opportunities for Petry's small market clients. There's more on this topic in the section about selling local television in Chapter 6.

At television stations, there are some operators who accept national advertising without a rep firm's involvement. A TVB study showed that direct business from national agencies was increasing at 69% of TV stations.[34] Only a few stations in the survey encouraged the practice; 80% actually *discouraged* it. Those who accepted the direct advertising did so because they feared losing the business.

Advertisers gained no benefits in terms of rate structures if they bought direct. All the station managers who TVB contacted agreed that national reps can arrange all the services and follow through work that a client needs, including promotional support.

New technology, such as computer-based avails systems, shortened the sales cycle from advertiser to rep to local media outlet. Television representatives like TeleRep, Blair Television, and Petry use electronic transfer of orders to smooth the process.

National Cable Communications, owned by Katz, offered a planning and buying service called CableTrack, which stored information on every ad-insertable cable system on a desktop computer. Buyers could create customized target areas by ZIP code, town, cable system, or Nielsen DMA.[35]

MARKET REVIEW CHECKLIST

To get the selling atmosphere of a market, regardless of size, collect the information on this checklist.

Statistical Data, Size, and Nature of the Market

Research the market and coverage area to determine the following:

- Population
- Households
- Consumer spendable dollars per capita, per household, and total
- Retail sales per capita, per household, and total
- National rankings of population, households, income, and retail sales
- Growth trends, past and future, of population, households, income, and retail sales
- Principal employers and other industries

From these basic measures of market strength, look for upward or downward trends that indicate future market shifts of population, income, and retail sales.

Advertising Data, Total Market

Research the station's market and coverage area to determine the following:

- Market's total annual advertising volume. Break down the total to determine the amount of national and local (if available).
- List all major media in the market.
- Break down all major media to include the annual dollar volume and then determine the amount that each received of national and local expenditures (if available).
- Break down all major media to include circulation, rates, and cost per thousand.

From this information, determine each medium's percentage of the market. Look for market trends in total advertising dollars and any medium that dominates. Observe carefully the broadcast and radio shares.

Broadcasting Data, Specific Stations

Determine or estimate the following data for each broadcast station:

- Revenues (network, national, local)
- Audience size and composition
- Time listening or viewing
- New stations: available, applications pending, granted applications
- Coverage, power, and frequency
- Programming
- Rate card
- Affiliation and representative
- Local public and client opinion of station

This checklist was written for investors who intend to purchase television or radio stations. I found it so useful in pinpointing a market's selling environment that I've always kept it with my sales materials. It's from the NAB publication, *Buying or Building a Broadcast Station*, by Erwin Krasnow, Geoffrey Bentley, and Robin Martin.

An online service called BuyMedia allows advertisers to buy time on radio and television stations in rated markets regardless of where the advertisers' offices may be located.[36] The service uses electronic data transfer (EDT) to process orders. Stations pay lower commissions: 7% for radio and 5% for TV. Agencies get a 2% rebate on the net total of advertising placed on participating stations. Proprietary software is unnecessary because users access the service via the Internet at *www.buymedia.com*.

Computer-based buying services are serious threats to the national rep firm.

Review Highlights and Discussion Points

1. The organizational structure of sales departments is directly related to the size of the market in which a station operates. Large-market TV stations may have several divisions: local sales manager, national sales manager, retail sales manager, and so forth. A small-market radio station may find the owner doubling as the sales manager and directing the efforts of a handful of salespeople.

2. The key functions of any sales department include selling ad time, delivering targeted audience to advertiser, developing promotions for advertiser, generating revenue and profit for the station, and adding to the station's asset value.

3. At the local cable system, subscriptions are the largest share of revenues, but the contribution of the advertising sales department is growing.

4. Effective leadership of the sales department maximizes both revenues and profits.

5. The director of sales (DOS) is a job function at the largest organizations, such as large-market television stations or clusters of multiple radio stations under one ownership. Most often the DOS coordinates the efforts of a group of sales managers.

6. In the absence of a DOS, the general sales manager (GSM) is at the top of the department's chain of command. The GSM must possess complete understanding of the ownership and management of the media outlet, of the marketplace and its competitive environment, of programming and the audience it reaches, of sales management techniques, and of the sales staff as individuals and as a team.

7. The national sales manager (NSM) answers to the GSM and coordinates the sale of national and regional advertisers through the station's national representative firm (rep).

8. The local sales manager (LSM) also reports to the GSM and is primarily responsible for the planning and administering of local sales activities.

9. Some sales organizations also have a co-op coordinator who provides information to salespeople about co-op advertising opportunities that may exist for their clients.

10. Television sales trainer Pat Shaughnessy calculates that between 1980 and 1992 at least one million additional 30-second commercial units became available for sale in most markets because of new radio, television, and cable outlets.

11. The first month or two at a new sales job may include a schedule of viewing video tapes and listening to audio tapes about basic selling and marketing techniques.

12. According to Ken Greenwood, the top skills needed to succeed include listening, people skills, questioning skills, presentation, handling objections, closing, and post-sales implementation and service.

13. Top broadcast executives have created several systems to aid in the sales process, including the SEES formula, the PAPA presentation, and the SKOAPP system.

14. Team selling became popular in the mid-1990s because of the intensifica-

tion of the selling efforts at all electronic media outlets.

15. The dearth of qualified sales personnel prompted some outlets to create teams of experienced sellers who don't want to work full-time. Job-sharing sales teams sell as one person would, but they split the workload and the commissions.

16. Sales meetings can be an opportunity to discuss strategy, gain knowledge, and create staff unity. Meetings are most productive when they are well-planned, agenda-driven, and action-oriented.

17. Selling has the rewards of the hunt (prospecting and closing) and also the reward of financial payoff. It is common for sellers to be the highest-paid employees in their companies.

18. Compensation strategies vary from company to company, even from outlet to outlet within a company. Local market conditions are the most important factor in any compensation package. From market to market, differences are also evident.

19. There are seven basic compensation methods: salary only, salary plus bonus, straight commission, draw against commission, salary plus commission, salary/commission/and bonus, and straight commission with bonus.

20. New compensation plans introduced since Telecom 96 use the basic approaches, but they show interesting mix-and-match combinations.

21. An incentive pool is the collected commissions for the entire sales team, combined so that each may share, depending on individual contributions. The pool concept rewards salespeople for selling the way the company wants them to sell and for reaching company goals, not individual goals.

22. Half of the radio stations managers interviewed by NAB said they used contests as part of their overall incentive plan. The larger the market, the more likely they were to use contests.

23. While not technically part of the compensation plan, some contest prizes are sufficient to augment compensation. The greatest benefit of contesting among sellers is to make them feel like winners personally.

24. Some companies constantly modify their pay plans, looking for the right mix of incentive, motivation, and staff stability.

25. Commissions are sometimes paid on billings, that is, on orders written. Most often, however, commissions are paid on collections, so you don't receive your money until your company receives its money.

26. The word "compensation" conjures visions of money, but sellers also seek rewards beyond financial remuneration. Approval, respect, and recognition are high on the list of employee hopes for any job. Salespeople are individuals, so incentive and motivation plans should reflect that individuality.

27. For electronic media, once overhead costs—rent, salaries, and so forth—are met there's no additional cost for selling more advertising. Each dollar beyond overhead costs is profit.

28. Digital delivery allows over-the-air television to expand the number of commercial units through multicasting. Cable systems increase the number of channels delivered. This expansion of inventory has the potential to inflate overall revenues by expanding the advertising base.

29. There are markets in which forms of electronic media are traditionally underpriced, often suppressed by a dominant newspaper whose selling tactics undermine competitors.

30. Commercial inventory exists to be sold. Unsold inventory is lost revenue, and that means lost forever. Commercial time is a perishable commodity.

31. The rate card describes pricing. Some say it sets the rate, but often the rate card simply suggests the opening rate for negotiation.

32. Base rates depend on the size of the audience a program or medium will deliver. The bigger the audience, the higher the rates and the higher the demand for inventory.

33. Grid cards are written versions of the rate fluctuations found in the electronic cards created by software systems. Grid cards are inventory- and marketplace-sensitive.

34. Maintaining revenue is a product of assessing and understanding demand. Maximizing revenue requires an additional step: manipulating supply in order to increase demand.

35. Inventory management is more critical in television than in radio or local cable, because TV time is generally bought in narrow dayparts or specific programs.

36. Broadcast outlets divide their days into segments roughly defined by the amount of viewership or listenership at that time of day. Thus the term daypart.

37. A unit is a commercial message regardless of length. In most situations, the more advertising a client buys, the less the average unit will cost.

38. Most advertisers buy packages, a custom plan they create with their sales representative or a plan developed by the outlet to maximize both exposure and revenue.

39. Most operations have policies that govern the amount of time that can be purchased, whether 30- or 60-second increments or longer; the number of commercial breaks per hour; the number of commercials in a break; and the total number of commercial minutes in an hour.

40. Salespeople should read the back of the rate card, and they should read and become familiar with the conditions that their operation imposes.

41. National reps are responsible for selling national spot advertising. That includes advertising that is bought on a national basis, but not distributed by a network.

42. New technology, such as computer-based avails systems have shortened the sales cycle from advertiser to rep to local media outlet. Many television reps use electronic transfer of orders to smooth the process.

Chapter Notes

[1] Duties of the general sales manager are from *Electronic Media Management*, 3rd ed., by Peter K. Pringle, Michael F. Starr, and William E. McCavitt, Newton, MA: Focal Press, 1995; and from *The Radio Book, Volume One: Management and Sales Management*, West Palm Beach, FL: Streamline Press, 1995.

[2] Duties of the national sales manager are from *Electronic Media Management* and from *The Small Market Television Manager's Guide II*, Washington, DC: National Association of Broadcasters, 1992.

[3] The typical tests from the first few weeks of a seller's job are from a training program by Chris Lytle of the Lytle Organization, 700 Regent Street, Suite 200, Madison, WI 53715.

[4] The SEES and PAPA formulas are quoted in Ken Greenwood's *High Performance Selling*, cited previously.

[5] SKOAPP is from Warner and Buchman's *Broadcast and Cable Selling*, cited previously.

[6] Michael Carter and Hal Smith offered their team selling experiences in *Radio Ink*, June 7, 1993.

[7] The KLIF twins were profiled in *The Dallas Morning News* in Diana Kunde's "Job Sharing Can Give Clients, Employers Double Benefits," September 3, 1997.

[8] The RAB-TVB joint study was reported in the 1991 paper, "Radio and Television Sales Staff Profiles, Compensation, and Practices," by Charles Warner and James Spencer, available from the University of Missouri School of Journalism, P.O. Box 838, Columbia, MO 65205.

[9] RAB's George Hyde was quoted in a *Radio Only* magazine article, "How to Get Salespeople to Work Harder for You," February 1993.

10 If you use a Daytimer® time management system, you know the name Charles Hobbs. Daytimer materials are full of Hobbs' quotations on goal setting and efficient use of time. The Hobbs Corporation number is (801) 278-5381. You can access Daytimers online at *www.daytimer.com*.

11 As Director of Audience Measurement and Policy Research for the NAB, Gerald G. Hartshorn collected the data and wrote the text for *Successful Radio Compensation Strategies*, Washington, DC: NAB, 1994. Gerry later did research for cable television.

12 The details of various compensation plans are collected from Gerry Hartshorn's NAB book, cited above; from *Electronic Media Management*, also cited previously; from Warner and Buchman's *Broadcast and Cable Selling*; and from Warner and Spencer's paper after the RAB-TVB study, cited above.

13 "Compensating Broadcast Salespeople: Some Recommendations," by Charles Warner, available from the University of Missouri School of Journalism.

14 "What Are Your Salespeople Worth?" asked Dick Chapin in *Radio Ink*, February 1, 1993. The subhead to the article answered the question: "Most likely much more than you believe."

15 The KMLE customer study was documented by *Radio Only* magazine in an article "What We Learned from Client Gripes," September 1993.

16 The mix-and-match compensation plans are from a session called "Compensation" at the RAB 1998 Marketing Leadership Conference in Dallas.

17 In addition to the paper I cited earlier by Charles Warner and James Spencer, Professor Warner wrote a paper called "Sales Contests," available online at *www.missouri.edu/~journcw/contests.html*.

18 Usually, when choosing between billings and collections, collections wins because payment is assured. See Chapter 2 for a chart that demonstrates the collections cycle.

19 In addition to the motivational ads in the July/August 1997, issue of *Selling Power* magazine, there was an article by Jeff Keller, "Picture Your Success: Put Yourself in the Role of Sales Superstar."

20 Dave Gifford's "Management Can't Motivate but You Can Activate" is in *The Radio Book, Volume One*, cited previously.

21 Marilyn Kushak was a panelist at RAB's 1998 "Compensation" session referred to above.

22 I first heard the comparison to the airline industry from Paul Fiddick when he was president of Heritage Media's radio division.

23 These are just a few examples of the seasonality of selling. You'll find more in the discussion of direct, or retail, selling in Chapter 5.

24 *Buying or Building a Broadcast Station: Everything You Want—and Need—to Know, But Didn't Know Who to Ask* is a big title. It's by Erwin G. Krasnow, J. Geoffrey Bentley, and Robin B. Martin, Washington DC: National Association of Broadcasters, 1988.

25 The math exercises are so simple, I thought I shouldn't use them. Then I checked with Dick Oppenheimer of Signature Broadcasting, who lectures at the University of Texas at Austin and conducts financial analyses for broadcasters. "That's the only way to approach it," he told me.

26 The discussion of rates, rate cards, and sellouts was enhanced greatly by my conversations with Dick Oppenheimer, with Gary Fries of the RAB, and with Diane Sutter of Shooting Star Broadcasting.

27 Michael Keith's Selling *Radio Direct* was cited previously.

28 Jim Taszarek's TazMedia no longer publishes *Large Market Radio Selling*, which is too bad because it applied to selling generally as well as to radio specifically. These tips were adapted from the January 1996 issue. Taz does provide sales tips online at *www.tazmedia.com*.

29 The standard dayparts are assembled from Nielsen Media Research, the Arbitron Company, and *Electronic Media Management*, cited previously.

30 The 1986 television buying market was documented in fine fashion by Ken

Auletta in *Three Blind Mice*, New York: Random House, 1991. Auletta's account introduces the discussion of national television sales in Chapter 6.

[31] Terms and conditions vary by outlet, by ownership, and by medium. National organizations such as TVB, RAB, and CAB offer standards to their member organizations that are guidelines, but members are by no means bound to use them. Michael Keith's *Selling Radio Direct* and *The Radio Station* examine terms and conditions for radio. Each book has been cited previously.

[32] For more on how the station rep and local station interact, see *Electronic Media Management, Broadcast and Cable Selling*, and *The Small Market Television Manager's Guide II*, all cited previously. Also, *Broadcast Programming*, by Susan Tyler Eastman, Sydney W. Head, and Lewis Klein offers a good view of the television rep's role in programming. Belmont, CA: Wadsworth, 1981.

[33] "ABC Ends Rep Contract with Katz," *Radio Business Report*, May 4, 1998.

[34] The TVB study, "Buying Direct vs. Rep Survey," is offered online at *www.tvb.org/research*.

[35] Information on national cable representatives came from the Cabletelevision Advertising Bureau's "Why National Spot Cable Advertising."

[36] Information about BuyMedia was supplied by the company.

Taking It Further

Here are a few Web sites that relate to this chapter and additional reading not included in the Chapter Notes.

www.ama.org/index.html—The American Marketing Association's site with a variety of sales and marketing tools

www.sellingpower.com—The site for *Selling Power* magazine

www.smartbiz.com—The Smart Business Supersite with books and articles on business subjects. Search: Sales, Marketing, Advertising, Media, etc.

Additional Reading

Connellan, Thomas K. *Inside the Magic Kingdom: Seven Keys to Disney's Success*. Austin, TX: Bard Press, 1997.

Fox, Shane. *Broadcast Revenue Management: Pricing and Inventory Management in Today's Broadcast Environment*. Washington, DC: National Association of Broadcasters, 1997.

Freiberg, Kevin, and Jackie Freiberg. *Nuts: Southwest Airlines' Crazy Recipe for Business and Personal Success*. Austin, TX: Bard Press, 1996.

Greenwood, Ken. *High Performance Leadership: The Search for Your Organizational Wizard*. West Palm Beach, FL: Streamline Press, 1998.

Kravetz, Dennis J. *Getting Noticed: A Manager's Success Kit*. New York: The Wiley Press, 1985.

National Association of Broadcasters and Broadcast Cable Financial Management Association. *Television Financial Report*, 1997. Washington, DC: NAB and BCFA, annual.

5

Casting the Net

Where do potential customers come from? You'll remember that I asked that question at the beginning of the discussion of prospecting. The answer is that ideas for a prospect list come from the newspaper, radio and TV ads, the Yellow Pages, new business registration at government agencies, and from your personal networking.

In theory, any business that wants to remain in business is a potential customer for an advertising medium. As you read in the chapter on prospecting, the more often you cast your net, the more possible customers you find to add to your list.

An account list is no more than a "hunting license," as sales trainer Chris Lytle calls it. The key, as you've learned, is the qualification process—discovering who is and who is not an appropriate target.

There are three typical sources for business for your medium:

1. *National advertisers*, who are agencies that buy in a variety of markets and place their orders through a network or a representative firm. These advertisers have very little direct contact, if any, with salespeople from the local station or outlet.

2. *Local and regional advertisers*, who place their schedules through advertising agencies. The sellers from local operations make presentations directly to the buyers at the agencies and sometimes to others in the agency hierarchy.

3. *Direct accounts*, who are usually local retailers and service establishments that place their orders themselves. They work directly with the sales representative of the outlets they wish to buy.

Other channels of revenue exist. Nontraditional revenue (NTR) for example, refers to dollars that are not committed specifically to media buying but to promotion or community service activities. There are also budgets that target ethnic or other specialized audiences. All are important sources of revenue, but not until the changes in radio and television ownership rules did they become as important as the big three mentioned above: national agency, local and regional agency, and direct or retail sales.

As you'll see, agency selling is ratings-oriented. Agencies tend to buy numbers, and their goal is to buy big numbers at the lowest possible prices. Agency buyers most often buy for efficiency.

Direct or retail selling is results-oriented. Retailers buy advertising in order to see customers come through the door and to hear the ringing cash registers. Direct account buyers most often buy for effectiveness.

Direct Selling

"Why I love to sell direct." Sales trainer Jim Taszarek stated it as if he were going to read a poem in a classroom exercise. Instead, he was in front of an audience at the Radio Advertising Bureau's Managing Sales Conference in Dallas to inform the assembled sellers about retail direct selling.[1] Here are a few of the reasons Taszarek loves to sell direct:

I don't need good demos.

I don't need to be efficient.

I don't have to "get on a buy."

I can sell an idea or a promotion.

Selling direct means calling on business owners and not on advertising agencies. It's the person-to-person part of the sales process, and it's the heart of selling electronic media in medium and small markets. Most beginning sellers call on direct accounts long before they call on ad agencies.

An agency may be involved in a direct account, but "the station and the client have control of the business," says Taszarek. "The principal money comes from the client. The principal decisions come from the client."

Most direct business is not affected by ratings. If the numbers go up or down, a direct advertiser cares less than an agency buyer would. The direct advertiser is more likely to measure the effectiveness of an ad by how many people came through the doors and, more important, how many pieces of product were sold as a result of the advertising.

The spectrum of direct accounts includes everything from mom-and-pop operations where the owner is manager, clerk, janitor, and advertising manager, to megastores such as Wal-Mart and K-Mart. In between are dry cleaners, fast-food operations, and any other business that sells directly to the public—thus the term "direct" accounts.

In contrast to direct sellers, agencies are hired by advertisers to provide a variety of services, including media planning and buying, creative copy writing and production, and consumer research and consultation on product positioning and imaging. Not every agency provides all services.

"The agency buyer is a commodity specifier." Taszarek equates agency business to the old industrial paradigm, buying screws in bulk at a factory. Instead of choosing a perfect screw, the buyer checks a few individual screws, then orders a ton of them. "Agencies don't understand the value of something that doesn't have a numeric aspect. They're not paid to listen to ideas."

He's right. Agency buyers are charged with getting the most coverage for their client's dollars—more spots for the least amount of money. As you'll read in the section on ad agencies later, the buyer executes the plan that someone higher in the pecking order has already laid out. The buyer is at the end of the process. If a seller wants to introduce an idea that changes the overall plan, it has to be done early in the planning, not at the time the schedule is in the buyer's hands.

The direct seller, however, typically works with the people who can make the decisions and is also called a "retail" seller, because most direct business comes from some sort of retail store. There's no succinct definition for "retail." It's a broad category and includes:

- Stores that sell both hard goods and soft goods
- Restaurants and drive-ins
- Services like insurance, banking, and dry cleaning
- Entertainment, such as theaters, night clubs, movie rental stores, skating rinks, and amusement parks

The people who operate these types of establishments know their customers personally and can measure response to advertising by counting the customers who enter their store and matching them to cash register receipts. For charts on how knowing your customer can aid your advertising, see Figures 5–1 through 5–4.

The purpose of retail advertising is to generate store traffic, increase sales volume, improve net profits, and build the store's image or reputation. Also, retail advertising is sometimes used to stabilize sales volume during slow sales periods.

The Radio Advertising Bureau (RAB) training program, titled "Welcome to Retail Sales," features a long primer called "Working with Retail Accounts." It includes a good introduction to retail for the seller of any electronic medium:

> Retailers want their advertising to reach the greatest number of people at the lowest possible cost. They design ads to bring people into the store to shop for advertised items, and to prompt impulse buying of unadvertised merchandise. Good advertising invites new customers (or noncustomers) to shop; simultaneously it encourages current customers to shop more often and buy more merchandise. Most retail operating expenses are fixed, which means that added sales volume, brought in by advertising, can mean greater profits for the retailer.
>
> Being known for quality advertising is also a good morale builder for the store's sales staff. Effective retail advertising can enhance a store's image or position by talking to the prospect one-on-one about the store's special features, the quality of its merchandise, unique services, and other special reasons why customers should shop there, such as free parking, easy credit, large sizes, etc.
>
> Retailers often conduct sales or other special events to maintain an adequate level of business during 'slow' periods. Retailers track sales on a day-to-day basis and they often adjust their prices to meet economic realities.[2]

Charles Nelson, the owner of Carolina Cleaners in Chapel Hill, North Carolina, is a typical example. He established his company in 1986. His first advertising appeared in the *Chapel Hill News*—3" × 4" ads once a week that invited his customers to "Come in and Try Us." The ads cost about $100 each.

After a year, Nelson did not see the increase in business he had hoped for, so the following year he tried direct mail with discount coupons sent to 30,000 area residents. Within a year, his sales had tripled.

In 1992 Nelson began advertising on WCHL radio, using 60-second commercials during the station's local morning talk show. A typical commercial featured Nelson himself discussing stains and how to remove them. By 1997 Carolina Cleaners was a $2 million business with 5% of its revenues reinvested in radio advertising and coupons.[3]

There are many media options for a small firm like a dry cleaner. As Nelson discovered, the key strategy is to choose the medium that the customers are most likely to use. The positive aspect of local direct advertising is that a dry cleaner like Nelson can ask his customers how they heard about his firm. While it's not the systematized market research we encountered in Chapter 3, it gives him a good indicator of how his advertising is working. He can see his business increase after his commercial airs. He can determine how effective his schedule and his copy are. A local retailer's cash register is the ultimate research.

The Carolina Cleaners example has an underlying message: direct selling takes time. That's why it's often referred to as "developmental" selling—the salesperson must nurture the prospects and help them develop positive attitudes toward not only the medium but also the advertising itself.

To some retail direct clients, your pitch could be their first excursion into advertising. If that's the case, you have to be knowledgeable about marketing in order to know how to get the prospect comfortable with the benefits of advertising. The next step is to outline the benefits of television, cable, radio, or whatever medium you're selling. Only then can you focus on your own operation and the audience you can deliver.

Keep in mind that you're selling an intangible in a highly tangible world. Retailers take inventory, stock shelves, bag their goods, count cash, greet customers—all very real.

As a seller, you must be patient and not expect a quick sale. It took Nelson several years to judge the inefficiencies of the newspaper and to realize that his best

CONSUMER PROFILE
Family Restaurant Users
PAST THREE MONTHS.

Gender

50 %Male   **50** %Female

Income (Adults 18+)

Over $50,000	37%
$25,000-$50,000	39%
Under $25,000	24%

Occupation (Adults 18+)

Professional/Managerial	20%
Technical, Sales, and Administrative Support	20%
Service	7%
Precision Production and Craft & Farming, Forestry and Fishing	7%
Operators, Fabricators and Laborers	6%

Education

19% High School or Less   **27%** Completed High School   **24%** Some College/ Trade School   **30%** Completed College or More

Sociographic Shoppers Profile

Brand Loyal	33%
Cautious	42%
Venturesome	25%

Own Home   **76%**

Households with Children   **37%**

Average Weekday Non-Newspaper Readers   **35%**

Demographic Breakout

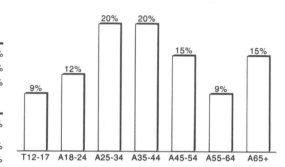

T12-17	A18-24	A25-34	A35-44	A45-54	A55-64	A65+
9%	12%	20%	20%	15%	9%	15%

Lifestyle Profile by PRIZM® Groups

GROUP	DESCRIPTION	
S2	The Affluentials	10.2%
C2	2nd City Centers	9.1%
R3	Rustic Living	9.1%
S1	Elite Suburbs	8.9%
T3	Working Towns	8.6%
T1	Landed Gentry	7.8%
S3	Inner Suburbs	7.1%
T2	Exurban Blues	6.5%
U2	Urban Midscale	5.8%
C3	2nd City Blues	5.4%
C1	2nd City Society	5.1%
R1	Country Families	4.7%
U3	Urban Cores	4.1%
R2	Heartlanders	3.9%
U1	Urban Uptown	3.7%

Family Restaurant Users
Consumer Profile

*Media Targeting 2000 — conducted by
The Arbitron Company in cooperation with
the Radio Advertising Bureau*

90-A

FIGURE 5–1 The more a seller knows about the customers who frequent the advertiser's place of business, the easier the sale. Let's say you're calling on a restaurant owner. Wouldn't it be nice to have this profile of the typical family restaurant user? It's from *Media Targeting 2000*, conducted by the Arbitron Company in cooperation with RAB. Used with permission from each organization.

MEDIA HABITS
Family Restaurant Users
PAST THREE MONTHS

Average Weekday Share of Time Spent with Each Medium

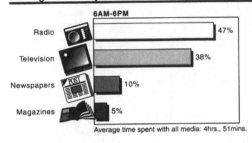

6AM-6PM

Radio	47%
Television	38%
Newspapers	10%
Magazines	5%

Average time spent with all media: 4hrs., 51mins.

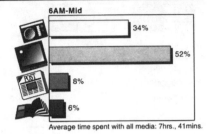

6AM-Mid

Radio	34%
Television	52%
Newspapers	8%
Magazines	6%

Average time spent with all media: 7hrs., 41mins.

Competitive Weekly Reach (percent exposed to medium)

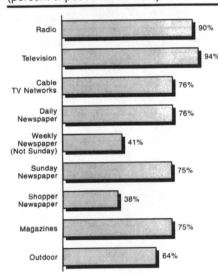

Radio	90%
Television	94%
Cable TV Networks	76%
Daily Newspaper	76%
Weekly Newspaper (Not Sunday)	41%
Sunday Newspaper	75%
Shopper Newspaper	38%
Magazines	75%
Outdoor	64%

Media Exposure Prior to Purchasing

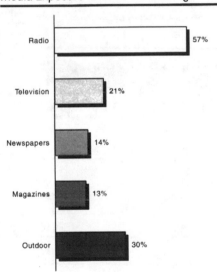

Radio	57%
Television	21%
Newspapers	14%
Magazines	13%
Outdoor	30%

**Percent of Shoppers Reached by Medium
Within 1 Hour of Largest Purchase**
*(Respondents reporting any purchase
within 24 hours prior to contact)*

90-B

*Media Targeting 2000 — conducted by
The Arbitron Company in cooperation with
the Radio Advertising Bureau*

Family Restaurant Users
Media Habits

FIGURE 5–2 The media habits of the family restaurant user profiled in Figure 5–1. Courtesy Arbitron and RAB. Used with permission.

CONSUMER PROFILE
Live Music Concert Attendees
PAST TWELVE MONTHS

A National Study of **Media Targeting 2000** Consumers & Media

Gender

54 % Male   **46** % Female

Income (Adults 18+)

Over $50,000	46%
$25,000-$50,000	37%
Under $25,000	17%

Occupation (Adults 18+)

Professional/Managerial	25%
Technical, Sales, and Administrative Support	19%
Service	9%
Precision Production and Craft & Farming, Forestry and Fishing	9%
Operators, Fabricators and Laborers	5%

Education

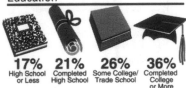

17% High School or Less   **21%** Completed High School   **26%** Some College/ Trade School   **36%** Completed College or More

Sociographic Shoppers Profile

Brand Loyal	28%
Cautious	46%
Venturesome	26%

Own Home   **71%**

Households with Children   **34%**

Average Weekday Non-Newspaper Readers   **35%**

Demographic Breakout

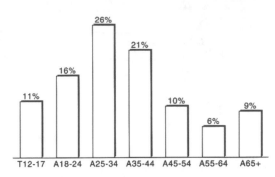

T12-17	A18-24	A25-34	A35-44	A45-54	A55-64	A65+
11%	16%	26%	21%	10%	6%	9%

Lifestyle Profile by PRIZM® Groups

GROUP	DESCRIPTION	
S2	The Affluentials	12.6%
C2	2nd City Centers	9.5%
T1	Landed Gentry	8.5%
T3	Working Towns	7.7%
R3	Rustic Living	7.6%
S1	Elite Suburbs	7.6%
T2	Exurban Blues	6.5%
U2	Urban Midscale	6.4%
S3	Inner Suburbs	6.4%
C1	2nd City Society	6.0%
U1	Urban Uptown	5.7%
C3	2nd City Blues	4.7%
U3	Urban Cores	4.5%
R1	Country Families	4.0%
R2	Heartlanders	2.2%

Live Music Concert Attendees
Consumer Profile

*Media Targeting 2000 — conducted by
The Arbitron Company in cooperation with
the Radio Advertising Bureau*

114-A

FIGURE 5–3 Here's an opportunity to see the differences in consumers. The restaurant users in Figure 5–1 are older than these concert goers. More concert goers are male than female. What other differences do you see? *Media Targeting 2000* was conducted by the Arbitron Company in cooperation with the RAB. Used with permission from each organization.

MEDIA HABITS
Live Music Concert Attendees
PAST TWELVE MONTHS

Average Weekday Share of Time Spent with Each Medium

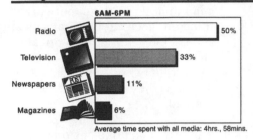

6AM-6PM

Radio	50%
Television	33%
Newspapers	11%
Magazines	6%

Average time spent with all media: 4hrs., 58mins.

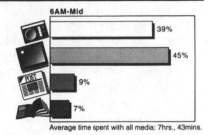

6AM-Mid

Radio	39%
Television	45%
Newspapers	9%
Magazines	7%

Average time spent with all media: 7hrs., 43mins.

Competitive Weekly Reach
(percent exposed to medium)

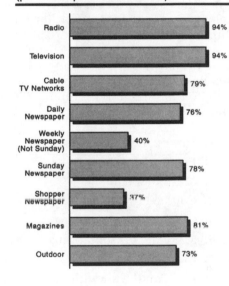

Radio	94%
Television	94%
Cable TV Networks	79%
Daily Newspaper	76%
Weekly Newspaper (Not Sunday)	40%
Sunday Newspaper	78%
Shopper Newspaper	37%
Magazines	81%
Outdoor	73%

Media Exposure Prior to Purchasing

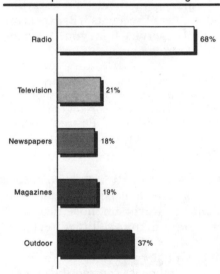

Radio	68%
Television	21%
Newspapers	18%
Magazines	19%
Outdoor	37%

**Percent of Shoppers Reached by Medium
Within 1 Hour of Largest Purchase**
(Respondents reporting any purchase
within 24 hours prior to contact)

114-B

*Media Targeting 2000 — conducted by
The Arbitron Company in cooperation with
the Radio Advertising Bureau*

Live Music Concert Attendees
Media Habits

FIGURE 5–4 Concert attendees are more radio-oriented and more likely to be influenced by outdoor media than are family restaurant users. This figure shows how valuable specific consumer information can be to your direct selling effort. If your outlet delivers the right mix of the advertiser's target, it helps you make the sale. *Media Targeting 2000*, conducted by the Arbitron Company in cooperation with the RAB. Used with permission from each organization.

attack was a mix of direct mail coupons and the local radio station. (We should assume a WCHL salesperson helped him see the light!)

You can bet that the WCHL seller was not the only one calling on Carolina Cleaners. There are more than 30 radio stations in the Raleigh-Durham-Chapel Hill market, plus nine television stations and a cable interconnect that covers that market plus the Greenville-New Bern area. Add to those options the Yellow Pages, local magazines, the University of North Carolina newspaper, outdoor advertising, bus cards, and direct mail. Lots of sellers compete for Charles Nelson's business. In retail selling, everybody's client is somebody else's prospect.

When you sell direct, you'll be most successful if you are knowledgeable about relationship management (discussed earlier in this book). Retail accounts will expect an intense level of service from you. Ad agency founder Fred Poppe puts it best:

> For some reason the out-of-sight, out-of-mind syndrome predominates the client psyche. It is therefore important that you make sure the client feels you are thinking only of him or her and their company 24 hours a day.[4]

Rules 4 and 5 in Poppe's *50 Rules to Keep a Client Happy* are "constant contact" and "more contact." Never are those two rules more important than in selling directly to the retailer.

Often the retailer you call on is the business owner, who is commonly hypersensitive about the dollars spent on advertising. Retailers often view advertising as a necessary evil, an expense to be avoided. As a business owner myself, I know that whatever money I spend means reduced income for me personally. Your pitch to a person like me has to be compelling enough to get me to part with my own money.

Retailers you encounter will want to see results from the schedule you sell them. They want to sense an increase in traffic, and they want to count the additional revenues. This point cannot be stressed enough. There are truisms about retailers:

- They want reassurance that they've done the right thing.
- They need attention and demand it in subtle ways, like asking for copy changes and schedule changes, usually at the last minute on Friday.
- They want details handled. For instance, if the retailer is using co-op money from a manufacturer, the paperwork must be filled out accurately. That's usually the seller's job. (More on co-op later in this chapter.)
- They want to know their schedule before it runs so they can see or hear their commercials.

In short, they act like customers.

The Direct Sales Process

The direct sales process is the same as the sales process you learned earlier, but since Jim Taszarek trains sellers to call on direct retail clients, I'm using a nine-step process that he teaches. It takes my seven-step selling cycle and adds a spin to make it specific to the retail environment. The nine steps are

1. Survey the categories.
2. Find target accounts.
3. Make first contact.
4. Conduct the needs analysis.
5. Confirm your facts.
6. Make the presentation.
7. Close the sale.
8. Put it on the air with ceremony.
9. Recycle and upgrade.

The first and second items on that list are the same as prospecting, but Taszarek suggests that for retail and direct selling, the prospecting net should not be spread across the whole market; rather, it should be focused. "Account lists are not strategic," he says. "Most lists have no target, no differentiation, nothing in common."

To improve on the typical list, Taszarek urges sales directors to survey categories that fit their medium best when it comes to delivering results. He asks, "What categories do we sell best? What fits with our audience composition?" For instance, in radio terms, home builders and grocery accounts are right for adult contemporary stations; autos and financial are right for news and talk stations; soft drinks and fast food for top-40 stations. Cable sellers can relate to the same differentiation selling VH-1, Headline News, or MTV.

In addition to asking "What are we good at?" Taszarek suggests asking "What are we not good at?" so sellers don't waste time selling to categories that don't fit. As an example, a CBS television affiliate will sell more banks and financial services than a WB or UPN affiliate will.

Another issue for direct selling is: what is the *seller* good at? A salesperson who calls on a lot of auto dealers learns more about the automotive industry with each client contact. Why not concentrate that seller's activity on the auto category so dealers know there's a specialist on their accounts? Taszarek adds, "If I'm good at automotive, then I have to be good at everything around autos. Let the category include auto alarms, driving schools, and service stations."

You'll recall in Chapter 2 that I made mention of the Phoenix Yellow Pages. There were 136 pages with the heading "automotive." That included the dealers, the car washes, muffler shops, wrecker services, and page after page of prospects—all in that one category. The Yellow Pages are organized by category, so you can identify immediately what a company does.

In Taszarek's list, "needs analysis" combines three items from my outline of the sales cycle, "qualifying," "needs analysis," and "answering objections." (I said there are lots of variations!)

"Confirm your facts" is a prelude to "presentation." Taszarek likes salespeople to go back to a prospect before the formal presentation and repeat what was said: "I heard you say you needed an extra $10,000 in sales next month. Is that correct?" From that second interview, the presentation is built using the customer's words.

"Recycle and upgrade" has an easy explanation: do it again. If there's a part of the cycle that didn't work, examine what you did during that step and make adjustments. Then do it again.

My favorite of Taszarek's steps is "Put it on the air with ceremony." This is something we seldom think about, but he saw it firsthand in a former communist country. He worked with a Polish broadcast company to develop their sales effort in the early days of capitalism. He told me he was amazed to see the management of a radio and television station gather in the conference room with newly signed clients.

Every third Friday, the director general (the equivalent of our general manager) conducted a signing ceremony among big advertisers, complete with lace tablecloths, silver coffee service, and photographers to capture the moment. The clients signed their contracts at the ceremony, and the photographers snapped away. The clients were then taken on a V.I.P. tour of the broadcast facility. Later in the day, the photographs were developed, printed, framed, and delivered to the advertisers to commemorate the occasion. Station personnel even hung the framed photographs on the wall if the client allowed. (They usually did.)

In the lobby of the station, where the typical U.S. radio or TV station displays pictures of air personalities, the Polish operation had framed logos of its clients. The clients were treated like royalty.

Building Partnerships

There are definite patterns to retailing. Merchandise bought by customers at this time this year will also be purchased by the same customers at this same time next year. Unless there's an aberrant weather pattern, snowblowers are bought in the winter, lawn and garden supplies in the spring, and barbecue utensils in the summer.

Spring sales are strong for fashion merchandise for women and children. Around Memorial Day each year, shoppers shift to summer merchandise and buy for their vacations. Summer buying includes gifts for graduates, for Father's Day, and for June weddings. By August and September, back-to-school buying means school supplies and clothing. Christmas season is the retailer's biggest selling period.

These highly predictable cycles happen each year, barring unforeseen circumstances like weather emergencies, recession, war, or international incidents.

Good advertisers plan ahead. Because of the patterns in the retail environment, stores will place orders for Christmas merchandise in the summer, preparing months in advance. As a seller of electronic media advertising, you cannot wait until November to pitch ideas for Christmas schedules. It's essential to become familiar with merchandise trends by product category so you'll know when planning is being done.

If all months were equal for retailers, the percentage of business each month would be 8.33%, or $\frac{1}{12}$ of the total annual revenues[5]. Since retail selling is seasonal, however, the percentages follow the seasonal cycles. For all retail stores and services the average is a low of 7.0% in January and February and a high of 10.4% in December. Even that range doesn't tell the specific seasonal story. Let's look at some examples of wide seasonal fluctuations:

- Lawn and garden stores are dormant in January (3.7%) and February (3.9%) and cultivate huge sales in May (16.8%).
- Mobile home dealers have their peak months in August (10.6%) and September (10.0%).
- Video stores show their best revenues in August (10.2%) and their lowest in October (6.5%) and November (6.7%).
- Children's clothing peaks in both August for back-to-school (11.0%) and December (11.2%).
- Book stores reach their best revenues in January (11.2%), August (11.1%), and December (13.5%).
- Florists have slow sales in January (6.7%) but blossoming sales in May for Mother's Day and proms (11.9%) and in December (11.6%).
- Department stores do only 5.9% of their business in January, as compared to 15.2% in December.
- Jewelry stores do only 4.9% of their business in January but they skyrocket to 23.3% in December.

You can understand why so many retail categories depend on December's Christmas buying. Only a rare category does not benefit from the holiday season shoppers. Such categories include: lawn and garden and video stores, auto dealers and auto repair, the bridal market, and real estate, all of which do not have big December revenue patterns.

Ideas for Sale

Every media outlet has commercials to sell. What your retail client wants is *ideas* to enhance business. Those ideas can take the form of intriguing copy concepts that make commercials more effective or a promotion that adds value to the commercial schedule and marketing punch for the retailer.

Promotion refers to an activity that gets viewers or listeners directly involved with an activity or event that enhances the image of your outlet and your advertiser's business. There are three basic types of promotion:

1. *Audience promotions*, which introduce your outlet to new users or extend the viewing or listening of existing users.

2. *Community promotions*, which are designed to support charity campaigns or large public events.

3. *Advertiser promotions or sales promotions*, which are designed to attract the attention of buyers and make them feel favorable toward your operation.

Effective promotion strategy combines the best elements of each type. An audience promotion can also involve one or more advertisers and become a sales promotion. CBS-TV created a contest with Minute Maid during their broadcast of the 1998 Winter Olympics: Minute Maid juice cartons promoted tuning in to the games to watch for a lucky number that won the viewer a prize.

Prize promotions are often constructed at the local retail level to build store traffic and audience participation at the same time. Radio stations often sell commercial schedules that include spots and give-aways of advertiser merchandise.

"The broadcaster who accepts the premise that the local advertiser needs marketing ideas rather than spot schedules has taken a giant step toward generating significant amounts of additional revenue from both new and existing clients," says Dave Donelson in *The Small Market Television Manager's Guide II*. Donelson, who heads his own sales promotion company, says, "Sales promotions . . . readily meet the advertiser's need for extra marketing muscle."

Promotional ideas come in a variety of shapes and sizes: contests, premiums and giveaways, special events, and special offers for customers who patronize the advertiser's business.

Donelson outlines the station's role in a promotion:

The station's role is to design the promotion and to help the advertiser execute it. The station may provide collateral material or merchandise as part of its package, with the cost built into the advertiser's total investment. Care must be taken that the client actually pays for the added value he/she is receiving from the station. The principal advantage of offering this type of promotion to one advertiser, of course, is that it puts the station in a consultant's role with the client, strongly cementing the relationship.

Stations typically mix an on-going program of promotions that are designed for one advertiser with occasional large-scale promotions in which multiple advertisers take part. Event marketing falls into the latter category. For instance, special-interest expositions such as bridal fairs and travel shows produce not only advertising revenues but also exhibitor fees and admissions.[6]

A Madison, Wisconsin, station, for example, rented a 20,000-square-foot coliseum to stage a weekend warehouse sale. Each advertiser received a 10' × 10' booth in exchange for a schedule on WMTV-TV that matched their first quarter expenditures on the station in the previous year. If they wanted a larger booth, they had to agree to spend more than they had spent in last year's first quarter. The public was invited to the two-day event at which WMTV advertisers sold items from their retail establishments. According to the station's Jacalyn Buesing, "Businesses that had smaller ticket items seemed to do better in sales than those with higher ticket items, although each of the retailers made sales and the exposure for all was terrific."

Many TV and radio stations create bridal showcases early in the year to focus on all the items a bride and groom will need for their big event. Bridal gowns, tuxedos, cakes, photographers, videographers, travel agents, and hotels are promoted in a weekend expo that features fashion shows and seminars. According to material from WLOX-TV, of Biloxi, Mississippi, one boutique sold five wedding gowns the week following a WLOX showcase.

92 ZOO radio in Lima, Ohio, uses its annual bridal show to accommodate advertisers who cannot otherwise afford schedules on the station. For example, a local singer wanted to buy radio time but found the pricing out of her range. She contracted for a booth at the bridal show to sell tapes and CDs, and to book singing appearances at upcoming weddings.

In Minot, North Dakota, KMOT-TV produces a cookbook each year. Recipes are solicited from viewers and compiled in *KMOT Favorite Recipes*. To be a part of the promotion, advertisers are required to run a schedule on KMOT. For that commitment, the advertiser gets a supply of the cookbooks to sell at its counters.

Local cable systems tap the resources of the networks they carry to stage promotional events. As you'll read in the chapter on selling cable, Nickelodeon, E! Entertainment Television, the Food Network, and others provide off-channel events that local systems can sell without sacrificing commercial inventory. In 1997, MTV Networks attracted an additional $3.5 million through promotions, according to the Cable Advertising Bureau (CAB).

The list could go on. In fact, it does: NAB, RAB, TVB, and CAB have assembled ideas for promotions that include case studies of how each idea works. The Broadcast Promotion and Marketing Executives

SALES PROMOTION

Advertisers are interested in getting their messages to the people most likely to use their products and services, and in the most economical way. Accordingly, sales promotion places heavy emphasis on the broadcast media's ability to reach targeted demographics at a competitive cost.

An effective sales promotion campaign is the result of careful planning based on the following considerations:

1. *Campaign purpose.* Is the primary purpose to project station image or to sell time? If the former, will it be attractive to the targeted advertisers? If the latter, will the focus be on particular programs or dayparts? What about the financial expectations?

2. *Target clients.* Will the campaign be directed toward existing advertisers and timebuyers, potential new clients, or both?

3. *Client benefits.* What benefits will the campaign stress? Demographics and the cost of reaching them? Exposure to potential new customers? Other benefits?

4. *Promotion methods.* Which medium or media will be used to reach the clients? Will the station's own air be used? What about the possibility of a joint promotion with an advertiser or advertisers?

5. *Content.* What content will best suit the medium or media selected? Can it be prepared by station staff or will outside services be required?

6. *Budget.* What costs will be incurred? Can they be justified by anticipated new business?

7. *Scheduling.* During which quarter of the year will the campaign benefit the station most? Will that period match advertisers' needs?

8. *Program impact.* Can the campaign be used to draw additional listeners or viewers to the station? Will it detract from programming?

9. *Evaluation.* Will the campaign be evaluated on the basis of dollars generated or will other criteria be used, also?

This checklist is from *Electronic Media Management*, second edition, by Peter K. Pringle, Michael F. Starr, and William E. McCavitt. ©1995, Focal Press. Used with permission.

---

group, BPME, is a terrific source of ideas for advertiser promotions. The publishers of *Radio Ink* magazine also have books on promotions. One three-volume series outlines more than 200 promotions that can be used by any advertiser in any medium.

As I said before, the ideas that retailers want to hear are not just promotions, although promotions tend to stretch the advertiser's dollar in positive ways. Clever copy ideas for commercials are also welcomed by many direct advertisers.

Advertisers, the Endangered Species

Jim Taszarek warns of a diminishing natural resource: advertisers. He looks at it this way:

Every town now has three banks. Walgreen's owns the drug business. Toys "Я" Us, Home Depot, Office Max, etc., are all names that own huge shares of market. [Wal-Mart founder] Sam Walton started it all. Mom and pop are going out of business in retail America.

They're being replaced by a diminishing number of entities who are being called on by more people with more new media than ever before.

The lesson for us: there is a natural void for a new role — idea suppliers to retailers.[7]

As a media seller, you can be one of those "idea suppliers." And through direct selling, you can present your ideas right to the person who counts. The good news about selling direct is that an idea can be presented to a decision-maker. Seldom are there layers of management or bureaucracy to delay an idea's implementation. For a glossary of industry terms that makes it easier to talk to retailers in their own language, see Figure 5–5.

Selling direct is an opportunity to demonstrate real selling skills by determining the best solutions for your client. The base, of course, is an effective advertising schedule that takes advantage of the audience your medium delivers. But what else? A contest or other promotional event? A live broadcast featuring station personalities? A joint marketing campaign with another advertiser? A mixed schedule on several co-owned radio stations? A combination of radio and television or of radio and cable?

As Diane Sutter of Shooting Star Broadcasting says, "Spots are easy. Everybody has spots to sell." When you provide marketing solutions to your client, you're going beyond spots to grow the client's business.

Co-op Dollars

The words "co-op" and "service" go hand-in-hand. Using co-op effectively requires research by the seller and exacting attention to paperwork details to make the program pay off for the advertiser. Of course, when it pays off for the advertiser, it also pays off for the seller.

In short, co-op is the shared cost of advertising by the retailer and a manufacturer or supplier. "Co-op" is short for "co-operative advertising" and is also called "vendor advertising" because the manufacturers or suppliers are referred to as "vendors" at retail.[8]

Co-op advertising traces its roots to the early 1900s when retailers looked for help in using the new, fast-growing advertising media: newspapers and magazines. The local shop owner asked manufacturers and distributors to underwrite advertising expenditures.

Newspapers tended to charge one rate for national advertisers like the manufacturers, and another lower rate to the local retailers. The newspapers also offered volume discounts to the local advertisers.

The retailer's rate advantage made co-op advertising a smart idea. The newspaper ad might cost the manufacturer $500, but it cost the retailer only $250. That math is easy. It gets better if the manufacturer provides co-op money at 50%, because the manufacturer pays $125 for an ad that would cost four times that amount. The retailer pays only half of what the newspaper charged.

There are as many co-op plans as there are manufacturers and distributors who maintain them. The percentages vary from plan to plan, and the strategies change with advertising strategy. The percentage of reimbursement is tied to the value of the product that the retailer purchases from the manufacturer.

Co-op plans often have "accrual" funds or "accrued amounts" tied to them. The fund (usually money, but it could also be merchandise) is reserved for the retailer and represents a percentage of the amount of merchandise that the retailer purchases from the manufacturer in a certain period. The period could be a calendar quarter, calendar year, a manufacturer's fiscal year, or a selling season, such as the lawn and garden season.

A plan that lists accrual "up to 3% of previous year's purchases" means that a retailer who spent $10,000 last year with the manufacturer has accrued a co-op fund of $300 for this year's advertising.

Each co-op plan has an "allowance," or a percentage of the advertising that the manufacturer agrees to pay. A typical allowance is 50–50, or 50%. You'll see that some co-op plans pay 100%. Remember, a 100% allowance means 100% of the accrued amount, not 100% of the cost of the schedule if the schedule is bigger than the accrual.

Here are typical co-op plans outlined to member stations by the RAB:[9]

- Teledyne Water Pik paid 100% co-op, up to 11% of the current year's net purchases by the retailer. One plan was in place until July 2, another through December 31.
- Stearns Manufacturing paid 100% co-op on children's wear, women's wear, and men's wear, up to 3% of the previous

GLOSSARY
OF INDUSTRY TERMS

- **MARKETING**
- **MERCHANDISING**
- **RETAILING**

FIGURE 5–5 The RAB is a remarkable resource for its member
stations. This glossary of industry terms allows
sellers to study the terminology used at the retail
level so conversation with direct accounts occurs in
the prospect's language. Used with permission from
RAB.

Account Specific: A product and/or promotion sold in to one store.

Accrual: Co-op money earned by a retailer as a percentage of purchases from a manufacturer.

Accrual Period: Retailer accrues co-op advertising funds on his purchases during a specific period of time set by the manufacturer.

All Commodities Volume: (ACV), basis for measuring retailer distribution which takes into account the relative importance of an operator. For example: Brand A has distribution in only one store. If that store does 10% of market sales, Brand A has 10% ACV distribution.

Alternative Retail Format: Deep Discounters, Mass Merchandisers, and Warehouse Club stores.

Amortization: The splitting of an investment between departments or budgets; the ability to take one investment and spread it over a longer period of time.

ANA/RAB Tear Sheet: Radio co-op documentation system combining script with affidavit.

Aperture: The height and width and depth of facings.

Assortment Plan: Sometimes referred to as a model stock. It is the required depth of stock by price, color, material, size, and classification to satisfy expected customer demand.

Audit or Survey: The checking of stores in a chain to verify how much product must be shipped to each store to fulfill distribution requirements.

Automatic Reorder: Setting up a reorder cycle whereby basic merchandise is ordered as the stock reaches a predetermined minimum level.

Back Card: A point of sale card affixed to the back of a Dump Bin or Floorstand, designed to present an advertising message at eye level above the product.

Bait & Switch: Illegal retail practice of advertising an unusually low-priced item, usually not even available, to lure customers into a retail store, where they can be sold a higher priced item.

Bedding: Mattresses.

Brand dollar: A budget that manufacturers use to promote the value of their brands to consumers.

Buyer: The individual who is responsible for purchasing products from a manufacturer or broker.

Buy-In: The procedure whereby a retailer is required to buy a new product or a certain amount to participate in a co-op schedule. Usually paid 100% by the manufacturer.

C-Store: Convenience store.

Case Allowance: Discount offered by a marketer to a retailer, based on a number of cases purchased.

Case Cards: Price cards that are used on displays, usually refrigerator and freezer cases.

Case Extender: Device used to extend shelf space from store case or bin into aisle. Extender is affixed to the case.

Case Commitment: The agreement by a retailer to buy a certain amount of product sold in cases from the manufacturer.

GLOSSARY OF INDUSTRY TERMS — 1

FIGURE 5–5 RAB's Glossary of Industry Terms, continued.

Case Deal: A price discount established by the manufacturer based on the volume of cases purchased by the retailer.

Ceiling Hanger: Type of point of purchase signage hanging from the ceiling above the product.

Chain: An operation of 11 or more retail stores, under corporate ownership.

Channel Marketing: A way of organizing marketing functions of a company to put individuals in charge of selling certain classes of trade.

Charge Back: Bill that store issues to vendors to collect money owed for co-op advertising or merchandise rebates.

Circular: Special advertising supplement (price/feature piece) inserted in the newspaper, picked up at the store, or mailed directly to the consumer.

Claim: The process and form used by the retailer to get reimbursement for advertising expenditures. (Sometimes known as the "proof of performance".)

Claim Period: The period of time after the advertising has run and before any deadline date in which claims can be filed, usually between 30-60 days after advertising schedule.

Coffin: Horizontal display in the frozen food section.

Commodity: Product sold by trades at less than price purchased for. Usually sold and promoted with product which has high margin. For example, coffee often is a commodity item sold at a loss, but sold and promoted with creamer, which holds a high margin.

Deductions: Incentives given/paid to trade from the manufacturer to motivate better display, space, reduction in prices, shelf facings, etc.

Delicatessen Buying: Sampling many lines of merchandise without providing sufficient depth to satisfy customer demand.

Demo: An demonstration of manufacturer's product.

Development Money: Funds outside the normal co-op budget that are based on proposals from the advertiser for such things as store openings, new products, or remote broadcasts.

DFI: Discount from invoice.

Direct Response: Non-store retailing. Consumers order products/service by mail, phone, fax or computer.

Disclaimer: Copy which is intended to limit a marketer's liability regarding promotional claims.

Discretionary Funds: All funds (vendor, promo, special event, market development) that a manufacturer may provide to a retailer.

DSD: (Direct Store Delivery) Marketer delivers direct to the store level without using wholesaler or warehouse. DSD's are products like chips, milk, and soft drinks, usually delivered by a rack jobber.

Display: Arrangement of product(s) usually accompanied by signage and special racks placed to attract a shopper's attention in the store.

Display Allowance: Incentive offered to retailer in return for off-shelf display of the marketer's products.

FIGURE 5–5 RAB's Glossary of Industry Terms, continued.

Display Funds: A budget used to pay for retail display.

Display Merchandiser: Permanent display provided by principal. Often includes some service attachment; i.e., battery tested, coffee grinder, etc.

Distributor: (Wholesaler) Business which warehouses products, provides a selling function to retailer, and ships/invoices goods. A distributor doesn't usually handle competing lines where a wholesaler usually does.

Distressed Product: Product that doesn't move off the shelf. Trade will sell at a loss to free shelf space for other products or return through agreement to principal. Often includes perishable products with dated shelf life so principal reimburses trade for distressed perishable product.

Feature: A highlighted product within a retailer's circular, newspaper ad, POP display, or even a radio or TV commercial.

Football: Product is price sensitive and product price is kicked up and down; i.e. Pepsi Cola, Coca-Cola.

Forward Buying: Buying excess product on deal to sell later at full price.

Franchise: Exclusive distribution agreement. Store may be company owned or individually owned. Examples; fast food, auto dealers, etc.

Free Standing Display: Portable display accessible from all sides positioned in open areas of stores to display product on promotion. Usually not placed at end of aisle.

FSI (Free Standing Insert): Coupon carrier usually delivered in Sunday edition paper.

Front End: The area of the front of the store (near the cash registers). Impulse items, high-profit items, and items that need to be watched are found here.

Front Loading: Requirement by principal for specific buy to qualify for promotion.

General Merchandise: Non-edible goods; i.e., automotive, baby needs, greeting cards, toys, batteries, photo needs, light bulbs, etc.

Generics: "No name" or "no frills" products.

GWP (Gift With Purchase): Promotional technique most often found in department stores; i.e., free eye shadow with fragrance purchase.

Gondola: Long narrow display case from which merchandise is accessible to customers on either side.

Gondola End: Product display designed for the end of a Gondola, a set of store shelving. Usually considered a prime, large display situation.

Graduated Percent Participation: A participation plan based on the number of ads the advertiser runs. For instance, the first ad may be 50% paid, the second ad may be 75% paid, and the third ad may be 100% paid.

Incremental Cases: Additional cases of product sold during specific promotion period.

Keystone: A method of applying markup whereby the cost price is doubled to arrive at the selling price.

Kiosk: A free standing, usually permanent display. Might be an information display for pamphlets or an actual selling space.

GLOSSARY OF INDUSTRY TERMS — 3

FIGURE 5–5 RAB's Glossary of Industry Terms, continued.

Launch: Roll-out new product introduction.

Leased Department: "Store within a store," Example; a shoe, cosmetics, or jewelry department in a department store. They pay rent and/or a percentage of sales to the larger store.

Length of Deal: Inclusive dates of case deal and promotion offered by principal.

Leverage: The tools the manufacturer uses to sell-in his/her product.

Limited Assortment Store: A store with under 1,500 items basically selling dry grocery and very few perishables. Very low margin and labor ratio. Practically no service offered.

Line Extension Allowance: Principal creates a new product that is really a variation of the old product; i.e., Liquid Tide, Tide with bleach, etc.

LMA (Local Marketing Allowance): The amount per case available to support the promotion at the local level. These funds traditionally have been used to lower prices, also for in-store Radio.

Loss Leader: Product featured at a low price, often below cost, in order to increase store traffic to sell additional profitable items.

LVP (Low Volume Product): Also called convenience items. Items stocked in a store purely for the consumer's convenience; i.e., shoe strings, kite string, etc.

Manufacturer's Accrual Notice: A notice to the retailer of amount of accrued earnings, sent by the manufacturer monthly, quarterly, or semi-annually.

Manufacturer's Claim Form: A specific form provided by the manufacturer that must be used in order to make claims upon that manufacturer for advertising reimbursement.

Manufacturer's Rep: A salesperson working directly for a manufacturer and calling on retailers and/or distributors.

Margin: Gross profit. The difference between the retail and wholesale price before expenses (other than costs of goods sold).

Markdown Pool: A budget from which manufacturer pays a percentage of the cost of selling goods at a marked down price.

Market Development Funds: Manufacturer funds available to boost product sales in a specific market.

Packaged Goods: Branded consumer products that are sold primarily via supermarkets, drug stores, convenience stores, and mass merchandising retailers.

Pass-Through Co-op: Co-op funds available to the retailer even though he/she purchases from the wholesaler or some other indirect source.

Performance Date: The last date by which an ad must run in order to qualify for co-op.

Performance Requirements: Rules and regulations set down by the manufacturer to which a retailer must adhere in order to be reimbursed for advertising costs.

Planogram: A space management tool. Layout of a store's floor space and shelf space as it pertains to store inventory, shelf stocking requirements, floor layout, and promotions.

POP (Point of Purchase): Display materials used at the point-of-sale to attract customer attention to a product.

GLOSSARY OF INDUSTRY TERMS — 4

FIGURE 5–5 RAB's Glossary of Industry Terms, continued.

POS (Point of Sale): Usually printed materials, but also electronic, designed to attract consumer attention and stimulate a purchase at the retail store. Also, Point-of-Purchase.

Prepack: Merchandise shipped already bundled in a size, it is either broken down further in the warehouse, or display is sold to the customer as the manufacturer packaged it.

Price Point: Price consumer pays.

Principal: Term used by trades and brokers for manufacturer.

Prior Approval: A term in some co-op plans that requires ads to be approved by the manufacturer before running.

Private Label: Packaged goods product similar to a nationally advertised brand, but priced lower. Trademark product usually regionally owned by the distributor/wholesaler or a chain common housebrand.

Product Introductory Allowance: Special trade allowance offered for new product, usually with a higher allowance than normal.

Product Turn: Selling out of total stocked inventory.

Proof of Product Purchase: Documentation used to claim pass-through co-op. Normally a document either filled out by the distributor or a copy of the retailer's invoice proving that he did purchase the product and indicating the amount of accrual he has earned.

Proof-of-Purchase: Sometimes a requirement by the marketer that must be remitted to qualify for his offering. Might be a box top, a UPC symbol, or a cash register tape.

Purchase Cycle: The frequency with which consumers buy a product or service.

Redemption Programs: Incentive offers such as free admission, product, or service that are made available with proof of purchase of a specific product.

Sampling: A form of consumer promotion in which the consumer receives free samples (often smaller sizes) either through the mail, in-store, or at an event.

Scanner: Cash register, or computerized checkout equipment which records transactions by reading the UPC code. Used to track consumer purchase of product, control inventory, and observe sales by category, brand, size, stores, and time periods. Can also measure effect of coupons and promotions.

Scanner Data: Data captured by the scanner process which can be used for inventory control, sales analysis, etc.

Sell-In: The process of the manufacturer selling goods to the retailer.

Sell-Through: The process of the retailer selling goods to the consumer.

Shelf Extender: A point-of-sale fixture which can hold additional product over and above normal shelf stock quantity to create extra product visibility and availability.

Shelf Talker: A small sign displayed with the product. It may give suggestions on usage of product, announce contests, or have tear offs for the customers.

Shipper: A free-standing display filled with the product sold as a package to trades. It is usually made of cardboard.

FIGURE 5–5 RAB's Glossary of Industry Terms, continued.

Shrink Allowance: Amount deducted from billing prior to shipment to cover anticipated loss or damage to products delivered to trades.

Shrinkage: Loss of merchandise due to theft.

Single: One display at the end of an aisle.

Sign Over: A process where the retailer releases his co-op funds to a wholesaler or manufacturer. These funds then go into a pool to be used for dealer group advertising.

Slotting Allowances: Set up charge billed to the principal by the trade. Fee includes entering items into the computer, self/fixture space, floor space, correspondence (i.e., shelf talker, POP, take-ones, etc).

Space Management: The science of analyzing product movement potential and allocating shelf inventory to best accommodate that potential. Also involves the decision of product location/position/facings on the shelf. See Planogram.

Split-Out/Force-Out: How a retailer distributes product among the stores in the chain. Example; a company with 20 stores in its chain may purchase 10,000 cases of toothpaste from a manufacturer, then "split-out" the product, sending maybe 500 cases to each of the individual stores.

Spread: Percentage difference between wholesale and retail price.

Street Money: Discretionary money given to specific retailers by manufacturers to "obtain their support" and obtain a higher sell-in of product or a better store position.

Trade: What a manufacturer calls his retail accounts.

Trade Dollar: Money paid by manufacturers to retailers to obtain price features, displays, and other trade-sponsored consumer-targeted promotions.

Vertical Co-op: A co-op program which combines a retailer's accruals from various manufacturers to fund a schedule.

Voluntary Group Retailer: Retailers who belong to a voluntary merchandising group sponsored by wholesalers who operate under a company name; i.e., Fleming Co., Super Valu, etc.

Warehouse Store: Large retail outlet that operates under a "no frills" theme. They carry everything from general merchandise to perishables. Usually stock a lot of private label items and don't have a big variety of products. Feature case-quantity pricing. Some charge a membership fee. Examples; Sam's Wholesale Clubs, Price Clubs, Costco, etc.

FIGURE 5–5 RAB's Glossary of Industry Terms, continued.

year's net purchases by the retailer. That program ended July 31.

- Melnor Industries paid 100% co-op, up to 2% of the current fiscal year's net purchases at retail for advertising its car wash system. That plan ended August 31.
- Black Leaf Products offered co-op at 100%, up to 3% of net purchases or the actual cost of advertising, whichever was less. Two of Black Leaf's popular lawn care products, Sevin Dust and Diazinon, were excluded from the co-op program.
- Gilmour Group offered 100% to distributors and a 50–50 split to dealers for up to 3% of the previous lawn and gardening season's net purchases.
- Celotex Corporation offered 100% co-op for up to 3% of the fiscal year's net purchases for commercials that mentioned four or more of their wall-covering patterns, 75% for three or more patterns, and 50% for mentioning only one pattern. They also required the retailer to sponsor a do-it-yourself clinic with their products.
- Ricoh Corporation offered 100% co-op, up to an amount in the retailer's accrual fund.

The differences in percentages, timing, and products makes co-op seem complex and daunting. Every one of those examples has a subtle difference. Since the manufacturers pay part, if not all, of the retailer's advertising schedule, everyone plays by the manufacturer's rules.

Rule one is submitting the manufacturer's co-op form to get permission to use the funds. Rule two is following the product specifications in the co-op program. For example, two Nike co-op plans I reviewed looked exactly the same, but there were subtle differences in the product categories. Rule three is to use the manufacturer's commercial if they supply one. And rule four is that retailers are expected to pay the media bills then get reimbursement from their co-op partners.

The complexity and subtlety of the system is why radio and television stations and the large cable interconnects hire "co-op coordinators." The coordinator's job is to research what's available from manufacturers and to keep salespeople apprised of how to help their retail customers. The key job of the co-op coordinator is to keep tabs on all those pesky details. Some co-op coordinators carry their own account lists, while others act as support personnel. You can read about a co-op specialist's job tasks in Figure 5–6.

The job of the co-op coordinator is truly servicing the accounts. In most cases, the coordinator will do the work that the retailer cannot or will not do. A small retailer may not have staff. A large retailer comes to expect the media outlet to provide the co-op service.

Whatever the size of the retail operation, you can imagine that the co-op world is confusing. Vendors inform their retailers of the plans available, but that doesn't mean the retailer understands how to apply the money to local media. Furthermore, one retailer may buy from dozens (sometimes hundreds) of manufacturers and suppliers. Each may have co-op money, and each has its own unique set of procedures. That's where the sales organization comes to the rescue. As Mark Monce of Multi-Ad Services says in *The Small Market Television Manager's Guide II*:

> The media can turn this frustration into a revenue-producing opportunity by offering to sort out a retailer's co-op for them. In most cases, co-op advertising is the last thing on a retailer's mind. A media representative who is able to build a trusting relationship with the retailer can take the headaches out of co-op advertising by organizing these facts and figures for them. In return, the retailer will be more likely to place his/her advertising with that medium.

RAB, TVB, and CAB maintain co-op files for their members to alert salespeople of vendor money available. They provide contact phone numbers, details of the allowances and accruals, and the expiration dates so sellers can take prompt action before monies are cut off. The co-op plans available in a given year require hundreds of pages of printed notes.

There are also co-op databases available by subscription with software tracking systems (including the Retail Co-op Advertising

CO-OP SPECIALISTS
Here are some of the duties a co-op specialist might handle at your station:
Develop co-op file systems to make information instantly accessible to the sales staff.
Establish a relationship with local manufacturer reps to promote co-op among client retailers – and use of the station by the manufacturer reps' retail customers.
Research the accruals of retail clients and provide analyses of the use of station salespeople in expanding advertiser budgets.
Accompany salespeople on client calls to orient advertisers about co-op and how it can impact their sales.
Educate station salespeople about using co-op and help them develop systems to monitor co-op activity on their accounts.
Organize dealer groups and other horizontal co-op campaigns.
Act as station liaison with manufacturers to verify plans and stimulate more Radio co-op programs.
Coordinate with traffic, accounting, continuity, and other departments to make sure all co-op business is handled and billed properly.

FIGURE 5–6
The differences in percentages, timing, and details of the hundreds of available vendor co-op programs prompts television and radio stations and some cable interconnects to add co-op coordinators—specialists who track the programs and service the accounts. Here's the co-op specialist's job, as defined by the RAB. Reprinted with permission.

System, sold by Mark Monce's company). The most basic source of co-op data is the *Co-op Source Directory*, published twice a year by Standard Rate and Data Service.

The key to success in capturing co-op dollars is to integrate a co-op plan into every retail sales proposal. Every proposal should address how a schedule will be funded. That's part of the qualifying process. Presentations to retailers should include an analysis of available co-op dollars and how they can make a proposed schedule possible.

As you collect information from a retail prospect, do a co-op audit. Ask for the top ten manufacturers they buy from, including account numbers. Then compare that to co-op information your operation keeps on file.

Monce says that retailers will respond in one of three ways: with immediate enthusiasm, with guarded enthusiasm, or with skepticism. "A portion of your client base will respond immediately and enthusiastically," he says. "Use these initial successes to motivate your co-op staff."

Retailers showing guarded enthusiasm are the most frustrating of the co-op clients. As the seller, you know the money's there waiting to be used, but it's not easy to convince the retailer to allocate it toward a co-op plan. The skeptical retailer may have had a bad experience in the past. "Don't pressure them," Monce advises. "The last thing you want to do is to appear threatening to your clients."

Once you've conducted the co-op audit, your next step is to approach the manufacturer. In the "Welcome to Radio Sales" program, RAB offers advice:

Understand that the person you are calling could receive hundreds of calls from media reps every week. As a rule, he or she wants to protect the manufacturer's best interests, which means that the co-op contact might be hesitant to release all of the information you are seeking.

Before releasing accrual totals, the manufacturer most likely will require some kind of proof that you are working with his/her customer. Sometimes the proof is as easy as giving them an account number, or you might have to fax them a release letter from the retailer. Once you provide the proper documentation, the accrual totals should be made available. At this point, you should ask the following questions:

Have the guidelines of your co-op program changed? Do you provide scripts? If not, does dealer copy need prior approval? Are you offering any one-time co-op opportunities? What kind of documentation is required after the schedule has run? Where should claims be sent?

That last question is essential. Manufacturers want proof that their schedules ran the way they were specified in the co-op plan. Proof includes an affidavit of performance and copies of scripts that were used in the program.

Newspapers always had it easy; a newspaper seller would send a copy of the ad as it appeared in the paper (a "tear sheet," torn from the page where the ad appeared). That practice is tougher in electronic media, so the Association of National Advertisers created (with RAB) a "radio tear sheet," a standardized form for documenting co-op advertising for the manufacturer's files.

Some manufacturers will refuse to pay co-op, even if they've established a co-op plan. It's their money, so they can spend it any way they choose. It's up to the seller to give the manufacturer the incentive to spend.

Estimates vary on how much money is available through co-op programs. I've seen figures as high as $15 billion. The consistent note with every estimate is that from 15% to 30% of co-op money goes unused!

Tapping into co-op funds is time-consuming and sometimes frustrating for both the retailer and the media seller. It requires more preparation than capturing straight advertising dollars. However, it's worth the while to bring in billing that might not have been placed on your outlet otherwise.

Special Selling Targets

In the early days of television, ethnic viewers rarely saw themselves represented on the screen. Lucy Ricardo's husband Ricky was the rare exception.[10] The options for nonwhite viewers were not just limited, but virtually nonexistent. With the explosion of media options generally came specific opportunities to claim a fast-growing, long-ignored market.

In an article called "Watching in Tongues" in *American Demographics* magazine, Marcia Mogelonsky sets the scene:

In America, non-English programs have been a casualty of mass-market broadcasting. As long as free-market competition led broadcasters to seek the largest audience possible, in-language television could not pay. Even today, the big four national networks (NBC, ABC, CBS, and Fox) broadcast only in English. That is because 86% of Americans speak English at home, according to the 1990 census.

That's changing quickly in markets where there are large numbers of non-English speakers. Hispanics, for example, watch about as much TV as the American average, but much of their TV time is spent with Spanish-language programming. Hispanics watch an average 15.3 hours of Spanish programming and 10 hours of English-language programming per week, according to Market Segment Research and Consulting (MSR) of Miami.

MSR's hometown leads the nation in Spanish-language television viewing: 17 hours per week in the average Hispanic household. Hispanics of Cuban and Puerto Rican descent tend to watch a higher-than-average amount of Spanish-language television. Compare Miami's numbers to Dallas's, for example: Hispanic viewers in Dallas watch Spanish-language television only about 12 hours a week. Most of Dallas's Hispanic population is of Mexican ancestry.

In Los Angeles, Univision's KMEX-TV has led the 6 p.m. time slot in viewers aged 18–34 by presenting a newscast that answers the specific needs of the Hispanic audience in Southern California. On a night when the NBC-owned TV station led with singer Michael Jackson's fatherhood, KMEX led with a story about a suspect in an area sex-abuse case fleeing to Mexico.

The same is true in Miami, where Univision's WLTV targets its newscasts to the local Spanish-speaking population and consistently beats the traditional English-language networks. (See Figure 5–7.)

In addition to owning stations like KMEX and WLTV, Univision operates the most-watched Spanish-language television network in the United States and Galavision, a leading Spanish-language cable network. Approximately 92% of U.S. Hispanic households can view Univision through 42 broadcast affiliates and 831 cable affiliates. They claim an 80% share of the Spanish-language network television audience, but sources outside the company attribute shares of 90% or more.

Univision programming looks like any network's programming: news, talk shows, comedy, and long-term mini-series called "novelas." One of the big stars of Univision is Cristina Saralegui, known simply as Cristina. Her daily talk show is seen by 100 million viewers worldwide and has been a ratings challenge to Oprah Winfrey.

Another is Don Francisco, whose "*Sabado Gigante*" is the highest-rated variety show on Spanish-language television. Univision is not using hyperbole when they call Don Francisco "charismatic." For three hours on Saturday night, he stages a spectacular with games, contests, comedy blackouts, and musical guests.[11]

The success of Univision led *Fortune* magazine to call them "the real fifth network" and *Broadcasting & Cable* notes that "stock analysts are rapidly exhausting superlatives to describe the performance of Univision." National advertising agencies understand: Univision scores well in TV's "upfront" selling market. You'll get the story of upfront in the next chapter.

Univision does so well that it's easy to forget that there's a second Spanish-language network, Telemundo. Despite a revamp of its prime-time schedule, the Telemundo audience declined from 26% of Spanish-language viewers in 1995 to 18% in 1997. The network restructured after bankruptcy in 1994 and, as *Broadcasting & Cable* puts it, "The network continues to appear helpless before the Univision programming onslaught."

National ratings show the same weakness at Telemundo. Of the top 20 Hispanic programs in September 1997, numbers 1 through 14 were on Univision, and numbers 15 through 20 were on Telemundo.

Hispanic Profile

A profile of the United States' Hispanic population is as follows:

- Population: 27 million, or one in nine Americans
- TV households: 7.74 million, including Spanish-dominant: 3.68 million (47.5%) (Spanish-dominant is based on language used by adults in the household, when two adults speak "mostly" or "only" Spanish)
- Income: 20% earn $50,000 or more
- Purchasing power: over $348 billion
- Advertising targeting Hispanics: $1.2 billion (1996)
- Radio stations: 476 broadcast in Spanish[12]

As strong a case as those statistics make for targeting Hispanics, the mainstream media outlets haven't caught up with the growth of the population and their buying power. One of the obstacles is understanding. What appeals to an audience of Puerto Rican ancestry in New York cannot attract an audience of Mexican ancestry in Houston or an audience of Cuban ancestry in Miami. It's not just a difference in country of origin: the words are different.

Since I live in Houston, I've watched the process firsthand as people from El Sal-

guess who's #1 in
prime time in miami?

nope.   **nope.**   **nope.**   **nope.**

yep.

WLTV/23. The first Spanish language television station
to rank #1 in prime time over the competition.
It Works!

Source: November 1996 Miami-Ft Lauderdale NSI Prime HH Rtg/Shr (M–Sa 8-11pm/Su 7-11pm)

FIGURE 5–7 Univision's WLTV in Miami was right to boast in this
ad in *Advertising Age*. The station targets local
newscasts to Miami's Cuban population and presents
the popular programming of the Univision network,
the most-watched Spanish-language network in the
United States. Courtesy Univision Television Group,
Inc., d.b.a. WLTV-Channel 23. Used with permission.

vador express needs that are totally different from people from Mexico. In Los Angeles, KLAX radio understands that their audience is from northwestern Mexico and addresses them with that in mind. The music mix on KLAX is totally different from the music mix on Houston's KQQK, which plays to a northeastern Mexican audience. To the uninitiated, "It's all Hispanic." To the Mexican-American, it's *norteño* or *ranchera* or *tejano*.

MIÉRCOLES/WEDNESDAY

	Hora/Time		Estación/Station			Lugar/Place			
			Letras o nombre de la estación (¿No sabe? Use el nombre del programa o número en que se sintonice.)	Marque uno (✓) Check one		Marque uno (✓) Check one			
	Comience <u>Start</u>	Termine <u>Stop</u>	Call letters or station name (Don't know? Use program name or dial setting.)	AM	FM	En su casa <u>At Home</u>	En un automóvil <u>In a Car</u>	En el trabajo <u>At Work</u>	En otro sitio <u>Other Place</u>
Temprano en la mañana *Early Morning* (desde 5 AM / from 5 AM)									
A mediodía *Midday*									
En la tarde *Late Afternoon*									
De noche *Night* (hasta las 5 AM jueves/ to 5 AM Thursday)									

Si usted no oyó la radio hoy, por favor, márquelo aquí. ☐
If you didn't hear a radio today, please check here.   7

FIGURE 5–8 "¡*Usted cuenta en los 'ratings' de la radio!*" says the first page of the bilingual Arbitron diary, or "You count in the radio ratings!" Courtesy the Arbitron Company. Used with permission.

Two of New York's ten highest-rated radio stations program in Spanish. So does Los Angeles's number one station. Radio attracts 33% of revenues spent in Hispanic radio and television, compared to the general market, where radio attracts less than 10% of broadcast ad dollars. (See Figures 5–8 and 5–9.)

Hispanic radio was primarily a local medium until the launch of Radio Unica, billed as "Hispanic-America's First—And Only—National Radio Network" in its advertising. Radio Unica was founded by Joaquin Blaya, former president of both Univision and Telemundo television networks. Broadcasts of World Cup '98 soccer was Radio Unica's first big win, attracting nearly one-third of men aged 18–54.

The cable industry has not yet reached as large a portion of the Hispanic market as they have the population in general. Only

Hispanic Language Preference Report
Summer 1997

Arbitron Hispanic-Controlled Metros	Total P12+ Metro Rank	Total P12+ Metro Population	Hispanic % of Population	Hispanic P12+ In-Tab	% of Hispanic P12+ In-Tab Classified as		
					Spanish Dominant	Bilingual	English Dominant
Albuquerque, NM	71	546,300	37.9	712	6%	25%	69%
Austin, TX	51	845,700	21.7	440	11%	26%	63%
Bakersfield, CA	86	424,400	32.7	471	33%	26%	41%
Boston, MA	10	3,264,900	5.6	239	15%	33%	53%
Chicago, IL	3	6,953,200	11.9	692	32%	35%	33%
Dallas-Ft. Worth, TX	7	3,621,500	14.7	535	31%	29%	41%
Denver-Boulder, CO	23	1,756,100	12.6	402	9%	19%	71%
El Paso, TX	69	553,700	75.5	912	31%	33%	36%
Fresno, CA	64	604,400	38.0	696	33%	25%	42%
Houston-Galveston, TX	9	3,393,100	22.9	893	27%	35%	38%
Las Vegas, NV	45	905,500	12.6	341	26%	35%	40%
Los Angeles, CA	2	9,741,200	38.1	2,797	37%	37%	27%
McAllen-Brownsville-Harlingen, TX	63	633,900	86.4	1,502	37%	34%	29%
Miami-Ft. Lauderdale-Hollywood, FL	11	2,984,300	38.9	2,019	42%	37%	20%
Monterey-Salinas-Santa Cruz, CA	78	484,900	29.7	470	35%	35%	30%
Nassau-Suffolk (Long Island), NY	15	2,247,200	7.6	204	20%	29%	51%
New York, NY	1	14,114,400	17.3	1,780	29%	40%	32%
Orlando, FL	38	1,042,800	11.9	323	19%	40%	41%
Philadelphia, PA	5	4,065,300	3.8	173	16%	35%	48%
Phoenix, AZ	18	2,074,000	16.7	577	25%	24%	51%
Riverside-San Bernardino, CA	26	1,363,300	29.4	861	25%	32%	43%
Sacramento, CA	28	1,358,400	12.1	268	11%	22%	68%
San Antonio, TX	34	1,203,100	49.0	1,195	13%	30%	57%
San Diego, CA	14	2,251,000	22.3	706	25%	35%	40%
San Francisco, CA	4	5,445,800	16.2	1,211	21%	31%	48%
San Jose, CA	30	1,339,500	22.0	598	21%	30%	49%
Tucson, AZ	60	652,900	25.3	342	15%	31%	54%
Washington, DC	8	3,535,000	6.9	268	15%	40%	45%

Metro Ranks as of Spring 1997; estimated populations as of 1/1/97 (all populations are for the Total Metro)

How to Read

■ The Albuquerque radio Metro ranks 71st in the U.S. among Total Persons age 12 and over.

■ Albuquerque has an estimated population of 546,300 Persons 12+.

■ Of those 546,300 Persons, 37.9% are estimated to be Hispanic.

■ Total Hispanic P12+ in-tab for the Summer 1997 survey was 712.

■ Of those 712 respondents, 6% were classified as Spanish Dominant; 25% were classified as Bilingual; and 69% were classified as English Dominant.

ARBITRON

FIGURE 5–9 Arbitron discovered that there was no right way to classify language preference among Hispanics. In the Arbitron radio diary, respondents are asked what language they speak at home and away from home, and what language they prefer. Here are the answers from Arbitron Hispanic markets. Courtesy the Arbitron Company. Used with permission.

4.4 million Hispanic households (56.6%) are wired, compared with 66.7% of the general population, according to Nielsen figures. CBS Cable, for example, delivers CBS TeleNoticias, a 24-hour news channel, to more than 10 million households in Latin America, 2 million in Canada, and fewer than 1 million in the United States. (See Figure 5–10.)

Cable operators' need to develop new revenue streams will cause them to look favorably at new networks aimed at the Hispanic population, and digital tiers will allow cable system operators to deliver more channels.

A Gallup Organization study released at a meeting of the National Hispanic Corporate Council in 1996 showed only 36% of U.S. marketers targeted Hispanic consumers, even though that population segment was growing at a rate five times that of the population in general. Of the 36% of marketers targeting Hispanics, less than 2% said they tracked results of their marketing efforts.[13]

Other notes from the study include the following:

1. One-fifth used dedicated Hispanic ad agencies; one-fourth used mainstream agencies.

2. Fewer than half of marketers who target Hispanics tracked ad reach or exposure levels.

3. Over 60% of marketers did not know the percentage of total market sales accounted for by Hispanic consumers.

4. Radio, newspaper, television, and special events were the most-used vehicles for reaching the Hispanic market.

The Asian-American Market

Asians are a smaller population group in the United States, and they also watch fewer hours of television in their own languages. The average Asian-American adult watches about 6 hours of native-language television, according to MSR. The largest number of hours watched is in San Francisco, just under 10 hours a week. The lowest is in Chicago, 4.6 hours a week.

I'm not surprised about the San Francisco totals. That city has not only a large Asian-American population but also an aggressive local television station, KTSF, that does for its Asian-American audience what KMEX and WLTV do for their Hispanic viewers.[14]

KTSF broadcasts programs in Cantonese and Mandarin, serving the Bay Area's large Chinese-American communities. The station also produces material in Korean, Japanese, Vietnamese, Tagalong, Farsi, Mon Khmer, and Hindi.

The daily, hour-long newscast in Cantonese is the cornerstone of KTSF programming. Managing editor Mei Ling Sze says her newscasts are aimed at recent immigrants. "Many of them have never voted or been involved in legislative issues before. We provide them with news and community information." The station has a satellite link to Hong Kong and covers breaking Asian news from that vantage point.

Many KTSF advertisers dub their English-language commercials in Cantonese, Mandarin, or Japanese. Some use subtitles over English commercials. A few large advertisers with a presence in Asia use the same commercials on KTSF that they use in Asian countries.

In Houston, a very ethnically diverse city, I have also watched the increase of Asian-American populations. It's a city where the ballots are in English and Spanish, but the street signs along Bellaire Boulevard on the southwest side are all in Chinese. Bellaire hosts one of two "Chinatowns" in Houston, although neither is strictly Chinese. You see lots of Korean and Japanese businesses, as well.

A large section near downtown is home to the city's Vietnamese-American population. This community is so strong economically that its businesses support three competing radio broadcast operations. None of the three owns a radio station, but each buys time on local stations to present news and feature programs in Vietnamese. To pay for the blocks of time, each organization resells the time to advertisers who want to target commercials to Vietnamese-American listeners.[15] Asian Americans have an annual purchasing power of $107 billion, according to MSR research.

FIGURE 5–10 When the Spanish-speaking population catches up
to the general population in cable connections, CBS
Cable will be ready. CBS provides TNN (The
Nashville Network), CMT (Country Music
Television), and *CBS Eye on People* to English-
speaking audiences in the United States.
TeleNoticias, owned in part by CBS, meets its
success outside the United States. Courtesy CBS
Cable. Used with permission.

The African-American Market

When electronic media thinks of ethnic markets, it usually thinks first of the African-American population, long served by black or "urban" radio formats. MSR figures show the African-American audience with a purchasing power of $469 billion, clearly the largest of the ethnic groups in the country.

My friend Dick Oppenheimer, now a lecturer at the University of Texas at Austin, was once the head of a chain of radio stations that served African-American audiences in Houston and New Orleans, among other cities. At some point in the early 1970s, he traveled to New York to call on national advertising agencies with sellers from his station group's rep firm. In a presentation to the agency for an underwear manufacturer, the buyer told Oppenheimer, "We don't buy black media." It wasn't the first time Dick (or any seller of nonwhite radio) had heard that phrase. Many advertisers at that time shunned any but the whitest, most mainstream advertising venues.

Oppenheimer's response was, "Listen to yourself. Do you know what you're saying?"

"What do you mean?" the buyer answered.

"You're telling me that black people don't wear underwear!" Dick claims that changed the buyer's mind, and he got the order.[16]

For many years, "black media" meant radio and only radio, and the stations that reflected the black experience often dominated their markets. It was common to see "urban" stations in the number-one positions in Atlanta, Houston, Memphis, Chicago, and other markets with large African-American populations. Few of the stations were owned by African-Americans, however.

"The advent of cable provided an opportunity for additional program content and formats," say Robert Hilliard and Michael Keith in *Global Broadcasting Systems*. "To some extent cable networks function like radio stations, not able to compete on an individual basis with broadcasting networks, but seeking to obtain a sizable share of targeted audience. For example, the Black Entertainment Network (BET) on cable provides programming to and about African Americans that is not available from any other source."[17]

BET was the first network with African-American programming 24 hours a day. What's more, BET was black-owned and black-operated, guided from the beginning by founder Robert L. Johnson. BET began in 1980 as a 2-hours-a-week service seen only on Friday evenings. In 1991, the company became publicly traded with its stock listed on the New York Stock Exchange. By 1998, the network had grown to 50.5 million cable households and 52% of television households, and was growing at about 10% per year.

Extending the BET brand are other media vehicles: *Emerge* and *B.E.T. Weekend* magazines. In 1996, BET launched a second cable channel, called "BET On Jazz," featuring jazz concerts and interviews with jazz musicians, with some rhythm and blues artists mixed in. BET On Jazz reprised *The Nat 'King' Cole Show*, an early effort at showcasing black talent on NBC in 1957. The vintage program's guests were the day's jazz greats: Pearl Bailey, Mel Torme, Peggy Lee, Sammy Davis, Jr., and Ella Fitzgerald.

The best of the BET stories is in their advertiser lists. No more do you hear "We don't buy black media." More than 85% of the commercials on BET are general market ads. The advertiser list they sent me was 14 pages long and had the names of almost 300 national companies and brands. Here are a few:

A. C. Delco, Adolph Coors Company, Allstate Insurance, America Online, American Express, Anheuser-Busch, AT&T, Avon, Bayer, Burger King, CBS, Coca-Cola, General Motors, Hallmark, Hanes, J. C. Penney, Jamaica Tourism, Lincoln-Mercury, M&M, MCA, MCI, MGM, NBC, Nike, Northwest Airlines, Walt Disney Company, Wendy's.[18]

Seeing Hanes on the list must make Dick Oppenheimer proud. (See Figure 5–11 for a comparison of radio listening by Hispanic and black audiences.)

Hispanic Radio Today

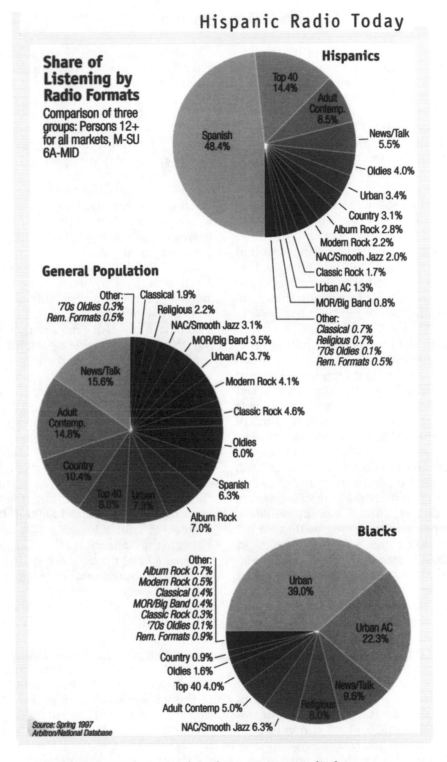

Share of Listening by Radio Formats

Comparison of three groups: Persons 12+ for all markets, M-SU 6A-MID

Hispanics

Top 40 14.4%
Adult Contemp. 8.5%
Spanish 48.4%
News/Talk 5.5%
Oldies 4.0%
Urban 3.4%
Country 3.1%
Album Rock 2.8%
Modern Rock 2.2%
NAC/Smooth Jazz 2.0%
Classic Rock 1.7%
Urban AC 1.3%
MOR/Big Band 0.8%
Other:
Classical 0.7%
Religious 0.7%
'70s Oldies 0.1%
Rem. Formats 0.5%

General Population

Other:
'70s Oldies 0.3%
Rem. Formats 0.5%
Classical 1.9%
Religious 2.2%
NAC/Smooth Jazz 3.1%
MOR/Big Band 3.5%
Urban AC 3.7%
Modern Rock 4.1%
Classic Rock 4.6%
Oldies 6.0%
Spanish 6.3%
Album Rock 7.0%
News/Talk 15.6%
Adult Contemp. 14.8%
Country 10.4%
Top 40 8.8%
Urban 7.9%

Blacks

Other:
Album Rock 0.7%
Modern Rock 0.5%
Classical 0.4%
MOR/Big Band 0.4%
Classic Rock 0.3%
'70s Oldies 0.1%
Rem. Formats 0.9%
Country 0.9%
Oldies 1.6%
Top 40 4.0%
Adult Contemp 5.0%
NAC/Smooth Jazz 6.3%
Urban 39.0%
Urban AC 22.3%
News/Talk 9.6%
Religious 8.0%

Source: Spring 1997 Arbitron/National Database

FIGURE 5–11 The general market response to radio formats compared to that of Hispanic listeners and black listeners. From "Hispanic Radio Today," ©1997, the Arbitron Company. Used with permission.

Selling Sports

To use a sports term, the stats are staggering. Rupert Murdoch's Fox network made sports history in 1993 when it preempted CBS TV's longtime NFL rights by paying $1.58 billion to broadcast football from 1994 through 1997. The total 4-year package for football rights included Fox, NBC, ABC, Turner, and ESPN and totaled $4.4 billion. That was a 20% increase over the previous contract and a new record price.

But wait! In sports, records are made to be broken. The next round of bidding took NFL rights to an unprecedented $18 billion—not just a percentage increase but *quadruple* the cost. All the networks that previously had football rights were caught in a well-choreographed negotiation conducted in mid-December 1997, by the NFL.

"Forget the price tag," said *The Wall Street Journal*. "The most surprising thing in last week's $18 billion TV deal for pro football is that, against a lineup the likes of Rupert Murdoch, Ted Turner, and Michael Eisner, the toughest corporate player turned out to be the National Football League." Instead of the genteel negotiation that went so far as to allow networks to reduce rights fees in the recession year 1987, the NFL went for the money and got it.[19]

CBS was first in the negotiations, according to *The Journal*, and immediately set new precedents by suggesting a $500 million per year bid. That put CBS back in the football business with an overall commitment of $4 billion for AFC games for eight seasons (the package NBC used to have) and the rights to two Super Bowls.

ABC retained its "Monday Night Football" franchise and NFL playoff games, and captured the rights to Super Bowl telecasts in 2000 and 2003. ABC's co-owned network, ESPN, stole Sunday night football telecasts from Turner Broadcasting. To capitalize on selling synergies, ABC introduced "NFL Prime," which combined the forces of the two networks so ABC games, ESPN games, and all the pregame shows and features could be sold as a package.[20]

CBS's challenge was to show the advertising world that the expensive rights purchase was worth more than the ego boost it gave the network and its affiliated stations. There was an advantage for CBS: radio. "Look for a team of radio salespeople who already sell the many NFL football games for CBS-owned radio stations to descend on New York to teach TV salespeople what works and what doesn't," said the newsletter *Inside Radio*.[21]

NFL rights are the most expensive, but not the only fees that are going up. In order to take the sting out of the loss of NFL programming, both NBC and Turner took aggressive (read "expensive") turns at rights to the National Basketball Association. Each promised to show more games, a move that eroded profitability.[22]

Because of escalating rights fees, cable aired more baseball games in the 1998 season than broadcast television, for the second year in a row. According to *Broadcasting & Cable*, the average number of broadcast games per team fell from 65.5 in 1996 to 59.6 in 1997 and to 55.2 in 1998. The average number of games on cable was 62 in 1997 and 68.6 in 1998.[23]

Hockey rights fees also doubled. As *Broadcasting & Cable* puts it, "With Nielsen ratings as ugly and rights fees as brutal as the action on ice, ABC and ESPN have stepped up to pay about $600 million for exclusive national broadcast TV and cable rights to the National Hockey League." The rights package for the Disney-owned networks was approximately twice the previous deal which divided NHL games between Fox and ESPN. Fox did not bid on the new rights package when it came up for renewal in 1998.

At some point, you'll sell *some* sporting event. It may not be a schedule for Anheuser-Busch in "Monday Night Football" (although *somebody* sold it—for $120 million), but there will be sports in your future. Sports and electronic media go hand-in-hand. Even on the local level, sports coverage is a valuable commodity.

The key to sports is affinity. Fans follow their teams with religious fervor. Some fans even paint their faces "Oilers blue" or

"Bengals orange" for football games. High school basketball in parts of the Midwest is a social event for towns large and small. In Texas, high school football games draw such large crowds, they are played in venues like the Astrodome. An advertiser that appears to support a favorite team gets the halo effect of being associated with that team. If you're a seller for local TV, local cable, or local radio, you'll want part of that fervor for your advertiser client.

The smaller the market you're in, the more likely you'll be selling sports packages within the network broadcast of a team that does well in your area, whether a major league franchise or a college team. Stations in Louisiana fight to get the rights to LSU Tiger broadcasts because there are so many alums who stay in the state after graduation. Notre Dame is a sought-after commodity due to its national following.

Unless there's that kind of undying, loyal affinity, your success could be in direct proportion to the team's success. After the Philadelphia Phillies' winning 1993 season, radio stations in Pennsylvania and Delaware had a big year selling spots in the 1994 baseball broadcasts. A radio general manager told me he netted $300,000 that year in Phillies business alone. When the team did less well in 1994, the same station attracted only $90,000 in Phillies revenue for the 1995 season.[24] (See Figures 5–12 and 5–13 for a look at radio broadcasting during the Houston Astros games.)

Sports selling means more than spots in games. A top-40 station in Lima, Ohio, sells weekly tailgate parties at high school football games. The station doesn't carry the play-by-play but stages personal appearances by its personalities. At each game, the station throws mini-footballs with the client's name imprinted on the side. (Yes, the station logo is on the other side!)

All-sports radio stations are on the air in most large markets and in many small markets. The closer they are to a major league team the better, but some all-sports stations survive if there's a strong local connection (like Ohio State in Columbus). Again, the sales pitch is one of affinity: sell to direct accounts who like sports, and sell to retailers who like the personalities on the station. (See Figure 5–14.) Sports stations carry more live endorsement commercials than almost any other type of radio station.

Nontraditional Revenue

Ideas for new ways to make money come and go as fast as new forms of media merge and converge. Because of that, I was hesitant to include a discussion about NTR. My fear was that if I led you to certain ideas, by the time you started selling electronic media, they might not be fashionable (or even practical). To the experienced seller, the next few pages may seem a cursory overview at best. That's my intention.

In the purest sense, NTR means revenue that does not come from traditional spot sales. This meaning has been stretched over recent years to mean dollars that haven't been in standard buys, such as co-op money, which you read about earlier in this chapter. (See Figures 5–15 and 5–16.)

Consolidation in the radio industry created the need for additional dollars to feed debt service and mega-mergers, so NTR sources were tapped by the new companies in that field. Nationwide Communications created the "Nationwide Marketing Information Center" to link the sellers in its various markets (before it was bought by Jacor Communications). It was an attempt to look for dollars beyond typical advertising sales. Chancellor Media bought an existing company that specialized in NTR.[25]

Nonspot revenue at radio is 11.8%, according to *Manager's Business Report*. Nonspot's importance is growing at both radio and TV as a way to add new revenue. It's not unusual for a station in a major market to generate $250,000 in NTR dollars with a large event.[26]

What constitutes NTR? Basically, NTR includes anything that makes money and doesn't eat up commercial inventory.

ASTROS RADIO COVERAGE

ASTROS RADIO AFFILIATES

Alpine, TX	KVLF	1240AM
Baton Rouge, LA	WIBR	1300AM
Beaumont, TX	KLVI	560AM
Brenham, TX	KWHI	1280AM
Bryan/College Station, TX	WTAW	1150AM
Columbus, TX	KULM	98.3FM
Conway, AR	KFCA	1330AM
Conway, AR	KTOD	92.7FM
Corpus Christi, TX	KSIX	1230AM
Crockett, TX	KIVY	92.7FM
Edinburg, TX	KURV	710AM
El Campo, TX	KULP	1390AM
Fredricksburg, TX	KNAF	910AM
Gonzales, TX	KCTI	1450AM
Houston, TX (Flagship)	KILT	610AM
Houston, TX (Spanish Flagship)	KXYZ	1320AM
Jacksonville, TX	KEBE	1400AM
Lake Charles, LA	KLCL	1470AM
Lampasas, TX	KCYL	1450AM
Livingston, TX	KETX	92.3FM
Lufkin, TX	KRBA	1340AM
Madisonville, TX	KMVL	1220AM
Monroe, LA	KMLB	1440AM
Morgan City, LA	KMRC	1440AM
Navasota, TX	KWBC	1550AM
New Iberia, LA	KANE	1240AM
New Orleans, LA	WLNO	1060AM
Orlando, FL	WWZN	1440AM
Rockdale, TX	KRXT	98.5FM
San Antonio, TX	KENS	1160AM
Shreveport, LA	KFLO	1300AM
Temple, TX	KTEM	1400AM
Texarkana, TX	KKYR	790AM
Thibodaux, LA	KTIB	640AM
Tyler, TX	KGLD	1330AM
Victoria, TX	KAMG	1340AM
Woodville, TX	KVLL	1490AM
Woodville, TX	KVLL	94.7FM
Armed Forces Radio Network		

As of 10/20/97. Subject to change.

FIGURE 5–12 At the top of every hour during Houston Astros radio broadcasts, Hall of Fame play-by-play announcer Milo Hamilton salutes three stations on the Astros network. Each station sells local commercials in pre- and post-game shows plus two positions in each Astros game. Courtesy of the Houston Astros. Used with permission.

IN-GAME SPONSORSHIPS – FULL NETWORK

Air your commercial over our entire network throughout Texas, Louisiana and Arkansas.

:60 SPONSORSHIP

	Unit Cost	Season Total
One :60 spot	$650	$121,550
Two :60 spots	$630	$235,620
Opening & Closing Billboards		
Three :60 Spots	$610	$342,210
Opening and Closing Billboards		
In-Game Product Exclusivity		
Four :60 spots	$600	$448,800
Opening and Closing Billboards		
In-Game Product Exclusivity		
Pre-game and Post-game Exclusivity		

:30 SPONSORSHIPS

60% of the applicable :60 rate

Billboards and product exclusivity for :30 sponsorships is based on :60 equivalencies (i.e. four :30 spots equal two :60 spots).

SCHEDULE INFORMATION

All English radio rates are net and based on a 187-game schedule, comprised of 162 regular season games plus a minimum of 25 spring training games. Full season sponsors will not be charged for additional spring training games that are aired. On average, 30 spring training games are scheduled. If fewer than 25 spring training games are played, "make good" spots will be aired during the regular season games. Radio sponsorships of fewer than 187 games are subject to an additional charge of 10% per unit. Ask about two-year and three-year sponsorship packages and partial network sponsorships.

All sponsorship packages are based upon inventory available and are subject to change without prior notification.

FIGURE 5-13 The Houston Astros own their own radio network and sell sponsorships for the full network, which gets the advertiser exposure on the Houston flagship station, KILT-Star 610. Here's the Astros Radio Network rate card from the beginning of the 1998 season. Courtesy the Houston Astros. Used with permission.

FIGURE 5–14

"I must admit that this is the first place I've worked where people constantly react to my business card," said Bruce Gilbert of KTCK in Dallas when I asked if I could use his card in this book. Using the look of a game ticket not only reinforces the station's name, The Ticket, but also adds to strong branding. Bruce credits Jeffrey Dunbar with the idea. Used with permission.

Events like the warehouse sale and the bridal showcase you read about earlier are examples. Others include: concerts with major artists who let your medium share the profits; concert promotions that allow you to sell additional sponsorship at the venue; mall promotions; station vehicles with advertiser logos; phone systems that allow commercials to play with specific information like a weather forecast or a movie schedule; telephone dating services; job lines that help both recruiters and candidates; loyalty clubs and "card-carrying viewers"; celebrity golf tournaments; food festivals; and Web sites.

T-shirts and other branded items like hats, Koozies, and key chains are popular giveaways for stations and have become lucrative at retail as well. Radio stations have sold their merchandise for some years, and the major networks sell their branded gear to tour groups and at sporting events. Now, local TV stations get into the act as well. "Such sales opportunities aren't limited to clothing and specialty items," says Dave Donelson.[27] "Consumer services such as bank credit cards and videos celebrating local events (produced from station news footage) have also been successfully marketed over the air by stations."

Also in the NTR category are tower leases and similar business deals. As I collected ideas for this section, I found radio and TV stations that leased the land under their towers for farms, cattle grazing, and shopping centers. FM stations lease their frequency's sideband to transmit background music or special programming like reading services for the visually impaired.

Print products like newspapers and magazines are also part of the NTR arsenal. Cox Communications, which owns newspapers, television, radio, cable, and Internet-based city sites, also sells to radio and TV stations a publication called *The Marketeer*, essentially a business journal published by the stations to take advantage of nonbroadcast revenues.[28] Many country music radio stations publish their own newspapers, full of features on country music stars and local club and concert information. Those who don't have staff to create their own publications call on com-

FIGURE 5–15A
Wal-Mart is the focal point of this presentation from the Sinclair stations in the Wilkes–Barre/Scranton market, but the bills are paid by Pennsylvania manufacturers who participate in the promotion. From the RAB's 1997 collection of NTR proposals. Used with permission.

panies that syndicate magazines, allowing each station to add a few pages of local copy to personalize the "national edition."

Television stations sell sponsorships of public interest campaigns that promote education, health, family values, safety, or other causes. Many, like the "For Kids' Sake" and "Teenagers & Tough Decisions" campaigns, are available on a syndicated basis, although stations with sufficient staff and commitment can create their own. Often stations develop a news quiz or weather feature to highlight a popular personality. The reason these ideas fit the NTR model is that instead of using regular inventory, they simply add sponsorship to public service messages.

Warren Wright, whose quarterly sales tracking forms appear in Chapter 4, has helped broadcasters exploit NTR through his association with several companies. As vice president of sales for 21st Century Communications, he helped stations set up interactive telephone systems that provide job listings and sponsorship opportunities. "If the problem is that unemployment is at a 24-year low, then the solution is to find qualified candidates," Wright says. "Recruiters are searching for alternative and effective means of finding workers."

"Where is the money?" he asks.[29] "In recruitment. In a recent Sunday edition of the *Cleveland Plain Dealer*, 8,200 column inches were dedicated to the Help Wanted

WAL*MART
SUPER CENTERS

CONCEPT

* *Best Of Pennsylvania is a program that offers many exciting sales increasing elements for Wal*Mart Super Centers and their Pennsylvania manufacturers. This program is created to direct consumer attention to buy Pennsylvania products. It will include the grocery and general merchandise departments of the West Hazleton and East Stroudsburg stores.*

* *It is designed to reach consumers in two ways:*

    1. *Through retail support with displays and special POS*
    2. *Through promotional support on nine key radio stations*

* *We want your shoppers to know that buying American is good, buying Pennsylvania is great!*

* *This program will run for five weeks and will include associations and manufacturers that produce Pennsylvania products.*

* *Products will be displayed and special POS will identify the participating products.*

* *Wal*Mart Super Center will host a "Best Of Pennsylvania" kick off event. This event will include a Live Action Broadcast, demos and sampling of featured products. A second Live Action Broadcast will take place during the fourth week of the program again with demos and sampling of featured products.*

TIMING

* *March 1 - April 4, 1997*

Property Of Sinclair Radio Of Wilkes-Barre, Inc.

WAL*MART SUPER CENTERS WILL RECEIVE

* *A complete marketing program designed to increase sales*
* *315 :60 second radio commercials per week on nine radio stations*
* *Complete orchestration of the program*
* *Two Live Action Broadcasts at each store*
* *POS and all collateral in store material*
* *Community involvement and goodwill*
* *Product demonstrations by a professional demo service*

THIS ENTIRE PROGRAM CAN BE FUNDED BY YOUR PENNSYLVANIA MANUFACTURERS PARTNERS

To fund this program, we will need 20 manufacturers. They will receive:

* *Special display during their one week promotional period*
* *81 radio commercials on nine radio stations during their one week promotional period*
* *Special POS identifying them as a Best Of Pennsylvania product*
* *Product demo/sampling*

TOTAL PROMOTIONAL VALUE: $48,000

TOTAL INVESTMENT PER PRODUCT: $2,400.00

TOTAL COST OF WAL*MART SUPER CENTERS: $00.00

Property Of Sinclair Radio Of Wilkes-Barre, Inc.

FIGURE 5–15B Inside the "Best of Pennsylvania" proposal. The radio stations take advantage of their co-ownership to involve nine stations. Wal-Mart helps to gather the Pennsylvania manufacturers. Wal-Mart gets the customer traffic. The stations do the leg work and the promotion work and collect NTR. (Note: POS stands for "point of sale.") Courtesy RAB. Used with permission.

section. At $100 per column inch, that is $820,000 in one day!" Wright likes radio because it "reaches people where they work, reaches people who are gainfully employed, and provides an alternative to the newspaper classified reader." His Job Line service disseminates detailed job information off the air and prescreens candidates for employers. Systems like the one Wright represents offer fax-back capabilities, the opportunity to transfer a caller directly to a sponsor's switchboard, and data collection programs.

Wright's first taste of NTR was at a Washington, D.C., radio station where he was sales manager. His station bought the billboards and banners at Washington's Merriweather Post Pavilion and resold them to advertisers.

Wright admits that NTR ideas are hard to assess. "There's no trackable system," he told me, "and there's not one entity track-

ing all of it." That means that what might be NTR to your operation could be considered standard revenue to your competitor.

The newest addition to the NTR arsenal is the Internet. Of all electronic media, NBC made the most extensive foray into the online world by forming a partnership with Microsoft to establish MSNBC and its *www.msnbc.com* Web site. NBC also sold promotions and advertising on its *www.nbc.com* site. General Motors' Oldsmobile division was integrated into a storyline for an NBC show, *The Pretender*.[30] In an online game on the NBC site, users were asked to click onto various parts of an Olds looking for clues to solve a mystery. E! Entertainment Television offered viewers a chance to chat online and get more information on E! programming.

CNN, Warner Brothers, Disney, and ESPN are described as "nearly in the black" with their online ventures by *Broadcasting*

EVERYONE WINS

Your Customers

*   *Will have another reason to come to Wal*Mart Super Centers for savings*

*   *Your customers will be able to help Pennsylvania by buying the advertised specials*

The Manufacturers

*   *Will secure valuable display space*

*   *Radio commercials will help them increase incremental sales*

Wal*Mart Super Centers

*   *Will increase stores' traffic and sell more of the store, not just the specials*

*   *Wal*Mart will promote goodwill within the community by providing a valuable service*

Property Of Sinclair Radio Of Wilkes-Barre, Inc.

FIGURE 5–15C This puts the whole program in customer-focused, win-win terms. Wal-Mart customers, Pennsylvania manufacturers, and Wal-Mart Super Centers are listed on the proposal as beneficiaries, but the involved stations win, too. Courtesy RAB. Used with permission.

& Cable. MTV is the sole major media Web presence that is reportedly making a profit, and MTV claims to have done so since their site's launch in 1994. "Otherwise, the list of sites claiming to be profitable is short and comprises uniquely positioned Web programmers with particular audience targets, niche interests or unusual formulas," says the magazine (noting that pornography was the only clear online winner).

ESPN's SportZone capitalized on what Web developers call the tiered approach, with some content—video clips, for example—available only for a monthly payment of $5 or a $40 annual subscription. To participate in a sports fantasy league, sports

THE KNIX CONNECTION

Find out why some callers are saying ...

The very next day you've got five or six possible matches on your answering machine.

This is the best way that I've ever seen to meet somebody.

I met somebody great on the KNIX Connection!

I'm really grateful that I made the call.

Probably the best thing about the whole system was the convenience of it.

❤ If you're single and over 21, you know how difficult it can be to meet someone you're compatible with. But now there's the **KNIX Connection**, a computerized singles matching system.

❤ Simply call and answer a few questions about what kind of person you'd like to meet and about yourself. The KNIX Connection selects only potential dates who you're 95% compatible with.

❤ It takes just a few minutes and you could be talking to your perfect match later this week!

Enroll FREE, call 1-800-KNIX-FM-1.

1-800-KNIX-FM-1

FIGURE 5–16
The calls are screened at a free 800 number, then there's a charge for the KNIX Connection dating service. That makes it NTR. This ad appeared in the monthly *KNIX Magazine*, another example of NTR for the Phoenix station. Courtesy KNIX. Reprinted with permission.

fans paid ESPN $19.95. Subscriptions accounted for 30% of ESPN's Web revenues in 1997, with advertising revenues over $4 million, according to *Broadcasting & Cable*.

Local outlets, too, created online presences or participated in Web ventures provided by their network affiliates. NBC created NBC-in (for "Interactive Neighborhood") so its local television affiliates could share resources.

The newsletter *iRADIO* claims that WNNX radio in Atlanta (known as "99X") made over one million dollars in advertising revenues during 1996.[31] Much of the 99X site is the same as any radio Web presence, with on-air program announcements, profiles of their disc jockeys, e-mail, and concert schedules. Some elements, however, stood out:

- The morning show page included the Coca-Cola logo.
- The live links sported a Blockbuster Video logo.
- A CD countdown page (the weekly top 30) had a McDonald's logo and link.
- The contest page displayed a Budweiser logo and link.

The big money on the 99X site was in streaming special-event audio programs, available only online. The sponsors mentioned above (and others) were part of the special-events programming. *iRADIO* claims that sponsors could "own" the live events, making the investment valuable. According to the newsletter, 99X was making $50,000 to $70,000 per "broadcast" in 1997.

Other stations, like Charlotte's WSOC, built and hosted Web sites for advertisers. "For the price of a full-page ad in the *Charlotte Observer*, we can build a Web site and host it for a year," WSOC'S Craig Hahn told *iRADIO*. The station built sites for Blockbuster Pavilion, a concert venue, and the Charlotte Checkers hockey team, among others.[32]

All of these opportunities are terrific NTR sources. This list cannot be comprehensive because there are so many untapped sources of revenue for electronic media sellers. Most organizations have begun NTR departments to maximize their efforts so sellers of advertising inventory do not have to change hats and sell nontraditional revenue as well.

In many outlets, NTRand Web selling comes under the heading of "new business development" or NBD. I think "NTR" states it best. After all, new business development could (and does) also mean calling on prospects who have never advertised.

Advertising Agencies

You read in the first chapter that the modern advertising agency can trace its history to a Philadelphia newspaper agent. Today advertising agencies are hired by businesses to provide a variety of services, including media planning and buying, creative copy writing and production, consumer research and product testing, and consultation on product positioning and imaging. Not every agency provides all services.

You'll find huge international agencies like the London-based Saatchi & Saatchi with offices and affiliates across the United States and around the world. At the other end of the spectrum are one-person agencies that handle just a few local clients. Some agencies are wholly owned by the company they work for and are responsible only for that company's advertising. Not surprisingly, they are called "house agencies."

Media organizations have to make a judgment about whether some small operations truly qualify as agencies. When that judgment is made, an outlet is said to recognize the agency: that is, it acknowledges that the agency in question is a good credit risk and fulfills requirements qualifying it for commission payments.

Traditionally, agencies took a 15% commission on the media buys they made. If a schedule on a local cable system cost $1,000, the agency would keep $150 and pay the system the remaining $850. Agencies also charged clients an additional 15% for materials purchased on the client's behalf. For example, an agency might hire a videographer for $1,000 and bill the client for $1,176.50. Basic math tells you that figure is 17.65%, not 15%. The agency arrives at the charge by working *backwards* from the total. In order to keep 15% as commission, the agency calculates a gross amount that yields the net price when 15% is deducted. That's called "grossing up" the charges.

Add 15% to the $1,000 fee and you get only $1,150. Subtracting the 15% agency commission from that figure leaves $977.50 (and an unhappy videographer!). For the videographer to get the full fee, the agency must add 17.65%. (Math purists will argue that the figure should be closer to 17.67% to be exact, but 17.65% is easier to calculate without messy rounding of pennies.)

I intentionally use the past tense when talking about the 15% and 17.65% standard commissions at advertising agencies. They became a negotiating tool as advertisers began to consolidate their businesses. An agency that agreed to a 12% or a 7% commission rate put itself in a better position to win new business.

Some advertisers demanded commission concessions from their agencies in the mid-1990s; some agencies volunteered concessions. The result was high turnover of accounts, or "churn," as clients moved from agency to agency looking for better deals and more effective use of advertising dollars.

Since agency earnings were traditionally governed by how much money was spent in media, advertisers questioned efficiency. Was the agency spending money to benefit the advertiser or to collect big commissions? The question led some advertisers to structure a fee arrangement with their agencies. Fees might be paid as monthly retainers on hourly time-and-charges billing.

Advertising Age reported that commissions accounted for 35% of agency compensation in 1997, and fees accounted for 58%. The magazine contrasted those numbers with figures from 1982 when 71% of agency compensation came from commissions and only 8% came from fees. (The remaining percentages were combinations of commissions and fees.) The change in compensation structure increased the profit margin for the typical agency from 13% in 1983 to 19% in 1997.[33]

In addition to the big, national agencies, you'll encounter marketing specialists who have been hired by advertisers to coordinate planning and media buying from inside the advertiser's operation. They're called "house agencies," as I mentioned earlier. Media outlets generally afford them the same commissions that an outside agency would get. The advantage to the advertiser is that the commission stays in house and is added to the bottom line of the company.

Just like the media they buy, ad agencies are evolving. At the 1998 meeting of the American Association of Advertising Agencies (the Four A's), the systemic changes in the industry were apparent. Four A's chair Jordan McGrath says that clients (advertisers) at one time perceived "immense value" in agency products and services. He laments "client CEOs who are so preoccupied with quarterly earnings that they remain detached from advertising—and of course from the ad agency—and view advertising as an expense, not an investment."

There was a time when agencies handled everything in the marketing and advertising process for an advertiser. The business consolidation of the 1980s and especially of the 1990s, converted agencies to niche vendors of specialized services. One agency might produce spots, another creates the buying plan, while yet another handles brand promotion. Specialty shops create radio commercials and not television commercials. Some agencies handle only online advertising.

That turn toward specialization has changed some of the terminology. "Agency of record," for example, once meant "the agency." Now it means the *leading* agency, the one that coordinates an advertiser's promotion of products handled by more than a single agency.

Agency Organization

The biggest agencies may have thousands of employees located all over the world. The smallest may be that one-person shop I mentioned earlier. The basic functions, regardless of size, are account management, creative copy and production, and media evaluation and planning. Here is a brief overview of each of these three functions:

1. Account management people, usually called account executives, are the contacts between the agency and the advertiser, which is the agency's client.

2. Creative people come up with the concepts and copy direction for ad campaigns.

3. Media evaluation involves planners who recommend what media to use for a campaign and what the media mix should be. Buyers then select the individual newspapers, magazines, radio and TV stations, and cable systems to buy.[34]

The last group, the buyers, are the agency people you'll encounter most often. They are the primary contact for electronic media sellers. You'll immediately note a stark contrast between the retail direct client and the agency buyer client:

- The retailer, as you read in the last section, wants impact, action, and response. The buyer wants efficiency.
- The retailer wants a solution to a problem, to take advantage of opportunity, and to see results firsthand. The buyer wants justification: proof that he or she bought the right thing.
- The retailer wants return on the investment, firsthand indication of dollars well invested. The buyer wants no hassle, no challenges.

Those are true opposites. Since most sellers of electronic media, especially at the local level, sell to both types of customers, you must get ready for the dichotomy.

The more skilled you become at dealing with agencies, the more you'll learn about working within multiple levels of the agency. Some people call it "getting around the buyer," but that's not the point at all. If you work with the buyer in order to get to the media planner, then you will be able to work with the people who respond to ideas, the decision-makers, and not just those who execute the plan. More about that later.

The largest agencies also have research departments, which conduct consumer studies on client products and evaluate commercials both before and after production. Some have sizable production departments to create and produce print and electronic ads in house. Some have traffic departments, which get the right commercial to the right media outlets.

Based on a 1963 discussion with Seymour Banks, then the vice-president and manager of media planning and research for the Leo Burnett Company in Chicago, Darrell B. Lucas and Steuart H. Britt arrived at three principles for advertising:

1. There is no one medium (or type of media) best for everything—all forms of media have their place, depending on the circumstances.

2. Media recommendations should be developed only after decisions have been made about both creative and marketing strategy.

3. The more that is known about audiences of advertisements, the better the media recommendations will be.[35]

Those principles still apply, almost 40 years later. They should guide both the advertising agency and the electronic media seller who calls on agencies.

What's Good for General Motors

"What's good for General Motors is good for America" was said often in the first half of the twentieth century. General Motors (GM) grew so rapidly that it seemed to pull the nation's economy along in its wake.

When GM announced its 1998 advertising budgets, *Broadcasting & Cable* used a twist on the old saying as a headline: "What's good for General Motors is good for TV." The company's $2.1 billion budget was shifting from print to television, according to the subject of the magazine's cover story, Philip Guarascio, marketing and advertising vice president for GM's North American operations.

As Guarascio puts it in *Broadcasting & Cable*'s interview:

> I can't foresee a time, at least in my career, when network television as we know it— and I mean the expanded version of network, including CBS, NBC, ABC, Fox, Warner Brothers, and Paramount—when they won't have the lion's share.
>
> When I came to GM we were spending almost no money in cable or syndication. Now we're spending a lot in both, and by ranking we're probably number one or two in those categories. And we're spending more money locally.

Asked by the magazine where GM spends most of its cable dollars, Guarascio answered,

> It's split pretty wide—TBS, TNT, USA, CNN. We're probably in 12 or 15 networks. We started to see some cable networks almost as reexpressions of some of the things we used to do in print: smaller, better-defined audiences.

About the decline of traditional network viewing:

> [I]f you look at network television, advertisers have paid more for a commodity that is decreasing in audience. . . . it doesn't mean it has less value. You could argue network television has more value than it did 15 years ago. On a cost-per-thousand basis it's not the same, but your ability to generate a large audience in a fragmented media spectrum in some ways is more valuable.[36]

That's great news for television and cable sellers. Those quotations from Guarascio should be in almost every TV selling presentation.

Just as GM's shift in media mix benefited TV and cable in 1998, burgers and fries were a boon to radio. McDonald's increased overall ad spending and doubled local promotional activity for its "Did somebody say McDonald's?" campaign.

At the same time, Burger King combined television and radio to launch its french fry "makeover." Burger King's director of advertising, Andy Bonaparte, told *Radio Business Report (RBR)* that TV took the lead because he believes consumers must be able to see a new food product, something he couldn't do with radio. The chain created radio advertising especially for the french fry campaign so TV and radio worked in concert.[37]

RBR reported that Burger King does 60% of its business at the drive-through window, thus radio has an advantage in delivering customers behind the wheel. RAB says that people make fast-food decisions 8 to 10 minutes before purchase, so it's not surprising that fast food is one of radio's largest advertising segments, since those customers are most likely driving in their cars and listening to the radio at that time.

Optimizers

With 98 million television households, the United States is a huge television market. Add to that the long history of commercial television and you can expect people in the TV industry to feel a sense of superiority over television and advertising in the rest of the world. That superiority was challenged, however, when a European data-modeling program was introduced to U.S. ad agencies with magic words as part of the presentation: "efficiency," "effective reach," and "optimization." What agency could resist?

In 1997, Procter & Gamble required agencies competing for its billion-dollar media buying assignments to include optimizing systems in their proposals. Two things happened immediately: other agencies began evaluating optimizers, and there was a feeling of culture clash among advertisers and television sellers.

First, an optimizer is a computer-based approach to evaluating media options and identifying the set of TV programs that best achieves the advertiser's objective. (It works for radio spots and print pages, too, but TV got most of the attention when optimizers were introduced in the United States.) Because most marketers attempt to maximize reach, the objective is to find the media schedule that achieves the target reach at the lowest cost. Optimizers are software programs that use algorithms to evaluate schedules and compare a variety of alternatives to arrive at the best one.

Here's the hitch: to work properly, optimizers require respondent-level data, that is, specific records of specific viewing choices made by specific viewers over time. In Europe, that information existed, so optimizers worked very well. In the United States, respondent-specific data did not exist when optimizers were introduced, although Nielsen planned to make it available.

Optimization systems first began in the United Kingdom when that nation's TV ratings authority began giving third-party analysis companies access to raw respondent data. The first two popular off-the-shelf optimization systems in Europe were Super Midas and X*pert, which are essentially the same except that Super Midas is more program-specific, while X*pert is daypart-specific.

Additional studies in Great Britain survey television viewers three times a year. These proprietary studies generate large databases of which programs people pay the greatest attention to. Media plans are based on that information, merged with the optimizer data.[38]

In the European markets, optimizers determine how the final schedule will look based on the number of spots needed to achieve a plan's goals, the costs of buying the spots, and the actual audience delivered by those spots.

Users of the optimizer software claim that there are too many "disconnects" between the creation of a plan and the ultimate purchase of a TV schedule. The execution of the plan looks nothing like the original, they claim, thus the need for the optimizer.

"All of the hype might make you think optimizers can magically increase the effectiveness of advertising," writes Neil Braun, president of the NBC television network in *Advertising Age*. "Optimizers can be useful tools, but not more. There is no magic—it's only computer software."

What Braun terms "optimizer mania" is caused by efficiency, effective reach, and optimization, "which made it easy to overlook the absence of the most important word: effectiveness. Optimizer software cannot optimize effectiveness. It can help you implement strategies, but it cannot design a strategy for you," Braun says.[39]

A regular commentator on national advertising, Erwin Ephron, partner in the media consultancy Ephron, Papazian & Ephron, says of optimizers: "The essential media planning problem is allocating a scarce resource, dollars, to achieve a maximum communication effect. That's the simple definition of optimization." Ephron notes that the key to success is knowing "what it is you want to optimize. Are you optimizing the reach of an advertising buy? Or, are you optimizing the reach against a set number of frequencies?"

Expect optimization software to spread, especially if Nielsen can deliver the respondent data needed to make the U.S. system more like the successful European model. Expect also that agency buyers will use optimization to effect the best (i.e., the lowest) media pricing while you, as a seller, are trying to demonstrate value and extract the highest dollar for your advertising.

Sellers of syndicated television hoped of optimization would demonstrate efficiencies in syndication that advertisers had not perceived. That view is supported by Jack Klues, chairman of Leo Burnett's media unit, Starcom, who says, "Optimizers break down the artificial barriers we've established over the years between broadcast [network], cable and syndication, and it deals with the way people watch TV: by program."

The television newsletter "*Spots 'n Dots*" calls optimizers "a way for agencies to buy cable with a clear conscience," reflecting the mood of their publication's audience at local TV stations. The newsletter reported, however, that two agencies, Western Media and Bates, were experimenting with optimizers on local buys. At a TVB research conference, Bruce Goerlich of Bates "assured the assembled station people that the optimizer was 'good news' for local stations," said "*Spots 'n Dots*."[40]

Reach or Frequency?

"How often should the target of the marketing plan be exposed to the message? At what level of frequency does this exposure operate with a maximum degree of effectiveness? How does one judge when the communications threshold has been crossed?"

Those questions opened a speech by Joseph Ostrow to a meeting of the Advertising Research Foundation in 1982.[41] At the time, Ostrow was executive vice president and director of communication services for Young & Rubicam advertising. Later he was the president and CEO of the CAB.

With all the types of analysis of advertising available, Ostrow's focus was on frequency. "Frequency values can be established by demography, geography, seasonality, etc., and as a result each one of these criteria becomes a more effective and specific element in the development of a media plan."

Ostrow foresaw today's highly segmented population. He also predicted that media alternatives would multiply, and the public's media habits would change as a result.

"Marketing campaigns are more frequently being directed to narrow groups of the population, making the ability to communicate even more important than with mass-directed marketing messages, because if you miss the narrow target you miss it all." Ostrow urged his ARF audience to use frequency distribution analysis, which allowed planners to examine alternatives related to frequency goals.

Until that time, media plans were often based on "average frequency." The goal might be "50% of the target . . . an average of four times." The danger with the average was that a number of targeted consumers might never hear the message, while another number might be overexposed to the message. Either was counter-productive.

Ostrow was not the first to suggest frequency as a key component in media planning, although his audience was an important one, and his remarks were reprinted in *Advertising Age*, which disseminated his thinking through the ad community quickly. Westinghouse Broadcasting introduced a slide rule in the 1960s to show the relationship between reach and frequency on its radio stations. Stated simply, it used a formula to show advertisers how many times a commercial had to be aired in order to be heard a certain number of times by the average listener. The idea was adopted widely and became known as "Westinghouse math."

In the 1970s, Ellen Hulleberg, research director at McGavren-Guild, the station representatives firm, promoted the idea of effective rating points, (ERPs), in addition to gross rating points (GRPs). And as head of marketing research for Lever Brothers Company, Mike Naples wrote *Effective Frequency: The Relationship Between Frequency and Advertising Effectiveness*. It was published in 1979 by the Association of National Advertisers, which gave the idea considerable clout.[42]

Ostrow's ARF speech had the benefit of quantifying specific criteria for advertisers in determining what level of effective frequency was most desired:

- An established brand needs lower frequency; a new entry into the market needs higher frequency.

- The greater the brand dominance, the greater the brand loyalty, the lower the frequency.
- Longer purchase cycles need lower frequency. Short purchase cycles need higher frequency for top-of-mind awareness.
- If the strategy is to overtake competition, higher frequency is needed.
- Different demographic groups have different learning curves and rates of forgetting.
- A simple message requires lower frequency; a complex message requires higher frequency.
- The continuation of an existing campaign requires lower frequency; a new campaign requires higher frequency.
- The more specific the product sell, the lower the required frequency. Imagery requires higher frequency for reinforcement.

Radio traditionally used "the theory of three": three exposures to a message was sufficient frequency. Ostrow's new approach indicated the need for greater sophistication in buying for frequency. Since radio is the medium best known for delivering frequency to an advertiser, a specific formula was developed to achieve effective frequency: the optimum effective scheduling (OES) system. The principle behind OES is to buy just the right number of spots to eliminate wasted reach. OES is covered in Chapter 8.

Review Highlights and Discussion Points

1. In theory, any business that wants to remain in business is a potential customer for an advertising medium.
2. The more often a seller casts his or her net, the more possible customers may be found to add to a list. An account list is no more than a hunting license. The key is the qualification process—discovering who is and who is not an appropriate target.

3. There are three typical sources for business: national advertisers, local and regional advertisers, and direct accounts. Other channels of revenue also exist.
4. Agency selling is ratings-oriented, while direct or retail selling is results-oriented. Selling direct means calling on business owners and not on advertising agencies.

5. Most direct business is not affected by ratings. The direct advertiser is more likely to measure effectiveness by how many people came through the door and how many pieces of product were sold as a result of the advertising.

6. Agencies are hired by advertisers to provide a variety of services, including media planning and buying, creative copy writing and production, and consumer research and consultation on product positioning and imaging. Not every agency provides all services.

7. Agency buyers are charged with getting the most coverage for their client's dollars: more spots for the least amount of money.

8. The direct seller is also called a retail seller, because most direct business comes from some sort of retail store. There is no succinct definition for "retail," because it is such a broad category.

9. The purpose of retail advertising is to generate store traffic, increase sales volume, improve net profits, and build the store's image and reputation.

10. Often the retailer is the business owner, who is hypersensitive about the dollars spent on advertising. Retailers often view advertising as a necessary evil and an expense to be avoided if possible.

11. Because of the patterns in the retail environment, stores will place orders for Christmas merchandise in the summer, preparing months in advance. These predictable cycles happen each year, barring unforeseen circumstances like weather emergencies, recession, war, or international incidents. Good advertisers plan ahead.

12. Promotion refers to an activity that gets viewers or listeners directly involved with an activity or event that enhances the image of your outlet and your advertiser's business.

13. There are three basic types of promotion: audience promotions, community promotions, and sales promotions. Effective promotion strategy combines the best elements of each type.

14. Promotional ideas come in a variety of shapes and sizes: contests, premiums and giveaways, special events, and special offers for customers who patronize the advertiser's business.

15. The ideas that retailers want to hear are not just promotions, although promotions tend to stretch the advertiser's dollar in positive ways. Clever copy ideas for commercials are also welcomed by many direct advertisers.

16. Advertisers are interested in getting their messages to the people most likely to use their products and services, and in the most economical way. Accordingly, sales promotion places emphasis on the medium's ability to reach targeted demographics at a competitive cost.

17. Co-op is the shared cost of advertising by the retailer and a manufacturer or supplier. The term is short for "cooperative advertising" and is also called "vendor advertising."

18. The options for nonwhite television viewers were traditionally limited, if not nonexistent, but with the explosion of media options generally came specific opportunities to claim a fast-growing, long-ignored market.

19. The need by cable operators to develop new revenue streams will cause them to look favorably at new networks aimed at the Hispanic population, and digital tiers will allow cable system operators to deliver more channels.

20. When electronic media thinks of ethnic markets, it usually thinks first of the African-American population, long served by black or "urban" radio formats.

21. Rights fees bring staggering prices to major sports leagues. NFL rights are most expensive, but they're not the only fees going up.

22. The key to selling sports is affinity. Fans follow their teams with religious fervor, and advertisers on sporting events get the "halo effect" of being associated with a favorite team.

23. The smaller the market you're in, the more likely you'll sell sports packages within the network broadcast of a major league or college team.

24. Nontraditional revenue is revenue that does not come from traditional spot sales. NTR includes anything that doesn't take up commercial inventory.

25. There's no tracking for NTR, so what might be classified as NTR by one outlet might be standard revenue for another.

26. Some advertisers demanded commission concessions from their agencies in the mid-1990s; some agencies volunteered concessions. The result was high turnover of accounts, or "churn," as clients moved from agency to agency looking for better deals.

27. The biggest agencies may have thousands of employees located around the world. The smallest may be one-person shops. The basic functions, regardless of size, are account management, cre-

ative copy and production, and media evaluation and planning.

28. With 98 million television households, the United States is a huge television market. Add to that the long history of commercial television and you can understand why people in the TV industry were reluctant to accept optimizers from Great Britain.

29. An optimizer is a software program that uses algorithms to evaluate schedules and compare a variety of alternatives to arrive at the best one.

30. Expect optimization to spread, especially if Nielsen can deliver the respondent data needed to make the U.S. system more like the successful European model.

31. Reach and frequency are central concepts to a successful advertising campaign and thus are an important consideration of media buyers.

Chapter Notes

[1] Jim Taszarek conducted a session called "Secrets to Successful Direct Prospecting and Selling" at the Radio Advertising Bureau 1998 Marketing Leadership Conference.

[2] What's more direct than radio? The material in the RAB's "Welcome to Radio Sales" applies to any electronic medium, especially the section called "Working with Retail Accounts."

[3] Charles Nelson's advertising story was told by Jan Alexander and Aimee L. Stern in "Avoid the Deadly Sins in Advertising," in *Your Company* magazine, August/September 1997.

[4] Fred Poppe's *50 Rules to Keep a Client Happy* are basic rules of courtesy and common sense. Cited in Chapter 2.

[5] Annual percentages of retail sales are from U.S. Department of Commerce figures provided by the RAB.

[6] Promotion ideas came from *The Small Market Television Manager's Guide II*, cited previously, and from *Money Mak-*

ers: Sales Promotions from the Hundred Plus Television Markets, Washington, DC: National Association of Broadcasters, 1992. The station in Lima, Ohio, 92 ZOO, is a Shane Media client.

[7] Jim Taszarek's warning of "diminishing natural resources" was in *Large Market Radio Selling*, the newsletter his company, TazMedia, used to publish.

[8] The description of how co-op advertising works comes from a combination of my own experience; from details outlined in *Electronic Media Management*, cited previously; from "Co-op Advertising: Making Something Big from Something Small" by Mark Monce of Multi-Ad Services, Inc., in *The Small Market Television Manager's Guide II*, available from the NAB, also cited previously; and from the RAB.

[9] RAB publishes material about co-op plans and alerts their membership about amounts available, what's needed to qualify, and the deadlines im-

posed by the manufacturers. TVB and CAB do the same for their members.

10 Using Ricky Ricardo of the "I Love Lucy" show as an example of one of the few nonwhite faces on early TV was lifted directly from "Watching in Tongues" by Marcia Mogelonsky in *American Demographics*, April 1998.

11 Specifics on Univision's history and programming are from the network's advertiser presentation materials, which include "The Univision Story," revised, December 1997.

12 *Broadcasting & Cable*'s "Special Report: Hispanic Television and Radio" provided information on the battle between Univision and Telemundo and on the Hispanic profile. The report appeared in *Broadcasting & Cable*, October 6, 1997.

13 The Gallup study was quoted in *Advertising Age*, November 4, 1996, in "Gallup: Few Targeting Hispanics," by Jeffrey D. Zbar. "The New Audience: Hispanics" seems an unlikely title, but that's what *USA Today* called a collection of articles on the Hispanic market on March 18, 1998.

14 The story of KTSF is from "Watching in Tongues."

15 I was asked to study Houston's Vietnamese media for a project and worked for one of the three competing radio operations.

16 Dick Oppenheimer told the underwear story to his class at the University of Texas at Austin the day I was a guest speaker in 1997.

17 Robert L. Hilliard and Michael C. Keith let us know that there are more perspectives on media and broadcasting than the U.S. view in *Global Broadcasting Systems*, Boston: Focal Press, 1996.

18 The story of Black Entertainment Television and the advertiser list came from sales presentation materials distributed by the network.

19 The feeding frenzy of football negotiation is described in detail in "TV Deal Shows How the NFL Plays Hardball," by Stefan Fatsis and Kyle Pope in *The Wall Street Journal*, January 19, 1998. Fatsis and Pope's first report on the new

rights package appeared the previous week: "NFLScores Nearly $18 Billion in TV Rights," *The Wall Street Journal*, January 14, 1998.

20 ABC's "NFL Prime" package was announced in a full-page advertisement in *Advertising Age*, May 11, 1998.

21 "Mel Sends Radio Salespeople to Teach CBS TV How to Sell the NFL," *Inside Radio*, February 17, 1998.

22 NBC's and Turner's NBA deals were covered in *The Wall Street Journal*'s "Marketing & Media" column on November 11 and November 12, 1997. Also see *Advertising Age*, October 27, 1997: "NBA Marketing Strategy Hinges on New TV Deal" by Jeff Jensen.

23 "Cable's Batting Average Keeps Climbing" by Kim McAvoy was one of several articles in "Baseball 1998," a special report in *Broadcasting & Cable*, March 30, 1998.

24 Pete Booker, president of Wilmington-based Delmarva Broadcasting shared stories of selling the Phillies broadcasts after the team's slump.

25 Nationwide's move was in *Inside Radio*, January 14, 1997. Chancellor's acquisition of Global Sales Development, Inc., was reported in *R&R Today*, May 1, 1998.

26 Estimates of NTR at radio appeared in *Manager's Business Report*, August 1998.

27 Donelson wrote in *The Small Market Television Manager's Guide II*, cited previously.

28 Information on the Cox Communications magazine, *The Marketeer*, came from an interview with the company's Tammy Kinzer, October 1, 1997.

29 Warren Wright assembled presentation materials for me that I have adapted for text. Warren is vice president of sales for 21st Century Communications.

30 The NBC Web site and the Oldsmobile promotion were cited in Chuck Ross's article, "Olds' Intrigue Stars in Web Game Based on NBC TV Show," *Advertising Age*, July 28, 1997.

31 WNNX's success on the Internet was described in "Stations Making Money on the Web: Part One" in the newsletter *iRADIO*, November 1996.

32 WSOC's Internet story was part two of the *iRADIO* series, December 1996.

33 The comparisons of commissions and fees in 1982 and 1983 with commissions and fees in 1997 came from *Advertising Age*, September 14, 1998. See "Price Becomes Prime Issue" by Mercedes M Cardona. In the same issue, *AdvertisingAge* reported that Ford Motor Co. would abandon commissions to its agencies in favor of a performance incentive payment system. Later, GM did the same.

34 Who knows better about the organization of an advertising agency than David Ogilvy? The brief outline is from *Ogilvy on Advertising*, cited previously.

35 The three principles for advertising that hold up 40 years later are from *Measuring Advertising Effectiveness* by Darrell Blaine Lucas and Steuart Henderson Britt. New York: McGraw-Hill, 1963.

36 The interview with GM's Philip Guarascio was called "What's Good for General Motors is Good for TV." *Broadcasting & Cable*, April 13, 1998.

37 The McDonald's and Burger King media plans were reported in *Manager's Business Report*, March 1998.

38 Optimizers confused me until I read "Cultures Clash as 'Optimizers' Sort Out U.S. Media" in *Advertising Age*, August 4, 1997. Details of SuperMidas and X*pert plus Erwin Ephron's comments came from that article.

39 Neil Braun of NBC TV in an editorial in *Advertising Age*, "There's No Magic in TV's Optimizers," May 11, 1998.

40 The *Spots 'n Dots* report from TVB's research conference appeared October 16, 1998.

41 Joe Ostrow's 1982 speech to the ARF was reprinted in *Radio's Missing Ingredient: The Optimum Effective Scheduling System*, by Steve Marx and Pierre Bouvard. Washington, DC: NAB, 1993. Read all about OES in Chapter 8.

42 Mike Naples' *Effective Frequency: The Relationship Between Frequency and Advertising Effectiveness* is called "the green book" in agency circles. New York: Association of National Advertisers, 1979. An updated book, *Advertising Reach and Frequency*, was released by Association of National Advertisers in 1995, contradicting some of the earlier conclusions about frequency. That caused an uproar in the ad agency world. Erwin Ephron examined the two theories in "The Bible, Lately Revised" in *Inside Media*, January 10, 1996.

Taking It Further

Here are a few Web sites that relate to this chapter and additional reading not included in the Chapter Notes.

www.adtalk.com—Online magazine aimed at agency and media people

www.buymedia.com—Online buying service connecting radio and television stations with advertising agencies and other media buyers

www.mediacentral.com—Cowles publications, including *American Demographics*, *CableWorld*, and other media titles

www.mediadaily.com—Advertising and media industry news

www.mediapost.com—Advertising resource and search engine

www.srds.com—Standard Rate and Data Services directories on every medium, including rates, coverage, and ownership companies

Additional Reading

Advertiser & Agency Red Books Plus. New Providence, NJ: National Register Publishing, annual.

Graham, Stedman, Joe Jeff Goldblatt, and Lisa Delpy. *The Ultimate Guide to Sport Event Management and Marketing*. Homewood, IL: Irwin Professional Publishing, 1995.

Guernica, Antonio, and Irene Kasperuk. *Reaching the Hispanic Market Effectively*. New York: McGraw-Hill, 1982.

Schultz, Don E., William A. Robinson, and Lisa A. Petrison. *Sales Promotion Essentials*. 3rd ed. Lincolnwood, IL: NTC Business Books, 1997.

Sissors, Jack Z., and Lincoln Bumba. *Advertising Media Planning*. 5th ed. Lincolnwood, IL: NTC Business Books, 1996.

Surmanek, Jim. *Introduction to Advertising Media: Research, Planning and Buying*. Lincolnwood, IL: NTC Business Books, 1992.

The Standard Directory of Advertising Agencies. New Providence, NJ: National Register Publishing, annual.

Wiechmann, Jack C. *NTC's Dictionary of Advertising*. 2nd ed. Lincolnwood, IL: NTC Business Books, 1993.

6

Selling Television Advertising

Network Television

The TV commercial is the most pervasive form of communication known, with a profound ability to influence both habit and thought.

TV commercials are so much a part of the American culture that they are often considered as entertaining as the programming during which they appear. A well-crafted national commercial often takes on an aura of its own, with stories and characters that viewers come to know and talk about in casual conversation.

Neil Postman estimates that "an American who has reached the age of 40 will have seen well over one million television commercials in his or her lifetime, and has close to another million to go before the first Social Security check arrives."[1]

In *Broadcast and Cable Selling*, Warner and Buchman call America's response to television "a passionate affair." They speak in both reverent and rhapsodic tones about the pageantry, intimacy, and escapism that makes America love television for its "vast mirrored mosaic of ephemeral reflections of ourselves and our dreams."[2] That's the kind of power that advertisers pay billions of dollars to tap.

The percentage of households with at least one TV set was at 98.3% in 1998, according to the Television Bureau of Adver-

tising (TVB). (See Table 6-1) Of those households, 99.3% have color sets and 72.2% have two or more sets. The average number of sets is 2.32. The typical American household spent 7 hours and 17 minutes a day with the television on in 1995, down by only 5 minutes in 1997.

TVB documents the public's perception of television as the most influential, authoritative, exciting, and believable advertising medium, based on a proprietary 1995 Bruskin–Goldring study.[3] For example, think of commercials in the annual Super Bowl telecast: by November 1997, NBC had sold out advertising time during Super Bowl XXXII at an average rate of $1.3 million for 30 seconds. The previous year, the Fox broadcast of the game had sold out early and approached the same unit cost.

The final episode of *Seinfeld* in May 1998 was such an event that the cost of commercials set records for prime time—more than $2.0 million for 30 seconds. *Advertising Age* reported that buyers told NBC-TV salespeople during the 1997 upfront buying season that if 1997–1998 were to be the last year of *Seinfeld*, they wanted to advertise during the finale. That was almost a year before comedian Jerry Seinfeld announced the end of the show.[4]

TABLE 6-1 Television Households

In 1950 television penetration of U.S. households was only 9.0%. It didnít take long to grow, however, and within five years it was up to 64.5%. By 1965 it reached 92.6%, and has grown steadily to its current 98.3% level.

Year	Total U.S. Households (000)	TV Households (000)	%HH with TV
1950	43,000	3,880	9.0
1955	47,620	30,700	64.5
1960	52,500	45,750	87.1
1965	56,900	52,700	92.6
1970	61,410	58,500	95.3
1975	70,520	68,500	97.1
1980	77,900	76,300	97.9
1985	86,530	84,900	98.1
1990	93,760	92,100	98.2
1995	97,060	95,400	98.3
1996	97,540	95,900	98.3
1997	98,610	97,000	98.4
1998	99,680	98,000	98.3

Source: Nielsen Media Research, January each year.

The advantage of big-event programs like the *Seinfeld* finale or the annual Super Bowl broadcast is that they get big ratings across all demographic groups. Day-to-day selling at the network level is based on demos, that is, how many 18–49s or 25–54s you can deliver.

The conflict between demos and ratings is a key part of the narrative in Ken Auletta's *Three Blind Mice*, a detailed look at the battle that the three original networks fought against declining share.[5] Auletta followed each of the "old" networks (ABC, CBS, and NBC) through the launch of the 1984–1985 season. The shows introduced then are long forgotten, but the pattern is the same: you need to sign new programs, re-sign previous programs, and convince the local affiliated stations that you've got hits on your hands

that will make money for them. Then you must sell advertisers on the same idea.

The importance of demographics is widespread and well-known today, but that was not the case when *Three Blind Mice* was written. Auletta observed an NBC affiliates' meeting in Burbank where NBC programming chief Warren Littlefield (later president of NBC's entertainment division) announced, "The message loud and clear is demographics," only to be followed by NBC research chief William Rubens, who said, "If you don't have good ratings, good demos don't matter. . . . It's a mistake for us to think of unmass appeal."

"This mini-debate," Auletta writes, "was but one of many [the president of NBC Entertainment, Brandon] Tartikoff would adjudicate this week—between Sales, which

YOUTH IS SERVED

The following table shows the median age of TV network viewers in the fourth quarter of 1996, and the first quarter of 1997, from BJK&E Media Group.

Network	Median Age
WB	24.8
Fox	32.3
UPN	34.3
ABC	40.7
NBC	41.1
CBS	51.5

cared about ratings but was preoccupied with urban-oriented demos, and Research, which cared about demos but first thought of ratings."

How things have changed from the mid-1980s to the twenty-first century! What Rubens called "unmass appeal" is exactly what the networks now sell, especially against encroaching cable and direct satellite operations that can focus demographics for optimum advertiser impact. The "Big Three" became the "Big Four" when Fox entered the race. The Big Four then became the less-than-big six (or so) with the launch of UPN (United Paramount Network) and "The WB" (Warner Bros. Network). Paxson Communications' Pax TV further complicates the count.

Fox led the way with targeted programming, showing the other networks how to make a living with 18–34 and 18–49 numbers, not the whole universe. Following suit were UPN and WB networks.

As *Business Week* put it, "Viewers are increasingly abandoning the Big Three for more interesting fare elsewhere. And where viewers go, so go advertisers—eventually." While the audience eroded, television kept selling, increasing network revenues by just over 6% a year, according to TVB.

Business Week attributed that revenue increase to "snobbery surrounding the broadcast networks [that] still holds with advertisers, which continue to pay huge premiums to place ads on broadcast versus

cable. Even with sharply reduced market share, the lure of reaching a huge audience in one shot still propelled the networks to $6 billion in advertising sales for the upcoming [1998] season."[6]

In 1997, basic cable edged out the major networks in shares during the summer re-run season. Basic pulled a combined 40 share in prime time versus a combined 39 share for the Big Three. TVB countered with information about television's average weekly cume, which showed broadcast affiliates with percentages more than double the individual cable networks. See Figure 6–1.

TVB also created an advertising campaign called the "TV Boxscore" which compared broadcast and cable ratings on a monthly and cumulative basis. To target national advertisers, TVB placed the comparisons in the *Ad Age Daily Fax* and later turned it into full-color, full-page ads in *Advertising Age*. In an announcement coinciding with the TV Boxscore campaign, TVB said, "With highly selective use of Nielsen data, the cable industry has misled the advertising community into believing cable has a larger audience than broadcast. [TV Boxscore] clearly demonstrates how Nielsen numbers, computed fairly, shows the Broadcast 'Airways' consistently beating the Cable 'Nets' in overall ratings."

The good news, of course, is that network television is still a viable—and valuable—medium for advertising. Like any other "mass medium," television is slowly becoming demassified not only by cable, but also by new and emerging interactive forms of media that nip away at time formerly used for watching television.

New networks like the WB are helping television keep dollars in the family, so to speak. The WB's *Buffy the Vampire Slayer* broke the $100,000 mark for 30-second spots in the 1997–1998 season. That was encouraging news for network managers. It meant ad dollars shifting away from the Big Four were staying in broadcast and not moving to cable.

But will there ever be a world without ABC, CBS, and NBC? "Don't count on it," says *Digital Home Entertainment* magazine.[7] "For all the doom and gloom fore-

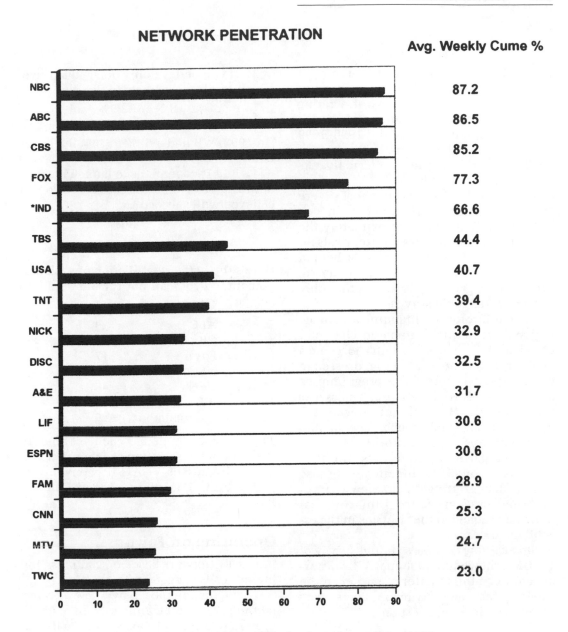

NETWORK PENETRATION

Avg. Weekly Cume %

Network	Avg. Weekly Cume %
NBC	87.2
ABC	86.5
CBS	85.2
FOX	77.3
*IND	66.6
TBS	44.4
USA	40.7
TNT	39.4
NICK	32.9
DISC	32.5
A&E	31.7
LIF	30.6
ESPN	30.6
FAM	28.9
CNN	25.3
MTV	24.7
TWC	23.0

FIGURE 6-1 In 1997, cable edged out the traditional TV networks in summer ratings. That prompted TV sellers to look for good news. They found it in the average weekly cume of the traditional networks against cable networks.

casts, the majors have proven surprisingly nimble through the years and there's no reason to think they won't adjust to the new terrain." The magazine quoted CBS senior vice president Martin Franks, "The news of the networks' demise is always premature."

The Netlets

Add *Dawson's Creek* to *Buffy the Vampire Slayer* and you have the makings of a network, if the early performance of The WB is any indicator. Those two shows helped WB edge out UPN for the first 21 weeks of the 1998 TV season. "Edged" is the right word, too. WB's victory party came because of a lead of only two-tenths of a rating point. UPN immediately announced a full week of programming for the 1998–1999 season and launched an updated version of the TV classic *Love Boat*, hoping to float its rating higher than WB's.[8]

Executives of the two networks were constantly sparring. The two launched onto the TV scene at approximately the same time and were seen as bitter rivals for the "Number Five" network spot behind Fox. WB CEO Jamie Kellner was quoted (in *Broadcasting & Cable*) as saying that only five networks could survive.

In an effort toward branding and imaging, WB created the animated character Michigan J. Frog to act as both a logo and a host for the network. Mr. Frog, dressed in top hat and tails, introduces programming and even delivers commercial messages for sponsors. He also introduced the phrase, "Dubba-Dubba-Dubba-Bee" to reinforce the name of the network.

By comparing affiliate lists online, I noted that some WB affiliates were also UPN affiliates during the first few years of each network's existence. I imagine that must have added to the rivalries in the executive offices.

Broadcasting & Cable's annual survey of TV GMs showed in 1998 that WB was expected to be the long-term winner in the battle of the new networks.[9] The survey asked the following questions:

1. WB and UPN have now been on since 1995. Do you believe that both of them will survive and expand in a manner similar to Fox?

Yes	45%
No	48%

2. Do you believe that at least one of them will survive and expand in a manner similar to Fox?

Yes	80%
No	17%

3. If you believe only one will survive, which one is more likely to survive?

UPN	32.5%
WB	60.0%

(In 1997, WB had a 52% to 48% lead over UPN.)

4. Bud Paxson plans to launch his new network, Pax Net, in August 1998. Do you believe it will succeed?

Yes	30%
No	57%

Here's the network affiliation of each participant, so you can put the answers into perspective:

ABC	23
CBS	22
Fox	17
NBC	19
UPN	8
WB	2
Independent	9

The study is conducted each year before the National Association of Television Program Executives (NATPE) convention, with 100 TV GMs interviewed by Cahners Research.

Operating on Faith

"Can a TV network based on godliness and infomercials get good ratings?"

That question, posed by *The Wall Street Journal*, greeted the announcement of the proposed launch of Pax Net, the national family-oriented network created by Lowell "Bud" Paxson. Described by *the Journal* as "a minor player in TV for decades," Paxson established the Home Shopping Network in the 1970s and operated a Christian cable channel that scrolled Bible verses on the screen while inspirational music played in the background.[10]

Paxson assembled a collection of UHF stations in large markets, all bought at low prices and operated on shoestring budgets. Revenues were generated from airing infomercials. When the U.S. Supreme Court ruled that cable systems were required to carry Paxson's local stations, the seeds of the new Pax Net network were sown.

Paxson contracted with CBS to air *Touched By An Angel* and *Promised Land* in syndication. Rights for *Touched* were almost $1 million per episode, which raised eyebrows at other networks and in the financial community. (Wall Street was undecided on Paxson, at one time calling him "the toast of TV" and at other times questioning his financial prowess.) Paxson also bought rights to *Dr. Quinn Medicine Woman* and *Dave's World*.

Pax Net's infomercial roots were showing: the original schedule included *The Mike Levey Show*, featuring the founder and board chair of Positive Response Television (PRTV). As host for the infomercial program "Amazing Discoveries" (on Paxson's stations and others), Levey was known in the industry as the "infomercial king." His company found likely products for sale on televison and developed the selling and marketing concepts.

Paxson's personal philosophy was underscored by an agreement with Focus on the Family Productions, headed by Christian radio personality Dr. James Dobson.

Ads announcing the launch of Pax Net read:

> It's about entertainment.
> It's about drama.

> It's about family.
> It's about life.
> Get the spirit.

The 1998 launch was slowed by a lack of affiliates in some large markets. Paxson's owned, operated, and affiliated stations combined reached only 68.2% of U.S. TV homes. To complete the coverage needed to qualify as a network, Paxson agreed to pay Tele-Communications, Inc. up to $27 million to carry Pax Net programming on its cable systems, calling the move "cheaper than buying stations."[11]

The deal was similar to one that WB entered with both TCI and Warner Cable to fill in "white areas"—locations where consumers cannot receive Grade B television signals off the air. (There was debate in Congress in 1997 to determine just how to judge picture quality of "white areas.") *Broadcasting & Cable* reported that Paxson agreed to a fee of $6 per subscriber for each cable system carrying his network on an analog tier to all subscribers and $2 for digital-tier carriage.

Weeks before the official launch of Pax Net, the company decided on a name change to "Pax TV" and retooled its logo and color scheme. The logo began as a white dove and cross against a sky blue background. At kickoff the new network called itself "the red, white, and blue Pax TV" both on the air and in its advertising.

The Benefits of Television as an Advertising Medium

Here's a run-down of the environment for selling TV advertising:

1. Total advertising volume in the United States in 1997 was $187.529 billion, a 7% increase over 1996. (See Table 6–2)

2. All U.S. TV advertising (including cable) totaled $44.519 billion in 1997, up 10.5% from 1996. Television accounted for 23.8% of advertising dollars.

3. There were 1,204 commercial TV stations on the air at the beginning of 1998, 642 UHF stations, and 562 VHF stations.

4. Seven-hundred-fifty advertisers and 3,496 brands used network television in 1995 (the last year for which I could get figures).

5. The same year (1995), 1,893 advertisers and 12,002 brands used spot television: national commercials bought on local stations.

TABLE 6–2 Advertising Volume

Advertising volume in the United States reached $187.5 billion in 1997 with televison accounting for $44.5 billion, almost one quarter of the total, the largest share of any medium. Total ad volume has increased about 75% every 10 years since 1955, except for the 240% jump between 1975 and 1985.

In Millions

Year	Total Volume	TV Ad Volume	% In TV
1950	$5,700	$171	3.0
1955	9,150	1,035	11.3
1960	11,960	1,627	13.6
1965	15,250	2,515	16.5
1970	19,550	3,596	18.4
1975	27,900	5,263	18.9
1980	53,570	11,488	21.4
1985	94,900	21,287	22.4
1990	129,590	29,073	22.4
1995	162,930	37,828	23.2
1996	175,230	42,484	24.3
1997	187,529	44,519	23.8

Source: McCann-Erickson annual report on U.S. advertising volume assembled by Robert Coen.

The primary attraction of television as an advertising medium is its visual appeal, its ability to grab the audience's attention with pictures and motion. Among advertising agency executives, television is often the first choice for product imaging and demonstration.

As chief creative officer for D'Arcy Masius Benton & Bowles (DMB&B) in Chicago, Gary Horton says, "There's no question that television provides an advantage because the viewer is able to see the product." At DMB&B, TV advertising comes first, followed by print, then radio.

Rick Berger, account supervisor at New York's Jordan, McGrath, Case & Taylor, offers a specific example: "I worked in skin care for some time, where the proof is in the face. You have to show that the product works by showing a beautiful woman. This is true of other categories as well, where you have to visualize your point."

For another example, Dick Halseth, media manager at Ford Motor Company, says the "vast majority" of Ford's advertising dollars are spent on television and print. "An automobile tends to be an action-oriented product, as opposed to say a tube of toothpaste. You can really demonstrate the product very nicely in television. Then, when we use the magazine, it gives us the opportunity to reinforce what we've said on television and really hone in on an audience."[12]

Berger says his agency's decisions are influenced by the competitive environment: "If you have 12 competitors and they're all doing television only, then obviously you're missing something there. Now, while you don't have to be where everybody else is, there is a school of thought that that's probably a good place to be."

Sellers should take note of that: "Your competitor's on television" is a strong selling point. Let's examine other strong points of advertising on television.

Visual: Television (both broadcast and cable) grabs the audience's attention and creates appeal by combining full-color pictures, sound, and motion.

Lifestyle: Almost everyone born after 1948 grew up with television and sees it as part of life, spending an average of 8.5 hours a day with television, cable, or a VCR. Women spend the most time with television, averaging 4 hours and 33 minutes a day.

Mass Appeal: Television reaches huge mass audiences with a single exposure and allows delivery to multiple household members simultaneously.

Ubiquitous: Over-the-air television reaches virtually all households in the United States. (98.3%). Television reaches people who are not exposed to other media.

Intrusive: Television does not require the viewer to seek the advertising.

Reach: Television is capable of producing high levels of reach into generalized consumer segments, (e.g., children, teens, women, men, adults 18–49, etc.) and of combining reach with high-frequency levels.

Immediacy: Television provides immediate and simultaneous delivery of advertiser messages 24 hours a day.

Variety: There's a broad array of program types, which allow ads to reach viewers while they're in a specific state of mind, creating a positive environment for advertising messages.

Multilevel: Advertising time can be purchased nationally, regionally, or locally.

Agency Interest: The creative environment of TV production offers revenue opportunity for advertising agencies, production companies, and creative directors.

Entertainment Value: TV commercials are part of the culture and are often as entertaining as the programs that carry them.[13]

The Case Against Television Advertising

Video rules Americans' leisure time, but over-the-air television does not. Shrinking shares at the major networks, channel surfing, and taping favorite programs for later viewing are all factors that complicate the sales of TV time.

In addition to audience erosion, there are some inherent downsides to TV advertising that as a seller you may hear from your prospective advertiser, including:

Clutter: The average network prime time hour contained eight minutes of commercials—as many as 24 commercial units—in 1993, and the numbers have increased since then. The average nonprime hour contained 13 minutes. Television's cluttered environment can affect viewer retention of messages.

Nonmobile: Over 90% of TV viewing is done in the home, making it difficult to reach consumers directly at the point of purchase.

Poorly Targeted: Television is not as demographically selective as other forms of media and is not cost-efficient for reaching narrowly defined target groups.

Not Upscale: U.S. adults who earn more than $60,000 watch 26% less television than the average viewer.

Zipping, Zapping, and Surfing: Commercials can be easily avoided by changing channels or by fast-forwarding a VCR after recording a program.

Limited Avails: In spite of clutter, there is a limit to television's inventory, which could preclude the purchase of specific programs.

Production Costs: In 1995, a typical 30-second national commercial cost more than $268,000 to produce.

Fragmentation: The average TV household could receive 43 channels of broadcast and cable in 1996, up from 11 in 1980. That adds to the declining share of the major networks and makes advertising choices more difficult.

Selling Network Television

The FCC defines a TV network as an entity providing more than 14 hours per week of prime time entertainment programming to interconnected affiliates on a regular basis.[14] In addition, to qualify as a network, the programming must reach at least 75% of the nation's TV households. Until 1990 Fox was a "syndicator," not a "network," even though it had a schedule of daily programs. Its national penetration was not enough to fit the "network" definition.

Salespeople at the network level are a small group, the best in the business. Because they deal with the largest dollars amounts, they face the most knowledgeable buyers in advertising. Since the buyers are usually at the top level of their agencies, they often demand to negotiate with people at the highest levels of network hierarchy.

Buyers stay up-to-date on the network marketplace on a daily basis. They know each network's inventory, demographics, and rates. They also have to be savvy enough about programming to evaluate new pilots for their advertisers and to estimate the potential audience and demographic reach.

Often buyers and sellers move from one side of the table to the other. A network seller might have agency experience while an agency buyer might have a background in network selling. Because of this association, they know each other well and learn to trust each other. Trust is important in an environment that uses verbal orders that often total hundreds of millions of dollars.

"Network sales people must be skilled negotiators who have built up solid reputations," say Warner and Buchman. "Their writing and research skills are not as important as their negotiating skills, because

the television networks give their sales people in-depth sales support." That means researchers are available to analyze ratings and demographics, as well as proposal writers to dress up presentations.

The sellers are responsible for offers and counteroffers, in other words, negotiation. As Warner and Buchman write: "Due to the limited amount of network inventory and the great demand for it, there is a constant and complicated juggling process that sales people go through to get advertisers the schedules they want."

There are three markets for network television: the upfront market, the scatter market, and the open or opportunistic market.

The Upfront Market

"Upfront" is the annual purchase of TV commercial time well in advance of the telecast time, usually for a one-year schedule. It's a relatively common practice among large advertisers for the purchase of prime time as well as other TV dayparts.

Ken Auletta calls upfront sales "a mating dance which begins sometime in March, when the networks invite the ad agency representatives out to Los Angeles for their first taste of the programs being developed for the new season."[15]

Erwin Ephron is not so kind. He calls upfront sales "Dodge City media. Pull the trigger and count the bodies later." Ephron is a partner in the New York agency Ephron, Papazian & Ephron, and is front and center as a buyer each year when the TV networks open what some agency people call a "feeding frenzy."[16]

The first of the upfront markets involves selling children's programming because of

TABLE 6–3 Top 25 Agencies by U.S. Network TV Billings

Rank			Network TV billings		
1995	1996	Agency	1995	1996	% Change
1	1	D'Arcy Masius Benton & Bowles	$1,190.0	$1,152.0	–3.2
5	2	McCann-Erickson Worldwide	794.0	1,051.3	32.4
11	3	Y & R Advertising	478.9	972.9	103.4
4	4	J. Walter Thompson Co.	813.0	967.1	19.0
7	5	BBDO Worldwide	751.4	941.4	25.3
6	6	Ogilvy & Mather Worldwide	767.3	909.3	18.5
2	7	Saatchi & Saatchi Advertising	838.3	886.2	5.7
3	8	Leo Burnett Co.	828.5	843.6	1.8
8	9	Foote, Cone & Belding	730.0	800.0	9.6
9	10	Grey Advertising	725.3	753.5	3.9
10	11	Bates Worldwide	514.8	548.8	6.6
12	12	Ammirati Puris Lintas	399.9	379.4	–5.1
15	13	TBWA Chiat/Day	276.2	340.5	23.3
13	14	DDB Needham Worldwide	370.6	328.2	–11.4
14	15	Campbell-Ewald	277.3	275.1	–0.8
16	16	Messner Vetere Berger McNamee Schmetterer/Euro RSCG	271.5	274.2	1.0
17	17	N.W. Ayer & Partners	263.9	218.0	–17.4
19	18	Bozell Worldwide	162.4	181.3	11.6
18	19	Hal Riney & Partners	165.0	180.4	9.0
29	20	Goodby, Silverstein & Partners	63.1	149.2	136.6
20	21	Jordan, McGrath, Case & Taylor	138.9	139.2	0.2
22	22	Temerlin McClain	116.7	121.7	4.3
21	23	Campbell Mithum Esty	124.1	120.4	–3.0
24	24	Rubin Postaer & Associates	100.3	119.5	19.2
37	25	GSD&M	39.9	109.5	174.6

Source: *Advertising Age.*

the limited amount of inventory. After children's upfront comes prime time, followed by daytime, news, and late night.

Prime time gets the most attention, because big money is involved. In the 1996–1997 season, for instance, one ad agency spent over $1 billion in national network TV and syndication time, leading the industry. That was Tele-Vest, the media buying unit of the MacManus Group.

The following season the stakes became even higher. Tele-Vest was eclipsed by an alliance between agency giants J. Walter Thompson and Ogilvy & Mather Worldwide. That combination was responsible for $1.8 billion of time on network TV alone, says *Advertising Age*. The publication quoted Arnold Semsky, executive vice president of BBDO Worldwide: "Bigger is better. You get the best prices." BBDO spent $941.4 million on network TV advertising in 1996, an increase of 25% over the previous year. Those figures get the attention of the networks. See Table 6–3.

The clout of big expenditures does no good, however, if the client's product doesn't get appropriate exposure. Irwin Gotlieb, president of Tele-Vest, says it's more than a matter of money: "The bulk of the work is how you translate your client's objectives to actual buys," he told *Advertising Age*.

Gene DeWitt of New York's DeWitt Media, a buying service, agrees, saying, "The guys who proclaim clout don't really negotiate with the networks. They make 'agency deals,' and then the networks buy the programs for them. Then they can go back to their clients and say, 'Yes, I got you a few 'Seinfelds,' but we had to take some other stuff.'"

The "other stuff" he refers to is less valuable programming. That means smaller audiences or demos that are not quite on target. But the lower prices help to balance the high cost of the premium shows. That balance comes with skillful negotiation on the part of the network sellers and sales management.

As I said before, the enormous sums involved in upfront buying prompt ad agencies to use their highest level people to negotiate. That means the network sellers are also selected from the highest level of management. As Warner and Buchman point out in *Broadcast and Cable Selling*, "Because these major network advertisers spend in the hundreds of millions of dollars, they prefer a high level, tightly controlled buying process to make sure nothing falls through the cracks—a 5% mistake could cost Procter & Gamble $20 million!"

Upfront buyers take the biggest risks, because they buy so far in advance. They also make the biggest commitments—usually a year's budget in one buy. About 70% of a network's prime time inventory and about 50% of the other dayparts is sold in the upfront market. In the days before the explosion of options for advertisers, the networks would sell as much as 90% of their inventory in the upfront market.

By pouring money into buying in the upfront market, an advertiser gambles that the early cost will be less than it would be when the season begins. The network guarantees that the advertiser will reach a specified minimum audience level.

The Scatter Market

Once upfront selling is finished, the scatter market begins. "Scatter" is the sales of the rest of network inventory not accounted for in upfront. Inventory is generally tight; therefore, rates go up. In the 1995–1996 selling season, scatter prices were 50% higher than upfront.

Advertisers usually buy about 60 days before the quarter in which they expect their commercials to run. Scatter buys are bought in shorter flights than upfront buys, and the buyer generally pays a premium rate compared to upfront's negotiated rate structure. There are no audience guarantees in the scatter market, and the advertiser could end up paying an even higher price if a show succeeds.

In some years, the scatter market can save an advertiser money. For instance, Elise Lawless of Atlanta's Fahlgren agency told *Advertising Age* that she had a client who wanted to make sports buys upfront in the 1995–1996 season. Since her client was on a calendar fiscal year, "we waited until January to make the buys." Lawless' client had not participated in upfront buying before, so "the networks really wanted our money," she said. "Since the market had softened somewhat since the upfront, I know we got some better buys than some advertisers who made upfront deals last year."

Scatter also refers to a commercial schedule that rotates the message through multiple dayparts. Most scatter plans are designed to meet an advertiser's specific audience target, such as men 18–49, women 18–49.

The Opportunistic Market

The opportunistic market is the last-minute buying involving commercial inventory that has been created by programming changes or changes in an advertiser's planning, like a move to another daypart.

Programs with controversial themes or plot lines make advertisers uneasy and anxious to disassociate themselves from that material. That also opens avails in the opportunistic market. Two examples from the 1997–1998 season that made advertisers skittish were ABC-TV's *Ellen*, featuring an openly gay lead character, and the same network's *Nothing Sacred*, about a Catholic priest who wanted his church to relate to contemporary needs instead of dogma.

The 30-second rate for *Ellen* that season was $180,000, much lower than the rates for the shows immediately before it on ABC: *Spin City*, $200,000; *Dharma & Greg*, $210,000; and *Drew Carey*, $275,000. *Nothing Sacred* had the least expensive 30-second rate among all the season's network programs at $55,000.[17]

When advertisers avoid programs like these, the commercial positions can go vacant unless the network sells them at bargain rates to recoup the loss.

Cancellations and Guarantees

Most network orders, once placed, are non-cancelable. If an agency commits to an upfront buy and its marketing strategy changes or it faces financial problems, it's the advertiser's responsibility to sell off the unused time, not the network's responsibility. Network sellers generally try to help, but they're not required to do so.

The networks, on the other hand, cancel programs with no notice to the advertiser, but with the provision that commercials will run in another program that delivers the same audience profile.

In spite of audience erosion, time on network television is a valuable commodity, and the prices increase each year. Only the national networks can deliver a truly national audience; therefore, gross rating points (GRPs) become commodities. The demand for network GRPs has not diminished even in the face of declining shares. That creates a negotiating point for buyers and sellers, so the cost of network time is based on guarantees of price against audience, computed in cost per thousand (CPM).

As you remember from the discussion of research and ratings in Chapter 3, cost per thousand is calculated this way:

$$\text{CPM} = \frac{\text{Cost of the spot or schedule}}{\text{Number of households or persons reached}} \times 1,000$$

(The following numbers are way too low for network spot rates and audiences, but they're easier to use as examples.) If a spot costs $200 and is aired on a program seen in 40,000 TV households, the household CPM is $5.00 (200 divided by 40,000 and multiplied by 1,000).

If the program reaches only 30,000 households, the CPM is $6.67. Let's say that the network guaranteed the advertiser the $5.00 CPM in the first calculation. That means the network will have to run the spot in other programs to accumulate the additional audience required to bring the CPM down to the promised level.

For example, a friend of mine who runs a regional sports network cautioned a small TV station about running his programming. The station's audience was so limited that the commercials would have to run in *all* the station's programming in order to satisfy the audience guarantees that the station had made. My friend feared that the TV station would have no time to sell its own commercials because it would be running the sports network's inventory 24 hours a day in order to satisfy the guarantees.

Clearances

Delivering enough households (or persons) to make the buys efficient is a product of two things: the popularity of the network's programming and the number of network affiliates that carry the program. When an affiliate carries a network program, it is said to "clear" the program, hence the term "clearance."

TABLE 6–4 Television Dayparts in 1997

Daypart	Households Viewing Minutes	Cost per 30 CPM	CPM
Daytime	3,830,000	$14,800	$3.85
Early evening	8,390,000	46,600	5.55
Nighttime	9,530,000	106,500	11.18
Late evening	3,270,000	24,500	7.48

Household viewing is expressed as "numbers viewing in the average minute of the average program."

Advertisers who buy network time rely on clearances that deliver a huge combined audience of all the network's affiliated stations. The stations, however, are not required to clear the programs. If local management feels a program does not suit the local marketplace, they may make a local substitution, a preemption. That decreases the potential audience for a program and reduces the advertiser's reach, and therefore the cost.

The prices for an average 30-second commercial on network television in prime time have generally risen over the years. For example, the cost in the 1965 season was $19,700, or $1.98 per 1000 homes. In 1979, the average cost was above $50,000 for the first time. By 1984, it had risen to its all-time high, $107,500. Averages in 1996 and 1997 were $101,400 and $106,500, respectively. The CPM rose to $11.18 in 1997. Table 6–4 shows how network television looked in 1997 in cost per thousand.

Syndication

The same year that *Seinfeld* broke records for the price of 30-second commercials, the show also broke records for single-episode pricing in syndication. Columbia TriStar Television sold *Seinfeld* in the New York market for $300,000 per episode. WNYW, New York's Fox-owned and operated station, paid the price in 1998 for programming that it could not air until spring 2001. The station paid record prices knowing that its competitor, WPIX, would broadcast *Seinfeld* episodes in the years before 2001. WPIX had bought the program for its first run in off-network syndication. WNYW's purchase was for the second run.

"By the time *Seinfeld* goes through a third, fourth, and possibly fifth run in syndication (a la *I Love Lucy*) it will likely wind up in the $2 billion range," wrote *Broad-*

casting & Cable after the 1998 convention of the National Association of Television Program Executives (NATPE), where syndicated shows are usually sold.

The $2 billion figure represents the combined license prices for all stations buying *Seinfeld* over the life of the series in syndication. Given the program's strong showing as a first-run sitcom on NBC and the demand for commercial time in the program's final episode, syndicators and station executives alike were confident about its future. "I don't think there is a station that doesn't want *Seinfeld*, said Michael Eigner, the general manager of WPIX.[19]

Before the *Seinfeld* pricing, the Advertiser Syndicated Television Association (ASTA) valued its industry at $4 billion, including sales per episode to stations and

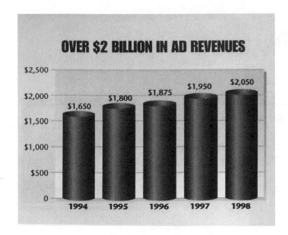

OVER $2 BILLION IN AD REVENUES

Year	Revenue
1994	$1,650
1995	$1,800
1996	$1,875
1997	$1,950
1998	$2,050

FIGURE 6–2
Half of television syndication revenues come from advertising (the other half come from selling rights to programs). Advertising revenues are on the rise because of "broadcast-sized ratings," according to the SNTA.

cable networks plus advertising sales. Half of syndication revenues come from advertising, which is just under $2.1 billion with expectations of continued increases. (See Figure 6–2.) The potential for additional revenues caused syndicators to change the structure and the name of their organization. In 1998, ASTA became SNTA, the Syndicated Network Television Association.

Syndication is the sale of programs on a station-by-station, market-by-market basis. Syndicated programs are those not produced by the local station or sent to the station via one of the networks (although some syndicated programs may have originated as network fare). Syndicated programs are sold to the stations on a market-exclusive basis for a certain length of time and for a certain number of broadcasts per episode. Once the syndicator has cleared a group of stations to carry its program, it sells advertising time in the program to national advertisers.[20]

Advertisers use syndication in combination with network buys to maximize their use of broadcast television against the declining shares of the networks. The biggest customers for syndication are the nation's big spenders in all electronic media: Procter & Gamble, General Motors, and Kraft General Foods.

"Syndication's use is on the rise because of what it delivers to advertisers," says Jon Barovick of Tribune Entertainment. "We've proven time and time again that we can develop fantastic programming that rivals what the networks have—and hands-down what cable has—in terms of original programming, U.S. coverage, daypart appeal, and demographic delivery."

Both the increase in the number of cable outlets and the opening of lucrative time periods in broadcast television have contributed to the boom in syndication. In 1996, the Federal Communications Commission eliminated the prime time access rule, which had prevented ABC-, CBS-, and NBC-owned or -affiliated stations from running off-network syndication in prime access (the period immediately before prime time, 7 p.m. to 8 p.m. Eastern).

In addition, that same year saw the end of financial interest and syndication rules, known in the industry as "fin/syn." Fin/syn forbade a TV network from owning or syndicating its own programming. The end of those rules meant that a network could now enter the syndication market. The first to capitalize on this situation was the Walt Disney Company, which bought Cap Cities/ABC (owner of the ABC-TV network) without having to divest its profitable syndication division.

The result of the rules changes was larger entities in both production and distribution of syndication. Some had feared that first-run programming would be pushed out of prime access in favor of off-network programming, but that did not happen, owing to the strength of first-run programs like *Wheel of Fortune*, *Entertainment Tonight*, and *Access Hollywood*.

How Syndication Works

Programs like *Seinfeld*, *Home Improvement*, and *The X-Files*, which originally ran as network series, are called "off-network syndication." Syndication also includes original programs like Tribune's *Geraldo Rivera Show*, Universal's *Xena: Warrior*

TABLE 6-5

Whether you sell on a national or a local level, you need to be familiar with standard TV dayparts. Table 6-5 lists each daypart and outlines the available audience and the typical programming strategy based on that daypart.[18]

Daypart (all times Eastern)	Available Audience
Early morning (6 a.m. to 9 a.m.)	Children, homemakers, adult men and women who work outside the home, retired persons. Schoolchildren and working adults are preparing to leave, and most have left by the end of the daypart.
Morning (9 a.m. to noon)	Mostly preschoolers, homemakers, retired persons, and shift workers
Afternoon (Noon to 4 p.m.)	Early in the daypart, working adults who eat lunch at home are added to the morning audience. They leave and are replaced from about 2 p.m. by children returning from school.
Early fringe (4 p.m. to 6 p.m.)	The return of most working adults begins and, in many small and medium markets, is complete.

Scheduling Strategies

Many affiliates start the daypart with local news and/or newsmagazine programs, and most join the network at 7 a.m. for their respective news magazines. In large markets, stations have found success with their own 2-hour magazine shows. Children and teenagers are not being served. Locally produced children's programs, syndicated cartoons, and off-network sitcoms or drama-adventure series offer alternatives for part or all of the period.

Homemakers are a principal target in this daypart. During the first hour or two, the networks do not provide programs. Options include syndicated talk, discussion, or magazine programs oriented toward women. Off-network situation comedies starring children or having slapstick elements may bring children as well as adults to the set. Starting at 10 a.m. or 11 a.m., the networks launch into talk shows or game shows, and most affiliates broadcast them through the end of the period.

Between noon and 12:30 p.m., many affiliates opt for local news or a newsmagazine, both of which provide an opportunity to promote later newscasts. Syndicated entertainment, such as quiz or game shows and situation comedies, is an alternative. From 12:30 p.m. to 4 p.m., ABC and CBS affiliates generally carry the network soap operas. NBC affiliates usually clear their network's 2-hour soap opera block and have an opportunity to counter-program starting at 3 p.m.. The alternatives include syndicated talk shows with strong appeal to women or cartoons and situation comedies with teenage and child appeal, to target returning schoolchildren.

This is the start of the longest period for which an affiliate has programming responsibility. At the same time, it offers a station the opportunity to generate significant advertising revenues and build the adult audience for its local news.

The growth in audience size and diversity allows stations to engage successfully in counter-programming. Thirty-minute and 1-hour off-network and first-run syndicated content fit easily into the period, and many stations have discovered that audiences respond well to blocks of programs of the same genre.

Placement of local news is a major strategic factor. Airing it at 5:30 p.m. rules out the possibility of back-to-back hour-long programs. However, a succession of three off-network situation comedies with increasingly older appeal can bring youngsters to the set first, followed by teenagers and adults. A block of 30-minute reality programs attracts the adult demographics desired for news. An alternative strategy for building a news audience involves the scheduling of 2 hour-long syndicated talk programs across this period. Movies may be considered, but their appeal varies. They also pose some scheduling problems because of their varying lengths. Made-for-television movies are consistent in length, but have proven less appealing than feature films.

TABLE 6–5 *continued*

Daypart (all times Eastern)	Available Audience
Early evening (6 p.m. to 7 p.m.)	In all but large markets, all segments of the audience are home.
Prime access (7 p.m. to 8 p.m.)	All audience segments are available to view.
Network prime time (8 p.m. to 11 p.m.)	During the first hour or so, the audience is the same as that for prime access. A decrease begins at about 9:30 p.m., chiefly among children, adults who have to get up early, and retired persons.
Late fringe (11 p.m. to 11:30 p.m.)	Mostly adults
Late night (11:30 p.m. to 2 a.m.)	Mostly adults, including shift workers.
Overnight (2 a.m. to 6 a.m.)	Shift workers comprise the largest part of the comparatively small available audience.

Scheduling Strategies

The length of the local newscast, in the periods selected both for local and network news, influences the schedule in this daypart. The 30-minute network newscast may be preceded or followed by a 30-minute local newscast. An hour-long local news program may be followed by network news in the first half hour of prime access, or a 90-minute news block may start with 30 minutes of local news, followed by network news, and a final 30 minutes of local news. In most major markets, longer news blocks are common. However, many affiliates air one hour of news from 6 p.m. to 7 p.m., comprising 30 minutes of local and 30 minutes of network.

In practice, the networks do not begin their prime time broadcasts until 8 p.m., leaving programming of the 7 p.m. to 8 p.m. period to affiliates. The prime time access rule used to influence program choices in this daypart. Until 1996, the rule forbade network-owned or -affiliated stations in the top-50 markets from broadcasting more than 3 hours of network or off-network programs between 7 p.m. and 11 p.m.

One of the goals of the rule was to encourage local production, but most stations filled the time slot with syndicated programs. Quiz and game shows proved very strong in this period. Reality programs and those built around entertainment news enabled stations to inherit adults from the preceding newscasts. With the end of the rule, some people in the syndication field feared that first-run programming would be eliminated from this most lucrative hour. It didn't happen.

Most affiliates carry network programming during this entire daypart. If a network program is not competitive, or if most of the network's schedule on a given night is doing poorly, the station may consider preempting and substituting its own programming. Syndicated entertainment programs can fill a 30- or 60-minute period, while movies may produce the desired audience for periods of 90 minutes or 2 hours.

NBC provides affiliates with programming for the entire period, and CBS programs all but 30 minutes. ABC fills only the 11:35 p.m. to 12:35 a.m. slot. Options for CBS and ABC affiliates include off-network situation comedies, syndicated talk or entertainment-based programs, off-network dramatic series, and movies.

Affiliated stations usually air their late local news in this time slot, which runs to 11:35 p.m. on affiliated stations and sets back the late-night daypart by 5 minutes.

Affiliates that remain on the air during this daypart usually carry news fed by the network.

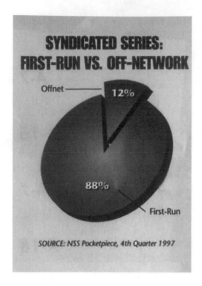

SOURCE: NSS Pocketpiece, 4th Quarter 1997

FIGURE 6–3

Syndication once meant reruns. Now 88% of TV syndication is first-run programming like *The Rosie O'Donnell Show* and *Entertainment Tonight*. From *1998 Guide to Advertiser Supported Syndication*. Used with permission.

Princess, and Warner Bros.' *The Rosie O'-Donnell Show*, which are "first-run syndication." (See Figure 6–3.)

Syndication is done on a "barter" basis. The local TV station agrees to run commercials sold by the syndicator within the program in exchange for the program itself. The more popular the program, the more likely the station will have to pay cash for each episode, as well as provide the syndicator with commercial positions, an arrangement called "cash-plus." The local station generally gets commercial time within the program, too. Whether pure barter or cash-plus, the term generally used is "barter syndication."

Warner Bros. Domestic Television's *Jenny Jones*, *The Rosie O'Donnell Show*, and *The People's Court* are examples of cash-plus syndication. The distribution company takes $3\frac{1}{2}$ minutes of commercial time for its national advertisers, and the local station gets $10\frac{1}{2}$ minutes to sell to local sponsors.

TV sales trainer Martin Antonelli calls barter syndication "one of the fastest-grow-

ing areas of the TV industry. It has created a marketplace for original programming as TV stations and cable networks seek to fill openings in their program schedules. Typically, a syndicated program appears in at least 70% of the country," Antonelli says, making it attractive to national advertisers.[21]

The Rosie O'Donnell Show claimed 99% coverage of Nielsen households in the 1997–1998 season, and the science fiction series *Babylon 5* claimed 95%.

A special report in both *Advertising Age* and *Electronic Media* described the impact of syndication:

> Broadcast television has long been the primary marketing tool of major national advertisers, because it can deliver large audiences, national coverage and broad reach. But fragmentation has been eroding the broadcast networks' ability to deliver these key benefits.
>
> But "broadcast" doesn't just mean "network." Advertiser-supported syndication is the other part of the national broadcast medium—a very major part, comprising about a third of the national broadcast audience, and dominating some key dayparts.

The daypart in which syndication has been most successful is daytime, driven by the proliferation of syndicated talk and entertainment shows. Syndicated programming generally reaches women 18–49 and 25–54 in daytime, and 66% of the audience is reached over a 4-week period.

National advertisers pay hefty unit prices for 30-second spots in syndication. Through 1997, *Home Improvement* was the most expensive of the programs offered in syndication, with a 30-second rate of $105,000. *The X-Files* was second and *Seinfeld* was third. Table 6–6 shows the top 25 prices for syndicated programming that year. Note that six of the top ten programs are off-network.

Syndicated TV buyers told *Advertising Age* that the prices paid in 1997 were somewhat below 1996 levels because of ratings slippage. Most talk shows, for example, dropped "dramatically" (*Advertising Age*'s word) in ratings and in revenues. Not one of the major advertising agencies surveyed for a special report in *Advertising Age* acknowledged buying the *Jerry Springer Show* or the *Maury Povich Show*, and only one said it bought *Jenny Jones* at an estimated average unit rate of $17,000 per 30-second spot. The exceptions to the talk show trend were *The Oprah Winfrey Show* and *The Rosie O'Donnell Show*.

Like the networks in upfront selling, the syndicators make audience delivery guarantees to their advertisers. If a program delivers less than the projected rating, the syndicator adjusts the rate with cash back to the advertiser. The prices in Table 6–6 reflect that adjustment.

Media buyers claim that syndication historically has the biggest "spread," or gap, between audience estimates forecast by buyers and those projected by the sellers.

Cable Syndication

Syndication finds a warm welcome at national cable networks as well as at broadcast TV stations. TBS paid $100 million for the rights to *Seinfeld* for its WTBS superstation. TNT agreed to pay $1.2 million per episode for *ER* in syndication. Warner Bros. sold the first-run rights to the hour-long emergency room drama to TNT for Monday through Friday programming and to

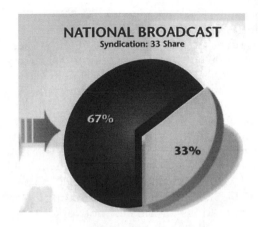

FIGURE 6–4

Syndication has 13% of total viewing, according to SNTA, and a third of national broadcast, as shown in this pie chart. In early fringe, syndication takes 77% of the pie. Courtesy SNTA. Used with permission.

local broadcast TV stations for weekend programming.

Why did a syndicated show command such a high price from cable? NBC-TV established value for *ER* in the wake of the end of *Seinfeld*. In order to keep its Thursday night lineup as stable as possible, NBC

SPECIAL FX

Like the networks, syndicators vie for the attention of national advertisers with costly and elaborate presentations.

Rysher Entertainment, the company that syndicates the very successful *Entertainment Tonight* magazine-style TV show, rolled out a new series called *FX* about a movie special effects expert teamed with a "tough-talking, head-banging, street-hustling" detective. The presentation materials themselves had "special effects" built in:

- Open the spiral-bound booklet to the picture of special effects man Rollie Tyler (actor Cameron Daddo), and there's a magnifying glass to distort his face.

- Open to the page just after the detective with the hyperbolic description, and there's a mirror to turn a backwards "FX" title so it can be read properly (or to distort the advertising buyer's face).

- And speaking of distorted faces, peel off a plastic overlay and what looks like an elderly, bald, and bristle-bearded street person turns into the lead character's winsome and hazel-eyed girlfriend (actress Lucinda Scott).

- The last effect in the booklet is a page of temperature-sensitive paper. Place your palm in the center, and you've made a hand print to cover the pouting face of Rollie Tyler's assistant and office manager (actress Christina Cox).

agreed to an unprecedented $13 million dollars per episode for the first run of *ER*. In turn, the network charged advertisers $565,000 per 30-second commercial during the 1998–1999 season, the highest price ever charged for airing in a prime time program. In addition, there were very few dramas available. Supply and demand drove prices up. Twentieth Television licensed its two top off-network dramas to the FX network. *The X-Files* and *NYPD Blue* were sold to FX for $600,000 and $400,000 respectively. The result was a doubling of its 18–49 ratings for the new network.

Cable also captured the rights to *Party of Five* (Lifetime), *Chicago Hope* (Lifetime), *Walker, Texas Ranger* (USA), and *New York Undercover* (USA).

Doug McCormick, president of Lifetime, told *Broadcasting & Cable* that the reason cable became a major player in off-network syndication was the lack of "real estate" (that is to say, air time) on broadcast stations:

> Years ago you had *Kojak*, *Cannon*, and all those shows in early fringe on stations, but that was pre-"Rosie," pre-"Oprah," pre-"Jerry Springer." So there's a crowding out in the syndication marketplace, and cable has become the best outlet. What we have done is make it impossible or very difficult for syndicated hours to be profitable on stations.[22]

Except for the largest TV markets like New York and Los Angeles, local stations cannot pay $500,000 for individual episodes of programs and expect to recoup that money from advertisers.

Advertisers on Syndicated Television

Food and food products were the leading advertising category in syndicated television in the mid-1990s. The total expenditures for food commercials in 1997 was $368.5 million, which is $70 million ahead of that year's number-two category, toiletries and toilet goods. The grand total for advertising on syndicated television in 1997 was $2.515 billion. The rankings were as follows:

TABLE 6-6 Top 25 Syndicated Shows Ranked By Ad Price

This table shows the cost of a 30-second commercial among the top barter syndicatd TV series.

TV Show	1997–1998
Home Improvement	$105,000
X-Files	92,000
Seinfeld	81,000
Entertainment Tonight	72,000
Wheel of Fortune	65,000
The Simpsons	65,000
Frasier	62,000
Star Trek: Deep Space 9	58,000
Mad About You	58,000
Jeopardy!	57,000
The Oprah Winfrey Show	52,000
Grace Under Fire	47,000
Xena	40,000
Hercules	40,000
Rosie O'Donnell Show	37,000
Extra	36,000
Living Single	30,000
Access Hollywood	29,000
NYPD Blue	29,000
Martin	29,000
Pensacola	26,000
Inside Edition	26,000
Earth: Final Conflict	25,000
Honey, I Shrunk the Kids	24,000

Source: 1998 *Advertising Age/Electronic Media* survey of national barter syndication buyers, based on Nielsen Media Research's 50 top-rated shows through November 11, 1997. Unit rates are based on average price paid for a 30-second unit, after audience adjustments are factored in for cash refunds.

FIGURE 6–5 This ad from Warner Bros. Domestic Television shows one company's diversity. Multiply that by 14 member companies of SNTA and you find lots of syndicated programming available.

1. Food and food products
2. Toiletries and toilet goods
3. Proprietary medicines
4. Confectionery, snacks, and soft drinks
5. Restaurants and drive-ins
6. Automotive
7. Sporting goods and toys
8. Movies
9. Consumer services, including telephone companies
10. Household equipment and supplies
11. Soaps, cleaners, and polishes
12. Home electronics
13. Personal services
14. Department stores
15. Apparel, footwear, and accessories
16. Pet foods and supplies
17. Jewelry, optical goods, and cameras
18. Publishing and media
19. Computers and office equipment
20. Loan and mortgage companies
21. Anti-smoking materials
22. Shoe stores
23. Insurance
24. Leisure time activities and services
25. Beer and wine

The biggest gainers in the list were loan and mortgage companies, up 255% from 1996 to 1997, and jewelry, optical goods, and cameras, up 113%. Sporting goods and toys were off by 29%.[23]

The top five advertisers in syndication were Procter & Gamble, General Motors, Johnson & Johnson, Diageo PLC, and Unilever.

Infomercials

A family on vacation demonstrates the ways each member uses their credit card. Not just any card, the Discover Card. On its tenth anniversary, Discover discovered the infomercial. It was the first credit card company to do so.[24]

Discover's entry into the infomercial field in 1996 demonstrated that long-form commercials were capable of selling more than exercise machines, contour pillows, and food choppers that slice and dice. The company chose the "storymercial" format, dramatizing the family's vacation in a playlet called "Give Me Some Credit."

In addition to the storymercial, infomercial formats include the "programercial," almost a documentary approach, but dramatized for the production, not collected from existing sources as a documentary would be. The Sled Dogs Company of Minneapolis used the programercial to demonstrate snow skates, which are a cross between inline skates and snow board boots. Their half hour followed a skating champion as he tried to escape an angry Rottweiler. Footage was edited MTV-style with spoofs of the Sled Dogs board of directors trying to decide how to market the new product.

Don't confuse the programercial with the "documercial," which is produced just like a documentary. For example, behind-the-scenes footage of the rock band the Grateful Dead on tour was used in an infomercial called "The Long Strange Trip Continues," which sold Dead videos, CDs, T-shirts, and screen savers. The seemingly laid-back Dead were one of the most aggressive database marketing organizations and used the infomercial to add names to their database.

Next, there's the "brandmercial," designed to deepen the image of a national brand. For example, Lexus introduced the

1997 LS 400 luxury car with a brandmercial titled, "Lexus Presents: Driven to Perfection."[25]

(The suffix, "-mercial," gets out of hand: Cruise Holidays International of San Diego called its scenes of happy vacationers a "cruise-mercial," which is *not* an official designation).

The original infomercial format was the "talk show," which for some reason escaped that "mercial" suffix. As its name indicates, the talk show walks a fine line between a typical TV talk show and a commercial. There's also an infomercial format called "demonstration," for obvious reasons. Sometimes, the demonstration includes an audience in order to simulate a typical talk show format.

Peter Spiegel, president of Kent & Spiegel Direct in Culver City, California, suggests letting the product decide the format: "Housewares are normally done in a demonstration format. Vanity/sex are generally done in talk-show or documentary styles, but, again, if it is an image piece, it could be done as a storymercial. Financial opportunities, personal improvement, and entertainment products are generally documentaries."[26]

Most of the early infomercials were seen late at night and featured books, seminars, and tapes from real estate consultants, and gadgets like juicers, vegetable slicers, and paint applicators. In his book, *The Age of Multimedia and Turbonews*, Jim Willis addresses the infomercial's nocturnal placement:

> Possibly the secret of these newly formatted infomercials is that they combine elements of popular talk shows featuring well-known faces in beautiful settings and direct-market home television shopping, where ordering products and services of-

fered is as easy as picking up the phone. Like other types of late-night media programming, such as radio call-in shows, these social gabfests greet insomniacs and other night people with friendly faces and urge the viewer to join in the fun by using the telephone.[27]

The infomercial grew up, so to speak, when major advertisers took advantage of TV's audience and their willingness to respond immediately. In addition to Discover and Lexus, Hoover Vacuum Cleaners, Phillips-Magnavox, Quaker State Motor Oil, MGM Home Entertainment, Nissan Motors, Apple Computer, and many others produced and aired long-form commercials.

In the 1996 presidential campaign, candidate Ross Perot raised the visibility of the half-hour infomercial format by airing programs in prime time on national networks.

Timothy Hawthorne, known in the field as "The Father of the Modern Infomercial," founded Hawthorne Communications in Fairfield, Iowa, in 1986. Since then the name has changed to "hawthorne direct", and revenues have risen to $50 million a year. Here's Hawthorne's definition of "infomercial":

> In essence, an infomercial, or long-form television commercial, is a $28\frac{1}{2}$-minute program designed to motivate viewers to request more product information, place an immediate order, or purchase the product at a retail outlet. The program informs, entertains, builds credibility, explains product benefits and addresses anticipated objections. Spaced within the program are several ads running 2 or 3 minutes that further explain the product, demonstrate the benefits, present the offer, and encourage viewers to call a toll-free number.[28]

There are also short-form infomercials, elongated commercials that usually run 2 minutes in length, although some are 60s and 90s. They are called "direct response television" (DRTV) because they ask the viewer to call a toll-free number and place an order.

Hawthorne says DRTV is "ideal for products generally under $30 that are easily and quickly understood such as CDs, videos, Ginsu knives. . . . Infomercial products, usually above $30, are those that require more time to fully explain the product's features and benefits or to create an emotional bond." An exception to the $30 rule was a DRTV campaign from Xerox Corporation in 1995 to introduce a line of digital copiers. (See Figure 6–6.)

In the early 1990s, infomercials accounted for $750 million in sales, according to *Direct Marketing*. By 1997, revenues were at $1.56 billion, according to Hawthorne, up from the $1.4 billion in 1996 and $1.1 billion in 1995, as reported by NIMA International, the trade association of infomercial producers.

"Infomercials give the buying public what it wants in an entertaining and interesting form that sells," Hawthorne says. However, he does not advocate replacing spot buys or print ads with infomercials:

> In our experience the media mix works well together, complementing one another. Infomercials bolster consumer awareness of your product and share the product story with millions of additional prospects at a cost per lead or cost per order that usually matches or beats other direct marketing channels such as direct mail or print ads.

Myrna Gardner, president of Hudson Street Partners, the New York–based infomercial unit of Saatchi & Saatchi advertising, produced the Lexus "brandmercial" as well as long-form commercials for Fidelity Investments, Florida Citrus, and Toyota.[29] She takes a practical approach to infomercials: "Advertisers are searching for the best way to deliver information about their products to consumers. If we want consumers to find out about our products, we have to present the information in an entertaining manner."

Jim Willis underscores Gardner's comments: "One way to avoid the viewer's predisposition to escape commercials is to make those commercials as interesting as other programming."

The more sophisticated the programming in the infomercial, the less relegated the shows are to late nights and odd hours. An infomercial for the New England Patriots

ITEMS PURCHASED via TELEVISION

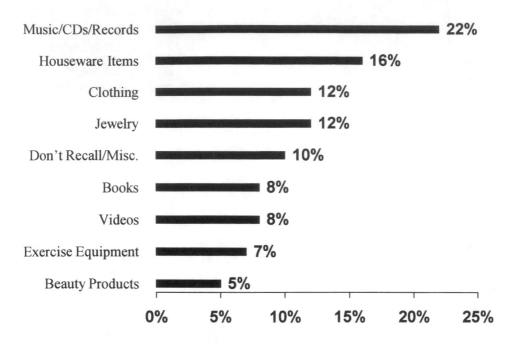

FIGURE 6-6 The father of the modern infomercial, Timothy H. Hawthorne says the infomercial is unparalleled in its ability to generate consumer demand. Here's what sells in infomercials. The data was collected from *Direct Marketing*, January 1998.

football team broadcast on Boston's WCVB, the ABC-TV affiliate, and other New England TV stations earned a 5.3 rating (better than basketball's Celtics and hockey's Bruins combined on that same day). The "Patriots Insider" infomercial highlighted Patriot and Pro Bowl star David Megget, beginning with him waking early in the morning and following him through a day. It also featured former Patriot Andre Tippet, who offered "Tippet's Tips for Kids." The athletes were portrayed as role models. Interspersed throughout the program were "great moments in Patriots' history." The remainder of the program sold NFL merchandise.

Rising media costs for infomercial placement created a new type of network—the infomercial network.

- Before Paxson Communications launched Pax TV, the company called its collection of TV stations "inTV, The Network of Infomercials." It was the largest of the infomercial broadcasters, airing infomercials for 15 hours on the average day and covering 59% of U.S. TV households.
- Access Television Network (ATN) fed programming on two unduplicated channels to cable systems covering about 37 million homes. Cable operators were able to plug ATN feeds into open time slots on networks or on public access channels.
- Guthy-Renker, a producer of infomercials, also owns GRTV Network, which buys unused time on cable systems owned by Tele-Communications, Inc., Time-Warner, and MediaOne. GRTV is

---

INFOMERCIALS

Broadcasting & Cable's 1998 survey of TV GMs showed that 92% of TV stations carried infomercials. Survey questions included the following:

1. Do you run infomercials of at least a half-hour length on your station?

Yes	92%
No	8%

2. Yes respondents only: How much of your total revenue do they account for?

5% or less	79.3%
6% to 10%	12.0%
Over 15%	3.3%

3. All respondents: Are you projecting more, less, or about the same revenue from infomercials in 1998?

More	13%
About the same	57.6%
Less	28.3%

The study is conducted each year in time to be released at the National Association of Television Program Executives (NATPE) convention in January. One hundred TV GMs are interviewed by Cahners Research.

---

also available on DirecTV satellite channels. Their ad in *Broadcasting & Cable* was headlined "Got Money?" The answer: "We do! We'll help you identify the underutilized airtime in your lineup and turn it into cash . . . today!"

- Product Information Network (PIN), owned by Jones Intercable, Cox Cable, and Adelphia Communications, covers 10.2 million homes and operates 24 hours a day.

The Next Generation

"As more cable channels appear, the need for innovative programming increases," says Andrew Miller, who hopes his company, MarkeTVision Direct, will be asked to fill it. "The key is to provide these channels with a program that looks like good network television and also incorporates the proper elements which make the consumer respond and buy the products being offered."

Miller's Boston-based operation produced "Patriots' Insider" and the Grateful Dead's "The Long Strange Trip Continues." Infomercials from MarkeTVision have a twist: they sell commercial time in the program as well as selling products directly to the viewer.[30] Miller calls it "revenue enhanced programming" (REP).

When General Cinema opened two theaters in the Chicago area, Miller produced an infomercial (i.e., a REP) to tell the story. Traditional movie marketing focuses on the stars and the action, not on the specific theater, so General Cinema was "breaking the mold," in Miller's words. The infomercial featured a tour through the state-of-the-art theater with behind-the-scenes looks at everything from the acoustics to the projection booth. Along with direct response pitches for gift certificates and ticket coupon books were commercials for Pepsi Cola products and M&M/Mars candies. "The direct response spots afford General Cinemas a revenue stream from the paid program and the placement of commercials from their vendors helps defray the production costs," Miller says. "By using direct response television and REP, a company can promote both its name and specific products and brands. As media time and general advertising become more expensive, REP becomes a viable and effective way of marketing that can actually bring a return on an investment."

Production costs for MarkeTVision's Grateful Dead program were paid by Maxell Corporation of America. Maxell's Scott Fain told *Advertising Age* that his company had a "long-standing relationship with the Grateful Dead and we have a very loyal following among their fans. It makes all the

sense in the world to be a sponsor of programming that revolves around the Grateful Dead and reaches the band's fans."

Selling Local Television

I didn't realize that television was already learning from radio until I got deep into the interviews for this book. Honestly, I anticipated a lot of questions. Specifically, "Why was a radio guy assigned to this project?"

Like a good seller, I was ready with information about myself and my background to answer any objections I encountered. Selling is selling, I was ready to say, whether it's selling radio time, cable

---

INFOMERCIAL FAQS

Peter Spiegel is president of Kent & Spiegel Direct in Culver City, California. Here are some questions his potential clients ask him about infomercials.

1. How much does it cost to produce an infomercial?

There is a very broad range here— $75,000 to $1 million—however, most fall in the $150,000 to $250,000 category. A typical demonstration show tends to fall in the lowest range of the spectrum. A typical talk-type show might cost $250,000, while an elaborate storymercial with actors and a story line would probably fall in the upper range.

　　Guard against budget overruns. You don't want to find that you have spent all your money on production and have nothing left for media or inventory. Location shoots, high-priced talent, special effects, reshoots, and overtime can all drive a budget out of control. The best advice is not to let your ego rule your pocketbook.

2. How much does it cost to air an infomercial?

Media is generally broken into two categories: the test and the rollout. Media tests run anywhere from $25,000 to $100,000. We usually get our feet wet with about $10,000 and start doubling it every week. You pretty much know what you have after you spend $50,000. A de

cent test should include a mix of broadcast and national cable.

　　The rollout is another story. Our bare minimum for a successful infomercial is $50,000 per week—generally we spend between $100,000 and $500,000 per week. . . . If we were to use baseball as an analogy, $100,000 is a single while $500,000 is a home run.

3. Do I need a celebrity?

When you hire a celebrity, you are entering the alien world of the entertainment industry. As I like to say, enter at your own risk. It is a world inhabited by agents, managers, and lawyers. Need I say more?

Once again, look at the categories:

- Housewares never require a celebrity.

- Financial opportunities and personal development depend on the charisma of the spokesperson and the credibility of the testimonials and also do not require a celebrity.

- Vanity/sex-appeal products may benefit from celebrities whose lives depend on vanity or sex appeal.

- Entertainment products generally feature celebrity-driven products and therefore don't necessarily require the additional panache of a celebrity host.

©1996 Direct Marketing Association

insertions, banners on Web pages, or products and services. (There's more about neutralizing objections in Chapter 2.)

As I pursued interviews of expert sellers, I was surprised that those questions in fact did not arise. I came to realize how lucky I was to approach the new environment of electronic media from a radio perspective.

Cable salespeople reminded me they had been emulating radio for quite a while by selling tight demographic niches or specific geographical areas. Sellers in broadcast television had recently discovered the need to change their approach, moving from transactional selling to creative, customer-focused sales.

Radio had been a scrappy, niche seller since the rise of television in the 1950s. Radio salespeople typically sold listener lifestyle, specific target audiences, and—most important—creative ideas.

In 1997, CBS paid tribute to radio when they named radio sales veteran Mel Karmazin to head the 14-station CBS TV group as well as the CBS radio group.[31] Karmazin had led Infinity Broadcasting to the prominence that made it a fit partner with Westinghouse and CBS in a three-way merger. Karmazin made immediate and dramatic changes in the way CBS sold time on its owned-and-operated stations, including a change in compensation structure from salary-plus-commission to commission-only. I use the word "dramatic" without hyperbole: the changes brought both an immediate jump in the price of CBS stock and positive reaction from Wall Street investment houses.

In a rare interview (in *Broadcasting & Cable*), Karmazin explained the move: "The reason to pay people a salary is to control the costs. My view is, if the sales person is making a ton of money at 3 percent, then I'm making a zillion dollars at 97 percent."

Karmazin felt his radio roots would serve him well at CBS-TV: "There are television people who look at a 12 rating and say, 'Oh my God, it's only a 12 rating.' I look at a 12 rating and say, 'Wow, it's a 12 rating!' I've never seen such big ratings. So there's a mindset where you're able to deal with

marketing and sell a lot more competitively than people in television historically have, where there are six competitors versus 30 in radio."

The results after one year of Karmazin's tenure at CBS prompted the company to name him president and chief operating officer responsible for CBS radio stations (there were 150 of them at the time of his appointment), CBS TV stations (there were 14 of those), the outdoor advertising company TDI, and the CBS TV network.[32]

Karmazin delivered a 12% gain in cash flow for CBS in the first quarter of 1998, his first as chief operating officer. Announcing those figures, he asked his managers for $1 billion in cash flow by the end of 1999. "Not an analyst we could find thinks he won't get it," said *Inside Radio*. Karmazin later rose to the top at CBS when the company's chairman, Michael Jordan, announced his retirement.

Karmazin was so well known in the radio industry that *Inside Radio* called him only by his first name. *Crain's New York Business* underscored that by saying, "In the world of radio, when they talk about a guy named Mel, there is little doubt who they mean." To those in the industry, the letters M-E-L were as well-known as the letters C-B-S.

When CBS-TV reclaimed the rights to NFL football's AFC games through the year 2005, salespeople from CBS radio properties were asked to work with network and station sellers on the TV side. The feeling was that radio's history of creative selling would help CBS recoup its $4 billion investment.

That idea is supported by Ron Aldridge, publisher and editorial director at *Electronic Media*. "If I were a TV GM, I'd find the best radio salespeople in my market and teach them TV. They already know how to compete. All media are converging and merging," he says. "The means of distribution is much less important."

Diane Sutter of Shooting Star Broadcasting refers to the first TV station she owned, KTAB in Abilene, Texas, when she says, "TV has to compete the way radio did before. Increased competition means (local) TV sales people have to become marketing consultants for their advertisers. They're problem-solvers instead of commodity brokers."[33] (See Figure 6–7.)

Local TV advertising dollars were $11.436 billion in 1997, according to McCann Erickson figures prepared for *Advertising Age*. That figure is virtually double the dollar level of just 10 years before. Still, some advertisers are reluctant to commit more than a fixed percentage of their budgets to television.

That's the mission of TVB, according to its president, Ave Butensky: "TVB's concern . . . is advertising and we try to talk to [clients] about the values of television, why they should use television and how it will work for them. There still is a major naiveté insofar as this business is concerned. Television is 52 years old. Its ad revenues passed newspapers for the first time only in 1995; it took 50 years to get there and not by a lot."

Butensky cites specifics: "[W]e still have a lot of people who don't know how to use television. The May Company, as an example, allegedly has a rule that says, thou shall not put more than 14% of your money in electronic media. Something we suspect was written some time during the Grant administration and never changed."[34]

While Butensky has his tongue in his cheek when he says that, it's true that some advertisers refuse to give in to electronic media. For example, the newspaper remains a formidable competitor to television, cable, and radio. See the discussion about selling against newspaper in Appendix A.

Classifieds

HELP WANTED SALES

WRAL-TV (CBS) in Raleigh, North Carolina. Experienced account executive to handle regional and local business. Strong negotiating and presentation skills, as well as the ability to sell promotional opportunities and develop new business consistently a must. A great station, and a great company in a dynamic market! If you can make a difference in representing the market leader, send your resume to Laura Stillman, Local Sales Manager, WRAL-TV, PO Box 12000, Raleigh, North Carolina 27605. An Equal Opportunity Employer.

Local ad sales with direct/advertising agency clients. A min. or 3-5 years experience in broadcast sales, excellent track record in new business development. Knowledge of Nielsen, Scarborough, TV Scan. Computer literate, college degree. Send letter/resume: Dept. #AE 202, WBFS, UPN 33, 16550 NW 52nd Avenue, Miami, FL 33014. EOE.

Sales Account Executive. FOX O&O in Houston is seeking a highly motivated Account Executive who really knows how to sell! Requires three to five years broadcast selling experience. Highly motivated achiever, team-oriented individual with the ability to work independently and as a part of a sales team while under pressure. Polished presentation skills and ability to organize professional client proposals and presentations. Must have knowledge of major market television sales. Knowledge of TVScan and other PC based broadcast sales programs. Interested applicants send resume to: Recruitment, KRIV FOX 26, PO Box 22810, Houston, Texas 77227. EOE/M/F/D/V.

FIGURE 6–7
These ads for TV sellers reinforce the skills needed: negotiating, new business development, and motivated, team-oriented, polished presentation skills. Thanks to WRAL-TV, Raleigh; to UPN-33, Miami; and to Fox 26 in Houston for permission to use their ads.

News as Focus

Networks are the most important source of programming in television, based on the number of hours scheduled in the typical week. Affiliated stations rely on their networks to fill important daytime and prime time programming slots. To cement an image in the local community, local broadcast television relies heavily on news. A strong news image allows the station to maintain overall visibility and to support advertising rates.

As you saw in the outline of TV dayparts, many affiliates program early-morning news broadcasts before the network morning shows, and a noontime newscast as well. They use the programming for its own merit and to promote their "big newscasts" (6 p.m. and 11 p.m. Eastern and Pa-

THE SIGNAL

In broadcast television, the lower the channel number, the better the signal and coverage area. Channels 2 through 6 are low-band VHF (very high frequency) stations. Channels 7 through 13 are high-band VHF stations. The low-band stations have a 100,000-watt power limit while the high-band stations are allowed 316,000 watts to accommodate for the differences in signal quality.

Channels 14 through 69 are UHF (ultra high frequency). These stations are subject to more interference than VHF channels. Even with transmission power up to 5 million watts, UHF signals tend to require special antenna treatment when received over the air.

cific time, 6 p.m. and 10 p.m. Central and Mountain).

The early evening daypart (6 p.m. to 7 p.m.) may include a 30-minute local newscast and a 30-minute network newscast. In many larger markets, stations produce an hour or more of local news, adjusting the time of the network newscasts as needed.

A stable, well-liked news team is one of the strongest selling points for local TV salespeople. The longer an anchor stays on the air with positive reaction from local viewers, the more the station's image and advertising rates are enhanced. The opposite is also true: a revolving door at the anchor desk reduces viewer confidence and, therefore, advertiser confidence.[35]

New York's Channel 7 News (WABC-TV) has featured anchor Bill Beutel for the adult lives of most of the station's viewers. At Channel 4 (WNBC-TV), anchor Chuck Scarborough has been a fixture at his station for almost as long. At the same time, Channel 2 (WCBS-TV) constantly churned anchors, reporters, and other on-air personnel for years. That left the station with the fourth-ranked local newscast at 6 a.m. (of four on the air at the time), third at 6 p.m. (of three),

and third at 11 p.m. (of three). That's the performance that led CBS to put radio's Mel Karmazin in charge of the TV station group.

I use New York as an example, but the principle applies to any market size. A well-loved local newscast is difficult to beat without long years of building a news image to counter. Working for a client in Savannah, Georgia, I saw firsthand how long-time and beloved Channel 11 anchor Doug Weathers outlasted many a challenger at the other stations. Local news is a franchise for local television.

The key to effective use of the news franchise is understanding the psychographic of the news viewer. Only in the late 1980s and early 1990s did television begin to research its product as thoroughly as other consumer products did. The pressure of competition and the decline of shares at the network level caused TV operators to employ positioning studies to learn more about news viewers.

Which stories are demographically driven? Which are driven psychographically? The answers allow stations to target more precisely with stories that attract older listeners at 6:00 p.m., for example, and younger females at 11:00 p.m..

Who Buys Local TV?

The first buyer of local TV time is the network, if the local station is an affiliate. Networks provide compensation to their affiliates at the rate of $200 million each for ABC, CBS, and NBC. Each local station gets some portion of the compensation pool based on the contractu-

al agreement between the station and the network and how many clearances the local affiliate provides. (See Table 6–7.)

Network compensation is in jeopardy, however. CBS affiliates were expected to return a total of $50 million in cash and advertising inventory to help the network cover the costs of acquiring NFL football rights. In markets smaller than the top 100, ABC-TV reduced compensation payments to affiliates that carry Monday Night Football. NBC network president Neil Braun proposed to his affiliates that instead of traditional compensation, the affiliated stations would be offered the chance to buy into programming and reap the profits of those investments.

Compensation plans are subject to change as the affiliates play tug-of-war with money that has flowed to local stations since the inception of the TV network concept. It's important to note that the sellers at local television stations will be asked to make up some of the difference if the compensation packages evaporate.

A range of buyers exists for local television.[36] At one end of the spectrum are bulk buyers. They demand that the TV station delivers x number of demo points by daypart, because their needs are driven by cost per point. If your points do not fit in a given week, they will be moved to another week or to another flight to match the points needed.

Bulk buyers cannot assure their advertisers about what part of the schedule will run until after it's on the air. If there's a need for make-goods, it's up to the TV station to find them and match them to the original points purchased.

Bulk buys are often made by advertising agencies that buy large blocks of time without a specific client in mind. They buy based on a favorable rate, then spread the opportunities among their clients once individual advertiser strategies are established.

The specific buyer is at the other end of the spectrum. Each spot is placed by time

TABLE 6–7 TV Station Sales

If the local station is a network affiliate, that network is an important "customer" because of network compensation. While compensation, or "comp," is endangered because of economics, it's still an important component for local TV. All of the figures in this table are in millions of dollars.

	Network Compensation	National Spot*	Local Spot	Total in Millions
1986	462.0	5,907.0	5,449.0	11,818.0
1987	456.0	6,155.0	5,716.0	12,327.0
1988	459.0	6,426.0	6,082.0	12,967.0
1989	473.0	6,574.0	6,356.0	13,403.0
1990	463.0	6,962.0	6,559.0	13,984.0
1991	417.0	6,356.0	6,316.0	13,086.0
1992	375.0	6,750.0	6,745.0	13,870.0
1993	370.0	6,973.0	7,102.0	14,445.0
1994	396.0	8,040.0	7,968.0	16,008.0
1995	632.0	8,152.0	8,406.0	17,190.0

*Before commissions to agencies, rep firms, etc.

Source: Estimates by TVB and available on their Web site at *www.tvb.org*.

TABLE 6–8 Television Activity by Length of Commercial

Originally the 60-second commercial was the standard length for TV, a carry-over from radio. By the mid 1960s the 30-second commercial was introduced, first as a 30/30 piggy-back on network, later as a stand-alone. The :30 soon replaced the :60 as the standard. While :15 second commercials grew at the networks in the 1990s, their growth has since leveled off. They have neber been a big factor at local stations.

Networks

% of Total

	:10's	:15's	:20's	:30's	:45's	:60's	:90's +
1965						100.0*	
1970				25.1		74.9*	
1975				79.0		21.0*	
1980	0.7			94.6	2.7	1.9	0.1
1985	1.3	10.1	0.8	83.5	1.7	2.2	0.4
1990	0.1	35.4	1.4	60.1	1.0	1.7	0.3
1995	0.2	31.5	0.9	64.8	0.6	1.2	0.8
1996	0.3	33.0	0.5	63.9	0.3	1.2	0.8
1997	0.2	33.1	0.2	64.2	0.3	1.3	0.7

Stations

% of Total

	:10's	:15's	:20's	:30's	:45's	:60's	:90's +
1965	16.1		13.3	0.8		69.8**	
1970	11.8		4.5	48.1		35.6**	
1975	9.1		0.5	79.2		11.2**	
1980	7.8		0.2	85.1	0.2	3.9	2.8
1985	5.5	1.3	0.1	88.0	0.6	2.7	1.8
1990	4.0	5.9	0.1	84.4	0.2	3.7	1.7
1995	3.3	7.3	0.2	84.9	0.1	3.3	0.9
1996	3.2	8.3	0.2	83.5	0.1	4.0	0.7
1997	2.7	9.0	0.1	83.1	0.1	4.4	0.6

* Includes piggy-backs.

** :60's and :90's +

Source: CMR-MediaWatch annual averages reported by TVB.

slot, daypart, and program to achieve demo points against the advertiser's target audience. Some people call this type of buy a "focused buy," but that's not an official term for it. The focused buyer sees each week as a complete schedule in itself, with specific goals. They believe that a single preemption can change the effectiveness of an entire week's schedule. When a spot is missed, they believe, it must be made good with a specific program that either meets or exceeds the established criteria.

Focused buys are developed around specific client needs: a new product rollout, the introduction of a brand name into a market, or a short-term but high-impact awareness campaign.

Many schedules fall in between these two types: not nearly so regimented as the focused buy, yet not nearly so loose as the bulk buy. For the length of the commericials they buy, see Table 6–8.

Review Highlights and Discussion Points

1. The TV commercial is the most pervasive form of communication known, with a profound ability to influence the audience's habits and thoughts.

2. Neil Postman estimates that the average American will have viewed two million TV commercials in his or her lifetime.

3. The percentage of households with at least one TV set was at 98.3% in 1998, according to the Television Bureau of Advertising.

4. The typical American household spent 7 hours and 17 minutes a day with the television on in 1995, down by only 5 minutes in 1997.

5. TVB documents the public's perception of television as the most influential, authoritative, exciting, and believable advertising medium.

6. In November 1997, NBC sold advertising time during the Super Bowl at an average rate of $1.3 million for a 30-second spot, and in 1998 the final episode of *Seinfeld* was such an event that the cost of commercials set records for prime time—more than $2 million for a 30-second announcement.

7. The advantage of big-event programs like those just mentioned is that they get big ratings across all demographic groups, and day-to-day selling at the networks is based on demos, that is, how many 18–49s or 25–54s can be delivered.

8. What NBC's William Rubens called "unmass appeal" is exactly what the networks now sell, especially against encroaching cable and direct satellite operations that can focus on demographics for optimum advertiser impact.

9. Fox led the way among the networks with targeted programming, showing the others how to make a living with 18–34 and 18–49 numbers, not the whole viewing universe.

10. WB and UPN have now been on the air since 1995, and in 1998, *Broadcasting & Cable*'s annual survey of television general managers showed that WB was expected to be the long-term winner in the battle of the new networks.

11. The launch of Pax TV, whose intended programming fare was to center around family values and infomercials, was greeted with skepticism by *The Wall Street Journal*.

12. The primary attraction of television as an advertising medium is its visual appeal, its ability to grab the audience's attention with pictures and motion. Among advertising agency executives, television is often the first choice for product imaging and demonstration.

13. Television also offers the advertiser other features: lifestyle, mass appeal, ubiquitousness, intrusiveness, reach, immediacy, variety, and value.

14. The inherent downsides of television for advertisers include clutter, nonmobility, inadequate targeting, channel surfing, fragmentation, and production costs.

15. The FCC defines a TV network as an entity providing more than four hours per week of prime time entertainment programming to interconnected affiliates on a regular basis and reaching more than 75% of the nation's TV households.

16. Salespeople at the network level are a small and talented group, and because they deal with the largest dollar amounts, they face the most knowledgeable buyers in advertising.

17. There are three markets for network television: the upfront market, the scatter market, and the open or opportunistic market.

18. Most network orders, once placed, are firm, that is, noncancelable. If an agency commits to an upfront buy and its marketing strategy changes or it faces financial problems, it's the advertiser's responsibility to sell off the unused time, not the network's responsibility.

19. The networks, on the other hand, cancel programs with no notice to the advertiser, but with the provision that commercials will run in another program that delivers the same audience profile.

20. Delivering enough households (or persons) to make the buys efficient is a product of two things: the popularity of the network's programming and the number of network affiliations that carry the program.

21. The same year that *Seinfeld* broke records for the price of airing 30-second commercials, the show also broke records for single-episode pricing in syndication.

22. Syndication is the sale of programs on a station-by-station, market-by-market basis. Advertisers use syndication in combination with network buys to maximize their use of broadcast television against the declining shares of the networks.

23. Fin/syn forbade TV networks from owning or syndicating their own programming. The end of these rules in 1996 meant that the networks could enter the lucrative syndication market.

24. National advertisers pay hefty unit prices for 30-second spots in syndication. Syndication finds a warm welcome at national cable networks as well as at broadcast TV stations.

25. Food and food products were the leading advertising category in syndicated television in the mid-1990s. The grand total for advertising on syndicated television in 1997 was over $2.1 billion.

26. Discover's entry in the infomercial field in 1996 demonstrated that long-form commercials were capable of selling more than exercise machines, contour pillows, and food choppers that slice and dice.

27. In addition to the storymercial, infomercial formats include the programercial, the documercial, and the brandmercial.

28. *Broadcasting & Cable*'s 1998 survey of TV GMs showed that 92% of TV stations carried infomercials.

29. Cable salespeople have been emulating radio for some time by selling tight demographic niches or specific geographical areas. Sellers in broadcast television have recently discovered the need to change their approach, moving from transactional selling to creative, customer-focused sales.

Chapter Notes

1 Neil Postman is troubled by commercials and their impact. He states his concern clearly in *Amusing Ourselves to Death*, cited in Chapter 1.

2 Warner and Buchman's description of a "passionate affair" is from *Broadcast and Cable Selling*, cited previously.

3 The TVB information is from the public-access section of *www.tvb.org*.

4 NBC's Super Bowl price was quoted in *Advertising Age*, November 24, 1997. The same magazine called the end of NBC's *Seinfeld* series a "Super Sein-off," in a front-page report, May 11, 1998.

Projections of *Seinfeld* earnings came as early as the February 23, 1997, issue of *Advertising Age*.

5   Ken Auletta's *Three Blind Mice* was cited in Chapter 4.

6   "Is It Prime Time for Cable?" asked *Business Week* in its September 8, 1997, issue. Yes, seemed to be the answer.

7   The article from *Digital Home Entertainment* was cited in Chapter 1.

8   "The Frog That Crowed" by Barry Garron in *Broadcasting & Cable*, January 12, 1998, showed WB pulling ahead of UPN.

9   The *Broadcasting & Cable* survey of TV GMs appeared in the January 12, 1998, issue.

10 The attitudes toward Bud Paxson swung wildly in *The Wall Street Journal*. In the April 22, 1997, issue the headline read, "From Near Outcast to Toast of TV." By the end of that year, a December 18 article about his new PaxNet network (later known as PaxTV) was peppered with words like "unorthodox" and a quotation from NBC's Robert Wright that Paxson was "taking an absolute flier."

11 "Paxson renders unto TCI" appeared in *Broadcasting & Cable*, May 4, 1998.

12 I should ask Eric Rhoads of *Radio Ink* magazine why he discontinued the old "Advertiser Q&A" column. I always read it and usually clipped and saved it. Gary Horton's interview ran on August 23, 1993; Dick Halseth's on March 1, 1993; and Rick Berger's on June 7, 1993.

13 Both the benefits and the case against television were assembled from a variety of sources. I recommend *Introduction to Advertising Media* by Jim Surmanek. Lincolnwood, IL: NTC Business Books, 1992. Figures for total advertising volume are from Robert J. Coen of McCann-Erickson, quoted in *Advertising Age*, May 18, 1998. Other information came from TVB's "TV Basics" online, from *Electronic Media Management*, and from *Broadcast and Cable Selling*, both cited previously.

14 The FCC's definition of a network is from the Telecommunications Act of 1996.

15 Ken Auletta's book has been cited previously. Other data about upfront buying came from: "TV's Upfront," *Advertising Age*, April 22, 1996, and *Broadcasting & Cable*, February 9, 1998.

16 Erwin Ephron was quoted in "How Do You Rate Your TV Buyer?" in *Advertising Age*, September 22, 1997.

17 *Advertising Age* lists network pricing each year, program by program. The figures I used are from the 1997 pricing survey that appeared in the September 15, 1997, issue.

18 The daypart audience makeup and programming strategies were originally two separate tables in the book *Electronic Media Management*. Putting them together made sense in this context so you can see what's available and what a programmer is likely to give you to sell.

19 *Broadcasting & Cable*'s Joe Schlosser wrote a long report on the syndication marketplace, "The Funny Money in Off Net," which appeared February 23, 1998. The cover of the issue had hundred dollar bills with comedians' faces in the place of the presidents'.

20 The story of syndication and how it works is from the 1997 and 1998 annual reports from ASTA, the Advertiser Syndicated Television Association, published each year in *Advertising Age* and *Electronic Media* magazines. ASTA's Tim Duncan offered me access to everything the organization prints. Sorry I don't have the space to take advantage of the kindness, but thanks. Syndicators decided to change the structure and the name of their trade organization and unveiled the Syndicated Network Television Association. A report of the change appeared in *Broadcasting & Cable*, August 10, 1998.

21 Information from Antonelli Media Training Center was provided by the center's Martin Antonelli.

22 Doug McCormick's comments about real estate appeared in the *Broadcasting & Cable* special report mentioned earlier.

23 Advertiser categories for syndication were released by TVB.

24 The Discover Card's family on vacation was the subject of *Advertising Age*'s "Discover Takes to Long Form with 'Storymercial,'" November 4, 1996.

25 The suffixes were collected from an advertising section from NIMA, the National Infomercial Marketing Association, in *Advertising Age*, September 8, 1997.

26 Peter Spiegel's "The Eight Most Frequently Asked Questions About Infomercials" was posted online at the Smart Business Supersite. ©1996, Direct Marketing Association.

27 Infomercials started at night, but later saw the light of day. Jim Willis' *The Age of Multimedia and Turbonews*. Westport, CT: Praeger, 1994.

28 In addition to Timothy Hawthorne's book (see Suggested Reading), see "Opening Doors to Retail Stores: Infomercials with Shelf Space for Your Products" in *Direct Marketing*, January 1998.

29 Myrna Gardner was quoted in the NIMA report, cited above.

30 MarkeTVision Direct was profiled in "The Next Generation of Direct Response Television," *Direct Marketing*, August 1997. That featured information on the company's "Patriots' Insider" as did "Infomercials Attracting Spots for Other Products" in *Advertising Age*, December 2, 1996.

31 Mel Karmazin became so synonymous with CBS that when an executive was promoted to a new position at CBS, trade publications led with Mel instead of giving the person credit for the new position.

32 This outline of Karmazin's move to CBS-TV is collected from "Mel Karmazin Makes (and Accepts) NO EXCUSES" by Steve McClellan in *Broadcasting & Cable*, which accompanied an interview with Karmazin in the same November 17, 1997, issue; from "Westinghouse to Focus on Broadcasting" by Kyle Pope in *The Wall Street Journal*, November 17, 1997; from *Inside Radio*, February 17, 1998; and from "To Infinity and Beyond: Mel Takes on CBS" by Robin Kamen in *Crain's New York Business*, November 24–30, 1997.

33 Ron Alridge's and Diane Sutter's remarks are from interviews cited previously.

34 On July 8, 1997, TVB president Ave Butensky interviewed Joel Brinkley of *The New York Times* and author of *Defining Vision: The Battle for the Future of Television* (New York: Harcourt, 1997). The entire conversation, which ranged from digital TV to PCs connected to the Internet, was posted online on the TVB Web site.

35 Diane Sutter offered me important background on local television's attitudes toward news. The New York battle was detailed in "Channel 2's history of anchors away finally cost general manager his job" in *Crain's New York Business*, November 24–30, 1997.

36 Information on "bulk buys" and "focused buys" came from Broadcast Marketing Group of Kansas City and their newsletter MEDIA PREP.

Taking It Further

Here are a few Web sites that relate to this chapter and additional reading not included in the Chapter Notes.

www.biacompanies.com—Research on television and radio industries including market-by-market revenue estimates

www.nab.org—The National Association of Broadcasters

www.nielsenmedia.com—Television's ratings company

www.spotsndots.com—*Spots 'n Dots* is a daily newsletter for TV sellers

www.tvb.ca—Canada's Television Advertising Bureau (Study your French at the same time!)

www.tvb.org—Television Advertising Bureau (U.S.A.)

www.ultimatetv.com—TV station search engine, TV news and information

Additional Reading

Eicoff, Alvin. *Direct Marketing Through Broadcast Media: TV, Radio, Cable, Infomercials, Home Shopping and More*. Lincolnwood, IL: NTC Business Books, 1995.

Hawthorne, Timothy R. *The Complete Guide to Infomercial Marketing*. Lincolnwood, IL: NTC Business Books, 1997.

The Television Industry: 1998 Market-By-Market Review. Washington, D.C.: National Association of Broadcasters, 1998.

Whitaker, Jerry. *DTV: The Revolution in Electronic Imaging*. New York: McGraw-Hill, 1997.

White, Hooper. *How to Produce Effective TV Commercials*. Lincolnwood, IL: NTC Business Books, 1994.

7

Selling Cable Advertising

When I was a kid in Atlanta, Georgia, we had all the television anyone could watch—three channels! That's all there was in 1952. And one of those (Channel 11) wasn't even on the air during the morning hours.

My own fascination with radio and television caused me to spend many afternoons of my 1953 summer vacation watching Channel 11's fuzzy raster turn to a test pattern and finally to programming. Unfortunately, "programming" meant the same black-and-white cartoons that the station repeated every day or so.

In the mid-1950s one of the local radio stations launched a UHF station from a room in the old house they occupied in Atlanta's Buckhead section. We didn't have a TV set that could receive those channels, so I rode the bus to the station to watch the broadcast. I may have been their only viewer: the station went dark within a year.

At that time, there was no cable. Cable was for those poor people "up north" whose two or three channels of over-the-air television were blocked by mountainous terrain. I read about them in *Popular Science* and *Mechanix Illustrated* magazines. I wish I could find the stories now. One showed what looked like a garage linked by a wire to a huge outdoor antenna on a mountaintop. The antenna captured signals from

Philadelphia and sent them into the garage. In the garage was the distribution system and a single video camera that was used for local programming. There was no editing gear, so the operator used a hat to cover the lens while changing shots.

What we take for granted in today's multichannel environment is a phenomenon that began in Manahoy City, Pennsylvania, in 1948. According to *Electronic Media Management*, what I remember as a garage was actually the back of an appliance store. The owner was having difficulty selling TV sets because the reception in his area was so poor, so he created a distribution system.[1]

My memory of the antenna on the mountaintop is correct. The store owner charged $100 for installation and $2 per month for the clear signals from the three Philadelphia TV stations. As a result of his "cable" service, sales of TV sets picked up quickly.

The same thing happened in Astoria, Oregon, and the idea spread to other rural or valley towns where TV reception was less than satisfactory. Thus, Community Antenna Television (CATV) was born.

According to *Electronic Media Management*, there were 800 such systems across the United States by 1962, serving 50,000 homes:

FIGURE 7–1
On Tuesday, May 5, 1998, delegates to the National Cable Television Association's Cable 98 conference in Atlanta blew out the candles on the industry's 50th birthday cake. Courtesy NCTA. Used with permission.

The visionaries predicted that, by 1970, half of American television homes would be served by cable. There was talk of a wired nation and a multiplicity of cable TV services. Included in those services were to be computerized libraries that would allow a viewer to order any book ever printed for transmission into their homes. Subscribers would be able to dial a movie, any movie, any time of the day or night; hold business conferences with participants scattered throughout the country; pay bills, shop, and do their banking—all without ever having to leave the comfort of their homes.

What happened? Cable operators showed little imagination in programming and less marketing savvy. Other than clear reception in areas where TV stations were fuzzy, cable offered no benefit to the consumer.

Programmers of cable systems—the local companies that held franchises to serve individual communities—played a role very different from that of the broadcast programmers. Sydney W. Head describes the role in the textbook, *Broadcast Programming*:

> Cable operators line up a smorgasbord of program sources, leaving it to their subscribers to pick and choose at will from a number of channels—anywhere from a half-dozen to thirty. On most of their channels, cable operators act merely as relayers of programming that arrives at the cable

headend already structured. Thus, when cable operators pass on the output of television or radio stations to their subscribers, the programming function has already been performed by the originating stations. Cable's own originations thus far have consisted mostly of automated readout services such as news tickers. Local cable public access programming is typically a first-come, first-served proposition, with cable operators exerting minimal controls.[2]

Not until 1975 was there an idea that would give cable the boost it needed. RCA launched the SATCOM I satellite, and Home Box Office (HBO) announced plans for a national pay cable network delivered by satellite. From that turning point, cable became more than a device for retransmission. Head comments: "With the development of national satellite distribution systems for cable programming, the line dividing cable and broadcast operations grew less sharply defined."

Prime Time for Cable

If 1975 was a benchmark year for cable because of satellite technology, then 1997 was cable's breakthrough year. By then, the medium had become so pervasive that it challenged network television for viewership and won.[3]

For years, executives at ABC, CBS, and NBC laughed at cable. *Business Week* said the Big Three viewed the upstarts as "poor cousins toiling in the obscurity of cable TV." Even as the networks lost share, no one questioned their ability to deliver mass audiences and to attract huge dollars, as we've seen in Chapter 6.

At the Television Critics Association summer tour in Pasadena, California, in July of 1997, USA Network founder Kay Koplovitz said the networks "conceded the summer to cable."[4]

That summer was a landmark for cable. For the week ending on July 20, 1997, basic cable drew a 40 share in prime time versus a 39 combined share for ABC, CBS, and NBC, according to Nielsen figures reported by *Cable World*. That gave cable three consecutive weeks edging out the networks. Further, it gave the "poor cousins" bragging rights and it finally made the networks take notice. (See Figure 7–2.)

During the first week of the 1997–1998 fall season, cable networks captured a combined 33.7 audience share, which was another record. The top four broadcast networks slipped to a prime time share of 62.5, down from 65 in September 1996, according to the Cabletelevision Advertising Bureau (CAB).

When the 1997–1998 season got underway, the broadcast networks felt the shock of cable's success, according to *Business Week*:

All the broadcast networks except CBS are aggressively trying to brand themselves with a specific identity—much the way cable networks MTV, ESPN, and CNN have done for years.

NBC is focusing on half-hour sitcoms, which will dominate four nights a week. WB, the fledgling network launched by Time Warner Inc., has recast itself as the family-friendly network. UPN, half-owned by Viacom Inc., is investing in sci-fi programs to complement its flagship *Star Trek: Voyager.*

And in a hugely expensive bid to appear hip and relevant, ABC is aping cable's attitude-heavy advertising in its new, $40 million "TV Is Good" campaign.

Fox had established itself as a brand already. Its rapid growth as the fourth network brought it attention. Fox scored desirable young adult viewers and matched that profile with aggressive acquisition of sports rights: NFL football, NHL hockey, and Major League Baseball. During the summer of 1997, Fox abandoned the usual summer reruns, debuted several new shows, and carefully scheduled specials. The result was a 9% improvement in viewership.

Branding came naturally to the national cable networks. But the early entries need-

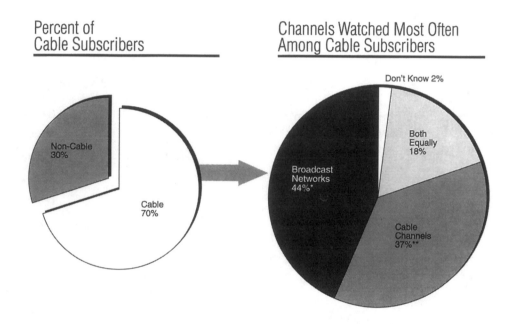

Cable Channel vs. Network Channel Viewing by Cable Subscribers

Percent of Cable Subscribers

Non-Cable 30%

Cable 70%

Channels Watched Most Often Among Cable Subscribers

Don't Know 2%

Both Equally 18%

Broadcast Networks 44%*

Cable Channels 37%**

* Broadcast Networks such as ABC, CBS, Fox, NBC.
** Cable Networks such as CNN, ESPN, Lifetime.

FIGURE 7–2 The summer of 1997 saw national cable networks edge out the traditional TV networks in ratings. Overall usage still goes to the "old" networks, but the percentages are close among cable subscribers. These charts are from *Media Targeting 2000*, conducted by the Arbitron Company in cooperation with the Radio Advertising Bureau. Used with permission from each organization.

ed to differentiate themselves from the other fare on the system, especially from the traditional networks. They chose clear positions and 24-hour formats much like radio station formats. Instead of a schedule of different programs, typical of the older networks, the cable networks created cohesive, easily identifiable niches, known as "vertical programming." CNN was all news. HBO was all movies. MTV was all music. ESPN was all sports.

1996-1997 KIDS SEASON HIGHLIGHTS

- Season-to-date, **NICKELODEON**'s 3.2 K2-11rating beats FOX's 3.1. **NICKELODEON** has led FOX on delivery since the end of Fourth Quarter 1996.

- **NICKELODEON** owns 56% of K2-11 GRPs and 58% of K6-11 GRPs: that's greater than all other sources combined.

- **NICKELODEON** also boasts the highest cume in kids' programming among major sources, reaching 58% of all K2-11. This is greater than FOX (45.6%) and ABC/CBS *combined* (44.4%). **NICKELODEON**'s 60% K6-11 cume is tops, too.

- **NICKELODEON** has 4 of the top 5 kids' dayparts and 79 of the top 100 kids' programs.

Source: Nielsen: NTI, NHI, 9/4/95-3/17/96 and NTI, NHI 9/2/96-3/16/97 and NSS 9/4/95-3/10/96 & 9/2/96-3/9/97; Nielsen Client Cume System, February 1997.
NOTE: Based on Nick Total Day and competitive kids' programming only

FIGURE 7-3 Effective targeting and clear segmentation make branding easier, as discussed in Chapter 3. Nickelodeon captures the whimsy of the network in a graphic that tells their success story. Used with permission. MTV Networks.

Cable networks were the first national media properties that *needed* specific positioning and branding in order to differentiate themselves. From the discussion of targeting in Chapter 3, you remember the references to Joseph Turow's *Breaking Up America*. Turow used General Motors as an example of targeting and segmentation to differentiate products.

That same logic led manufacturers to support magazines and radio stations that reached the consumer segments they wanted to reach. Radio became the ideal demographic and psychographic segmentation medium, with cable close behind. Segmentation makes branding easier when the media resonates with the viewers' personal beliefs and helps them chart their position in the larger world. In Turow's words:

Nickelodeon and MTV were pioneer attempts to establish this sort of ad-sponsored community on cable television. Owned by media giant Viacom, they are lifestyle parades that invite their target audiences (relatively upscale children and young adults, respectively) into a sense of belonging that ranges across a panoply of outlets, from cable to magazines, to books, videotapes, and outdoor events that their owners control or license.

The idea of these sorts of "programming services" is to cultivate a must-see, must-read, must-share mentality that makes the audience feel like they belong to a family, attached to the program hosts, other viewers, and sponsors.

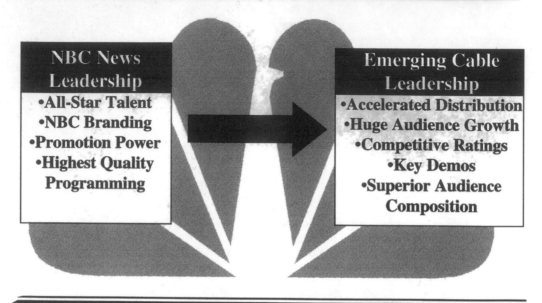

Now More than Ever...MSNBC is a Must Buy!

NBC News Leadership
- All-Star Talent
- NBC Branding
- Promotion Power
- Highest Quality Programming

Emerging Cable Leadership
- Accelerated Distribution
- Huge Audience Growth
- Competitive Ratings
- Key Demos
- Superior Audience Composition

FIGURE 7–4 "Must-See TV" becomes "Must Buy" cable. To ward off erosion at the main network, NBC extended its brand to cable and to the Internet and gave MSNBC "emerging cable leadership." Courtesy of NBC Cable Networks, Ad Sales Department, April 1998. © 1998.

Nickelodeon is an exercise in branding, both on screen and off. Each show attempts to establish its own brand. Even the consumer products division of that network has a branded hit in Gak, the slimy green goo that gets dumped on unsuspecting performers.

Fast Company magazine[5] explored the Nickelodeon attitude, calling it a "smart-aleck personality that gives the brand its trademark irreverence." Behind the scenes, each department gets its own "look." Visitors to Nickelodeon headquarters in New York get a taste of one such "look" when they are met in a room decorated with scenes from the network's hit show *Rugrats*. Similarly, the staff of Nick at Nite works in conference rooms with blowups of characters from classic TV sitcoms looking over their shoulders: Buddy, Rob, and Sally from

the *Dick Van Dyke Show* on one wall, Samantha from *Bewitched* and Cindy from *The Brady Bunch* on another. At Nick Jr., where programs for younger kids are developed, the offices have low ceilings so the adults who work there are constantly reminded of the audience's point of view.

All of Nickelodeon's walls have chalkboards for staffers to work out ideas spontaneously. The hallways are dotted with sofas and conversation areas for instant brainstorming. It's not the regimented Dorfsman design from the old days at CBS, but it's reflective of Nickelodeon: "a direct connection between play and work," as *Fast Company* put it.

In addition to Nickelodeon, I listed its sister network, MTV, as one of cable's original brands. MTV became so much a part of the life of its viewers that it took on even greater significance. In *Future Radio Programming Strategies*, David McFarland wrote, "For people under 21, and certainly for those under 18, one of the most powerful 'editorial' voices in the United States is MTV—because of the lifestyles and the attitudes the network portrays." McFarland classified MTV as a "significant part of the young generation's ritual drama entertainment" in an increasingly visual age.[6]

In a special section in *Advertising Age* and *Electronic Media* magazines in 1997,[7] the CAB pointed with pride at cable's success in branding: "Just 14 years ago, the cultural icons of television were the exclusive domain of the three broadcast networks. No more. Today, numerous cable networks are as firmly implanted in the viewers' mind as ABC, CBS, and NBC."

The name CNN is certainly "firmly implanted" in the world of television. The news network has extended its name to CNN Airport Network (found at passenger gates of major airports), CNN Better Health Network (in doctors' offices), CNNvention News (at large conventions and trade shows), and online with CNN Interactive and CNNfn (breaking financial news).

Like many of the cable networks, the Sci-Fi Channel offers branded clothing, gifts, and accessories through a direct mail catalog. There are Sci-Fi Channel interactive trivia games on CD-ROM; Sci-Fi Channel presence at science fiction conventions and fan fests; and a magazine, *Sci-Fi Entertainment*.

A&E also has a magazine, named after the network's signature series, *Biography*. Like *People*, but upscale and reflective, A&E's publication is designed to promote personalities featured on the *Biography* se-

FIGURE 7–5
Lifetime Television's target is women, so weddings are right in line. The series title, *Weddings of a Lifetime*, underscores the target and the Lifetime brand. Courtesy Lifetime Television and Lifetime Entertainment Services. Used with permission.

ries and to reinforce the overall A&E schedule.

The greater the success in branding cable channels, the greater the opportunity for top-of-mind awareness among members of the public. That in turn increases the acceptance at the advertiser level.

Advertising Age underscored the advances in branding by cable networks by naming ESPN its "Cable Marketer of the Year" in 1996. ESPN developed its branding with a channel that was termed "somewhat addictive to its core audience" by ESPN senior vice president Judy Fearing. The network added two additional cable channels, ESPN2 and ESPNEWS, the ESPN Radio Network, the online SportsZone Web site, and *ESPN Total Sports* magazine. There are also ESPN Sports Clubs, the first at Walt Disney World in Florida.

Selling Cable Nationally

Cable itself is part of the American lifestyle, with cable television in just under 70% of households with a television. CAB reported cable homes at 93.2 million at the end of the 1995–1996 season, or 68.1%. Of those cable homes, 30.5 million receive 54 or more channels.[8] If you add alternate de-livery of national cable networks—Satellite Master Antenna Systems (SMATV), Direct Broadcast Satellites (DBS), and Multi-Media Distribution Systems (MMDS)—basic cable programming is available in three out of four U.S. TV homes.

The sheer numbers are good news for cable sellers. And the continued erosion of broadcast network audiences makes the news even better. CAB noted smugly that noncable homes were watching less television, further reinforcing the decline of the major networks.

The bad news for cable sellers is that in 1998 there were 40 advertiser-supported national cable networks competing for dollars. *Broadcasting & Cable* listed 109 new networks that planned to launch before the end of 1998.[9] Digital technology has created the opportunities for the new entrants, even though digital set-top boxes are not expected to be universally available until 2002 or later.

Like selling the broadcast networks, selling the national cable networks requires dealing with sophisticated buyers at the highest levels of the advertising business. "The bulk of the money is placed in transactional business," said Lee Masters, when he was president of E! Entertainment Television.[10] "You don't see a whole lot of creativity (at that level)." Masters was not being unkind, only realistic. "If you're buying Coca-Cola commercials, you'll buy MTV. Buyers look at size of the target audience and cost per thousand.

"Selling skills come into play if the buyer's on the fence," he said. For example, there may be enough money in a buy for only a handful of networks. "If somebody's buying seven deep, selling skills determine how much money I get and at what price." The successful salesperson makes sure the network is in the top seven by demonstrating audience levels and cost efficiencies.

When Masters began his sales presentation for E!, he used the word "incredible" and focused on the network's demographics. "There are very few under 18 and very few over 49." Then he talked about the quality of the E! audience: "They are more affluent, even than the average cable viewer. They're pop culture people, early adopters, well-educated, easier to move with advertising."

The networks that get the highest cost per thousand (CPM), according to Masters, are MTV and ESPN. "It's not a matter of being 'best,' unless you're talking about doing the best job of maximizing ratings points. There's a myth that if MTV or ESPN sales people sold USA or Turner, they'd get more money. That's not the case. Ultimately every buy comes down to demo."

The Benefits of Cable as an Advertising Medium

In Chapter 6, I outlined the pros and cons of selling network television. Many of them also apply to cable selling because the visual aspect of the medium is the same; only the distribution is different. For example:

Visual: Both broadcast and cable television grab the audience's attention and create appeal by combining full-color pictures, sound, and motion.

Lifestyle: Almost everyone born after 1948 grew up with television and sees it as part of life, spending an average of 8.5 hours a day with television, cable, or a VCR.

Intrusive: Cable television does not require the viewer to seek the advertising.

Variety: There's a broad array of program types, so ads are able to reach viewers while they're in a specific state of mind, which gives advertisers a positive environment for their messages.

Sydney Head asks (and answers) this question about cable versus broadcast:

> To what extent does cable television share the attributes ascribed to over-the-air broadcasting?
> Cable can afford to devote entire channels to services aimed at limited audiences. A children's channel, for example, can offer uninterrupted programs designed exclusively for children throughout the day instead of just on Saturday mornings. Such

dedicated channels offer novel challenges to program strategists. Certainly cable is also capable of realism. Live sportscasts form a major element in cable's repertoire.

However, by its nature, cable lacks broadcasting's distinctive attribute of wirelessness at the delivery point. Absent, too is broadcasting's unique ability to reach every home in a service area at no more cost or trouble than it takes to reach one home. In contrast, each cable customer must be connected individually to the cable distribution network. Cable becomes prohibitively expensive in thinly populated rural areas that can be served easily at no added cost by broadcasting.

Cable has additional positive aspects as a medium, including the remarkable growth spurt of homes connected to cable (now 68%). With alternate delivery systems such as DBS, cable networks reach 76% of U.S. households, according to Nielsen figures released by CAB. Add to that the fact that there's greater growth of cable among households with an annual income of $60,000 or more.

Cable subscribers are "early adopters," which means that they are more likely to acquire new communications and entertainment technologies. (See Figure 7–6.) Cable subscribers have a higher propensity to use online services, laptop and personal computers, car and cellular telephones, and large-screen televisions.

The "limited audiences" that Sydney Head referred to create a strength for cable: the medium's targetability. Advertisers can reach specific target audiences using programs of interest to each group. MTV targets teens. ESPN targets men. Lifetime targets women. Nickelodeon targets kids. Cable can be targeted geographically, too.

A key point in cable's favor is that Americans spent more than $29.8 billion subscribing to cable services in 1997, according to the National Cable Television Association (NCTA). That's a large vote *for* cable.[11]

The Case Against Cable

For every strength, there is a weakness, and cable television is no exception. If cable is highly targeted, that means it doesn't reach a huge national audience all at once. Between 25% and 30% of U.S. households are missed in a cable buy. Also, some advertisers think of cable as "low-cost television," which casts a negative spin on a positive attribute of the medium.

Cable sellers face two of the major objections that broadcast television sellers face: clutter and lack of mobility. The average broadcast network prime time hour contains 8 minutes of commercials, as many as 24 commercial units. Cable often carries even more commercial units, making messages more susceptible to zipping, zapping, and timeshifting.

Another downside is that over 90% of television viewing is done in the home, making it difficult to reach consumers at the point of purchase. And the wire that delivers cable programming ties the viewer even more tightly to the home.

Local cable systems are affected by "churn" or turnover in subscribers. Old subscribers drop out of the system, and new ones are added on a regular basis. The industry attempts to remedy this problem with improved marketing and customer service, but churn slows the growth of many systems.

Market penetration is also a factor. The effectiveness of an advertising campaign depends on who can see the message. The national average of 68% penetration is just that, an average. In the 50 largest cable markets, the highest penetration is 83% in Hartford–New Haven and the lowest is 51% in Minneapolis–St. Paul.[12]

{ 🅴 }

E! Viewers are
Early Adopters

	CableIndex	E! Index
Home Computing Equipment	114	135
On-line Services	121	206
Personal Communications Services	108	134
High End Audio and Video	110	142

SOURCE: MRI 1996 Doublebase
Index based on national average for Adults 18+

FIGURE 7–6 Cable TV subscribers are early adopters, willing (and financially able) to try new things first, especially if technology's involved. This page from E! Entertainment Television shows that E! viewers are even more prone to be early adopters. © E! Entertainment Television, Inc. Used with permission.

Cable Upfront

Like the broadcast networks, cable joins the annual "ritual dance" of early selling—the upfront. By June of each year, the upfront buying season winds down. In 1997, cable attracted $2.3 billion, up about 28% from the year before. That's an indication of the increasing power of cable as part of the national advertising mix.[13]

At the same time, CPM showed only a minimal increase. For the second year in a row, average CPM on national cable networks was up 3%. That would be good news if it weren't for the 12% and 10% increases the broadcast networks enjoyed during the same 2 years.

As you read in Chapter 6 about selling the traditional broadcast television networks, the upfront cable market begins with children's programming—kids upfront. Nickelodeon has such a hold on young audiences (2–11 years old) that the network captures about 30% of the dollars in kids' upfront.

Some cable sales executives grumbled to *Advertising Age* that Turner entertainment networks (TBS and TNT, but not CNN) sacrificed CPM in order to increase their share of upfront dollars. Turner networks (including CNN) and USA Network together account for about a third of cable's upfront market.

USA also sold upfront advertising with low CPM increases, but for reasons other than share of the dollar. Like the broadcast networks, cable networks make guarantees of audience delivery against the dollars that ad agencies expend to buy in the upfront market. In 1997, USA was forced to take all of its daytime inventory off the scatter market for second and third quarters to accommodate make-goods to advertisers because of ratings shortfalls. *Advertising Age* reported that guarantees of USA audiences were off 15% by some accounts, and as much as 25% by others.

John Silvestri, vice president of advertising for USA Network, says, "This kind of thing happens from time to time, both at broadcast networks and cable networks." He says some shows on USA were just "not

working." For example, the network's *Murder She Wrote*, traditionally a good performer, was off in audience delivery.

In an environment of increased audiences for cable, the USA shortfall was a surprise to agency executives. However, it underscores the importance of accurate projections of audience to avoid costly make-goods.

Making It Easier

The Wall Street Journal compared buying ads on cable to going to the dentist with a toothache: "You have got to do it, and it isn't much fun, agency media buyers say."[14]

With 40 established national advertiser-supported cable networks and more being launched regularly, buyers have problems sorting out what to buy and how to keep up with the paperwork once they've made their choices. As valuable as audiences are, once cable achieved parity with the broadcast networks, advertisers still spent less per CPM in cable than they did in broadcast during the last quarter of 1997.

Enter electronic data interchange (EDI), modeled after "e-commerce," which is already used by the automotive, insurance, and retail industries to send purchase orders and invoices to each other electronically, rather than on paper.

For cable, EDI allows a network to transmit contracts, orders, and invoices from its own computers to those of an ad agency. At the same time, it allows agencies to transmit brand allocations and copy instructions to the networks. It also eliminates the need for paper documents, which can get lost, and for a buyer or seller to rekey all the information that's already been keyed in by its trading partner.

According to CAB, most cable networks and agencies have established electronic connections for contracts, and for master orders and invoices, which are the beginning and end, or "bookends," of any transaction. The next step will cover the much more challenging task of keeping up with all the changes that occur during the life of an advertising contract, which may last a year or longer.

The best that agencies and cable networks can do today is to keep one another up-to-date with faxes and phone calls, says Marylouise White-Petteruti, vice president and director of Media Systems at Leo Burnett Co., in a special report on EDI sponsored by CAB. "Brands go in and out of flight, budgets can be cut and shows get dropped and added," she says. "It's quite a dynamic relationship."

A lost fax, an unreturned phone call, or a typo on a document can mean discrepancies that slow the agency down when it tries to verify that its campaign is running as planned. In addition to tying up the back rooms of both agencies and cable networks, discrepancies that aren't caught in time can mean an advertiser isn't getting the media weight it has counted on.

"Once full EDI is in place," says Ron Schneier, senior vice president of advertising sales at A&E Television Networks, "people will be able to spend more time on the front-end, buy-sell process and less on processing the order." Schneier, along with White-Petteruti, chairs an executive steering committee of cable and industry representatives.

To put EDI into practice, agencies and cable networks worked to agree on "unit serialization," in which computer systems track each commercial with its own serial number. Unit serialization was a relatively simple matter for agencies because their systems already identified individual commercials. For cable networks, however, serialization required new traffic, billing, and sales software, an investment that could cost between $2 million and $6 million dollars.

A J. Walter Thompson executive told *The Wall Street Journal* that every one of her clients had increased their cable spending by a substantial amount because EDI "makes it much easier to buy." In fact, the *Journal* reported that media buyers contended that broadcast television should follow cable's lead into EDI.

Two Constituencies

The national cable network has two separate and distinct selling targets—the advertiser and the local cable system. (See Figures 7–7 and 7–8.)

Selling to the Multiple Systems Operators, or MSOs (most own more than one) is a long-term proposition. It involves relationship-building from the beginning, which is a highly social, one-on-one interaction that transcends the deal itself. Unlike selling CPM to an advertising buyer, the seller to a local system has no leverage to change the pricing.

Until digital transmission, local operators had limited channel space. So there had to be a substantial reason to add a new network—public demand, the failure of another network, or cash payments from the network—to make it worthwhile. Many cable networks had to stand in line until a channel opened up and to hope that they had made the kind of impression that would cause a market to welcome them by paying additional subscriber fees.

Selling Local Cable

About two blocks from the Atlantic Ocean off highway A1A in the town of Cape Canaveral, Florida, was a cinderblock building whose lobby would fill every Saturday morning. It was an amazing sight: faithful followers forming long lines, waiting patiently. The procession moved slowly. Those in line outside in the Florida sun made their way into the cavernous lobby and finally to a counter behind which loomed an unsmiling clerk. That's where they paid their cable bill. Most paid in cash, some with a check, and a few with a credit card. That was in 1986, a time when cable television was the only way consumers could get CNN, ESPN, and the other networks that gave cable its cachet. So cable had little incentive to improve its interaction with its public.

There's no vote that demonstrates the power of cable stronger than those lines of people waiting to *pay* for the service. Along with their fellow cable subscribers, they spent $29.8 billion in 1997 to attach coaxial cable or fiber-optic wires to their homes to give them an array of programming not available over the air. Those without cable usually cited poor customer service and high rates as reasons not to connect.

But even the faithful began to notice those high rates. When city officials asked what problems their communities faced, 72% of their constituents cited cable rates in 1997, up from 62% in 1996 and 47% in 1995, according to a study by the National League of Cities cited in *USA Today*.[15] Federal Communications Commission (FCC) figures confirm rate increases, from an average basic service rate of $23.50 in 1994 to $28.83 in 1997.[16] (The FCC watches the issues and tracks the numbers, but yields final control of cable to local governments with jurisdiction.)

The emergence of DBS and other alternative delivery systems forced local cable operators to take notice of the public mood. For the first time in history, they faced competition in the programming distribution business. The DBS business aggressively marketed its services with advertising that advised subscribers to unplug the cable in favor of their dish receivers.

An FCC assessment of video programming delivery showed that alternatives to cable had increased at an annual rate of 22% between 1990 and 1997. DirecTV/USSB, the big home satellite company, added almost 1.7 million subscribers during 1996 and the first 9e months of 1997.

The National Cable Television Association (NCTA), the industry group concerned with technical and mechanical operations of cable systems, warned members that by the end of 1998, 10-million consumers would be served by noncable, multichannel providers. (See Figure 7–9.)

The first positive moves came within the corporate structures of the largest MSOs such as Post-Newsweek Cable, Jones Intercable, and the largest systems operator in the United States, Tele-Communications, Inc. (TCI). Each company hired expert marketing help from outside the cable industry, specifically acquiring people with experience in marketing to consumers. TCI hired two people: a Procter & Gamble veteran and the person credited with creating American Airlines' frequent flyer program. Jones lured back a company alumna who spent 10 years marketing Citibank's credit cards. Post-Newsweek recruited a consumer expert from RJR Nabisco.

The next step was a 1996 joint campaign from NCTA and CTAM, a marketing and research organization. They offered cable operators customizable television, print, and radio ads advertising cable's "On-Time Guarantee" for installation and repair.

Subscribers First

You've been reading about local cable with no mention yet of selling advertising. Cable made so much money for so many years simply by connecting subscribers to the systems that advertising revenues were insignificant by comparison.

Furthermore, cable operators traditionally were technically and mechanically oriented. "They could string cable, but very few knew how to sell commercials, much less produce them," says Ronald Kaatz in *Cable: An Advertiser's Guide to the New Electronic Media*.[17] Kaatz describes the 1972 meeting of NCTA: "There was little to indicate that cable operators were interested in the national advertising dollar in 1972 . . . There was discussion of CATV's potential on a PI (per inquiry) basis as electronic direct mail."

Into the 1990s, cable's advertising revenues accounted for only 5% of system revenues. In 1992, national and spot sales on cable systems approached $1 billion, according to *Electronic Media Management*. That caught the attention of MSOs, who became aggressive in developing advertising as a revenue source. They connected individual systems in contiguous geographic areas to deliver more homes to advertisers. In large metropolitan areas, systems owned by different MSOs connected to-

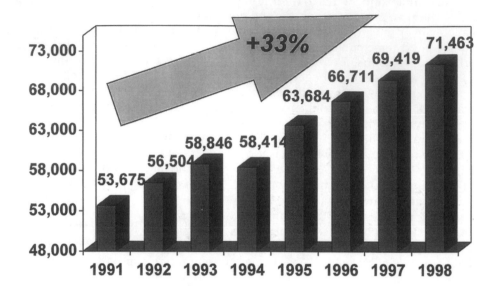

Lifetime's Subscriber Base Has Grown 33% Since 1991

(000)
Source: Nielsen (December 1991-1997 and May 1998)

FIGURE 7-7 Cable networks have to sell to cable operators in order to deliver advertising messages. Lifetime's success at collecting subscribers is a selling point to advertisers. Courtesy Lifetime Television and Lifetime Entertainment Services. Used with permission.

gether to make buying local cable easier. These combinations of systems are called "interconnects."

Just as EDI simplifies national cable buying, the local interconnects make it possible for advertisers to do what amounts to one-stop shopping.[18] The New York Interconnect, managed by Rainbow Advertising Sales, represents Time-Warner, Cablevision Systems, Comcast, MediaOne, and Adelphia Communications. It links 43 cable systems and offers access to 15% of the local advertising inventory on the top ten cable networks, according to *The Wall Street Journal*.

Interconnects deliver commercials from a central point either to individual cable systems or to all the systems in the combination by using satellite technology or fiber-optic lines. Revenues from the satellite-delivered portion of New York Interconnect's business increased by 40% in 1997 to $21 million. The Los Angeles interconnect, called Adlink, increased revenues by 52% in 1997. Chicago's interconnect was up 35%, according to CAB.

The interconnects have paid off in a new attitude toward cable among advertisers. "Once a market is interconnected, advertisers really understand and believe in

Distribution Growth Beyond Expectation!

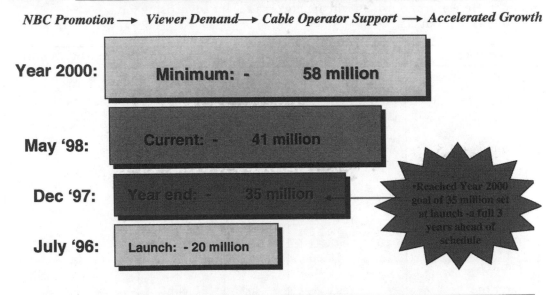

NBC Promotion → *Viewer Demand* → *Cable Operator Support* → *Accelerated Growth*

Year 2000: Minimum: - 58 million

May '98: Current: - 41 million

Dec '97: Year end: - 35 million

•Reached Year 2000 goal of 35 million set at launch –a full 3 years ahead of schedule

July '96: Launch: - 20 million

FIGURE 7–8 MSNBC projected its subscriber level to be at 35 million by the year 2000 and is proud to point out the fact that they are ahead of schedule. The network's two constituencies— cable operators and advertisers—had both been served. Courtesy of NBC Cable Networks, Ad Sales Department, April 1998. © 1998.

the value of cable," says Filemon Lopez, senior vice president of advertising sales at Comcast. "They put their money where their mouth is and they really spend," he said in the Cable Advertising Annual Report, prepared by CAB and published in *Broadcasting & Cable*.

"Cable operators today are more equipped to take advantage of broadcast audience erosion than they would have been even a year or two ago," says Jim Klunder, director of local advertising sales for Turner Network Sales. "Because of digital insertion, they can get advertisers on the air really quickly now, and that's a big deal to agencies."

The company that supplied three-quarters of the digital insert equipment to cable in 1997, SeaChange International, estimated that 65 to 70% of operations in major markets were using digital insertion technology "aggressively," adding commercials to 20 or more channels, and offering advertisers several geographic zones within a cable system's coverage area.

TABLE 7–1 Scoreboard for "Unmentionables"
The national cable networks can relax their commercial codes since
they are not over-th- air broadcasters. Some hold the line on certain
types of ads. Others allow their advertisers leeway on content and
product. Here's a rundown on which networks accept advertising for
controversial products.

Network	Contraceptives	Liquor	Gambling	Firearms/Ammo
A&E	No	No	No	No
BET	Yes	Yes	No	No
CMT/TNN	No	No	No	No
Comedy	Yes	Yes**	Yes*	No
Court TV	Yes	No	Yes*	No
Discovery	N.A.	No	No	N.A.
E!	Yes	No	No	No
ESPN/ESPN2	Yes	No	Yes*	Yes
Family	No	No	No	No
Lifetime	Yes	No	No	No
MSNBC/CNBC	No	No	No	No
MTV	Yes	No	No	No
Nick/Nick at Nite	No	No	No	No
Travel	N.A.	No	Yes	No
TBS/TNT/CNN/ Headline News	Yes	No	Yes*	No
USA/SCI FI	Yes	No	No	No
VH-1	Yes	No	No	No
Weather	N.A.	No	No	No

* Resort-oriented spots
** For premixed drinks
N.A.: Not available

Source: *Advertising Age*, April 14, 1997.

Advantages of Local Cable

In addition to the benefits of cable in general, local cable has specific advantages for advertisers.[20] Geography is number one. For example, if an auto dealer in a northwestern Chicago suburb wants to target potential customers in DuPage, Kane, and western Cook counties, what are the choices? Chicago's broadcast television covers not only the dealer's trading area, say Schaumburg, Napierville, and Batavia, but also Gary, Indiana. Most Chicago radio stations have the same broad coverage, al-

National Cable Television Association

FIGURE 7-9 The NCTA traces its roots to cable's origins as a distribution system for folks who couldn't receive over-the-air television broadcasts. Today, NCTA spearheads programs like "Cable in the Classroom" and "Tune In to Kids and Family," urging subscribers to use cable wisely. "Cable in the Classroom" has wired more than 70,000 schools since 1989. "Tune In to Kids and Family" prompted 75 cable networks to devote a night of prime time programming to family programming. Courtesy NCTA. Used with permission.

though there are a few western suburban signals to choose. So the dealer might be served best by a targeted geographic buy on cable.

CAB agrees about geographic targets and also highlights the demographic targetability of local cable:

These areas can correspond to a "trading zone," i.e., an area adjacent to a location where most customers come from, or a demographically concentrated area where many households have similar demographic characteristics such as age, income, occupation, or lifestyle.

With local cable advertising you can have your name and location appear in commercials in desired locations.

Cable advertising also has the ability to reach potential customers by using "targeted" programming (news, sports, children's, documentaries, home mprovement, etc.) with an audience of similar demographic characteristics.

CONSUMER PROFILE
Cable Subscribers

A National Study of **Media Targeting 2000** Consumers & Media

Gender

| 49 % Male | 51 % Female |

Income (Adults 18+)

Over $50,000	37%
$25,000-$50,000	41%
Under $25,000	22%

Occupation (Adults 18+)

Professional/Managerial	18%
Technical, Sales, and Administrative Support	21%
Service	7%
Precision Production and Craft & Farming, Forestry and Fishing	7%
Operators, Fabricators and Laborers	7%

Education

| 19% High School or Less | 27% Completed High School | 25% Some College/ Trade School | 29% Completed College or More |

Sociographic Shoppers Profile

Brand Loyal	35%
Cautious	40%
Venturesome	25%

Own Home	**74%**
Households with Children	**37%**
Average Weekday Non-Newspaper Readers	**35%**

Demographic Breakout

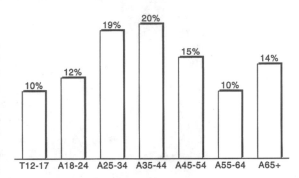

| T12-17 | A18-24 | A25-34 | A35-44 | A45-54 | A55-64 | A65+ |
| 10% | 12% | 19% | 20% | 15% | 10% | 14% |

Lifestyle Profile by PRIZM® Groups

GROUP	DESCRIPTION	
S2	The Affluentials	10.4%
C2	2nd City Centers	10.4%
T3	Working Towns	9.8%
S1	Elite Suburbs	9.0%
T1	Landed Gentry	8.6%
T2	Exurban Blues	7.3%
S3	Inner Suburbs	6.7%
R3	Rustic Living	6.2%
C1	2nd City Society	6.2%
U2	Urban Midscale	6.1%
C3	2nd City Blues	5.1%
U3	Urban Cores	4.1%
R2	Heartlanders	3.5%
U1	Urban Uptown	3.4%
R1	Country Families	3.3%

Cable Subscribers
Consumer Profile

Media Targeting 2000 — conducted by The Arbitron Company in cooperation with the Radio Advertising Bureau

16-A

FIGURE 7–10 You saw profiles like this one earlier in the book. Here's the cable subscriber profile. It's from *Media Targeting 2000*, conducted by the Arbitron Company in cooperation with RAB. Used with permission from each organization.

MEDIA HABITS
Cable Subscribers

Average Weekday Share of Time Spent with Each Medium

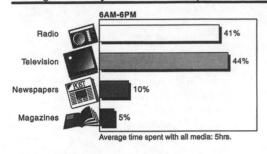

6AM-6PM

Radio	41%
Television	44%
Newspapers	10%
Magazines	5%

Average time spent with all media: 5hrs.

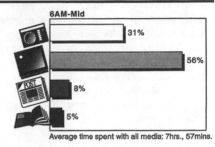

6AM-Mid

Radio	31%
Television	56%
Newspapers	8%
Magazines	5%

Average time spent with all media: 7hrs., 57mins.

Competitive Weekly Reach
(percent exposed to medium)

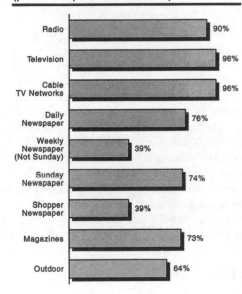

Radio	90%
Television	96%
Cable TV Networks	96%
Daily Newspaper	76%
Weekly Newspaper (Not Sunday)	39%
Sunday Newspaper	74%
Shopper Newspaper	39%
Magazines	73%
Outdoor	64%

Media Exposure Prior to Purchasing

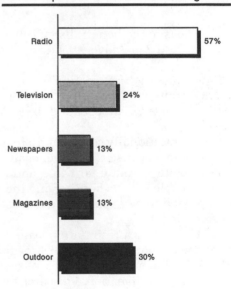

Radio	57%
Television	24%
Newspapers	13%
Magazines	13%
Outdoor	30%

**Percent of Shoppers Reached by Medium
Within 1 Hour of Largest Purchase**
*(Respondents reporting any purchase
within 24 hours prior to contact)*

16-B

*Media Targeting 2000 — conducted by
The Arbitron Company in cooperation with
the Radio Advertising Bureau*

Cable Subscribers
Media Habits

FIGURE 7–11 Not surprising, TV is the most-used medium by the cable subscriber. *Media Targeting 2000* was conducted by the Arbitron Company in cooperation with RAB. Used with permission from each organization.

DIGITAL UPDATE

Cable's digital upgrade is a priority. Here's how the NCTA reported progress in 1997:[19]

Presently, cable is transitioning from analog to digital programming and distribution systems, which are crucial to the cable industry plans to increase customer satisfaction and meet the competition posed by DBS, wireless cable, broadcasters, and telephone companies.

Cable operators are replacing some analog channels with a digital tier of new channels at compression ratios as high as 12:1. These companies receive digital programming either from TCI's National Digital Television Center via Headend in the Sky (HITS) or directly from the programmers. HITS customers can choose from 12 digital tiers that offer up to 155 digital networks.

In 1997, cable companies ordered over 300 digital cable headends that will serve nearly 16 million cable homes across the United States. More than 10.3 million cable customers were capable of receiving digital cable services.

In 1997, TCI offered TCI Digital Cable TV to 65% of its 14 million cable customers.

Adelphia offered digital cable to 1.2 million of its 1.8 million cable customers.

Cox, Comcast, MediaOne, Bresnan, Jones, Marcus, Buford, Time Warner, and Century are all in various stages of digital cable deployment.

Add these ideas to the benefit list of cable advertising, and you have a persuasive story to tell.

CAB adds one more attraction of local cable: it's "the most affordable television advertising vehicle for all types and sizes of advertisers."

Cable was traditionally considered a frequency medium because of its lower costs. With the growth of national cable audiences, local cable got the benefit, and the medium proved to be capable of reach as well as frequency.

Using a traveling presentation called "Media at the Millennium," Turner Broadcasting Sales demonstrated to local affiliate sales teams how to tap national research to show advertisers that cable can deliver reach that's the equivalent of the broadcast networks' reach.

Turner Sales used national Nielsen ratings to compare ratings, share, and cost-per-point results for ad schedules purchased on the top four broadcast networks. Turner's Rick North then shifted 20% of the buys earmarked for broadcast across the fully distributed cable channels CNN, ESPN, A&E, USA, and others. North claimed that advertisers achieved the same or better reach with the cable buy.

The national cable salespeople who grumbled about Turner entertainment networks sacrificing CPM in order to increase share of the upfront dollars did so because Turner had been at the forefront of this move to increase dollars for local cable.

An indication of the high stakes at the network selling level was a counter by CBS television that heavy cable viewers are less educated and have lower incomes than the cable universe overall. In the 1998 upfront market, CBS used their study to claim that cable networks *overdeliver* viewers, which seems more a vote *for* cable than against![21]

Direct Selling

Tune to Channel 6 on the Cable One system in Santa Rosa, California, and you'll see a smiling picture of Cheryl Vannucchi, along with her phone number. Vannucchi is the salesperson who calls on real estate agents, restaurateurs, and bridal shops, and she uses the on-screen photo to open doors. "When I make a sales call, I look familiar," she says. "It breaks the first barrier. It also gets me phone calls from owners of businesses and personalizes the photo channel."

"Santa Rosa 6," as the channel is called, features several different "programming" areas that are largely commercial photo-ads: real estate, weddings, dining, and entertainment. "Real estate is the easiest to sell because the agents get calls; they know it's working," Vannucchi says. Her clients get 17 exposures a day on *The Real Estate Show* at what Cable One calls "pennies per exposure." (See Figures 7–12 and 7–13.)

"People looking for real estate know to check Channel 6," Vannucchi says. "The real estate agents qualify their prospects by the prices of the homes that prompt the calls." (See Figure 7–14.)

The *Wedding Boutique* targets bakeries, florists, caterers, photographers, and other businesses that help brides and grooms plan weddings. The wedding portion of Channel 6 programming offers a "Bride & Groom Calendar," a planner that couples and their families can use to know when to hire a caterer, when to mail invitations, and when to purchase travelers checks for the honeymoon. Each request for a calendar was a prospect for a wedding advertiser. (See Figure 7–15.)

Dining and entertainment sales are more difficult, according to Vannucchi. "Individual restaurant owners who do the cooking themselves and greet the guests at the door are more likely to trade for advertising or rely on word of mouth. Some restaurants do believe in advertising, using a coupon in the paper and regular ads on Channel 6."

Video is not only effective, but at the local level it's usually more affordable than clients think it will be. Professional business coach Robert Imbriale underscores that fact in his articles for the Smart Business Supersite (*www.SmartBiz.com*):

> I love to see the reactions on people's faces when I ask them what they think the cost of the average 30-second television commercial is on a local cable station. Many will guess in the thousands of dollars while others will say in the hundreds. The truth is today, with so many cable stations and so much airtime to fill with advertising, the cost per 30-second spot is as low as $5 each!
>
> Having your ad on television means that you are a healthy business to most viewers. That fact alone makes this the most powerful advertising medium. You see, the key is that your market has no idea of how affordable cable television advertising can be. That works to your advantage because when your ad appears on television, time and time again, your prospects think that you are doing so very well that you can afford to drop millions on television ads—and everybody wants to do business with a winning company!

Local News Now

Interconnects are not the only way cable operators join together. Local programming channels are great unifiers of disparate systems. Pittsburgh's Cable News Channel (PCNC) and ChicagoLand's Regional News Channel (CLTV) are but two examples.[23]

PCNC claims 565,200 households through 19 local systems owned by six different MSOs. Cox Television's local broadcast station, WPXI-TV, is home base for PCNC and provides news coverage. The PCNC programming grid shows both live newscasts and repeat broadcasts of 6 a.m., noon, and 6 p.m. news hours. The channel originates a 10 p.m. newscast. Filling out the grid are shows like *Pittsburgh's Cooking*, *Steelers Huddle* or *Pirates Extra Innings* (depending on the sports season), *The Doctor Is In*, and live talk shows each evening.

For our second example, ChicagoLand's CLTV claims to be "easy to use":

> One call to one account executive.
> One dub to one place—any video format.
> One invoice.
> 24-hour time lead.
> Quality and service you expect from Tribune.

"Tribune" refers to the Tribune Company, the owner of WGN Radio and TV (among other radio and TV properties nationwide), the *Chicago Tribune* (among other newspapers nationwide), the Chicago Cubs baseball team, and Tribune Entertainment, which you read about in the section on syndicated TV sales.

CLTV News is among the largest of the 24-hour regional news channels in the United States. It claims 100% coverage on Chica-

SANTA ROSA'S BEST ADVERTISING ADVANTAGE!

Cable TV viewership is growing every day.
And, audience is expected to grow at unprecedented velocity for years to come. Why? Change.

People's tastes and interests are constantly changing.
Today, viewers want variety in programming. Post-Newsweek Cable Advertising gives it to them every day, 24 hours a day, 7 days a week. More to choose from so they can be more selective.

Choice means target marketing.
Unlike other media, Post-Newsweek Cable Advertising lets you focus your advertising dollars on your customers, in your own market, with the shows, events, news and special interest programming they choose to watch.

Targeting your customers is one part of the advertising equation.
Frequency is the other. Repetition is key. PNC's affordable rates allow you the frequency you need to reach your customers over and over again within the proven power of national network programming!

That's powerful marketing.
PNC Advertising combines the high impact of television, the demographic targeting of radio, the geographic selection of direct mail and the appeal of a local newspaper all in one medium.

#1. Target specific audiences.
Viewers have choices, so do you. PNC offers the most watched cable networks in the country. There is literally "something for everyone." Targeting your market maximizes results and minimizes your advertising costs. Great concept and it works.

#2. Upscale customers.
Cable viewers tend to be smarter. It's a fact. They are better educated, have better jobs, are more likely to own their homes and have families. They enjoy a better income, too, with more purchasing power. Cable viewers are your customers. Talk to them.

#3. Delivers more audience.
Cable television households watch more television than non-cable households. They also watch less regular network TV and independent television stations. Again, it gets back to choice. Subscribers watch cable TV. More audience. More potential buyers. Cable advertising is a numbers game pure and simple.

FIGURE 7–12 Post-Newsweek's Cable One in Santa Rosa, California, is where I found Cheryl Vannucchi's smiling face and her invitation to advertise on "Santa Rosa 6." The presentation begins by outlining the benefits of cable. © 1997 Cable One., Inc. All rights reserved. Reprinted with permission.

#4. Greater frequency, lower cost.

Frequency equals IMPACT. For the price of local radio, you can advertise on local network television just like the big national advertisers. Nothing motivates like television.

#5. Provides flexibility.

The breadth of networks allows Post-Newsweek Cable Advertising to package a sensible, cost-effective program for any advertiser regardless of the product or service. Through sponsorships of national programs, sporting events and tie-ins, you can substantially increase your audience delivery adding tremendous impact and awareness to your promotions.

#6. Pure advertising value.

Combining the strength of national network programming with strong local viewership, affordable cost, and a variety of different networks to target your advertising dollar, Post-Newsweek Cable Advertising is the most effective and efficient advertising medium in the Santa Rosa, north county area.

COMPARE POST-NEWSWEEK CABLE ADVERTISING DELIVERY WITH ANY OTHER LOCAL ADVERTISING.

NOTHING COMES CLOSE.

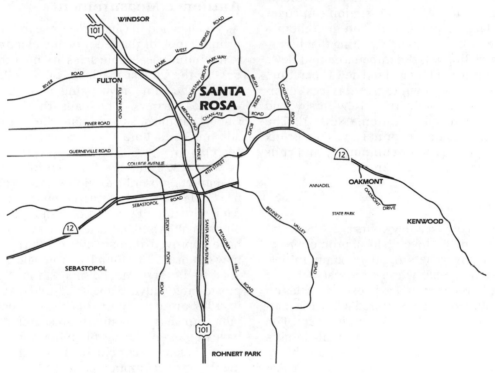

FIGURE 7–12 continued.

go area cable systems. CLTV originates local news programming most of the day. ("Around Chicago. Around The Clock." is the channel's positioning slogan.)

Ownership by the Tribune Company creates synergy: CLTV uses the resources of WGN-TV and repeats WGN's noon news-

cast. *Chicago Tribune* writers appear regularly, and the paper's suburban bureaus contribute neighborhood stories. Local weather is updated every quarter hour on CLTV and is also heard on WGN Radio.

On Wednesday nights, when Major League broadcast rules prevent WGN-TV from carrying Chicago Cubs games, CLTV fills the gap with play-by-play by the regular Cubs announce staff.

A seller for CLTV has the opportunity to introduce new clients to cable television with a special rate that offers not only a 30-second commercial but also production assistance in one package. A total of 40 commercial exposures plus production costs $5,000 on CLTV, a unit rate of $125.00, which is well below Chicago radio and just a fraction of Chicago broadcast TV.

For another example, people who live just outside of New York City have traditionally had to rely on Manhattan-based TV stations for their local news coverage. Needless to say, no TV station can cover that large a population and give them a sense of "hometown." Creating that hometown feeling was the impetus behind News 12. Begun as a Long Island news operation, News 12 has grown to five services covering areas in Connecticut, New Jersey, and the most recent addition, "News 12 The Bronx." The new channel gives the Bronx borough a sense of community and runs some newscasts in Spanish.

Promotions

Unheard of just a few years ago, MSOs and interconnects develop local promotions to benefit advertisers and their communities.

For instance, when Comcast Cable of Philadelphia wanted to boost local sales on Nickelodeon, it partnered with the network to create *Nick Nite at the 76ers*. The goal was to draw families to Philadelphia 76ers basketball games and to spotlight animated characters like Nickelodeon's *Ren and Stimpy*. The event was sponsored by Boscov's department stores. (Cooperation by the 76ers was easy to arrange: Comcast owns the team.)

Comcast also staged shopping mall promotions with Nickelodeon animated characters, which is something the network encourages. Jason Malamud, national director of affiliates advertising sales for MTV Networks, which owns Nickelodeon, says: "With its ratings increase, Nick is beginning to sell out at the system and interconnect level, so we're trying to create more opportunities to sell promotions and off-channel events."

Affiliates of the various MTV networks generated $3.5 million in extra revenue in 1997 through merchandising programs, according to CAB. Included in the value-added promotions were local associations with the MTV's Music Video Awards, E! Entertainment Television's "Hollywood Party in a Bag" kits that encourage restaurant business, and Food Network's "Cooking Across America" tour, which sends around the country four well-known cooks from the network's programs.

Audience Measurement

As you learned in Chapter 3, research is a primary tool for the seller of any electronic medium. Local cable sales are no different. In the largest markets, cable sellers call on the same advertising agencies as the broadcasters. The calls that go to Cheryl Vannucchi's real estate clients from ads on Santa Rosa 6 are considered research, too.

Most MSOs and interconnects in the top 50 markets subscribe to Nielsen. Many also use Cablescan, which marries quantitative data with qualitative information about buying habits and lifestyles. Research tools have improved dramatically, driven by the new opportunities for advertiser sales.

At TCI, Jerry Machovina, senior vice president for advertising sales, told CAB in its 1997 annual report that his company puts emphasis on qualitative research. "We have deployed Claritas mapping software, which is geo-coded cluster research that identifies consumption patterns."

TCI also subscribes to Nielsen and Arbitron data, but Machovina claims disappointment at "the limits of the Nielsen methodology, which is designed for a broadcast environment and highly underreports our audience." The Boston Nielsen Station Index (Chapter 3) listed only ten cable channels.

Larry Zipin, Machovina's counterpart at Time Warner Cable, says, "If our business depended on the data, we'd have no business at all. A good, reliable neutral and totally objective local cable ratings service

Subscriber Profile

ZIP CODES	City	Homes with CableONE Cable
95401	Santa Rosa	9,853
95403	Santa Rosa	9,416
95404	Santa Rosa	9,993
95405	Santa Rosa	8,036
95407	Santa Rosa	662
95409	Oakmont	9,742
95439	Fulton	151
95452	Kenwood	455
95492	Windsor	43
Other		16
Subscriber Homes		**48,367**

Total Household Penetration: 82%

3242 Airway Drive • Santa Rosa, California 95403 • 707.575.1320 • FAX: 707.575.1374

FIGURE 7–13 If an advertiser buys a schedule on Cable One overall or Santa Rosa 6 specifically, who sees it? Here's the breakdown. ©1997 Cable One., Inc. All rights reserved. Reprinted with permission.

Benefits to the Real Estate Show Advertiser

Colored-High Quality TV Advertising
Eye catching, informative and effective.

Affordable TV Advertising
All we need is a picture, no costly production involved.

Great Flexibility
When a house sells, we can insert a <u>new ad within 48 hours</u>.

Qualified Customers
Viewers watching your advertisement <u>want to buy</u> what you are selling.

Response Oriented
Television is proven in generating response from viewers.

Buyers See What You're Selling
Full~color pictures are the best way to show prospective buyers what you're selling.

Low Cost
Ads run for pennies per exposure.

The REAL ESTATE SHOW reaches 47,000 cable subscribers in the Santa Rosa area and is on all day, EVERY DAY ~ you can count on it.

Your ad can be viewed up to 2 times an hour in the convenience and comfort of the viewer's home.

Cheryl Vannucchi
Cable*ONE* Advertising
3242 Airway Drive
Santa Rosa, California
707/541-3585   Fax: 707/575-1374

FIGURE 7–14 When the agents get calls, they know their advertising is working. It's nice to have that direct feedback on an investment. Here's the one-sheet Santa Rosa 6 uses for the *Real Estate Show*. ©1997 Cable One., Inc. All rights reserved. Reprinted with permission.

doesn't exist." He feels that it won't happen until "advertisers and their agencies decide that they'd like to have better information than is currently available."

Arbitron no longer studies the TV market, so cable sellers referring to "Arbitron" research mean either RetailDirect Lite or Scarborough qualitative data, which is sold by Arbitron.[25] RetailDirect Lite is provided in 132 markets that are 100-plus in size. Arbitron added qualitative questions to the radio diary in those markets in the spring survey of 1997. Beginning in July 1997, the company sold the data to radio subscribers, cable systems, advertisers, and agencies.

RetailDirect Lite provides the following:

- Personal viewing information on 15 national cable networks. A seller can match networks with prospects' customers.
- Enough depth to show viewing beyond the major players. A seller can demonstrate that there's enough traffic on the Weather Channel, VH1, and the Family Channel to convince a customer to allow spots to rotate beyond CNN or ESPN.
- A demonstration of value. Arbitron uses this example: "Let's say that 1,000 ESPN viewers report they are going to buy or lease a car. The average car costs about $15,000. Multiply your car buyers against the price of the typical car ($15,000) and you discover your audience will spend $15 million on cars!"
- Newspaper readership information: who does and who does not read the paper; what cable channels reach them.
- Fast food consumption. Banking services. Leisure activities like nightclubs and concerts. Plans to buy carpeting, furniture, major appliances. Grocery expenditures.

Scarborough information includes much more detailed qualitative data available in the large markets. A good example of Scarborough's advantage comes from Bob Keeton of Keynote Advertising in Tampa.[26] He approached a Caribbean tourism agency about doing a co-op campaign with a large Northeastern tour operator. The tourism agency was concerned that sales in Baltimore were well below average. "The consensus of the meeting," Keeton says, "was to raise sales in this market over a four-to-six week period."

Using Scarborough information, he searched for people who traveled to the Caribbean from Baltimore. He found that they were in the 35–64 demographic and had household incomes over $50,000. He examined the area based on those criteria and focused media dollars in only one county using cable:

> Based on this information, network TV would obviously not be an efficient use of the client's dollars, since 90 percent of the people it would reach could not afford the trip. So, using Scarborough, I looked at cable programming — including specific shows as well as networks — and put together a six-week, very-high-frequency, fixed-position cable campaign.

Advertiser Quiz

What can cable do for the advertiser? In *Cable: An Advertiser's Guide*, Ronald Kaatz suggests a quiz that helps a prospect evaluate an existing media program.[27] The first section requires a true-or-false response to each statement:

ADVERTISER QUIZ

I am basically satisfied with my advertising and with my media plan.

It appears to showcase my product (or service) well.

Research shows that it is conveying to my customers pretty much what I want to tell them.

It seems to be efficient.

I believe that it is doing an effective job.

Introducing The Wedding Boutique !

Bakeries	Photographers	Florists
Fashions	Limousines	Music
Honeymoons	Videographers	Rentals
Caterers	Wedding Shows	Jewelers

The Wedding Boutique show gives Santa Rosa viewers the latest and greatest local information about planning your wedding day. What better way to tune in to what is going on in the wedding world!

Benefits to Santa Rosa 6 Advertisers

Full-Color High Quality TV Advertising
Eye catching, informative and effective.

Qualified Customers
Viewers watching your advertisement
want to buy what you are selling.

Affordable TV Advertising
No costly production involved.

Great Flexibility
In most cases we can insert a new ad within 48 hours.

Response Oriented
Television is proven in generating response from viewers.

Buyers See What You're Selling
Full-**Color** pictures are the best way to show prospective buyers what you're selling.

CABLE ONE

3242 Airway Drive △   Santa Rosa △   95403
707-541-3585

FIGURE 7–15 This is the second graphic about weddings in this chapter! (If you've ever dealt with one, you know they're big business.) The Santa Rosa 6 *Wedding Boutique* uses photo ads to demonstrate services needed for the big event. ©1997 Cable One., Inc. All rights reserved. Reprinted with permission.

This part requires some soul-searching by the advertiser:

I only wish that _____.

The result of that question is the basis for developing a campaign. Kaatz says the answer can take a variety of forms:

I only wish the media conveyed my messages in a more compatible environment and acted as more than just a commercial "carrier."

I wish I could afford to sponsor something where I could get some real identity.

I wish I had more time to tell my story. Thirty seconds is not enough, but that's all my television budget can afford.

I wish I could have the advantages of television, but with the ability to say everything I now say in my print ad.

I wish I could advertise somewhere that appealed more to the people that buy my product.

I wish I could afford the high frequency of exposure I need but can now get only in radio.

I wish I could zero-in more closely on some of the small towns where my dealers are located.

I wish I could run a dozen or more different commercials, but I can't afford to spend all the money it takes to produce them for broadcast television.

I wish I could experiment a bit and explore some new commercial ideas—maybe even try some direct response options.

Examined in the context of all media, cable offers a variety of highly specialized programming options that allow advertisers to zero-in on highly targeted audiences that would be difficult to reach otherwise.

As Kaatz describes it: "Cable offers: the visualization of television, the targeted formats and specialization of magazines, the low unit costs and frequency of radio, and the local interests and appeals of newspapers."

Stringing Cable

As I said earlier, local cable's heritage is mechanical and technical. Advertising sales is a recent addition to the cable cul-ture. As a seller of advertising on an MSO, local system, or interconnect, you will find yourself talking about the technical upgrades both in your system and in cable nationally. It's part of the benefit package that cable brings to the community.

NCTA represents hardware vendors and technical suppliers. Just as CAB measures cable's advertising revenue each year, NCTA measures the outlay for equipment and system upgrades. Here's an overview from NCTA's 1997 Year-End Review:[28]

Cable companies invested heavily in infrastructure improvements—$5.38 billion this year alone—bringing our customers higher-quality pictures and sound, more programming, and two-way capable systems.

Operators upgraded facilities to 550 MHz-750 MHz, creating more bandwidth for the delivery of more channels and two-way interactive services.

Industry analysts estimate that equipment in 20% of all cable homes allows for the deployment of interactive online services and telephony. Cable companies accelerated their deployment of fiber optics in 1997 by 27% over 1996.

Cable greatly expanded its digital capability by deploying digital cable technologies—digital headends and set-top boxes—which allow for as many as 12 high-quality digital channels to be compressed into the space of one analog channel.

Channel capacity increased resulting in the average customer receiving an average of 78 channels, an increase of 14.7% over 1996.

Cable companies expanded commercial cable modem services into 67 markets in 29 states. Nearly 75,000 cable customers subscribe to this brand-new way of accessing the Internet and online services at speeds 50 to 100 times faster than telephone-based modem technologies.

Cable operators continue to create new online services that take advantage of cable's high speed and bandwidth: @Home, Road Runner, Optimum Online, MediaOne Express, PowerLink, and Charter Pipeline.

The ultimate combination of cable and Internet was prefaced by the 1998 announcement that AT&T and cable MSO TCI would merge. *Broadcasting & Cable* announced the merger under the headline, "Convergence II."

Review Highlights and Discussion Points

1. Community Antenna Television (CATV) was born in 1948; by the early 1960s some 50,000 homes were served by 800 of these systems.

2. Initially, all that cable brought to its subscribers was standard over-the-air broadcasts that could not reach their TV receivers because of distance and terrain problems.

3. In 1975 RCA launched the SATCOM I satellite, and Home Box Office (HBO) announced plans for a national pay cable network delivered by satellite.

4. Cable's breakthrough year was 1997. By that time the medium had become so pervasive that it challenged network television and won.

5. Although the traditional TV networks lost share, no one questioned their ability to deliver mass audiences and to attract huge dollars.

6. Branding came naturally to the national cable networks. The early entries needed to differentiate themselves from the other fare on the system, especially from the traditional networks. They chose clear positions and 24-hour formats much like radio station formats.

7. Cable networks were the first national media properties that needed specific positioning and branding in order to differentiate themselves.

8. Segmentation makes branding easier when various forms of media resonate with the viewers' personal beliefs and help them chart their position in the larger world.

9. Cable itself is part of the American lifestyle today, with audience penetration at about 70%. The numbers are good news for cable sellers, and the continued erosion of broadcast network audiences makes the news even better.

10. The bad news for cable systems is that in 1998 there were 40 advertiser-supported national cable networks, all of which are competing for the same dollars.

11. Like selling the broadcast networks, selling national cable networks requires dealing with sophisticated buyers at the highest levels of the advertising business.

12. Cable subscribers are early adopters, more likely to acquire new communications and entertainment technologies as they become available.

13. Americans spend nearly $30 billion subscribing to cable services, according to the National Cable Television Association (NCTA).

14. Local cable systems are affected by churn, or turnover, in subscribers. In other words, old subscribers drop out of the system, and new ones are added on a regular basis.

15. Like the broadcast networks, cable joins the annual "ritual dance" of early selling: the upfront. In 1997, cable attracted $2.3 billion, which was up dramatically from the year before.

16. According to the Cabletelevision Advertising Bureau (CAB), most cable networks and agencies have established electronic connections for contracts, master orders, and invoices.

17. The national cable network has two separate and distinct selling targets—the advertiser and the viewers—and that means selling to local cable systems.

18. Federal Communications Commission (FCC) figures confirm cable rate increases, from an average basic service rate of $23.50 in 1994 to $28.83 in 1997. The FCC watches the issues and tracks the numbers but yields final control to local governments with jurisdiction.

19. The NCTA warned members that by the end of 1998, ten million consumers would be served by noncable, multichannel providers.

20. Cable made so much money for so many years simply by connecting subscribers to the systems that advertising revenues were insignificant by comparison. As advertising revenues increased in the 1990s, many MSOs

became aggressive in developing advertising as a key revenue source.

21. Interconnects deliver commercials from a central point either to individual cable systems or to all the systems in the combination by using satellite technology or fiber-optic lines.

22. Cable is making a transition from analog to digital programming and distribution systems, which are crucial to the cable industry plans to increase customer satisfaction and meet the competition posed by Direct Broadcast Satellite (DBS), wireless cable, broadcasters, and telephone companies.

23. Cable was traditionally considered a frequency medium because of lower costs. With the growth of national cable audiences, local cable got the benefit, and the medium proved to be capable of reach as well as frequency.

24. Affiliates of the national cable networks generated $3.5 million in extra revenue in 1997 through merchandising programs.

25. In the largest markets, cable sellers call on the same advertising agencies as broadcasters. Most MSOs and interconnects in the top 50 markets subscribe to Nielsen. Many also use Cablescan and other available ratings analysis services.

Chapter Notes

[1] My memory of the antenna on the mountaintop was clarified by *Electronic Media Management*, cited previously, and by Ronald B. Kaatz's *Cable: An Advertiser's Guide to the New Electronic Media*. Chicago: Crain Books, 1982.

[2] The early cable "smorgasbord" was described by Sydney W. Head in *Broadcast Programming*, which he co-authored with Susan Tyler Eastman and Lewis Klein. Belmont, CA: Wadsworth, 1981.

[3] The headline "Prime Time for Cable" was inspired by the title "Is It Prime Time for Cable?" in *Business Week*, cited previously.

[4] Kay Koplovitz's announcement appeared in *Cable World*, cited in Chapter 1. Additional information on cable's win in the summer of 1997 and in the summer of 1998 came from the Cabletelevision Advertising Bureau (CAB).

[5] The *Fast Company* article, "Nick Tunes In to Kids," captured the spirit of Nickelodeon with pictures of their offbeat offices. February/March 1998.

[6] David McFarland's MTV comparison is in *Future Radio Programming Strategies: Cultivating Listenership in the Digital Age*, 2nd ed. Mahwah, NJ: Lawrence Erlbaum Associates, 1997.

[7] The special report from CAB appeared in *Advertising Age* and *Electronic Media* on September 22, 1997.

[8] The statistics about cable are from *Cable Facts 1997*, published by CAB.

[9] In "New Cable Networks," January 26, 1998, *Broadcasting & Cable* announced a remarkable number of new entries into the national cable fray. They were listed alphabetically from Air & Space Network to ZDTV.

[10] Thanks again to E!'s Lee Masters for sharing insights in an interview, cited in Chapter 1.

[11] The subscription dollars paid for cable came with membership application materials from NCTA.

[12] For the benefits of cable, start with the benefits of all television. For the case against cable, I looked at materials used by sellers of other media, especially over-the-air television and radio.

[13] The data for cable's upfront came from *Advertising Age*, February 3, June 16, June 23, and July 7, 1997.

[14] *The Wall Street Journal* article about electronic data interchange (EDI) was "Buying Cable-TV Ads Gets Easier Thanks to New Computer System," March 12, 1998. EDI was explained in some detail in a supplement to *Adver-*

tising Age, February 17, 1997, sponsored by CAB.

15 *USA Today* was not kind to cable in "Cable's Cash Cow," by David Lieberman, March 16, 1998. CTAM, the cable marketing society, and NCTA joined in a cooperative image advertising campaign several years before that article. The "On-time Guarantee" campaign was reported in *Advertising Age*, December 9, 1996.

16 FCC figures were provided by NCTA.

17 Ronald Kaatz's book was cited previously.

18 The same *Wall Street Journal* cited above for the story about EDI contained the references to the New York Interconnect. Additional quotations about interconnects are from "Cable Advertising Annual Report, 1997," CAB.

19 "Digital Update" is from "Cable Television Industry Year-End Review: 1997," ©1997, NCTA.

20 More from CAB's "Cable Advertising Annual Report, 1997."

21 Turner's "Media at the Millennium" presentation was reported by Donna Petrozello: "Does Cable Reach Exceed Sales' Grasp?" in *Broadcasting & Cable*, March 23, 1998. The spat between Turn-er and CBS was reported in *Advertising Age*, April 6, 1998.

22 I saw the slide with Cheryl Vannucchi's picture while channel surfing at a hotel in Santa Rosa, California. I interviewed Cheryl about her selling techniques on January 6, 1998.

23 PCNC and CLTV information came from their presentation kits. "News 12, The Bronx," is from *Broadcasting & Cable*, April 20, 1998.

24 Details of cable promotions and audience measurement are in CAB's "Cable Advertising Annual Report, 1997."

25 A "New Media" page on Arbitron's Web site *www.arbitron.com* has information on RetailDirect Lite. Link to Scarborough through Arbitron, too.

26 Bob Keeton's story about his travel client appeared in *Arbitron Advertising News*, 1997, Issue No. 6.

27 The advertiser quiz developed by Ronald Kaatz for cable can be applied to any medium. Ron's book was cited previously.

28 More from "Cable Television Industry Year-End Review: 1997" from NCTA. Thanks again, NCTA, for the support with this book. Since I am writing this book in 1998: Happy birthday, cable!

Taking It Further

Here are a few Web sites that relate to this chapter and additional reading not included in the Chapter Notes.

www.cabletvadbureau.com—Cable Advertising Bureau

www.ctam.com—Marketing society for the cable and telecommunications industries

www.ncta.com—National Cable Television Association

www.prevue.com—Previews of new fare from all networks

Additional Reading

Dominick, Joseph R., et al. *Broadcasting, Cable, and Beyond: An Introduction to Modern Electronic Media*. New York: McGraw-Hill, 1993.

Heighton, Elizabeth J. *Advertising in the Broadcast and Cable Media*. Belmont, CA: Wadsworth, 1984.

Parsons, Patrick, and Robert M. Freida. *The Cable and Satellite Television Industries*. Needham Heights, MA: Allyn & Bacon, 1998.

8

Selling Radio Advertising

In the fall of 1962, there was a big parade in Griffin, Georgia, then a town of about 15,000 people located about 40 miles south of Atlanta. I don't remember the occasion, but there must have been a football game that weekend. High school bands, clowns, and city dignitaries filed from Highway 75 around the town's main street, where the pool hall, the variety store, and the radio station were located.

It's the radio station that counts in this story. WRIX wanted to serve the citizens of Griffin who couldn't make it to the big parade, so we snaked a long mike cable to the front of the building, giving us a second-floor vantage point. The station's sales manager sat in the window, watched the activity, and described the scene to the listening audience.

At the back of the building, with a view of only the alley between our building and the town's movie theater, I ran the control board, inserted the commercials (for the variety store), and experienced the parade—by radio.

My wife, Pam, had a similar experience at baseball's spring training in 1998. I was working with the Astros radio network as a talent coach for members of the broadcast team. Pam joined us for a few innings in the broadcast booth. She quickly discovered that, unless you're calling the play-by-play and seated right at the window of the booth, you can't see the field or the players from the booth. She had to rely on the commentary by Astros announcers Bill Brown and Alan Ashby.

"Sorry you can't see more," said Bill. "That's OK," Pam replied. "This is the way I hear the games on the radio. I'm able to tell what's going on."

That fall day in Griffin when I was 16 and the spring day 30-something years later are terrific examples of radio at its best: descriptive commentary that's a real service to listeners stuck in back rooms, unable to watch the clowns or the cheerleaders or the home run.

Theater of the Mind

Call it "theater of the mind;" it's radio's unique contribution to mass media. Television and cable services show the pictures, while various forms of interactive media mix and match sounds, pictures, text, and animation. But only radio leaves it to the listener to create the image conjured by the words.

Before television, the "pictures" that entertained America were on the radio. A man named Raymond opened a squeaking door on the drama *Inner Sanctum*, and the stories told behind the door made spines tingle for a half hour. The main character of *The Shadow* was a mental projection against a foggy night full of smoke from coal-burning furnaces. Those pictures were drawn with words and sound effects in the radio of the 1930s to the 1950s.[1]

"Radio is pure sound," says Jack Trout, the man who gave the marketing world the positioning concept. "To do good radio you have to understand how to use sound and sound effects. Unfortunately, most creative types are picture-oriented, not sound-oriented."[2]

"Radio is an ideal sales vehicle to stretch the imagination as well as the mind," says Bill Burton, president of the Detroit Radio Advertising Group. He continues:

> What better medium to sell the great aromas of perfume, shaving lotion, a warm vegetable soup for lunch or the smell of turkey and ham cooking? There's no way you could convert these wonderful aromas to picture or film—but the visualization in the mind can be overwhelming. All great radio takes place in your mind. The characters and situations you identify with, the taste, smells, emotion, all come to life through the power of your imagination.

Advertising legend David Ogilvy called radio "the Cinderella of advertising media," because it often was left behind by major agencies.[3] In 1983, when he published *Ogilvy on Advertising*, radio represented only 6% of total advertising in the United States. Radio's share of the advertising pie has grown only slightly since Ogilvy's remark, capturing 7.1% of advertising dollars in 1997.

"Have the big agencies discovered that radio is a lousy way to advertise?" asked John Emmerling of New York's John Emmerling, Inc., in *Advertising Age*. Emmerling answered his own question: No. "[T]he large shops are scared stiff of radio." He explained:

Consider the account executive who has the temerity to suggest a radio campaign and must face the wrath of the creative director (probably reached at poolside in Beverly Hills where he is attending yet another TV shoot).

"Radio?" the CD sputters, "my top people are all too busy creating world-famous TV spots." After this initial outburst he might deign to assign a junior producer to adapt the national TV jingle to a 60-second length. "If you need some announcer copy," he allows, "one of the copy typists can whip something out."

The rewards of selling radio in the age of television's 10-, 15-, and 30-second "spotlets" (Emmerling's word) include the fact that radio still offers "an affordable 60 seconds. And in that long, luxurious time span," he wrote, "you can *involve* a listener. For when consumers perk up and actively imagine the radio spot's situation, an enduring 'mind picture' is created—and your product's name and position can be indelibly stamped on a receptive mind."

Emmerling also cited radio's audience segmentation, low production costs, and speed of production as key benefits to the medium. "They add up to flexibility that lets you take quick advantage of momentary changes in a marketing situation."[4] (See Figure 8–1.)

The Benefits of Radio as an Advertising Medium

Radio's two major selling points are:

- *Flexibility*. If an advertiser has a change of price, a new location, or a special shipment, radio is ready to create an announcement at a moment's notice to help the advertiser who missed the newspaper's deadline or who cannot afford to produce new video for commercials on television or cable.
- *Mind Pictures*. The "theater of the mind" is a concept that we discussed earlier in this chapter. Only radio leaves it to the hearer to create the image conjured by the words.

ACCOUNT EXECUTIVES
Sell for the #1 Station in Dallas-Fort Worth

106.1 KISS-FM, KHKS, the #1 station in 11 different demos, has immediate openings for experienced Account Executives. If you have a minimum of three years of radio sales experience and a proven track record of top billing status at your current station, WE WANT TO TALK TO YOU!!

You must demonstrate creativity, the ability to sell high rates, experience with non-traditional revenue and a thorough understanding of Promotions and Marketing.

Join a team of winners making top dollar in an aggressive and fun working environment.

Call Shawn Nunn, Local Sales Manager at 214-891-3484 for an appointment. Chancellor Media is an equal opportunity employer.

FIGURE 8–1 Creativity, high rates, winners. This ad sounds like the description of sellers in Chapter 2, doesn't it? It looks uniquely like an ad for a radio salesperson with the emphasis on promotions. Courtesy Chancellor Media's KHKS. Used with permission.

"Radio's unique attribute is intimacy with the customer," says Gary Fries, president of the Radio Advertising Bureau (RAB). "We're an extra member of everybody's family. Our job is to market the relationship between radio and the listener through events, through concern about the safety of children, through involvement in listener lifestyles."

- Virtually everybody in America listens to radio at some point during the average week. That fact leads the RAB to outline these benefits of radio as a medium.
- Radio reaches 76.5% of all consumers every day and 95.1% every week.
- Radio reaches 57% of customers within an hour of making their purchase decision.
- Radio reaches newspaper readers and television viewers.
- The average person spends 3 hours and 18 minutes listening to the radio on an average weekday. On the weekend that increases to 5 hours and 45 minutes.
- Radio reaches 95.9% of Hispanics and 95.9% of African Americans weekly.
- Radio reaches 82.3% of adults in their cars in the typical week.

RAB also touts the percentages of people who typically listen to the radio while they're working, running errands, or relaxing, including grocery shoppers, automobile buyers, financial customers, computer users, wine drinkers, restaurant customers, and a long list of other positive associations. (See Figure 8–2.)

In addition to the RAB's list of radio's benefits, there are other attributes that make radio attractive to advertisers:

- There's a wide array of formats to reach listeners during a receptive state of mind, which can complement a specific advertising message.
- Radio allows delivery of its messages to multiple household members simultaneously and can deliver them 24 hours a day.

CONSUMER PROFILE
Heavy Radio Listeners
AVERAGE WEEKDAY/TOP TWO QUINTILES

Gender

| **51** % Male | **49** % Female |

Income (Adults 18+)

Over $50,000	35%
$25,000-$50,000	42%
Under $25,000	23%

Occupation (Adults 18+)

Professional/Managerial	20%
Technical, Sales, and Administrative Support	21%
Service	9%
Precision Production and Craft & Farming, Forestry and Fishing	13%
Operators, Fabricators and Laborers	6%

Education

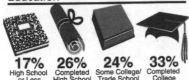

| **17%** High School or Less | **26%** Completed High School | **24%** Some College/ Trade School | **33%** Completed College or More |

Sociographic Shoppers Profile

Brand Loyal	33%
Cautious	39%
Venturesome	28%

| Own Home | **74%** |

| Households with Children | **36%** |

| Average Weekday Non-Newspaper Readers | **35%** |

Demographic Breakout

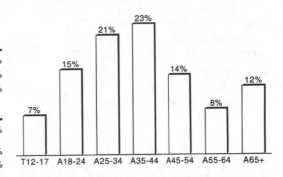

T12-17 (7%) A18-24 (15%) A25-34 (21%) A35-44 (23%) A45-54 (14%) A55-64 (8%) A65+ (12%)

Lifestyle Profile by PRIZM® Groups

GROUP	DESCRIPTION	
S2	The Affluentials	12.4%
R3	Rustic Living	10.1%
C2	2nd City Centers	9.1%
S3	Inner Suburbs	8.5%
T2	Exurban Blues	7.8%
T3	Working Towns	7.2%
S1	Elite Suburbs	7.1%
U3	Urban Cores	6.7%
T1	Landed Gentry	6.3%
U2	Urban Midscale	5.1%
C3	2nd City Blues	4.8%
R1	Country Families	4.7%
U1	Urban Uptown	4.6%
R2	Heartlanders	3.0%
C1	2nd City Society	2.6%

Heavy Radio Listeners
Consumer Profile

*Media Targeting 2000 — conducted by
The Arbitron Company in cooperation with
the Radio Advertising Bureau*

12-A

FIGURE 8–2 I hope these profiles are as helpful to you as they are to me when I try to visualize just who uses either a medium or a product. The one thing to be said about a profile of radio users: it includes everybody! This profile is from *Media Targeting 2000*, a study conducted by the Arbitron Company in cooperation with the RAB. Used with permission from each organization.

- Radio is advertiser-driven, that is, it's intrusive. Listeners have to make a conscious effort *not* to hear a radio commercial.
- Radio advertising can be purchased nationally, regionally, or locally.
- Radio produces high-frequency levels, which enhance effective reach.
- It's one of the most cost-efficient of the major media forms. Radio offers a proportionately low cost per commercial announcement as well as the lowest production cost of any medium.
- A radio commercial conjures the visual elements of a television commercial using imagery transfer; that is, reminding listeners of an image they've seen on television.
- The radio commercial can produce images not physically executable in other media forms by using the listener's imagination.

On the other hand, there are also some negatives about advertising on the radio:

- Radio is often considered a "background" medium because the listener can do something else at the same time.
- Radio requires high levels of frequency in a schedule.
- The listener is not always able to take immediate physical action, such as calling an 800 number, depending on the listening location.
- There are high costs to purchase time on multiple stations in order to accumulate high levels of reach.
- Radio offers none of the visual or motion elements found in television.[5]

Advertisers React

"I've always thought radio is a terrific medium," says Bob Rose, vice president and media director for the Hal Riney & Partners New York office. "On paper, it's a dream come true for a media planner. It's efficient and it cumes a very broad reach over time, yet it has the ability to deliver more focused audiences as well."

Rose was one of many ad agency executives interviewed by *Radio Ink* over a period of years. He told the magazine that his agency used radio for a variety of reasons: "We've used it to supplement television network under-delivery; we've used it as a stand-alone to deliver a campaign where other clients didn't have money to be in television; and we've used it to hit specialized audiences as well."

When Alec Gerster took over Grey Advertising's media department in the early 1980s, it was the largest in New York. Later, as Grey's executive vice president and director of media and programming services, he told *Radio Ink* that he found it "ironic" that "every account guy, media person, client, and creative team uses or listens to [radio] in some way, yet it's not, by any means, one of the high top-of-mind media options."

As late as the early 1990s, radio was still a difficult buy for a national advertiser. In 1993, Sean Fitzpatrick was vice-chairman and area manager for McCann-Erickson in Detroit. In another *Radio Ink* interview, he said, "The fact is that radio does a great job on the local level. Programming is extremely good, and the effectiveness of radio as a buy is very good. What's totally stupid—and without measure in the media industry—is radio's inability to sit down and create for itself a national sales platform. Radio makes it too difficult for the big-time advertiser to buy radio. On the other hand, you make it an easy local buy by cutting any kind of deal."[6]

But just as he was saying those words in 1993, radio was changing. Gary Fries had assumed presidency of RAB and was creating the "national platform" that Fitzpatrick suggested. Trying to recover from a deep national recession, local radio stations were creating partnerships, local marketing agreements (LMAs), which linked the selling efforts of several stations. The stage was being set for the changes that reshaped the industry after the Telecommunications Act of 1996 (referred to later in this chapter as Telecom 96).

Let the Deals Begin!

"Let the Deals Begin!" was the headline in *Radio & Records* in its first issue after Congress passed the new legislation that shifted media paradigms. "It's buy, sell, or get out of the way," *Radio & Records* said, as it reported on the first of what would be many consolidation moves after Telecom 96: Jacor Communications' purchase of CitiCasters, Inc., and SFX Broadcasting's acquisition of Prism Radio Partners. A harbinger of those purchases was the announcement that Group W and CBS would merge and create the largest group of radio stations in the country ("at least as of this week," *Radio and Records* said).[7]

The 1996 changes meant that one company could own as many as eight radio stations in a single major market—more than could be controlled nationally under the old seven-station limit, which had lasted for decades. In the 1980s, the FCC expanded those limits to 12, then 18, then 20 stations. The new law set no upper limit to the number of radio stations one company could own.

Radio & Records' joke about the biggest company "as of this week" became a reality quickly. Within 2 years of Telecom 96, CBS was eclipsed by Chancellor Media, which would control almost 500 stations. Jacor agreed to a merger with Clear Channel Communications, giving Clear Channel ownership of more than 450 stations.[8]

Here is a list of what any one company could own:

In a market with:	A single entity can control up to this many stations:
45 or more stations	Up to 8, no more than 5 in the same service (AM or FM)
30 to 44 stations	Up to 7, no more than 4 in the same service
15 to 29 stations	Up to 6, no more than 4 in the same service
14 or fewer stations	Up to 5, no more than 3 in the same service

In no case could a single owner control more than half of the stations in any market, regardless of size. The Antitrust Division of the U.S. Department of Justice decided that no single market radio ownership combination could exceed half of that market's radio advertising revenue.

Writing in the *Journal of Radio Studies*, Christopher Sterling reminded us of a 1949 doctoral dissertation at Harvard University:

> Nearly half a century ago, a young economist theorized that a single owner with five stations would provide more program diversity in a given market than would five separate owners. The owner of several stations would achieve a larger audience by providing five different formats appealing to five different audiences. The separate owners would duplicate the most popular formats in an effort to share the largest portion of the audience. Thanks to the 1996 amendments, we are already testing the theory under real market conditions.[9]

Radio found itself more viable than ever as an advertising medium after deregulation. Marketing consultant Jack Trout proclaimed, "The industry finally grows up" and offered congratulations to radio for "fast outgrowing its fragmented, almost cottage-industry status." Trout addressed his advice to radio in a management article in *Radio Ink*:

> **1.** *Sell the medium, not your stations.*
> As a highly fragmented medium, just about all your energy and money was spent on beating up your direct competitors. Now that there's some critical mass in many markets, perhaps we'll begin to see some "my-medium-is-better-than-their-medium" efforts.
> **2.** *Make the medium easier to buy.*
> Buying television or newspapers is a snap compared to buying radio. Putting together a major buy usually entails having to deal with a parade of salespeople that spend a lot of time bad-mouthing other stations on the list.

RADIO'S NEW ENVIRONMENT

How many stations can one radio operator own? As many as the company can acquire and operate, as long as the market by market rules are followed. That fact led to ownership numbers that were astonishing to anyone who remembered the previous limits. Chancellor Media's proposed merger with Capstar Communications would mean 488 stations owned by one company, including stations in all of the top ten markets and in 17 of the top 20.

Here are the top ten radio owners, ranked by revenues, from *Broadcasting & Cable*, October 12, 1998:

	Number Owned	Estimated 1998 Revenues
Chancellor Media	488	$1,765,421,000
CBS, Inc.	164	1,687,457,000
Clear Channel Communications	453	1,240,644,000
ABC, Inc.	35	339,822,000
Cox Broadcasting	59	279,279,000
Entercom	41	193,564,000
Heftel Broadcasting	39	184,748,000
Emmis Communications	16	171,538,000
Cumulus Media	207	167,209,000
Susquehanna Radio	22	152,475,000

Owning stations in the largest markets is the key to large revenue figures. Cumulus Media has a large station component, but since all but two of the company's markets are ranked below 100, their revenues are less than a tenth of Chancellor's. Emmis Communications, on the other hand, owns stations in New York, Los Angeles, and Chicago, giving their much smaller group considerable revenue clout.

---

3. *Educate the users.*
Radio is pure sound. To do good radio you have to understand how to use sound and sound effects. Unfortunately, most creative types are picture-oriented, not sound-oriented. Many are happy just to run the soundtracks from their TV commercials.

Paradigm Shift

I've tried so hard not to use the word "paradigm" in this book, but I can't hold back, especially when describing the new landscape of radio. The industry experienced a seismic paradigm shift after Telecom 96.

David Pearlman called radio's new paradigm a "format change." Pearlman, co-chief operating officer of American Radio Systems, leads a company that "changed formats." It developed as one of the fastest-growing radio companies and then sold to CBS.

Rapid consolidation and mergers of radio companies was so difficult to track that the newsletter *Inside Radio* began publishing a weekly edition called "Who Owns What" to rank station ownership groups, their estimated revenues, numbers of stations owned, and estimated national audiences. The weekly scorecard ran 20 to 25 pages some weeks, listing individual stations figured in the station group totals based on that previous week's buying, selling, and swapping. The top 50 markets were outlined with percentages of revenue controlled by each group with a cluster in that market. (See Figure 8–3.)

The pace of change was so rapid that when Sean Ross, editor of *Billboard*, was asked to appear at a regional radio conference and deliver the same speech he had presented just a few weeks before, Ross accepted the invitation but declined to use the same address. "None of it would be true," he said. "That's how fast things are changing."[10]

Who Owns What.

The Weekly Scorecard of Radio Consolidation
June 15, 1998

Forever Broadcasting moves up to No. 45 in revenue. From No. 49. Moves up to No. 11 from No. 24 in top groups by stations. Numbers for Forever updated.

Sunburst Media up to No. 43 in revenue. Bought one station — KAGG-FM — in Madisonville, TX from OARA Inc. For $3 million in cash. Sunburst moves from No. 44. Also up to No. 39 in number of stations.

Mortenson Broadcasting enters top groups by stations at No. 39. Bought two stations: WHBN-AM/FM simulcast in Harrodsburg, KY. Bought for $1.2 million cash from Channel Chek Inc. Channel Chek still owns two radio stations. Mortenson owns 18 stations now.

Jacor and Capstar swap AMs to satisfy DOJ. Jacor gets WTAE-AM, Pittsburgh. Capstar gets WKNR-AM. Both stations enter each market with standalone stations. *(Follow the ✓ for all of this week's changes).*

Top Groups by Revenue

This Week	Last Week	Groups	Estimated(000)	This Week	Last Week	Groups	Estimated(000)
1	1	CBS Radio	1,529,380	26	26	Sandusky	38,900
2	2	Chancellor	995,950	27	27	Triathlon	37,280
3	3	Jacor	605,430	28	28	Buckley	36,710
4	4	Capstar	534,050	29	29	Bcast Partners Hldgs	35,575
5	5	Clear Channel	452,400	30	30	Renda	32,730
6	6	ABC Radio	310,350	31	31	Inner City	30,600
7	7	Cox	246,850	32	32	Connoisseur	29,910
8	8	Emmis	156,730	33	33	Barnstable	29,830
9	9	Heftel	155,500	34	34	Lotus	29,290
10	10	Susquehanna	141,400	35	35	Bloomington	25,400
11	11	Entercom	139,900	36	36	Fisher	23,800
12	12	Sinclair	127,300	37	37	Simmons Family	22,710
13	13	Citadel	112,540	38	38	Great Empire	22,230
14	14	Cumulus	110,095	39	39	Midwest TV	22,180
15	15	Bonneville	109,600	40	40	Dame Media	21,590
16	16	Greater Media	103,200	41	41	EXCL	21,480
17	17	Jefferson-Pilot	92,300	42	42	South Central	20,130
18	18	Beasley	79,250	43	49	✓ Forever Broadcasting	19,920
19	19	Spanish Broadcast	75,500	44	44	Sunburst Media	19,810
20	20	Saga	64,690	45	43	✓ Midwestern Bcastg	19,000
21	21	Radio One	56,800	46	45	✓ M.L. Media	18,950
22	22	Tribune	54,550	47	46	✓ Buck Owens	18,650
23	23	Hearst	40,900	48	47	✓ Midwest Comm	18,080
24	24	Journal	40,600	49	48	✓ Ackerley Group	18,000
25	25	Dick	40,200	50	50	Mid-West Family	17,575

To subscribe to *Who Owns What* call 609-424-6800

FIGURE 8–3 You can't tell the players without a scorecard. Radio's daily newsletter *Inside Radio* introduced this weekly edition to document the rapid changes in the industry with mergers and station consolidation. ©1998 *Inside Radio*. Used with permission.

By the end of 1998, 71.4% of commercial radio stations were in some sort of consolidated clustering. The figures were over 75% in the largest (top 50) markets.[11] This activity was revolutionary in a business where, as recently as 1992, no one was allowed to own more than two stations in any market.

The business outcome of deregulation was very positive for radio:

- Advertising revenues topped $13 billion in 1997, giving radio 7.1% of total advertising dollars.
- Marginal signals were saved by combining sales with other stations to yield efficiencies.
- Companies gained additional inventory to sell by combining stations.

- The value of the inventory was increased with more sophisticated selling.
- Asset values and stockholder values of radio companies grew at exponential rates.

In fact, if you apply the measures that Tom Peters used in his 1982 book, *In Search of Excellence*, to radio companies after Telecom 96, most would show favorably. You'll recall that Peters measured (1) compound asset growth, (2) compound equity growth, (3) average ratio of market value to book value, (4) average return on total capital, (5) average return on equity, and (6) average return on sales.[12]

The Radio Network Environment

Radio networks underwent the same revolutionary changes that local station operations experienced, thanks to a consolidating industry. Here comes that phrase "paradigm shift" again.

Paradigm Shift, Version One: Combine Forces

The first to merge were Westwood One Networks and CBS Radio Networks. Westwood already had a stable of brands to sell. It had its own long-form music networks with 24-hour country, rock, adult contemporary, and talk programming. Also in its stable were NBC Radio Network, CNN Radio, CNBC Business Radio, and Mutual News. The company added Fox News late in 1998 and announced the development of the Fox Radio Network.

By combining resources with CBS Radio, Westwood sold advertising for all the radio brands but ABC. The merger with CBS made Westwood the largest radio network. Mel Karmazin, CEO for both CBS and Westwood, used that fact to their advantage. "All we do is radio," he told *Manager's Business Report*. "We think that having a company that is a dedicated radio company has al-

ways been good for every industry. For [ABC owner] Disney, radio isn't their first priority."

Karmazin entered the network business in 1993 when his Infinity Broadcasting bought Unistar Networks. Unistar, producer of 24-hour music formats, later merged with Westwood One, producer of weekend programs and specials. At the time Karmazin told *Broadcasting & Cable*, "I'm a little surprised it took us so long to get into the network business. It's definitely a business we're going to stay in and expand in." When Karmazin merged Infinity with Westinghouse and CBS in 1996, his words rang truer than ever.[13]

Paradigm Shift, Version Two: Create a New Network

The launch of the AMFM Networks, created by Chancellor Media at the beginning of 1998, was one of the largest new network debuts ever. (See Figure 8–4). It was made possible by designating inventory at the stations owned by Chancellor and its merger with Evergreen Media. Other stations owned by Capstar Partners also pledged inventory.[14]

The available commercial time was the linchpin. No other radio network delivered the top 10 markets the way AMFM could with their owned stations in those markets.

"Another benefit is the number of stations that we bring to the network radio pie that previously were unaffiliated with any other network," AMFM senior vice president David Kantor, told *Hitmakers*. "In the past, network radio reached only about 65 percent of the United States Now, with us coming in, we anticipate that number will be in the mid-80s. It makes it a more viable national medium and hopefully will help us to bring in more dollars to network radio."

In addition to spot inventories at key stations, AMFM signed Kasey Casem for a reincarnation of his *American Top 40* radio show, which meant a defection by Casem from Westwood One. To staff the new AMFM Networks, Kantor hired personnel who had worked with him at ABC Radio when he was president of that network. AMFM launched with clout.

Paradigm Shift, Version Three: Own the Programming

Premiere had been in the network business for ten years before its merger with Jacor Communications in 1997. Premiere's base was unlike most networks, however: it provided radio production services, Web site development, and Mediabase music monitoring services. The fact that Premiere provided those services in exchange for inventory at affiliated stations made their model resemble the traditional network model.

Premiere's first long-form program was *After MidNite*, an all-night program for country stations, originating in Los Angeles. That program did not join the Premiere fold until January 1997. With the Jacor merger, Premiere created a programming powerhouse by combining Premiere products with the syndicators of Rush Limbaugh, Dr. Laura Schlessinger, Art Bell, Jim Rome, Michael Reagan, and Dr. Dean Edell—the biggest names in talk radio. (See Figure 8–5.)

While Premiere sold network inventory, the big money for those shows came from licensing fees paid by affiliates. Premiere walked a fine line between being a syndicator and being a network.[15]

The Old Paradigm: ABC

"Old" is not bad. In referring to ABC, "old" means that ABC's network configuration is more traditional than the others.

ABC's *Paul Harvey News and Comment* was radio's number-one rated program year after year. ABC had ten of the top ten programs and 19 of the top 20 in the fall 1997 RADAR (Radio's All Dimension Audience Research, conducted by Statistical Research, Inc.). ABC offered top-of-the-hour news networks, 24-hour music formats, ESPN Sports, and specialty programs. They did some minor paradigm shifting of their own when they introduced *The Tom Joyner Show*, a live wake-up show aimed at African-American audiences.[16]

The Unchanging Paradigm: Selling Network Commercials

Radio network buying is generally done by the same high-level agency negotiators who buy network television. Just like TV sales, selling for a radio network requires patience and good negotiating skills. Oral skills are essential, since the seller of network radio time often makes sales presentations to groups of high-level advertising agency executives and their clients.

Warner and Buchman make this suggestion in *Broadcast and Cable Selling*:

> Buying time on a radio network is a good way to introduce national advertisers to broadcast advertising, especially if they cannot afford network television. Agencies often encourage this type of developmental selling because the addition of network radio to an advertising plan often involves an increase in an overall advertising budget, on which the agency makes more money.

The real difference between selling radio network time and selling TV network time is the agency's willingness to hear ideas about how to enhance a schedule at radio with value-added promotion. This difference can be a real selling point for radio.

New Reach
With The Top Stations

AMFM Radio Networks delivers many of the top FM radio stations in the top 10 markets,
that were previously unaffiliated with *any* network.

Adult Network – Adults 25-54	DMA	Youth Network – Adults 18-34
WLTW-FM #1, WAXQ-FM	New York	WKTU-FM #2, WHTZ-FM, WBIX-FM
KYSR-FM, KBIG-FM	Los Angeles	KKBT-FM #3, KIBB-FM
WLIT-FM #2, WVAZ-FM #3, WNUA-FM #4	Chicago	WGCI-FM #1, WRCX-FM #3
WDAS-FM #2, WJJZ-FM, WYXR-FM	Philadelphia	WUSL-FM #2, WIOQ-FM #4, WAEB-FM
KKSF-FM #2, KISQ-FM #4	San Francisco	KYLD-FM #1, KMEL-FM #2, KIOI-FM
WGIR-FM	Boston	WJMN-FM #1, WXKS-FM #3
WMZQ-FM #2, WBIG-FM #4, WGAY-FM	Washington DC	WASH-FM
KZPS-FM #4	Dallas	KHKS-FM #1, KDGE-FM
WNIC-FM #1, WMXD-FM #4, WWWW-FM	Detroit	WJLB-FM #1, WKQI-FM #4
WFOX-FM	Atlanta	

...along with the rest of the great affiliate stations of Chancellor Media and Capstar Broadcast Partners across America.

A New Network For A New Millennium

Call Now For Advertising Opportunities

Los Angeles	Dallas	Chicago	Detroit	New York
213-852-3002	972-239-6220	312-202-8850	248-614-7064	212-373-8180

A Division of Chancellor Media Corporation

Rankers based on Arbitron, FA, '97, M-S, 6A-Mid, AQH

FIGURE 8-4 The launch of AMFM Radio Networks brought
major stations in the largest markets into the
network radio fold. This ad listed 41 stations,
but the combination of stations owned by
Chancellor Media and Capstar Broadcast
Partners totaled more than 500 outlets.
Courtesy AMFM Networks. Used with
permission.

FIGURE 8–5 Premiere Radio Network touted its all-star lineup of personality talk shows with ads like this in radio trade publications. Used with permission.

Radio time and production cost so little compared to buying TV time and producing TV commercials. As Karmazin of CBS says, "General Motors spends more money buying yellow pads than its does in network radio. That's the opportunity."

Network or Syndication?

There's a fine line between network radio and syndicated radio. Some syndicators sell commercials to advertisers, some sell programming to stations, and some do both. (See Figure 8–7.)

The advent of computer-based wide area networks (WANs) allowed local station groups to create ad hoc networks of their own, sharing morning shows or other air talent. When they do that are they actually a network? Well, it's *networked*, isn't it? The phrases to use are "programming supplier" and "program service," whether the discussion is about ABC, Westwood, or a true syndicator like SupeRadio, which provides weekly specials for contemporary music stations, a live morning show, and a long-form classical format. (See Figure 8–6.)

The United Stations Radio Networks have "networks" in their name, and they sell commercials like a network. At the station level, they're seen as a programming supplier with a catalog of comedy services that morning personalities like to use and a line-up of weekend special programs, including some hosted by Dick Clark, a partner in United Stations. The company tried a series of daily talk shows, but decided to shift the affiliation burden to another company while retaining the rights to sell commercials in the shows.

"Network radio can be a complex medium to buy," says Maureen Whyte, vice president of McCann-Erickson, who looks at both network buys and syndication buys for her national clients. She continues:

> For adult buys (generally 18–49 and older), it is likely that the line networks will take up at least 50 percent of the gross rating points (GRPs) with the balance going to syndication. The older the target demographic group is, the more important the line networks are to the mix, due to sheer ratings strength.
> For youth and young adult targets (12–34), it is likely that syndication will be used to reach the majority of the GRPs, with the balance going to the line networks.[17]

Whyte claims that the complexity of buying syndication comes in establishing exact clearance times. For example, a station might run a program in morning drive, but then clear the attached commercial in another daypart. Or a commercial that runs from 7 p.m. to midnight is classified as a 6 a.m. to midnight clearance.

"In spite of the nuances involved in evaluating syndicated properties, we believe that it is a vital part of the network radio marketplace," Whyte says. That's why networks and syndicators are sometimes difficult to distinguish.

In the September 1998 RADAR, Premiere Radio Networks was measured for the first time with four network configurations, covering a cumulative total of more than 2,200 stations. "Dr. Laura," a Premiere program classified as syndication, was included in the measurement. Advertising agencies cheered because it was the first opportunity for accountability in radio syndication.

Selling Radio to Planners

In Chapter 5 you learned that by the time an agency's advertising schedule gets to the buyer, it's too late to influence anything but cost per point. Sellers who call on agencies are most effective when they work the planners (who can make the decisions) as well as the buyers. Radio salespeople discovered that idea later than their colleagues in newspaper and print. To radio's credit, the lesson was learned, and it benefited the industry overall.

Karen Ritchie raised eyebrows in the radio world in March 1993, when *Radio Ink* magazine quoted her blunt assessment: "Radio is doing a dreadful job, primarily because of the way it's sold. . . . There has

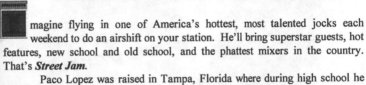

Street Jam

WITH PACO LOPEZ!

Paco Lopez
Latino on the loose

THIS IS NOT A MIX SHOW!
THIS IS NOT A COUNTDOWN!

magine flying in one of America's hottest, most talented jocks each weekend to do an airshift on your station. He'll bring superstar guests, hot features, new school and old school, and the phattest mixers in the country. That's *Street Jam*.

Paco Lopez was raised in Tampa, Florida where during high school he started deejaying parties. His first radio job at WFLA/Tampa led to major market gigs in Miami, Phoenix, Tampa, Houston, Washington, D.C. and New York, where Paco was rated **number one** in afternoon drive. The award winning Paco Lopez is now **number one** in mornings at WJHM-102 JAMZ/Orlando.

HOT FEATURES, SUPERSTAR GUESTS

You get a fresh station promotion every weekend. Your jocks can talk about promoting the biggest artists in the business with interviews from:

112	Keith Sweat
BLACKstreet	LL Cool J
Bone Thugs 'n Harmony	Mary J. Blige
Changing Faces	Montell Jordan
Coolio	Patty LaBelle
Dru Hill	Puff Daddy
En Vogue	R. Kelly
Fugees	Salt 'n Pepa
Faith	SWV
Ginuwine	Total
Heavy D	Will Smith

LET THE PARTY BEGIN

Replace weak part time talent with the charisma and excitement of Paco Lopez every weekend. *Your call letters* are the first words out of Paco's mouth out of every song, making you sound local and live. *Low commercial load.* We take one third less inventory than those boring canned countdown shows. *Phat mixes every week* of the freshest jams and old school. *Increase sales* by packaging *Street Jam* as a premium station event.

YOU DESERVE THE BEST

Street Jam has twice been nominated as *Billboard Syndicated Program of the Year* in '96 and '97! *Street Jam* is delivered live in CD quality on digital satellite. Only one station per market can have *Street Jam*. To lock it up in your market, contact Superadio now at 1.508.480.9000.

FIGURE 8–6 It may not be a mix show or a countdown, but it *is* a syndicated show. *Street Jam* from syndicator SupeRadio, is designed for weekly play on contemporary stations. Courtesy SupeRadio. Used with permission.

FIGURE 8–7 The WOR Radio Network rides that fine line between network and syndicator. The company syndicates the talk shows from New York's WOR and sells advertising like a network. This flyer touts the return of New York talker Bob Grant to WOR and to the WOR Network after his dismissal by WABC. Courtesy WOR Radio Network. Used with permission.

been absolutely no attention ever given to marketing or planning disciplines."

At the time, Ritchie was senior vice president and director of media services at Mc-Cann-Erickson Worldwide, Detroit, and group media director for General Motors (GM) Worldwide. (Later she would gain notice as an expert in marketing to "Generation X" and publish a book on the subject.)

One radio organization that took Ritchie's challenge seriously was the Detroit Radio Advertising Group (DRAG). First, they restructured their membership into "target teams" to broaden their work with ad agencies in Detroit, which control most of the automotive buys nationally. Second, they invited Ritchie to be the speaker at one of their breakfast meetings in June 1993. I was there to hear Ritchie issue her marketing challenge to the DRAG membership and again urge radio to take its message to media planners, not just buyers. Her example: Buick's 1993 allocation for radio was 6% of the total budget. That figure could have been doubled, she said, if radio had sold her client on its industry as a whole.

For the Detroit meeting, Ritchie charted the changes in ad agencies from simple departmentalized functions to specialization with input at all levels. "Specialization in brands means not 'food guys,' but 'hamburger guys,'" she says. "Specialization in media means someone who does great outdoor, someone else who does breakthrough television."

Based on her experience handling GM accounts, Ritchie found radio salespeople in the early 1990s to be below par in knowledge of her client's product. "It's important to know that Buick doesn't make Grand Am," she joked. She was perfectly serious, however, describing print sellers (primarily magazine reps) as very knowledgeable in the client business. Is that why print gets almost 30% of the GM budget? Yes, she admitted.[18]

Here are Karen Ritchie's rules for meeting with media planners:

1. *Follow protocol.* Let the buyer know you're meeting with the planners.

2. *No surprises.* Let the buyer know what you'll do.

3. *No sneak attacks.* A meeting with the planner is no time to circumvent or embarrass the buyer.

4. *Sell radio.* Your station is secondary to the overall medium. Your business will benefit.

5. *Bring ideas.* Ideas and questions get planners involved.

DRAG's target teams idea was an early response to radio's need to show its sophisticated side. Led by DRAG president and COO Bill Burton, the organization developed teams for each of Detroit's 21 major agencies. Each target team had a captain from a member radio station, station rep firm, or network. Team members worked with the captain to sell radio, not the individual stations, to the agencies. Burton is an ex-officio member of any team that needs him.

Burton outlined DRAG's target team objectives:

1. Get more radio dollars.

2. Get a larger share of the budget for radio.

3. Effectively sell client's products using radio.

The Detroit group's story is just one example. Other local radio organizations combined their forces to sell the medium, not just the individual stations. Accelerated efforts by the RAB accomplished the same ends on a national basis.

It worked! By 1997, perceptions at agencies had changed. There was such a change, in fact, that after a study of 200 ad agency media planners, Arbitron called radio "a planner's best friend." Specifically, the study referred to spot radio bought on a national basis. Two-thirds of the respondents to that study put spot radio at the top of a list of 14 different national media. Radio's 66% score was followed by spot television and newspaper, both at 57%. (See Figure 8–8.) Planners who use radio for their clients tend to use it often, including radio as a regular component of their media mix. Only 12% of the planners surveyed said they rarely use spot radio.

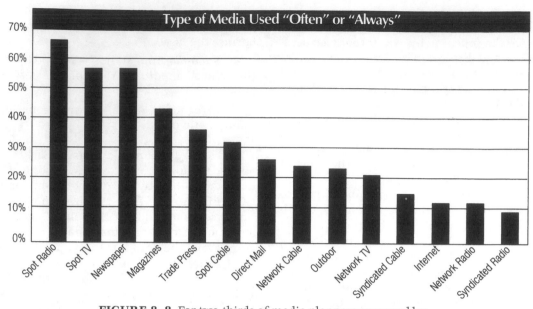

FIGURE 8–8 For two-thirds of media planners surveyed by Arbitron, radio is at the top of the list as the medium they used "often" or "always." The chart is from *Arbitron Advertising News*, May/June 1997. Used with permission.

Why radio? The planners liked the following benefits the most:

- The ability to target specific demos
- High frequency
- Creativity
- Short lead time with the ability to change messages
- Availability of both qualitative and quantitative data
- Superior cost alternative to television

On the other hand, planners criticized spot radio for not being as effective as they'd like in reach, which was a surprise in the study since reach is usually accepted as a strength of the medium. They also gave radio low marks because of lack of visuals.

The study was developed by Arbitron and conducted by Direct Marketing Results. It explored perceptions among planners of every available advertising medium and asked them to list their priorities when planning campaigns. To participate in the study, planners needed at least two years' media planning experience and had to have used spot radio in a plan within the previous 6-month period.

Compared to Karen Ritchie's deserved criticism just a few years before, the Arbitron study was good news for radio as an industry. The increase in national spot business in 1996 and 1997 and the robust revenue gains at radio generally also spoke well for radio's improved selling efforts.[19]

Selling Local Radio

Gary Fries tells his audiences, "We think we're in the radio business, but we're a bridge between the advertiser and the listener." Fries carries the banner for radio to advertisers, radio station sales staffs, and broadcast conventions.

His mission is to help radio increase its advertising dollars. "We're ahead of Yellow

Pages, but still behind newspapers, magazines, and television in share of the dollar," he reported to a group of Arkansas radio operators in 1997. (He made the speech many times, and I was his "opening act" on several occasions that year as we addressed the same groups.)

Fries credits consolidation with allowing failing stations to add new, niche formats "to raise the level of good, quality inventory." Don't discount timing: "Radio opened new inventory during a strong economy. If it had happened in 1989, we might not see the same results," he said.[20]

What results we saw! Radio revenues from 1997 reached $13.646 billion dollars, by RAB count, which was $1.2 billion more than the previous year. That was the year radio broke through the 7% mark, capturing 7.1% of all advertising dollars in McCann-Erickson's annual tally.

How can we increase that share? Fries' answer: "Solve the problems of the advertiser. Become part of the marketing team of our advertisers."

"What drives a radio station is localization," said Charlie Colombo when he was president of Banner Radio, the New York–based sales representative firm. "Local personalities and local promotion make a station win in its market. The same thing makes an advertiser successful." Colombo called radio "the pulse of the market."[21]

So many local radio stations depend on local accounts for their livelihoods because local advertisers depend on the local stations to get messages to their customers. The smaller the market, the higher the percentage of local business on the station.

When I wrote the section in Chapter 5 about direct (or "retail") selling, I really wanted to tout radio over all the other electronic media. To be fair to sellers of television, cable, and new media I didn't. Now that I'm writing about radio, I can. Selling direct is radio's great strength. Yes, my roots are in radio and that makes me partial to the medium. The majority of radio stations are in small towns, and that makes direct selling radio's forte more than any other medium's with the possible exception of newspaper.

Nowhere is the need for customer focus greater than in direct selling. The radio seller has to know enough about the advertiser's business to get customers through the advertiser's doors. The typical way to get to know the advertiser's business is simply to ask. Next is to read trade journals in the advertiser's field. Radio sellers have an additional advantage. If your station is an RAB member, that organization maintains remarkable resources on a variety of businesses.

Selling Ideas

Some radio sellers call agencies and ask "Do you have a buy for me?" or they call a direct account and ask "How many spots do you want?" If you believe in customer focus, you won't be one of them.

Kerby Confer, chairman of Sinclair Communications' radio division, says he was a 30-year-old disc jockey in Baltimore when sales representatives from his station would ask him to accompany them on sales calls. They liked Kerby's presence because he was creative off the air as well as on.

"With the advertiser, I did my on-air bits and the salesperson just sat there," he says.

"I thought, hey, I can do my bits and ask for the order, too. This is show business, and we should be in show business in the client's office as well as on the air."

That realization started Confer on a sales career that expanded to include ownership of stations and running two national chains in radio's consolidated environment. He continued to ask if he could go on sales calls with his local staff, to address the sales staff, and to lead creativity sessions. (It was Kerby's "big deal pen" you read about in Chapter 2.)

"Advertisers see nothing but a shuffle of papers with rankers and other station de-

HELP IS ON THE WAY

Mike Bass was a client service representative for the Radio Advertising Bureau in Dallas when I spent the day exploring the resources they maintain for their 5,000 radio station clients.

The first call Mike fielded while I eavesdropped was from a salesperson in Milwaukee. She wanted information about indoor rock climbing so she could work up a proposal for a new health and fitness prospect at WXPT. Mike said he knew he had something and would try to find it quickly in the RAB's computerized database.

He checked keywords: "Amusement park." No luck. Then, "Rock climbing." Still no luck. He tried a few others, but couldn't locate the information while the lady from Milwaukee was still on the phone.

"I'll have to send that one to research," he told me, visibly disappointed in himself. "I know we've got it, though."

A few more calls came in. Valerie from WGGY in Wilkes Barre wanted to know what RAB had on file about banking, about beepers and pagers, and about selling to a local university. Mike found what she needed immediately and sent her articles from the database by fax while she was still on the phone with him.

Another call came in, this one from Hopper at a station in Guilford, New Hampshire, who wanted Simmons Research information on appliance purchase habits. A keystroke or two and that information was on its way.

Another client representative told Mike to try "health and fitness" for the indoor rock climbing articles. Sure enough, up came the information he had remembered. The seller from Milwaukee had waited only 7 minutes or so.

Mike fields 50 such requests on an average day and has logged as many as 121 in a single day. Mike and his cohorts are the research department for RAB-member radio salespeople who want to be customer-focused.

RAB's "Instant Background" service alone covers hundreds of industries with two-page summaries of activity. Add to that the in-depth research on virtually any industry a radio sales representative might call on, and the organization provides radio with a staggering amount of information.

Most users talk to a client representative like Mike Bass and wait by their fax machines for only a few minutes for the data they need. RAB also maintains a huge Web presence with most of the information accessible by password only at *www.rab.com*.

How does the organization keep up with the businesses like the indoor rock climbing industry? It stays in the know by reading and clipping industry trade publications and by spotting related items from the consumer and business press. The research department (there are four people) reads more than 250 publications on a regular basis and adds data retrieved from Internet sites to add about 400 other sources.

---

scriptions," Confer says. "Better to call a bicycle shop and say to the owner, 'There's a bike shop in Memphis that doubled its business with this commercial.' If you give ideas to increase business, you'll own him."[22]

Sales trainer Jim Taszarek agrees. "Leave your rankers in the car," he says, advising against reams of research data that show your station a tenth of a point away from your competitor in the ratings. "Advertisers have tons of information, what they need is ideas. They're looking for a great spot, a great campaign. They're looking for an edge."[23]

To demonstrate that you or your station is a resource for ideas, start with your presentation: attract attention. It takes creativity, an idea that sets your proposal apart as something special. Here are some good examples:

- *The cake chart.* A sales rep at KCCY Radio in Pueblo, Colorado, wanted to show the station's audience with a pie chart. Instead, she used a "cake chart." The prospect was presented with a round cake, with the station's share graphically shown in the icing.

- *The weakness.* A Chattanooga seller presented a contest idea to a hamburger chain. He told the client that it was a great promotion that the station really believed in, but there was a weakness in it. He said he would describe the weakness at the end of the presentation, and maybe the client could help.

  At the end of the presentation, the client was interested, but before he signed, he wanted to know the weakness. The seller replied, "We're only asking $35,000 for this. It's such a reasonable price you might not think we're really serious about how good a promotion it is!"

- *The punchline.* GulfStar Communications' Chris Wegmann tells the story of a one-sided game of telephone tag with a one-person agency when he managed a station in Pittsburgh. When there was no reply to his messages, Chris called the agency's voice mail and recorded the setup to an intriguing joke. "Want the punch line? Call me."

- *A model sale.* A Seattle sales manager couldn't get a Nissan dealer to respond to a presentation, so he went to a hobby shop and bought a model truck kit. Once

the model was built, it was delivered with a note: "If you're interested in selling more of these, please call."

- *The homing pigeon.* A friend of mine at an Atlanta station delivered a homing pigeon to a Buick dealer with a note: "I've been trying to see you with an excellent media campaign. Please put a time for an appointment in the capsule on the bird's leg." In a few days, my friend got a call from the owner of the bird. The car dealer was ready to meet.

- *In the can.* The presentations had been made, but KHFI in Austin was having trouble closing on the Coors account. Account Executive Peggy McCormick went to a costume shop and was "fitted" for a Coors can costume. Wearing it, she made one last presentation. And she got the order.

- *Know when you're whipped.* A seller for our long-time client KFRG, in San Bernardino, California, presented a bullwhip to a buyer with a proposal, saying, "You're going to beat me up on rates anyway!" That was the seller's way of anticipating an objection and getting ready to neutralize it.[24]

Looking Good

In Chapter 1, I suggested that the presentation kits strewn on the floor of my office were a metaphor for the explosion of media options available for the audience. That same littered floor was also a metaphor for the options available to advertisers. An important consideration for radio sellers is how good do your presentation materials look?

Jim Taszarek reminds audiences at industry conferences that "We're competing with everybody who does business with our clients. Not just other radio stations or media outlets." That means your prospect or client will judge your media kit against national magazines, appliance brochures, and graphics from their local printer. If the local cable salesperson has access to the media kits for each of the networks on the system, that advertiser—your prospect—

will have seen some of the glitzy presentations I mentioned earlier.

Now how good do your station's presentation materials look?

So many radio stations I've encountered use photocopied presentations that *look* like they were photocopied. A Xerox salesperson would be embarrassed because they not only show the station in bad light, but they also show the station's copier to be in bad repair.

No radio station needs to spend the kind of money that the national networks spend on their kits, but every station owes it to its clients (and to its sales staff) to look good. With the technology of desktop publishing, there's no reason to look anything but professional.

Next, put the presentation in *client* terms. As Mike Mahone, executive vice president of RAB says, "Start from the prospect's perception of reality (not our opinion of how it is or ought to be), and use those perceptions as the foundation of the entire proposal." Like other sellers, Mahone uses the prospect's logo on the cover of presentations. He suggests that it should be the "largest item on the page, demonstrating right up front that the subject of the proposal is going to be the client—that the *client* will be the most important entity in the discourse that will follow."[25]

In the "Get Wet & Win!!" proposal in Figures 8–9 through 8–11, you see that the promotion idea, the name Sea Doo, and the picture of the Sea Doo craft are prominent. Furthermore, every page is headlined with the Sea Doo name. The proposal is not

elaborate, but it looks good (even in this black-and-white rendition). The typeface makes it very clear and readable.

Jim Taszarek takes presentations beyond the "logo on the cover" idea and suggests a "client-based title" on the presentation as well. He uses "Full Boat Monday Night" as an example. "'Full Boat' means a car loaded with accessories at a maximum profit for the dealer. Monday night is the worst selling night of the week," says Taszarek. Put those two together, and you have the attention of an auto dealer.

To be completely customer-focused, Taszarek suggests avoiding the words "pitch" or "presentation." "That's what it is for us," he says. "Let's use words with client

GET WET & WIN!!

Sea Doo Makes a Splash in Cleveland!
Ride the Wave into Sales in the Summer of '97!!

Presented to: Dan Proffer, Sea Doo Account Manager
and Karen Neal, HT Marketing/Hawaiian Tropic
Presented by: Annemarie Heasley, MRM, Nationwide Communications

April 16, 1997

FIGURE 8–9 Putting the client first is important for any presentation or proposal. Here you have to read the entire cover to see that this proposal is from Nationwide Communications. This is from "Nontraditional Revenue Proposals" collected by RAB and is used with permission.

Sea Doo

PROGRAM THEME:
Get Wet and Win!

PROGRAM CONCEPT:
Buy two Hawaiian Tropic sun care products and receive $5 discount at Sea World with proof of purchase. Purchase and redemption also qualify consumer for a chance to win a Sea Doo.

PROGRAM STRATEGY:
Six week promotional window
~$5 off admission to Sea World
~Four week radio campaign on WGAR
~In store display for Sea Doo at Hawaiian Tropic display

PROGRAM TIMING
June 16 through July 31
June 16: Program Kickoff (in-store & radio)
July 13: Radio Campaign Complete
July 20: In store offer ends (if using tear pads)
July 31: Last day for Sea World Discount

Nationwide Communications*phone 216-642-5304*fax 216-328-9951

Sea Doo

HOW IT WORKS:
GET WET & WIN!

Consumer Incentive: Consumers will purchase two specially marked packages of Hawaiian Tropic and show proof of purchase at Sea World for a $5 discount on admission. This redemption qualifies them to win a Sea Doo at the end of the promotion. Alternate method of entry will be available.

Benefits to Involved Parties:
*Sea Doo- receives market wide exposure on a designated product (w/ blown on sticker), a hot summer time product at a North East Ohio grocery store or department store. Receives additional advertising exposure from product, third party tie-in, and Sea World. Has opportunity to display in store.

*Sea World- receives exposure on Sea Doo and third party tie-in advertising.

*Third Party- receives exposure on Sea Doo advertising which generates sales of product and provides traffic to key account/trade.

MEDIA SUPPORT
WGAR Radio 100 (:60) commercial messages M-Sun 6am to 7p and 140 (:60) commercial messages evenings 7pm-mid/weekends 6a-mid.

POP (if necessary)
One 25" x 14" 2 color poster w/ tear off pads per store. POP includes Sea Doo logo and watercraft, Sea World logo & Hawaiian Tropic logo.

FIGURE 8–10 This proposal ties several sponsors together. Sea Doo is an obvious one. Read carefully and you find Hawaiian Tropic sun care products and Sea World amusement park, too. Not until you get to the third panel of the presentation do you see that Nationwide's WGAR is the station sponsor. Courtesy RAB. Used with permission.

benefits, what it'll do for them, the people with the money." His suggestions include, "a plan," "an advertising blueprint," and "a radio advertising flow chart."

I won't embarrass the station by using call letters, but a station in a small, Arbitron-rated market sent me a presentation package that demonstrates what *not* to do. First of all, the station talked about itself and about nothing else. The presentation was stacked this way:

- The power (50,000 watts) and tower height (500 feet)
- The name of the family business that runs the station
- The programming consultant they hired
- The fact that they play country music
- The fact that they are committed to assisting area businesses to develop an effective overall marketing plan

Finally! The last point is all that the customer cares about.

The points about the power and the tower in the list should be in customer terms: how many of the advertiser's customers can hear the station? How wide a coverage area can the client draw customers from? The consultant is irrelevant to the advertiser. Country music is an important point, but how does that relate to the advertiser? In this particular case, the whole area loved country music. That means the station is able to target the very people who would visit the advertiser's store, which is a point they should have included.

You get the idea: customer first. The radio station is a conduit for the message between the advertiser and the people who will buy the advertiser's product or service.

Sea Doo

WGAR to provide: Radio commercials
Radio production
POP Production
Logo'd tear pads
Securing of third party tie-in
20 tickets to Sea World for trade
Logistics of implementing program at trade
Logistics of implementing program at Sea World

Sea World to provide: Redemption offer
Mention of promotion in ads
Display area for Sea Doo vehicle

Third Party Tie to provide: Sea Doo logo on product
Incentive to trade
Funds to promote promotion

Sea Doo to provide: Program funding
Vehicle for display at trade(s) and
Sea World
Camera Ready artwork

Total Investment for Sea Doo

$39,500

Nationwide Communications*phone 216-642-5304*fax 216-328-9951

FIGURE 8-11 Here's what each party has to do to participate in the promotion. Sea Doo's investment was in radio time and in the Sea Doo watercraft. (Note: "POP" is retail-speak for "point of purchase.") Courtesy RAB. Used with permission.

Targeting with Radio

People spend more time with radio than with any other medium. (See Figure 8–12.) You saw among radio's strengths the ability to target certain listener groups through formatting. A Top 40 station will deliver 18- to 34-year-old listeners. A news and talk station will deliver listeners 35 and older. Adult contemporary stations tend to attract women, while rock stations typically attract men.

Format differences are of tremendous advantage to advertisers who target their buys and their messages to the specific audiences of each station. For example, adult contem-

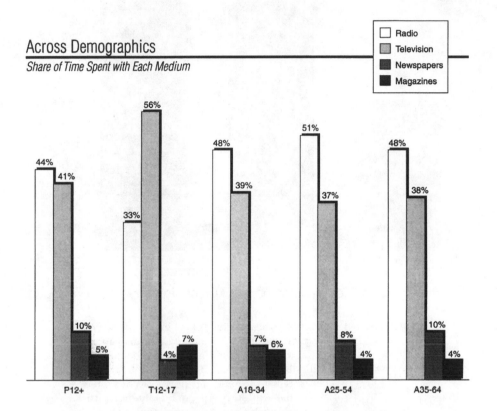

People Spend More Time with RADIO!
Average Weekday 6AM-6PM

A National Study of **Media Targeting 2000** *Consumers & Media*

Across Demographics
Share of Time Spent with Each Medium

Legend:
- ☐ Radio
- Television
- Newspapers
- Magazines

P12+: 44%, 41%, 10%, 5%
T12-17: 33%, 56%, 4%, 7%
A18-34: 48%, 39%, 7%, 6%
A25-54: 51%, 37%, 8%, 4%
A35-64: 48%, 38%, 10%, 4%

FIGURE 8-12 As a radio guy, I hope the headline remains true for a long time. Because television captures attention in the evening hours, RAB tends to use 6 a.m. to 6 p.m. figures for radio. Except for teens 12 to 17 (the second graph), radio leads. From *Media Targeting 2000*, conducted by the Arbitron Company in cooperation with RAB. Used with permission from each organization.

porary stations are proven to deliver clients for medical offices, home builders, and grocery stores. News and talk stations deliver customers for cell phone companies, auto dealers, and financial services.

Listeners are generally in a positive frame of mind when they've chosen their favorite music or radio personality for companionship. The radio commercial uses that environment to transfer positive feelings to the product or service being advertised. (See Figure 8-13.)

"I believe that the best commercials nearly always make people feel that the ad-

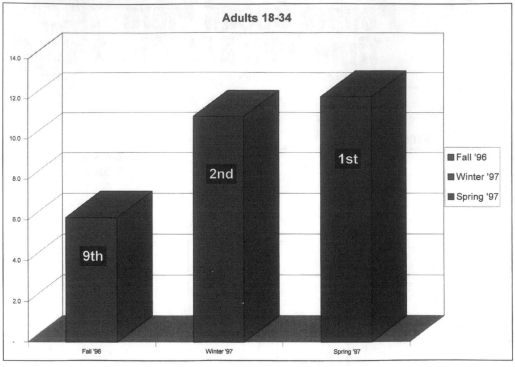

FIGURE 8–13   To show radio's targetability, here's a chart of
the growth of the syndicated morning show
"Steve and D. C." and the impact it had on
adults 18 to 34 on KIX 106 (WKKX) in St.
Louis in just three ratings periods. With radio,
any demographic group can be targeted with
positive effect. Courtesy SupeRadio. Used
with permission.

vertiser is talking directly to them," says
Tony Schwartz in *Media: The Second God*.
Schwartz is one of the best practitioners of
the radio advertising craft. He calls commercials a form of narrowcasting:

An advertiser . . . is only interested in that
part of the audience that has a need for his
product or may become interested in it. To
this end, he studies the distribution pattern
of his product, selects stations that can
reach his potential audience in that distribution area and tries to determine the most
cost-effective way of doing this.
    One of the most fruitful uses of radio,
from an advertiser's standpoint, is narrow-

casting (as opposed to broadcasting). For instance, if we want to reach the elderly, we
buy time on Station A. We reach teenagers
on Station B, young blacks on Station C,
Hispanics on Station D, jazz buffs on
Station F, news hounds on Station G.
Analyzing an audience along a different dimension, we may learn that 69 percent of
Station H's listeners read the *Daily News*,
while 65 percent of Station I's listeners read
The New York Times. During the morning,
80 percent of Station J's listeners are in
their cars, most of them driving to work.[26]

Those two paragraphs are the best short
course in selling radio I've ever read!

TALK RADIO SALES SPECIALISTS

Clear Channel - South Florida is looking for the best Talk Radio Sales Specialists in the country. Candidates should have at least 2 years experience selling Talk Radio, and a real passion for the format! Move to Miami and help us launch our 3-station SuperTalk network. We are moving quickly, so serious candidates should FAX resume today to:

Dave Harris
General Sales Manager
WINZ/WFTL/WIOD
FAX: 305-654-0094
EOE

FIGURE 8–14
Not only does radio target specifically by demographic and by format, but stations look for sellers who are experienced in specific formats. Courtesy Clear Channel, South Florida. Used with permission.

Schwartz believes so much in the narrowcasting aspect of radio that he has bought time on stations to reach only *one person*! In one instance, he designed a commercial to reach *only* the president of a major automobile company who did not believe in using radio advertising. The purpose of the campaign was to change the man's mind. They found out what station he listened to on his drive to work and bought a highly targeted spot that said people think more consciously about automobiles when they are driving automobiles.

"He listened," Schwartz says, "because we discussed *his* concerns, *his* aims, *his* problems. He must have felt these commercials were talking to him, even though it probably never entered his mind that he was the only person we were interested in talking to." The campaign worked: someone from the automobile company called the phone number listed in the commercial. Six other companies also called!

Schwartz was able to target his audience of one by finding out the man's favorite radio station. Everybody has at least one favorite station, and often they choose two or more favorites depending on their mood or activity. Arbitron indicates that the average listener over 12 years of age listens to 4.1 stations over the course of a week. That number varies by format. Listeners who prefer country stations, for example, listen to only 3.7 total stations; those who prefer sports stations listen to 4.4 total stations. The more loyal a listener is to any one station, the fewer total stations they use.

Billboard lists 17 distinct radio formats. Arbitron uses 38 different format designations. Because *Billboard* serves the music industry as well as the radio industry, their divisions are more music based. *Billboard*, for example, combines any station that deals in news, talk, or information into one category. Arbitron separates them into all news, news/talk/information, talk/personality, and all sports. Arbitron also separates adult contemporary, soft adult contemporary, hot adult contemporary, modern adult contemporary, urban adult contemporary, and easy listening. *Billboard* uses only two designations, adult contemporary and urban adult contemporary (*Billboard* used "Easy Listening" until early 1996.)[27]

Arbitron's categorization is more exact than *Billboard*'s simply because Arbitron shows the greater diversity. Even Arbitron's designations cannot show the differences between Spanish contemporary stations in Miami, Houston, and Los Angeles, although Arbitron does separate urban oldies from rhythm & blues. The point here is not to find fault with the categorization but to demonstrate that there are lots of radio formats and lots of subsets to each format.

The major formats, found in virtually every market, are adult contemporary, country, contemporary hits (also called CHR and Top 40), oldies, and news/talk. (See Figure 8–14.) The more varied the makeup of the market, the more permutations you'll find on the air. That's when formats begin to split into smaller niches. For instance, "oldies" might mean the early

Top 40

Emphasizes current hit music. Also known as CHR (Contemporary Hit Radio). Includes stations specializing in "adult," "rhythm" or "rock"—based on Top 40 formats.

A Few Format Highlights

Top 40 has 16 percent more Women 18+ (58 percent) in its audience than Men 18+ (42 percent).

Seventy-five percent of Top 40's audience is made up of Persons 12-34. And, of all formats, Top 40 has the highest percentage of teenage listeners (24.1 percent).

Out of all dayparts, Top 40 gets its largest share of listening 7PM to Midnight (11.6 percent).

Top 40 Stations
412

Total Stations
12,472

Source: Arbitron, September 1997

Listeners 18+

Men 42%

Women 58%

Mon-Sun, 6AM-Mid

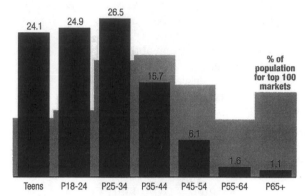

% of population for top 100 markets

| Teens | P18-24 | P25-34 | P35-44 | P45-54 | P55-64 | P65+ |

24.1 24.9 26.5 15.7 6.1 1.6 1.1

Audience Composition
Percent of Format Audience by Demographic
Mon-Sun, 6AM-Mid

	Summer '96	Fall '96	Winter '97	Spring '97
P12+	8.8	8.4	8.6	8.6
P18-34	13.4	12.9	13.2	13.3
P25-54	7.2	7.0	6.9	7.0
P35-64	4.4	4.4	4.2	4.2
M18+	6.2	6.0	5.9	6.3
W18+	8.1	7.8	8.0	7.9
Teens	28.9	27.8	29.1	26.9

AQH Share of Listening by Season
Mon-Sun, 6AM-Mid

Source: Format definitions are from Billboard and are used in the Arbitron National Database. All data come from Arbitron National Database, 94 Continuously Measured markets, Spring '97 survey.

FIGURE 8–15 The Top 40 format was most popular in New England with the West Coast second in this analysis from 1997 Arbitron surveys. The audience profile is primarily teens to 34, and the audience is 58% women. The graph in the upper right shows that nighttime is prime time for Top 40 radio. The information is from Arbitron's *Radio Today: How America Listens to Radio*, 1997 edition. ©1997 The Arbitron Company, and used with permission.

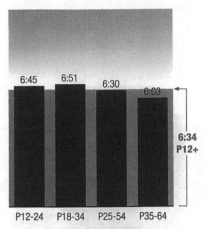

**Time Spent Listening
by Demographic**
Mon-Sun, 6AM-Mid, HH:MM

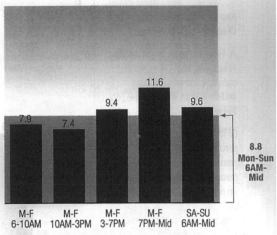

AQH Share of Listening by Daypart
Persons 12+

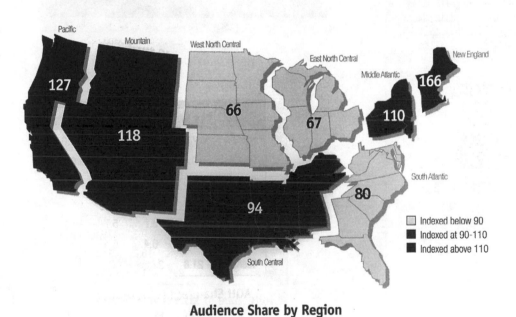

Audience Share by Region
Index Based on 94 Markets; 100 = National Average
Mon-Sun, 6AM-Mid, Persons 12+, AQH Shares

FIGURE 8–15 continued.

News/ Talk

Includes news, business news, talk, sports and children's formats.

A Few Format Highlights
Fifty-six percent of News/Talk's listeners are Men 18+ and a marginally smaller 44 percent are Women 18+.

Tops in morning drive, News/Talk has the largest share of listeners tuning in at 6AM to 10AM.

This format performs well in many regions across the country, indexing above average in New England (123), Middle Atlantic (119), East North Central (110), West North Central (112) and Pacific (114) regions.

News/Talk Stations

1,228

Total Stations

12,472

Source: Arbitron,
September 1997

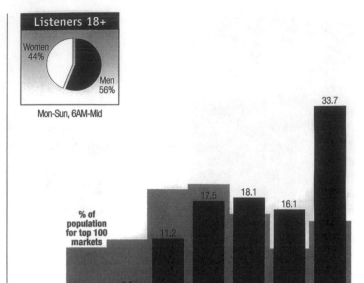

Audience Composition
Percent of Format Audience by Demographic
Mon-Sun, 6AM-Mid

	Summer '96	Fall '96	Winter '97	Spring '97
P12+	15.6	16.6	16.8	16.2
P18-34	6.4	7.2	7.2	6.2
P25-54	12.4	13.3	13.7	12.7
P35-64	17.5	18.5	19.0	18.4
M18+	19.0	20.0	20.9	19.8
W18+	14.6	15.4	15.2	15.2
Teens	1.8	2.8	1.4	1.8

AQH Share of Listening by Season
Mon-Sun, 6AM-Mid

Source: Format definitions are from Billboard and are used in the Arbitron National Database. All data come from Arbitron National Database, 94 Continuously Measured markets, Spring '97 survey.

FIGURE 8–16 Here's the same analysis for the news/talk format. For ease of demonstration, this category includes the all-news, news/talk/information, talk/personality, and all-sports formats. This is quite a contrast to the Top 40 analysis at Figure 8–15. The audience is substantially older and 56% male. The largest shares are in morning drive. The only similarity to the Top 40 graph is the high index of listeners in New England.

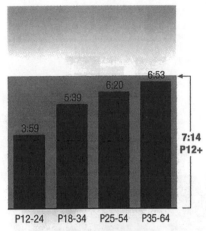

Time Spent Listening
by Demographic
Mon-Sun, 6AM-Mid, HH:MM

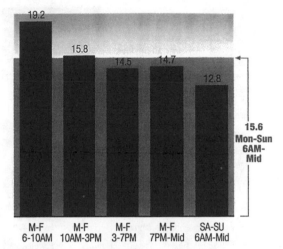

AQH Share of Listening by Daypart
Persons 12+

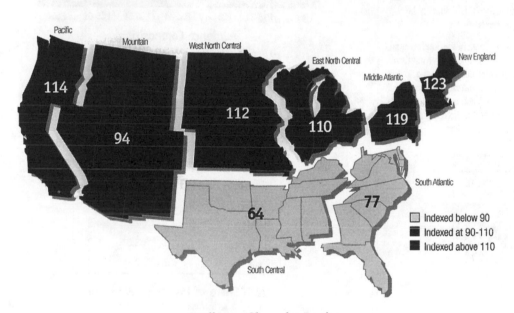

Audience Share by Region
Index Based on 94 Markets; 100 = National Average
Mon-Sun, 6AM-Mid, Persons 12+, AQH Shares

FIGURE 8–16 continued.

Religious

Includes Gospel and "Contemporary Christian" formats as well as non-music based religious stations specializing in "teaching programs."

A Few Format Highlights

Religious claims the number one spot among formats for having the greatest percentage—67 percent—of its listening audience as Women 18+.

Older listeners spend more time listening each week. Adults 35-64 listen four hours more than 12- to 24-year-olds do.

A slightly larger share of listeners tune in to this format on the weekends.

More people in the South Central region listen to this format than any other. Listeners in the South Central region are 86 percent more likely to listen to Religious-formatted stations compared to the rest of the country.

Religious Stations
1,205

Total Stations
12,472

Source: Arbitron, September 1997

Listeners 18+

Men 33%

Women 67%

Mon-Sun, 6AM-Mid

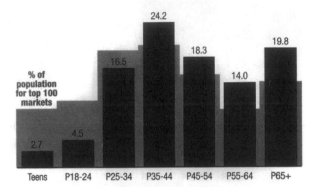

% of population for top 100 markets

Teens	P18-24	P25-34	P35-44	P45-54	P55-64	P65+
2.7	4.5	16.5	24.2	18.3	14.0	19.8

Audience Composition
Percent of Format Audience by Demographic
Mon-Sun, 6AM-Mid

	Summer '96	Fall '96	Winter '97	Spring '97
P12+	2.2	2.2	2.1	2.1
P18-34	1.3	1.5	1.4	1.3
P25-54	2.2	2.2	2.1	2.1
P35-64	2.6	2.7	2.6	2.5
M18+	1.5	1.5	1.5	1.5
W18+	3.0	3.1	3.0	2.8
Teens	0.8	0.7	0.8	0.8

AQH Share of Listening by Season
Mon-Sun, 6AM-Mid

Source: Format definitions are from Billboard and are used in the Arbitron National Database. All data come from Arbitron National Database, 94 Continuously Measured markets, Spring '97 survey.

FIGURE 8–17 Here you can see real differences again. The largest audience appeal for the religious format is in the Southwest and the Southeast, while the lowest is in New England and the Mountain regions. The audience is made up of two-thirds women, mostly 25 and older, but the shares are very low. In this analysis, the religious format includes stations with preachers and teaching programs as well as those with Christian music formats.

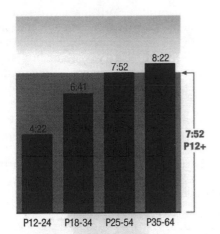

**Time Spent Listening
by Demographic**
Mon-Sun, 6AM-Mid, HH:MM

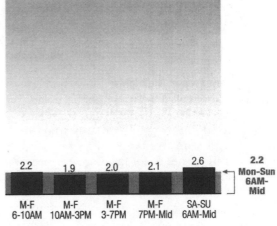

AQH Share of Listening by Daypart
Persons 12+

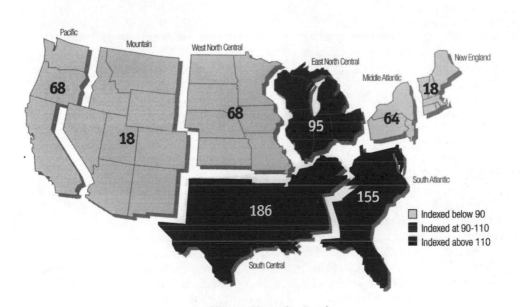

Audience Share by Region
Index Based on 94 Markets; 100 = National Average
Mon-Sun, 6AM-Mid, Persons 12+, AQH Shares

FIGURE 8–17 continued.

days of rock and roll from the late 1950s, the Beatles-based 1960s, or the 1970s.

The further into the 70s the sound gets, the more likely the station will call itself "classic hits." Please don't confuse "classic hits" with "classic rock," no matter how subtle the difference in sound to your ears. (It's like asking your parents to get the difference between house and industrial music, which are too narrow individually to base radio formats on. As targeted as radio is, there's still a need for audiences large enough to be of value to advertisers.)

Formats vary by region, too. There are fewer country stations in the Northeast than there are in the Southeast and Southwest because the audience base is not as strong. In Figures 8–15 through 8–17, I've used three Arbitron analyses that show the differences in the top-40, news/talk, and religious formats by audience profile and by region.

Every format shows this type of regional difference. Many will have differences from city to city, even when the cities are close together. For example, the top 40 station in Houston, KRBE, is very mainstream in its sound, which is radically different from the sultry rhythms of KTFM in San Antonio, just 185 miles west on Interstate 10.

Radio at Work

Good news from Arbitron about radio usage at work: during the average quarter hour, 40% of full-time employees are listening to radio. Of those, 65% say they are more likely to listen to radio at work than they are to read a newspaper (39%), surf the Internet (16%), or watch television (11%). Although the boss chooses the station in 48% of work places, 43% say they typically listen alone and choose their own station. Another 13% listen in groups of ten or more. Of those, 49% make a group decision about the station.

Almost 80% choose the station they listen to based on the kind of music it plays. The amount of music also comes into play for almost 60% of respondents. Most (61%) say their office is tuned to one station all through the day. (See Figure 8–18.)

There are assumptions about listening at work that the study countered:

- "9 to 5" is a fiction. Only 4% of workers begin and end their workday at those times.
- "At work" does not mean at the "office." Only 42% were at an office. Another 42% were indoors but not in an office setting.
- Adult contemporary formats do well in the workplace, but they don't have an exclusive hold. Only urban and news talk score below an index of 100. (See Figures 8–19 and 8–20.)
- People are not forced to listen to stations they wouldn't choose on their own.

The Arbitron Company and Edison Media Research conducted the study in 1997 by reinterviewing Arbitron diary keepers.[2829]

A real selling point for radio in the work place is the fact that almost 60% of the respondents say that listening to radio while working improves their productivity. (See Figure 8–21.)

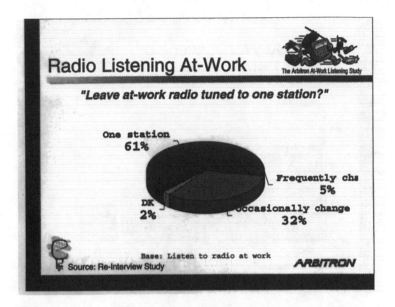

FIGURE 8–18 People listening to radio at work tune to one station and leave it there, according to "Radio Goes to Work, the Arbitron At-Work Listening Study." That's good news for radio. Courtesy the Arbitron Company. Used with permission.

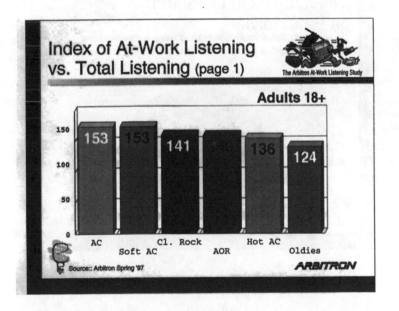

FIGURE 8–19 The myth was that adult contemporary formats work best in the workplace, but Arbitron's at-work study indicated otherwise. With the average at 100, you can see the impact each format has on adults 18 and over. Courtesy the Arbitron Company. Used with permission.

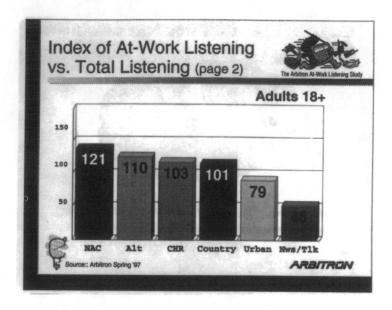

FIGURE 8–20   Only urban and news/talk score below the average for at-work listening. Courtesy the Arbitron Company. Used with permission.

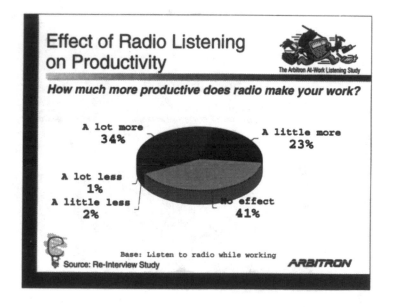

FIGURE 8–21   Bosses all over America should love this news: radio makes workers more productive. At least workers think so and told the Arbitron at-work study so. Courtesy the Arbitron Company. Used with permission.

Points Versus Value

As you visit advertising agencies, you might encounter a sign on the wall in a buyer's office: "Torture numbers and they'll tell you anything." It's a way to put some fun into an otherwise serious business: buying efficiency through ratings points. Television's phrase, "spots and dots," is sometimes applied to radio when selling becomes meeting cost-per-point (CPP) or cost-per-thousand (CPM) goals. Agencies like to "torture the numbers."

Buying "by the numbers" is the worst way to purchase time on radio. Radio's inherent targetability should prompt agencies to buy audiences, but some agencies just don't take the time to learn the subtle differences. (That's what sellers are for, after all.) The typical Arbitron ranker might show 20 or more radio stations with what looks on the surface like the same shares. What buyer can make good sense of it?

"Sooner or later all selling comes down to eyeball-to-eyeball, mind-to-mind, person-to-person communication," says Wayne Cornils in the foreword to Michael Keith's *Selling Radio Direct*. Cornils, a former RAB and NAB executive, continued:

> In advertising, and especially radio, there is a fringe which would reduce the profession to a pseudo-science of computer generated numbers.
>
> Computer-driven robots build cars, but people sell cars. Computer software programs design and build computers, but men and women still sell computers.
>
> Radio stations, like people, have individual personalities, and personalities don't compute very well. The subtle differences between stations, markets, on-air talent, and promotion and marketing support are difficult—if not impossible—to accurately portray in computer language.

Computer systems such as the optimizers that agencies use to buy TV time (you read about them in Chapter 5) are not nearly so effective in radio. They may make a buy efficient, but they cannot make the buy practical. Using gross rating points (GRPs) to buy radio does not take into consideration whether the schedule can achieve results for the advertiser, only whether enough bodies will be reached by the commercial.

GRPs are useful in television because they relate directly to the number of viewers of a program. Advertisers who buy television know that the ratings apply to specific programs and that importance of time spent with a program is minimal. Television is measured in one dimension: household rating points.

Radio is measured in broad dayparts, and time spent listening is vital to radio ratings. The longer the listening time, the higher the share. Radio is measured in two dimensions: cume and average quarter hour.

GRPs are calculated one of two ways:

1. Multiply the number of spots by the average quarter hour rating, such as 20 spots running on a station with a 2 rating gets you 40 GRPs.

2. Multiply the total reach of the schedule, expressed as a percentage, by the average frequency.

It's good math, but it's bad buying because GRPs conceal valuable information about reach and frequency. In *Radio Advertising's Missing Ingredient: The Optimum Effective Scheduling System*, Steve Marx and Pierre Bouvard use this example of how four radically different schedules can each produce 100 GRPs:

	Market Reach	**Frequency**	**GRPs**
Schedule A	100%	1 time	100
Schedule B	50%	2 times	100
Schedule C	25%	4 times	100
Schedule D	1%	100 times	100

Schedule A will have virtually no impact, and Schedule D will make 1% of the market annoyed at hearing the commercial too many times!

CPP buys create the same danger for advertisers because CPP is based on GRP measurements. CPP calculations take into account only two factors—audience size and spot rate—not who is reached and not the value of the audience in terms of potential buying.

Marx and Bouvard reacted to CPP buys this way:

> Imagine if the sole criterion in buying a new car was the average cost per part! Or if the determining criterion on your next clothes shopping trip were the average cost per thread! Would you decide on a college education just by looking at the average cost per book?
>
> Sounds pretty silly, doesn't it? So why do we allow radio to be bought and sold this way? Cost Per Point is a bean-counting exercise that misses the only important issue: will this schedule generate results?![30]

Early in my radio career, stories circulated in the industry about agency buyers who bought only "by the numbers" and accidentally ordered schedules for suntan lotions on stations targeted to African-American audiences. I don't know if the stories were true, but they reinforced the point of radio's unique targetability. The audience of any station will have enough in common that effective (and studied) placement of commercials should deliver results.

Jim Taszarek's training to his clients' sales departments suggests three points to offset CPP or CPM buys: he uses the letters "CPI," for "cume, profile, and ideas." Taszarek feels that each presentation should show the station's cume, a profile of how that cume fits with the product the buyer wants to advertise, and an idea that gives the station value beyond its numbers.

Seven Dirty Words

"I tried it once. It didn't work."

At some time in your selling career, you'll hear those seven words. In Chapter 2, you learned to answer and neutralize objections, and you'll recognize that as one of them. Your first response is to probe for more information. Explore the likely causes of disappointment.

"Disappointment" is the key word here. Often "It didn't work" translates into "It didn't meet my expectations." A variety of factors determine the success or failure of a schedule in any medium, and advertiser expectations is first among them. Others are the marketing strategy, the competitive environment, the copy concept, and the medium chosen to carry the message.

According to Steve Marx and Pierre Bouvard, one more factor was long overlooked in radio: scheduling. Marx is president of the Tampa-based Center for Sales Strategy. Bouvard is general manager, radio, at the Arbitron Company. Together they created the Optimum Effective Scheduling System (OES), which "opened the eyes of thousands of advertisers (and radio salespeople) to the awesome marketing power of

the world's most pervasive medium," according to Gary Fries of the RAB.

In their OES book, published by the NAB, Marx and Bouvard reported on an NAB study "that points clearly to the fact that the vast majority of radio schedules purchased today either contain too few announcements or they're spread over too long a period to generate the bang necessary to create a profitable return on investment for the advertiser."

As far back as I can remember (mid-1960s or so), radio commercial schedules used increments of 6, 12, and 18 spots per week. Twenty-four spots per week was termed a "saturation plan." No one seems to know why those numbers were chosen, although it may be a product of accommodating budgets of small businesses in small towns. Other mass media have traditionally used a high unit count per schedule. Television, for example, schedules two spots for the same client in a single commercial pod to double the frequency.

Marx and Bouvard called radio's low unit count "a strange quirk of fate" and set out to create a more effective plan. To do

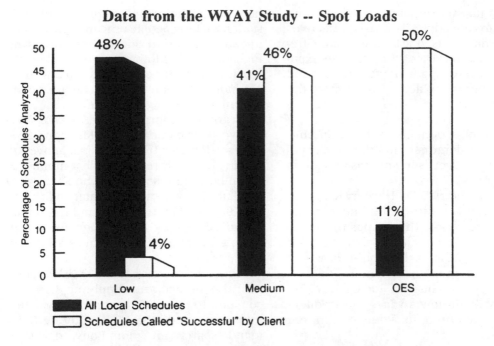

Data from the WYAY Study -- Spot Loads

FIGURE 8–22 When Steve Marx and Pierre Bouvard studied advertiser schedules on Atlanta's WYAY, they discovered that only 11% of the spot schedules resulted in 50% of the claims of success from advertisers. That prompted them to maximize radio's reach and frequency with the Optimum Effective Scheduling (OES) formula. Courtesy NAB. Used with permission.

so, they analyzed the schedules of WYAY-FM in Atlanta, a station owned at the time by New City Communications, the company that founded Marx's Center for Sales Strategy. (See Figure 8–22.) They discovered that of all the commercial schedules run on WYAY, 48% had low spot loads. Those with low spot loads accounted for only 4% of schedules described as "successful" by the clients. Schedules with medium spot loads accounted for 41% of all schedules and 46% of success claims.

The numbers that made them take notice were the schedules with high spot loads (the OES schedules, as they defined them). They accounted for only 11% of all schedules, but were responsible for 50% of claims of success.

"Our particular research approach at WYAY was not designed to find every success story," Marx and Bouvard write, "but it did clearly demonstrate that Optimum Effective Schedules were more than *8 times as likely* to produce impressive results for the advertiser." (That's their emphasis.)

Two factors for advertising in electronic media are *reach* and *frequency*. Reach is the head count of how many people are exposed to a message; frequency is the measure of how many times the average person is exposed to the message. Before the erosion of TV shares, television was considered the reach medium, and radio was the frequency medium.

In radio, there's a delicate balance between reach and frequency. To get more reach, you may have to sacrifice frequency. By boosting frequency, you lose reach. Marx and Bouvard attempted to find a real number they called "effective reach," which is just those people reached often enough for the advertising to be effective.

Advertising has long believed in the frequency of three theory: that three exposures to a message achieves the desired effect. There's evidence to support the idea:

- Mike Naples' benchmark book *Effective Frequency* demonstrated that one exposure of an advertisement "has little or no effect."
- General Electric's Dr. Herbert Krugman measured the difference between the first, second, and third exposures to advertising and concluded that the third exposure is the earliest point at which the human mind takes action.
- In Chapter 6, you read Joe Ostrow's remarks about how a variety of frequencies is required to achieve different strategies.

So Marx and Bouvard added an important element to frequency: frequency over time. They recommended a minimum of three exposures within a week's time. The number of exposures needed to accomplish that goal "is at a different weekly spot level for any given station, daypart, audience target, and survey period," they said.

The essential number in their OES formula is the station's turnover ratio, which is the mathematical comparison of cume and average quarter hour. Divide cume by AQH to yield the turnover:

$$\frac{\text{cume}}{\text{AQH}} = \text{T}/0$$

Marx and Bouvard relate turnover to a library and a convenience store. The library has low turnover, in that a few people come in and stay a while. The convenience store, on the other hand, has lots of people coming in for brief stays. "If you were to broadcast advertising inside each of these locations, you might want to repeat the message more frequently inside the convenience store, right?" they say.

Compare that to radio stations: a station with high cume and a low average quarter hour has a high turnover (such as all news stations, where people tune in to get a quick update). A station with a low cume and high AQH has a low turnover (a classical music station, for example). You'd want to use more commercials in a schedule on the station with the high turnover.

To arrive at a formula to make OES as effective as its name implies, Marx and Bouvard settled on a frequency just above the magic number three: 3.29. That number is based both on research by the Katz Radio and Katz Television representative firms in the 1980s and on the reach-and-frequency formula developed by Westinghouse Broadcasting in the 1960s (known as "Westinghouse math").

Marx and Bouvard added their own empirical evidence after applying 3.29 as a constant to their OES formula. It was further confirmed by a NAB study by Coleman Research (for whom Bouvard worked when the study was conducted).

The number 3.29 is a point on a graph where total reach and effective reach begin to separate. The total reach becomes wasted against the effective numbers of listeners who will hear the commercial often enough to be motivated by it. Figure 8–23 makes this clear.

What's needed for an OES schedule? Figures 8–24 and 8–25 give you specifics. The formula is turnover multiplied by 3.29 to yield the number of commercials needed to effectively reach the station's audience and create a success story for the advertiser. For example:

You can see that a station whose cume turns over often needs considerably more units in a schedule to effectively reach its target audience with a message.

Stations that do not subscribe to ratings services and have no access to their specific turnover ratios can use national averages for their specific format. The averages are published from time to time by Arbitron and are also available from national station representative firms. Usually the radio trade publications carry the national average turnover when it's released.

Optimum Effective Scheduling
Radio's "Secret Formula"
For Advertising Success

Here's a typical schedule reach curve for a radio station. The OES spot level for this particular station is 44 commercials, evenly dispersed throughout a seven-day week. Note that the listeners reached _effectively_ (three or more times) comprise the majority of the station's weekly cume, and two-thirds of the schedule reach.
Optimum Effective Scheduling harnesses radio's power as _the_ Effective Reach Medium.

The Elements of An Optimum Effective Schedule:

- Broad-daypart (preferably Monday-Sunday 6AM-Midnight) time period
- Spots evenly dispersed throughout the schedule.
- Weekly spot level matched to station's audience characteristics, using the OES formula: **Weekly Schedule = Audience Turnover times 3.29.**

The Operative Word Here is "Effective"...
Here's What An Optimum Effective Schedule Will Deliver On Any Station:

- Over 50% of the station's weekly audience (cume) will hear the message _at least three times._
- _Two-thirds_ of the people exposed to the message (the total schedule reach) will hear it _at least three times._
- Almost half of the people reached will hear the message _five or more_ times.

 TAPSCAN INCORPORATED

3000 Riverchase Galleria
Suite 850
Birmingham, Alabama 35244
205-987-7456

© 1991, TAPSCAN, Incorporated

Source material: NAB's "Radio Advertising's Missing Ingredient: The Optimum Effective Scheduling System."
By Steve Marx and Pierre Bouvard. Copyright 1991 National Association of Broadcasters.

FIGURE 8–23 The difference between total reach and effective reach is clear in this graph of an OES schedule from Tapscan, one of the software providers for radio sales. The OES level for this particular station is 44 commercials. Tapscan provides this graphic for radio sellers to add to their presentations to illustrate the OES concept.

OES

Calculating the Optimum Effective Schedule requires only a rating book which shows Cume and Average Quarter-Hour, a pocket calculator, and these three simple steps:

1 Calculate the Turnover Ratio $\left(\dfrac{\text{CUME}}{\text{AQH}}\right)$ for a broad demographic, Mon–Sun 6AM-12MID.

The only reasons to select a daypart other than total week are marketing reasons, not budget limitations. We review these marketing considerations, as well as the issue of budget limitations, in the book *Radio Advertising's Missing Ingredient: The Optimum Effective Scheduling System,* published by NAB.

2 Multiply the Turnover Ratio times

3.29

to determine the number of spots per week.

3 Run the spots with a *guaranteed even distribution* across all days and dayparts, Mon–Sun 6AM-12MID, as shown in this example:

Daypart	MON	TUE	WED	THU	FRI	SAT	SUN	Total
AMD	2	2	2	1	2	2	2	13
MID	1	2	2	2	1	2	2	12
PMD	2	1	2	2	2	1	2	12
EVE	2	2	1	2	2	2	1	12
Total	7	7	7	7	7	7	7	49

FIGURE 8–24 A one-page summary on how to calculate an OES for radio. Authors Steve Marx and Pierre Bouvard urge buyers of their NAB book to photocopy the summary and distribute it to staff and clients. Courtesy NAB. Used with permission.

The Ten Steps

for buying multi-station OES schedules

① Begin by drawing up a list of all the stations which merit consideration for the buy. Take into account all your usual factors: audience characteristics and size, lifestyle, qualitative data, programming environment, unique station benefits, value-added services, etc. List the stations in the left-hand column of the table below.

STATION	CUME	AQH	TURNOVER	OES	COST	EFF REACH	CPMER	ORDER

② Select your demographic target, survey area, and the daypart Mon-Sun 6AM-12MID. For each station, record the Cume and Average Quarter-Hour (AQH) Audience estimate in the columns provided.

③ For each station on the chart, divide the Cume by the AQH to determine the Turnover Ratio and record it in the appropriate column.

④ Now multiply the Turnover Ratio times 3.29 to determine how many spots per week are required for the Optimum Effective Schedule on each station, and record the answer in the OES column.

⑤ Check the rates for the OES schedule on each station. Calculate what it would cost to buy the OES schedule on each station and record that amount in the Cost column.

⑥ Determine the Effective Reach of the OES (in thousands) by using whichever Reach & Frequency software system you have available to you, and record that number in the Effective Reach column.

⑦ If you need to calculate a measure of relative cost-efficiency -- which allows for a crude and incomplete comparison of schedules -- use the CPMER, the *Cost Per Thousand Effectively Reached.* You calculate it by dividing the Cost by the Effective Reach (in

thousands). Record your answer in the CPMER column.

⑧ This is the media decision step. Consider all the data you've gathered and calculated in the table above, think about each station's unique benefits, factor in the value of the station's total proposal in meeting the advertiser's marketing objectives, and finally determine your overall *rank order of desirability* for this buy. With *total value* in mind, rank the stations, using the right-hand column, from most desirable for the buy down to least desirable.

⑨ This is the actual buying step. You've got the stations in order of desirability, you know how many spots to buy on each one and what the schedule costs, so the buying is simple. Start at the top and order the schedule on each station in order, until your budget is exhausted. Never go below the OES on one station in order to "free up the budget" to add a station which you have already determined to be less desirable.

⑩ Take care to ensure that the OES you place on each station will run with a *guaranteed even distribution* across all days and all dayparts. If you allow a rate negotiation to cause your schedule to skew into specific days or specific dayparts, you no longer have an Optimum Effective Schedule.

FIGURE 8-25 An OES worksheet from *Radio's Missing Ingredient: The Optimum Effective Scheduling System* by Steve Marx and Pierre Bouvard. Courtesy NAB. Used with permission.

Turnover		OES Constant		Spots per Week
7	×	3.29	=	23
10	×	3.29	=	33
13	×	3.29	=	43
15	×	3.29	=	49
18	×	3.29	=	59
20	×	3.29	=	66

Show and Tell

Radio salespeople should take advantage of the medium's greatest strength and play commercials for potential clients. By using what radio does best—provide interesting sound—the seller has the opportunity to engage the imagination of the retailer with a commercial for that advertiser's store. This type of commercial is called a "spec spot" because it is truly speculative.

Rarely do clients buy on the spec spot alone, but it has happened, says Michael Keith in *Selling Radio Direct*: "A spec spot should never (or rarely) be the plan itself but rather an element of the plan. In other words, design a package you know will do the job for the client, then use the spec spot to seal the deal."

Using a spec spot after the needs analysis interview shows the prospect that you've understood what was said. It also demonstrates the skills of your station in turning out imaginative copy and effective audio production.

The best context for a spec spot is your station, so include a brief sample of the station's sound with the spot. Let the client or prospect hear the way their commercial will actually be heard on the air.

Maureen Bulley, president of the Radio Store, a creative consulting firm, suggests rewarding everyone involved in the production of a spec spot when the spot results in new business. "The writer, producer, and voice-over talent—as well as sales reps—should be compensated for their contribution to the successful new business pitch," she wrote in *Radio Ink*.[31]

"It's fair and it makes them more willing to contribute in the future. Encourage friendly competition and reward the team that generates the most new business each quarter." Bulley acknowledges that producers and writers are often disappointed when a spec spot is sold because the salesperson comes back to the station asking for revisions. Make sure that producers and writers know that rewriting is part of the process. Remind them that when a spot needs to be recut, that's a sign of success not failure.

Another suggestion from Bulley is to organize commercials by category or style. For example, one generic spec tape shows ideas that can be used for auto dealers, another contains lawn-and-garden ideas, and another is geared to banks and financial advisors. You might show a particular strength of your station's production team: comedy spots or dialog spots.

"Don't leave the tape behind," Bulley advises. "The prospect will share it with friends and colleagues and you won't be there to handle objections. Add a verbal or written disclaimer so prospects understand that you own the idea until they buy it."

More on Commercials

You'll recall from the beginning of this chapter that advertising great David Ogilvy called radio "the Cinderella medium" because radio is often left behind by ad agencies. Herschell Gordon Lewis echoes that sentiment, calling radio "the misunderstood, misused medium." Lewis is a direct marketing expert who, as chairman of both

Communicomp and BJK&E Direct in Fort Lauderdale, Florida, has crafted copy for First Union Bank, Omaha Steaks, *National Geographic*, Oxmoor Books, and a long list of other direct marketers. (I've cited studies from BJK&E in several previous chapters.)

Lewis believes that radio can be the most flexible and economical weapon in an advertiser's communications arsenal. The good news is, he says that "radio does work, if one uses it properly. And using it properly begins with language.

"With radio," Lewis wrote in *Direct Marketing* magazine, "words (plus occasional music and sound effects, both accessories) have to carry the message without assistance." If we have any reverence for clarity, we'll follow eight rules Lewis developed for generating radio messages:

1. Place the subject before the verb.

2. Short sentences are clearer than two sentences tied together with "and." For example, "They've done this. They're considering that." is clearer than "They've done this and are considering that."

3. Use music as a mood-setter, not as an end in itself.

4. Narration followed by a jingle is clearer than a longer jingle by itself.

5. Give ample instructions, within the script, to the announcer. Instructions should be all caps, and nothing else in the script should be all caps.

6. Come to an inflectional stop before starting a new concept. Inflectional doesn't mean temporal. Time is precious, and a long pause lets the listener's interest sag.

7. Spell out numbers. This prevents stupid mistakes and is your assurance that the performer will read the numbers the way you want them read. So it's "eleven-twenty-nine," not "$11.29." The year is

"twenty-oh-four," not "2004." The amount is "a thousand dollars," not "$1,000."

8. Don't leave pronunciation and emphasis to the announcer's imagination. Your script might read: ". . . headquartered in Chickasha [CHICK-A-SHAY], Oklahoma," or "Ask for John Taliaferro [TOLLEVER]." It might read "Call *right now* and be a hero to your family," or you might prefer "Call right now and be a *hero* to your family."

There's one more rule from Lewis:

> Don't let the desire to be clever override clarity. . . . Many inexperienced radio writers think of entertainment first and "sell" second. Cleverness becomes the message instead of the carrier, and what happens is that sell never does enter into the carrier, and what happens is that sell never does enter into the mixture. Marketing messages of any type, for any product or service, in any medium, should tell the reader, viewer, or listener what to do. Never is this more true (and more valuable) than in radio.[32]

Roy H. Williams, whose Austin, Texas-based agency places radio buys on more than 500 stations, weighs in on the same subject:

> Too many ads today are creative without being persuasive. "Slick, clever, funny, creative, and different" are poor substitutes for "informative, believable, memorable, and persuasive."[33]

Once again I end a chapter with David Ogilvy's thoughts on the subject:

> In my opinion—and it is nothing more than that—the first thing your radio commercial has to do is to get people to listen. Surprise them. Arouse their curiosity. Wake them up. Once they are awake, talk to them as one human being to another. Involve them. Charm them. Make them laugh.

Review Highlights and Discussion Points

1. Radio is "theater of the mind." Television and cable show pictures, while various forms of interactive media mix and match sounds, pictures, text, and animation. Only radio leaves it to the listener to create the image conjured by the words.

2. The rewards of selling radio in the age of 10-, 15-, and 30-second "spotlets" (John Emmerling's word) include the fact that radio still offers an affordable 60 seconds.

3. Says RAB president Gary Fries, "Radio's unique attribute is intimacy with the customer. We're an extra member of everybody's family."

4. Virtually everybody in America listens to radio at some point during the average week, and the average person spends 3 hours and 18 minutes listening to radio on an average day.

5. Radio is one of the most cost-efficient of the major media forms. It offers a proportionately low cost per commercial announcement and the lowest production cost of any medium.

6. Trying to recover from a deep national recession in the early 1990s, local radio stations were creating partnerships, local marketing agreements called LMAs, that linked the selling efforts of several stations.

7 The stage was being set for the changes that reshaped the industry after the Telecommunications Act of 1996. "Let the deals begin!" was the headline in the first issue of *Radio & Records* after Congress passed the new legislation that shifted media paradigms.

8. The 1996 changes meant that one company could own as many as eight radio stations in a single major market— more than could be controlled nationally under the old seven-station limit, which lasted for decades. The new law set no upper limits to the number of stations any one company could own.

9. The Antitrust Division of the U.S. Department of Justice decided that no single market radio ownership combination could exceed half that market's advertising revenues. Radio found itself more viable than ever as an advertising medium after deregulation.

10. Rapid consolidation and mergers of radio companies was so difficult to track after Telecom 96 that the newsletter *Inside Radio* began publishing a weekly edition called "Who Owns What?" to rank station ownership groups, their estimated revenues, numbers of stations owned, and estimated national audiences.

11. On average, 71.4% of commercial radio stations were in some sort of consolidated clustering in late 1998, and the figures were over 75% in the largest (top 50) markets.

12. Radio networks underwent the same revolutionary changes that local station operations did thanks to a consolidating industry. The first to consolidate resources were Westwood One Networks and CBS Radio Networks.

13. The launch of the AMFM Networks, created by Chancellor Media at the beginning of 1998, was one of the largest new network debuts ever.

14. Radio network buying is generally done by the same high-level agency negotiators who buy network television. Just like TV sales, selling for a radio network requires patience and good negotiating skills.

15. The real difference between selling radio network time and selling TV network time is the agency's willingness to hear ideas about how to enhance a schedule at radio with value-added promotion.

16. There is a fine line between network radio and syndicated radio. Some syndicators sell commercials to advertisers, some sell programming to stations, some do both.

17. The advent of computer-based wide area networks (WANs) allowed local station groups to create their own networks, sharing morning shows or other air talent.

18. Radio salespeople were late to discover that they could sell to media planners as well as to buyers. Working with planners requires full knowledge of the (planner's) client's product.

19. Buyers don't like surprises, so an approach to the media planner should be done with the buyer's knowledge.

20. Two-thirds of agency media planners put spot radio at the top of a list of 14 different forms of national media, and planners who use radio tend to use it often.

21. RAB's Gary Fries notes that radio is "ahead of Yellow Pages, but still behind newspapers, magazines, and television in share of the dollar."
22. "What drives a radio station is localization," says Charlie Colombo. Local radio stations depend on local accounts who want to get commercial messages to their customers. Selling direct is radio's great strength.
23. Kerby Confer of Sinclair Communications says, "This is show business, and we should be in show business in the client's office as well as on the air." He suggests selling *ideas*, not just spots.
24. With the technology of desktop publishing, stations can make presentation materials look professional with little effort.
25. Putting your presentation in *client* terms makes the client the most important part of the discourse. Use language that the client or prospect uses every day.
26. Format differences are of tremendous advantage to advertisers who target their buys and their messages to the specific audiences of each station. Listeners are generally in a positive frame of mind when they choose their favorite music or favorite personality. That enhances their feelings toward commercials.
27. *Billboard* lists 17 distinct radio formats. Arbitron uses 38 different format designations. There are many styles that become subsets to each major format.
28. During the average quarter hour, 40% of full-time workers are listening to radio. An Arbitron study of radio usage at work countered assumptions made about the workplace and workplace listening.
29. Buying "by the numbers" is the worst way to purchase time on radio. Radio's inherent targetability should prompt agencies to buy audiences, but some don't take the time to learn subtle differences.
30. Radio is measured in two dimensions, cume and average quarter hour. GRPs are useful in television, not radio, because television is measured in one dimension: household rating points.
31. Radio's seven dirty words are "I tried it once. It didn't work." Usually that phrase translates into "It didn't meet my expectations." The solution is effective scheduling.
32. In radio, there's a delicate balance between reach and frequency. Steve Marx and Pierre Bouvard sought "effective reach"—those people reached often enough for advertising to be effective.
33. The number 3.29 is a point on a graph where total reach and effective reach begin to separate. Turnover times 3.29 yields Optimum Effective Scheduling (OES).
34. Radio salespeople should take advantage of the medium's greatest strength and play commercials for potential customers. By using what radio does best—provide interesting sound—the seller has the opportunity to engage the imagination of the retailer with a commercial for the advertiser's own store.
35. Michael Keith writes, "A spec spot should never (or rarely) be the plan itself but rather an element of the plan. In other words, design a package you know will do the job for the client, then use the spec spot to seal the deal."

Chapter Notes

1 Recycling is good for the environment and helpful to authors, too. The big parade in Griffin, Georgia, was lifted from "Lessons from Small Town Radio" in *LPTV* magazine, January/February 1984. Other pictures in the theater of my own mind were recalled in my foreword to Michael C. Keith's *The Radio Station*, cited in Chapter 1.
2 Jack Trout's comments appear in "The Industry Finally Grows Up," *Radio Ink*, July 8–21, 1996.

3 *Ogilvy on Advertising* has been cited previously.

4 John Emmerling attacked timid agency people and coined the word "spotlets" in "Agencies Fear Radio?" in *Advertising Age*, November 11, 1984.

5 Benefits of radio are top-of-mind with me, of course. I also referred to *Introduction to Advertising Media* by Jim Surmanek, cited previously, and to materials from the RAB, including *Media Facts, A Comprehensive Media Guide*, ©1996 by RAB.

6 More from *Radio Ink*'s long-gone "Advertiser Q&A" column. Bob Rose was interviewed May 24, 1993; Alec Gerster, February 1, 1993; and Sean Fitzpatrick, September 6, 1993.

7 The *Radio & Records* headline appeared February 16, 1996.

8 Station totals for Chancellor Media and Clear Channel Communications were updated after a tally published in *Broadcasting & Cable*, October 12, 1998.

9 Christopher H. Sterling outlined the Telecommunications Act of 1996 as it applied to radio in *Journal of Radio Studies*, IV, 1997.

10 *Billboard*'s Sean Ross told me his story when we were together at the Country Radio Seminar regional meeting in Kansas City in 1996.

11 Consolidation figures are from *Radio Business Report*, October 12, 1998.

12 *In Search of Excellence* was cited in Chapter 1.

13 Mel Karmazin on networks was in *Managers Business Report*, June 1997, and in "The Infinite Possibilities of Radio," *Broadcasting & Cable*, September 6, 1993.

14 First word of AMFM Networks came in *Inside Radio*, November 6, 1997. Also see "Kantor's 'net' move" by Katy Bachman in *Radio Business Report*, January 12, 1998, and the interview in *Hitmakers*, March 13, 1998.

15 "Premiere's Steve Lehman: From the 'Boonies' to the Board Room" by Katy Bachman appeared in *Radio Business Report*, June 9, 1997.

16 Presentations from Premiere, AMFM, ABC, and Westwood One radio networks contributed to this chapter.

17 Maureen Whyte of McCann-Erickson wrote an article about syndicated radio that was reprinted by United Stations Radio Network in its *News Update*, September 1997.

18 I was at the Detroit Radio Advertising Group's meeting when Karen Ritchie spoke and issued her challenge to radio. We covered it in information reports to Shane Media clients. Later, Karen participated in a project for our company as we introduced a music format called Radio X™.

19 Details of the Arbitron study of media planners came from *Arbitron Advertiser News*, May–June 1997.

20 The ideas from Gary Fries are combined from Gary's speeches to various industry groups and from my interview with Gary at the NAB's Radio Show, September 18, 1997.

21 I interviewed Charlie Colombo for "Playing the Local Song," *American Demographics*, September 1989. Charlie later became part of the United Stations Radio Network.

22 Kerby Confer spoke to the annual management conference of Forever Broadcasting, October 11, 1997, in Hidden Valley, Pennsylvania. In addition to his role at Sinclair Communications, Kerby founded Forever Broadcasting.

23 Jim Taszarek's comments from his session at the RAB conference were cited in Chapter 5.

24 The proposal ideas are from *Power Selling Tactics*, cited previously.

25 In the RAB's study guide, *Welcome to Radio Sales*, you'll find "Preparing Effective Presentations" by Mike Mahone.

26 Tony Schwartz was cited enviously in Chapter 1.

27 Just to confuse the format issue further, Arbitron uses *Billboard* format descriptors for its quarterly recap of share trends by format.

28 "Radio Goes to Work: The Arbitron At-Work Listening Study," © 1997, The Arbitron Company.

29 *Selling Radio Direct* was cited previously.

30 *Radio's Missing Ingredient* was cited previously. If you're a radio seller, you

should buy that book from the NAB and use it to your advantage. Also see "OES: One Step Beyond CPP" by Reed Bunzel in *The Radio Book*, cited previously.

31 Maureen Bulley of the Radio Store wrote "Generate Business with Spec Spots: Six Tips for Success" in *Radio Ink*, June 8, 1998.

32 Herschel Gordon Lewis wrote "Radio: The Misunderstood, Misused Medium" in *Direct Marketing*, July 1997.

33 Roy Williams' "12 Reasons for Advertising Failure" appeared in RAB's *Radio Sales Meeting*, September 1997.

Taking It Further

Here are a few Web sites that relate to this chapter and additional reading not included in the Chapter Notes.

www.arbitron.com—The Arbitron Company's homepage

www.biacompanies.com—Radio and TV industry figures

www.broadcast.com—Live audio of hundreds of radio stations

www.duncanradio.com—*Duncan's American Radio* with Arbitron information and ownership data

www.iradio.com—Radio marketing on the Internet

www.nab.org—The National Association of Broadcasters

www.onradio.electricvillage.com—A "syndicator" of Web sites for radio stations

www.rab.com—Radio Advertising Bureau

www.radioinfo.com—A directory and searchable database of radio stations and suppliers to the radio industry

www.radiowave.com—A subsidiary of Motorola, Inc., providing visuals along with live streaming of audio from radio stations

www.supertrends.com—Arbitron help from a non-Arbitron source

www.webradio.com—A service designed to distribute radio stations on the Internet and to take advantage of marketing opportunities

Additional Reading

Ditingo, Vincent M. *The Remaking of Radio*. Boston, MA: Focal Press, 1995.

Heath, Julie, and Gerald G. Hartshorn. *Numbers to Dollars: Using Audience Estimates to Sell Radio*. Washington, DC: National Association of Broadcasters, 1991.

Herweg, Godfrey W., and Ashley Page Herweg. *Radio Niche Marketing Revolution: FutureSell*. Boston, MA: Focal Press, 1997.

Radio 101: Radio Sales Ideas & Promotions That Will Make You Money! Washington, DC: National Association of Broadcasters, 1989.

Think Big: Event Marketing for Radio. Washington, DC: National Association of Broadcasters, 1994.

The Radio Book—Sales and Marketing. West Palm Beach, FL: Streamline Press, 1995.

Williams, Roy H. *The Wizard of Ads: Turning Words to Magic and Dreamers into Millionaires*. Austin, TX: Bard Press, 1998.

9

The Interactive Interim

Nobody knows what to call new media. Lots of people have tried to come up with just the right words.[1]

- *Broadcasting & Cable* adopted "Telemedia" as a weekly section heading.
- *Advertising Age* simply called their new media section "Interactive."
- *Wired* suggested the phrases "alternative media" and "Internet media." They seemed very old-fashioned and not up to *Wired*'s pithy style.
- The most-wired of *Wired*'s writers, Nicholas Negroponte, founder of MIT's Media Lab, called it, simply, "multimedia."
- "Merging" and "converging" were the favorite words during the waning years of the 1990s when things were, indeed, merging and converging. I use those words more often than the others.

To "merging" and "converging," I add "emerging." I like that it rhymes. But, more importantly, it also has meaning: "emerging" covers media that we haven't quite finished inventing, the ones that synthesize "old" media and morph ideas into new ones. Each seems to create its own starting point.

A good example of morphed media is MSNBC, the marriage of "old" NBC and "new" Microsoft Network (MSN). (See Figure 9–1). The media kit I received from them shows not only information about the programming on the MSNBC cable channel and a profile of the channel's viewers (very upscale) but also a Microsoft Network CD-ROM and a free one-month trial on MSN.

MSNBC Interactive (*www.msnbc.com*) differs from other "brand extension" Web sites in that it's not repackaged material from the major network but in-depth enhancements of the content on the MSNBC cable channel. "Converging" fits MSNBC perfectly, given the combination of NBC-TV, that network's affiliated stations, CNBC Cable, MSNBC Cable, and *msnbc.com* online. (See Figure 9–2.) The television network also maintained a Web content provider called "Interactive Neighborhood" for its affiliated stations.

Is there a definition for "new media"? This one is from the Direct Marketing Association's 1996 study "Marketing in the Interactive Age":

> Any electronic, interactive communications media that allow the user to request or receive delivery of information, entertainment, marketing materials, products, and services.

Get On Board with the Emerging Cable News Leader

NBC NEWS on Cable and the Internet
When You Really Want to Know

FIGURE 9–1 "Merging" and "converging" were among the first words you read in this book and one of the backdrops to selling electronic media of any kind. "Converging" fits MSNBC perfectly, although they prefer "emerging." Courtesy of NBC Cable Networks, Ad Sales Department, April 1998. ©1998, NBC Cable Networks.

New media are generally accepted quickly by early adopters who want to be the first with the latest. Then the new media spread slowly through the population, although "slowly" is not a word that really fits with merging, converging, and emerging new media.

Internet technology expanded so quickly that people began talking about "Web years" the same way they would about "dog years." *The Wall Street Journal* interactive edition celebrated its first birthday with artwork of a cake and a single candle. The headline said "Thanks for the First Seven Years (Web Years, That Is)." The newsletter *iRADIO* said on its masthead: "Since 1995 (that's 30 in Net years)."

That perception distracts us from the fact that even the newest media have history. The timeline is not as long or as deep as the histories of advertising, radio, and video, but there is history.

The History of New Media

The explosive growth of the Internet since 1995 belies its beginnings in 1969 when the Pentagon established it to link government and university computers. At first, the Internet simply reserved phone lines for joint research projects. In 1975, the National Science Foundation took over maintenance of the Internet. When funding ended in 1995, there was a rush to add commercial entities to the World Wide Web to maintain the worldwide connections. Commercial users of the Internet were the new source of funding.

Paralleling the Internet's quiet academic beginnings was the growth of interactive multimedia.[2] It began with the Pong video arcade game, introduced in 1972. That's the Stone Age in digital terms. More sophisti-

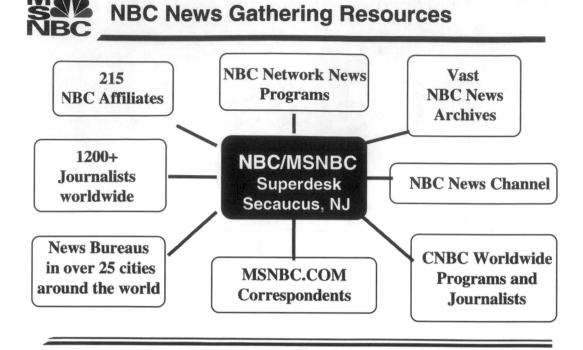

FIGURE 9–2 MSNBC combines the resources of its parent, NBC-TV, its sister cable network, CNBC, and its online presence at *www.msnbc.com* to give us a perfect metaphor for converging media. Courtesy of NBC Cable Networks, Ad Sales Department, April 1998. ©1998, NBC Cable Networks.

cated games followed. Atari's "Demon Attack" sold 2.6 million copies after its introduction in 1977. It was played on a $200 unit categorized as "a toy."

The years after Pong saw remarkable advances in digital multimedia: the Apple II with floppy drive (1978), the IBM PC with Microsoft's DOS (1981), the Macintosh (1984), Windows 1.0 (remarkable for 1985, but the digerati chose DOS), the Commodore Amiga computer (1986), and Harvard Graphics (1986).

The 1990s accelerated the pace of discovery of new ways to manipulate images, twist text, and connect ourselves with ever faster, ever more dazzling technology.

In a promotion for its annual convention and technical exhibition, the National Association of Broadcasters (NAB) in 1998 suggested that we were "living in the interactive interim." That's a very apt phrase that conjures what the NAB called "the Digital Halfway House—halfway between PC-TVs and TV-PCs, halfway between waveforms and bitstreams, halfway between Milton Berle and Virtual Vanna. . . ."

"With digital TV, you're not just a viewer anymore, you're part of the action," said an ad for Canal+ Technologies' set-top box called Mediahighway. (See Figures 9–3 and 9–4.)Touting that 2 million European households had already gone digital, Canal+ showed its wares at the same NAB convention. The theme of the gathering that year was "The Convergence Marketplace."

Research by Arbitron revealed that more than one-third of TV households in the United States had an interest in using their TV sets for some PC functions. A third

INFORMATION FIRST

Plain old news and information were the leading reasons consumers went online, according to a study by Market Facts for *Advertising Age*. The magazine noted in its 1996 report of the study: "[C]yber experts said entertainment would drive the nation to the information superhighway. . . but people are logging on for information, communication, and research much more than for entertainment."

In the 1998 study, the numbers of Net users seeking information was up, not down. *Advertising Age* said one of the key online activities is searching for product information on company home pages.[3]

Of those respondents who had been online in the 6 months before the 1998 study, 91.2% said they were there to gather news and information (up from 82.0% in 1996), 88.2% used e-mail, 79.4% conducted research, and 68.5% surfed various sites. The percentages of users who were surfing, playing games, or joining online chat sessions was down in 1998 compared to the two previous years.

Newspapers were an early staple on the World Wide Web, probably to attract some of the cachet of electronic media for the oldest commercial medium. *The New York Times* on the Web created a database of 1.7 million registrants in order to customize advertising messages to online users.[4] Some Web sites might as well be print, considering all the information they provide. Publishing on the Web is a cost-efficient way to distribute information.

A step above the publishing site is the self-service site where customers can do things for themselves, like check their bank balances or trace a FedEx package. The third step up is transaction-based and fully interactive, the real payoff for online users. IBM summed it up in a headline for its e-business services:

What's the Difference Between a Little Kid with a Web Site and a Major Corporation with One? Nothing. That's the Problem.[5]

I kept a copy of the *Kiplinger Washington Letter* from 1995 that asked the question, "Who runs the Internet?" The answer amused me: "No one in particular."[6] In fact, we all do. That's why there's a frenzied rush for Internet presence by huge corporations and by 8-year-olds, too.

of TV households said they'd like to use such a system for e-mail. A quarter said they'd like to do shopping online. Another quarter said they'd order tickets online.[7]

Internet use at the time that study was released (1998) was just ahead of where TV usage stood in 1969, but online activity was growing at an exponential rate. Simmons Market Research in 1997 showed Internet penetration at 20% of American households, up from 12.5% in only 2 years' time. *Advertising Age*'s sixth annual Interactive Media Study conducted in 1998 showed that 44.7% of a national sample had used the Internet. That compared with 30.2% the previous year.

"I was absolutely stunned by the increase in online usage," says Tom Mularz, vice president and general manager of Market Facts, the company that conducted the *Advertising Age* study. He said that the increase in online usage was the largest year-to-year increase since the research company started doing the survey in 1993.

The U.S. Department of Commerce reported in April, 1998, that online traffic was doubling every 100 days and that electronic commerce would likely reach $300 billion by 2002.[8] More than 100 million people were online, and the digital economy was growing at double the overall economy, representing more than 8% of the gross domestic product.

The Morgan Stanley publication, *The Internet Advertising Report*, which I quoted in Chapter 1, was also used in the Commerce Department data: radio took 30 years to reach an audience of 50 million; television took 13 years. The Internet took just four years.

Who knew it would grow that fast?

This is a TV-set...

FIGURE 9–3
Is it a TV or is it a PC? This one's a TV, and that's all.

Nicholas Negroponte did. He predicted at a meeting of Internet founders in 1994 that there would be one billion Internet users worldwide by 2000. His audience laughed or rolled their eyes. "Those who knew the most about the Net were the most conservative," he said.[9]

New Competition

There was debate in the late 1990s about whether the World Wide Web was cutting into TV viewing levels. For the Web to be the villain to television, said a study by J. Walter Thompson advertising, medium and heavy users of TV would have to change their behavior drastically. It could happen, if there were compelling content to lure them away.

It happened in Fall 1997. Nielsen Media Research reviewed its people meter panel from the October TV sweeps and found a decline in TV viewing in Internet households in certain dayparts. From 10 a.m. to 4:30 p.m., Internet households in Nielsen's sample watched 25% less television than the total TV universe.[10]

Networks that showed affinity for the Internet (ABC, Fox, NBC, and WB) had *higher* ratings in Internet households than in the TV universe generally. Could the marriage of TV

Set top box
run by Mediahighway

This is a phone, a supermarket, a computer, a movie theater, a bank, a game station, a radio, a video club, a mail box

and also a TV-set.

FIGURE 9–4
TV or PC? The answer is "yes." This advertisement for Canal + Technologies' Mediahighway System is a perfect metaphor for merging, converging, and emerging new media. Mediahighway is a trademark of Canal +. The ads are used with permission.

and the Web be far behind? *NewMedia* thinks that time will come:

> Someday, an online Lucy Ricardo will send the planet into hysterics with her wacky, interactive hijinks; a cyberspace Johnny Carson will colonize a corner of the American evening; and a Net-bred Ted Koppel will make presidential candidates squirm with his laserlike questions—fed to him in real time by a nation of plugged-in voters.[11]

This paragraph was the preface for an article called "The Web's Fall Season," an overview of the pioneering efforts of interactive producers who hoped to make a mark in cyberspace. America Online and Microsoft Network hunted for new ideas from multimedia developers working on shoestring budgets. Smaller players like WebTV and C/NET were going Hollywood with the big guys. Traditional entertainment companies—HBO and Sony Pictures were cited in the article—hoped to take their TV and movie business interactive.

A dilemma arose: how to provide programming that satisfies two types of audiences—the "sit back and watch" people and those who want to interact online. Were the Hollywood people deluding themselves? No, they were just looking for something they might not recognize if they saw it.

"There's a great opportunity to blend television and the online experience, but I don't think anyone's cracked the code on that yet," says Rob Jennings of America Online to *NewMedia*. "The buzz in Hollywood is how to actually make that bridge."

Madeline Kirbach of M3P, Microsoft Multimedia Productions, said, "We've probably seen a couple of thousand proposals, we've taken to development a couple of hundred, then to production a couple of dozen. That gives you an idea."

For all the TV talk—even Microsoft was calling its programming "shows" and referring to "channels"—the Web is not television. Television, like print, is a one-way medium. That's not value judgment; that's fact. The telephone and the Internet are two-way media. That doesn't make them better, only different. And different is what punches new ideas through.

In Fall 1997, AOL found the bridge Jennings was talking about and launched its AOL Network with "infotainment" shows, interactive sci-fi, comedy, and Hollywood themes.[12] At that time, there was no streaming video, but the programming used TV-style titles ("The Hub," "Kids Only," and "Newsstand," for example) and TV celebrity Joan Lunden hosting chat sessions and updated content sections on "AOL Today."

By February 1998, AOL was averaging 600,000 users. A media tracking study released in May of that year by McCann-Erickson advertising agency called the AOL Network "the fastest growing network." McCann charted AOL on a timeline that included ESPN, CNN, and MTV. The agency concluded: "Not only is AOL the fastest-growing network; but, at its current rate of growth, it will soon be the number-one cable network."

AOL president (and former MTV executive) Bob Pittman told the online magazine *Adtalk*: "The TV experience is very different from the PC experience. We are confident that we will play a leadership role when the time is right."

When's the time right? The week before the McCann-Erickson study was released, AOL had agreed to acquire NetChannel, once a competitor to Microsoft's WebTV, which enables TV users to view online content on their TV sets. NetChannel would allow AOL to expand beyond the users-only base to the 98 million TV households in the United States.

The ground for new channels was fertile as AOL made its move. Cable had whittled away at the shares of the traditional TV networks. The original Big Three had become the Big Four (by adding Fox), then the Big Six (with UPN and WB in the mix), with others testing the traditional TV network waters. When NBC-TV's *Seinfeld* aired its last episode in the series, the network also promoted the last seasonal episode of *ER* on the same night. Focusing on the end of the TV seasons indicated that, at least at the network level, NBC was working on the old TV paradigm.

"Seasons" came from the days of TV as a truly mass, national, homogenizing medium. That was a time when all school systems worked on a September-to-May schedule, all moms stayed at home and baked bread and apple pies, and all families vacationed at the same time, reducing summer TV viewing.

This is no longer the case. The new paradigm is the viewer's ability to watch anything at any time, whether it's distributed by traditional mass media, individualized media like video rentals, or one-on-one online downloads.

Even though NBC-TV followed the old paradigm, as a company NBC was first among the conventional broadcast networks to embrace the idea of media convergence. As *Wired* put it, "NBC has staked its entire future on convergence—on the assumption that unlimited choices in en-

tertainment, information, and transactions, in video, audio, and text, are moving inexorably onto a single home appliance, in a way that undermines traditional media economics."

Wired pointed out that at the time NBC entered its agreements to mine cyberspace, the NBC-TV network was on track for a record $1 billion in annual profits while five other broadcast networks were at best barely breaking even. When he first joined the network, NBC president and CEO Robert Wright "would grimly tell advertisers, competitors, and underlings that the networks had to re-make themselves—or die," reported *Wired*. Sure enough, NBC did so, making itself ready for new media.[13]

Net Gain

"New media" has so many meanings. It's the CD-ROM dictionary that allows you to virtually examine the quality of *aba* or to speak Komi like a Zyrian[14]. It's the digital downlink that helps you bypass cable or broadcast television. Most often, "new media" means the Internet generally and the World Wide Web specifically.

I concentrate on the Internet because of its rapid impact and its potential as an advertising medium. In *The Internet Advertising Report*,[15] Morgan Stanley's Mary Meeker suggests that "the Web may be the single most important development in technology since the debut of the PC, and that, in time, it should have a pervasive effect on our daily lives." The Internet was growing at an unprecedented pace, "creating enormous opportunities for investment and wealth creation," Meeker says.

Interviewed by *Time Digital*, she outlines six major issues facing the Internet:

1. Figuring out the appropriate company valuations. (In *The Internet Advertising Report,* she says that investors like subscription- and transaction-based companies more than advertising supported companies.)

2. Determining which companies provide the best portals to the Web. The con-

tenders were Yahoo!, America Online, Netscape, Microsoft, Excite, and C/Net. "These companies are creating assets like those created by NBC, CBS, and ABC in the early days of TV broadcasting."

3. The growth of Web commerce and advertising revenue. "We think Web retailing will grow dramatically and Web advertising will grow three-ish times the 1997 level."

4. How quickly enterprises launch Web sites, create in-house online resources for their employees, and develop direct online links with other businesses.

5. How successful America Online will be with its transition to the Internet.

6. How Microsoft's "relentless effort" to gain market share in all categories will impact other players.[16]

When my company applied for *www.shanemedia.com* back in 1994, we were one of 22,511 who requested a URL that year. That seemed like a lot at the time. But compare that figure to 1996, when a staggering 657,000 domain names were registered. When InterNIC began registering names, in 1985, there were only 29. Now the numbers are in the 6,000-plus range *per day*!

About 50% of U.S. companies had their own Web sites by the end of 1997. Of those, about 66% used them mostly for advertising, marketing, and public relations, according to RHI Consulting, which commissioned the study among 1,400 chief information officers. The best indication I had that the Web was to be ubiquitous was when Frank, the Exxon dealer across from our office, told me to log on to his site for coupons.

As part of a wide-ranging survey on a variety of media issues, the American Association of Advertising Agencies reported in 1998 that 55% of advertisers were buying interactive media to advertise their brands. (See Figure 9–5.) Jake Winebaum of Disney Online told *Wired* that eight car companies were advertising with *Disney.com*.[17] "I've called on car companies for 12 years, selling print ads, television shows, and now sponsorships on the Internet. The difference in the meetings I've had vis-á-vis the Internet and all other media has been profound: In the Internet meetings, they're saying, 'Jake, we're selling cars online—lots of them.'"

Benefits and Drawbacks of Online Advertising

Earlier we looked at the benefits of other electronic media: television's visual appeal, the way it permeates American life, its mass appeal, its reach, and its variety. Cable has similarities with broadcast TV as well as its own unique attributes: vertical niches, geographic targeting, and upscale viewers. Radio offers flexibility, ubiquitous reach, cost-efficiency, and the "theater of the mind." Advertising on the Internet has its own assets and liabilities. The main assets are:[18]

- Advertising is accessible, on demand, 24 hours a day.
- Distribution costs are low, so reaching a million targets is the same as reaching one.
- Content drives access, so opportunities for market segmentation are great.
- A one-on-one, direct marketing relationship can be created with the consumer.
- Content can be updated, supplemented, or changed at any time.
- Responses are highly measurable.
- Navigation is easy. The consumer controls the destination and spends as much time as desired.

The case against Internet advertising presents these objections:

- There's no clear standard for measuring success.

- The variety of advertising formats on the Internet is so great that comparisons from ad to ad are difficult.
- Traditional advertising needs—ratings, share, reach, and frequency—are difficult to assess.
- The audience is still small.
- Online service providers store, or cache, Web pages to speed up delivery to subscribers. The original site's server doesn't record page views properly.
- Text-only browsing allows images to be turned off and advertising is not viewed.
- If the page is longer than the browser viewing space, advertiser content at the bottom of the page may not be seen.
- Users may leave a page before an ad downloads.

Like advertising in any traditional medium, Internet advertising is all about reaching potential customers and making an impression on them. Web publishers are responsible for attracting traffic, and advertisers are challenged to develop a creative experience to capitalize on that traffic.

"Well-designed advertising creative, delivered in the right environment with complementary content, is a key driver of advertising success," says *The Internet Advertising Report*. "It is important that ads not be too intrusive, and we believe the more an advertisement seems like a value-added

FIGURE 9–5 The Internet and the World Wide Web generate new ideas just by being there. The Property Channel, a Web site for the real estate industry, ran this ad for sellers in *Advertising Age*. Used with permission.

service to the user and less like an invasion of privacy, the more successful that ad will be in driving traffic or business to wherever it is connected."

The *Report* suggests that a Web site should be an advertisement in itself and uses Absolut Vodka (*www.absolutvodka.com*) and Clinique (*www.clinique.com*) as examples. Those sites "have attempted to create compelling content and interesting and informative resources for users about their products, industry, or even content (through games, and so forth)."

What to Sell?

Revenues for Internet advertising increased 200% per year between 1996 and 1997 with no expectations that the increas-es would level off. What brought in all that money? Here are some answers:[19]

- *Links.* Anything on a Web page that drives traffic to another site is a link, also known as a "hyperlink." A link can be a button, hypertext, or a banner. To understand the importance of links, consider the fact that Yahoo!, Excite, Infoseek, and Lycos spent $5 million to be on Netscape's search page. That positioning puts them in the way of an enormous amount of traffic that comes through the Netscape site.
- *Banners.* Typically, a banner is a horizontal rectangle that looks like a little billboard. (Some advertisers actually call them billboards.) Typical size is 468 × 60 pixels. The banner contains text, usually the advertiser's slogan. GIF, Java, or other animation tends to increase response rates.

Many banners house an imbedded link to the sponsor's site. That link creates a "click-through" and is called a "nonenhanced" banner. With an "enhanced" banner, the user never leaves the original page. All the advertising appears on the banner.

The most effective banners are targeted specifically to the user viewing the page, based on registration at the site, a previous link, the browser, affiliation (AOL, Prodigy), and domain (*.edu*, *.com*, *.org*, etc.).

- *Click-throughs.* Some banners are sold by impression, others by the number of times users click on the ad and link to the advertiser's Web site. The advertiser gets a sense of the results of the campaign rather than estimates that resemble radio or TV ratings.

Not surprising, one of the basic rules of selling and copywriting works in the multimedia environment: banners with the words "Click Here" increase click-through rates from 40% to 300%. It pays to ask for the order!

- *Buttons.* Like banners, buttons offer a click-through, but usually to a software download site. Buttons are typically 120 × 90 pixels or 120 × 60 pixels. Some buttons allow users to download software directly, while others link to a product page with descriptive text.

- *Key words.* When a search engine looks for a topic, it does so by key word. Advertisers to buy key words that relate to products or services. The advertiser's banner is shown when the user searches for the advertiser's word.
- *Portals.* Yahoo!'s Tim Koogle calls portals "the only place where someone has to come to connect to anything or anybody in the world." Yahoo! is a portal, so Koogle spoke in hyperbolic terms. An advertising portal is a linkable graphic in the tool bar area of a site that links to another site specified by the advertisers.
- *Interstitials.* The most old-media-like of new media advertising, interstitials are flashes of imagery or branding information that appear between pages of a site. They're comparable to single frames of a TV commercial.

The online magazine *MediaCentral Digest* predicts, "As sites become increasingly application-like, for example *Blender.com* and BeZerk's NetShows, interstitial advertising will contribute to the goal of making the Web more like television by interrupting the content with an ad." (There was no indication of whose "goal" that might have been.)

- *Pop-up windows.* Separate windows that appear over site content while a page is loading are called pop-up windows and are approximately 245 × 245 pixels (that's my imprecise count). The idea is to increase impact without slowing down the user's Web experience.

CondeNet Marketing created the five-second pop-up window for its food and travel sites in 1997, and they were embraced by the industry because they increased click-throughs by 200%.

- *Offline ads.* These are coupled with "push" content, where the user requests tailored news or information. As an example, if a customer subscribes to Point-Cast in order to get CNN news, PointCast automatically begins running when the customer's computer is not in use, replacing the screensaver with CNN headlines. (The viewer selects up to ten channels of content.)

Animated ads are delivered to each content screen with links to the advertisers' Web sites. The service allows advertisers to customize delivery based on content requested, demographics, or psychographics.

- *Inline ads.* This type of ad is an online "advertorial" positioned within a site, thereby adding credibility to an advertising message. Auto manufacturers have used this idea to great advantage to create online "showrooms" for vehicles.
- *Sponsored content.* Another variation on old media, sponsored content refers to an advertiser's "ownership" of a site the same way a TV advertiser "owns" a show or a sporting event by purchasing sponsorship rights.

What works? The Internet Advertising Bureau (IAB) reported that banners were responsible for 96% ad awareness. The same study showed real weakness for click-throughs in the same awareness category.[20] In contrast, Berkeley Systems, the operators of the BeZerk games site *www.bezerk.com*, claimed that interstitials generate even higher brand awareness than banners.

Whom do we believe? Since Berkeley is home of "You Don't Know Jack" and other interactive games, their findings about interstitials are true more for their site than for others.

A Grey Advertising study cosponsored by SOFTBANK Interactive and the Advertising Research Foundation found that the size of an ad is important when the advertiser wants to be noticed (why advertise otherwise?). Large-format ads produced higher recall than banners. Over three-quarters of respondents (76%) remembered seeing interstitials; 71% recalled split-screen ads. In contrast, 51% recalled banner ads.

In questions about whether the ads were irritating, 15% said interstitials were; 11% said split-screens were; and 9% said banner ads were. Respondents favored enhanced banners, which do not take them off the site they had chosen to visit.

The 1998 *Advertising Age* Interactive Media Study indicated a decrease in response to online advertising compared to 1997 figures. The survey asked, "How often do you look at banner ads?" In 1998, 48.5% said "never," up from 38.7% in 1997. On the other hand, more than a quarter (26.5%) of online users said they'd be more likely to click on video ads, and 24.5% said they would download special software to view video ads. The drop in interest in banner ads could be a product of online users becoming bored with banners and looking for something new.

All indications are that response to banners drops dramatically after the first or second viewing, so the best response rates come from banners bought for reach, not frequency. Thunder Lizard Productions, presenters of Web advertising conferences, advised, "Buy small (for larger sites, less than 10% of inventory) and buy wide (lots of sites)."

HotWired Network translated "buy small and buy wide" into a service called "reach-frequency management." Their system allowed targeted visitors to see an ad for only a specified number of times before the ad rotated on to different visitors. In this way, an advertiser could show an ad to 50,000 unique Web visitors no more than four times, thus creating 200,000 impressions.

DoubleClick introduced a similar frequency management feature when they launched their service in March 1996. DoubleClick claimed that few Net surfers will click on an ad banner after seeing it more than four times (less than 1%, they said). By comparison, nearly 3% click on first impression.

Internet Profiles Corp., the company that provides I/PRO Web audits, also introduced an automated buying service, called "Dispatch." The goal was to help media buyers compare advertising buys across a variety of sites. Until I/PRO's announcement, there had been no standard way to submit online campaign data to Web sites and track ad performance across all the sites in a buy.

While selling banners and other online advertising, GeoCities developed what they called "neighborhoods" for their mil-

FIGURE 9–6
Note the need for experience in national media sales or an ad agency. When this ad ran in late 1997, few people had experience in new media selling. Courtesy *mplayer.com*. Used with permission.

Internet Ad Director/Sales Positions

Mplayer.com, one of the top entertainment communities on the net, has advertising management and senior sales positions available across the country. Our rapidly growing service offers some of the net's most desirable target groups and media options. All salaries commensurate with experience. Excellent benefits, including 401(k) and stock options.

Western Advertising Sales Director
The successful candidate will establish relationships and build revenue for the Western Region while managing the Bay Area HQ sales team. Strong persuasive communication skills are essential. Minimum 5+ years national media sales required. Internet and agency experience a plus.

Regional Sales Representatives
Positions available in NY, Chicago and SF/Bay Area. 2-5 years proven track record in national media sales or 4+ years agency experience. Internet sales a plus. Self-starter with strong communication/presentation skills a must.

Please send/fax resume and cover letter to:
**Mplayer.com
Att: Ad Recruitment
665 Clyde Avenue
Mountain View, CA 94043
FAX (650) 429-3911
Or e-mail resumes to: ad_jobs@mplayer.com**

lion plus "homesteaders," the name GeoCities gives their online visitors. The concept combined GeoCities advertisers into 40 special interest areas, like "Napa Valley," which covered food, wine, dining out, and "the gourmet lifestyle," as they termed it.

For the Visa credit card company, GeoCities added a section to Napa Valley called "Restaurant Row," where users could read recipes and restaurant reviews and post their own if they wanted. The site also offered to build free Web sites for epicureans.

Web Networks

GeoCities, HotWired Network, and DoubleClick are distant cousins of traditional networks like ABC, CBS, and NBC, linking advertisers rather than local media outlets. Each operation provides one-stop shopping for an advertiser trying to reach large numbers of Web users one at a time.

LinkExchange, on the other hand, is an all-new model based on the specific needs of the Web. It is a banner-swapping network of more than 100,000 sites that deliver about four million ad views per day, according to statistics from I/PRO. Telling the LinkExchange story, *Wired* calls it "a good old-fashioned Web success story—youth,

idealism, a good idea, 24-hour workdays, and, somewhere down the road, the possibility of making lots and lots of money." Two Harvard computer science graduates, Sanjay Madan and Tony Hsieh, started LinkExchange as a side business during their first post-collegiate jobs at Oracle.[21]

The idea behind LinkExchange is to help small business clients generate traffic by linking sites. "We want to bring banner advertising to everyone on the Web, not just the big corporations," says Madan. From that goal was born the world's largest ad network, identifying 1,600 narrowly defined interest groups so advertisers can target precisely.

Because LinkExchange is supported by sponsors, members of the network advertise their sites for free. Members determine where they want their banners shown and what type of targeting will work best—by category, by rating level, and by business status. Here's how LinkExchange describes the process in their online media kit:

> Our rating system and filtering technology helps ensure that the banners appearing on your site are appropriate for your audience, and that your banners appear on sites that would appeal to your potential visitors.
>
> Please Note: LinkExchange does not accept sites containing adult material, links to adult material, or other inappropriate content as outlined in our Terms and Conditions.
>
> You can view your stats in a summary or daily format. We provide you with up-to-the-minute statistics about:

- The number of times your site is visited
- The number of times your banner is displayed
- The number of times your banner is clicked on
- Your display-to-click ratio

LinkExchange also maintains a searchable directory of all of its members, with each site's target categories. Precision targeting is the most powerful aspect of the Internet as an advertising medium. The advertiser has the ability to filter messages to selected audiences based on exacting criteria and thus dictate the composition of an advertisement's audience.

Making Money

Projections developed by Forrester Research and quoted in *The Internet Advertising Report* show newspapers to be the long-term victims of Web advertising. More than 10% of newspaper revenues will be funneled to online advertising by 2001, compared to 5.1% from Yellow Pages, 0.8% from radio, and 0.3% from television. (See Figure 9–7.)

Advertisers have to approach the Web the way they would approach any form of traditional media, by asking, "What's the best way to reach the prospects for my goods or services?" Morgan Stanley's *The Internet Advertising Report* outlines it this way:

> When advertisers make media buying decisions, they use a rate card supplied by each of the potential sites, magazines, and the like. The rate card lists the rate (most likely in CPMs) that the publisher charges for each type of advertising product it offers....Web sites might list the CPM for their banners, along with prices for products like buttons or key words, all tailored to the particular vehicle that site might provide.

In a discussion of Web pricing, Thunder Lizard, the conference production company, relied on old-fashioned imagery: "Ad rates on the Web are like laws in the wild west—they're tough to enforce, every town is different, and it helps if you're carrying a big gun. The most common model charges between 20 and 50 dollars per thousand impressions, but variables include type of buy, targeting, duration, and number of impressions per month."

An unnamed Tribune Ventures executive mused to *MediaCentral Digest*, "When your ad rates are $50 per thousand and you only have 10% to 50% sell-through, do you take a lower price? Or do you drop your CPM? No one has the right answer yet."

At Web Advertising '98, a conference sponsored by *Advertising Age*, the response was, essentially, take the lower price: "It's a buyer's market at this point—more than 50% of inventory goes unsold—so the bargains are definitely out there."

Revenue Lost to the Internet

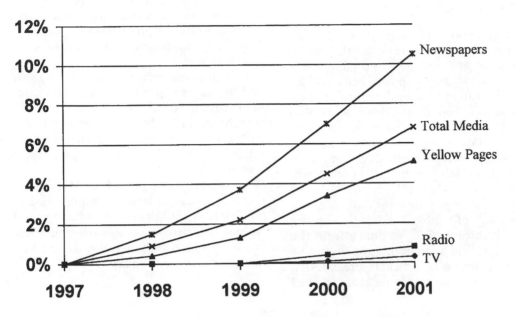

FIGURE 9–7 Traditional media stand to lose 6.8% of revenues to Internet advertising by 2001, if projections by Forrester Research, quoted in *The Internet Advertising Report*, are accurate. Newspapers stand to be the biggest losers.

The Cost-per-Thousand (CPM) Myth

CPMs vary widely on the Web, much to the consternation of advertisers used to traditional media. To the national or network television buyer, eyeballs are eyeballs; the more eyeballs, the more efficient the buy. They look at Internet advertising as costly, as much as 66% higher than television. That's true. Television is, after all, a mass-reach medium.

The Internet advertiser must remember first that while the Net reaches large audiences in terms of numbers, each audience member is reachable in a one-on-one setting. LinkExchange identified 1,600 audience categories, and that's just a start! There are potentially as many categories as there are users.

This takes the discussion about CPM in Chapter 8 on selling radio and magnifies the absurdity. New media are about true "demassification" (to borrow Alvin Toffler's word) and "1:1" communication (using Don Peppers' ratio).

"Most of what is published by the analyst community promulgates the Web CPM myth," wrote Rick Boyce in a special report for advertisers published by the IAB. "As any media planner will tell you, it is impossible to compare CPM objectively across different media without accounting for the level of targeting the advertiser wants to reach."

Boyce illustrated his idea with this example:

A 30-second network prime time spot delivered a $12 CPM against all U.S. households.

Refine that audience to adults 18–49 with a household income of $50,000 a year and the head of household with a year or more of college, and the CPM jumps to $49.15.

"As a single point of reference," Boyce said, "consider that a banner schedule can be purchased on *Quote.com*—which delivers an audience with an average household income of $110K and 70% college graduates—for under a $50 CPM. Once television CPMs are adjusted to account for reaching a specific target audience, the economies of Web advertising—particularly for reaching discreet [sic], affluent target audiences—becomes clear."

Pricing strategy for most sites is based on a variety of factors: market conditions, research information, feedback from the sales force, and availability of advertising opportunities on a particular site. C/NET, for example, operated nine sites in 1997 with price ranges from $15 CPM to $100 CPM. The company's shareware download service increased pricing from $20 CPM to $30 CPM that year based on supply and demand.

Run-of-site advertising on C/NET's search engine was decreased that same year from $20 CPM to $15 CPM to stimulate demand, according to MediaCentral's *Online Tactics*.

Mecklermedia vice president and general manager Chris Elwell told the same publication: "Content sites are not like search engines. There's a cost associated with creating content, and therefore, ad rates have to reflect continuing costs of content creation."

Elwell suggested that the CPM for an online magazine for consumers might be $35, while a trade publication can justify $100. "If you can prove to the advertisers that you have a good audience, you should have to charge more," he said.

NOTICEABLE ADVERTISING

In a 1997 study for the IAB, MBinteractive concluded that "online advertising is more likely to be noticed than television advertising."

First, Web users are actively using the medium instead of passively receiving it.

Second, there's less advertising online. The typical ad banner is 468 × 60 pixels, a total of 28,080 square pixels. A typical default screen is 640 × 480 pixels, or 307,200 square pixels.

That's 91.4% content against 8.6% advertising, something no other electronic medium can claim!

City Sites

The battle for local community information on the Internet has been heating up since America Online created Digital City with localized information for cities across the United States. Other entries in the local market were Microsoft with *Sidewalk.com*, CitySearch, CityWeb, and NBC's Interactive Neighborhood, created for NBC-TV affiliated stations.

Cox Interactive Media was actually one of the first, but received little national notice because they approached the idea conservatively, establishing Access Atlanta and refining the site *accessatlanta.com* before launching other city services. Cox took pains to go deeper than the typical information. Any site can report a weather emergency, but Cox sites add road conditions and life-saving information. As the newsletter *iRADIO* pointed out, the Cox sites are more than simply "community bulletin boards."

Cox owns plenty of media outlets, but, as Cox Interactive's Michael Parker put it,

"We're not putting our newspaper, radio, and television stations online, that is the formula for sporadic visits." Instead, Parker told *Advertising Age,* Cox wants to communicate that their local sites "provide information [and] emotional attachment."

Cox sites do use their media outlets well. Access Atlanta, for example, gets weather information and lottery numbers from WSB-TV. There's access to editorials from the *Atlanta Journal–Constitution* newspaper. "Do research in the Journal–Constitution's archives," says a link. Traffic information comes from WSB Radio. But the site is self-contained.

Tribune Ventures, the interactive arm of Chicago's Tribune Company, maintains Web presence for its newspapers in Chicago, Orlando, Fort Lauderdale, and Newport News, Virginia. The company also owns 20% of Digital City, which has sites in each area where Tribune owns papers. (The other 80% of Digital City is owned by AOL, and the service began in 14 cities.)

The Virtual Marketplace

I received an advertisement from a promotion company in Pennsylvania with copy that sums up the new media paradigm: "This is America. You're allowed to shop for 200 pens at 1 a.m. if you want to."

This is the point where all of life merges and converges with media—online commerce. People want to check their account balances, transfer funds, and book flights when they want to. Time zones are irrelevant. The nine-to-five office is irrelevant.

IBM's advertising for its e-business (electronic-business) systems seemed hyperbolic at first: "E-business will transform the economy, alter the rules of competition, and shake up the status quo."[22]

Hyperbole faded as predictions were made of $176 billion worth of goods expected to be purchased online in 2001. Those numbers were revised upward by Forrester Research in 1998 when they projected business-to-business electronic commerce at $183 billion in 2001 and online retail revenues at $17 billion. The predictions came after 1996 figures reached $1.3 billion and the Department of Commerce projections of $300 billion.

Fueling the unprecedented totals were online trading of stocks and mutual funds by Charles Schwab, which opened over one million new accounts online. Cisco Connection Online, a business-to-business site, reported selling $11 million in networking equipment *per day*! Dell Computers claimed $5 million a day from its Web site. Microsoft's Expedia travel service sells airline tickets at the rate of $4 million a week from its site.

Ticketmaster sold $35 million in concert and event tickets from its Web site in 1997, approximately 3% of its total ticket sales.[23]

Electronic banking was available to 60% of households in North America through a network of 16 banks and VISA USA. The collaboration established a standard for Internet bank card security, overcoming a deterrent to e-commerce: consumer fear of credit information being stolen online.

The most prominent story in e-commerce was Amazon.com, Inc., billed as "Earth's Biggest Bookstore." Founded in 1995, Amazon quickly became the leading online seller of books. (While the company sold compact discs, videotapes, and audiotapes, books comprised more than 90% of sales in 1997.) All Amazon purchases are made on the Web at *www.amazon.com* and are delivered via third party services such as UPS and FedEx.[24]

At retail, the total book market is about $26 billion in the United States and $82 billion worldwide. By comparison, Amazon online sales are insignificant: a cumulative total of $98 million through the third quarter of 1997, to approximately 610,000 customers.

The difference between Amazon and a retail bookseller is space. The size of the retail store limits its inventory, which is why many booksellers create niches based on the population available to them (i.e., the University bookstore) or categories of books (business books, mystery books, etc.). As a Web-based business, Amazon has no such limitations, and offers most of the 1.5 mil-

410   THE INTERACTIVE INTERIM

lion English-language books believed to be in print, with a total of 2.5 million titles. Amazon's success attracted national bookstore chains Barnes & Noble and Borders Group to enter online retailing.

A report on Amazon's performance by Everen Securities gave a glimpse into the future of online selling: "On the basis of our analysis of retailing costs, we believe the efficiency of the Web site as a retailing mechanism should lead to significant cost advantages over even the most efficient of location-based retailers."

The investment community responded also to K-Tel International, the direct marketer of music CDs and tapes, when it said it would launch online sales; to CDNow, when the online music seller went public; and to N2K when it sold stock shares to an underwriting group.[25] Music sellers are expected to gain even further ground in e-commerce once encryption technology allows downloading music to consumers without fear of copyright violation.

User's Guide

When you're selling online advertising, you're probably going to be regarded as the expert. Users of traditional media will ask for help in presenting their messages online. On the other hand, new media is a field full of experts—the users themselves—some of whom have had a mouse in their hands since infancy.

The basic rules for creating an Internet marketing plan and implementing it with creative messaging follow:[26]

View the Internet as an Adjunct

"Online and offline media are a perfect couple," says Kim Bayne in *The Internet Marketing Plan*. Building Web presence is not enough. Advertisers need to be reminded to use traditional media to drive traffic to a Web site.

"If your direct mail campaign is working, don't trade it for the Internet," Bayne advises. "If your TV campaign is working, don't trade it for the Internet. Use the Internet to enhance programs that are already working. If you notice a shift in how customers are gathering your literature and how they are contacting you, then it's time to regroup—but not before."

Think Quality, Not Quantity

The "eyeballs are eyeballs" theory of media buying does not apply to the Internet. Evan Schwartz, author of *Webonomics*, suggests creating a "sense of community among a group of ultradesirable clients."

Reciprocate

Give the customer advantages that are as good as what you'd like to get from the customer. If you're asking for personal demographic information, make it worth the customer's while by offering incentives such as gifts, advice, discounts, or entertainment information. For example, Chrysler offered its vehicle owners free wiper blades for participating in an online survey, according to Schwartz. Others offer online users credits against airline frequent flyer miles, stays at hotels, and other noncash incentives.

Use E-Mail Strategically

Advertisers can communicate with one, two, three, or thousands of customers at once. E-mail can provide customer service, build relationships, distribute newsletters, and so forth. "If you choose to contact your customers via e-mail," Bayne warns, "do so with caution, incorporating business ethics and professional courtesy. If someone has contacted you, you know they are already interested in your company. This is the time to ask them if they would like to receive regular news through either e-mail or another method."

Create Extra Value

Why do customers come back to a Web site? Because they perceive that the site offers continuing benefits. New and updated information is a key benefit online. Bayne suggests adding to every update a note of the date and the person who updated the files.

In *Selling on the Net,* Herschell Gordon Lewis tells us to highlight whatever's new. "It can be new product or new uses for product. Healthy Choice offers a new healthy recipe, using their products of course, every day."

Schwartz reminds us that "there's no such thing as a completed Web site. Even at the best-designed Web location, information is as perishable as a baker's goods. Today's aromatic loaves are tomorrow's day-old bread. Don't let your site get stale."

Plan for the Long Term

"Don't sign up for an Internet account intending to try it for a while," Bayne advises. "Take your Internet opportunity seriously. Creating and maintaining an Internet presence takes dedication, time, ingenuity, time, resources, and time."

Design with Online in Mind

Ads in cyberspace are not print ads, and they're not television ads. They're interactive online ads. Advise advertisers to investigate the unique features of the Internet and to take advantage of them.

Lewis advises Net copywriters to "never be the bottleneck. Use a computer powerful enough to handle your site's load with adequate speed connecting to the Internet so the bits aren't waiting in line on your end."

He also suggests using "grabbers" early in your text. Since text loads before graphics, the text should make the visitor want to wait for the graphics. He says the word "free" still works in spite of overuse and abuse.

One more rule from Lewis: Offer interactivity early in the text. "Give them something to do."

The Attention Economy

Early in the book, I tied advertising to the economy of abundance, saying advertising is impossible to separate from the economy as a whole. When supply outstrips demand (as in the U.S. economic system, for example), advertising fulfills an essential function: moving merchandise from the manufacturer to the consumer.

Where does supply outstrip demand even more than in the general economy of abundance? It happens in nations like ours that find an increasing number of workers working not in production or transportation of goods but in managing information. It's been called "the information glut" and "the information explosion." It's even called "the information economy," but that's a misnomer if you define economics as the study of how a society uses scarce resources. In our lives, there's certainly no scarcity of information!

In cyberspace, information is not only abundant, it's overflowing. In traditional media there's just as much. You may call it "data" rather than "information," but it overflows regardless of its name.

What is scarce is enough attention to attend to all the information that tempts us. "Attention has its own behavior, its own dynamics, its own consequences," says writer Michael Goldhaber of the University of California at Berkeley.[27]

Because attention is a limited resource, Goldhaber's theory is that ours is—or will be—an "attention economy." Attention is scarce, Goldhaber wrote in *Wired*, "and the total amount per capita is strictly limited . . . . The size of the attention pie can grow as more and more people join the world audience, but the size of the average slice can't."

The Internet creates an unusual context for the attention economy. Goldhaber writes:

In cyberspace, there is nothing natural about large-scale divisions like cities, nations, bureaucracies, and corporations. The only divisions, and rough ones at that, are among audiences, entourages, and what could be called attention communities. Each community is centered on some topic and usually includes a number of stars, along with their fans. Attention flows from community to community. Below this primary exchange will flow the less important exchange of goods and materials.

He says the attention economy changes advertising, too, since "ads will exist only to attract and direct attention."

That information provides a good background for understanding the function of advertising on the Internet.

Review Highlights and Discussion Points

1. Nobody knows what to call new media. Lots of people have tried to come up with just the right words. "Merging and converging" were the favorite words during the waning years of the 1990s when things were, indeed, merging and converging. Add to this the word "emerging."

2. A good example of morphed media is MSNBC, the marriage of "old" NBC and "new" Microsoft Network (MSN). "Converging" fits MSNBC perfectly, given the combination of NBC-TV, that network's affiliated stations, CNBC Cable, and *msnbc.com* online.

3. New media are generally accepted quickly by "early adopters" who want to be the first with the latest. Then the new media spread slowly through the population.

4. "Slowly" is not a word that fits with merging, converging, and emerging new media. Internet technology expanded so quickly that people began talking about "Web years" the same way they would about "dog years."

5. The explosive growth of the Internet since 1995 belies its beginnings in 1969 when the Pentagon established it to link government and university computers. At first, the Internet simply reserved phone lines for joint research projects.

6. Paralleling the Internet's quiet academic beginnings was the growth of interactive multimedia. It began with the Pong video arcade game, introduced in 1972—which was the Stone Age in digital terms.

7. Plain old news and information were the leading reasons consumers went online. In 1998, the numbers of Net users seeking information was up, not down.

8. Newspapers were an early staple on the World Wide Web, probably to attract some of the cachet of electronic media for the oldest commercial medium.

9. In a promotion for its annual convention and technical exhibition, the National Association of Broadcasters in 1998 suggested that we were "living in the interactive interim."

10. Research by Arbitron revealed that more than one-third of television households in the United States had an interest in using their TV sets for some PC functions.

11. The U.S. Department of Commerce reported, in April 1998, that online traffic was doubling every 100 days and that electronic commerce would likely reach $300 billion by 2002.

12. There was a debate in the late 1990s about whether the World Wide Web was cutting into TV viewing levels. BJK&E Media Group indicated that early adopters of the Internet gave up their TV habits in favor of online activity.

13. The dilemma for online content producers was how to provide programming that satisfies two types of audiences—the "sit back and watch" people and those who wanted to interact online.

14. In the fall 1997, AOL found the link between "sit back" and "interact" and

launched its AOL Network with "info-tainment" shows, interactive sci-fi, comedy, and Hollywood themes. By February 1998, AOL was averaging 600,000 users.

15. "New media" has so many meanings. It is the CD-ROM dictionary. It is the digital downlink that helps you bypass cable or broadcast television. Most often, "new media" means the Internet, generally, and the World Wide Web, specifically.

16. About 50% of U.S. companies had their own Web sites by the end of 1997.

17. Revenues for Internet advertising increased 200% per year between 1996 and 1997, with no expectations that the increase would level off anytime soon.

18. The Internet Advertising Bureau (IAB) reported that banners were responsible for 96% ad awareness. The same study showed real weakness for click-throughs in the same awareness category.

19. Large-format ads produced higher recall than banners. Over three-quarters of respondents (76%) remembered seeing interstitials; 71% recalled seeing split-screen ads. In contrast, 51% recalled banner ads.

20. GeoCities, HotWired Network, and DoubleClick are distant cousins of traditional networks, like ABC, CBS, and NBC. They link advertisers together rather than local media outlets.

21. Projections developed by Forrester Research and quoted in *The Internet Advertising Report* show newspapers to be the long-term victims of Web advertising.

22. CPMs vary widely on the Web, much to the consternation of advertisers used to traditional media. The Internet advertiser must remember first that while the Net reaches a large audience in terms of numbers, each audience member is reachable in a one-on-one setting.

23. Pricing strategy for most Web sites is based on a variety of factors: market conditions, research information, feedback from the sales force, and availability of advertising opportunities on a particular site.

24. In a 1997 study for the IAB, MBinteractive concluded that "online advertising is more likely to be noticed than television advertising."

25. The battle for local community information on the Internet has been heating up since America Online created Digital City with localized information for cities across the United States.

26. Hyperbole faded as predictions were made of up to $300 billion worth of goods expected to be purchased online in 2001.

27. When you are selling online advertising, you are likely to be perceived as the expert. Users of traditional media will ask for help in presenting their messages online.

28. Ads in cyberspace are not print ads, and they are not television ads. They are interactive online ads. Sellers should advise advertisers to investigate the unique features of the Internet and to take advantage of them.

29. Like advertising in any traditional medium, Internet advertising is all about reaching potential customers and making an impression.

30. When supply outstrips demand (as in the U.S. economic system, for example), advertising fulfills an essential function: moving merchandise from the manufacturer to consumer.

31. There is no scarcity of information, but there is scarcity of attention. The result is that advertising will be used to attract and direct attention.

Chapter Notes

1 The title of this chapter is borrowed from "Living in the Interactive Interim," by Robert L. Lindstrom in the NAB's magazine, *On the Verge*, March 1998, a promotion for the 1998 NAB Convention.

2   There was a new media timeline in "When Did You Get Multimedia?" in *New Media*, January 2, 1996.

3   The Market Facts studies were reported in *Advertising Age* in "Online Users Go for Facts over Fun" by Adrienne W. Fawcett, October 14, 1996. The following year it was "Information Still Killer App on the Internet" by Kate Maddox, October 6, 1997. The latest data I had before publication deadline was from "Survey Shows Increase in Online Usage, Shopping" by Kate Maddox, October 26, 1998. Check *Advertising Age* each year in October for the latest results.

4   "*The New York Times* on the Web," *Direct Marketing*, August 1997.

5   A photograph of what looked like a little girl with her prize duck at a pet show or FFA awards program illustrated the "What's the difference?" headline in an ad for IBM in *Wired*, December 1997.

6   *The Kiplinger Washington Letter*, February 17, 1995.

7   The Arbitron research was in "Living in the Interactive Interim," cited above.

8   The U.S. Department of Commerce report in *USA Today* was cited in Chapter 1.

9   In my opinion, Nicholas Negroponte knows everything. Fortunately, he writes about some of it. See "The Third Shall Be First: The Net Leverages Latecomers in the Developing World," *Wired*, January 1998.

10 The Nielsen review of Internet households was cited in Chapter 1. An Arbitron study showed that radio usage was also reduced by online activity an average of two hours per week.

11 The idea of an online Lucy Ricardo is from *New Media*, August 4, 1994. The article was "The Web's Fall Season" by Paul Karon. That's also the source of Hollywood's quest for the bridge between "sit back and watch" and interactivity.

12 AOL's new lineup was described in *Broadcasting & Cable*, October 13, 1997.

13 Randall Rothenberg interviewed NBC's Robert Wright for "Go Ahead, Kill Your Television. NBC Is Ready," in *Wired*, December 1998.

14 "The quality of *aba*" and speaking "Komi like a Zyrian" are for people who like to play with words.

15 *The Internet Advertising Report* was cited in Chapter 1.

16 "Morgan's Mary Meeker: Look for the Net's 'Top Dogs'" by Maryanne Murray Buechner appeared in *Time Digital*, a supplement to *Time*, March 23, 1998.

17 Disney Online's Jake Winebaum was interviewed in *Wired*, June 1998. The article was called, "The New Mouseketeer," and it appeared just before Disney agreed to buy Infoseek and merge Disney Online with Starwave. The result of the Disney moves was an all-new Web presence called *go.com*.

18 I was surprised to find few examples of either benefits or liabilities of advertising online, so I assembled some for you from a variety of sources, most of them mentioned in the text. *The Internet Advertising Report*, cited previously, was the starting point.

19 The discussion of links, banners, and other online advertising opportunities also had to be collected from a number of sources: *The Internet Advertising Report*; advertising for GeoCities and *www.geocities.com* online; presentation materials for "CNN on Pointcast"; LinkExchange *www.linkexchange.com*; MediaCentral's "Online Tactics"; and *Online Media Strategies for Advertisers*, published by the Internet Advertising Bureau in Spring 1998.

20 The IAB study was reported in *Advertising Age*, September 28, 1997, and in MediaCentral's "Direct Newsline," September 25, 1997.

21 Sanjay Madan and Tony Hsieh of LinkExchange were featured in "Barter for Banners," *Wired*, October 1997. I added promotional information from LinkExchange.

22 The IBM ads ran in *The Wall Street Journal*, December 8, 1997.

23 The remarkable online sales totals are from "E-commerce Becoming Reality" by Kate Maddox in a special report on interactive media and marketing in *Advertising Age*, October 26, 1998.

24 Amazon's story is from Everen Securities' *Investor News*, January–February 1998.

25 K-Tel, CDNow, and N2K were the subjects of "Internet, Music CDs Hit Right Key" by David Lieberman in *USA Today*, April 16, 1998.

26 For the "users guide," I combined Kim M. Bayne's ideas from *The Internet Marketing Plan*. New York: John Wiley & Sons, 1997, and Herschell Gordon Lewis' columns in *Direct Marketing*, October, November, and December 1996, and January and February 1997. Lewis' book is listed under Additional Reading.

27 The attention economy is real. Michael Goldhaber's "Attention Shoppers!" appeared in *Wired*, December 1997, and was a prelude to a book he was working on. I can't wait to read it.

Taking It Further

Here are a few Web sites that relate to this chapter and additional reading not included in the Chapter Notes.

www.100hot.com—Tracks 100 top Web sites and groups high-usage sites by category, e.g., autos, books, etc.

www.cimedia.com—Cox Interactive Media and links to their city sites

www.clickz.com—Newsletters covering interactive agencies

www.cnet.com—Updates on interactive news from C/NET

www.electricvillage.com—Syndicators of Web sites

www.focalink.com—An online rep

www.forrester.com—Forrester Research is quoted often in Internet and new media stories. Forrester provides research data to subscribers. This site offers limited detail, but is helpful.

www.gossipcentral.com—Media updates and links to a variety of news sources. A source for "The Buzz" online newsletters (also at *www.adtalk.com*)

www.home.net—The @Home Network from Cox Interactive

www.iconocast.com—Internet marketing, market research, and e-commerce

www.mediametrix.com—Statistics on Internet usage

www.netlingo.com—An Internet language dictionary with a guide to online culture and technology

newmarket.net—They are Web developers and marketers. Their CEO, Tom Lix, coined the phrase "audience attention deficit disorder" to describe the effects of fragmentation on user loyalty.

www.sidewalk.com—City sites from Microsoft Network

www.zdnet.com—Ziff Davis publications site that is parent to cable channel ZDTV

Additional Reading

Lewis, Herschell Gordon, and Robert D. Lewis. *Selling on the Net: The Complete Guide*. Lincolnwood, IL: NTC Business Books, 1996.

McKenna, Regis. *Real Time*. Boston: Harvard Business School Press, 1997.

Miles, Peggy, and Dean Sakai. *Internet Age Broadcaster: Broadcasting, Marketing, and Business Models on the Net*. Washington, DC: National Association of Broadcasters, 1998.

Maddox, Kate, and Dana Blankenhorn. *Web Commerce: Building a Digital Business*. New York: John Wiley & Sons, 1998.

Negroponte, Nicholas. *Being Digital*. New York: Alfred A. Knopf, 1995.

Peppers, Don, and Martha Rogers. *The One to One Future*. New York: Doubleday Currency, 1993.

Tapscott, Don. *Growing Up Digital: The Rise of the Net Generation*. New York: McGraw-Hill, 1998.

Epilogue

One of the disadvantages of a book like this is that technology changes without regard to publication schedules, the timing of semesters, or the ability to get information about change disseminated rapidly.

I've written, rewritten, and unwritten many segments of this book, trying to keep up with the merging and converging of traditional media and the constant invention of new ideas.

The newspaper industry did a smart thing while I was preparing *Selling Electronic Media*. They combined 130 or so major newspaper Web sites into a consortium designed to be a "national rep" of sorts. Instantly, newspapers appeared to be keeping up with electronic media. They were able to use their marketplace clout coupled with a cutting edge perception.

It was called NewsWorks and was billed as "the very first network on the Web grown from the local affiliate level." There was monthly traffic of more than 200 million page views. The top 50 DMAs were covered (and lots more, too). Big newspapers were involved and all their editorial content was available online at one location. An early profile of the site's users showed very salable demographics.

If you've read this book carefully and completely, you're probably thinking that you don't recall reading a word about News-Works until now. You're right. Not quite a year after NewsWorks launched, the project was shut down. So I deleted the copy.

Apparently, the nine companies who put the project together couldn't agree on anything except that they had a good idea. One source said they probably wasted as much as $30 million arguing about structure.

That's how quickly things changed in the electronic media environment in the year that I wrote this book. Some of those changes I could catch, some I couldn't. While we all want to predict the future well enough to avoid being caught by changes that occur after the type is set in a book or after the final edit of a video, we must realize that it's just not possible.

All my life, I've heard predictions about the future. Some came true, and some I'm still waiting on. The "interactive future" was predicted, but I can't say that it looks like any of the predictions I heard about it in the 1950s and 1960s.

I tried to construct this book without predictions because the one I wanted to make was troublesome: at what point will digital creation and delivery be so ubiquitous that the television and the PC are forever merged? I realized that like the NewsWorks story, the answer may happen before I finished. I'm also realist enough to know that it may happen without our noticing entirely. The merger of AT&T and TCI might bring it closer to reality but only when TCI has full digital capability system-wide. When the merger was announced in 1998, TCI was behind the digital curve. With technology, it's easy to catch up.

It's fun to make predictions, because there's a chance that I'll be correct and you'll call me a genius. But it's just as easy to be wrong. Then what do you say about me? Peter Drucker warned us about the danger of predictions in an interview in *Wired*:

It's not given to mortals to see the future. All one can do is analyze the present, especially those parts that do not fit what everybody knows and takes for granted. Then one can apply to this analysis the lessons of history and come out with a few possible scenarios. Then one comes out with a few possibilities.

That statement reflects something from Drucker's 1964 book *Managing for Results* : "The best we can hope to do is to anticipate *future effects of events* which have already irrevocably happened."

The World Future Society uses the phrase "successful anticipations" instead of "predictions." It urges its members to "suggest things that *might* happen in the future." I like to use the term "projections" rather than "predictions"; so, here are some projections—anticipations based on what we know now. These projections will help you see a positive future in selling electronic media. Retail sales continue to rise in these projections. And population statistics indicate more money being spent in the future on advertised products.

By projecting birth rates and potential movement across demographic groups (see Table E–1), we see future baby booms and baby busts that affect every industry. From that, we can make some assumptions: the 75-year-old of the year 2020 will still listen to the Rolling Stones just as he or she did in the 1970s. Think of what that means for entertainment, for housing, and for retirement homes.

TABLE E–1 U.S. Population Projections (Expressed in millions)

Age	2005	2010	2015	2020
0–4	19.1	20.9	21.2	22.0
5–13	35.9	35.6	36.7	38.7
14–17	17.0	16.9	16.7	17.0
18–24	28.3	30.1	30.5	29.9
25–34	36.3	38.3	41.1	42.9
35–44	42.2	38.5	37.6	39.6
45–54	41.5	43.6	41.2	37.7
55–64	29.6	35.3	39.7	41.7
65–74	18.4	21.1	26.2	31.4
75+	17.8	18.4	19.3	21.8
TOTAL	286.1	298.7	310.2	322.7

Source: U.S. Department of the Census figures "Middle Series" projections made in 1996 from the 1990 Census base.

Diagonal Thinking

A chart like the one in Table E–1 is distracting. Your eye wants to follow each straight line, watching the numbers grow or decline. But population groups don't move in straight lines across the page. Rather, they move diagonally downward and to the right. Today's 0-to 4-year-olds are the 5- to 13-year-olds of the year 2005. The printed page doesn't give me the chance to show that clearly.

If you read across, begin with the 45–54 line, and note the peak at 2010 and the decline toward 2020. Then follow the 55–64, 65–74, and 75 + lines as they increase from now to 2020. That's the effect of the baby boom moving through the chart.

You can see an all-new baby boom emerging by 2015. It extends diagonally downward to 2020 (and, of course, beyond). The new century's boom won't be as large as the baby boom we've chronicled for the past 40 years, but it will be a welcome sight to marketers and employers of 2020.

Educators geared up in the late 1990s for increased enrollment because kids born in the late 1980s and early 1990s were heading to school. Enrollments will flatten again until 2015 or 2020.

Marketers who target 18- to 24-year-olds for a living are stuck with flat numbers. Dominance by the 35 to 44 group ends in 2005. My remarks about elderly Rolling Stones fans is supported by the increases in the 65 to 74 and over 75 populations. They'll listen to the Stones, to Kenny G, to Aretha Franklin, or to Garth Brooks, just as they did when they were younger. And they'll eat pizza and wear designer jeans while they do it, just as they did when they were younger.

The elderly population of 2020 will be a most unusual group. They will have seen the wealthiest period of American history. They will have been the most culturally diverse. They'll be the healthiest group of old folks ever, jogging, running, and hardening their abdominals (and complaining about it more than they did when they were 45). The reason 75 + will be so important in 2020 is that there will be so many of them expecting to continue demographic dominance.

Not shown in these figures will be major changes in the workforce: fewer males, more females; fewer whites, more blacks, Hispanics, and Asians. More than 80% of retirees will be white. A third of new workers will be minorities. Civilian employment is projected at 171 million in 2020.

The workplace itself won't be a *place* at all, but a portable electronic terminal used to communicate with co-workers and to download and upload information.

Retail

By 2010, the average household income will have increased by 22%, according to Woods and Poole Economics. During the same period, the number of households will have grown by only 14% and the population by only 13%. Read that projection as a windfall for retailers. With money outpacing people, retail sales are projected to increase 24%. Any increase in retail sales spells an increase in advertising sales in all media, and electronic media will be dominant. (See Table E–2.)

I first used these projections in a series of speeches that celebrated my company's twentieth anniversary (in 1997). Not liking to dwell on the past, I thought it might be a nice twist to look forward instead of backward at an anniversary. Broadcast managers groups and several state association meetings heard about this very positive future. That resulted in a booklet called *2020 Visions* which my company created and distributed to radio stations nationally.

It's exciting to see projections like these because they say the future is secure for the field of electronic media. With a larger population spending more money in retail, there should be plenty of opportunities for

TABLE E–2 Retail Sales Projections*

	2000	2005	2010
Income per capita	$18,097	$19,416	$20,801
Total personal income	4,972	5,556	6,195
General merchandise	234	259	289
Food stores	310	318	332
Auto dealers	420	454	498
Eating out	199	224	256
Total retail	$1,847	$1,997	$2,183

*Income per capita is expressed in 1987 dollars. All other figures are in billions of dollars.

Source: Woods and Poole Economics, quoted in *American Demographics*.

sellers of advertising to capitalize. Of course, there also will be more media fighting for those increased dollars.

Some things, however, will not change: the need for talented people, for example, or the need for coherent messages delivered effectively to the audiences the advertiser wants to reach.

The key will still be how we focus on the customer. Instead of managing products in the future, corporations will manage customers. If that sounds manipulative, it's not. An automobile dealer told direct marketing guru Lester Wunderman that one customer who buys cars from one dealership over a lifetime represents $332,000. That makes that dealer want to work on "share of customer" as well as "share of market."

In the long term, share of customer will win. If the dealer has a 100% share of cus-tomer, the customer relies on the dealer for *all* auto purchases, not just the next one. Companies that advertise must reach the target in a virtually one-on-one setting, whether using mass media or interactive online services.

One final note, if I might. Throughout this book, I've been reasonably successful at avoiding highway metaphors, as in the "Information Superhighway." The highway analogy raises questions for me: do we live on highways? No. Do we create relationships with highways? No. We use highways to get to our destinations. The destination is much more important than the road. Sure, we want the shortest, most direct route to the audiences we serve. But some information highways are really dirt roads, while others are autobahns. The customer tells you which is which.

Appendix A

Selling Against Newspapers

The year was 1690. The first newspaper was printed in the United States. In the 300-plus years since, the newspaper has been a cornerstone of the culture, so important that "freedom of the press" is written into our essential law.

Newspapers are sources of massive amounts of information. In his book, *Information Anxiety*, Richard Saul Wurman points out, "A weekday edition of *The New York Times* contains more information than the average person was likely to come across in a lifetime in seventeenth-century England."

Fueling the American economy, newspapers have been the key advertising medium in years of both boom and bust. Local advertisers trust their newspaper campaigns almost to a fault. The traditional reach is enormous. And newspapers are tangible. They literally can be seen and touched. Retailers love to see their ads, cut them out of the paper, and tape them to the cash register.

Newspapers do get results. But the growth of electronic media has rendered newspaper advertising less effective than it was. In 1995, television (including cable) inched past the newspaper for the first time as the largest advertising medium in terms of dollar volume. Figures from 1997 showed television with 23.8% of the advertising pie and newspaper with 22.2%. There was a time when newspaper's percentage was 50% or more on a consistent basis. According to *Editor & Publisher* magazine, 15 of the nation's 25 largest metropolitan dailies reported declines in circulation from 1995 to 1996.

For TV, cable, radio, and Internet-based media selling, I outlined both benefits and liabilities so that you would know how to position advertising sales for each medium.

More often than not, you'll run across advertisers who are sold on the newspaper. Your job will be to (a) un-sell them or (b) add your medium to the campaign to maximize impact.

The information presented in this appendix will help you counter objections and sell against the newspaper.

The Case for Newspapers

The newspaper is one of the oldest, most highly regarded forms of media in the United States. Among its loyal readers it enjoys a high degree of acceptance, credibility, and respect. Other benefits in favor of newspaper include the following:

1. It creates visual appeal through pictures and graphics.

2. It reaches a relatively large mass audience with one exposure. (See Figure A–1.)

3. It immediately delivers its reading audience, generally 100% within one day.

4. It offers a variety of editorial environments: national news, international, food, entertainment, sports, etc.

5. It offers a variety of ad sizes to match budget needs.

6. It has the ability to communicate lengthy, complex, or detailed information.

7. It is easy to track response, primarily through couponing.

8. It holds a perception of permanence: ads and articles can be clipped for reference. Advertising remains in place for a second reader. There is a record of the date and copy.

9. It provides retail information for shopping purposes: what's on sale, which movie is playing, etc.

10. Its production costs are relatively low compared to magazines and television.

11. It accommodates preprinted materials, such as free-standing inserts (FSIs).

12. Its ads can be targeted geographically by zone, zip code, or block code.

NEWSPAPER REACH

	1st Day	2nd Day*	3rd Day*	4th Day*	5th Day*
Number of Persons Reached by Newspaper	924,850	1,072,826	1,146,814	1,202,305	1,230,051
Newspaper's Reach Rating (% of Population)	28.5	33.1	35.4	37.1	37.9
Frequency	1	1.7	2.4	3.1	3.8

REACH & DELIVERY

Section	Read Regularly		% of Population Reached; Persons Reached; Average Exposure Frequency; GRPs				
Section 1	55%	Reach (#)	508,668	590,054	630,748	661,268	676,528
		Reach (%)	15.7%	18.2%	19.4%	20.4%	20.9%
		GRPs	15.7	30.9	46.7	63.2	79.3
Sports	32%	Reach (#)	295,952	343,304	366,981	384,738	393,616
		Reach	9.1%	10.6%	11.3%	11.9%	12.1%
		GRPs	9.1	18.0	27.2	36.8	46.1
Business	30%	Reach (#)	277,455	321,848	344,044	360,692	369,015
		Reach (%)	8.6%	9.9%	10.6%	11.1%	11.4%
		GRPs	8.6	16.9	25.5	34.5	43.2
Editorial	27%	Reach (#)	249,710	289,663	309,640	324,622	332,114
		Reach	7.7%	8.9%	9.5%	10.0%	10.2%
		GRPs	7.7	15.2	22.9	31.0	38.9
Food	27%	Reach (#)	249,710	289,663	309,640	324,622	332,114
		Reach	7.7%	8.9%	9.5%	10.0%	10.2%
		GRPs	7.7	15.2	22.9	31.0	38.9
Classified	17%	Reach (#)	157,225	182,380	194,958	204,392	209,109
		Reach	4.8%	5.6%	6.0%	6.3%	6.4%
		GRPs	4.8	9.6	14.4	19.5	24.5

Sources:

Circulation - Audit Bureau Circulations, 6 mo. report ending 3/31/97
Households/Population - Sales & Marketing Mgmt: Arbitron
Sectional Readership - Media Audit 1996
NDM=Newspaper Designated Market (defined by newspaper)
Rates: SRDS, Standard Advertising Unit Open Per Inch Rate

Duplication Formula - Newspaper Association of America
Readers per Copy - Simmons Research
Gross Circulation - Total copies sold inside and outside NDM
Net Circulation - Total copies sold inside NDM

Prepared by the Radio Advertising Bureau   1320 Greenway Drive, #500 Dallas, TX 75038

PH: 972-753-6700
FX: 972-753-6727

FIGURE A–1 Want to hit 28.5% of the Dallas Metroplex population? Buy space in *The Dallas Morning News*. Want your ad to be seen? Read the "Reach and Delivery" chart for each section of the paper. Prepared by RAB. Used with permission.

The Case Against Newspapers

In addition to its benefits, newspaper also has its drawbacks, including these:

1. Circulation is dropping. In many markets, circulation is below 50% of households.

2. Most people don't read all sections of the paper every day. An ad in a specific section reaches only those people who read that section.

3. Readers must make a conscious effort to read an ad.

4. It does not produce as high a frequency level as other media.

5. It does not offer the total reach potential of other media.

6. It can't target specifically; for instance, newspapers cannot reach nonadult audiences as effectively as other media.

7. It charges high premiums for less than full-run purchases.

8. There is no sound or motion in the advertising message.

9. It is difficult to get high-resolution color reproduction.

10. The newspaper usually does not expose an advertising message to more than one person at a time.

11. It is short-lived. Advertising impact lasts for one day.

12. A pass-along audience cannot be assured.

13. Rates are determined by circulation, not readership.

14. Newspapers are cluttered. A typical daily paper consists of 60% to 62% advertising. The Sunday edition averages 68% advertising, not counting FSIs.

15. Ads for competitors are often placed side by side. In that environment, an ad is effective only if the price is lower, the location is more convenient, or the comparison is favorable.

16. Newspapers have only 15% exposure prior to purchase.

Getting Clipped

Couponing is declining. While coupon face values increased 24% from 1992 to 1995 (from an average of 54 to 67 cents), redemptions began to drop in 1993.

Year	% of Redeemed Coupons
1992	2.5%
1993	2.1%
1994	2.0%
1995	1.9%

Buying Less for a Higher Price

As newspaper circulation goes down, costs go up. Table A–1 presents a 10-year analysis of circulation figures (in millions) and the cost of a half-page ad in enough newspapers to cover a national audience.

TABLE A–1

	Total Daily Circulation (000)	Cost Half Page Each Daily	Cost per 1,000 Circulation
1987	62,826	$1,580,006	$25.15
1988	62,695	1,803,335	28.76
1989	62,649	1,830,572	29.22
1990	62,328	1,907,600	30.61
1991	60,687	2,137,266	35.22
1992	60,164	2,118,873	35.22
1993	59,812	2,294,384	38.36
1994	59,305	2,430,568	40.98
1995	58,193	2,715,677	46.67
1996	56,983	3,054,014	53.60

The figures in Table A–1 were gathered by Television Bureau of Advertising (TVB) for its member stations, based on the national open rates. (Local, or retail, rates would be approximately 60% of the national rates, according to TVB.) A half page was defined as 63 column inches, based on guidelines from *Editor & Publisher*.

Appendix B

The SAFECO Media Example

Media plans are often so complex that they don't lend themselves to learning. This one for SAFECO Insurance Companies does. It's written from the advertiser's point of view showing the mix of media that achieved the company's goals in three distinct markets: Chicago, one of the nation's three largest markets; Dayton, in the top 50; and Springfield, Illinois, a small market.

I discovered the article through the Smart Business Supersite, www.smart-biz.com, a terrific resource for sales and marketing people. Nanette Straw had written the article for the Direct Marketing Association. She secured permission through SAFECO Insurance Companies for me to share it with you.

Selecting the Proper Media to Reach Your Target Audience

by Nanette Straw

The product is auto insurance. The objective in each market was to generate company and product awareness by general advertising and responses primarily by direct mail and telemarketing. Our goal is to have advertising build awareness and to have direct marketing provide the measurable response or action.

As an example of how this works, we can use SAFECO and the media selection strategies we used in three different-sized cities of our Key Market program: Chicago, one of our large markets; Dayton, a medium-sized market; and Springfield, Illinois a small market.

Chicago

We evaluated which media to use to best reach our audience in the most cost-effective manner. Using the media characteristics resulted in the following marketing plan.

Television

Television in Chicago and the suburbs is difficult to target, with 30–40 cable stations causing clutter. Due to the size of the market, Television is cost-prohibitive. We simply would need to buy too much airtime to make this an effective medium and to fit our budget and needs. The "disadvantages" of difficulty to target and cost outweighed the advantages. Any consideration of television as a major driving media was dismissed.

Radio

On the other hand, in radio we knew which stations appealed to our target audience of age 35+ homeowners. Also the stations reached an audience that matched the demographics of our agents' book of business and target market. Radio also had local appeal and the ability to tag the agent's name, address, and phone number along with an 800 number. The "advantages" of low-cost multimedia support outweighed the disadvantages. We selected a number of stations to reach the various listening tastes of our audience. Commercials were aired on drive time as our prospects were primarily commuters.

Newspaper

Newspaper was the next medium added to the mix. Newspaper inserts with 800 numbers were placed in selected papers. These are highly measurable, tied well into the radio advertising, and were very inexpensive. We used a suburban newspaper network and targeted zip codes in each agent's marketing area.

We advertised in papers the week prior to the mailings. Agents participating in the program were highlighted in our full- and half-page ads. The suburban editions of the Chicago newspapers were used. The newspapers provided excellent multimedia support, concentrated coverage, local appeal, and low cost.

Co-op Direct Mail

At the conclusion of the 2-month radio campaign with a small amount of TV image advertising in select areas, co-op direct mail was used. This was a low-cost and targeted medium. Through our experience, cooperative mail also provided a very good response both in quantity and quality of leads. Mailings were targeted by zip code and included a brochure with information listing the agents representing SAFECO. Based on our experience, we were able to guarantee agents a minimum response rate and cost lead. They knew the minimum number of prospects (leads) they would receive.

In summary, a large market necessitated the use of more targeted media to avoid wasted advertising dollars while still generating high response.

Dayton

For our medium-sized market, we again looked at how to best reach our audience in a cost-effective way.

Television

In Dayton, most of our audience members watch TV news. As most of our audience was unfamiliar with SAFECO, TV fit our needs. The advantage of broad immediate reach with our image advertising was of utmost importance and outweighed the disadvantages of television. In addition, there was no need to target our message to a specific area, and airtime for this size market was affordable.

Radio

While television built image, we used radio to emphasize product differentiation. Radio again gave us the ability to tag the agent's name, address, and phone number and was also low cost and highly supportive of television.

Newspaper

Inserts were targeted to specific zip codes through suburban newspaper delivery and were very inexpensive and highly measurable. Although the response rate for 800-number inserts was lower than co-op direct mail, the sales conversion potential of each lead was much higher.

Half-page newspaper ads were used for tagging agents. These ads were timed to coincide with our mailing. Newspaper gave us local appeal and provided excellent multimedia support.

Direct Mail

We did direct mail targeted to prospects with the most desirable demographics. Then direct mail allowed us to target our efforts into the agents' specific markets. Targeted co-op mailing was not available in Dayton. The radio, television, newspaper, and insert support lifted direct mail response 25%.

The major difference between Chicago and Dayton was the fact that TV became the foundation for our marketing efforts in Dayton. We also experienced a much higher response rate in Dayton mainly due to its size, lack of mailbox clutter, and consumer awareness of the company products.

Springfield

The basic principles of media evaluation applied.

Television

Television often becomes difficult in a small market, and the costs can be prohibitive or have "cable clutter." Although cable is available, it did not fit our needs in Springfield and was discounted from our media plan.

Radio

We felt our advertising dollar could be more wisely used with other media, so we purchased airtime on the two major radio stations to reach our target audience. Radio gave us local appeal, excellent agent and advertising tie-in for this type of market, and was very low cost.

Direct Mail

Again, direct mail was used to target the appropriate audience at the end of our advertising campaign. Based on market size and strong consumer awareness, our lead cost was extremely low while the quality of lead was excellent.

There is really nothing new or groundbreaking about SAFECO's approach; the markets were reviewed, and media was evaluated and tested. We found that the results of testing media in similar-sized markets could be successfully applied to markets of the same size and demographics in all areas of the country. In all cases, general advertising was incorporated into an effective direct marketing program. The combination proved very beneficial to our agents and the company.

Nanette Straw is the direct marketing production manager for SAFECO Insurance Company, in Seattle, WA. ©1996 by Nanette Straw and the SAFECO Insurance Companies. Used with permission.

Appendix C

The Chally Test

In Chapter 2, you read about the testing procedures used to qualify candidates for sales positions. Here's the result of a test administered by the H. R. Chally Group of Dayton.

The name of the candidate and the company affiliation have been changed, but the analysis is real. Your employer will probably see a profile like this that offers insight into you and your selling skills.

500 Lincoln Park Blvd.
Dayton, OH 45429-3479
Telephone: 937-299-1255
Fax: 937-299-0630
E-mail: chally@worldnet.att.net

Personal & Confidential

January 14, 1997

Mr. David Smith
President
ABC Services
500 Nelson St.
Columbus, OH 43219

Bottom-Line Recommendation	
Candidate:	Robert H. Burks
Branch:	Columbus, OH
Position:	Sales Producer
Bottom-line:	Recommended

The validity scales from the Self-Descriptive Index indicate that Mr. Burks completed the questionnaires in an honest manner. Therefore, the test results accurately represent his pattern of motivation and style of approaching work.

Summary of Candidate's Critical Selling Skills Potential

According to Chally's analysis of ABC Services' position information, we have agreed that the following Sales Skills are most critical to success in this position:

Agreed-Upon Skills	Candidate Score	Agreed-Upon Skills	Candidate Score
IMAGE BUILDING	98%	CLOSING	45%
LEAD GENERATING	61%	CUSTOMER RELATIONS	78%
QUALIFYING	83%	CUSTOMER SERVICE	75%
MAKING PRESENTATIONS	99%	RESALE	94%
ANSWERING OBJECTIONS	42%		

Summary

Based on the assessment results, we recommend Mr. Burks for Sales Producer. Overall, he demonstrates strong sales skill potential. You can enhance his potential for this position by helping him understand that answering objections is like talking with customers on a personal level. Role-play with him to give him a feel for the art of follow-up questioning. Demonstrate proper closing techniques, and insist on repeated practice before live coaching calls are made. In addition, since his display sales style is not a match with your relationship market, incentives may be necessary to motivate him to use a relationship approach with customers.

Candidate's Preferred Sales Style and Knowledge of Selling Principles

The results describe Mr. Burks as a display salesperson. People with this style accommodate customers in a friendly and low-key manner, are reactive, and see little need for personal involvement. Price and convenience are the key factors in this type of sales. He may find it difficult to develop strong business relationships.

On the Sales Attitude Check List, he placed at the 99th percentile compared to applicants for sales and sales management positions. His knowledge of sales techniques is excellent. Keep in mind, however, that the SAC does not measure motivation or ability to succeed in a sales situation.

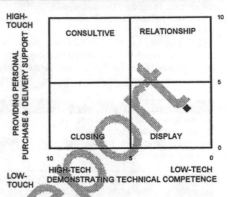

In-Depth Evaluation of Critical Selling Skills Potential

IMAGE BUILDING	SCORE	
Tailors image to fit customer expectations; adapts to new situations; does not allow personal preferences to limit the range of approaches used; favorably distinguishes product benefits through style and language	98%	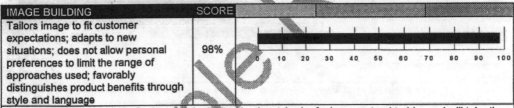

Skill/Capability Level: Mr. Burks won't be limited by the styles he feels are natural to him and will take the approach he feels his prospect would expect. Before approaching new sales situations, he makes a conscious effort to modify his personal style and language to fit in with each customer's expectation. He can reactively tailor his personal approach and overall image to address changing customer preferences and changing or different types of selling situations.

LEAD GENERATION	SCORE	
Demonstrates initiative to uncover new sales opportunities; networks to increase contacts; actively attracts interest of potential customers; prioritizes prospects; stays on top of market conditions	61%	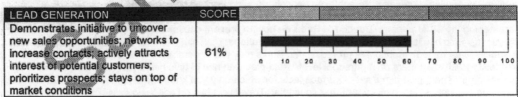

Skill/Capability Level: He is reasonably comfortable with the interpersonal communication needed to build his sales contacts. Mr. Burks is fairly consistent in generating new leads because he typically takes a disciplined approach to this routine task.

QUALIFYING	SCORE	
Determines company's ability to profitably satisfy customer needs; understands product and its application well enough to recognize compatibility; determines prospects' readiness to consider product	83%	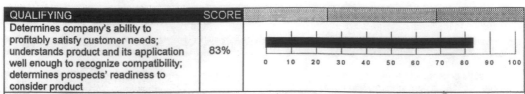

Skill/Capability Level: Because Mr. Burks stays up-to-date on the company's product and applications, he can determine the fit needed to meet a prospect's needs. He will sound out prospects to determine the profit potential from their business. He is fairly careful to observe the cues that allow him to weed out less likely prospects and maximize the time he spends with more serious prospects.

MAKING PRESENTATIONS	SCORE	
Projects interest and competence in fulfilling customer needs; illustrates value of the product or service; actively promotes the company's product	99%	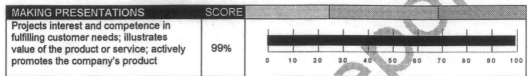

Skill/Capability Level: He is a proficient presenter who makes known his genuine interest in helping the customer and his capacity to get it done. He tailors each presentation so that it clearly demonstrates the benefit of a product or service to the prospect. Mr. Burks' presentation style demonstrates a rich enthusiasm that he uses to actively promote his company and its products and services.

ANSWERING OBJECTIONS	SCORE	
Probes for concerns that may create a barrier to the sale; resolves customer problems without putting them on the defensive; does not become defensive over objections; remains open to suggestions	42%	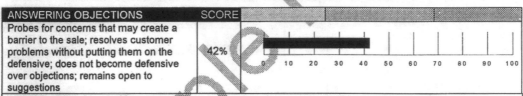

Skill/Capability Level: He may not always delve into the more in-depth concerns blocking a sale. Mr. Burks may not always provide useful solutions to a prospect's objections, provoking hostility and hindering progress on the sales track. He may sometimes regard the objections of difficult customers as personal attacks and resist their ideas for producing mutually beneficial solutions.

Coaching Suggestions: Mr. Burks will need to learn that objections signal the start of a meaningful discussion. Use role-play to show how to turn an objection to a fact-gathering process. Stress that objections, perceived or real, relate to products or services and not to him personally. Give examples of sales that you or a sales representative achieved only after finding the real source of the objection(s). Explain the concept of win-win solutions. Show him how to ask open-ended questions to avoid guiding or threatening the other person. Coach Mr. Burks on how to present causes of problems before he presents solutions. Help him learn more about customers' hot buttons. Ask him to watch seasoned salespeople for a specific time period. Monitor his progress. Mr. Burks may not understand that answering objections is like talking with customers on a personal level. Role-play with him to give him a feel for the art of follow-up questioning. Then, give him a set of surface facts for which only you know the true motivation. Have him question you until he uncovers your other concerns. Travel with him on coaching calls where you demonstrate this process. When he is ready, go with him on sales calls. Hold "curbstone conferences" following each call. Ask him to tell you what went well and what needs improvement. Interject specifics of your observations as to the good and bad points.

CLOSING	SCORE	
Motivates and reinforces a decision to buy without later buyer remorse; demonstrates effective timing and degree of urgency	45%	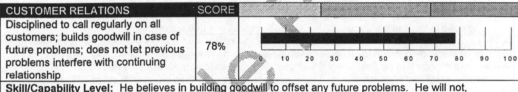

Skill/Capability Level: He may sometimes experience difficulty in asking for customer orders because he may not be able to determine either their readiness to buy or the right time to ask for the order. Mr. Burks may not always provide prospects with adequate rationale to support the buying decision.
Coaching Suggestions: Role-play to give Mr. Burks a better feel for timing the closing process. Assure him that once all objections have been resolved or minimized, customers will be ready to buy. Demonstrate proper closing techniques, and insist on repeated practice before live coaching calls are made. Have him observe successful closing presentations before he attempts to approach his own customers. When he is ready to go on live calls, take note of any times when he does not handle the close effectively. Coach Mr. Burks to slow down and talk with customers in a more relaxed fashion. Ask him to restate all accepted benefits, and suggest that he ask the customer if there is anything else to discuss before attempting to close. As part of his close, have him lay out an action plan for both parties. Practice this process in role-play situations before going on coaching calls. Assure him that, even when he does everything right, some sales will stall for unknown reasons. When this happens, he should revert to probing and answering objections until, once again, the prospect signals a readiness to end this process.

CUSTOMER RELATIONS	SCORE	
Disciplined to call regularly on all customers; builds goodwill in case of future problems; does not let previous problems interfere with continuing relationship	78%	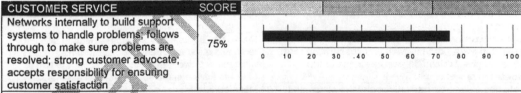

Skill/Capability Level: He believes in building goodwill to offset any future problems. He will not, ordinarily, let past problems with certain customers affect his willingness to maintain contact with them. Mr. Burks will keep up reasonably regular contact with customers.

CUSTOMER SERVICE	SCORE	
Networks internally to build support systems to handle problems; follows through to make sure problems are resolved; strong customer advocate; accepts responsibility for ensuring customer satisfaction	75%	

Skill/Capability Level: Mr. Burks will serve as an advocate and channel for customer complaints. He will carefully follow up on customer problems to make sure they are settled. For the most part, he will try to establish and maintain thorough alliances with company personnel who can handle customer problems.

RESALE	SCORE	
Develops a sales plan for each customer and works to increase use of products and services; demonstrates effective timing when seeking additional purchase decisions	94%	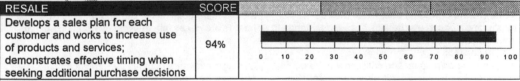

Skill/Capability Level: Mr. Burks stays abreast of the products and services his customers are using and seeks reorders in a timely manner. He will develop detailed sales plans for his customers and press to increase their usage of current products and services.

Mental Ability and Critical Thinking Skills

While at least minimal mental ability and critical thinking skills are important, we have no statistical evidence that higher scores predict better job performance for this particular position. A selection decision, therefore, should not be influenced by the Mental Abilities Test or Watson-Glaser Critical Thinking Appraisal scores.

Mr. Burks will learn quickly and broaden his depth of expertise on a wide array of topics. He will pursue academic, theoretical, or research-based information. His score on the Watson-Glaser Critical Thinking Appraisal is at the 99th percentile when compared to typical salespeople. His scores indicate that he takes a very logical and analytical approach to problem-solving. His deductive reasoning skills are excellent, and his conclusions are likely to be accurate and incisive.

Key Motivational Characteristics

The motivational characteristics described below measure Mr. Burks' preferences, wants, or desires. However, they DO NOT necessarily indicate that he currently has developed the habits or skills to satisfy them entirely on his own. A manager may wish to note these specific motivational needs and utilize the suggested tips to enhance Mr. Burks' potential

MOTIVATIONAL CHARACTERISTICS:	MANAGER'S TIPS:
He enjoys being in the limelight. At times, he may not listen to others' concerns or ideas because of his strong need to dominate a discussion.	Help him learn more about active listening. Show him how to organize others' ideas by asking questions and summarizing thoughts.
He will work to increase his knowledge and skill level because he wants recognition as an expert in areas he considers important in his field. He will welcome opportunities to mentor or coach others.	Ask him to lead an apprenticeship program or to become responsible for monitoring the work of a junior associate. Make sure he has sufficient time for this project so his other responsibilities do not suffer.
He has a strong need to spend time with people he likes and will avoid those with whom he is not comfortable. He might spend too much time with his favorite people and avoid those who are less congenial.	Mr. Burks' tendency to favor some people over others may interfere with his effectiveness in difficult situations. Assist him in learning how to stay objective and focused on the problem at hand rather than the people involved.
When working with others, he will actively try to develop a spirit of teamwork and cooperation. He likes to give advice and believes in the group-decision process.	Praise Mr. Burks for balancing his need to be recognized as an expert influence with his willingness to work with others. Encourage him to offer his advice in the spirit of mutual assistance.
He has a need for recognition and the status and perqs of success, but may feel that there is something improper about calling attention to his accomplishments.	Make sure to recognize his efforts or he will feel taken advantage of or unrewarded.
Mr. Burks is sensitive to sources of pressure and is keenly aware of when it builds. He may be unprepared for some situations because he tends to act on intuition, but he also seems to respond to this kind of challenge.	It is important that his coping abilities not be tried to the breaking point. Planning and realistic time frames are necessary to avoid overburdening him.
Constructive comments and criticism will have little impact on him because he is already comfortable with his achievements.	Constructive criticism of his performance should be prefaced by a positive comment on his overall value and potential. This way, the criticism is seen as a suggestion for improving his potential rather than a reproach.

Glossary

Access The locally programmed time period, 7 to 8 p.m. EST, immediately preceding television network prime time. See also Prime Access.

Ad Clicks On the Internet, the number of times a user clicks on an online ad, often measured as a function of time ("ad clicks per day"). Also called click-throughs.

Ad Click Rate On the Internet, the number of ad clicks as a percentage of ad views, or the number of times an ad is clicked on by users as a percentage of the number of times an ad was downloaded and viewed by users.

Addressability The ability of a cable system to send a program to a designated home converter (address). Made possible by a microchip in the TV set converter box.

(ADI) Area of Dominant Influence Arbitron Company's definition of a TV market during the period when that company provided TV ratings. It's the same as Nielsen's Designated Market Area (DMA).

Adjacency A commercial time period that is scheduled immediately preceding or following a scheduled program. Opposite of an in-program placement. Also called a break position.

Advances A ratings company service that provides to the subscriber immediate ratings information electronically several days in advance of publication of a rating book.

Advertorial A print advertisement styled to resemble the editorial format and type face of the publication in which it runs.

Ad Views On the Internet, the number of times an online ad is downloaded by users, often measured as a function of time ("ad views per day"). The actual number of times the ad is seen by users may differ because of caching (which increases the real number of ad views) and browsers that view documents as text-only (which decreases the number of ad views).

Affidavit A notarized statement from a broadcast station that confirms the commercial actually ran at the time shown on the station's invoice.

Affiliate A broadcast station bound to a contractual relationship with one or more networks to carry network-originated programs and commercial announcements.

Affinity Group People with a common interest. On the Internet, typically a subject-oriented mailing list, newsgroup, or a conference on a Web site.

Afternoon Drive A radio daypart, 3 to 7 p.m.

Agency-of-Record (AOR) An advertising agency or independent media buying company that purchases media on behalf of another agency or group of agencies serving the same advertiser. Sometimes also refers to a full-service advertising agency that performs all the services for a particular advertiser.

AM (Amplitude Modulation) The transmission of sound in radio broadcasting in which the amplitude (power) of a transmitting wave is modulated (changed) to stimulate the original sound; a type of radio signal. How far a signal travels depends on dial position (signals at lower positions on the AM band travel farther) and how much power a station has (50,000 watts is the maximum authorized power for AM stations operating in the United States).

American Association of Advertising Agencies (A.A.A.A.) serves as a national lobbying organization for the advertising agency industry. Also called the 4 As.

American Federation of Television and Radio Artists (AFTRA) Union comprised of broadcast performers, announcers, deejays, and newscasters.

American Women in Radio and Television (AWRT) A national, nonprofit organization dedicated to advancing women in electronic media and related fields.

Announcement An advertising message in broadcast media, commonly 10, 15, 30, or 60 seconds in length. Synonymous with the word commercial and usually referred to as a spot.

AQH The average quarter-hour rating for broadcast programs as reported by several media research suppliers. Ratings services calculate station ratings based on the average number of persons listening for at least 5 continuous minutes within a 15-minute (quarter hour) time period. AQH estimates may be reported as AQH persons, AQH shares, and AQH ratings.

Arbitrends A 3-month average of radio station ratings that is given to stations during each of the2 months between the full quarterly Arbitron ratings reports.

Arbitron A media research supplier. Radio's primary ratings supplier. Also provides data to advertising agencies and cable systems.

(ASCAP) The American Society of Composers, Authors, and Publishers A music licensing organization.

Association of National Advertisers (ANA) Pledged to meeting the needs of advertisers, agencies, and the media.

Audience Composition The demographic profile of media audiences, usually expressed in percentages of components by age and sex.

Audience Flow The analysis of the transition periods between programs. Audience flow is maximized when a given program's audience stays tuned for later programming.

Audience Turnover The ratio of cumulative audience listening or viewing to the average audience listening or viewing.

Availability/Avails The commercial position in a program or between programs on a given station or network that is available for purchase by an advertiser.

Average Persons Rating A rating based on the average number of persons listening or viewing. Radio ratings are expressed as average persons ratings; television ratings are based on either households or persons.

Away from Home Listening Estimates of radio listening that occurs at work, in the car, while shopping, or in other locations outside of the respondent's home.

Bandwidth The capacity of a channel to dictate the range of frequencies and the amount of data the channel can carry in a short amount of time. A wider bandwidth allows for faster communication of more data.

Banner Advertising Advertising on a Web site that promotes a product or service and allows the user to link to the advertiser's site for additional information. Typically a banner is a horizontal rectangle that looks like a miniature billboard.

Barter The exchange of goods and services without the use of cash. Usually the acquisition of media time or space in exchange for merchandise. Also called a trade out.

Barter House An advertising agency or other intermediary that specializes in trading various types of merchandise to radio and television stations in return for time and then resells the time to advertisers.

Barter Syndication Radio or television syndicated programming that stations pay for in part or in whole by giving the syndicator an agreed-upon amount of commercial time to sell within the program.

Basic Cable The offering to subscribers of broadcast- and cable-originated programs as part of a basic service agreement in which a subscriber pays a cable TV operator or system a monthly fee. Does not include pay or premium services that might be offered by the cable operator.

Billboard In radio, television, and cable, a billboard is a brief opening or closing sponsor identification announcement that may also contain a brief product benefit or slogan description. On the Internet, another name for a banner ad.

Black Out The option for a national network advertiser to keep an advertisement from airing in specified markets. The local affiliates in those markets may then sell the availability or substitute a promotional announcement or public service announcement.

(BMI) Broadcast Music Incorporated music licensing service.

Bonus Spots Commercials given to an advertiser at no cost as a consideration for buying other commercials.

Break An interruption in programming, usually for commercials. Also a station identification announcement or station break.

Break Position A commercial aired between programs as opposed to in-program. Also called Adjacency.

Broadcast Education Association (BEA) The organization for professors, students, and professionals involved in teaching and research related to ratio, television and electronic media.

Broadcast Promotion and Management Executives (BPME) The former name of Promax International.

(BTA) Best Time Available A package of commercial announcements in which a station or system promises to place an advertiser's spots in the highest-rated time periods that remain available at the time the schedule runs.

(CAB) Cabletelevision Advertising Bureau A national membership organization of system operators, cable networks, sales representatives, and industry associates devoted to increasing the value and viability of cable as a national, regional, and local advertising medium. Services include research information, cable data and sales tools, and presentations to advertisers and agencies.

Cable Penetration The percentage of homes within a given area that subscribe to cable.

Cable-Ready Television sets that have built-in circuitry enabling them to receive and translate cable signals without the use of separate converters.

Cable Television Reception of TV signals via cable (wires) rather than over the air (i.e., via a TV antenna).

Caching The practice by Internet access providers or browsers of storing Web page data in a temporary location on their networks or in their disk space to speed access and reduce traffic. Reduces the number of measured page views at the original content site.

Call Letters Station identification signs. In the United States, call letters begin with W east of the Mississippi River and K west. In Canada, call letters begin with C, in Mexico, with X.

Cash Discount A discount granted by the media supplier to an advertiser for payment within a certain period of time, for example, "a 2-percent discount if payment is made within 10 days of invoice."

(CATV) Community Antenna Television An early form of cable system that merely retransmitted existing over-the-air television signals. The term CATV is still sometimes used to refer to cable systems.

CD-ROM (compact disc read-only memory) A nonerasable, prerecorded digital optical disc system that is used to store and play back computer compatible data. A CD-ROM can hold text as well as graphics.

Chain Break An outdated term for the time between network programs when a network-affiliated station identifies itself to viewers and during which commercial announcements air. More often called, simply, break.

Checkerboard Programming Scheduling a different TV program in the same time period each day.

Circulation In print media, the number of copies sold or distributed by a publication. In broadcast, the number of homes owning a TV or radio set within a station's coverage area. In cable television, the number of households that subscribe to cable services for a given network. In out-of-home media, the number of people passing an advertisement who have an opportunity to see it.

Clearance Broadcast stations' agreement to carry network or syndicated programs. This list is usually accompanied by a coverage percentage indicating the percent of U.S. TV homes or radio listeners in markets in which the program airs, or clears.

Clear Channel Station Class IA and IB AM radio stations operating with 50,000 watts on their assigned frequency at night.

Click-Throughs On the Internet, the number of times a user clicks on an on-line ad, often measured as a function of time ("click-throughs per day").

Cluster A group of commercial or promotional announcements, in television, also known as a pod. In radio, a group of stations in one market owned by the same company.

ClusterPLUS A geodemographic clustering system offered by Strategic Mapping.

Cluster Systems/Geodemographic Segmentation Developed by data companies to create meaningful segments based on residence and the assumption that people live in areas where there are a lot of other people just like them. This geographic element is one thing that distinguishes clusters from psychographic segments. Another difference is that cluster categories are virtually always based on socioeconomic and consumer data rather than attitudinal information. Each system has at least several dozen clusters. The four major cluster systems are Claritas' PRIZM, National Decision System's MicroVision, CACI's ACORN, and Strategic Mapping's ClusterPLUS 2000.

Clutter A condition that occurs when too many commercials, promotional announcements, and public service announcements appear in the same venue.

Coincidental A research methodology that requires respondents to report listening and viewing activity at the moment the survey is being conducted. Most coincidental studies are conducted by telephone.

Compact Disc (CD) A nonerasable, prerecorded digital optical disc system that is used to store and playback music and/or data. Playback is produced by a laser, which reads the information stored on the disc. Also see CD-ROM.

Compensation Payments made by networks to affiliates in exchange for carrying programs. Compensation rates depend on station ratings, clearance rates, and affiliate bargaining power.

Competitive Media Reporting (CMR) An organization that monitors TV commercials to verify that advertising schedules were run as ordered by their clients. CMR monitors the largest markets on a weekly basis and smaller markets each month.

Compression A technical term for reducing the representation of information but not the information itself or for reducing the bandwidth or bits necessary to encode information. Full standard coding of broadcast-quality television typically requires 45 to 90 megabits per second. Compressed video includes signals from 3 megabits per second down to 56 kilobits per second.

Continuity The department within a broadcast station or cable system that is responsible for writing commercial copy.

Converter A device that translates cable signals into TV signals and allows the viewer to select individual channels.

Cooperative Advertising (Co-op) The agreement by a manufacturer to reimburse a retail outlet for a predetermined percentage of a retailer's advertising expenditure that promotes the manufacturer's product.

County Size Designation of all U.S. counties into one of four categories originally defined by A. C. Nielsen based on population density and labor force concentration. Commonly referred to as *A*, *B*, *C*, and *D* counties. Still used in television ratings by Nielsen Media Research.

Coverage The percentage of a population group covered by a medium, akin to a rating.

(CPM) Cost-per-Thousand The cost per 1,000 people (or homes) delivered by a medium or media schedule. The "M" is from the Latin"milia," thousand.

(CPP) Cost-per-Point The cost of an advertising unit (e.g., a 30-second commercial) divided by the average rating of a specific demographic group (e.g., women 18–49).

Creative The name given to the art, design, or copy within an advertisement.

(CRMC) Certified Radio Marketing Consultant A certification granted by RAB to radio salespeople who successfully complete training and examination.

Cume The number of cumulative, different, or unduplicated people who are reached by a station, program, or advertising schedule. For example, when estimating an advertising schedule's cume, a ratings company counts each listener only once no matter how many times a listener may see or hear a commercial.

Cume Duplication The percentage of a given station's audience that also listened to another given station during a specified time.

Cut-in A local commercial that preempts a network spot. Frequently used by the national advertiser to test new commercials.

Dayparts Broadcast time periods or segments (e.g., television's daytime, 10 a.m. to 4 p.m. EST, or radio's p.m. Drive, 3 p.m. to 7 p.m.)

Delayed Broadcast (db) The term given to a network radio or TV program that is delayed for airing in a given market at a different time than the time it airs nationally.

Demographics The classification of an audience by social and economic characteristics. Among the characteristics commonly used for demographic classification are age, gender, race, income, education, and employment status.

Diary A self-administered rating technique used to record radio listening and TV viewing. Called a diary because the respondent writes down each listening or viewing occasion in a booklet.

Digital In telecommunications, in recording, or in computing, digital is the use of a binary code to represent information.

Digital Audio Broadcasting (DAB) A technology that transmits audio with CD-quality sound.

Direct Broadcast Satellite (DBS) A system for relaying programming directly to home receiving dishes by way of satellites, bypassing TV and radio stations and cable systems.

(DMA™) Designated Market Area Nielsen's definition of a TV market.

Domain Name The unique name that identifies an Internet site, such as *microsoft.com*. A domain name always has two or more parts, separated by periods. A given server may have more than one domain name, but a given domain name points to only one machine.

Double Billing A fraudulent business practice in which a station bills a retailer at twice (or more) the normal rate charged. The retailer then sends the bill back to a manufacturer (or vendor) for reimbursement through a co-op plan. If the co-op plan was designed to reimburse the retailer for 50% of the cost of the advertising, the advertiser would be reimbursed for the full cost of the campaign, and the station would be reimbursed at its normal rate.

Downlink Part of a satellite transmission in which signals are sent from the satellite to earth. Also used as the name of the receiving dish.

Draw A partial payment advanced to new salespeople and later charged back against commissions earned on sales for a particular month.

Drive Time The morning and afternoon hours of radio broadcasting: morning drive is from 6 to 10 a.m.; afternoon drive is from 3 to 7 p.m.

Dub (dupe) Making one or more copies of an audio or video recording.

Duopoly Ownership of more than one radio station in the same market broadcasting in the same service, such as more than one AM station or more than one FM station.

Duplication The number or percentage of a medium's audience, or of those reached with a media schedule, who are exposed to more than one media vehicle or to more than one advertising message.

Early Fringe The TV daypart between daytime and prime access, generally from 4 to 7:30 p.m. EST.

Early Morning A television daypart, usually 6 to 10 a.m. EST.

Effective Frequency The number of times a commercial has to be exposed to reach sufficient numbers of the target audience effectively. See also Effective Reach.

Effective Reach The number or percentage of a population group reached by a media schedule at a given level of frequency.

Efficiency Generally refers to the relative costs of delivering media audiences. See also Cost-per-Point and Cost-per-Thousand.

End Rate The lowest rate charged for commercial time.

Enhanced Banner Online advertising that allows the user to receive information on the banner itself without leaving the Web site.

(ESF) Expanded Sample Frame A technique used to sample households that are not listed in telephone directories, including households without telephones and households with unlisted telephone numbers.

Exclusive Cume Listeners The number of different people who listen to a given radio station and to no other radio station during a specific daypart.

Exposure A person's contact (visual and/or audio) with an advertising medium or message.

Fact Sheet List of pertinent information about a sponsor, used by a copywriter to create a commercial.

FAQs (Frequently Asked Questions) Short lists of common questions and their answers provided to users of an Internet site. Pronounced "facks," FAQs are designed to explain to a novice user the scope of information available at the site.

Federal Communications Commission (FCC) The government agency that regulates the broadcasting, cable, and telephone industries.

Fiber Optics A transmission vehicle composed of hair-thin glass cables through which data such as text, voices, or images can be reduced to pulses of light and transmitted with great speed and clarity. Fiber-optic lines permit the transmission of more data at a much faster speed than do conventional copper telephone lines or even coaxial cable.

Financial Interest and Syndication Rules (Fin-Syn) Rules set by the FCC that prohibited networks from ownership of or syndication of their prime-time entertainment programs. The rules were relaxed in the early 1990s but some syndication restrictions remained.

First-Run Syndication The sale to TV stations of programming produced for syndication, not previous network showings.

Fixed Position A commercial position that a station or system guarantees will run at the exact time ordered by an advertiser. In broadcast, a commercial unit purchased with nonpreemption guarantees.

Flat Rate A rate without any discounts.

Flight The length of time during which the advertiser places commercials on a station or system (e.g., a 4-week flight).

Flighting A media buying strategy that involves airing commercials in short time periods several times a year rather than airing commercials continuously over the time period.

FM (frequency modulation) A radio signal, without static or fading, that results from the adjustment of the frequency of the transmitting wave to the originating sound.

Fragmentation A term used to describe smaller audiences size caused by the increase in the number of media outlets available to consumers.

Franchise/Franchise Agreement A contract between a cable television company and a municipal government authorizing and defining the terms under which the company may install cable television service within the community.

Franchise Area The specific geographic area in which a cable television company may offer service, as defined by the cable company or by local government.

Frequency In a research context, frequency refers to the average number of times an advertising message, an advertising campaign, or a specific media vehicle is heard by the average viewer or listener. In a technical context, frequency refers to the portion of the electronic spectrum on which the station's signal is broadcast.

Frequency Discount A rate of discount allowed to an advertiser who purchases a specific schedule within a specific period of time, such as six ads within one week.

Fringe Time Television dayparts immediately before and after prime time. See Early Fringe and Late Fringe.

Grazing The process of watching two or more TV programs at the same time. Grazers flip back and forth among the stations during both the programs and commercial breaks. Related to surfing, a more popular term.

Grid Card A rate card that features several prices for spots in each daypart (6 to 10 a.m. in radio or 8 to 11 p.m. in television, for example) and that provides salespeople with the flexibility to respond to market demand more easily. In periods of low demand, the cost is lower, or at a lower grid. When demand is high, the cost increases to a higher grid level.

Gross Impressions The total number of advertising impressions made by a schedule of commercials. Calculated by multiplying the average persons reached in a time period by the number of spots in that time period. If more than one time period is used, the impressions in each time period are added together.

(GRP) Gross Rating Points The sum of all ratings delivered by a given list of media vehicles. Although synonymous with target rating points, GRPs generally refer to a household base in television.

Headend The originating point of programming in a cable system where the signal is received from satellites is amplified, and sent down the line to subscribers.

Hiatus A period of nonactivity; the period between advertising campaigns or flights.

High-Definition Television (HDTV) A television system that offers a sharpness and clarity of image that is far beyond the range of conventional television. With HDTV, the number of lines of vertical resolution is as high as 1080, more than double the standard 525. HDTV screens are wider, changing the standard 4:3 aspect ratio of the screen to a 16:9 ratio.

Hit On the Internet, any request for data from a Web page or file. Often used to measure popularity or traffic of a site.

Homes Passed The number of homes in which a cable television service is available because feeder cables are already in place.

(HTML) Hypertext Markup Language A simple coding system used to format documents for viewing by Web clients. Web pages are written in this standard specification.

(HTTP) Hypertext Transfer Protocol One of the sets of rules that computers use to communicate with each other.

(HUT) Homes Using Television The total number of homes that have TV sets turned on at any given time. Calculated by adding up the numbers of households viewing all stations in a market at a given time.

HUT Level HUT expressed as a percentage of the 98 million U.S. TV households (TVHH). HUT Level is calculated by dividing HUT by TVHH.

Hypertext Generally, any text on a Web page that contains links to other documents. Words or phrases in a document that can be chosen by a user and that cause another document to be retrieved or displayed.

Identification (ID) A 10-second TV commercial (10 seconds visual and 8 seconds audio). Also station identification that is required of radio and television by the FCC.

Impressions The gross sum of all media exposures (numbers of people or homes) without regard to duplication. See also Gross Impressions.

Independent Station A TV broadcast station not affiliated with a network.

Index A number indicating change in magnitude relative to the magnitude of some other number (the base, usually an average) taken as representing 100. A 110 index indicates a 10% positive change in magnitude; a 90 index indicates a 10% negative change.

Infomercial A long-form broadcast commercial (usually a half-hour in length) that provides much more information than can be supplied in a typical 30- or 60-second commercial.

In-Line Ads Advertorials positioned within a Web site designed to add credibility to an online advertising message.

Institutional Advertising Advertisements that promote a corporation's image rather than specific products or services sold by the corporation.

In-Tab Sample Returned, usable diaries that are used to calculate the ratings in a radio or television rating report.

Interactive Media Media with two-way capabilities between service or information provider and user. A number of different media formats are mixed together, and the user can access any or all of them, from text to graphics (moving or still) to audio formats.

Interactive Multimedia Computer-based programs that incorporate audio, video, animation, still images, photographs, and text—all controlled by the user. CD-ROM and videodisk are the most common distribution channels.

Interconnect Two or more cable systems that are linked together to air commercials simultaneously (if possible). A hard interconnect is linked by cable or microwave. A soft interconnect is a group of systems with an agreement to insert commercials into programs or time periods, but not necessarily simultaneously.

Internet A worldwide network established by the U.S. Department of Defense in 1969 to link government and university computers and to share information among researchers.

Interstitial Advertising Flashes of branding information or imagery that appear between the pages of a Web site. Also, brief advertisements that appear between interactive experiences on a Web site such as between plays of an online game.

Interstitial Programming In television, the placement of short programs between full-length programs. For example, Home Box Office (HBO) and other movie channels schedule programs of about 2 to 25 minutes between the full-length movies.

INTV (Association of Independent Television Stations) An organization representing independent, or non affiliated, stations before Congress.

Inventory In broadcast advertising, the number of commercial positions available for sale. In actual use, inventory refers to the unsold time that a station or network has available for advertisers. On the Internet, a site's inventory is the number of page views it will deliver in a given period of time, thus the amount of product that can be sold to advertisers.

ISDN The Integrated Services Digital Network created by AT&T as it moved to become a major player in the age of interactive media. With ISDN, voice and data can travel side by side over the same wires, which are being upgraded to fiber-optic lines in many parts of the country.

(JSA) Joint Sales Agreement A contractual agreement that allows the sales staff of one medium to sell the commercial inventory of another medium as well as their own.

Killer App Short for "killer application." A creative or breakthrough software program that drives the demand for the hardware that runs it. Also applied to uses of technology not specifically related to software.

Kilohertz (kHz) One thousand cycles per second; AM frequency measurement, kilocycles.

Late Fringe A TV daypart that immediately follows prime time, usually 11 p.m. to 1 a.m. (or later) EST.

Lead-in A program preceding the time period of the program being analyzed.

Lead-out A program following the time period of the program being analyzed.

Lifestyle Pertains to the nondemographic characteristics of people in describing their behavior (e.g., recreational habits). See also Psychographics.

Link The path between two documents that associates an object, such as a button or hypertext, on a Web page with another Web address. The link allows a user to point and click on an object and thereby "move" to the location associated with that object by loading the Web page at that address. Also referred to as a hyperlink.

(LMA) Local Marketing Agreement A contractual agreement in which a radio or television station sells a block of airtime to a programmer that uses the time to broadcast content, including commercials, on the station. Also, a licensee selling only its commercial inventory to a third party while maintaining programming control.

Low Power Television (LPTV) Television stations licensed by the FCC to serve a small geographic area, ideally to audiences desiring specialized programming.

Make-good In broadcasting, a commercial position offered in lieu of an announcement that was (or will be) missed due either to station error, preemption by another advertiser, or movement of the program purchased from one time slot to another.

Mean The sum of all items divided by the number of items. Commonly called average. See also Median.

Media Audit A qualitative research report published by International Demographics, Inc.

Mediamark Research, Inc. (MRI) A media research supplier.

Media Mix The use of two or more media forms, such as television and magazines; or radio, outdoor, and newspapers.

Median The middle number in a sequence of numbers. See also Mean.

Megahertz (MHz) Million cycles per second; FM and TV frequency measurement, megacycles.

Merchandising Promotional activities that complement advertising and that are provided free or at a nominal charge to advertisers when advertising time is purchased.

Metro Area A geographic area defined by the U.S. Government's Office of Management and Budget. Also called a Standard Metropolitan Statistical Area (SMSA) or a Metropolitan Statistical Area (MSA).

Metro Survey Area A geographic area defined by subscribers to Arbitron Radio reports as their trading area. One or more counties may be the same as the government's MSA or SMSA, but they do not necessarily match exactly.

Morning Drive A radio daypart, generally 6 to 10 a.m.

(MSO) Multiple System Operator A company that owns more than one cable system.

Multimedia An all-embracing term reflecting the combination of media forms and presentations resulting when different forms of print and electronic media couple with the computer, CD-ROM technology, and the telephone system to offer the user one all-purpose, interactive media system.

Multimedia Buys The purchase of advertising in more than one medium owned by a media supplier, or by media suppliers who have a cooperative agreement. Multimedia buys can include multiple media vehicles within a media form (e.g., several magazines) or a mix of different media forms (e.g., magazines and television).

Must-Carry The FCC rule requiring cable systems to carry all local broadcast television signals in their markets. Also, the stations carried under the rule, commonly called must-carries.

(NAB) National Association of Broadcasters An organization of broadcast stations designed to represent the industry's position on matters of importance to Congress, the public, and the FCC. Also conducts original research on new technologies and other issues of concern to radio and television broadcasters.

Narrowcasting Programming designed to reach a specific group defined by demographics and/or program content.

National Association of Television Progam Executives (NATPE) The non-profit organization made up of production companies, program distributors, networks, group owners, local cable systems, local television stations, and advertisers. Best known for the NATPE Annual Program Conference and Exhibition, the world's largest marketplace for syndicated TV programming.

(NCTA) National Cable Television Association NCTA is the major trade association representing the cable industry before legislative, regulatory, and judicial bodies on issues primarily related to franchising and technical operations.

Netiquette Etiquette on the Internet, following the conventions of the Web page or user group, such as avoiding redundancy, histrionics, profane language, or personal attacks in chat sessions.

Network A broadcast entity that provides programming and sells commercial time in programs aired nationally via affiliated and/or licensed local stations, such as ABC TV network, ESPN cable network, or Westwood One radio network. On the Internet, an aggregator/broker of advertising inventory from many sites.

(NHSI) Nielsen Hispanic Station Index From Nielsen Media Research. It gathers viewing information in markets with significant Hispanic population.

(NHTI) Nielsen Hispanic Television Index From Nielsen Media Research. It was the first electronic metered service to report Hispanic audiences on a national basis.

(NHVI™) Nielsen Homevideo Index From Nielsen Media Research. It measures cable-delivered networks, pay cable, VCRs, and video discs.

Nielsen, A. C. The man who founded thecompany and the company that originated television and national cable ratings. Now A. C. Nielsen provides ratings in countries outside the United States and Canada.

Nielsen Media Research "Nielsen" in the United States. The company provides television information for networks, stations, cable systems, syndicators, and advertising agencies in the United States and Canada.

Nielsen Ratings One of a variety of services provided by Nielsen Media Research depending on the medium being measured. See also NHTI, NHVI, NSI, NSS, and NTI.

(NSI™) Nielsen Station Index From Nielsen Media Research. The local ratings for 44 major markets and more than 200 designated market areas (DMAs).

(NSS) Nielsen Syndicated Service Nielsen Media Research's measurement of syndicated television programming on both the national and local levels.

(NTI™) Nielsen Television Index Network television's rating report. Established in 1950, NTI provides continuous audience estimates for all national broadcast network programs. Nielsen gathers information every day from approximately 5,000 households using an electronic "people meter" that instantaneously measures viewing.

O & O A radio or TV station owned and operated by a broadcast network.

Off-Network Syndication The sale to local television stations of programming that originally aired on a network.

Online Magazine A magazine produced only on the Internet, never using a printing press. Also known as a zine.

Open Rate The maximum rate charged for one commercial aired one time.

Out-of-Home Media Those forms of media meant to be consumed only outside of one's home, such as outdoor billboards, transit advertising, or in-store media.

Overnights Daily ratings provided to the television networks and their advertisers for programs that aired the previous evening.

Package A combination of commercial spots sold as a whole unit.

Page An HTML document that may contain text, images, and other online elements. See also Web page.

Page View The number of times a page was downloaded by users, often measured as a function of time ("page views per day"). The actual number of times the page was seen by users may be higher because of caching.

Participation A commercial that appears in-program, as opposed to between programs during a break.

Pay Cable Programs and/or services provided to basic cable subscribers for an additional fee (e.g., HBO).

Pay-Per-View A telecast, usually of a special event, like a boxing match or a concert, for which subscribers pay a one-time fee to view.

Penetration In cable, the proportion of homes subscribing to cable measured as a percentage of the total number of TV households in a specific area.

People Meter An electronic device for instantaneously measuring television viewing. Since the fall of 1987, people meters have been used to generate the NTI.

PI (per inquiry) Advertisements for which the outlet airing them is paid a fee that is based on the number of units sold by the ad. These advertisements use a phone number or post office box number for ordering that is unique to each station airing the advertisement.

Piggyback Scheduling two commercials back-to-back in one purchase. Typically, an advertiser will buy one 60-second position to piggyback two 30-second spots for two different brands within the advertiser's product line.

Pod A grouping of commercials and non-program material in which more than one advertiser's commercials air. Also referred to as a commercial interruption or commercial break, but airing in-program.

Point-of-Purchase Display (POP) An advertising display at the place where consumers purchase goods or services (e.g., a counter card at a retail outlet).

Pop-Up Windows Separate windows that appear at the top of a Web site while a page loads to increase advertising impact without slowing the Web user's experience.

Post, or Postbuy Analysis The process of comparing the CPM and CPPs actually generated by a campaign with those that were projected at the time a buy was made. Sometimes used as a verb, as in "How did the schedule post?"

Preemption The displacement of a regularly scheduled program or commercial announcement by the station or network.

Prime Access A TV daypart immediately preceding prime time in which local stations were originally charged by the FCC to broadcast programs in the interest of the local community, but which now contains various local or syndicated programs. Generally, the half hour from 7 to 7:30 p.m. or 7:30 to 8 p.m. EST.

Prime Time In broadcast, the general reference is to the time period that attracts the most viewers or listeners. Specifically, in television, generally 8 to 11 p.m. EST, Monday through Saturday, and 7:30 to 11 p.m. EST, Sunday; in radio, generally 6 to 10 a.m. (morning drive) and 3 to 7 p.m. (afternoon drive).

PRIZM A geodemographic clustering system offered by Claritas.

Promax International A nonprofit organizationof advertising, promotion and marketing executives in electronic media, formerly known as BPME, Broadcast Promotion and Marketing Executives.

Promo An announcement promoting a station, a network, or a specific program or feature. Short for "promotional announcement."

Prime Time Access Rule (PTAR) A rule preventing network affiliated television stations in the top 50 markets from airing more than 3 hours of network programming between 7 and 11:00 p.m. EST. The ruling created the Prime Access daypart.

Psychographics Pertains to the identification of personality characteristics and attitudes that affect a person's lifestyle and purchasing behavior. Usually refers to a formal classification system such as SRI's VALS™ (values and lifestyles) that categorizes people into specific types (achievers, belongers, etc.). Lifestyle is a more vague term, and many lifestyle types or segments have been defined in various market studies. Generally speaking, these systems organize people according to their attitudes or consumer behavior, such as their involvement with and spending on golf.

Public Access A noncommercial channel set aside by a cable system for use by the public.

Public Service Announcement (PSA) An announcement on TV or radio aired at no charge by a station or system and usually promoting some charitable, nonprofit organization. PSAs are often used to fill unsold avails, but some stations or systems may reserve avails specifically for PSA use.

Pulsing A media buying strategy that combines elements of flighting and continuity scheduling. Some minimal level of exposure is maintained throughout the campaign, with additional spots being scheduled on a flighting basis.

PUR (persons using radio) The percentage of people using radio at a particular time.

PUT (persons using television) The percentage of people using television at a particular time. Sometimes called PVT for people viewing television, but the term PUT is more common.

Quintile Distribution In research, a display of frequency (or related data) among audiences grouped into equal fifths of reach.

(RAB) Radio Advertising Bureau An educational and promotional organization for the radio industry. Provides training materials and information resources for radio salespeople.

(RADAR) Radio All Dimension Audience Research Radio network ratings report issued by Statistical Research, Inc., and measuring listening to network radio programs.

Radio and Television News Directors Association (RTNDA) An organization of journalists in electronic media which issues a code of ethics for broadcast news personnel.

Random Sample In research, a type of sample in which every element within the sample has an equal probability of being selected.

Rate Card Written statement of advertising fees and terms.

Rate Holder A commercial aired only to maintain the conditions of a contract that allows for a discounted rate. Usually this requires placing a single commercial in each of 52 weeks to obtain an annual discount. The remainder of the schedule is flighted. Rate holders fell out of favor in demand-driven rate negotiations.

Rating The percentage of a given population group using a medium at a particular moment. Generally used for broadcast media, but can be used for any medium. One rating point equals 1%.

Radio Broadcast Data System (RBDS) Technology that enables AM and FM stations to send data to "smart" receivers, allowing them to perform several automatic functions, including displaying station name, format, song title, and artist.

Reach The number or percentage of a population group exposed to a media schedule within a given period of time.

Rebate A payment to the advertiser by a medium when the advertising schedule exceeds the contractual commitments originally agreed to and the advertising schedule earns a lower rate.

Remote A broadcast that originates outside of the station's studios, including live coverage of concerts, sports events or a program from a client's place of business. Remotes may be full remotes, where all programming originates outside the studios (music and commercials), or partial remotes, where only some commercials originate outside of the station's studios. When speaking with clients, salespeople should refer to remotes as "live broadcasts" because the term "remote" is an engineering term that has no meaning to clients or the public.

Rep National sales representative firm or salesperson. National sales reps are salespeople who specialize in selling avails on many stations in different markets to national or regional advertisers.

Return on Investment (ROI) Generally refers to the advertiser's desire to have a return on the advertising funds invested in media.

Roadblock A scheduling device used with broadcast media to increase reach at a given point in time (e.g., scheduling a commercial on all local market stations at 9 p.m., or all the local positions in a network program).

Roll-out A marketing procedure where advertising begins in one area and is progressively expanded into more geographic areas over time.

(ROS) Run of Station Scheduling commercials throughout the day and night at the discretion of the station or network, as opposed to time periods designated by the advertiser.

Sample In research, the portion of a population selected, usually on a random basis, to represent the population as a whole, so that inferences can be made about characteristics of the population.

Sampling Error In research, the possible deviation in the reported finding of media audience research based on a sample from what might be the actual finding had a complete census been done. Usually reported as "plus or minus" some percentage of the reported number.

Satellite Station A broadcast station that rebroadcasts the transmission of another station (generally operating in a nearby market) to an area that cannot otherwise be served by that station.

Saturation Schedule A heavy commercial buy aired when targeted homes or persons are tuned in.

Scarborough A media research supplier specializing in qualitative information.

Scatter Purchasing commercial time in broadcast media in many different programs. Also refers to the purchasing of network TV time that is not purchased during an upfront media buy.

Separate Audio Program (SAP) A third audio channel that can be received by some stereo televisions that allows for the transmission of specialized audio like language translations or descriptive audio for the visually impaired.

Session A series of consecutive visits made by a visitor to a series of Web sites.

Sets in Use Antiquated term replaced by HUT. Referred to the number of TV sets in use (turned on) at a given time.

Share Share of audience is the percentage of people tuned to a particular program or station. Share of market is the percentage of advertising impressions generated by all brands in a category accounted for by a particular brand. Also refers to the share of media spending such as radio's 7% share of advertising dollars.

Short Rate An extra charge passed on to an advertiser who purchases fewer spots than originally contracted and thus fails to qualify for the lower spot rate that was originally charged. Also see Rebate.

Simmons Market and Research Bureau A media research supplier and publisher of an annual nationwide survey of media usage and product purchase behavior.

Simulcast To broadcast simultaneously on more than one medium: AM and FM radio, radio and television, radio and cable, and so forth.

(SMSA) Standard Metropolitan Statistical Area A geographic area defined by the U.S. Government's Office of Management and Budget.

Spec-Spot A speculative commercial that is produced for a prospective client before the client has purchased a spot schedule. The spec spot is used as a sales tool.

Spill-in/Spill-out Spill-in refers to an audience viewing a TV broadcast from a different market (e.g., people in San Diego viewing Los Angeles stations). Spill-out refers to a station's attempt to deliver an audience from outside the originating TV market (e.g., Los Angeles stations selling the audiences they deliver in San Diego).

Sponsorship The purchase of more than one commercial within a program, allowing advertisers to receive bonus time via opening and closing billboards, or exclusivity of advertising within the brand's product category, or both.

Spot A word commonly used in lieu of "commercial announcement." Also refers to the purchase of national TV or radio commercial time on a market-by-market basis as opposed to network purchases.

Standard Error See Sampling Error.

Standard Rate and Data Service (SRDS) Publications that list data (e.g., costs, circulation) for all media vehicles that accept advertising.

Strategy Research Corporation (SRC) A media research supplier concentrating on the Hispanic market.

Strip Programming Scheduling a TV program at the same time each day. Sometimes called horizontal programming.

Subcarrier Authorization (SCA) A technology that allows broadcast stations to transmit additional information that can be received only by specially equipped radios. For example, most FM stations use one of their two subcarriers to transmit in stereo. The other subcarrier may be used to transmit financial news, Muzak, or some other specialized programming.

Subliminal Advertising or programming not consciously perceived; below normal range of awareness, background.

Superduopoly A word coined by *Radio Business Report* to indicate ownership of multiple radio stations in the same market broadcasting in the same service, that is, multiple AM stations or multiple FM stations.

Superstation An independent TV station whose signal is transmitted throughout the United States via satellite. Technically refers specifically to WTBS, Atlanta, and WGN, Chicago, both of which promote themselves to cable systems, but is also used to describe other stations.

Surfing Moving quickly from channel to channel using a remote or moving from Web site to Web site using hyperlinks or hypertext transfer protocol.

Sweep The period when local market TV ratings are studied. Originally coined to represent the time when Nielsen would sweep the country to obtain ratings in all markets. Sweeps are now issued four times a year in all markets and more frequently in top markets.

Syndication In broadcast, a program carried on selected stations which may or may not air at the same time in all markets. The sale and distribution of programming directly to television stations, radio stations, or cable systems. Off-network syndication involves the sale of programming that has previously aired on network television. First-run syndication involves the sale of programming that has been produced specifically for airing on local stations or systems. National advertisers may sometimes purchase advertising time directly from the syndicators or distributors of the program.

(TAP) Total Audience Plan A scheduling strategy that involves placing spots in several of a station's or system's dayparts.

Target Audience The demographic an advertiser is most interested in reaching, such as adults 25–54 or men 18–34.

Target Rating Points (TRPs) The sum of all ratings delivered by a given list of media vehicles. Essentially synonymous with GRPs, which is the more common term.

Television Market An unduplicated television area to which a U.S. county is assigned based on the highest share of viewing of originating TV stations.

Television Network By FCC definition in the Telecommunications Act of 1996, an entity providing more than 4 hours a week of prime-time entertainment programming to interconnected affiliates on a regular basis and reaching at least 75% of the nation's TV households.

Test Market A market (or markets) chosen for the purpose of conducting a media test.

Tier A cable service in addition to basic service that a subscriber can pay extra for monthly and receive. Some cable systems have two or more pay tiers available. HBO is an example of a service on a pay tier. Each additional price increment for service offered is called a tier.

'Til Forbid Instructions by an advertiser to run a purchased schedule or advertisement(s) until notified to stop. Also referred to as TFN—'til further notice.

Time Shifting Videotaping television programs and viewing them at a later, more convenient time.

Traffic The department in a broadcast station or cable system that administers the scheduling of commercials and other program material on a daily operation schedule and produces the schedule or log.

Translator A low-power transmitter that is used to retransmit the signal of a radio or television station to areas that would otherwise have poor reception.

(TSL) Time Spent Listening An estimate of the amount of time the average person spends listening to radio during a given time period.

(TVB) Television Bureau of Advertising An educational and promotional organization for the television industry. Provides training and other resource materials for television salespeople with the goal of helping advertisers make effective use of local and national spot television.

UHF (ultra high frequency) Television channels 14 to 69. UHF channels require high-power transmitters which are expensive to operate. UHF signals received over the air are often of poorer quality than those of VHF stations on channels 2 to 13.

Universe The total population within a defined demographic, psychographic, or product consumption segment against which media audiences are calculated to determine ratings, coverage, reach, and so forth.

Unwired Network Applicable to either radio or television, the purchase of advertising on pre-selected local stations not connected by wire or satellite, through a sales organization representing the stations.

Upfront Purchasing TV commercial time well in advance of the telecast time of the programs and generally for a protracted period, such as for a 1-year schedule. A relatively common practice among many advertisers for the purchase of network prime-time television.

Uplink Part of a satellite transmission in which signals are sent from Earth to a satellite.

URL (universal resource locator) The information on the protocol, the system, and the file name of an Internet site so that the user's system can find a particular document. An example of a URL is *http://www.bh.com/focalpress*, which is the Butterworth–Heinemann Web server with a file name for Focal Press. This indicates that "hypertext transfer protocol" is the protocol and that the information is located on a system named *www.bh.com*. Most Web servers are set up to point to a home page if no additional file name is used.

VALS 2 A research study developed by SRI International, which describes eight distinct population groups according to their values and lifestyles. VALS is a trade mark of SRI International.

VHF (very high frequency) TV channels 2 to 13. More desirable than UHF channels 14 to 69 because VHF signals carry farther.

Viewers per 1,000 Households The number of people within a specific population group tuned to a TV program in each 1,000 viewing households.

Visit A sequence of hits made by one user at a Web site. Internet technology does not maintain a continuous connection (like a radio signal) to a site; rather, data is sent in packets. If a user makes no request for data from the site during a predetermined (and discretionary) period of time, the user's next hit would constitute a new visit.

(VPVH) Viewers per Viewer Household Households don't watch television, people do. How many people per household? The answer is expressed as VPVH.

Web Page An HTML document on the World Wide Web, usually one of many that together make up a Web site.

Web Server A system capable of continuous access to the Internet, retrieving and displaying documents and files via hypertext transfer protocol (http).

Web Site The virtual location for an organization's presence on the World Wide Web, usually made up of several Web pages and a single home page designated by a unique URL.

Willhight A radio research provider supplying ratings information primarily to stations in small- to medium-sized markets in states in the northwestern United States.

World Wide Web The mechanism originally developed for physicists to be able to share documents via the Internet. The Web allows computer users to access information across systems around the world using URLs to identify files and systems and hypertext links to move between files on the same or different systems.

Zapping Deliberate removal by a viewer of nonprogram material (e.g., a commercial) while recording on a video cassette recorder so as to play back program(s) without commercial interruptions.

Zipping Fast-forwarding through commercials and/or programs while playing back a VCR recording.

Index

T